# BARBARISM AND RELIGION
## Volume Three
### *The First Decline and Fall*

'Barbarism and Religion' – Edward Gibbon's own phrase – is the title of a sequence of works by John Pocock designed to situate Gibbon, and his *Decline and Fall of the Roman Empire*, in a series of contexts in the history of eighteenth-century Europe. This is a major intervention from one of the world's leading historians, challenging the notion of any one 'Enlightenment' and positing instead a plurality of Enlightenments, of which the English was one. The first two volumes of *Barbarism and Religion* were warmly and widely reviewed, and won the Jacques Barzun Prize in Cultural History of the American Philosophical Society.

In this third volume in the sequence, *The First Decline and Fall*, John Pocock offers a historical introduction to the first fourteen chapters of Gibbon's great work. He argues that this first Decline and Fall is a phenomenon of specifically 'ancient' history in which Christianity played no part, and whose problems were those of liberty and empire. The first Decline and Fall is that of ancient, imperial and polytheist Rome, and Gibbon's first fourteen chapters recount the end of classical civilisation, a civilisation with which Gibbon and his readers were vastly more familiar than with its late-antique successor. Only towards the end of this present volume do the Christians appear, and Gibbon's history begins to move towards its dominant themes.

Born in London and brought up in Christchurch, New Zealand, J. G. A. POCOCK was educated at the Universities of Canterbury and Cambridge, and is now Harry C. Black Emeritus Professor of History at The Johns Hopkins University. His many seminal works on intellectual history include *The Ancient Constitution and the Feudal Law* (1957, Second Edition 1987), *Politics, Language and Time* (1971), *The Machiavellian Moment* (1975), and *Virtue, Commerce and History* (1985). He has also edited *The Political Works of James Harrington* (1977) and Burke's *Reflections on the Revolution in France* (1987), as well as the collaborative study *The Varieties of British Political Thought* (1995). A Corresponding Fellow of the British Academy and of the Royal Historical Society, Professor Pocock is also a member of the American Academy of Arts and Sciences and of the American Philosophical Society. He was appointed an Officer of the Order of New Zealand Merit in 2002.

# BARBARISM AND RELIGION

## Volume Three

*The First Decline and Fall*

J. G. A. POCOCK

CAMBRIDGE
UNIVERSITY PRESS

PUBLISHED BY THE PRESS SYNDICATE OF THE UNIVERSITY OF CAMBRIDGE
The Pitt Building, Trumpington Street, Cambridge, United Kingdom

CAMBRIDGE UNIVERSITY PRESS
The Edinburgh Building, Cambridge, CB2 2RU, UK
40 West 20th Street, New York, NY 10011–4211, USA
477 Williamstown Road, Port Melbourne, VIC 3027, Australia
Ruiz de Alarcón 13, 28014 Madrid, Spain
Dock House, The Waterfront, Cape Town 8001, South Africa

http://www.cambridge.org

First published 2003

Printed in the United Kingdom at the University Press, Cambridge

*Typeface* Baskerville Monotype 11/12.5 pt      *System* LaTeX 2ε   [TB]

*A catalogue record for this book is available from the British Library*

ISBN 0 521 82445 1 hardback

*On ne peut jamais quitter les Romains*
Montesquieu

# Contents

# *Acknowledgements*

This volume bears no dedication like those to Franco Venturi and Arnaldo Momigliano, prefixed to *The Enlightenments of Edward Gibbon* and *Narratives of Civil Government*. There is no single historian with whose theses the volume is engaged throughout, in ways that render him a guiding light even when I have steered away from the paths he illuminated; not even Hans Baron who, whatever his overstatements, established Leonardo Bruni and Niccolo Machiavelli in the crucial roles I have continued to accord them. I therefore simply mention his name at this point, together with that of Ronald Syme, another great figure of a past generation, whose interpretation of Tacitus casts a dazzling light on Gibbon's understanding of the same figure. Among historians yet living, and even of age-groups that will succeed my own, I should like to mention Peter Miller for his incomparable depiction of *Peiresc's Europe*, while the debt of all Gibbonian scholars to David Womersley is not only inexhaustible but increasing.

The institutions whose help I acknowledged in presenting my former volumes have continued, directly and indirectly, to contribute to the making of this one. Many of the chapters that follow were typed in a former draft by David Mene; others by Ellen Pearson and Catherine Cardno; the final typescript was predominantly the work of Jason Kuznicki, with late revisions by Caleb McDaniel. I should like to thank them all, and the History Department of the Johns Hopkins University for supporting their work. My thanks go also to many colleagues, at Johns Hopkins and elsewhere, who have helped me by conversation and comment: in particular, Thomas Izbicki, Richard Kagan, Peter Miller, Orest Ranum, Melvin Richter, Matthew Roller, Teofilo Ruiz, Quentin Skinner, Gabrielle Spiegel, and James Tully. They are not to blame for any errors that have survived the scrutiny they encouraged me to undertake.

Thanks also to the anonymous readers for the Cambridge University Press, and above all to Richard Fisher, who have surpassed the generosity and patience they accorded to the preceding volumes of *Barbarism and Religion*.

Felicity Pocock again read the whole thing aloud for the correction of proofs. This volume is presented to our grand children, Charlotte, Henry and Rowan, who were born while it was in the making.

# Note on usages

I have not attempted in this volume the earlier practise of supplying eighteenth-century English translations of quoted texts. The translations given are those of modern editors, with the exception of two cases where they were written *circa* 1600 and two where I have been obliged to supply my own. Matthew Roller helped with these, but responsibility for them is my own. In transcribing languages other than English, I have followed the typographic conventions of the editions I use. This has entailed differences both between ancient and modern editions, and between the conventions preferred by modern editors. The bibliography at the end of the volume contains a separate section for modern editions and translations. The *Decline and Fall* (*DF*) is cited by volume, chapter and footnotes; all page references are to the edition by David Womersley.

# *Abbreviations*

The following abbreviations are used throughout the volume. Those in separate chapters are listed in the bibliography.

| | |
|---|---|
| *EE* | Patricia B. Craddock (ed.), *The English Essays of Edward Gibbon*. Oxford: at the Clarendon Press, 1972 |
| *EEG* | J. G. A. Pocock, *Barbarism and Religion. Volume I: The Enlightenments of Edward Gibbon*. Cambridge: Cambridge University Press, 1999 |
| *EGLH* | Patricia B. Craddock, *Edward Gibbon: Luminous Historian, 1772–1794*. Baltimore: The Johns Hopkins University Press, 1989 |
| *Letters* | J. E. Norton (ed.), *The Letters of Edward Gibbon*. In three volumes. London: Cassell and Company, 1956 |
| *Library* | Geoffrey Keynes (ed.), *The Library of Edward Gibbon*. Second edition. N.P.: St Paul's Bibliographies, 1980 |
| *Memoirs* | Georges A. Bonnard (ed.), *Edward Gibbon: Memoirs of My Life*. New York: Funk and Wagnalls, 1969 |
| *MGH*, xx | G. H. Pertz (ed.), *Monumenta Germaniae Historica Scriptorum Tomus XX*. Hanover, *impensis bibliopoli aulici Hahniani*, 1868. |
| *MW* | Lord Sheffield (ed.), *The Miscellaneous Works of Edward Gibbon, Esq. With Memoirs of his Life and Writings, Composed by Himself: Illustrated from his Letters, with Occasional Notes and Narrative. A new edition, with considerable additions, in five volumes*. London, John Murray, 1814. |

| | |
|---|---|
| *NCG* | J. G. A. Pocock, *Barbarism and Religion. Volume II: Narratives of Civil Government.* Cambridge: Cambridge University Press, 1999 |
| Womersley, 1994 | David Womersley (ed.), *Edward Gibbon: The History of the Decline and Fall of the Roman Empire.* In three volumes. London: Allen Lane, The Penguin Press, 1994 |
| *YEG* | Patricia B. Craddock, *Young Edward Gibbon, Gentleman of Letters.* Baltimore and London, The Johns Hopkins University Press, 1982 |

# Introduction

This is the third volume of *Barbarism and Religion*, a series intended to exhibit Edward Gibbon and his *Decline and Fall of the Roman Empire* in historical contexts to which they belong and which illuminate their significance. The two volumes so far published have brought Gibbon to the verge of writing his master work. *The Enlightenments of Edward Gibbon* concluded with his intention to write a history which was to have been primarily a history of the city of Rome as it was deserted by its own empire, and only by degrees came to be intended as a history of that empire's decline and transformation. *Narratives of Civil Government* concluded with the prospectus Gibbon prefixed to the first volume of the *Decline and Fall*, and isolated as problematic a series of decisions then explicitly or implicitly announced, which were to determine the future character of the work. One of these was the decision to bypass the history of the Latin middle ages, already recounted by Robertson and Voltaire, and pursue the history of the eastern Roman empire to the Turkish conquest of 1453; perhaps the strangest of all Gibbon's decisions and that which perplexed him most. Implicit in it was the further decision that the *Decline and Fall* would not be, like other great Enlightened histories, a history of the 'Christian millennium' leading to the 'Enlightened narrative' of the emergence from 'barbarism and religion' – these are terms used in constructing the second volume of this series – but a history of late antiquity leading into the 'Christian millennium'; a history, as Gibbon came to see, of the 'triumph of barbarism and religion'. More deeply implicit still – and perhaps in 1776 not fully apparent to Gibbon himself – was the decision that the history of the late empire must also be a history of the Christian church and its theology. Gibbon indicated the persistence of his original conception by announcing – a decision in due course executed – that he would conclude his planned work by a study of the city of Rome during the Latin middle ages which he had treated only marginally.

I

The two volumes so far published are thus preliminary to the history of Gibbon's text. The third, now presented, will begin an engagement with that text, but not until the last of this volume's six sections. The preceding five conduct a survey of the idea of Decline and Fall itself, beginning long before the events held to constitute that catastrophe, at a time at which the decline of Rome's empire was being predicted by writers before it had reached its height; and the survey includes a view of late-antique and medieval Christian historical concepts, in particular the Augustinian concept of the 'two cities' and the Latin, papal and imperial concept of the *translatio imperii*. These are prominent in the volume for more than one reason. For many centuries they outweighed and submerged the notion of Decline and Fall itself, which in some ways may be said to have returned to the surface only with the humanist recovery of ancient texts and ancient virtues, including the political; this volume conducts a re-assessment of that recovery. In the ages when *translatio imperii* counted for more than Decline and Fall, it indicated the presence of that competition between ecclesiastical and imperial authority, Christian and classical values and culture, which for Gibbon marked the difference between ancient and modern history and was in his mind when he wrote that a history of the decline and fall of the Roman empire had become one of 'the triumph of barbarism and religion'. The historiography of church and empire supplied so many of the events and themes of the *Decline and Fall*'s third through sixth volumes that it has been necessary to give it equal prominence with the historiography of *libertas et imperium*, republic and principate, that supplies the narrative of what the title of this volume terms 'the first Decline and Fall'.

That narrative is the theme of the first fourteen of the sixteen chapters composing the volume which Gibbon published at the beginning of 1776. The decision to devote the third volume of *Barbarism and Religion* to a historical introduction and close study of chapters 1 through 14, deferring the study of chapters 15 and 16 to another place, entails the assertion, to be defended in due course, that there is a sharp and profound breach in the continuity of Gibbon's narrative, separating these two chapters from their predecessors and plunging them in a larger caesura, involving the five years (1776–81) which separate the first volume of the *Decline and Fall* from the second. During the lapse of time bridged, in the reader's eye, by chapters 15 to 21, Gibbon had to address the challenge, scarcely confronted in the preface he wrote in 1776, of making his way from an ancient history, whose problems were those of empire and liberty, to a modern history whose problems were those of empire and church; in the terms of our earlier volumes, the 'Christian millennium' preceding the 'Enlightened narrative'. How he met that challenge will come to preoccupy us, but does not appear in Chapters 1 through 14. The First Decline and Fall is that of ancient, imperial and polytheist Rome: the history of how the *libertas* and *virtus* which had extended *imperium* failed to sustain the weight of the empire they had built up. It will be argued here that this Decline and Fall is a phenomenon of 'ancient' history, in which the Christian religion plays no significant part; its role is yet to come; but to situate Gibbon in the *moyenne durée* of the history of historiography, we must set classical and Christian histories side by side and consider Enlightened historiography as the partial escape from both. The present volume will enter the world of the Enlightenments only towards its close. If there is a single historian at the centre of the First Decline and Fall, he is Tacitus, followed in modernity by Montesquieu; for what is meant by 'followed' in this context the reader is referred to the book. Writing shortly after the murder of Domitian in AD 98, Tacitus examined events at the death of Nero in AD 70, and then turned back to the foundation of the principate by Augustus and the calamitous reigns of his successors. Commencing the narrative of the Decline and Fall at the murder of Commodus in AD 180, Gibbon employed an explanatory structure so exactly Tacitean as to compel an even longer retrospect; he once wrote that he should have begun where Tacitus began instead of long after he ended, and it was possible to base Tacitus' analysis of the ills of the principate on a remoter narrative of the fall of the republic, beginning as early as Tiberius Gracchus. The first decision by Gibbon which *The First Decline and Fall* seeks to explore is the decision to begin with this Tacitean retrospect; the second, already inspected, is the imposition of a caesura at the accession of Constantine. These two have had the paradoxical effect of making his first volume better known to readers than the five to which it is essentially a preliminary. Chapters 1 to 14 recount the end of classical civilisation, with which readers including Gibbon were, and long remained, more familiar than with the late-antique figures and culture that succeeded them. Chapters 15 and 16, dealing with the Christian church before Constantine, provoked – as Gibbon may or may not have intended – such a furore that they have ever since been read as the principal index to Gibbon's attitude towards Christianity; though it can be argued that they too are no more than preliminary, and that the history of the church in the empire, and of the philosophy underlying its theology, does not begin until chapter 21, five years as well as five chapters later.

Chapters 1–14 belong in a historiography that treated the Decline and Fall of Roman empire as continuing the history of the republic, the theme of the present book. Chapters 15 and 16 belong in, and at the same time rebel against, the very different historiography of the Christian church. How they do so, and how they were read in this context by a public whose culture was clerical as well as humanist, must be the subject of a separate volume, perhaps to be entitled *The Unbelieving Historian*; it may then be possible to consider whether the reading of these two chapters in any way alters that, already complete, of their fourteen predecessors. There is, however, one more omission and postponement that must now be acknowledged. Chapters 7 and 8, dealing with the Persians and Germans respectively, do not form part of the explanatory narrative presented here of the First Decline and Fall; the peoples whom they present are rather the beneficiaries of Roman military decay than its principal cause. For this reason, the two chapters which depict their manners and customs rather than their actions have been reserved for future treatment, entitled perhaps 'the history and theory of barbarism', or more ambitiously still, *Barbarians, Savages and Empires*. When these two omissions have been made good we shall be embarked upon the journey from 'the decline and fall of the Roman Empire' to 'the triumph of barbarism and religion'. Among many generous observations for which I am grateful, reviewers of my Volumes I and II have wondered how *Barbarism and Religion* is to be further developed and whether it is planned to reach a definite end; some of them have asked for a prospectus of the volumes yet to appear. Like Gibbon himself, presenting the *Decline and Fall* when he did not quite know how it would turn out, I am prepared to enter into an 'engagement with the public'[1] to produce this and the next volumes;[2] what may follow must be determined by the interest of the public and the longevity of the historian.

---

[1] For Gibbon's use of this phrase, see Womersley, 1994, 1, pp. 2–3; *NCG* p. 373.

[2] I may be permitted to record that since Volumes I and II appeared in 1999, I have published five essays relative to the future of my enterprise: 'Gibbon and the Primitive Church', in Stefan Collini, Richard Whatmore and Brian Young (eds.), *History, Religion and Culture: British Intellectual History, 1750–1950* (Cambridge: Cambridge University Press, 2000), pp. 48–68; 'Commerce, Settlement and History: a reading of the *Histoire des Deux Indes*', in Rebecca Starr (ed.), *Anticipating America: Fashioning a National Political Culture in Early America. Essays in Honour of J. R. Pole* (Lanham, MD: Rowman and Littlefield, 2000), pp. 15–44; '*The Outlines of the History of the World*: a Problematic Essay by Edward Gibbon', in Anthony J. Grafton and J. H. M. Salmon (eds.) *Historians and Ideologues: Essays in Honour of Donald R. Kelley* (Rochester, NY: University of Rochester Press, 2001), pp. 211–30; 'Tangata whenua and Enlightenment Anthropology', in Judith Binney (ed.), *The Shaping of History: Essays from the New Zealand Journal of History* (Wellington: Bridget Williams Books, 2001), pp. 38–61; 'Gibbon and the History of Heresy', in John Christian Laursen (ed.), *Histories of Heresy in Early Modern Europe: For, Against and Beyond Persecution and Toleration* (New York and Houndsmills: Palgrave, 2002), pp. 205–20.

# Prologue

# CHAPTER I

# *Gibbon's first volume: the problem of the Antonine moment*

(1)

Gibbon published the first volume of *The History of the Decline and Fall of the Roman Empire* on 17 February 1776.[1] He was in his thirty-ninth year and, once his father's death in 1770 had left him in a condition of independence, had moved to London and taken a house in Bentinck Street in search of what he termed 'study and society'.[2] The paired terms indicate that the *Decline and Fall* was to be a work of Enlightenment, in the primary sense that the life of the mind was to be, freely but inescapably, a life in society. Though Gibbon liked to be considered a virtuoso – 'a gentleman who wrote for his amusement'[3] – he knew very well that he was pursuing a vocation; from infancy, he believed, he had been formed to be a historian. This vocation, however, was not to be a profession, in either the clerical-academic or the nineteenth-century sense of that word; Gibbon pursued it in the company of urban and urbane gentry, gentlemen of letters in a sense differing from the French *gens de lettres*. He was a member of the Literary Club,[4] formed by Joshua Reynolds with the intent of elevating painting – as David Garrick sought to elevate acting – from a trade to a high art conducted in high society. It was here that Gibbon met, but did not much like, Samuel Johnson, who remembered the literary life before some of its practitioners had been rescued from Grub Street desperation by the expansion of genteel publishing (the London and Edinburgh 'business of Enlightenment') which enabled Hume, Robertson and Gibbon to live in affluence off the sale of their copyrights, independent of either patrons or booksellers.[5] It was also through the Literary Club that Gibbon became a friend of Adam Smith, representing with David Hume that group of Scottish

---

[1] *EGLH*, p. 67.   [2] *Letters*, I, pp. 362, 364; II, p. 63.   [3] *Memoirs*, p. 126.
[4] Rogers, 1997, is a detailed study of the Club and of Gibbon's membership.
[5] Brewer, 1997, chs. 3 and 4; Darnton, 1979.

'philosophers' – this word too has other resonances than those of the French word *philosophes* – with whom Gibbon associated, but did not identify, the writing of history. Smith published *The Wealth of Nations* in March 1776, and Hume died in the following August, after reading and approving the *Decline and Fall*'s first volume. Gibbon valued Smith's conversation and Hume's correspondence; at the latter's death he was consulted about Hume's surviving manuscripts, and seems to have approved of the *Dialogues of Natural Religion*, though there is nothing to connect him with Smith's refusal to be associated with their publication.[6]

As Gibbon prepared his first volume – it was a difficult process of composition – he was drawn into London public life as well as social. One morning in September 1774, 'as I was destroying an army of Barbarians', he was invited to accept a seat in Parliament controlled by a family friend.[7] He held this until 1780, when his patron went into opposition and Gibbon did not wish to follow him; he was a steady if silent supporter of the North ministry, though his letters reveal disquiet and even dismay at the disasters of 1778–81 and he later wrote that in the dispute with the American colonies he had upheld 'the rights, though not, perhaps, the interest of the mother country'.[8] There is a letter of 1779 in which he remarks 'la décadence de Deux Empires, le Romain et le Britannique, s'avancent à pas égaux',[9] but facile connections are to be avoided; Gibbon understood the differences between an ancient land empire of appropriation and a modern maritime empire of commerce, and he would know that whereas the institutions of Roman freedom had been subverted and replaced by the institutions of empire, the British were engaged in losing an empire rather than extend their institutions of self-government to include it. He would agree with Adam Smith that they would survive this loss with no more than emotional damage.[10] Nevertheless, it is to be remembered, and may be examined, that the first three volumes of the *Decline and Fall* were written and published during that major crisis of the Hanoverian monarchy and the Europe it upheld which Venturi termed *la prima crisi dell' Antico Regime*. On the

---

[6] See William Strahan's letter to Suard of December 1776; Baridon, 1971 (I am indebted to Patricia Craddock and David Raynor for help with this reference) and Ross, 1995, pp. 290–1, 299–301, 304; Mossner and Ross, 1987, pp. 205–7, 208, 210–13, 215, 216–17, 223–4. These letters do not mention Gibbon as playing any role in the affair. He bought the *Dialogues* when they were published in the following year; *Library*, p. 156.

[7] *Letters*, 11, p. 32.　　[8] *Memoirs*, p. 156.

[9] *Letters*, 11, p. 218. The singular noun and plural verb are Gibbon's.

[10] *Letters*, 11, p. 326 (20 May 1783: 'Notre chute cependant a été plus douce . . . Il nous reste de quoi vivre contens, et heureux'). An echo of Adam Smith's 'the real mediocrity of their condition'?

authorial level, Gibbon converted his seat in Parliament into a place under government, and it was after losing the latter at the hands of the reformer Edmund Burke – his fellow member of the Literary Club – that he removed to Lausanne in 1783, to finish the *Decline and Fall* five years later.[11]

## (11)

So much, at this point, for the context of personal and historical circumstances in which Gibbon's first volume may be situated. He had been at work on this volume for perhaps four years, and both its contents and the preface he affixed to it can be read as indicating his understanding of his project at the end of the year 1775. This preface[12] – considered in a preceding chapter of this series[13] – lays out a plan for future volumes not remote from that finally executed; it indicates an intention of carrying on to the fall of Constantinople in 1453, and concluding with a study of the city of Rome in the middle ages. From this it has been inferred, first that Gibbon's original vision of a history of the city within that of the empire was still alive beneath the many layers of intention that had been superimposed upon it; second, that he had already decided to bypass the Latin middle ages (treated by Robertson in his *View of the Progress of Society in Europe*[14]) and treat them as marginal to a history of New Rome and the eastern empire, reserving the ruins of the ancient city as a coda to which he would return. This is a very remarkable decision, which will call for a great deal of examination. Concealed beneath it is a further decision, not announced in the 1776 preface and perhaps not yet visible in all its complexity to Gibbon himself: the decision that the history of the empire after Constantine would have to be 'a history as well ecclesiastical as civil',[15] a history of the Christian Church and in particular of the rise of Christian theology, a principal motor of the challenge of ecclesiastical to civil authority. This decision, however momentous, is not made explicit in Chapters 1 through 14 and is only partly visible in Chapters 15 and 16. It can be examined, like its predecessor, only as it takes effect; and the preface of 1776 says nothing about it.

That preface, however, announces in the clearest terms a further decision, not yet considered, which must furnish the present volume with

---

[11] *Memoirs*, pp. 163–5.    [12] Womersley, 1994, I, pp. 1–3.
[13] *NCG*, ch. 25.    [14] *NCG*, pp. 275–88.
[15] A term regularly used in English historiography on either side of the year 1700.

its principal theme and enquiry. Gibbon pronounces that the complete history of the Decline and Fall

> may with some propriety, be divided into the three following periods. I. The first of these periods may be traced from the age of Trajan and the Antonines, when the Roman monarchy, having attained its full strength and maturity, began to verge towards its decline; and will extend to the subversion of the Western Empire, by the barbarians of Germany and Scythia, the rude ancestors of the most polished nations of modern Europe.[16]

Gibbon here announces the theme of barbarism and indicates its centrality in a history of Europe which it helps to define. The second period is to run from the reign of Justinian to that of Charlemagne, and the third from the re-foundation of the western empire to the extinction of the eastern. With that the history of the Roman empire is concluded, and we are left to infer that the history of 'modern Europe' is constructed on other foundations; perhaps, given the role of the papacy in founding, and then subverting, the empire of Charlemagne and his successors, a history of religion alongside that of barbarism and civility. But the Gibbon of 1776 is not yet ready to tell us, and perhaps has not yet fully decided, how to present a medieval history he is committed to viewing through Constantinopolitan lenses. We are more immediately concerned with his third decision, that to commence the narrative of Decline and Fall with the Antonine monarchy at the height of its power and wealth. 'Decline and Fall' conventionally refers to events of the fifth century, when the western empire was partitioned into a patchwork of barbarian kingdoms; why is Gibbon writing so proleptically as to begin his narrative three centuries earlier? This is his subject in Chapters 1 through 14, and it is the initial problem of the present volume.

His decision may be defended, which is not the same thing as explained, by pointing out that it was a convention of rhetorical and moral historiography that revolutions were rotations of Fortune's wheel and that decline invariably began from the zenith of power and success. Gibbon accordingly began with a *peinture* – as Sainte-Palaye would have called it[17] – of Antonine civilisation at its height, which occupies the first three chapters of his history; and he detected at its heart a 'secret poison'[18] which ultimately produced its decline. What this was we must in due course consider; but first we must note that Gibbon has switched from the key of cyclical rotation to that of systemic transformation. The

---

[16] Womersley, 1994, I, p. 1.    [17] For the dictum of La Curne de Sainte-Palaye, see *EEG*, p. 155.
[18] *DF*, I, ch. 2; Womersley, 1994, I, p. 83.

Antonine empire was a generalised condition of circumstances, which in time was replaced by some other, and what was to be replaced was classical civilisation itself, not yet challenged by Christianity and existing in a condition which was the product of its own history. The Decline and Fall is the breakup of a civilisation as well as an empire, both described in great richness of detail, and the 'secret poison' must be something generated within its systemic completeness. Here is the moment at which Gibbon is writing a prehistory to 'the Enlightened narrative'; where the latter began with 'the triumph of barbarism and religion' and traced its ultimate reversal, Gibbon is approaching that triumph from a starting-point in classical antiquity, the last moment of its existence in completeness.

If the description of Antonine civilisation is a *peinture*, the narrative of its decay must be a *récit*. That *récit* starts with the murder of the emperor Commodus by his domestics in AD 180, a palace revolution which touches off a series of interventions by the frontier armies. This phenomenon is not new; Gibbon has already isolated a period of benign rule by responsible emperors, beginning in 98, when the murder of Domitian in similar circumstances had led his successor Nerva to nominate the frontier general Trajan to succeed him, thus inaugurating that age in which Antonine civilisation had been at its height and the happiness of 'the human race' nearly complete. But 98 was also the moment at which the historian Tacitus had been moved by what was happening before him to write a history of events in AD 69–70, when the suicide of Nero had produced interventions by the frontier armies and wars in the streets of Rome, and to follow it with a history of events since the time of Augustus, when dissensions within the imperial household, and between that household and the senate, had produced conditions tending to the murders and suicides of emperors and the consequent interventions of the armies. This narrative was recyclable; the deaths of Caligula, Nero, Domitian (the exceptional case) and Commodus had led to the re-enactment of a scenario in which that of 180 was the last act only in the sense that it precipitated Antonine decay and led – in some sense yet to be explained – towards Decline and Fall. In deciding to start as far back as the Antonines, Gibbon committed himself to a Tacitean historiography of explanation, and it was to be a problem for him that this narrative was retrospective, equally valid for the fall of the Antonines, the Flavians, the Julio-Claudians, the Augustan principate and even (as we shall see) the Roman republic itself. He once wrote that he should have commenced the *Decline and Fall* from AD 70 where Tacitus had ended his history, or even AD 14 where it began, rather than 180, the collapse of the system which Tacitus had examined.[19]

The problem here encountered by Gibbon merges into a problem for us rather than for him. Why the Antonine moment at all; why the premise that imperial decay began in the late second century? What connection can exist between the crisis following the death of Commodus and what we ordinarily term the Decline and Fall, namely the loss of control over the western provinces by an empire centred on Constantinople two and a half centuries later? If Gibbon saw the Roman world as a single civilisational system, could the 'secret poison' afflicting it in the second century have remained operative in the fifth? He once wrote that the imagination was able to connect the most distant revolutions by a regular series of causes and effects;[20] but what impelled him to begin his series at a point not only distant in itself, but driving the imagination to seek its origins in a past more distant still? These problems have led at least one distinguished historian to contend that Tacitus was Gibbon's 'great evil genius', fascination with whom set the *Decline and Fall* on a wrong path that Gibbon recognised but could not escape.[21]

It seems indeed to be the case that Gibbon thought of the ancient Roman world as a unified system whose decay might be the result of general causes; but we have to take some account of an earlier, deeper and never quite superseded pattern in his thinking about the Decline and Fall. He had initially conceived a history of the decay of the city of Rome as the centres of imperial power moved away from it;[22] and the sense that there was a critical relationship between city and empire survived after his project had become that of writing a history of the decay of the latter. At the beginning as at the end of his completed volumes, his thought focussed on the city and the failure of its politics. The city, which is to say the republic, had conquered an empire, but failed to rule it; history thus became that of the empire divorced from the city, and consequently of the decline of both. We shall see that he found in Tacitus an explanation – entailing a retrospective of the history of the republic – of how power

---

[19]  *EE*, p. 338: 'Should I not have deduced the decline of the Empire from the civil wars, that ensued after the fall of Nero or even from the tyranny which succeeded the reign of Augustus? Alas! I should: but of what avail is this tardy knowledge?' Just what Gibbon means by 'tardy knowledge' may be debated; he cannot refer to his knowledge of Roman history in general.

[20]  *DF*, III, 33; Womersley, 1994, II, p. 293.

[21]  Bowersock, 1977, p. 67. He interprets the words quoted in n. 19 as Gibbon's confession of this error. Cf. Shaw, in Bowersock, Brown and Grabar, 1999, p. 164, for a development of Bowersock's point.

[22]  *EEG*, pp. 272–4.

had moved away from the city, to points in Tacitus' phrase *alibi quam Romae*.[23] This enabled him to begin the narrative, sustained through Chapters 1–14, of the wars of frontier generals with one another, and with the increasingly dangerous barbarians, until Constantine emerges as sole victor like Augustus three centuries before him, and like him embarks on an altogether new system of rule.

There are several senses in which Constantine marks completion of the movement *alibi quam Romae* – though it is vital to remember that Gibbon in 1776 reached only a point at which they were about to become actual, and that five years were to pass before he published his treatment of them in his second volume. By founding New Rome the emperor had rendered final and visible the abandonment of the old city, which began its long journey into the picturesque; by his alliance with the Christian religion he created both the empire which was to endure for a millennium in the east, and the force which was to replace, rather than renew, empire in the west. The failure of the sons of Theodosius to control the barbarian irruptions after 400 led to the end of empire in the Latin provinces and old Rome itself; the limited success of Justinian's attempt to resume control of Italy left the bishops of Rome free, and necessitated, to form alliances with the barbarian kingdoms in Gaul and elsewhere. Here we enter on the second period of Gibbon's 1776 preface: that from Justinian to Charlemagne, at the end of which Rome has become the capital of Peter and his Church, and the ghost of the deceased empire has seated itself on the grave thereof. The abandonment of Rome by empire has come full circle. The 'Enlightened narrative' may now embark on the history of the 'Christian millennium' – a process, and its premises, rather western than eastern, Latin than Greek.

All these processes take place in the history of Christian empire. Five of Gibbon's six volumes deal with the decline and fall – and in the west the post-history – of the system founded by Constantine. We therefore return to the problems set us by Gibbon's first volume, which introduces that figure but does not engage with his work. Chapters 1 through 14 bring him only to the Milvian bridge; Chapters 15 and 16 deal only with the Church before him; it will be 1781 before Gibbon tells us how Constantine in his new capital is obliged to repair to Nicaea by a theological dispute originating in Alexandria. We return to the problem of the Antonine moment. In what ways do weaknesses in the imperial system, detected by Tacitus in the first century and continued by Gibbon

---

[23] Below, p. 25.

into the second, serve to explain the failures of the fourth and fifth? If there was a 'secret poison' in the Antonine system, was it operative in the Constantinean? Here we may take up the belief, well established by Gibbon's time, that Constantine's military reforms, separating the frontier *limitanei* from a mass of reserves quartered in the cities, were fatal to legionary culture and led to its corruption. We must also confront the question whether the Christian religion, of which nothing has been said in the first fourteen chapters, figures in this process as cause or effect; but this must be the matter of a future volume.

Whatever the answers that emerge to these questions, it is evident that a Tacitean historiography, presenting the problems of the principate as the consequence of republican decay, was of enormous importance to Gibbon, who placed it at the outset of his narrative of Decline and Fall. He did not do so simply because he had read the works of Tacitus and become obsessed with their philosophic possibilities. There existed a long tradition of Tacitism, which had made him part of a European consciousness of history and philosophy, as an authority on Decline and Fall and the place in it of the barbarians, Batavian and British as well as German, who are prominent in his writings. But Decline and Fall, at first sight a fifth-century narrative, had arisen as a concept both before and after Tacitus, writing at the end of the first century. If we are to understand what Gibbon in his text was doing with the linked but non-identical concepts of Tacitean historiography and the Decline and Fall of the Roman Empire, we must trace their origins and transmissions through ancient, Christian and Enlightened historiography to the points at which they were inherited by Gibbon with such mixed consequences. Ancient predictions, which later became explanations, of Roman decline must be studied in the ancient setting where they took shape, and then pursued through the long silences of what Gibbon termed 'modern history' and we 'the Christian millennium', until they re-emerge in early modern Europe to constitute the Decline and Fall.

PART I

*The First Decline and Fall: Ancient perceptions*

CHAPTER 2

# Alibi quam Romae: *the Tacitean narrative*

(I)

Gibbon's narrative of Antonine decline – following his portrayal of Antonine efflorescence – begins from the murder of Commodus in the year 180. For the ensuing period he lacks the guidance of any classical historian, and it is a question whether he will meet with another deserving that name. The emperors from Commodus to Diocletian were known to him initially through the Greek Dio Cassius, writing under the later Severi, whom he came to consider a 'slavish historian',[1] and subsequently through the *Historia Augusta*, a compilation of the time of Diocletian, of which he held an even lower opinion.[2] These were indeed his main sources for the earlier period, that from Nerva through Marcus Aurelius, which he was resolved to consider the happiest in the history of mankind (his horizon not extending south of Mediterranean Africa or east of the Persian empire). It is significant, as he himself remarked, that no historian had dealt with this age of prosperity; history itself might be no more than 'a register of the crimes, follies and misfortunes of mankind',[3] and when mankind was for once happy, other skills were needed to report it. The great – at least the classical – historians, furthermore, had recorded the crimes, follies and misfortunes of the rulers of mankind. Nothing could be less true of Roman historiography than the cliché that history is written only in the service of the ruling order. The classical historians had written in semi-opposition, rendering immortal the grumbles of a dying senatorial elite, and they had ceased their labours about the time when Nerva instituted that eighty years' peace between the senators on the Capitoline hill and the Caesars on the Palatine which was part of the secret of Antonine prosperity. Suetonius' lives of the 'twelve Caesars' run from Julius to Domitian, and it was the crisis at the murder of the

---

[1] *DF*, IV, ch. 44, n. 38; Womersley, 1994, II, p. 787.
[2] *EEG*, p. 131.    [3] *DF*, I, ch. 3; Womersley, 1994, I, p. 102.

latter which moved Tacitus to write histories looking back to Nero, and beyond Nero to Tiberius, remarking that he would carry the story to the happier days of Nerva and Trajan if he lived so long and if it remained safe to do so[4] – conditions of which at least one must have remained unfulfilled.

Classical historiography therefore told a dark story of the negation of its own values; it was a problem for Tacitus and his successors that an art which should flourish only in freedom attained greatness in recording its loss. It was a problem, and at the same time a stimulus and an opportunity, for Gibbon that he had no classical guide to the periods with which he resolved to deal. Antonine decay was recorded by historians he on the whole despised, but if historiography ranked among the classical arts, Antonine prosperity was in a sense post-classical – a beginning of decline? In his autobiographies written later, Gibbon recalled how he had followed 'the classics as low as Tacitus', and thereafter 'plunged into the ocean of the Augustan history, and in the descending series' journeyed 'from Dion Cassius to Ammianus Marcellinus . . . the last age of the western Caesars'.[5] None of these writers after Tacitus ranked as a master (though he did not lack respect for Ammianus) and since Gibbon was himself a neo-classical and early-modern historian, he was under some obligation to seek out a master and begin where he had left off. Tacitus was that master for a complex of reasons. He had written in the time of Nerva, where Suetonius too had left off and the lost books of Ammianus Marcellinus (as Gibbon would know) had begun. His writings marked an end of classical Latinity, and indicated reasons why it could no longer flourish; even the post-Nervan peace might not have been free – or unhappy? – enough for historiography to flourish, and might be no more than a sunset of ancient literature. Finally, Tacitus was in Gibbon's eyes the greatest, and most philosophical, of the Latin historians. In earlier chapters we considered how he was held to have travelled furthest into the arcana of power and the human heart.[6] His writings on barbarism and barbarians (to be considered later) were classical accounts of that state of society. We have next to examine how it was that he supplied Gibbon with an almost over-satisfactory explanation of the weaknesses in

---

[4] '*Quod si vita suppeditet, principatum divi Nervae et imperium Traiani, uberiorem securioremque materiam, senectuti reposui*' (*Histories*, 1, i). ['Yet, if my life but last, I have reserved for my old age the history of the deified Nerva's reign and of Trajan's rule, a richer and less perilous subject,'; trans. Clifford H. Moore, 1968, pp. 4–5]. It may be asked whether 'reign' and 'rule' adequately convey the force of '*principatus*' and '*imperium*'.

[5] *Memoirs*, pp. 146–7. Cf. *NCG*, pp. 399–400.     [6] *EEG*, pp. 232–4; *NCG*, pp. 9–10.

imperial structure which were to begin accounting for the First Decline and Fall.

(II)

Tacitus was the chief, but by no means the only Roman historian of the classical period in Gibbon's intellectual field. In assessing their presence, and the accounts of their own history which they left in European minds, the modern reader has constantly to contend with two problems. The first is the incomplete and accidentally selected condition of their textual legacy. Many histories are known to have existed but have disappeared, and most texts that we have are imperfect and incomplete, derived from medieval Latin or Byzantine collections. There arose in the nineteenth century – and were quite unknown to Gibbon – the fearsome sciences of *Quellenkritik* and *Quellenforschung*, consisting in part of the minute reconstruction of vanished texts from quotations, allusions and philological evidence. This aside, and only partly checked by it, European reading has over the centuries necessarily put together a selective image of Roman historiography, based on interpretations and collocations of the texts that survive. When we ask what accounts of their own history Romans constructed and transmitted to Renaissance and Enlightened scholars, it is on these we are forced to rely. The second obstacle between us and Roman historiography is its incurably rhetorical and moralist character. Designed by and for orators expounding the virtues and failings of great men, it is not only confined as to subject-matter to the political and military (sometimes the philosophical) elites who produced and consumed it; it tells its stories primarily in terms of the moral (and political) goodness or wickedness, strength or weakness, virtue or corruption, of its principal actors, and only secondarily, if at all, in terms of changes in the political, or processes in the social or cultural, structures of the worlds in which they acted.

It is possible, however, to overstate this antithesis to the mindset of the modern historian. The orators and moralists of antiquity were citizens, conscious that they were members of political societies held together by laws and institutions, manners and religious observances; we shall find at least one case of awareness that the city had a material substructure. From Athenian philosophy they had acquired the knowledge that political society could be differentiated into form and substance, *politeia* and *politeuma*, and that it was theoretically conceivable, as well as painfully obvious to experience, that a *politeia* might undergo change and decay, might disappear or be transformed into some other. Ancient historiography is anything but lacking in that sense of macronarrative and systemic change which holds the great modern histories together; what is lacking, or only occasionally present, is the archival and philological research which transforms historiography into the archaeological pursuit of past states of society. When we find a Roman historian engrossed in the disappearance of a past system, therefore, it is likely that his awareness of it originates in rhetoric and the speech among citizens, rather than in research into their recorded past; we must enquire into the capacity of such speech to collect, organise and transmit the information out of which the image of a past could be created.

It seems fair to state that in the two series of histories we have from Tacitus there is very little political history, if by that we mean the history of human actions in a working and legitimised political system. Tacitus supplies histories of human behaviour after the breakdown of such a system, when there are no legitimate means of contestation for power and it is concentrated in the irresponsible hands of a few, from which the only appeal is to violence and the intervention of military force. He offers a series of studies in behaviour under these conditions, its deviousness, perversity, brutality and recurrently suicidal folly, which have made him renowned in the historiography of the human heart as we wish it were not but know that it is. But, it could still be said, this is not politics but the breakdown of politics (though if we look at the history of politics we shall find the Tacitean dimension always present). It is the history of humans desiring power and struggling for it, at a point where the intrigues of the palace mesh with the brutality of military force. There no longer exists, but it is believed and remembered that there recently did exist, a political system in which the contest could be carried on according to rules and with some sense of shared values and mutual respect. Tacitus is the first historian of unmitigated corruption, of a world in which such a politics has existed but exists no longer; as Gibbon remarked, a consequence is that one lives under a tyranny defined, and rendered more intolerable, by the knowledge that there was once such a thing as liberty.[7]

The absence of politics from the *Histories* and the *Annals* is underlined when we contrast Tacitus with the historian who has become his classical opposite. Titus Livius known to us as Livy, from Patavium known to us as Padua, lived in Rome in the days of Caesar Augustus and – not being of the elite engaged in active politics – devoted his life to writing

---

[7] *DF*, 1, 3; Womersley, 1994, 1, p. 107.

a history of Rome *ab urbe condita*, since the foundation of the city to days near his own.[8] He disregarded whatever convention may have enjoined that the historian should write of events in which he had participated or known the participants and witnesses, and was therefore as much archaeologist (in the ancient sense) as historian; but his genre is that of heroic and exemplary narrative throughout. Like others of his time, he saw himself as holding up the mirror of ancient virtue before the eyes of degenerate moderns, who could endure neither their vices nor the remedies for them; but whether this made him a critic or an apologist of the Augustan principate is not easy to tell. More than half of his text has been lost, and it so happens that what we have is the more ancient part of the narrative, from the legendary days of the kings and the founding fathers of the republic, through the wars against the Samnites for supremacy in central Italy, the Carthaginians for supremacy in Spain and Africa, and the Macedonians for supremacy in Greece and the Hellenised kingdoms of Alexander's successors. Livy is a historian of empire and of the republican virtue which made empire possible. His defective text does not reach the civil wars in which the republic's control of empire broke down and the republic came under the rule of emperors, but we know he knew that was the end of the story. Perhaps this is one reason why he wrote the sentence which Gibbon, who admired Tacitus above Livy, nevertheless placed on the title page of the *Decline and Fall's* first volume.

Jam provideo animo, velut qui, proximis littori vadis inducti, mare pedibus ingrediuntur, quicquid progredior, in vastiorem me altitudinem, ac velut profundum invehi; et crescere pene opus, quod prima quaeque perficiendo minui videbatur.

[I feel like someone who has been introduced into shallow waters near the shore and is now advancing into the sea. I picture myself being led on into vaster, one might say unplumbable, depths with every forward step. The task undertaken seemed to grow less with the completion of each of the early stages; now, in anticipation, it seems almost to increase as I proceed.][9]

Livy prefixed these words to his thirty-first book, Gibbon to his first volume. The Latin author had reached the end of the Carthaginian wars and was about to embark on the Macedonian. He was therefore daunted by an immense expansion of both narrative and empire; but

---

[8] Syme, 1958, I, pp. 137–41, for Livy in his Roman setting; Kelley, 1998, pp. 56–60, for his place in grand tradition (pp. 283–4 for bibliography).

[9] Livy, XXXI; McDonald, trans. Henry Bettenson, 1976, I, p. 23. Womersley, 1994, I, p. [29].

the destruction of Carthage was the occasion of a famous prophecy that Rome's greatness also would come to an end,[10] and there was a rhetoric which equated the expansion of empire with its self-destruction. If Gibbon, fixing himself at the unsteady date of AD 180, was daunted by the prospect of relating the decline and fall of the empire, Livy had before him, though he does not here mention, the decline and fall of the republic, and we do not know how far he was reassured by Augustus as saviour of society.

If it has been possible to regard Livy as something of a complacent Augustan,[11] it has been and is easier to think of him as an idealist republican. His surviving texts reach the point where the republic was about to become a Mediterranean and Syrian-Egyptian world empire, but we have not his account of the disruption of the republic that began in the second century BC; we must guess at it from uninstructive summaries which survive of his lost later books.[12] What we have is history *ab urbe condita*, from the legendary beginnings to the triumph over Macedon, and it narrates deeds of republican virtue: those of the founders and the early heroes, leading to the extraordinary solidarity which – as Polybius had already argued – held the republic together in the face of internal strife and external defeats, and gave it the resilience that enabled conquest and empire. This virtue was military and political, actualised in deeds of war, speech, legislation and decision; it was senatorial, though displayed by plebeians as well as patricians, and Livy is never really able to advance tribunes to an exemplary role. The word exemplary is of course crucial; the tales he has to tell display a virtue which is to be imitated, and a great many of them are without doubt legendary – as Livy himself may have been aware – intended to generate virtue rather than to display the arcana of statecraft. There is reason to suppose that Livy aimed to exhibit virtue to an age which had lost it, so that only the benign tutelage of Augustus could preserve what of it could be preserved, and it has always been thought that his history of the republic is ideal, concerned with its public face rather than its inner machinations.

It is possible, however, to overstate this interpretation. The reader may find in Livy, as far back as the exemplary tales of Brutus and Virginius, accounts of situations which are recognisably political: encounters between opposed attitudes and interests – patrician and plebeian, Roman and Samnite – in which something not only can be said for each side,

[10]  Below, p. 35.
[11]  Syme, 1958, 1, p. 141; Syme, 1939, pp. 463–4; evaluations of Livy which do not go quite so far.
[12]  Schlesinger, 1959.

but actually is said by it in the pairs of opposed speeches, dear to the rhetorical historian, where the motives of the protagonists are seen to be not unmixed. This is so, in the first place, because Livy is giving us the history, no doubt idealised, of a political society in which such encounters were possible, antagonists could respect one another, and the historian could see both sides of a question if the political actors themselves had failed to do so. Such a society was deemed to have disappeared by the time of Tacitus, and this is what is meant by saying that the idealist Livy writes a political history which the realist Tacitus despairs of seeing again.[13] In the second place, Livy can write these narratives because rhetoric is the instrument of the historian, as it is the medium of speech and action in the republic. In debate, either side states its own case and gives its own counsel; in narrative, the historian exercises the privilege of stating it for them. Rhetoric in action can be brutally unfair, distorting, mendacious, even murderous; in historiography, the author who uses it to state both sides of a question can slant it in favour of one answer. The senators usually have the last word against the tribunes, the Romans against the Samnites; and there are those excluded from the world of free speech altogether. If the Samnites speak to the Romans as their moral equals and almost their other selves, the Gauls are irrational barbarians and the Carthaginians sinister aliens, while within the city the voices of craftsmen, women and slaves are heard as seldom and as distortedly as one would expect. For all of this, rhetoric is the instrument of narrative and even dialectic, as far as these things emerge. Two voices are heard, two actions are attempted, and the narrative is the outcome of this encounter, from which neither actor may emerge unchanged. The historian meanwhile has exercised the privilege of stating both cases and narrating both initiatives, and may consider his own judgement of the actions and speeches he has imagined. There is a kind of historiography which presupposes a society open enough to speak with two voices.

## (III)

It is this kind of historiography, of rhetoric, and of politics which Tacitus tells us no longer exists in his own time. Both the *Histories* and the *Annals* open by stating that historians formerly wrote with freedom and

---

[13] See however Syme, 1958 (n. 11 above) for the point that Livy had no experience of political action.

impartiality, but have since succumbed to fear and flattery, so that the latter-day historian faces the problem of establishing his own credentials.

Nam post conditam urbem octingentos et viginti prioris aevi multi auctores rettulerunt, dum res populi Romani memorabantur pari eloquentia ac libertate: postquam bellatum apud Actium atque omnem potentiam ad unum conferri pacis interfuit, magna illa ingenia cessere; simul veritas pluribus modis infracta, primum inscitia rei publicae ut alienae, mox libidine adsentandi aut rursus odio adversus dominantis. Ita neutris cura posteritatis inter infensos vel obnoxios.

[Many historians have treated of the earlier period of eight hundred and twenty years from the founding of Rome, and while dealing with the Republic they have written with equal eloquence and freedom. But after the battle of Actium, when the interests of peace required that all power should be concentrated in the hands of one man, writers of like ability disappeared; and at the same time historical truth was impaired in many ways: first, because men were ignorant of politics as not being any concern of theirs; later, because of their passionate desire to flatter; or again, because of their hatred of their masters. So between the hostility of the one class and the servility of the other, posterity was disregarded.][4]

Tacitus goes on to say that he has lived under too many emperors to be committed for or against any one of them, while under Nerva and Trajan the prince can endure to hear free speech and truth. But it is not enough for the historian to convince others of his integrity; he must also find ways of writing a new kind of narrative. The question is not only how he is to write history under a monopoly of power; it is how citizens are to perform actions, and what manner of actions can be performed, to furnish the matter of historical narrative. If actions are no longer plural, public, contentious, expressed in rhetoric and analysable by constructing it, how are they performed and how may they be narrated? Tacitus gives us to understand that under monopolised power rhetoric itself decays; instead of Cicero and Cato debating opposite courses in a free assembly, we have the noble but unreal Stoic Helvidius Priscus accusing Eprius Marcellus of subservience to the dead Domitian and Marcellus defending himself successfully before an assembly at once corrupt and realistic.[5] But if historiography is a branch of rhetoric, and depends upon a politics of rhetoric for both its subject-matter and its discourse, what kind of history can be written in a world deprived of public speech and action?

There might be a narrative of how this deprivation had occurred; but it could not be confined to a narrative of the loss of liberty alone. Freedom of speech – if that is an adequate term for a political culture based on speech

[4]  Tacitus, *Histories*, I, i; trans. Moore, 1968, p. 3. Cf. *Annals*, I, i.
[5]  Tacitus, *Histories*, IV, vi; Syme, 1958, I, pp. 101, 187, 212.

and action – had existed in a republic; that republic had disappeared by the time of Actium, when the civil wars of the republic and its empire had made necessary the monarchy known as the principate. Under that form of rule, free action and free historiography had been impaired; but this did not mean the disappearance of events and processes whose calamitous history needed to be written. The spectacle of Domitian's last years, and the crisis following his death which had obliged Nerva to nominate Trajan as his successor – it was not yet known that this would inaugurate eighty years of peace – had moved Tacitus to begin writing a history[16] whose centre-piece as we have it is an earlier crisis of the same order: that of AD 69–70, when the suicide of the emperor Nero had brought an end of the Julio-Claudian succession of rulers descending from Augustus the founder of the principate, and had touched off a series of pronunciamentos by provincial commanders and civil wars in Italy and Rome itself, settled by the victory of Flavius Vespasianus, whose sons had succeeded him until the misconduct of the younger, Domitian, brought about the crisis resolved by Nerva and Trajan. Tacitus had declared his intention of carrying his narrative as far as this happy final outcome, but if he ever did his text is lost; we have only those sections which reach the victory of Vespasian. The mutilated condition of his work emphasises the importance of his decision to begin his narrative with the downfall of Nero and the wars following it.

What had happened at the death of Nero, had been averted at the death of Domitian, and unknown to Tacitus was to happen again at the death of Commodus, was the murder or suicide of a degenerate prince incompetent in palace politics, followed by the intervention, first of the praetorian guards – who had acted earlier still, at the death of Caligula – then of the frontier armies in a struggle over the succession which the senate was powerless to resolve. It was of this that Tacitus had written words that may contain the heart of his meaning for Gibbon:

> evulgato imperii arcano posse principem alibi quam Romae fieri;[17]

[There was revealed that *arcanum* of state, the discovery that emperors might be made elsewhere than at Rome;][18]

that is, by proclamation on the part of a provincial army, which must then fight it out with rival armies as far as Rome itself.

---

[16] Syme, 1958, I, chs. i–ii, vi, xi, for a study of Nerva, Trajan and Tacitus' decision to write. He suggests that Nerva's position was insecure and the adoption of Trajan a means of satisfying the legions and neutralising the praetorians.

[17] *Histories*, I, iv, Moore, 1968, pp. 8–9.   [18] Moore, 1968, pp. 10–11.

This *arcanum*, though cited nowhere in Gibbon's early chapters,[19] was of central importance to Gibbon, as one key to the process by which the city was ruined and abandoned by its own empire; the historical process he had resolved to write. Of no less importance was Tacitus' decision to explain, or approach, 96–98 by going back to 69–70, since Gibbon's knowledge of later history informed him that the happy age of Trajan and the Antonines had ended with the death of Commodus and a third crisis more like the first than the second. The *arcanum* had operated to produce a fresh cycle of wars among provincial commanders, ending not with a Vespasian or a Trajan, but with a decisive transformation in the empire's structure and its capacity to defend its frontiers against external as well as internal enemies. Tacitus had therefore supplied Gibbon with a key explanation of the first Decline and Fall, but at the same time with an irresolvable problem in deciding when to begin narrating it. The *arcanum* offered an explanation equally valid of all three crises – 180, 96–98, 69–70 – and of others after them. Gibbon had resolved to begin at 180, not at the end of Tacitus' surviving narrative or at the end of the process he had witnessed and intended to narrate, but at the end of the phase in Roman history of which his writing marked the beginning. Tacitus had made this possible for Gibbon, but his was a treacherous gift. Gibbon must constantly ask himself why he had begun at the end of a narrative whose causal structure explained earlier crises, any one of which might be deemed the beginning of Decline and Fall. As we know, he once declared that he should have begun at the fall of Nero – or, for reasons we shall presently explore, earlier still – but had he done so, the same *arcanum* would have operated, and the story of Decline and Fall might begin anywhere.

The case for 180 as point of departure lies elsewhere. It offered, not a peculiar explanation of the Decline, but an opportunity to portray the happiness and prosperity of a world that declined and fell for reasons – a 'secret poison' – inherent in its own structure. The question is whether Tacitus' *arcanum* and Gibbon's secret poison are one and the same. The eighty years from Nerva to Marcus Aurelius represented a suspension of the *arcanum*, but the life and death of Commodus showed that it continued to operate. If its causes could be carried back to Augustus – and there emerged a narrative carrying them back even further – the seeds of decline and fall were there from the beginning, and it was possible

---

[19] He cited it, apparently for the first time, in a chapter published in 1788, with reference to the struggles among the successors. *DF*, v, ch. 50, n. 178.

to relate the whole history of the empire as that of their latency and increasing agency; as if the empire at its most prosperous had been aboriginally engaged in its own decline. This was the problem faced, and found insoluble, by Gibbon in deciding where he ought to begin, and it might be argued that in the end he could escape it only by transforming 'the decline and fall of the empire' into 'the triumph of barbarism and religion'. The legacy of Tacitus was hugely stimulating and hugely problematic; while in ensuing chapters we shall see medieval and Renaissance historians wrestling with the no less problematic legacy of Sallust.

(IV)

The 'year of the four emperors' had a prehistory which could and should be written. Tacitus therefore turned back in time and in his next work, known to us as the *Annals*, constructed a history (most of which we have) running from the death of Augustus to the death of Nero, when the earlier-written *Histories* take up the story. It is a history of Augustus' four successors in his own family, whom we call the Julio-Claudians; it is also a history of the principate, the ruling institution he founded, and of what went wrong with it; a history of moral failure due to a flawed institution. The root of the evil could be said to lie in the *imperator*'s monopoly of military power, exercised without reference to the senate. This reduced the senators to a position of privileged impotence which they deeply resented, and at the same time undermined the efforts of the *imperator* to legitimise himself as *princeps*, holding a variety of republican magistracies which amounted to another kind of monopoly, but was robbed of meaning and the power to legitimise by the impotence of the senate. This led to corruption all round, itself reducible to the hypocrisy imposed on all parties by the pretence that the republic was still in existence. The senators combined servility with resentment; the *princeps* (who was also *imperator*) was unable to endure their mingled flattery and hatred, or the knowledge that his role lacked the legitimacy which alone could have reassured him in exercising it. Tacitus' Tiberius may be a semi-tragic figure, corrupted and destroyed by the hypocrisy imposed upon him, which he fully recognises for what it is. The situation was worsened by the circumstance that the office of *princeps et imperator*, being unprecedented, was neither elective nor hereditary. Since it rested on an abdication of power by the senate, that body could determine neither how the office should pass from dead hands to living, nor whether it should in fact continue; and the senate lacked control over the legions, which might act as agents

in the succession. On the other hand, the principate was not in law
what it was in fact, the *dynasteia* of a single family. Roman politics were
nothing if not familial, and soldiers were disposed to favour the sons of
respected commanders; but there was no rule of primogeniture, nor any
body of customs regulating familial succession; nor could one such have
been recognised by republican law had it existed. In these circumstances,
competition to determine the succession to supreme authority must go
on within the complex structure of marriages, offspring and intimates
inhabiting the Julio-Claudian household on the Palatine hill; and as we
derive the words 'emperor' and 'prince' from *imperator* and *princeps*, so
*palatinum* has given us 'palace', another key term in the vocabulary of
European kingship – though the word 'king' is itself deeply un-Roman.

The concept of the palace is older than the word. Deioces the Mede
in Herodotus passes from giving judgements in the open air to secluding
himself within a ring of buildings, where he can be reached only through
written messages and sends out agents to execute his will and inform him
of what his subjects are doing, saying and thinking. The palace is both
a grandiose sign of power and a system of chambers and corridors that
determine access to the prince – as they still do in the White House – and
may be used by the prince to control his counsellors and ministers, or
by them to control him. A literature of the palace exists in most monar-
chically governed empires – Han Fei Tzu, Kautilya; Tacitus is unusual
in writing it from the standpoint of a vanished republican alternative.
There is a common assumption that as one draws closer to the inner-
most sanctum, the competition for power grows more ungoverned and
homicidal. It is of course no accident that Deioces is a Mede, and the
western imagination has long peopled the palace with viziers, harems,
eunuchs and the sexual trappings of 'oriental despotism'. This image is
without doubt unjust to those it designates 'orientals'; it is not necessarily
so to despots, a species otherwise identifiable; and in Tacitus we have an
account of them which owes little to images of the 'orient'. The sexual
component of which harems and eunuchs remind us comes into being
when the prince is expected to beget those who may succeed him, and
there arises competition between women intriguing on behalf of their
sons; in Tacitus the sinister matriarch Livia, the wife of Augustus, who
may go as far as poison in the interests of Tiberius, her son by a previous
marriage. The idea that the intervention of women is a malignant in-
trusion of the sexual upon the political is of course part of the literature
of patriarchy; Tacitus, however, sees it arising as a consequence, not a
cause, of the divorce of the principate from republican legitimacy.

It is because of this divorce that succession becomes uncontrollably important, and heirs presumptive and competitive develop personalities shaped in an environment at once secluded, over-privileged and insecure. The combination of unmitigated power and perpetual fear may disorder their exercise of office should they succeed to it; their conduct may be manic, as with Caligula or Nero, or depressive as with Tiberius or perhaps Domitian, tending to the exhibitionism of power in the former case or to gloom, suspicion and withdrawal in the latter. In both cases they fit the classical portrait of the tyrant, and there may occur reigns of terror among the inhabitants of the palace and the senatorial aristocracy with whom convention obliges the *princeps* to live on terms of apparent social equality. These waves of unpredictable homicide further undermine the prince's personality and leave him isolated; he may end in murder or suicide, and it will occur to the armies of which he is nominally the head that there is a vacancy of power and that no agency but their own is capable of filling it. This is the point at which Tacitus' *arcanum* is revealed; but we can now see that *posse principem alibi quam Romae fieri* condenses the reality by omitting some of it. An army may indeed proclaim an *imperator* wherever it happens to be; but to make him a *princeps* it must still march to Rome, do battle with its competitors, deal with the praetorians and overawe the senate. The empire still has a centre, and the history of how power came to be exercised from points to which Rome became increasingly irrelevant has yet to begin. Gibbon will need a post-Tacitean narrative to continue the history of Decline and Fall. The *arcanum imperii* turns our attention towards the provinces, where the legions were encamped and which were the reason for their existence; empire returns to the story, and we remember that it was because of empire that there was a principate at all. The Tacitean narrative's weakness in our eyes is that it equates Roman history with history at Rome; neither Tacitus nor Gibbon will quite overcome this, but with the *arcanum imperii* we begin to see Rome at the mercy of its provinces, though this may not be enough to endow the provinces with a history of their own. By 'the provinces' we in fact still mean 'the provincial armies'; it is they who make the fatal discovery; and there are two passages from Book I of the *Histories* which underline what is happening in history and to it. In Chapters viii–xi there is a survey of the state of the provinces at the moment when Galba declared himself emperor. Sir Ronald Syme, a great Tacitean scholar of the twentieth century, observed that this was the first survey of its kind in Roman historiography, and we shall find Gibbon conducting one of his own in the first chapter of the *Decline and Fall*.[20] Tacitus' objective, however, was simply to say that Galba ought to have considered the state of the provincial armies; he had himself been proclaimed *imperator* by the legions in Spain, Vitellius would come against Otho with the legions of Germany, and Vespasian against Vitellius with those of Syria and the Danubian frontier. Each of these armies had discovered the *arcanum* in its own way. In Chapter lxxxiv the transitory emperor Otho, appealing to the troops at Rome for their support against Vitellius, makes use of language suicidally mistaken according to Tacitus, unconsciously prophetic according to Gibbon. He says:

Nationes aliquas occupavit Vitellius, imaginem quandam exercitus habet, senatus nobiscum est: sic fit ut hinc res publica, inde hostes rei publicae constiterint. Quid? Vos pulcherrimam hanc urbem domibus et tectis et congestu lapidum stare creditis? Muta ista et inanima intercidere ac reparari promisca sunt: aeternitas rerum et pax gentium et mea cum vestra salus incolumitate senatus firmatur. Hunc auspicato a parente et conditore urbis nostrae institutum et a regibus usque ad principes continuum et immortalem, sicut a maioribus accepimus, sic posteris tradamus; nam ut ex vobis senatores, ita ex senatoribus principes nascuntur.

[Vitellius has won over some peoples; he has a certain shadow of an army, but the senate is with us. And so it is that on our side stands the state, on theirs the enemies of the state. Tell me, do you think that this fairest city consists of houses and buildings and heaps of stone? Those dumb and inanimate things can perish and readily be replaced. The eternity of our power, the peace of the world, my safety and yours, are secured by the welfare of the senate. This senate, which was established under auspices by the Father and Founder of our city and which has continued in unbroken line from the time of the kings even down to the time of the emperors, let us hand over to posterity even as we received it from our fathers. For as senators spring from your number, so emperors spring from senators.][21]

Otho could not be more wrong, Tacitus is indicating, if he believes the soldiers will fight for the senate, or that they think every soldier carries a toga in his knapsack and emperors are made by the senate. The *arcanum imperii* is out of the bottle, and Otho has helped to release it. But he is half right – Gibbon might have added – in perceiving that without the majesty of empire the city of Rome is no more than *domibus et tectis et congestu lapidum*. This was the spectacle that had moved Gibbon to begin writing the history of city and empire. What neither Otho nor Tacitus

[20] Syme, 1958, 1, p. 147; *DF*, 1, ch. 1; Womersley, 1994, 1, pp. 47–55; below, pp. 430–2.
[21] *Histories*, 1, lxxxiv; Moore, 1968, pp. 144–5.

knew was that armies and emperors would desert both city and senate, or that the ruined buildings would outlast the empire and its history. The implications of the Tacitean phrase, *alibi quam Romae*, provide the key to the *Histories*, the *Annals*, and the *Decline and Fall* alike.

The primary Tacitean narrative, that of senatorial servility and imperial delinquency, is now at the end of its usefulness. There remains to be written the full history of the *arcanum imperii*, that of how the armies came to be the determinant of events. It is a history of both civil war and empire, in which Augustus himself appears so late that he can be seen as trying less than successfully to bring it to an end. As Tacitus went back from Vespasian to Augustus, so we must go back from Augustus and Tacitus to the decline and fall of the Roman republic, of which that of the principate and the empire was a continuation.

# CHAPTER 3

# The Gracchan explanation: Appian of Alexandria and the unknown historian

(I)

We know that ancient historiography was a rhetorical art, built around the eloquent narrative and exposition of military, political and moral action. We also know that Gibbon inhabited a neo-classical culture, in which the same idea of narrative exercised great authority over the writing of history; but we have been exploring and elaborating the scheme proposed by Arnaldo Momigliano, in which narrative was joined by two other kinds of history, the philosophic and the antiquarian. The last of these may be further subdivided, into the critical apparatus proposed by philology and erudition, and the archaeology of past states of language, law and culture uncovered by grammarians, jurists and humanists. Out of these in particular, we suggested, emerged narratives of systemic change which provided historiography with general patterns of change and causation, and so became part of what we mean by philosophic history.[1] In studying the Greco-Roman historians of whom Gibbon made use, it is of some importance to decide how far such patterns can be found in them, how far these were read into them by early modern historians of whom Gibbon was one.

Patterns of general change imported into history were certainly not unknown in antiquity; it has been usual to think of them as Greek, imported into Roman history, and it happens that most surviving accounts of the Roman civil wars and the end of the republic are in Greek. Before that catastrophic process began, a Greek observer and witness, Polybius of Megalopolis, had made it his business to narrate, and in so doing to explain, the victory over Carthage which led to Roman control over Macedon, Hellas and Hellenised Syria and Egypt: the entire civilised world as Polybius and his Mediterranean hearers and readers understood

---

[1] For this see *NCG* at large.

it. He remarked that this was a phenomenon unknown in all previous history as seen by the Greek intellect, and in doing so may remind us of Thucydides declaring that the war between Athens and Sparta was other in character, and greater in scale, than any war preceding it. The Peloponnesian struggle, however, had led to the exhaustion of both parties and a new phase in history, imposed on the Greeks by non-Greek actors. Polybius knew that he was living in the last phase of that history, in which the Romans' conquest of the Macedonian successor-kingdoms was leaving them without an external rival – a condition of west Eurasian civilisation which was to endure until late in the history of Decline and Fall. Perhaps this is one reason why Polybius, with momentous consequences for European political theory, chose to explain the rise of Roman empire by the peculiar structure of Roman politics, finding in *libertas* the explanation of *imperium*, and situating Roman history itself within a philosophical topos of the necessary evolution of cities through greatness to decline: the famous *anakuklōsis politeiōn*. As is well known – though not of immediate importance to Gibbon – he expounded this process in terms of a theory of mixed government. There were three forms of government known to mankind, monarchy, aristocracy and democracy; each contained imperfections and must corrode and decline if left to itself; but the Romans had successfully combined all three, and this explained the astonishing resilience of their city, which survived every defeat and returned to victory and the extension of *imperium*. Rigorously applied, this formula might be made to predict the immortality of the Roman constitution; Polybius, however, declined this option and insisted on the inevitability of decline. He had explained external empire by internal stability; it was a question whether the primacy of internal causes would ensure stability when empire had become universal. Polybius held that it would not.

Ὅτι μὲν οὖν πᾶσι τοῖς οὖσιν ὑπόκειται φθορὰ καὶ μεταβολὴ σχεδὸν οὐ προσδεῖ λόγων· ἱκανὴ γὰρ ἡ τῆς φύσεως ἀνάγκη παραστῆσαι τὴν τοιαύτην πίστιν. δυεῖν δὲ τρόπων ὄντων, καθ' οὓς φθείρεσθαι πέφυκε πᾶν γένος πολιτείας, τοῦ μὲν ἔξωθεν, τοῦ δ' ἐν αὐτοῖς φυομένου, τὸν μὲν ἐκτὸς ἄστατον ἔχειν συμβαίνει τὴν θεωρίαν, τὸν δ' ἐξ αὐτῶν τεταγμένην. τί μὲν δὴ πρῶτον φύεται γένος πολιτείας καὶ τί δεύτερον, καὶ πῶς εἰς ἄλληλα μεταπίπτουσιν, εἴρηται πρόσθεν ἡμῖν, ὥστε τοὺς δυναμένους τὰς ἀρχὰς τῷ τέλει συνάπτειν τῆς ἐνεστώσης ὑποθέσεως κἂν αὐτοὺς ἤδη προειπεῖν ὑπὲρ τοῦ μέλλοντος. ἔστι δ', ὡς ἐγῷμαι, δῆλον. ὅταν γὰρ πολλοὺς καὶ μεγάλους κινδύνους διωσαμένη πολιτεία μετὰ ταῦτα εἰς ὑπεροχὴν καὶ δυναστείαν ἀδήριτον ἀφίκηται, φανερὸν ὡς εἰσοικιζομένης εἰς αὐτὴν ἐπὶ πολὺ τῆς εὐδαιμονίας συμβαίνει τοὺς μὲν βίους γίνεσθαι πολυτελεστέρους, τοὺς δ' ἄνδρας φιλονεικοτέρους τοῦ δέοντος περί τε τὰς ἀρχὰς καὶ τὰς ἄλλας ἐπιβολάς. οὗ γενομένου τῶν μὲν ὀνομάτων τὸ κάλλιστον ἡ πολιτεία μεταλήψεται, τὴν ἐλευθερίαν καὶ δημοκρατίαν, τῶν δὲ πραγμάτων τὸ χείριστον, τὴν ὀχλοκρατίαν

[That all existing things are subject to decay and change is a truth that scarcely needs proof; for the course of nature is sufficient to force this conviction on us. There being two agencies by which every kind of state is liable to decay, the one external and the other a growth of the state itself, we can lay down no fixed rule about the former, but the latter is a regular process. I have already stated what kind of state is the first to come into being, and what the next, and how the one is transformed into the other; so that those who are capable of connecting the opening propositions of this inquiry with its conclusion will now be able to foretell the future unaided. And what will happen is, I think, evident. When a state has weathered many great perils and subsequently attains to supremacy and uncontested sovereignty, it is evident that under the influence of long established prosperity, life will become more extravagant and the citizens themselves more fierce in their rivalry regarding office and other objects than they ought to be . . . When this happens, the state will change its name to the finest sounding of all, freedom and democracy, but will change its nature to the worst of all, mob-rule][2]

preparing the way, should the *anakuklōsis* repeat itself, for a return to monarchy, though a monarchy unlike that of the primeval kings. Polybius' philosophical history has enlarged the rhetorical narrative without transforming it, since the replacement of virtue by corruption and luxury has been described many times before and all that is new here is that we are at the end of a cycle and must return to its starting point. It is noteworthy, however, that when the mixed constitution becomes an empire and perishes, the cause is luxury, desire without restraint, and that the one of the three forms of government which now breaks free, becomes supreme and corrupts itself, should be democracy. Here, we may want to say, Polybius was the victim of his conceptual scheme and his class prejudices. Romans would very soon find themselves living in a process which historians would describe in very different terms: one of civil war, faction and brutal armed force, which would go on until the last surviving warlord set about rendering his power perpetual by preventing a return to war. The aristocratic critique of democracy, as ancient in rhetoric and philosophy as the Old Oligarch and Plato's *Republic*, would of course survive but has little relevance to Roman politics. The historians would have to construct a different narrative.

---

[2] Polybius, vi, lvii; trans. Paton, 1923, iii, pp. 396–9.

It is of course important that Polybius identifies universal empire, the condition of unchecked external sovereignty, as the immediate cause why the passions break free from restraint and begin the demolition of the internal balance. A hero of his narrative whom he served as philosopher and friend is Scipio Aemilianus the destroyer of Carthage, and we have – in other texts but clearly from Polybius – an account of how Scipio shed tears over the ruin he had made and quoted a verse foretelling the ruin of Troy, and when Polybius asked him why, he replied that he was thinking of the end of all great cities.[3] It is not clear whether they were foreseeing that the destruction of a rival would bring luxury and corruption to Rome, but it was open to posterity to read this into their exchange. From Carthage the Romans went on to establish hegemony over the Greek cities – Polybius, himself a Greek statesman, acted in this process as well as writing its history – to wars against Macedon and the Hellenistic dynasties – this was the point at which Livy felt himself advancing into a bottomless and boundless sea – and to renewed conquests in the far west against the Celtic and Iberian peoples of Spain, in which Scipio took a leading and dreadful part. Just as we do not know whether Tacitus outlived Trajan, we do not know whether Polybius witnessed the later episodes of his hero's career; but when their joint lives ended, Rome was already plunging into a crisis the consequence of empire, but not that which Polybius had foretold. Scipio Aemilianus was a close family relative of Tiberius and Gaius Gracchus; he died after the murder of the former, in circumstances which gave rise to rumour.[4]

We turn from a Greek to a historian both Roman and senatorial. From the time of the Gracchi, the history of Rome came to be written, and must have been widely experienced, as a history of civic violence, leading to civil war and the end of the republican government. Living towards the end of that process, the historian Gaius Sallustius Crispus, known to us as Sallust, left two short books which, through the accidents of textual survival, were to furnish late-antique, medieval and early modern culture[5] with a durable and even fundamental account of the 'first decline and fall' and the 'decline and fall' itself. Writing a fairly conventional prelude to his history of the conspiracy of Catiline in 64–63 BC,

---

[3] The story is in Appian and Diodorus, following Polybius, xxxviii, xxi, 1–2 (Walbank, 1972, pp. ii, 173–6; 1979, iii, pp. 722–4). Walbank differs from Eckstein, 1995, p. 268, as to how far Polybius thought of Fortune as a moral force.

[4] Appian, *Civil Wars*, iii, xx; White, 1912–13, iii, pp. 39–40.

[5] For Sallust in medieval culture see Smalley, 1971; for his role as late as the eighteenth century, Armitage 2000, ch. 5.

Sallust provided posterity with an account, more classically brief if less
analytically penetrating than Polybius', of the complex relations between *libertas*, *virtus* and *imperium*. Following the expulsion of the kings, he
says,

coepere se quisque magis extollere magisque ingenium in promptu habere.
Nam regibus boni quam mali suspectiores sunt semperque eis aliena virtus
formidulosa est. Sed civitas incredibile memoratu est adepta libertate quantum
brevi creverit; tanta cupido gloriae incesserat.[6]

[every man began to lift his head higher and to have his talents more in readiness.
For kings hold the good in greater suspicion than the wicked, and to them the
merit of others is always fraught with danger; still the free state, once liberty was
won, waxed incredibly strong and great in a remarkably short time, such was
the thirst for glory that had filled men's minds.][7]

It is the heroic ideal of citizenship; the purely agonistic ideal criticised
by Athenian philosophers and Christian saints. The function of liberty is
to release heroic energy; the condition of liberty is the free enjoyment and
pursuit of that energy. The free man, citizen and warrior, is consumed
by the thirst for glory, and will accept the harshest discipline and the
strictest frugality to fit himself for the exercise of freedom to pursue it.
In consequence, the free city becomes great in the exercise of empire
over others, but remains subject to fortune, the capricious power which
rules all things, even the memory of glory which seems to defy her (the
gender should be noted). The deeds of the Athenians were less glorious
than those of the Romans, and it is an accident of fortune that Athenian
writers had the genius to record them.[8] Fortune also has power to ensure
that not even the virtue born of freedom and the pursuit of glory will
endure.

Sed ubi labore atque iustitia res publica creavit, reges magni bello domiti,
nationes ferae et populi ingentes vi subacti, Carthago aemula imperii Romani
ab stirpe interiit, cuncta maria terraeque patebant, saevire fortuna et miscere
omnia coepit. Qui labores, pericula, dubias atque asperas res facile toleraverant,
eis otium, divitiae, optanda alias, oneri miseriaeque fuere.[9]

[But when our country had grown great through toil and the practice of justice,
when great kings had been vanquished in war, savage tribes and mighty peoples
subdued by force of arms, when Carthage, the rival of Rome's sway, had perished
root and branch, and all seas and lands were open, then Fortune began to grow

---

[6] Sallust, *Bellum Catilinae*, VII, 1–3, text in Rolfe, 1980, pp. 12–14.
[7] Trans. Rolfe, 1980, pp. 13–15.     [8] VIII, 3–5, Rolfe, 1980, pp. 14–17.
[9] X, 1–3, Rolfe, 1980, pp. 16–18.

cruel and to bring confusion into all our affairs. Those who had found it easy to bear hardships and dangers, anxiety and adversity, found leisure and wealth, desirable under other circumstances, a burden and a curse.][10]

We are looking at what became a 'first decline and fall' long antedating Tacitus or the events he described. Sallust goes on to a lengthy denunciation of corruption and luxury in the Roman nobles, which he clearly associates with the attainment of universal empire and sees as underlying both the conspiracy of Catiline – who attacks the corruption he intends to share – and the initial failures of the war against the North African king Jugurtha, who thinks the whole city of Rome is for sale. He does not analyse the problems of empire as conducive to republican decay, and his account is even more moralist than that of Polybius. Living at the time he did, Sallust is not a witness of the transformation of republic into principate, nor of course of the decay of empire itself; it was his readers in succeeding centuries who saw him as foretelling and explaining these effects. A minor lieutenant of Julius Caesar, he sympathises with Marius against Sulla, and his indictment of a corrupt nobility is probably directed against the faction of the *optimates* by a member of the no less corrupt faction of the *populares*.[11] But a series of textual accidents caused his history of the minor civil war against Catiline to become a 'Sallustian moment' typifying the republican decay and the rise of the Caesars. Alongside his history there survived the copious literature in which Cicero, the medieval and Renaissance archetype of republican virtue, eloquence and philosophy, glorified his own role in detecting and suppressing the conspiracy; and Sallust constructed speeches in which Cicero, Cato and Caesar debated whether Catiline's accomplices should be summarily executed (as Cato advocated and Cicero effected) or detained in prison (as Caesar proposed). This literary exercise, whatever its purpose, became in later centuries a contest between three great symbolic figures of the republic's final crisis; and though Sallust may have intended to clear his leader Caesar of complicity with Catiline, the soft line he attributed to him in the matter of the prisoners generally had the reverse effect, and contributed to the un-Tacitean view that Julius rather than Augustus Caesar was the first of the usurping emperors. It is the antithesis between glory and corruption, however, with the acquisition of empire at its hinge, that was to render Sallust a key figure in the shaping of 'decline and fall'.

[10] Trans. Rolfe, 1980, pp. 17–19.
[11] For Sallust's career in politics and war see Rolfe, 1980, pp. x–xii.

(11)

From this point we must pursue the narrative of the republic's self-destruction with the aid of historians writing once more in Greek, far from Rome and up to two and a half centuries later. Plutarch of Chaeronea, a contemporary of Tacitus, was more a biographer than a historian; Appian of Alexandria, a contemporary of Hadrian, was a historian of some originality of mind;[12] both are visibly turning into Greek an account of history shaped by Romans who knew Rome at first hand, presumably the authors of a Latin historiography now lost to us. The surviving epitomes or summaries of the lost books of Livy make it clear that he had covered in annalistic narrative form the entire period from Gracchus to Augustus with which Appian set out to deal;[13] but there is no evidence that Appian was using Livy, and we do not know who constructed the account of history he considered and relayed (as it happened) to us. It has been suggested that it was Asinius Pollio,[14] believed to have written a history of Augustus' coming to power in terms the reverse of complacent or supportive.[15] Whoever the unknown author, he supplied Appian with a remarkable narrative, analysing the history of the civil wars and the apparent triumph of the principate by means of a study of underlying social causes: the decay of the Roman republic's system of military colonisation and expansion.

Appian of Alexandria possessed a mind of his own. Somewhat unusually for his time, he concludes his introduction by informing his readers that if they wish to know any more about him, he has written an autobiography which is available to the public.[16] He also makes it known that his history is to relate the Roman conquest of the Mediterranean and European world, and begins it with a topographic survey of the empire by provinces, proceeding from Britain through the Pillars of Hercules and then – as befits a native of Egypt – along the African littoral, turning north and west through Asia and Europe to complete the circuit in Italy, Gaul and lower Germany.[17] This is more ambitious than the comparable survey in Tacitus; it is a survey of provinces rather than armies, and we shall be reminded of it when we study Gibbon's first chapter. It leads to Appian's further statement that his history is to have no unified chronology, but to proceed by regions; from the early history of Rome under the kings he will proceed to an Italian history, a Punic

---

[12] Gibbon owned two editions and an Italian translation of Appian's works (*Library*, p. 53). His citations are indexed by Womersley (1994, III, p. 1192).

[13] Schlesinger, 1959.      [14] Gabba, 1956, pp. 10–115; McCuaig, 1989, p. 156.

[15] Syme, 1939, *passim*.      [16] White, 1912–13, I, pp. 24–5.      [17] White, 1912–13, I, pp. 2–9.

history, a Greek history and so forth, dealing with each region as the Romans dealt with it and allowing the narratives to overlap with each other for the sake of completing each before turning to its successor.[18] Since we do not have the whole of his work, we cannot say how this worked out in practice. We have, almost in full, five books on the Civil Wars of Rome, which were to have ended with the defeat of Antony and Cleopatra at Actium; and this, says Appian, will serve as prelude to his history of Egypt[19] – which, again, we do not have but which was presumably a full history of Roman dealings with the Ptolemaic dynasty.

The narrative and the point of view would certainly have been Roman throughout, but Appian's willingness to tell each story separately gives some hint that he was aware of the experience of the conquered as well as the conquerors. In the Spanish history that has survived, he has his own way of presenting Scipio Aemilianus, Polybius' hero and the conqueror of Carthage and the Spanish town of Numantia.

Ἐμοὶ μὲν δὴ ταῦτα περὶ Νομαντίνων εἰπεῖν ἐπῆλθεν, ἐς τὴν ὀλιγότητα αὐτῶν καὶ φερεπονίαν ἀφορῶντι, καὶ ἔργα πολλά, καὶ χρόνον ὅσον διεκαρτέρησαν· οἱ δὲ πρῶτα μὲν αὐτούς, οἱ βουλόμενοι, διεχρῶντο, ἕτερος ἑτέρως· οἱ λοιποὶ δ᾽ ἐξῆεσαν τρίτης ἡμέρας ἐς τὸ δεδομένον χωρίον, δυσόρα-τοί τε καὶ ἀλλόκοτοι πάμπαν ὀφθῆναι, οἷς τὰ μὲν σώματα ἦν ἀκάθαρτα καὶ τριχῶν καὶ ὀνύχων καὶ ῥύπου μεστά, ὠδώδεσαν δὲ χαλεπώτατον, καὶ ἐσθὴς αὐτοῖς ἐπέκειτο πιναρὰ καὶ ἥδε καὶ οὐχ ἧσσον δυσώδης. ἐφαίνοντο δὲ τοῖς πολεμίοις ἐλεεινοὶ μὲν ἀπὸ τῶνδε, φοβεροὶ δ᾽ ἀπὸ τῶν βλεμμάτων· ἔτι γὰρ αὐτοὺς ἐνεώρων ἔκ τε ὀργῆς καὶ λύπης καὶ πόνου καὶ συνειδότος ἀλληλο-φαγίας.

Ἐπιλεξάμενος δ᾽ αὐτῶν πεντήκοντα ὁ Σκιπίων ἐς θρίαμβον, τοὺς λοιποὺς ἀπέδοτο, καὶ τὴν πόλιν κατέσκαψε, δύο μὲν τάσδε πόλεις δυσμαχωτάτας ἑλὼν στρατηγὸς ὅδε Ῥωμαίων, Καρχηδόνα μὲν αὐτῶν Ῥωμαίων ψηφισαμένων διὰ μέγεθος πόλεως τε καὶ ἀρχῆς καὶ εὐκαιρίαν γῆς καὶ θαλάσσης, Νομαντίαν δὲ σμικράν τε καὶ ὀλιγάνθρωπον, οὔπω τι Ῥωμαίων περὶ αὐτῆς ἐγνωκότων, αὐτός, εἴτε συμφέρειν Ῥωμαίοις ἡγούμενος, εἴτε ἄκρος ὢν ὀργὴν καὶ φιλόνεικος ἐς τὰ λαμβανόμενα, εἴθ᾽ ὡς ἔνιοι νομίζουσι, τὴν δόξαν ἡγούμενος διώνυμον ἐπὶ τοῖς μεγάλοις γίγνεσθαι κακοῖς· καλοῦσι γοῦν αὐτὸν οἱ Ῥωμαῖοι μέχρι νῦν, ἀπὸ τῶν συμφορῶν ἃς ἐπέθηκε ταῖς πόλεσιν, Ἀφρικανόν τε καὶ Νομαντῖνον. τότε δὲ τὴν γῆν τὴν Νομαντίνων τοῖς ἐγγὺς οἰκοῦσι διελών, καὶ ταῖς ἄλ-λαις πόλεσι χρηματίσας, καὶ εἴ τι ἦν ὕποπτον, ἐπιπλήξας τε καὶ ζημιώσας χρήμασιν, ἀπέπλευσεν ἐπ᾽ οἴκου.

[Reflecting upon their small numbers and their endurance, their valiant deeds and the long time for which they held out, it has occurred to me to relate these

---

[18]  White, 1912–13, I, pp. 18–23. The word translated as 'history' is the Greek *syngraphē*.
[19]  White, 1912–13, III, pp. 12–13.

particulars of the Numantine history. First of all, those who wished to do so killed themselves in various ways. Then the rest went out on the third day to the appointed place, a strange and shocking spectacle. Their bodies were foul, their hair and nails long, and they were smeared with dirt. They smelt most horribly, and the clothes they wore were likewise squalid and emitted an equally foul odour. For these reasons they appeared pitiable to their enemies, but at the same time there was something fearful in the expression of their eyes – an expression of anger, pain, weariness, and the consciousness of having eaten human flesh.

Having chosen fifty of them for his triumph, Scipio sold the rest and razed the city to the ground. So this Roman general overthrew two most powerful cities – Carthage, by decree of the Senate, on account of its greatness as a city and as an imperial power, and its advantages by land and sea; Numantia, small and with a sparse population, on his own responsibility, the Romans knowing nothing about the transaction as yet. He destroyed it either because he thought that it would be for the advantage of the Romans, or because he was a man of passionate nature and vindictive towards captives, or, some hold, because he thought that great calamities are the foundation of great glory. At any rate, the Romans to this day call him Africanus and Numantinus from the ruin he brought to these two places. Having divided the territory of the Numantines among their near neighbours and transacted certain business in the other cities, censuring or fining any whom he suspected, he sailed for home.][20]

Whatever the source Appian is using, the ancient world was not humanitarian by sentiment, and it is unusual to find descriptions of human suffering carried to the point of dehumanisation. This passage is not transcribed simply in order to add to the literature of anti-imperialism. Appian means something by including it, and it is reasonable to ask whether his intentions go beyond the rhetorical to the structural; does he mean us to infer some connection between empire and the fate of Rome? Scipio's triumphs are close in time to the failed reforms of the Gracchi, but these are recounted at a quite different point in the text – as we have it; it has been excerpted and reassembled, and we do not know how Appian's multi-faceted original may have presented itself. The Gracchan programme is concerned with the organisation of empire, in the homelands and at the grassroots from which it grew.

The five books of Appian's history of the Roman civil wars are the longest of those composing his multiplex history which have survived; it would be rash to say whether he made them the centrepiece of the whole work, or whether his Byzantine editors preserved them complete for this or some other reason. His work as a whole opens with a prelude

[20] White, 1912–13, I, pp. 292–5.

summarising the course of events from Tiberius Gracchus to Augustus, whose victory at Actium transforms the Roman *politeia* into a *monarchia* under *basileis* (Appian is unabashed by this equivalent of the Latin *reges*, which Romans refuse)[21] and marks the transition from Appian's Roman history (*syngraphē*) to his Egyptian, which we do not possess.[22] We know, then, that he thought of the civil wars as a single narrative, running from the Gracchi through Marius and Sulla, Pompey and Caesar, to Antony and Augustus, and having a recognisable outcome. What we do not yet know, and must be careful not to presuppose, is whether he thought, or his language allowed him to say, that this narrative related the effects of a single set of causes, and whether these were those that he seems to us to isolate in his opening sentences.

Ῥωμαίοις ὁ δῆμος καὶ ἡ βουλὴ πολλάκις ἐς ἀλλήλους περί τε νόμων θέσεως καὶ χρεῶν ἀποκοπῆς ἢ γῆς διαδατουμένης ἢ ἐν ἀρχαιρεσίαις ἐστασίασαν· οὐ μήν τι χειρῶν ἔργον ἔμφυλον ἦν, ἀλλὰ διαφοραὶ μόναι καὶ ἔριδες ἔννομοι, καὶ τάδε μετὰ πολλῆς αἰδοῦς εἴκοντες ἀλλήλοις διετίθεντο.

[The plebeians and Senate of Rome were often at strife with each other concerning the enactment of laws, the cancelling of debts, the division of lands, or the election of magistrates. Internal discord did not, however, bring them to blows; there were dissensions merely and contests within the limits of the law, which they composed by making mutual concessions, and with much respect for each other.][23]

Appian goes on to tell us that the secession to the Mons Sacer was non-violent, that Coriolanus' march on Rome was the act of an exile, and that both were peaceably settled. His point, which was to be dear to Machiavelli centuries later, might have been drawn from Livy or, if Appian did not read him, from some other history of Roman antiquity. It is noteworthy that this Alexandrian Greek thinks the course of Roman history needs to be known, and that there is no overt sign he was addressing the peoples of his ethnically and savagely divided city (he was a contemporary of the Bar-Kochba rebellion and the violence that it brought in the diaspora.)[24] His purpose is rhetorical and antithetical; he goes on:

ξίφος δὲ οὐδέν πω παρενεχθὲν ἐς ἐκκλησίαν οὐδὲ φόνον ἔμφυλον, πρίν γε Τιβέριος Γράκχος δημαρχῶν καὶ νόμους ἐσφέρων πρῶτος ὅδε ἐν στά-σει ἀπώλετο καὶ ἐπ' αὐτῷ πολλοὶ κατὰ τὸ Καπιτώλιον εἰλούμενοι περὶ τὸν νεὼν ἀνηρέθησαν. καὶ οὐκ ἀνέσχον ἔτι αἱ στάσεις ἐπὶ τῷδε τῷ μύσει,

[21] White, 1912–13, I, pp. 10–11.   [22] White, 1912–13, I, pp. 22–3.
[23] *Civil Wars*, introduction, 1, i; White, 1912–13, III, pp. 2–3.   [24] White, 1912–13, I, p. vii.

διαιρουμένων ἑκάστοτε σαφῶς ἐπ' ἀλλήλοις καὶ ἐγχειρίδια πολλάκις φερόν-
των κτιννυμένης τέ τινος ἀρχῆς ἐκ διαστήματος ἐν ἱεροῖς ἢ ἐκκλησίαις ἢ ἀγο-
ραῖς, δημάρχων ἢ στρατηγῶν ἢ ὑπάτων ἢ τῶν ἐς ταῦτα παραγγελλόντων ἢ
τῶν ἄλλως ἐπιφανῶν. ὕβρις τε ἄκοσμος ἐπεῖχεν αἰεὶ δι' ὀλίγου καὶ νόμων καὶ
δίκης αἰσχρὰ καταφρόνησις. προϊόντος δ' ἐς μέγα τοῦ κακοῦ, ἐπαναστάσεις
ἐπὶ τὴν πολιτείαν φανεραὶ καὶ στρατεῖαι μεγάλαι καὶ βίαιοι κατὰ τῆς πατρίδος
ἐγίγνοντο φυγάδων ἀνδρῶν ἢ καταδίκων ἢ περὶ ἀρχῆς τινος ἢ στρατοπέ-
δου φιλονικούντων ἐς ἀλλήλους. δυναστεῖαί τε ἦσαν ἤδη κατὰ πολλὰ καὶ
στασίαρχοι μοναρχικοί, οἱ μὲν οὐ μεθιέντες ἔτι τὰ πιστευθέντα σφίσιν ὑπὸ
τοῦ δήμου στρατόπεδα, οἱ δὲ καὶ κατὰ σφᾶς ἄνευ τοῦ κοινοῦ κατ' ἀλλήλων
ξενολογοῦντες. ὁπότεροι δ' αὐτῶν τὴν πόλιν προλάβοιεν, τοῖς ἑτέροις ἦν ὁ
ἀγὼν λόγῳ μὲν ἐπὶ τοὺς ἀντιστασιώτας, ἔργῳ δ' ἐπὶ τὴν πατρίδα.

[The sword was never carried into the assembly, and there was no civil butchery
until Tiberius Gracchus, while serving as tribune and bringing forward new
laws, was the first to fall a victim to internal commotion; and with him many
others, who were crowded together at the Capitol round the temple, were also
slain. Sedition did not end with this abominable deed. Repeatedly the parties
came into open conflict, often carrying daggers; and from time to time in the
temples, the assemblies or the forum, some tribune, or praetor, or consul, or
candidate for those offices, or some person otherwise distinguished, would be
slain. Unseemly violence prevailed almost constantly, together with shameful
contempt for law and justice. As the evil gained in magnitude open insurrections
against the government and large warlike expeditions against their country were
undertaken by exiles, or criminals, or persons contending against each other for
some office or military command. There arose chiefs of factions, quite frequently
aspiring to supreme power, some of them refusing to disband the troops entrusted
to them by the people, others even hiring forces against each other on their own
account, without public authority. Whenever either side first got possession of
the city, the opposition party made war nominally against their own adversaries,
but actually against their own country.][25]

Appian or his source or sources – the originality of this passage is
not the issue – is narrating a progressive degeneration. The massacre of
Tiberius and his followers was a lynching, but the violence escalates to
a point where it involves the use of armies, and these forces raised by
public authority are being employed not in the pursuit of faction or class
struggles within the city, but in the pursuit of ambitions for high command
which used to be sought by lawful means. Sulla, one of the most ruthless
of these chieftains, attempts a permanent settlement and lays down his
power as though it were a public office; but Pompey and Caesar resume
the story, and it is reserved for Augustus to impose monarchy, by which
time marches on Rome by disobedient armies have become wars fought

---

[25] *Civil Wars*, introduction, I, ii; White, 1912–13, III, pp. 4–7.

in the provinces for control of the whole empire. If Appian was involved in a *bellum Judaicum* under Trajan, he would be aware that it was a long way from being a *bellum Actiacum*.

This was to become – and may have remained – a crucial explanatory structure and narrative. If ambitious office-seekers refuse to disband the armies entrusted to them by the republic, the armies obey their commanders and not the republic. We pass from a moment, very likely ideal, at which the armies were composed of citizens, to one in which they no longer act as such, and the republic dissolves into a mere cockpit of political (or post-political) competition pursued by military means. To our eyes, the central problem is to explain how this happened to the armies, and we shall find, from Machiavelli and Harrington to Montesquieu and Gibbon, a narrative taking shape – and operating as substructure to the *Decline and Fall* – which explained it as the consequence of the defeat of Tiberius Gracchus, who had proposed measures to rectify a social problem, the maldistribution of lands occupied by the republic in Italy. It is right to ask how far this narrative explanation operated in ancient historiography, how far it was constructed by the early modern historians and theorists who then read it into the ancients; and we must read Appian's text, and enquire what texts may have preceded it, in search of answers to this question, relevant to our understanding of Gibbon.

At this point we should remind ourselves that this book is a history of historiography, not a history of Rome. We are concerned to see what patterns of historical explanation arose in Greco-Roman historical writing, not whether these reinforce our own efforts to understand what processes were taking place in Roman imperial society. For good or ill, we no longer employ the social-realist assumption that, if a process was taking place in social relations, it must automatically have found expression or been 'reflected' in the minds and language of articulate members of that society. The historiography therefore forms a field of study of its own; we enquire what was in it, not whether it conveyed a 'reality' which has not at this point been grasped. It does not follow, however, that we know nothing about ancient society but what its historians have to tell us; it was the achievement of archaeology and erudition to inform us that there are other sources. Nor is it the case that ancient historians had nothing to tell their hearers but what their rhetorical and linguistic structures told them. The authority of these structures was inordinate, and it may very well be that nothing could be inscribed in the texts which could not be mediated through rhetorical convention. But ancient as well as post-ancient societies possessed means of gathering and verbalising information about what was going on in the worlds they perceived and inhabited, means not reducible to rhetoric; this was certainly the case in a legalist and institutionalist society like that of the Roman republic; and it is an open question whether perceptions of change in society could be organised, expressed and blended with the language of rhetoric, to the point where narrative explanations could take shape and might resemble those constructed by the early moderns.

Appian had access to such an explanatory structure as regards the reforms proposed by Tiberius Gracchus. He begins his first book on the civil wars, once the prologue is completed, by telling us without further introduction that the context is that of an agrarian problem.

Ῥωμαῖοι τὴν Ἰταλίαν πολέμῳ κατὰ μέρη χειρούμενοι γῆς μέρος ἐλάμβανον καὶ πόλεις ἐνῴκιζον ἢ ἐς τὰς πρότερον οὔσας κληρούχους ἀπὸ σφῶν κατέλεγον. καὶ τάδε μὲν ἀντὶ φρουρίων ἐπενόουν, τῆς δὲ γῆς τῆς δορικτήτου σφίσιν ἑκάστοτε γιγνομένης τὴν μὲν ἐξειργασμένην αὐτίκα τοῖς οἰκιζομένοις ἐπιδιήρουν ἢ ἐπίπρασκον ἢ ἐξεμίσθουν, τὴν δ᾽ ἀργὸν ἐκ τοῦ πολέμου τότε οὖσαν, ἣ δὴ καὶ μάλιστα ἐπλήθυεν, οὐκ ἄγοντές πω σχολὴν διαλαχεῖν ἐπεκήρυττον ἐν τοσῷδε τοῖς ἐθέλουσιν ἐκπονεῖν ἐπὶ τέλει τῶν ἐτησίων καρπῶν, δεκάτη μὲν τῶν σπειρομένων, πέμπτη δὲ τῶν φυτευομένων. ὥριστο δὲ καὶ τοῖς προβατεύουσι τέλη μειζόνων τε καὶ ἐλαττόνων ζῴων. καὶ τάδε ἔπραττον ἐς πολυανδρίαν τοῦ Ἰταλικοῦ γένους, φερεπονωτάτου σφίσιν ὀφθέντος, ἵνα συμμάχους οἰκείους ἔχοιεν.

[The Romans, as they subdued the Italian peoples successively in war, used to seize a part of their lands and build towns there, or enrol colonists of their own to occupy those already existing, and their idea was to use these as outposts; but of the land acquired by war they assigned the cultivated part forthwith to the colonists, or sold or leased it. Since they had no leisure as yet to allot the part which then lay desolated by war (this was generally the greater part), they made proclamation that in the meantime those who were willing to work it might do so for a toll of the yearly crops, a tenth of the grain and a fifth of the fruit. From those who kept flocks was required a toll of the animals, both oxen and small cattle. They did these things in order to multiply the Italian race, which they considered the most laborious of peoples, so that they might have plenty of allies at home.][26]

Appian is simplifying the complicated world of the Roman colonies, of which some (this is itself a simplification) were Roman garrisons settled among resentful Italians, while others were composed of Italians admitted, by alliance or annexation, to various approaches to the condition of

---

[26] *Civil Wars*, i, i, 7; White, 1912–13, iii, pp. 14–15.

Roman citizens. His account of the settlement of sharecroppers on waste lands, however, leaves no doubt that this part of the process was intended to multiply an Italian population who would serve in the Roman armies, and that there was going on an annexation and assimilation of central Italy (not yet wholly Latin by speech) to the Roman military state, otherwise known as the republic. This was a difficult and contentious piece of imperialism, and part of Appian's narrative was to be devoted to the Social War of 91–88 BC, when the Italians rebelled against Roman domination, demanding either independence or a full and equal incorporation in the Roman state (a demand not without its resonances in the late eighteenth century of our era). Appian made it clear that he considered – no doubt he had Latin sources which agreed – that the Social War was an episode in the Civil Wars, that these followed the failure of the Gracchan reforms, and that these were intended to deal with an agrarian problem that arose from the failure of settlement by sharecropping.

ἐς δὲ τοὐναντίον αὐτοῖς περιήει. οἱ γὰρ πλούσιοι τῆσδε τῆς ἀνεμήτου γῆς τὴν πολλὴν καταλαβόντες καὶ χρόνῳ θαρροῦντες οὔ τινα σφᾶς ἔτι ἀφαιρήσεσθαι τά τε ἀγχοῦ σφίσιν ὅσα τε ἦν ἄλλα βραχέα πενήτων, τὰ μὲν ὠνούμενοι πειθοῖ, τὰ δὲ βίᾳ λαμβάνοντες, πεδία μακρὰ ἀντὶ χωρίων ἐγεώργουν, ὠνητοῖς ἐς αὐτὰ γεωργοῖς καὶ ποιμέσι χρώμενοι τοῦ μὴ τοὺς ἐλευθέρους ἐς τὰς στρατείας ἀπὸ τῆς γεωργίας περισπᾶν, φερούσης ἅμα καὶ τῆσδε τῆς κτήσεως αὐτοῖς πολὺ κέρδος ἐκ πολυπαιδίας θεραπόντων ἀκινδύνως αὐξομένων διὰ τὰς ἀστρατείας. ἀπὸ δὲ τούτων οἱ μὲν δυνατοὶ πάμπαν ἐπλούτουν, καὶ τὸ τῶν θεραπόντων γένος ἀνὰ τὴν χώραν ἐπλήθυε, τοὺς δ' Ἰταλιώτας ὀλιγότης καὶ δυσανδρία κατελάμβανε, τρυχομένους πενίᾳ τε καὶ ἐσφοραῖς καὶ στρατείαις. εἰ δὲ καὶ σχολάσειαν ἀπὸ τούτων, ἐπὶ ἀργίας διετίθεντο, τῆς γῆς ὑπὸ τῶν πλουσίων ἐχομένης καὶ γεωργοῖς χρωμένων θεράπουσιν ἀντὶ ἐλευθέρων.

Ἐφ' οἷς ὁ δῆμος ἐδυσφόρει μὲν ὡς οὔτε συμμάχων ἐξ Ἰταλίας ἔτι εὐπορήσων οὔτε τῆς ἡγεμονίας οἱ γενησομένης ἀκινδύνου διὰ πλῆθος τοσόνδε θεραπόν-των·

[But the very opposite thing happened; for the rich, getting possession of the greater part of the undistributed lands, and being emboldened by the lapse of time to believe that they would never be dispossessed, absorbing any adjacent strips and their poor neighbours' allotments, partly by purchase under persuasion and partly by force, came to cultivate vast tracts instead of single estates, using slaves as labourers and herdsmen, lest free labourers should be drawn from agriculture into the army. At the same time the ownership of slaves brought them great gain from the multitude of their progeny, who increased because they were exempt from military service. Thus certain powerful men became extremely rich and the race of slaves multiplied throughout the country, while the Italian people dwindled in numbers and strength, being oppressed by penury, taxes, and military service. If they had any respite from these evils, they passed their time in idleness, because the land was held by the rich, who employed slaves instead of freemen as cultivators.

For these reasons the people became troubled lest they should no longer have sufficient allies of the Italian stock, and lest the government itself should be endangered by such a vast number of slaves.][27]

We need not ask whether this account is accepted by modern historians in order to see that Appian is furnished with a complex social and political narrative analysis. The problem is both Italian and Roman. The 'people' (*dēmos*) 'troubled' in the last sentence is the *populus* rather than the *senatus* of Roman political language, and what troubles them is their apparent failure to create an allied state in central Italy. They are failing to create a 'people' who will serve in the armies as second- or first-class citizens; impoverished smallholders competing with slaves and shepherds can no longer furnish these in sufficient numbers. Tiberius Gracchus, appealing to the voters of Rome on the subject, finds that the urban poor are divided between their dislike of the rich and their increasing dependency on them. He must rely for support on a 'country party' consisting of Roman citizens more or less recently of that status, who live near enough to town to intervene in its politics, but share the insecurities of remoter peasant populations. It is a shaky power base, and he is obliged to make it clear that what he wants, and asks Rome to want, is a warrior peasantry who will join in further imperial expansion.

Γράκχῳ δ᾽ ὁ μὲν νοῦς τοῦ βουλεύματος ἦν οὐκ ἐς εὐπορίαν, ἀλλ᾽ ἐς εὐανδρίαν, τοῦ δὲ ἔργου τῇ ὠφελείᾳ μάλιστα αἰωρούμενος, ὡς οὔ τι μεῖζον οὐδὲ λαμπρότερον δυναμένης ποτὲ παθεῖν τῆς Ἰταλίας, τοῦ περὶ αὐτὸ δυσχεροῦς οὐδὲν ἐνεθυμεῖτο. ἐνστάσης δὲ τῆς χειροτονίας πολλὰ μὲν ἄλλα προεῖπεν ἐπαγωγὰ καὶ μακρά, διηρώτα δ᾽ ἐπ᾽ ἐκείνοις, εἰ δίκαιον τὰ κοινὰ κοινῇ διανέμεσθαι καὶ εἰ γνησιώτερος αἰεὶ θεράποντος ὁ πολίτης καὶ χρησιμώτερος ὁ στρατιώτης ἀπολέμου καὶ τοῖς δημοσίοις εὐνούστερος ὁ κοινωνός. οὐκ ἐς πολὺ δὲ τὴν σύγκρισιν ὡς ἄδοξον ἐπενεγκὼν αὖθις ἐπῄει τὰς τῆς πατρίδος ἐλπίδας καὶ φόβους διεξιών, ὅτι πλείστης γῆς ἐκ πολέμου βίᾳ κατέχοντες καὶ τὴν λοιπὴν τῆς οἰκουμένης χώραν ἐν ἐλπίδι ἔχοντες κινδυνεύουσιν ἐν τῷδε περὶ ἁπάντων, ἢ κτήσασθαι καὶ τὰ λοιπὰ δι᾽ εὐανδρίαν ἢ καὶ τάδε δι᾽ ἀσθένειαν καὶ φθόνον ὑπ᾽ ἐχθρῶν ἀφαιρεθῆναι.

[What Gracchus had in his mind in proposing the measure was not money, but men. Inspired greatly by the usefulness of the work, and believing that nothing more advantageous or admirable could ever happen to Italy, he took no account of the difficulties surrounding it. When the time for voting came he advanced

---

[27] *Ibidem*; continuous with the passage last quoted.

many other arguments at considerable length and also asked them whether it was not just to let the commons divide the common property; whether a citizen was not worthy of more consideration at all times than a slave; whether a man who served in the army was not more useful than one who did not; and whether one who had a share in the country was not more likely to be devoted to the public interests. He did not dwell long on this comparison between freemen and slaves, which he considered degrading, but proceeded at once to a review of their hopes and fears for the country, saying that the Romans possessed most of their territory by conquest, and that they had hopes of occupying the rest of the habitable world; but now the question of greatest hazard was, whether they should gain the rest by having plenty of brave men, or whether, through their weakness and mutual jealousy, their enemies should take away what they already possessed.][28]

Free land, free soil, free labour and free men! Appian is criticising the rhetoric he ascribes to Gracchus, and the modern eye can read a great deal into this passage. In the first place, we see here the makings of the case both ancient and modern against sweeping reforms by means of a *lex agraria*; that in fact it is not just to let the common voice redistribute the common property, if this means that the rights of occupancy however acquired will not be respected; behind which lie the massive class fears that the propertied entertain of the poor. In the second place, Gracchus is made to express the classic doctrine that public virtue depends upon the liberty to bear arms, and this in turn upon security of tenure; the slave appearing less as a human being deprived of liberty than as an instrument threatening the liberty of those who have it. In the third place, the association between liberty and the acquisition of further empire opened the way in the eighteenth century – though this would hardly have been apparent to Appian himself – to the contention that liberty and democracy so defined condemned the free to go on forever seizing the lands of their neighbours and settling them with smallholders. There must be something wrong with a liberty dependent on an economy of primitive appropriation, and the antithesis between liberty and slavery might have something to do with it. A reader of Appian in Gibbon's generation was concerned with the debate between ancient and modern liberty.

(III)

Appian's narrative of the civil wars begins with the failure of Tiberius Gracchus' reform programme. What is less clear is how far it narrates

---

[28] *Civil Wars*, I, i, II; White, 1912–13, III, pp. 22–3.

them as a series of effects directly caused by that failure. Tiberius is that familiar figure, the young nobleman turning to radical action out of idealism, ambition and an unlimited faith in his own privileged position;[29] later to be typecast as the criminal adventurer Catiline and not unknown to the contemporaries of Lord Edward Fitzgerald and Charles James Fox. He typically underestimates the fury of his class's reactions against him, but in the Gracchan case fails through his readiness to go outside legitimate measures. Tiberius deposes a fellow tribune who has persistently opposed him, and is slain by a quickly formed execution squad of senators and their clients. Twelve years later, his brother Gaius takes up the cause, but attacks the senatorial class directly by placing their actions under the jurisdiction of courts composed of *equites* (a class equally ill translated as 'knights' and 'middle class'). Since they include most of the *publicani* or tax-gatherers,[30] they have their own involvement in the confused land situation in central Italy, and Gaius can hardly be seen as seeking to restore a virtuous yeomanry; he has enlisted one class of landsharks against another. His actions point in two directions. One is towards the Social War a generation later, a rebellion of the semi-independent Italians who see no future for themselves in the increasingly violent and divided politics of Rome, and seek either independence from it or incorporation and a full voice within it. The other is towards the increase of domestic political violence, leading to cynical manipulation or brutal disregard of all laws and sanctions; Gaius and his followers are put down by means involving armed force,[31] far more like war within the city than the lynch-law visited on his brother. This is moral and political degeneration, a condition of violence, stasis and nihilism which Greek historiography – Appian mentions Thucydides in another context[32] – has often fully described. It can be depicted, and to that extent explained, by a rhetoric of virtue and its opposites which readily becomes independent of specific historical and social contexts; one does not need the Italian land problem if one's aim is to depict *homo homini lupus*.

But alongside the escalating nihilism of the Roman power struggle – which rhetorical narrative permits to act as its own explanation – there is mounting another phenomenon for which it does not altogether account. This is the increasing willingness of competitors for power and office to use the provinces and commands with which politics entrusts them, and

---

[29] Stockton, 1979, pp. 29–33, 82–6.     [30] Badian, 1972.
[31] *Civil Wars*, I, iii; White, 1912–13, III, pp. 52–3; Stockton, 1979, p. 197.
[32] *Civil Wars*, II, xxxix; White, 1912–13, III, pp. 300–1.

which are the prizes of political competition, as sources of military power with which to intervene in the political process itself. The competition for provinces becomes a competition *à l'outrance*, and commander after commander – Marius and Sulla, Pompey and Caesar, Antony and the future Augustus – marches his army to Rome, fights battles at or within its gates, and enters to destroy his enemies; not to make himself monarch, but to attempt some final determination of a process he does not know how to stop. New provinces are conquered – Caesar in Gaul, Pompey in Syria – with the intention of increasing the warlord's resources, either directly or through forcing the senate to shoulder and then grant new responsibilities; Roman politics remain yoked to the extension of empire. The ferocities of faction impel those who march on Rome to destroy their enemies, and proscriptions, or reigns of terror, twice rise to apocalyptic heights: first under Sulla, who imposes a dictatorship from which he can retire with safety, then under the Second Triumvirate, when Antony and Octavian (Augustus) conduct a bloodbath which can result in settlement only after a war between them has eliminated Antony on ground as far from Rome as Appian's home in Egypt. By this time the struggle for provinces as a source of war-making power has turned into a series of wars for the control of provinces fought from one end of the empire to the other: Spain, Africa, Sicily, Epirus, Egypt.

A Rome-centred historiography can recount this process through a series of rhetorical devices depicting the progressive degeneration of Roman public virtue. This need not be a succession of moral clichés; Rome was a legalist, procedural and customary society, and there was a Latin vocabulary – to be sensed at the back of all our Greek histories – eminently capable of describing how the sanctions of society had worked and how they had gone wrong. There was a steady flow of information from context into rhetoric, and the narrative of systemic decay was well in place in antiquity. Modern historians, wielding the resources of source-criticism, archaeology and prosopography, have added a *peinture* and *récit* of provincial power – families, clientages, inheritances, investments – supplying Roman politics with a context into which it is at times absorbed, and going far towards explaining the civil wars as the actions of regional magnates and adventurers. There remains one problem which may tempt us to glance back to our Gracchan point of departure. We know a great deal, as did the ancient writers, about why Romans in search of hegemony led their armies against each other and against the city. What do we know, and what did the ancients know, about why their soldiers followed them into these civil wars?

Let it be repeated that we are looking for the origins of a historical explanation, not seeking to explain the events to which it might have been applied. It would be possible to suppose that the primeval Roman – the inhabitant of the heroic age of the first ten books of Livy – was a citizen, an arms-bearer and a smallholder, farming lands acquired by the republic through appropriation, conquest and treaty, and particularly through the establishment of colonies (in Greek cleruchies) among peoples willingly or unwillingly allied with Rome. As the territory of the republic expanded, the legionary class grew with it, enlarged by non-Romans acquiring some or all of the rights of citizenship, though down to the Social War there persisted Italian elites resentful of Roman hegemony and anxious either to overthrow it or to gain admission to it. Tiberius Gracchus is credited with two propositions: one that the legionary class is not stable but dynamic – it conquers new lands which are settled in their turn, and there is no end to this process short of domination of the whole world; the other that this class is threatened at its roots in the land by the spread of large estates worked by slaves and tending to pasture rather than arable farming. His reforms are intended to remedy this danger, but they fail; and both the manner in which he attempts them and the means by which they and he are destroyed begin the destruction of the republic whose authority is necessary if soldiers are to be citizens.

A double narrative now becomes possible. One relates the disruption of public authority, the increasing violence and lawlessness of political conflict, and the process by which the legions find themselves no longer the armies of the republic, but the military instruments of ambitious chiefs, engaged in civil wars which are, increasingly, conflicts less between citizens than between factions. This narrative is overt; it is related in detail by Appian, by the Caesarian authors, and assuredly by all the sources on which Appian drew. A second narrative is possible, arrived at by accepting the original diagnosis of the problem faced by Gracchus and working out the consequences of his failure to remedy it. In this narrative the soldier-farmer class is increasingly threatened by social causes akin to those originally diagnosed, with the result that the armies move towards being composed of landless adventurers in search of lands on which to settle. It becomes the business of the political adventurer who leads them to find lands for them, and he employs the political conventions of the republic to that end, in particular the custom which made provincial command the reward of magistracy. The dynamic of republican empire is redoubled, and the decay of Italian smallholding is directly linked to the dramatic expansion of empire east and west accompanying the breakdown of the republic. New lands are needed for new colonies, new armies – which must be rewarded with colonies – to acquire new lands. The demand for new provinces to satisfy political adventurers becomes a demand for military power for use in political competition, and the legions find themselves fighting one another in the interests of their commanders. Since the land-hungry soldiers are still mainly Italian, it is in Italy that their leaders want to settle them, and the civil wars entail both the dispossession of Italian populations and the increasing scale of proscriptions at Rome. The outward thrust of empire turns inward on Italy and Rome; and all may be explained through the Gracchan thesis of depopulation.

The elements of this narrative explanation may all be found in texts such as Appian's, and we may presume that Appian found them in texts on which he drew. The question is whether they are brought together in an explicit structure of explanation, or whether we are obliged to find them in the histories for ourselves; and if the latter, whether we are rendering explicit what the historian chose to leave implicit in awareness of what he was doing, or whether we are reading into Appian what our historically formed minds dispose us to find there. The problem is not simply that of the hermeneutic cycle, since it is possible to differentiate historically between the mindset of ancient historiography and that of the early modern or modern; this differentiation, however, leaves open the question of what kinds of information made their way into ancient rhetorical structures, and how they were domiciled there. Does Appian spell out a Gracchan explanation of the civil wars, does he leave us to infer it, or do we read it into him of ourselves?

What can be stated by way of reply is that, as his narrative of the civil wars proceeds, we hear more and more about the demands of both leaders and soldiers for lands on which the latter can be settled in colonies. Livius Drusus is found proposing colonies as a political measure in 91 BC,[33] but the first military leader we hear of settling his own men on the land is Sulla, who can hope to render his dictatorship perpetual, and even retire into private life in the expectation that it will survive his death, by establishing colonies of soldiers who will be compelled to uphold it by their own insecurity.[34] It does not last and new wars ensue, because provinces are still granted and armies raised which need satisfying; Caesar is found buying popular support by proposing land

[33] *Civil Wars*, I, v, 35–6; White, 1912–13, III, pp. 68–71.
[34] *Civil Wars*, I, xi, 96, and xii, 104; White, 1912–13, III, pp. 176–9 and 194–5.

settlements around Capua.[35] This is civilian politics, but he and Pompey are soon found raising great armies for service in Gaul and Syria, attached to them and not the republic by the promise of gain. We are not to think of these legionaries solely as mercenaries and adventurers; they are personally attached to their leaders as men they know, judge and trust; they have pride in themselves and their fidelity; and precisely because the public authority is disrupted, it is open to them to see themselves as citizens seeking to restore it. This is real, but cannot be carried too far. We read of no Roman Levellers or Putney Debates, and a reason that may be assigned – but seems not to be mentioned – is their landlessness and the fact that land is the only means of rewarding them. They are soldiers in the sense that they are *soldati*, living by their pay, and can be bought by sudden cash donatives (references to these occur in statistically significant quantity); but there is no republican fiscal machinery that can make them a true standing army. The New Model regiments were offered lands by the conquest of Ireland and in some cases declined the proposal; the legions of the civil wars were not able to avoid fighting one another for lands in Italy. At Pharsalus they are described as appalled by what they cannot help doing,[36] but after it they mutiny because they have not been rewarded; Caesar quells them by means of charisma, cash and promises.

δώσω δὲ καὶ γῆν ἅπασιν ἐκτελεσθέντων τῶν πολέμων, οὐ καθάπερ Σύλλας, ἀφαιρούμενος ἑτέρων ἣν ἔχουσι καὶ τοῖς ἀφαιρεθεῖσι τοὺς λαβόντας συνοικίζων καὶ ποιῶν ἀλλήλοις ἐς αἰεὶ πολεμίους, ἀλλὰ τὴν τοῦ δήμου γῆν ἐπινέμων καὶ τὴν ἐμαυτοῦ, καὶ τὰ δέοντα προσωνούμενος.

[And when the wars are ended I will give lands to all, not as Sulla did by taking it from the present holders and uniting present and past holders in a colony, and so making them everlasting enemies to each other, but I will give the public land, and my own, and will purchase as well the necessary implements.][37]

He does not live till the promise can be tested. Brutus and Cassius fail to revive the republic because they over-estimate the *faeces Romuli*.

καὶ αὐτοῖς βουλευομένοις ἔδοξεν ἐπὶ τὰ πλήθη μισθώματα περιπέμπειν· ἤλπιζον γάρ, ἀρξαμένων τινῶν ἐπαινεῖν τὰ γεγενημένα, καὶ τοὺς ἄλλους συνεπιλήψεσθαι λογισμῷ τε τῆς ἐλευθερίας καὶ πόθῳ τῆς πολιτείας. ἔτι γὰρ ᾤοντο τὸν δῆμον εἶναι Ῥωμαῖον ἀκριβῶς, οἷον ἐπὶ τοῦ πάλαι Βρούτου τὴν τότε βασιλείαν καθαιροῦντος ἐπυνθάνοντο γενέσθαι· καὶ οὐ συνίεσαν

---

35  *Civil Wars*, II, ii, 10; White, 1912–13, III, pp. 246–7.
36  *Civil Wars*, II, xi, 77; White, 1912–13, III, pp. 368–9.
37  *Civil Wars*, II, xiii, 94; White, 1912–13, III, pp. 400–1.

δύο τάδε ἀλλήλοις ἐναντία προσδοκῶντες, φιλελευθέρους ὁμοῦ καὶ μισθω-
τοὺς σφίσιν ἔσεσθαι χρησίμως τοὺς παρόντας. ὧν θάτερον εὐχερέστερον ἦν,
διεφθαρμένης ἐκ πολλοῦ τῆς πολιτείας. παμμιγές τε γάρ ἐστιν ἤδη τὸ πλῆθος
ὑπὸ ξενίας, καὶ ὁ ἐξελεύθερος αὐτοῖς ἰσοπολίτης ἐστὶ καὶ ὁ δουλεύων ἔτι τὸ
σχῆμα τοῖς δεσπόταις ὅμοιος· χωρὶς γὰρ τῆς βουλευτικῆς ἡ ἄλλη στολὴ τοῖς
θεράπουσίν ἐστιν ἐπίκοινος. τό τε σιτηρέσιον τοῖς πένησι χορηγούμενον ἐν
μόνῃ Ῥώμῃ τὸν ἀργὸν καὶ πτωχεύοντα καὶ ταχυεργὸν τῆς Ἰταλίας λεὼν ἐς
τὴν Ῥώμην ἐπάγεται.

[They took counsel and decided to bribe the populace, hoping that if some
would begin to praise the deed others would join in from love of liberty and
longing for the republic. They thought that the genuinely Roman people
were still as they had learned that they were when the elder Brutus expelled
the kings. They did not perceive that they were counting on two incompatible
things, namely that people could be lovers of liberty and bribe-takers at the
same time. The latter class were much easier to find of the two, because the
government had been corrupt for a long time. For the plebeians are now much
mixed with foreign blood, freedmen have equal rights of citizenship with them,
and slaves are dressed in the same fashion as their masters. Except in the case of
the senatorial rank the same costume is common to slaves and to free citizens.
Moreover the distribution of corn to the poor, which takes place in Rome only,
draws thither the lazy, the beggars, the vagrants of all Italy.][38]

So far the standard rhetoric of decline; but now comes a change of
tone.

τό
τε πλῆθος τῶν ἀποστρατευομένων, οὐ διαλυόμενον ἐς τὰς πατρίδας ἔτι ὡς
πάλαι καθ᾽ ἕνα ἄνδρα δέει τοῦ μὴ δικαίους πολέμους ἐνίους πεπολεμηκέναι,
κοινῇ δὲ ἐς κληρουχίας ἀδίκους ἀλλοτρίας τε γῆς καὶ ἀλλοτρίων οἰκιῶν ἐξιόν,
ἄθρουν τότε ἐστάθμευεν ἐν τοῖς ἱεροῖς καὶ τεμένεσιν ὑφ᾽ ἑνὶ σημείῳ καὶ ὑφ᾽ ἑνὶ
ἄρχοντι τῆς ἀποικίας, τὰ μὲν ὄντα σφίσιν ὡς ἐπὶ ἔξοδον ἤδη διαπεπρακότες,
εὔωνοι δ᾽ ἐς ὅ τι μισθοῖντο.

[The multitude, too, of discharged soldiers who were no longer dispersed one by
one to their native places as formerly, through fear lest some of them might have
engaged in unjustifiable wars, but were sent in groups to unjust allotments of
lands and confiscated houses, was at this time encamped in temples and sacred
enclosures under one standard, and one person appointed to lead them to their
colony, and as they had already sold their own belongings preparatory to their
departure they were in readiness to be bought for any purpose.][39]

Thus the text, but the narrative makes it clear that they knew exactly what they wanted. The competition for support between Brutus
and Antony, and their funeral orations, is determined less by the

---

[38] *Civil Wars*, II, xvii, 120; White, 1912–13, III, pp. 448–51.     [39] *Ibidem*, pp. 450–1.

Shakespearean fickleness of the mob than by the determination of the organised veterans to have their colonies and the senate's fear of what they may do to get them.[40] Brutus makes a long speech,[41] in which he tells them that colonisation was once an extension (by conquest) of the public land and settlement in colonies a public action which made citizens of those who performed it. Sulla and Caesar, however, made it an instrument of civil war and private spoliation, and deliberately entailed insecurity of tenure on the veterans Brutus is addressing, in order to make their usurping regimes perpetual.

Ἀλλ' ἐκεῖνοι μὲν ὑμᾶς ἐξεπίτηδες ἐχθροὺς ἐποίουν τοῖς ὁμοεθνέσιν ὑπὲρ τοῦ σφετέρου συμφέροντος· ἡμεῖς δέ, οὓς οἱ νῦν τῆς πατρίδος προστάται φασὶν ἐλέῳ περισῴζειν, τήν τε γῆν ὑμῖν τήνδε αὐτὴν ἐσαεὶ βεβαιοῦμεν καὶ βεβαιώσομεν καὶ μάρτυρα τὸν θεὸν τῶνδε ποιούμεθα. καὶ ἔχετε καὶ ἕξετε, ἃ εἰλήφατε· καὶ οὐ μή τις ὑμᾶς ἀφέληται ταῦτα, οὐ Βροῦτος, οὐ Κάσσιος, οὐχ οἵδε πάντες, οἳ τῆς ὑμετέρας ἐλευθερίας προεκινδυνεύσαμεν. ὃ δ' ἐν τῷ ἔργῳ μόνον ἐστὶν ἐπίμεπτον, ἰασόμεθα ἡμεῖς, διαλλακτήριον ὑμῖν ἅμα ἐς τοὺς ὁμοεθνεῖς ἐσόμενον καὶ ἥδιστον ἤδη πυθομένοις. οἷς τὴν τιμὴν τῆσδε τῆς γῆς τοῖς ἀφῃρημένοις ἡμεῖς ἐκ τῶν δημοσίων χρημάτων εὐθὺς ἐκ πρώτης ἀφορμῆς ἀποδώσομεν, ἵνα μὴ βέβαιον ἔχητε μόνον ὑμεῖς τὴν κληρουχίαν, ἀλλὰ καὶ ἄφθονον.

[They purposely made you enemies to your countrymen for their own advantage. We, the defenders of the republic, to whom our opponents say they grant safety out of pity, confirm this very same land to you and will confirm it forever; and to this promise we call to witness the god of this temple. You have and shall keep what you have received. No man assuredly shall take it from you, neither Brutus, nor Cassius, nor any of us who have incurred danger for your freedom. The one thing which is faulty in this business we will remedy, and that remedy will at once reconcile you with your fellow-countrymen and prove most agreeable to them as soon as they hear of it. We shall at once pay them out of the public money the price of this land of which they have been deprived; so that not only shall your colony be secure, but it shall not even be exposed to hatred.][42]

Brutus' speech is for the moment so successful that Antony is driven to all the theatrics of the Funeral Oration to recover ground. One wonders what Shakespeare might have achieved by including veterans among his citizens and allowing them to speak in the tones of Bates, Court and Williams in *Henry V*. Brutus is trying to restore the *ager publicum* and the public authority that gives security of tenure, but was the chief casualty of the post-Gracchan reforms; it is a higher objective than any

[40] *Civil Wars*, II, xvii, 125; White, 1912–13, III, pp. 458–9.
[41] *Civil Wars*, II, xix, 139–41; White, 1912–13, III, pp. 485–9.    [42] *Ibidem*, pp. 488–9.

redistribution of lands between smallholders and great estates. Needless to say, he comes too late; there is neither enough money in the public treasury to compensate all the victims of colonisation, nor the will to use it. We find Brutus enabling colonists to sell their allotments instead of retaining them for the twenty years which the policy of republican colonisation once required.[43] He and Cassius depart to their provinces, and in their absence the young Octavius, who will be Augustus, appears in Italy and is tumultuously welcomed by the colonised veterans.[44] The self-perpetuating politics of insecurity have returned, and Brutus and Cassius will find themselves exploiting their provinces as resources for renewed civil war. There is a grim tale of how Brutus destroyed the Greek city of Xanthos, whose inhabitants fought to the last 'on account of their love of liberty'.[45]

Appian's narrative continues through the formation of the second triumvirate, the proscriptions, and the destruction of Brutus and Cassius at Philippi. It is increasingly clear that the wars are being driven by a process of escalation; new armies command new spoliations and new spoliations command new wars. The primary victims of the process are the Italians, among whom most of the colonies are established,[46] but the dynasts themselves are in danger of imprisonment in what they have started.

καταλέγοντι δ᾽ αὐτῷ τὸν στρατὸν ἐς τὰς ἀποικίας καὶ τὴν γῆν ἐπινέμοντι δυσεργὲς ἦν. οἵ τε γὰρ στρατιῶται τὰς πόλεις ᾔτουν, αἳ αὐτοῖς ἀριστίνδην ἦσαν ἐπειλεγμέναι πρὸ τοῦ πολέμου, καὶ αἱ πόλεις ἠξίουν τὴν Ἰταλίαν ἅπασαν ἐπινείμασθαι τὸ ἔργον ἢ ἐν ἀλλήλαις διαλαχεῖν τῆς τε γῆς τὴν τιμὴν τοὺς δωρουμένους ᾔτουν, καὶ ἀργύριον οὐκ ἦν, ἀλλὰ συνιόντες ἀνὰ μέρος ἐς τὴν Ῥώμην οἵ τε νέοι καὶ γέροντες ἢ αἱ γυναῖκες ἅμα τοῖς παιδίοις, ἐς τὴν ἀγορὰν ἢ τὰ ἱερά, ἐθρήνουν, οὐδὲν μὲν ἀδικῆσαι λέγοντες, Ἰταλιῶται δὲ ὄντες ἀνίστασθαι γῆς τε καὶ ἑστίας οἷα δορίληπτοι. ἐφ᾽ οἷς οἱ Ῥωμαῖοι συνήχθοντο καί ἐπεδάκρυον, καὶ μάλιστα, ὅτε ἐνθυμηθεῖεν οὐχ ὑπὲρ τῆς πόλεως, ἀλλ᾽ ἐπὶ σφίσιν αὐτοῖς καὶ τῇ μεταβολῇ τῆς πολιτείας τόν τε πόλεμον γεγονότα καὶ τὰ ἐπινίκια διδόμενα καὶ τὰς ἀποικίας συνισταμένας τοῦ μηδ᾽ αὖθις ἀνακῦψαι τὴν δημοκρατίαν, παρῳκισμένων τοῖς ἄρχουσι μισθοφόρων ἑτοίμων, ἐς ὅ τι χρήζοιεν.
Ὁ δὲ Καῖσαρ ταῖς πόλεσιν ἐξελογεῖτο τὴν ἀνάγκην, καὶ ἐδόκουν οὐδ᾽ ὡς ἀρκέσειν. οὐδ᾽ ἤρκουν, ἀλλὰ ὁ στρατὸς καὶ τοῖς γείτοσιν ἐπέβαινε σὺν ὕβρει,

---

[43] *Civil Wars*, III, i, 2; White, 1912–13, III, pp. 520–1.
[44] *Civil Wars*, III, ii, 12; White, 1912–13, III, pp. 536–7.
[45] *Civil Wars*, IV, x, 76–80; White, 1912–13, IV, pp. 269–75.
[46] 'To expropriate Italy, if we must speak plainly', says Antony to his soldiers (v, i, 6; White, 1912–13, IV, pp. 384–5).

πλέονά τε τῶν διδομένων σφίσι περισπώμενοι καὶ τὸ ἄμεινον ἐκλεγόμενοι. οὐδὲ
ἐπιπλήσσοντος αὐτοῖς καὶ δωρουμένου πολλὰ ἄλλα τοῦ Καίσαρος ἐπαύοντο,
ἐπεὶ καὶ τῶν ἀρχόντων, ὡς δεομένων σφῶν ἐς τὸ ἐγκρατὲς τῆς ἀρχῆς, κατεφρό-
νουν. καὶ γὰρ αὐτοῖς ἡ πενταετία παρώδευε, καὶ τὸ ἀσφαλὲς ἡ χρεία συνῆγεν
ἀμφοτέροις παρ᾽ ἀλλήλων, τοῖς μὲν ἡγεμόσιν ἐς τὴν ἀρχὴν παρὰ τοῦ στρατοῦ, τῷ στρατῷ δὲ ἐς τὴν ἐπικράτησιν ὧν ἔλαβον, ἡ τῶν δεδωκότων ἀρχὴ
παραμένουσα. ὡς γὰρ αὐτῶν οὐ βεβαίως ἐπικρατήσοντες, εἰ μὴ βεβαίως ἄρ-
χοιεν οἱ δόντες, ὑπερεμάχουν ἀπ᾽ εὐνοίας ἀναγκαίου. πολλὰ δὲ καὶ ἄλλα τοῖς
ἀπορουμένοις αὐτῶν ἐδωρεῖτο, δανειζόμενος ἐκ τῶν ἱερῶν, ὁ Καῖσαρ. ὅθεν τὴν
γνώμην ὁ στρατὸς ἐς αὐτὸν ἐπέστρεφε, καὶ πλείων ὑπήντα χάρις ὡς γῆν ἅμα
καὶ πόλεις καὶ χρήματα καὶ οἰκήματα δωρουμένῳ καὶ καταβοωμένῳ μὲν ἐπι-
φθόνως ὑπὸ τῶν ἀφαιρουμένων, φέροντι δὲ τὴν ὕβριν ἐς χάριν τοῦ στρατοῦ.

[The task of assigning the soldiers to their colonies and dividing the land was one of exceeding difficulty. For the soldiers demanded the cities which had been selected for them before the war as prizes for their valour, and the cities demanded that the whole of Italy should share the burden, or that the cities should cast lots with the other cities, and that those who gave the land should be paid the value of it; and there was no money. They came to Rome in crowds, young and old, women and children, to the forum and the temples, uttering lamentations, saying that they had done no wrong for which they, Italians, should be driven from their fields and their hearthstones, like people conquered in war. The Romans mourned and wept with them, especially when they reflected that the war had been waged, and the rewards of victory given, not in behalf of the commonwealth, but against themselves and for a change in the form of government; that the colonies were established to the end that democracy[47] should never again lift its head – colonies composed of hirelings settled there by the rulers to be in readiness for whatever purpose they might be wanted.

Octavian[48] explained to the cities the necessity of the case, but he knew that it would not satisfy them; and it did not. The soldiers encroached upon their neighbours in an insolent manner, seizing more than had been given to them and choosing the best lands; nor did they cease even when Octavian rebuked them and made them numerous other presents, since they were contemptuous of their rulers in the knowledge that they needed them to confirm their power, for the five years' term of the triumvirate was passing away, and army and rulers needed the services of each other for mutual security. The chiefs depended on the soldiers for the continuance of their government, while, for the possession of what they had received, the soldiers depended on the permanence of the government of those who had given it. Believing that they could not keep a

---

[47] Appian seems to employ *dēmokratia* to denote the rule of *senatus populusque* at Rome, and perhaps local assemblies in the Italian cities. He does not deal with the negative connotation the word bore among philosophers and orators in antiquity and early modernity.

[48] Octavius, Octavianus and Augustus were names he bore at different times of his life. There is a convention among moderns of using the second of these. Appian refers to him by the Greek spelling of 'Caesar'.

firm hold unless the givers had a strong government, they fought for them, from necessity, with good-will. Octavian made many other gifts to the indigent soldiers, borrowing from the temples for that purpose, for which reason the affections of the army were turned toward him, and the greater thanks were bestowed upon him, both as the giver of the land, the cities, the money, and the houses, and as the object of denunciation on the part of the despoiled, and as one who bore this contumely for the army's sake.][49]

If we were to develop the Gracchan analysis in a Rostovtseffian direction,[50] we might present all this as class war, the revenge of the land-less classes on the citizens as landed proprietors. (No doubt we should then learn that things were not as bad as here depicted. 'Consanguin-ity and affinity will mar all,' it was once said of confiscations attempted during the English civil wars, and the very geography of Italy seems to lend itself to the construction of protective affinities.) Appian does not take us in this direction; the soldiers are not said to be landless as the result of the consolidation of large estates; their rapacity is simply the effect and then the cause of the failure of public authority to com-mand and control its armies. Nevertheless, the rhetoric offers a classic account of the wolf Augustus once said he held by the ears, and we are left wondering how the beast was ever to find its trainer. Faced with one mutiny, he tells them the civil wars are coming to an end and he will send them against the Illyrians and other barbarians, to find the rewards of victory there; they reply that they will obey orders when they have got the colonies they want.[51] The need to make an end of competitive colonisation figures in the rhetoric accompanying the rebellion – it is really a *grido* – of Antony's brother Lucius, a not irresponsible character who wants to end the triumvirate and restore the republic; but he makes his submission when he decides that the only way out of triumvirate is monarchy.[52] Here, to our deprivation, Appian's surviving text is incom-plete; it breaks off at the suppression of Sextus Pompeius, and does not make its way to Actium and Alexandria. There is therefore much that we do not know about how Appian completed his *oeuvre*: how he treated Egyptian history as the sequel to Roman, for example, and what he said

[49] *Civil Wars*, v, ii, 12–13; White, 1912–13, IV, pp. 394–9.
[50] Rostovtseff, 1926; a work famous for its argument that the armies of the third century were engaged in a class revolt against the cities.
[51] *Civil Wars*, v, xiii, 128; White, 1912–13, IV, pp. 588–9.
[52] This episode is recounted in *Civil Wars* v, iii, 18 and v, 49 (White, 1912–13, IV, pp. 407–59). For a modern reading including the observation that Appian has idealised the role of Lucius Antonius, see Syme, 1939, pp. 207–12, in particular p. 208, n. 1. Appian perhaps wanted a last voice of republican honesty, which he could scarcely ascribe to brother Marcus.

of the Augustan settlement. What would have become of the soldiers'
inexhaustible land hunger when there were no more war-leaders sum-
moning them to competitive spoliation? Would it have been tamed by
the mere act of proclaiming a single man *imperator* of all the armies and
rendering his *imperium* public by surrounding it with all the emblems of
republican legitimacy and calling the *imperator* a *princeps*? Is the willingness to obey commands as strong a motor of military behaviour as the
appetite for loot and a safe retirement? Finally, would Appian have told
us that peace refilled the treasury and made it possible to manage the soldiers as *soldati*, living by their pay instead of by confiscation of lands and
resembling the standing army which Enlightened historians thought a
turning-point of modern history? Justus Lipsius in the sixteenth century
will be found asking this question.[53]


(IV)

'In our larger experience of history,' Gibbon wrote at a later date, 'the
imagination is accustomed, by a perpetual series of causes and effects,
to unite the most distant revolutions.'[54] It is possible that this is not quite
how the ancient historians operated. They could confront remote with
later moments for the rhetorical and instructive value of doing so, and
their sense of the relation between them might approach the causal; but
'a perpetual series of causes and effects', operating continuously over
long periods of time, required a species of narrative hard to combine
with the narrative of selected human actions, and it is possible that the
latter inhibited the development of the former; though to say this would
require us to explain how the obstacle was overcome by neo-classical
early-modern historians, as heavily committed as the ancients to narrative of the latter kind. In Appian's case, there may be a serial connection
between the actions of Tiberius Gracchus and those of the second triumvirate; but if it exists, it is the relation of how the former brought about
a violent disregard of public authority, which escalated by degrees into
the civil wars and proscriptions which were to follow. The succession of
violent and lawless acts forms a series, in which we see the disruption
of the *res publica*, a term connoting both liberty and authority, whose
decay is both produced by actions and forms the context in which the
acts take place. The work is a history of a political system as well as
of the acts of men. But if this is a serial narrative, another is present

---

[53] Below, pp. 282–4, 290–5.    [54] *DF*, III, 33 (1781); Womersley, 1994, II, p. 293.

to our eyes, and there is difficulty in deciding how far it is placed before them by Appian. The distant revolutions it seems to unite are, first, the decay of the smallholder farmer-warriors described as furnishing Gracchus with his concerns; second, the unappeasable land-hunger of the legions settled in colonies on confiscated lands by faction-leaders from Sulla to Augustus. Both in their several ways represent the breakdown of the republic's policy of dominating and assimilating Italy by means of colonies, and we desire to know whether a series of causes and effects exists between them. Is it because there are fewer land-holding citizens, following Gracchus' failure to preserve them, that the legions come to be composed of landless men – still preponderantly Italians and Roman citizens – whose demands for land must be met by their leaders, acting outside the republic's lawful procedures, thus escalating the conflict between parties into civil wars for control of the provinces constituting empire? Is there a history of property, as the foundation of liberty and public virtue, and the disastrous effects of its decay, to be read into the deep background of Appian's narrative? To us it is tempting, almost obligatory, to look for such a narrative and find it; but it is far from certain that Appian has placed it there. If it is present, it may be in the form of two rhetorical set-pieces, one the background to the reforms of Tiberius Gracchus, the other woven into the narrative of the later civil wars, between which there is illustrative antithesis rather than a series of causes and effects. To adopt this reading is to oblige ourselves to explain a greater capacity for narrative explanation in the early-modern historians.

To go as far as we have gone with Appian, furthermore, is to raise a new set of questions regarding Tacitus. It is common ground to both historians that Augustus ended the civil wars by leaving no competitor alive in the known world, and that he put an end to the disastrous competition for provinces by making himself sole *imperator* of all the armies and uniting all major republican magistracies in his own person as *princeps*. Tacitus' *Annals* and *Histories* address the question of how Augustus' monarchy was to be transmitted to successors. Appian was born about forty years after Tacitus, and there is no evidence of what he thought about the history of empire from Augustus to Hadrian. But there is a sense in which the climax of all Tacitus' history is the discovery by the armies of the *arcanum imperii*, that a *princeps* can be made elsewhere than at Rome, though an army which has made an *imperator* must still march to Rome and instal him as *princeps*. There is no sign that Appian has read Tacitus, but his history raises the question whether this is an *arcanum* at all. To armies of the first century BC, it was no secret that they might march to Rome and instal their commander in semi-legal power. They indeed had confronted the dying *auctoritas* of the republic; Vitellius and Vespasian confronted that of the principate, whose character was subverted by the *arcanum* they discovered; but did that mean that the principate differed essentially from the republic, or had solved its problem of maintaining *auctoritas* over the armies?

When civil authority broke down, the armies marched on Rome. There had been some connection between the breakdown of the republic and its failure to maintain a stable Italian land settlement. The legions of the civil wars had been made up of Italians avid to be settled on the land, who had flung the world of Italian property into insecurity and chaos; but the legions intervening in the succession-crises described by Tacitus and Gibbon came from German and Syrian frontiers far away, and it has not appeared that their motive was the expropriation of Italy. Are cash donatives now a sufficient motive, and are the soldiers severed from the land? If there is a difference between the world described by Appian and that described by Tacitus, it lies in the economics of the Roman military structure, the social composition and the ambitions of the legionaries, rather than in the success of Augustus' revolutionary transformation of political power at Rome. This problem should have been faced by Renaissance and Enlightened historical writers, convinced as they were of the intimate connection between property, liberty and arms.

# CHAPTER 4

# *The construction of Christian empire*

(1)

We are now possessed of two narratives that were to be crucial in the making of Gibbon's account of the disintegration of the Antonine monarchy. The Tacitean narrative portrayed the Augustan principate as imperfect and unstable, exposed to interventions by the armies that moved power away from control by the governing elites at Rome; the 'Gracchan explanation' set out in the narrative of Appian surveyed the whole course of the Roman civil wars, down to the victory of Augustus, as the product of the republic's inability to satisfy its growing armies with grants of Italian land. If the two narratives could be linked, the principate would appear an imperfect solution to the problems that had destroyed the republic, and there would be a pattern of explanations capable of dealing with the crises of the first century before Christ and the first, perhaps also the second, centuries after him.

This explanation could be extended – as we know before pursuing Gibbon's narrative further, because it is already implanted in our minds – to deal with 'the decline and fall of the Roman empire' conceived as the conquest and settlement of Roman provinces by invading barbarians. The intervention of the armies in the recurrent crises of succession to the principate could be made to seem destructive of their military discipline and their control by the imperial state, so that they became increasingly incapable of resisting the fluctuating but persistent barbarian pressure on the frontiers. 'The barbarians' are a presence but not yet a menace in Tacitus' narrative. He tells his readers about the defeat of Augustus' armies in Germany, the revolt of the Batavian auxiliaries in the key area of the lower Rhine, and formidable rebellions in a Britain not yet pacified by his father-in-law Agricola.[1] He is also the author of a

---

[1] Tacitus, *Annals*, I, 49–11, 26; *Histories*, IV, 12–37, 54–80; II, 45–6; *Agricola, passim.*

work not yet considered, the *De moribus Germanorum*, which was to prove of central importance in the re-evaluation of barbarism carried out in Renaissance Europe; but he does not envisage, as his humanist readers took for granted, the massive if partial replacement of Roman by barbarian culture as a central event in European history. He is still a Roman, not a European,[2] and the extension of 'the first Decline and Fall' to cover the concept as a whole – implicit as Gibbon began planning the volumes of his history – has yet to occur.

The problem before us is that of tracing the *Begriffsgeschichte* of 'the decline and fall of the Roman empire': of what events and processes came to be known by that name, of how the concept took shape and was applied to happenings in the remembered past, and of how it was elaborated to the point where we confront the problem of seeing how Gibbon connected the failures of the principate with the collapse of the western empire some centuries later. Since this *Begriffsgeschichte* must connect Roman texts written in the first century AD with European readings of them seventeen centuries later, it is evident that its narrative must be long, complex and at times tenuous, and that it can only be summarised in the chapters to come. Yet without a history of the concept of Decline and Fall we cannot understand what it meant to Gibbon, or how Gibbon's understanding of it was situated in history. It is necessary to begin, then, by observing that when we ourselves think of 'the decline and fall of the Roman empire', we think primarily of events in the fifth century: the collapse of the Rhine frontier in 406, the sack of Rome by Alaric in 410, the extinction of the succession of western emperors in 476. From these points we begin to think of a Europe formed by barbarian settlements and kingdoms; and we face, as Gibbon did, the problem of why, setting out to narrate these events and processes, he chose to begin much earlier in time (and to concede that he could have begun earlier than he did).

The happenings of the fifth century are not always those which have seemed crucial to writers who figure in the history of 'decline and fall'; we emphasise them partly because they seemed crucial to Gibbon and because he set about explaining them as he did. It is evident to us, as it was to him, that they occurred in a world very different from that of the Antonine monarchy described and diagnosed in his opening chapters,

---

[2] I use 'Europe' in a modern sense, denoting the successor-states of the western empire, established in Italy and north and west of the Alps, subsequently expanding eastward into Germany, Hungary and Poland. The ancient use of the term denoted the Balkan peninsula and by extension the lands north and west of it.

and linked with a history of the principate looking back to that of the civil wars. It was the sons of Theodosius who failed to deal with the crisis of 406–10, and Theodosius had been the restorer of the monarchy of Constantine after the crises brought on by the failures of Julian and Valens. Constantine had erected a monarchy on foundations laid by Diocletian at the end of the military rule of the third century, itself a sequel to the anarchy which had succeeded the Severi who had displaced the Antonines. Not only were these successive systems radically unlike the Augustan principate which the Antonines had endeavoured to maintain; Constantine had been the author of two profound transformations of empire, the foundation of New Rome on the site of Byzantium and the adoption of the Christian faith as the empire's religion. From the former had stemmed the division of the empire into a Greek east where it survived until 1453, and a Latin west where it had failed a millennium earlier; from the latter arose the replacement of classical by Christian culture, and in the west by the ascendancy of a papal church which furnished the starting-point of both the 'Enlightened narrative' of 'the Christian millennium'[3] and Gibbon's 'triumph of barbarism and religion'. It was from the actions of Constantine, preceding the disasters of the fifth century, that the chief themes and problems of the *Decline and Fall* originated. Gibbon's first fourteen chapters bring us to the point where Constantine is about to take these decisive steps; but both the volumes published in 1781 are needed to bring us to the point at which the Decline and Fall can be seen as occurring in the world shaped by his actions and constructed by minds shaped by his values.

(II)

Alaric's sack of 410 was beheld and commented on by intelligences steeped in the ideology of Constantinean monarchy. This had been in the making for close on a century, and was far removed from the mindset of Antonine or Augustan Rome. Gibbon, and following him ourselves, could not but think of the defeat of empire as the defeat of the pre-Christian values and virtues that had built it up, but we shall need to consider how this perception came to be established in the European mind. It was not unknown in the fifth century, and the great discourses we shall study were framed to combat it; they, however, were the work of minds trained in the rhetoric of Christian empire. This rhetoric in turn

---

[3] For these terms see *NCG, passim.*

was the convergence of two streams indicated by the name given to it, and we may begin its analysis by considering the rhetoric of empire. The histories of the principate, as we have seen, were as often as not written by intelligences deeply hostile to it, voicing the grievances of a displaced senatorial elite against a system of government that had destroyed *libertas* and made history hard to write; Tacitus is perhaps the first to indicate a doubt whether the principate will be able to uphold the empire that has made it necessary. But where historiography was critical and subversive, there were other discourses powerfully upholding an imperial and Augustan ideal. One of these was poetic; Virgil was to endure through centuries as the bard and almost prophet of an empire which should bring peace to mankind and, under an emperor who restored the virtues of antiquity, bring about a golden age of divine return. His imagery was ecumenical where Tacitus' was metropolitan; it emphasised the peace of the provinces rather than the wars of the frontiers and the civil wars at Rome; and this came near to solving the problem, perplexing to European humanists, of how poetry could have risen to great heights when history was stifled by the lack of liberty. The image of imperial peace co-existed with the image of imperial decline, and this was to drive Gibbon to the assertion that the causes of the latter were 'a secret poison'.[4]

The discourse of empire – we have already seen that it was in part self-problematising and self-critical – was at least as old as the extension of the republic's power beyond Italy; Polybius had situated Roman power in a context made up of Persian, Macedonian and Carthaginian 'empires', and had argued that it was more universal than its predecessors. It is desirable, however, to place the word within quotation marks, reminding ourselves that it is not a given reality but has a complex etymological history. This is the history of how the term *imperium*, originally denoting the authority of a magistrate or military commander, became sharply distinguished into *imperium domi*, exercised within the city, and *imperium militiae*, exercised beyond it.[5] The appellation *imperator* could properly be employed only in the latter context, and came to be a recognition conferred on a commander by his soldiers, acting in a way not altogether detached from the civic; in the civil wars, however, and in the crises of the principate, this recognition became illegitimate, dangerous and in the Tacitean sense an *arcanum*. The rule of Rome came to be exercised by those we call 'emperors' when *imperium domi et militiae* came to be

---

[4] *DF*, 1, ch. 2; Womersley, 1994, 1, p. 83.    [5] Richardson, 1998.

permanently vested in a single person, both *princeps* and *imperator*; the history of the principate as written by Tacitus is the history of the instability of this compound. There is a parallel history, however, in which the *imperium militiae* comes to be identified with the *provinciae* to which it gives rise, and certain of these *provinciae* become means of perpetual domination over peoples beyond Rome, beyond Italy and even – as we would say, though the term was not of cardinal importance to the Romans – beyond Europe. The subject territories become provinces – equally, the *provinciae* of those exercising *imperium* become territories – and their indigenous inhabitants and Roman colonists become provincials. In this way *imperium* comes to mean 'empire'; a term denoting an allocated authority changes to denoting a chain or system of dominated provinces, an oecumene outside which exist only 'barbarians', in one or another of the meanings of that elastic term. It now becomes possible for Romans to say that the *imperium romanum* was the cause of the rule of Rome by *imperatores*, and for us to distinguish between 'the Roman republic' and 'the Roman empire', though we know that 'empire' preceded and occasioned the rule of 'emperors'.

The idea that Rome's quasi-universal dominion over other peoples could be represented as benign, protective and even civilising was of course older than the Caesars. Cicero had described it as having been a *patrocinium*[6] rather than a *dominium*, more akin to the rule of a patron over his clients than to that of a master over his slaves; and clients, though obliged to obedience, were human and social beings to whom protection was due even if they had no enforceable claim to it. They were in addition free, in the sense that they were not slaves; and there were liberties of action and guarantees of property which were theirs under, and in consequence of, the *patrocinium* of their powerful protector. The latter role could be ascribed to the *populus romanus*, and so to the *princeps* in whom *imperium* was concentrated; this is clearly a key concept in the Virgilian ideology of empire. We confront an important difference, at certain points a change, in the concept of liberty; from the *libertas* to exercise *imperium* which had mattered to the Romans, the equality in the exercise of rule which had mattered in Aristotle's theory of citizenship, it comes to mean the freedom of social action which *imperium* recognises in, and extends to, those who have no share in *imperium* themselves.[7] This is the freedom claimed by Paul of Tarsus, Hellenised Jew and apostle of

---

[6] *Ibidem.*, p. 7. He says it became an *imperium* in the time of Sulla.
[7] Wirszubski, 1950, chs. 4 and 5.

Christ, in uttering such formulae as *civis romanus sum* and *appello Caesarem* (it is better to give them in Latin than in the Greek in which they are first recorded), and Paul's claims are more effective than those of Thrasea Paetus and Helvidius Priscus, Stoic philosophers seeking to recover the *libertas* proper to Roman senators. We confront the distinction between the political and the social, the positive and the negative, concepts of freedom and personality, a distinction which is to be as important in the history of historiography as in that of political philosophy. The concept of civil society begins to appear as 'republic' is replaced by 'empire'.

If we begin to move – as far as the state of things under Roman empire permits us – towards the concept of liberty as the enjoyment of protection by the law, we can see the development of codes of ecumenical jurisprudence as vital to the legitimation of both empire and emperor. Paul appealing to Caesar was securing Caesar as well as himself; he was contributing to the image of Caesar as universal protector, assisting the *princeps* to move away from the jealously insecure tyrant which lack of republican legitimacy made him and become a 'prince' in the later European sense of the term, *legibus solutus* but *ille cui quod placuit habebat legis vigorem*, conditioned yet secured by the codified law of which he was the ultimate determinant. This was an imperial and provincial rather than a metropolitan conception of empire and emperor. Caesar might be at the same time a tyrant at Rome and a lawgiver to the provinces, and the only danger inherent in Paul's action was that appeal to Caesar obliged him to remove to Rome, where (it was said) he underwent martyrdom, long after the success of his appeal, at the hands of Nero. Decline and Fall might appear an outcome of either the corruption of provincial by metropolitan government, or (as to Gibbon) the abandonment of the metropolis by the provinces; but neither perception was known to antiquity. Roman law equated Caesar with universal justice and (in the social sense) universal liberty; it made him the guardian and the embodiment of the *felicitas* and *fortuna* of the ecumenical empire, and permitted him the veneration of all the cults by which a sophisticated polytheism ascribed divinity to him as embodying all these values.

This was the religion of empire – a political theology in ancient terms, a civil religion in modern – in which Christians were invited to join, and persecuted when they did not. The stumbling block was perhaps less their refusal of any sacrifice but that already performed by Christ – their offer to pray for Caesar instead of sacrificing to the gods might have been negotiated with magistrates in search of a solution – than their insistence that the legion of deities with whom Caesar associated were all of them false, and not merely illusions but active and malignant demons. Caesar's apparently minimal demand for a token sacrifice thus brought into the open what seemed to ancient minds the atheism of Christians, their entire rejection of the natural and supernatural world; and this is thought to account for the hatred in which, the martyrologies insist, their urban neighbours often outdistanced the unwilling (and therefore brutal) magistrates. The Christian issue became one of all or nothing. When Caesar chose to adopt Christianity as the religion of the empire he found – even though he did this by steps – that, no longer the associate of all the gods, he must be the associate of one only. This is a central fact behind the growth of ecclesiastical historiography, which changed the meaning of what it was to write history.

(III)

The history of the church is – or more properly includes – that of a human society like no other, in that it exists and can be narrated in a human time generated by the social order, but claims to transcend that order and exist simultaneously in a history which is that of the interventions in time of the divine and eternal. This is the point at which the church becomes Voltaire's *l'infâme*, a society existing within the social order but claiming an authority above and beyond it; Voltaire's perception may be thought of as a secularisation of that of the ancient persecutors whom he rejected. We are in search of a structure for Christian historiography, and have reached a point where sacred history – the narrative of God's actions upon and in time – can be seen as including, but especially visible in, ecclesiastical history: the history of a society at once human and transcending the human, both continuing the divine action of which it is the vehicle and endeavouring, by means human and fallible, to maintain the authority by which it vicariously performs that action. The church finds itself in a world fallen and haunted by evil, which it acts to redeem but which constantly threatens its capacity for redemption. There is a history of agonistic struggle, which is the primary history of the church under the rule of pagan magistrates, from Pontius Pilate to the competitors overthrown by Constantine.

This history – almost the civil history of the redemptive society – has to be set in the larger context of sacred history since the creation of the world. In one perspective the church begins its history at the ascension of Christ; in another, it is a fellowship with the divine that exists beyond time and has existed since time began. Its sacred history is a retelling of that of Israel; originally a Jewish sect, it lays hold of the Hebrew scriptures and re-narrates them as an Old Testament foretelling and typifying a New. It constructs a history of humanity in two ways. First, as it extends itself beyond the Jews to the Gentiles, it is necessitated to associate Gentile history – especially Greek and Roman – with that of Israel as the church retells it. There arise a number of interpretative techniques, of which that of comparative chronology is the most prominent, designed to harmonise the history and creation narratives of peoples other than Israel with that of Israel conceived as antetype to that of the church, so as to associate Gentile history with the history of redemption. This enterprise is important to the history of historiography in a number of ways. It obliges historians to provide documentation as well as narrative; it perpetuates Christian concern with the narrative histories of the Greeks and Romans; and in extending itself to the less classically narrated histories of Babylonians, Medians and Persians – to say nothing of Egyptians – it contributes to that complex relation between antiquarian scholarship and narrative history which we know remained crucial as late as the time of Gibbon. This may be termed the Gentile dimension of Christian sacred history.

It was Israel, however, that provided the dimension vitally important. The Christian narrative was committed to presenting Jesus as the Christ or Messiah, prophesied in the Davidic and Exilic writings, but come in a shape the Jews had not expected, bringing a redemption extensible to the Gentiles. It followed, first, that the Old Testament must be annexed to a New, and made to foretell it by means of interpretation not indeed esoteric or secret, but accessible only to believing Christians. Not all, but many of these entailed the use of analogy or typology; one event or saying was proved the shadow of another, by which it would be perfected or fulfilled in the course of sacred time, and the management of this interpretative skill came to be vastly important in the Christian management of history, culminating in the demonstration that the church was itself the second Israel and everything said of the first proved true of the second. Type and antetype were metaphor raised to the height of sacred power; the language of prophecy where it became the language of God himself. There will come a point where this proves crucial in constructing the discourse of empire. In the second place, however, the annexation of the first Israel by the second entailed the rejection of the first as surviving it. Jesus had been the Messiah promised to the Jews, but they had crowned a long history of backslidings from their mission as a chosen people by rejecting and killing him. The history of their apostasy became central to sacred history, which in some recensions could not culminate until they should recognise him at the end of time. Their downfall and ejection from history became essential to the validation of the church as successor to their role, which is why, from Eusebius to Bossuet, we meet with historians for whom the fall of Jerusalem is incomparably more significant than the fall of Rome, and Josephus' narrative of actions performed by Vespasian and Titus in AD 70–71 more important than that of Tacitus. What they did at Jerusalem was, though they did not know it, a turning point in sacred history; what they did at Rome was not.

It should follow that the fall of Rome – whenever such an event might be held to have occurred – was not an apocalyptic climax; it did not occur in sacred history, but merely in the history of the Gentiles. But once the redemptive mission was extended to the Gentiles, they entered into sacred history and might be the subject of its narrative; how were they to have a sacred history of their own? Here we encounter the fact that the writers of Christian history were, almost without exception, subjects or citizens of the Roman oecumene (or 'empire') and partakers in its Greek and Latin culture; and 'the Gentiles' become sharply subdivided into those who were 'barbarians' and the Greeks and Romans who were not. There is a high correlation between acceptance of Greco-Latin culture and acceptance of the Christian message, and the former must be assimilated to the latter by means altogether different from the annexation of the Old Testament to a created New. No Greek or Latin could be said to have prophesied the coming of Christ, because the word of the Lord did not come to any Gentile and command him to speak as a prophet; the classical and the Christian must be connected through an altogether different history. This was profane, even if it could be related to the sacred; even if its cultural prestige was very nearly the rival of the sacred.

Here we should observe – whenever and by what stages it happened – that Christians annexed the Virgilian myth of empire and assimilated it as closely as they could to their own sacred history. The ecumenical peace brought in by Augustus, under which Virgil looked for a golden age inaugurating a new historical cycle, became a peaceable order, conducive to the dissemination of the gospel. Under it God had consented to be born as man, when Augustus decreed that all the world should be taxed, and to suffer a redeeming death at the hands of Roman magistrates, who were almost the agents of redemption. Christians thus adopted the image of the *imperium* as a benign *patrocinium*, and extended to the Romans as its creators a role almost that of a chosen people. Christ had been born into, and by virtue of, a world of social order, exercising what might almost be called an *imperium* through his divinity; and this idea was to be crucial for perhaps a millennium and a half, in applying an imperial character to the church and a sacred character to the empire. But the Romans could never be a chosen people in the same way as the Jews. The latter had been chosen by covenant, by messages revealed to the patriarchs and laws revealed to the people; they had been given a direct charge and command, to which it was possible that they might prove disobedient and apostate. The fall of Jerusalem had been punishment for the ultimate apostasy of rejecting Christ; but Vespasian and Titus in AD 70, like Augustus forty years before, had not known that they were doing what they had been chosen to do. Apostasy was not possible for them, since they were not peoples of the covenant, and to say that they had been chosen for a certain role was to alter the meaning of the verb. In the place of covenant and revelation, there arose a new concept, that of providence: the mysterious power of God to arrange the circumstances in which humans act, so that the consequences of their acts are not those which they intend and perceive, but those conducive to his purposes. The notion of providence was to prove of great importance to histori-ography, as enlarging, mystifying and at the same time rationalising the multiplicity of contexts in which history goes on. It was also to heighten the bitterness and perplexity with which Gibbon's Christian contem-poraries read his account of the rise of the church in his fifteenth and sixteenth chapters. The array of secondary causes he adduced seemed to eliminate all need of a special providence arranging human affairs; yet the more providence was said to be special, the less it resembled the mere divine manipulation of historical circumstances, and the more it implied the direct action and immediate presence of the Holy Spirit. The real issue between Gibbon and his contemporaries was whether the first dissemination of Christianity had been pentecostal, an effect of the powers given the apostles in the upper room and continuing throughout their lives and perhaps those of others.[8] The issue for us in this chapter is that the adoption of the Romans into sacred history required new techniques of historical narration.

One of these was metaphor; providence was a way of saying that the Romans acted as if they had been chosen to perform certain tasks. But we have already seen that metaphor could be extended into typology; a given action or construction could be the mirror in anticipation of one yet

---

[8]  Womersley, 1997a; Pocock, 2000 (see p. 4, n. 2).

to come, in which its full meaning would become known. We are looking at a construct in which empire is the precondition of church and may be said to anticipate it. Neither Jesus nor Paul had been legislators of empire; they had been subjects – Paul a citizen – of an *imperium romanum*, and had commanded obedience to both the Roman Caesar and the Jewish law (until the latter had ceased to deserve it). But Jesus had been the founder, by authority of the divine nature that was his, of a new society, the church, which he left behind him to act as his person until the end of days; we are still at the point where incarnation makes metaphor an actuality. The spread of empire, which he had endorsed, was in ways sometimes mysterious conducive to the spread of the church; and once the empire had become even nominally a Christian society, it was possible to sacralise it by making it the antetype of the church, not so much preceding it in time as co-existing with it until the end of days, when antetype should give way to type. We have next to consider how the idea was constructed of a sacred empire, almost if never quite a church, and what became of that idea when the empire lost control of its further western provinces.

## (IV)

Eusebius of Caesarea – one of the entourage of the emperor Constantine – is acknowledged, though he had predecessors, to have given ecclesiastical history its enduring shape. Commenting on his work under that title, Arnaldo Momigliano found it most remarkable that Eusebius had recounted the history of the church – still a limited segment of late Roman society – side by side with the history of the empire, and had given it equal if not greater importance.[9] No other religious society of the period, except the Jewish, is known to have done this, and Jews did not write the history of the diaspora. We have to set aside a medieval Latin perspective which tempts us to take ecclesiastical history for granted, and consider just how it was possible for Eusebius to do this. The church was both a human society no older than the reign of Augustus, and a fellowship of humans with God as old as the creation. It had therefore two histories: one universal, organised around the Mosaic and Gentile chronologies and the adoption of Jewish history as forerunner of Christian; the other ecclesiastical in the specific sense that it was the narrative of the organisation and vicissitudes of the Christian society since

---

[9] For modern translations of Eusebius, see Williamson, 1965, and Cameron and Hall, 1999. For his place in the history of historiography, see Momigliano, 1990, pp. 132–52. There is a detailed analysis of his writings in Barnes, 1981, chs. 7–10, 13–15.

the ascension of Christ and the acts of the apostles (Paul and Peter in particular). This history had two faces: the one institutional, relating the succession of consecrated bishops since the apostles, and displaying the continuity of the church as the presence of Christ; the other triumphal, relating the suffering and glory of Christ's followers in a world of spiritual evil (not much present in the Gospels and only beginning to appear in the Acts). Since its exit from a purely Jewish ambience, Christianity had confronted a world of hostile gods and had undergone persecution by an imperial regime reliant on polytheist support. It had characterised these gods as demons, increasing the vehemence of its persecutors, and the history which Eusebius set out to describe – filling the uncanonically documented gap between Paul's departure for Rome and the time at which he was writing – was a history of combat with demons, assailing the church from without in the shape of persecutors and from within in the shape of heretics. These had been resisted by means spiritual in the former case – the sufferings of martyrs transformed into heavenly triumph – and intellectual in the latter: the disputations in which the heresies had been confuted. But persecution had been imperial as well as demonic, an act of state to which emperors had repeatedly resorted; and ecclesiastical history – as Gibbon found from Lactantius' *De mortibus persecutorum* to Tillemont's *Histoire des empereurs*[10] – had written the history of the pagan emperors as a history of those who were persecutors or were not. The Christian writers did not condemn the principate or the empire as a simply heathen or demonic engine of persecution, though they possessed the means of presenting it in this light; in the sequence of four empires laid down by the prophet Daniel, the Roman might be identified either with Babylon, the first, or with the fourth, a mystical empire which should endure till the end of the sequence and of time itself. The latter could be exalted into a prophetic role; either the antithesis or the antetype of the heavenly kingdom to come. Even under the fiercest persecution, however, Christians were not anxious to prophesy the fall of Rome as a godless Babylon; they wished to live as Romans and co-opt the empire to their cause, and by the time of Eusebius they could achieve this, by recounting the history of Constantine as the triumph of a godly emperor over both persecutors and the policy of persecution. At this point the history of the church, as that of a society both human and divine, both limited and eternal, merged with the history of the empire, and the two re-wrote one another.

[10] Womersley, 1994, III, pp. 1232, 1268–9.

They were essentially distinct, yet could converge. The history of the pagan and persecuting empire was a history of demonic possession overthrown by Christ at the victory of Constantine; but it was a history of transformation, not of decline and fall. Assuming the empire to be, potentially or actually, the vehicle of the church, the decision that the empire should become Christian could be presented as the moment when empire and church became one. The demons had not been banished, since the heresies persisted; the emperor had a role to play in combating them, from which he might lapse to a degree approaching apostasy; yet apostasy from a role is no proof that the role does not exist. The image of the empire as church was present as metaphor, and therefore as typified reality; and in this image the emperor reigned over the church and its bishops, in a capacity approaching that of a type of Christ. Constantine saw himself as equal to the apostles, the bishop of those not yet within the church; and if he planned a tomb for himself surrounded by twelve symbolic catafalques, it would be hard to deny that he claimed to anticipate the return of the pantocrator. The act may be seen as evidence of a surviving paganism; perhaps Caesar was treating Christ as he might treat other gods; but as the person of Christ came to be accorded full equality within the Trinity, the role of his type was exalted with him. A realistic churchman might enquire which of the twelve tombs was that of Judas, or his replacement Mathias; but even a bishop who rebuked Caesar, as Ambrose of Milan did Theodosius, for acts unworthy of his sacred position did not deny that the position was sacred.

Milan was far off, left behind in the west by the foundation of Constantinople; and even if it took time to empty the new Rome of all symbols of pre-Christian authority, and to Christianise those which remained, the city could figure as exclusively the theatre of sacred empire, in which the church was distinct but not independent. The rule of an emperor who was the primary figure symbolising or typifying Christ became an image accompanying a military, administrative and cultural system which continued to govern the provinces immediately dependent upon it, and did not undergo Decline and Fall in the sense of losing them to barbarian control. This is the difference between history east and west, Greek and Latin, Orthodox and Catholic; but the difference occurs within the history of the sacred monarchy outlined by Eusebius. We have previously identified the problem of connecting the decline of the Antonines in the second century with the collapse of western empire in the fifth. We now encounter the problems arising from the premise that the latter crisis occurred not in the history of Augustus' principate, but in that of Constantine's Christian monarchy; and in provinces, furthermore, which that monarchy could be said to have left behind it. Decline and Fall is a Latin problem, not constructed or confronted in the thought of the Constantinopolitan empire. We have next to discover that even in the abandoned and half-barbarised west, where popes usurped the role of emperors and Gibbon could locate the 'triumph of barbarism and religion', the imagery of Eusebian sacred empire remained so powerful that it was a thousand years before the concept of Decline and Fall, and the Roman thinking that had begun to explain it before it happened, became a central necessity to a historical intelligence.

# PART II

# *The ambivalence and survival of Christian empire*

# CHAPTER 5

# Orosius and Augustine: the formation of a Christian anti-history

## (I)

Ammianus Marcellinus, the last of the classical Roman historians, is thought to have completed his history about the year 395, fifteen years before the sack of Rome by Alaric, and a little more than twenty before Orosius wrote his *Historiarum adversum paganos libri VII*, at a moment when Augustine had completed the first ten books of *De civitate Dei contra paganos*.[1] Ammianus seems to have begun his history – the first thirteen books are lost – with the reign of Nerva, perhaps rather because this was the point at which Tacitus and Suetonius had left off than because he thought it marked a new phase in the history of the principate.[2] He once refers to the earliest emperors as *civiles principes*, as if this distinguished them from the military and hieratic figures of his own time;[3] but because the books that survive begin late in the reign of Constantine's successor Gallus (a historiographically tyrannical figure), we cannot say that he thinks the principate transformed by the adoption of Christianity, and he is more concerned to relate the actions of those who held the office than to narrate changes in the office's character. What may be read as situating his history in a linear structure linking Tacitus with Gibbon is a passage in Book 14, the first we have, contrasting the magnificence and awesome size of the buildings of Rome with the egoism, luxury and pettiness of their present inhabitants. Once the empire of Rome included the known world, he says, it was right that the ancient city should entrust its government to a monarchy, remaining itself venerable as the image of an empire it no longer exercised.[4] Here Ammianus takes his place among the historians of the sequence that so impressed Gibbon, that of

---

[1] Markus, 1970, p. i.
[2] Hamilton and Wallace-Hadrill, 1986, pp. 20–2, 443 (the closing sentences of the history; Book 31, 16:7).
[3] Book 15, 1:3 (Hamilton and Wallace-Hadrill, 1986, p. 65); Matthews, 1989, p. 235.
[4] Book 14, 5:6 (Hamilton and Wallace-Hadrill, 1986, pp. 45–50, in particular 46).

the movement of power away from the city and the status of the buildings left behind; but he does not quite say, as a Roman moralist would, that the departure of power accounts for the degeneracy of a citizenry left with nothing but luxury. Ammianus was a Greek from Antioch who had learned to write in Latin; the *urbs Roma* and *populus Romanus*, however powerful a symbol, were not his *patria* and he was writing the history of the armies, happening *alibi quam Romae*.

Nor can he be called a historian of Christian empire. His surviving narrative encompasses the reign of Julian, who tried and failed to reverse the work of Constantine, and events to which Christianity is central figure in it prominently; but the problems caused by the new religion, before and after its adoption by the emperors, are dealt with simply as aspects and incidents of their reigns. We feel confident in saying that Ammianus was a philosophic pagan;[5] but perhaps this too is unnecessary, and we are faced simply with two historiographical discourses, that of history and that of ecclesiastical history, which had yet to establish any ground whatever common to both.[6] The short interval of time separating Ammianus from Augustine may be used to dramatise this disjunction; but Augustine was rejecting not Ammianus, but the historiography of Christian empire as an aspect of ecclesiastical history.

(II)

It was sacred empire as it existed under the sons of Theodosius which suffered the shock of 410, when a Gothic warband in a disintegrating imperial service entered Rome and looted it. This event remains central in our image of Decline and Fall, as do many of the immediate responses of contemporaries to it, but we must beware of supposing that the empire it befell was a single body with a shared consciousness. The Dalmatian church father Jerome, living as far from Rome as Bethlehem, indeed recalled how the news of the sack devastated his sense of personal security;[7] yet Jerome wrote his recollections into a commentary on the prophet Ezekiel and organised them into a vision of the two cities. There was the destruction of the mystical Babylon typified by a Rome still heathen; there were the sufferings of the Christian community at

---

[5] For the very strong case that Ammianus' standpoint, and probably his personal beliefs, are pagan, see Wallace-Hadrill, in Hamilton and Wallace-Hadrill, 1986, pp. 31–3.

[6] Markus, 1970, pp. 1–21; Momigliano, 1963, pp. 79–99; Averil Cameron in Bowersock, Brown and Grabar, 1999. I rely heavily on these works in what follows.

[7] Pelikan, 1987, pp. 43–52.

Rome, whose members Jerome vividly remembered. He must wonder whether the world was ending and the Antichrist was at hand; but he could not do this without experiencing, and expressing, intense veneration for the violated city that ambivalently signified all history, pagan as well as Christian. Decline and Fall – if we are to take Jerome's agonised language as beginning to utter such a concept – therefore expressed a nostalgia for the old Rome from a standpoint that included the new. He was physically closer to Constantinople as he heard the news from Italy and wrote his letters and commentaries; and although he might wonder whether the new Rome could sustain the world in being, those at the centre of its power were in fewer doubts. To the heirs of Eusebius – the authoritative ecclesiastical historians Socrates Scholasticus, Sozomen and Theodoret – Alaric's sack of Rome was a far-off provincial event, a local setback to a world in which *ubi Caesar, ibi imperium*.[8]

The literature of Decline and Fall is conventionally held to begin with the responses of west Roman intellects to the news of the sack of the city in 410. Jerome in Bethlehem is a background figure in the construction of this literature. Orosius seems to have travelled as Augustine's emissary to co-ordinate with him the condemnation of Pelagius' teachings,[9] and we have to remember that the western authors were no less concerned with conflicts interior to the church than with the fall of the city to the Goths. As well as the perceived heresy of Pelagius from Britain, the Donatists in Africa had carried to the point of schism their contention that the imperially protected church, under leadership they considered apostate, had become a false church and instrument of Satan, and this might have appeared a greater crisis in the history of the church and empire than Alaric's symbolically loaded but transitory assault on Rome. Orosius and Augustine, however, wrote *contra paganos*, not *contra hereticos*. Among the Roman and Italian refugees arriving in Africa were not a few adherents of the old religions and their attendant philosophies, who declared that the disaster was due to the empire's abandonment of the gods of the city. To an eighteenth- and very likely to a fifth-century ear, this would mean that the old religions had been civic religions and that the city and empire would have been stronger if still practising cults rooted in their history. The Enlightened 'rebirth of modern paganism' – to employ that knotty phrase[10] – concurred that the ancient gods were civic fictions, but held that civil society did better to worship itself and its own myths, rather than abstractions from experience situated outside it. The study

---

[8] Pelikan, 1987, pp. 67–78.    [9] Raymond, 1936, pp. 6–9.    [10] Gay, 1966.

of history was in itself a re-institution of civil society, and it can have been no surprise to Gibbon to find Augustine and Orosius engaged in a deconstruction of history and a denial that it was a central location of human experience.

Both writers – Orosius from Roman Spain, Augustine in Roman Africa, two provinces under Vandal attack – were faced with pagans blaming Christianity for the disasters of the times and responded with lengthy demonstrations that there had been just as many disasters in the ages before Christian revelation. This tactic was not as puerile as it may seem and was something more than a rhetorical exercise. It entailed the contention that Roman empire had not in fact brought peace to mankind, or been necessary to the coming of Christ and the growth of his salvific church. In both its pagan and its Christian, its imperial and its ecclesiastical forms, the empire had left history 'little more than the register of the crimes, follies and misfortunes of mankind'.[11] The language of course is Gibbon's; he thought the uneventful reign of Antoninus Pius one of the few exceptions, during which the peace of civil society had left the historian of human actions no significant crimes and follies to record. His position is of course the reverse of that taken up by Orosius and Augustine, since they held that not even civil society and imperial peace could save history – the word is ours, not theirs – from being what it was, and that one must withdraw from it into the peace of Christ. Whether Gibbon thought withdrawal from the world a principal cause of worldly disasters is a problem to be revisited elsewhere.

Since this volume is a study of historiography, it gives the *Historiarum adversum paganos libri VII* priority over the *De civitate Dei contra paganos*. The latter is by far the greater work and ten books of it had been completed when Orosius presented his achievement to Augustine.[12] We are concerned here with an abandonment of historiography, and of the Tacitean narrative in particular; and from that standpoint we shall see that Orosius, merely because he conceived his work as a history, was bound to fail by the more far-reaching criteria set forth by Augustine. The *De civitate Dei* is a critique of history itself. As we study the rejection of history, however, we must have an eye to the extent to which history survived that rejection, in forms capable of being revived at later dates; and here the lesser mind and enterprise may have as much to tell us as the greater. Orosius attempts, with debatable success, to reconcile two positions: that history records the crimes and sufferings of unredeemed humanity, and

---

[11] *DF*, i, ch. 3; Womersley, 1994, i, p. 102.    [12] Raymond, 1936, p. 30.

that, in respect of the history of Christian empire, it is providentially directed towards universal good. Dedicating his work to Augustine, he says:

praeceperas ergo, ut ex omnibus qui haberi ad praesens possunt historiarum atque annalium fastis, quaecumque aut bellis grauia aut corrupta morbis aut fame tristia aut terrarum motibus terribilia aut inundationibus aquarum in-solita aut eruptionibus ignium metuenda aut ictibus fulminum plagisque grand-inum saeua uel etiam parricidiis flagitiisque misera per transacta retro saecula repperissem, ordinato breuiter uoluminis textu explicarem . . . Nanctus sum enim praeteritos dies non solum aeque ut hos graues, uerum etiam tanta atro-cius miseros quanto longius a remedio uerae religionis alienos: ut merito hac scrutatione claruerit regnasse mortem auidam sanguinis, dum ignoratur religio quae prohiberet a sanguine; ista inlucescente, illam constupuisse; illam con-cludi, cum ista iam praeualet; illam penitus nullam futuram, cum haec sola regnabit.[13]

[You bade me, therefore, discover from all the available data of histories and annals whatever instances past ages have afforded of the burdens of war, the ravages of disease, the horrors of famine, of terrible earthquakes, extraordinary floods, dreadful eruptions of fire, thunderbolts and hailstorms, and also instances of the cruel miseries caused by parricides and disgusting crimes. I was to set these forth systematically and briefly in the course of my book . . . But now I have discovered that the days of the past were not only as oppressive as those of the present but that they were the more terribly wretched the further they were removed from the consolation of true religion. My investigation has shown, as was proper it should, that death and a thirst for bloodshed prevailed during the time in which the religion that forbids bloodshed was unknown; that as the new faith dawned, the old grew faint; that while the old neared its end, the new was already victorious; that the old beliefs will be dead and gone when the new religion shall reign alone.][14]

Natural as well as human calamities are to be recorded, because Oro-sius is in search of evidences of divine punishment as well as human crime (it was in the age of the Lisbon earthquake that Voltaire denied any connection between the two). His exercise, however, is more than a mere heaping up of disaster narratives in a crude score-sheet between past and present. What renders Orosius interesting in the history of his-toriography is his systematic rejection of the narrative of republican and imperial virtue, and therefore of the premises and principles on which all Roman and nearly all classical history had been written. Addressing Augustine in the preface to his third book, he says:

[13] Orosius, 1889, pp. 2–3.  [14] Capitalisation added. Raymond, 1936, pp. 30–1.

Et superiore iam libro contestatus sum et nunc necessarie repeto secundum praeceptum tuum de anteactis conflictationibus saeculi: nec omnia nec per omnia posse quae gesta et sicut gesta sunt explicari, quoniam magna atque innumera copiosissime et a plurimis scripta sunt, scriptores autem etsi non easdem causas, easdem tamen res habuere propositas, quippe cum illi bella, nos bellorum miserias euoluamus.[5]

[In an earlier book I began my argument and now, in accordance with your instructions, I must resume the story of the struggles of bygone ages. I cannot here relate in full detail everything that has happened and how it came to pass, since many authors have already written at great length about innumerable matters of importance. These historians, however, came to no agreement in their interpretations, despite the fact that they had at their disposal the same materials; for they were describing wars, whereas I for my part am more concerned with the miseries caused by wars.][6]

He goes on to state the classical dilemma (not unknown to Gibbon) between too much prolixity in describing causes and too much brevity in relating events. Any of his predecessors could have, and most had, said as much, and Orosius is not unique when he claims: *nos uim rerum, non imaginem commendare curemus* [I am concerned with . . . the meaning of events rather than their description.][7] The word *miserias*, however, is a key to his intention. By *uim rerum* he intends no political *verità effettuale* or *eigentlich gewesen*; he is concerned to show that pre-Christian action was not only warlike and the occasion of miseries, but the action of depraved and unredeemed men, causing misery to the conquerors as well as the conquered. This must magnify his encounter with the difficulties faced by all historians, for in re-telling the narratives of others he must reverse the values according to which previous narratives were written. Orosius is a fierce critic of what we should term imperialism; the values of his criticism are not the same as ours, but he shares with contemporary post-colonial writers a determination to tell the story of empire from the bottom up. This lends his writing an air curiously postmodern, perhaps we should say postantique; it is as if we were reading the subaltern studies of the ancient world. At the opening of Book v he says:

Ecce quam feliciter Roma uincit tam infeliciter quidquid extra Romam est uincitur . . . An forte aliud tunc Carthagini uidebatur, cum post annos centum uiginti, quibus modo bellorum clades modo pacis condiciones perhorrescens, nunc rebelli intentione nunc supplici bellis pacem, pace bella mutabat, nouissime miseris ciuibus passim se in ignem ultima desperatione iacientibus unus rogus tota ciuitas fuit? Cui etiam nunc, situ paruae, moenibus destitutae, pars

---

[5] Orosius, 1889, p. 63.    [6] Raymond, 1936, p. 107.    [7] *Ibidem.*

miseriarum est audire quid fuerit. Edat Hispania sententiam suam: cum per annos ducentos ubique agros suos sanguine suo rigabat importunumque hostem
ultro ostiatim inquietantem nec repellere potebat nec sustinere . . . quid tunc de
suis temporibus sentiebat? Ipsa postremo dicat Italia: cur per annos quadrin-
gentos Romanis utique suis contradixit obstitit repugnauit, si eorum felicitas sua
infelicitas non erat Romanosque fieri rerum dominos bonis communibus non
obstabat?[18]

[It will then appear that whenever Rome conquers and is happy the rest of
the world is unhappy and conquered . . . Did Carthage perhaps not view the
situation differently at that time? Over a period of one hundred and twenty
years the city alternately dreaded the disasters of war and the terms of peace.
At one time deciding to renew war and at another to sue humbly for peace,
Carthage was continually exchanging peace for war and war for peace. In the
end her wretched citizens throughout the city were driven to desperation and
threw themselves into the flames. The whole city became one funeral pyre. The
city is now small and destitute of walls, and it is part of her unhappy lot to hear
of her glorious past.

Let Spain present her opinion. For two hundred years Spanish fields were
drenched with her own blood. The country was unable either to drive back
or to withstand a troublesome enemy that was persistently attacking on every
side . . . What was Spain, then, to think about her own condition?

And now let Italy speak. Why should Italy have oppressed, resisted, and
placed all sorts of obstacles in the way of her own Romans over a period of four
hundred years? She certainly could not have acted in this way had the happiness
of the Romans not spelled her own disaster and had she not felt that she was
promoting the welfare of all by preventing the Romans from becoming masters
of the entire world.][19]

At another point Orosius imagines a personified Gaul complaining
that Caesar's conquest has left her so exhausted that she is unable to
resist the Goths four or five centuries later.[20] Machiavelli and Robertson
were to agree that Rome had destroyed the virtue of all other peoples
in using up her own, but they were able to imagine secular alternatives:
republican freedom and civil society. What renders Orosius intelligible
in a postmodern perspective is his insistence that civic freedom is itself
destructive and self-destructive, and that outside it there is nothing in the
world but alienation and suffering. He subverts history because the only
history he knows is civic and conquering, and because he can imagine
no other history springing from civic values.

He goes on, at a number of points, to describe conquest itself as destructive to the conquerors and a species of misery to them. There is

---

[18] Orosius, 1889, pp. 141–2.    [19] Capitalisation added. Raymond, 1936, pp. 205–6.
[20] Raymond, 1936, pp. 290–1.

an account of how, at the end of the wars among Sparta, Athens, and Thebes,

tanta fatigatio omnium per totam Graeciam populorum corda corporaque oppresserit, quae efferos animos ignoto adquiescere otio tam facile persuasit.[21]

[a great lassitude oppressed the minds and bodies of all peoples throughout Greece and persuaded their fierce spirits to accept an inactivity hitherto unknown to them.][22]

Orosius is neither unwilling nor unable to expand his narrative into an explanation of general causes.

Contextui indigestae historiae inextricabilem cratem atque incertas bellorum orbes huc et illuc lymphatico furore gestorum uerbis e uestigio secutus inplicui, quoniam tanto, ut uideo, inordinatius scripsi, quanto magis ordinem custodiui.[23]

[I have woven together strands of unrelated events into a historical wickerwork that cannot be unravelled, and following the evidence closely, I have worked in a description of the uncertain cycles of wars waged here and there with uncontrolled fury. I could do this because, as I see it, the more I retained the order of events, the more was my account without order.][24]

We stand here at an important crux. If political narrative imposes no order on history, how far is it capable of supplying general causes of its own self-destruction? This is the point at which Orosius may or may not have had need of what we have termed the Tacitean narrative and the Gracchan explanation, those to us paradigmatic accounts of how the Roman republic and the Augustan principate had been destroyed by the consequences of the conquest of empire. It was open to him not to use them, falling back on the narrative of human misery as a necessary effect of the fallen condition, or to take the step – in which Thucydides and Tacitus had been before him – of using political history to explicate the causes of political catastrophe (whether or not there existed a political means of escaping it).

A version of the Gracchan explanation is distributed through Orosius' chapters. After an account of Scipio's destruction of both Carthage and Numantia, where he goes beyond what we have found in Appian in describing it as unnecessary and presenting it from the point of view of the victims,[25] we hear of the successive seditions of the brothers Gracchus and the suspicious death of Scipio himself.[26] The narrative continues through the Social War, at the end of which

---

[21] Orosius, 1889, p. 64.     [22] Raymond, 1936, p. 108.     [23] Orosius, 1889, p. 68.
[24] Raymond, 1936, p. 114.     [25] Raymond, 1936, pp. 215, 219–21.
[26] Raymond, 1936, pp. 221–2, 225, 227–8.

cum penitus exhaustum esset aerarium et ad stipendium frumenti deesset
expensa, loca publica quae in circuitu Capitolii pontificibus auguribus de-
cemuiris et flaminibus in possessionem tradita erant, cogente inopia uen-
dita sunt et sufficiens pecuniae modus, qui ad tempus inopiae subsidio esset,
acceptus est. Equidem tunc in sinus ipsius ciuitatis euersarum omnium urbium
nudatarumque terrarum abrasae undique opes congerebantur, cum ipsa Roma
turpi adigente inopia praecipuas sui partes auctionabatur. Quamobrem con-
sideret tunc tempora sua, cum quasi inexplebilis uenter cuncta consumens et
semper esuriens cunctis urbibus, quas miseras faciebat, pisa miserior nihil re-
linquens nihil habebat et stimulo domesticae famis ad continuationem bellicae
inquietudinis trudebatur.[27]

[The treasury at that time was thoroughly depleted and funds for the payment
of grain were lacking. The public properties within the circuit of the Capitol,
the ancient possessions of the pontifices, augurs, decemvirs and flamines, were
therefore sold under the pressure of necessity. These brought enough money to
relieve the deficit for the time being. Indeed all the wealth that had been seized
from conquered cities and from lands stripped bare was heaped up in the lap
of Rome at the time when the City herself, compelled by the urgency of her
shameful need, was putting up at auction her own most valuable properties.
Therefore let Rome now reflect upon her own past. Like an insatiable stomach
that consumes everything and yet remains always hungry, the City herself, more
wretched than other cities that she was making wretched, left nothing; and she
was forced by the pinch of hunger at home to continue in that state of unrest
which war engenders.][28]

We may see in this passage a material kernel to Orosius' moral account of how *libido dominandi*, the universal wolf, at last eats up itself; he
constantly insists on the desperation and insecurity in which even conquering cities exist from year to year. But the analysis is not carried on,
as in Appian it is, into a narrative of the wars of the second triumvirate
and the *bellum Actiacum*; these events are not presented as aspects of the
fate of Rome. There is little mention of Catiline, whose conspiracy is not
the turning point it was to become. Nor is there any Tacitean analysis of
the rule of Tiberius or the wars at the death of Nero; these events, and
Roman history in general, are being caught up in narrative of an altogether new kind. Orosius now changes key, and sets out to show that
the victory of Augustus, and the cessation of wars (other than on the
frontiers) which followed from it, were providentially ordained, constituting that world order under which Christ condescended to be born and
commence the work of salvation.[29] This does not mean an end to the

---

[27] Orosius, 1889, p. 172.
[28] Raymond, 1936, pp. 244–5. 'Stipendium frumenti' might have been translated as 'the distribution
    of grain' – i.e., to the city populace – since it is to this that Orosius seems to refer.
[29] Raymond, 1936, pp. 310–12, 316–17, 322–3.

history of pride, empire and misery; the history of the four empires is still at work; but the history of the church has begun and will converge with that of Roman empire. It is three hundred years from Augustus to Constantine, and much unredeemed history is still to be recounted; but the wicked acts that fill it are not those of sin in general but of persecution in particular, and the sufferings of martyrs give victimhood a new meaning, which is not that of simple misery. To recount this history *contra paganos* is to teach the heathen a new lesson.

(III)

The history of empire has now been enlisted, though not assimilated, by history sacred and ecclesiastical, but the terms in which this has been done are not immediately evident. Augustus entered Rome in triumph and closed the gates of Janus in token of perpetual peace on the sixth of January, which is the day of the Epiphany. It must take time before this sign could be read and understood; but the significance of the miraculous darkness at the moment of Christ's death – that one of all miracles which Gibbon laboured to refute[30] – was that in covering the whole earth it declared itself to the whole space of the Roman empire. Orosius insists, as Gibbon denied, that Roman historians mention the occurrence.[31] The fall of Jerusalem and the destruction of the Temple constituted an event of a different order: in sacred history the dispersal of a people once covenanted and now apostate, and the moment at which the first Israel gave place to the second which was the church.[32]

The history of Rome, before and after Christian empire, is linked with sacred history and the history of the church through providence. This means less that its political, imperial or secular history proceeds autonomously and can be viewed as acted upon by providence, than that there are two ways of viewing it in the scheme of sacred history. The earthly city is fallen and pagan, the empire of pride; Rome therefore continues to play the role of Babylon in the sequence of four empires. In this scenario Babylonian and Roman history mirror one another and share the same mortality.

Exaggerare hoc loco mutabilium rerum instabiles status non opus est: quidquid enim est opere et manu factum, labi et consumi uetustate, Babylon capta confirmat: cuius ut primum imperium ac potentissimum exstitit ita et primum cessit, ut ueluti quodam iure succedentis aetatis debita posteris traderetur

---

[30] *DF*, ch. 15; Womersley, 1994, I, pp. 512–13; *Memoirs*, p. 147.
[31] Raymond, 1936, pp. 326–7.     [32] Raymond, 1936, pp. 324, 336–8.

hereditas, ipsi quoque eandem tradendi formulam seruaturis. ita ad proxima
aduentantis Cyri temptamenta succubuit magna Babylon et ingens Lydia, am-
plissima orientis cum capite suo bracchia unius proelii expeditione ceciderunt:
et nostri in circumspecta anxietate causantur, si potentissimae illae quondam
Romanae reipublicae moles nunc magis imbecillitate propriae senectutis quam
alienis concussae uiribus contremescunt.[33]

[It is unnecessary to add here further instances of the unstable conditions that
have followed the changing events of history; for whatever has been built up
by the hand of man falls and comes to an end through the passage of time.
This truth is illustrated by the capture of Babylon. Her empire began to decline
just as it had reached the height of its power, so that, in accordance with a
certain law of succession which runs through the ages, posterity might receive
the inheritance due to it – posterity which was fated to hand on the inheritance
according to the same law. Thus great Babylon and vast Lydia fell at the first
attacks that Cyrus made after his arrival. The mightiest arms of the East and also
the head succumbed in a campaign of a single battle; and now we ourselves, as
we anxiously watch the structure of the once powerful Roman republic, debate
whether it is trembling more from the weakness common to old age or from the
blows struck by foreign invaders.][34]

If decline and fall is simply the effect of mutability, it needs no particular
secular explanation; at most we may detail the particular sins that were
punished in particular instances. In the framework of history, however,
events may either repeat one another or signify a typological sequence.
The Goths may capture Rome as the Medes did Babylon; but the Medes
were the founders of the second of four empires. If (it is not certain) Rome
is the last of the four, the Goths will not found a fifth, but presage, and
perhaps precipitate, the coming of Antichrist and the end of days. There
exists, however, another possibility: that Christian Rome, church as well
as empire, is not another human creation doomed to mutability, but
will last until the coming of Antichrist and withstand him. There may
be a Rome which is not Babylon as well as a Rome which is. When
Orosius takes up this possibility, it has consequences for secular as well
as sacred history. He can suggest that Christian empire from Augustus to
Constantine is less proud and destructive, and to that extent more stable,
than it was in the era of republican expansion; though persecutions and
their punishment recur to remind us that Rome as Babylon is by no
means extinct. He can further suggest that the Goths in their sack of
410 are less destructive than the Gauls at Rome after the *dies Alliensis*.[35]
Towards the end of his work he narrates the events of 410 as the actions

---

[33] Orosius, 1889, p. 43.     [34] Raymond, 1936, p. 82.     [35] Raymond, 1936, pp. 105–6, 143.

of Radagaisus, Stilicho and Alaric, in which the Goth appears a not dishonourable figure, less savage than the one and less treacherous than the other.[36] This leads to a position which may be that which Orosius finally adopts: that the Goths in Italy, and the Vandals in Spain and Africa, constitute a major but still local disturbance in the fabric of an empire still persisting in a history guaranteed by providence. He can mention his own frightening adventures in escaping a barbarian raid, but he can also write:

Mihi autem prima qualiscunque motus perturbatione fugienti, quia de confugiendi statione securo, ubique patria, ubique lex et religio mea est. Nunc me Africa tam libenter excepit quam confidenter accessi . . .

Latitudo orientis, septentrionis copiositas, meridiana diffusio, magnarum insularum largissimae tutissimaeque sedes mei iuris et nominis sunt, quia ad Christianos et Romanos Romanus et Christianus accedo. non timeo deos hospitis mei, non timeo religionem eius necem meam, non habeo talem quem pertimescam locum . . . Ubi sit ius hospitis quod meum non sit; unus Deus, qui temporibus, quibus ipse innotescere uoluit, hanc regni statuit unitatem, ab omnibus et diligitur et timetur; eadem leges, quae uni Deo subiectae sunt, ubique dominantur . . . Inter Romanos, ut dixi, Romanus, inter Christianos Christianus, inter homines homo, legibus inploro rempublicam, religione conscientiam, communione naturam. utor temporarie omni terra quasi patria, quia quae uera est et illa quam amo patria in terra penitus non est. Nihil perdidi, ubi nihil amaui, totumque habeo, quando quem diligo mecum est . . . quia ipsius est terra et plenitudo eius, ex qua omnibus omnia iusit esse communia. Haec sunt nostrorum temporum bona: quae . . . non habuere maiores, ac per hoc incessabilia bella gesserunt, quia, mutandarum sedium communione non libera, persistendo in sedibus suis aut infeliciter necati sunt aut turpiter servierunt.[37]

[At the present, however, I feel no apprehension over the outbreak of any disturbance, since I can take refuge anywhere. No matter where I flee, I find my native land, my law, and my religion. Just now Africa has welcomed me with a warmth of spirit that matched the confidence I felt when I came here . . .[38]

The width of the East, the vastness of the North, the great stretches of the South, and the largest and most secure settlements on great islands, all have the same law and nationality as I, since I come there as a Roman and Christian to Christians and Romans. I do not fear the gods of my host. Neither do I fear that his religion will bring death to me. Nor am I afraid of any place . . . where my host's law will not be my own. One God, Who established the unity of this realm in the days when He willed himself to become known, is loved and feared by all. The same laws, which are subject to this one God, hold sway everywhere . . . Among Romans, as I have said, I am a Roman, among Christians, a Christian; among men, a man. The state comes to my aid through its laws,

---

[36] Raymond, 1936, pp. 383–90.     [37] Capitalisation added. Orosius, 1889, p. 144.
[38] Raymond, 1936, p. 208.

religion through its appeal to the conscience, and nature through its claim to
universality.

For a time I enjoy any country as if it were my own, because that native land,
which is my real home and the one which I love, is not wholly on this earth. I
have lost nothing where I have loved nothing. I have everything when I have with
me Him whom I love . . . because the earth is His and its fullness, whereof He
has ordered all things to be common to all men. These are the blessings of our
age . . . Our ancestors had to wage incessant wars, because, not feeling free to
move as a body and to change their abodes, they continued to remain at home,
where they had the misfortune to be slaughtered or to be basely enslaved.][39]

Decline and Fall is here altogether denied. Barbarian disorders are local disturbances, and there persists a great cosmopolitan and monotheist
civilisation permitting free movement between Spain, Africa and Bethlehem. The unstated premise is that the empire of the new Rome has
survived the sack of the old, and this would be endorsed by all modern
historians of late antiquity, who see Latin, Celtic and German history
as marginal to that of the real Roman empire. It was Rutilius, writing
after the sack of 410, who introduced Gibbon to the idea that Decline
and Fall was that of the city whose empire had deserted it. But Orosius
is not celebrating simply as a Roman the survival of the secular empire
exercised from its capital on the Bosphorus. He declares his citizenship
of the heavenly city, and claims to be at home anywhere because the
earth is the Lord's and the fullness thereof. It is stated with a high degree
of explicitness, however, that the heavenly city guarantees the earthly;
Christ appears to have authorised the universal empire of Augustus in
consenting to be born under it, and though he makes no covenant with
Rome he extends his providence to it. It is because the heavenly city is
universal that Christian universal empire can persist, and it is not altogether true that Orosius has no love for the secular goods that go with
his heavenly citizenship. Christ brings an earthly peace where the pagan
ancestors knew only the sword, and the barbarians at their worst do not
equal the wars of heroic and miserable Rome. Orosius, in short, maintains the providential unity of empire with church, and this is exactly
where he falls short of what Augustine may have wanted from him.

(IV)

There is no lack of distinguished historians to assure us that Augustine,
who makes no reference to the work which Orosius says he assigned to

[39] Raymond, 1936, p. 210.

him, probably read it with feelings of disappointment if not disapproval.[40] Orosius says that ten books of *De civitate Dei* have been written as he is completing his history,[41] and Augustine begins book XI with words suggesting an interval and a resumption.

De ea parte qua duarum civitatum, id est caelestis atque terrenae, initia et fines incipient demonstrari.[42]

[Of the next part of this work, in which we begin to demonstrate the origin and end of the two cities, that is the heavenly and the earthly.][43]

This heading introduces a second part of *De civitate Dei*, which contains philosophy of history but not history itself; that is, a meditation on the metahistorical existence of the soul and the two cities, to which historical processes taking place in the earthly city are increasingly shown to be irrelevant or marginal. What Augustine has to say about the history of Rome, last and greatest of the four empires, is to be found in the ten books already completed, and is not as far as it goes much unlike the account given by Orosius. He points out that Christians do not live by the heroic code of pagan antiquity. A Christian woman who has been raped is aware of her inner chastity, and is not compelled to suicide like the pagan Lucretia, inhabitant of a culture of shame and honour;[44] it may, though it need not, follow that both rape and suicide are less common in a culture living by Christian values. The virtues of pagan Rome – the freedom, discipline, legality and often death-pursuing courage – were driven by a thirst for glory and conquest, a *libido dominandi* which left Rome at its most heroic a prey to fear and the deepest insecurity, and may be considered from the standpoint of the conquered as well as the conquerors. This virtue moreover was self-corrupting. Augustine here introduces the trope which had been central to the understanding of the first Decline and Fall since that process had been anticipated by Polybius: that virtue conquered an empire, but empire corrupted virtue. His text here relies upon Sallust – already a classic source for the associations between *libertas* and *imperium*, *virtus* and *gloria* – whose accounts of Roman degeneracy after the destruction of Carthage and Numantia introduce narrations of the Civil and Social Wars from the sedition of the Gracchi to the final victory of Augustus.[45] It is important to recall that Sallust recounts only two episodes, the war with Jugurtha and the conspiracy

[40] Mommsen, 1959; Brown, 1967, p. 296; Markus, 1970, pp. 161–2.   [41] Raymond, 1936, p. 30.
[42] McCracken et al., 1966, III, p. 425 (Book XI, c.1, title).   [43] Dyson, 1998, p. 449.
[44] McCracken et al., 1966, I, pp. 82–90 (Book I, c. 19); Dyson, 1998, pp. 29–31.
[45] Dyson, 1998, pp. 71–3 (Book II, c. 18), 81 (II, c. 22), 103–5 (III, c. 10), 118–19 (III, c. 17), 129–31 (III, c. 21), 208–12 (V, c. 12).

of Catiline, and that the *peinture* of a corrupt magistracy and citizenry on which these rest matters more to Augustine than the histories they serve to introduce. His purposes are moral, rhetorical and controversial, the denunciation of false morals and the false gods (demons rather than fictions) who promote them. Of the pagan authors whom he cites, Varro's analysis of Roman religion receives more attention than any historical narrative,[46] and a modern reader may feel that here Augustine is writing like a modern historian. This perception is probably misleading, since the replacement of ancient by Christian religion does not, for Augustine, take place in a time dominated by historic processes, but in the intersection of divine action with that time. He does not need to be unaware of such processes in order to be uninterested in them.

Sallust provides him with a model account of the degeneration of the earthly city's values, which sufficiently explains a sequence of occurrences down to the defeat of Mark Antony. It is therefore a reiterated explanation, and we have begun to see that Gibbon employs the Tacitean narrative in a similar way, reiterating it down to the civil wars at the death of Commodus. The two explanations, however, function in very different ways. For Gibbon, Tacitus and other Roman historians, what matters is the disintegration of a political system from causes contained within its own structure. Augustine recounts the fate of the earthly city founded on false values and false gods; it is the downfall of the last-named which matters the most. He does not therefore employ – though it is quite possible that he knows – the complex account of the decay of the military landholding structure which we have found in Appian, and he does not go beyond Sallust to Tacitus. For this we may assign two reasons: one that he is not interested in explanations of this material and secular character, the other, that his interest in Roman decay stops at the decline of the republic and does not extend to that of principate and empire – to Decline and Fall in our understanding of the term. He may seem to be moving towards an Orosian or Eusebian acceptance of the empire as legitimated by the rise of the Christian church.

It does not follow from this that Augustine gives a benign account of the founding of the principate.

Hoc toto tempore usque ad Caesarem Augustum, qui videtur non adhuc vel ipsorum opinione gloriosam, sed contentiosam et exitiosam et plane iam enervem ac languidam libertatem omni modo extortisse Romanis et ad regale arbitrium cuncta revocasse et quas morbida vetustate conlapsam veluti instaurasse ac renovasse rem publicam; toto ergo isto tempore omitto ex aliis atque aliis causis

---

[46] Dyson, 1998, pp. 182–4 (IV, c. 31), 241–51 (VI, cc. 2–6).

etiam atque etiam bellicas clades et Numantinum foedus horrenda ignominia maculosum.[47]

[We come next to the period down to the time of Augustus Caesar. Augustus seems in every way to have wrested their liberty from the Romans; but that liberty was in any case no longer glorious even in their own judgement, but full of contention and danger, and now deeply weakened and depleted. He once more submitted all things to the will of a monarch, and, in doing so, seemed to restore the commonwealth to health in its feeble old age. In the whole of the period down to his time, however, military disasters were sustained again and again for one reason or another. But I omit these. I also omit the treaty of Numantia, marred by such terrible disgrace.][48]

Augustine is not saying that monarchy is inherently superior to republican liberty; the defeat of Varus in Germany shows that Caesar's rule was not free from the military disasters which occur in all empires. He is evidently capable of historical generalisations about a series of bad times beginning with the Numantine war (though here it is a Roman defeat rather than an iniquitous victory that he is stressing). Augustus only seems (*veluti instaurasse*) to have restored the commonwealth and empire, and he is not incapable of brutal actions.

Nam et ipse Augustus cum multis gessit bella civilia, et in eis multi clarissimi viri perierunt inter quos et Cicero disertus ille artifex regendae rei publicae ... Tunc emerserat mirabilis indolis adulescens ille alius Caesar, illius Gai Caesaris filius adoptivus, qui, ut dixi, postea est appellatus Augustus. Huic adulescenti Caesari, ut eius potentia contra Antonium nutriretur, Cicero favebat, sperans eum depulsa et oppressa Antonii dominatione instauraturum rei publicae libertatem, usque adeo caecus atque inprovidus futurorum, uti ille ipse iuvenis, cuius dignitatem ac potestatem fovebat, et eundem Ciceronem occidendum Antonio quadam quasi concordiae pactione permitteret et ipsam libertatem rei publicae, pro qua multum ille clamaverat, dicioni propriae subiugaret.[49]

[Augustus himself waged many civil wars, and in these also there perished many men of the greatest renown, among them Cicero, a man most skilled in the art of governing a commonwealth ... Then emerged a young man of remarkable character: that other Caesar, the adopted son of Gaius Caesar, who was afterwards, as I said, called Augustus. This youthful Caesar was favoured by Cicero, in order that his power might be nurtured in opposition to Antony. So blind and unable to foresee the future was Cicero that he hoped that, when the dominion of Antony had been repulsed and crushed, Augustus Caesar would restore liberty to the commonwealth. But when that young man whose honour and power Cicero had promoted had made a kind of alliance with Antony and

---

[47] McCracken et al., 1966, I, p. 366 (III, c. 21).
[48] Dyson, 1998, p. 130.    [49] McCracken et al., 1966, I, p. 392 (III, c. 30).

subdued to his own rule that very liberty of the commonwealth on behalf of which Cicero had issued so many warnings, he allowed Cicero himself to be slain.][50]

It is the blindness of Cicero's virtue, and indeed of republican liberty itself, that interests Augustine, rather than the perfidy of Augustus. Nor has he much of the historian's concern with tracing the *arcana imperii*, the twists and turns of circumstance and character, that led Cicero to his death. The incident is exemplary, not because Augustine is a classical rhetor seeking lessons from the lives of famous men, but because it is one in a long recital of the disasters and deceptions to which the earthly city is prone by its nature. The rise of Augustus to sole power is the end of Roman liberty, as of the imperial conquests and civil wars to which liberty gave rise, but it is not the culmination of anything more than an episode in human history. We approach here the parting of the ways between Augustine and Orosius. They agree that Augustus brought peace and closed the gates of Janus, but where Orosius holds it to have been the work of providence that the world was at peace, and of grace that Christ chose to be born under that peace, Augustine depicts empire as the work of providence in very different terms.

Sic etiam hominibus: qui Mario, ipse Gaio Caesari; qui Augusto, ipse et Neroni; qui Vespasianis, vel patri vel filio, suavissimis imperatoribus, ipse et Domitiano crudelissimo; et ne per singulis ire necesse sit, qui Constantino Christiano, ipse apostate Iuliano, cuius egregiam indolem decepit amore dominandi sacrilega et detestanda curiositas . . . Haec plane Deus unus et verus regit et gubernat ut placet; et si occultis causis, numquid iniustis?[51]

[So also in the case of individual men. He who gave power to Marius also gave it to Gaius Caesar; He who gave it to Augustus also gave it to Nero; He who gave it to the Vespasiani, father and son, the gentlest of emperors, also gave it to Domitian, the cruellest; and – although it is not necessary to name them all – He who gave it to the Christian Constantine also gave it to the apostate Julian. This last, though a gifted intellect, loved mastery, and was seduced by a sacrilegious and detestable curiosity . . . Clearly, all these things are ruled and governed as it pleases the one true God. Though the causes be hidden, are they unjust?][52]

Augustine negates – he disregards rather than denies – Orosius' expressed belief that providence may confer legitimacy, even a kind of sanctity, on an aspect of the earthly city such as the empire of Augustus

---

[50] Dyson, 1998, pp. 139–40.  [51] McCracken et al., 1966, II, pp. 250–2 (V, c. 21).
[52] Dyson, 1998, p. 228. 'Gaius Caesar' is our Gaius Julius Caesar, not the emperor Gaius Caligula. The antithesis between Marius and Caesar is not clear.

or even Constantine. He does this less because he aims to deny legitimacy to earthly institutions than because he thinks them of infinitely less
importance than the human relation to God. The passage just quoted re-
places the application of providence to empire by the statement that the
ways of providence are utterly inscrutable – Julian's sin was curiosity –
and yet are righteous altogether. The Augustine we encounter here is
the adversary of Pelagius and the inflexible believer in the absolute decrees of grace. Orosius was certainly no Pelagian, but Augustine may
well have mistrusted his suggestion that the earthly city and its history
could play a narratable part in the work of salvation; Gibbon, who could
have seen Pelagius as a forerunner of Arminius, made the history of society independent of that of salvation.[53] Augustine might not have been
surprised by this outcome, but he is concerned less with history in the
sense of social and secular process than with refuting the contention that
the history of Rome in past and present owes anything to the worship
of the pagan gods. There are several layers of reasons why he does not
employ Sallust, or Tacitus, in arguing that the degeneracy of the earthly
city explains the crises of the years around 400 or constitutes them a
Decline and Fall. One is his preoccupation with refuting pagan theodicy. Another is his identification of the pagan virtues with the heroic
and ultimately self-destructive history of the republic. The history this
provides ends with the advent of Augustus, and there is no reason for
Augustine to take up the analysis of the principate as self-destructive in
consequence of the partial overthrow of republican values. Though he
clearly does not share Orosius' belief that the Augustan peace was providentially appointed as the time for the birth of Christ, there is room in
the writings for the belief that the history of the church, as the vehicle of
sacred history in this world, began its action under the earliest emperors,
and it is a fair question whether he assigns to the empire any positive
role in that history.

There is one decisive action: the destruction of Jerusalem in
AD 70–71,[54] in which Rome, like Babylon before it, was the instrument
of God's punishment of his people grown apostate. The Captivity that
followed the overthrow of the First Temple was the occasion of the Exilic
prophecies of Christ's coming, whereas – to a Christian mind – the
Diaspora after the fall of the Second was the far more terrible punishment of a people who had rejected him and now vanished from sacred

---

[53] *DF*, pp. 150–1: 'These idle disputants overlooked the invariable laws of nature, which have
connected peace with innocence, plenty with industry, and safety with valour.'
[54] Book XVIII, cc. 45–6.

and (as far as could be told) secular history until his return. Vespasian and Titus, however, did not know what they were doing; as agents of the earthly city their role was appointed but by no means sanctified, and though it might be no accident that they were benevolent rulers (towards all but Jews, and pitied even them) they would be succeeded by Domitian, and the will of providence towards their empire remained beyond our finding out. The alternation of good and bad emperors, even of patrons and persecutors of the church, and therefore – for all the mention that Augustine ever makes of it – of emperors capable and incapable of dealing with invading barbarians, did not form a history in which the Christian should seek for the process of his salvation. He was a pilgrim passing through history, not a participant in its processes. Providence was inscrutable; it demanded faith, not curiosity or action.

Roman history is scrutinised, in Books XI–XXII forming the second half of *De civitate Dei*, for evidence as to how far Rome is a second or mystical Babylon concluding the sequence of the four empires. Augustine is aware of the possibility that Rome is figured in that role in the *Apocalypse of John*, but the conclusion at which he means to arrive is anti-apocalyptic and anti-millenarian. Supposing that Rome is indeed the second Babylon and the history of the earthly city's organisation into empires is coming to an end, this is no more than a climactic moment at which the Christian should seek citizenship in the heavenly city, as he should have been doing from the beginning; it is not a moment whose significance in sacred history is to be sought as if it were of salvific importance. Augustine may have been moved here by thoughts of the Donatist schism, in which African purists had proclaimed that a church they considered corrupt was a false church under the rule of Antichrist, and had been replaced by their own church as the true one.[55] False church and true church might well become moments in an apocalyptic sequence, and it would be a consequence that an empire upholding the former was another Babylon. Augustine set himself against the entire apocalyptic mindset.[56] It was not for the Christian to display curiosity concerning the sequences of sacred history, but to define his salvation in obedience to a will he did not know. There remained the question of the church militant, that segment of the heavenly city on pilgrimage through a time including the history of the earthly; if it exercised an authority the Christian obeyed, did that authority exist in history and how was that history defined?

[55] See, however, Markus, 1970, pp. 115–22, for the role of the Donatist theologian Tyconius in shaping Augustine's thought.
[56] Book XX of *De civitate Dei* contains most on this subject.

(v)

We have found that two authors who wrote in response to the sack of Rome and the barbarian incursions into the western provinces in and after 410 had need of Sallust but not of Tacitus, of the end of the republic but not of the crisis of the principate, and of Gibbon's 'first Decline and Fall' – meaning a link between the insecurity of the principate and the collapse of the frontiers – not at all. The reasons for its absence centre upon their understanding of the empire as increasingly bound up with sacred and ecclesiastical history, following Christ's birth under the peace of Augustus, down to Constantine's alliance with the church and Theodosius' restoration of orthodoxy after the interlude of Julian's apostasy and the Arian turmoil. The history of persecution by pagan emperors displayed the empire as potentially Babylon, but did not necessitate any theory of its structural weakness as successor to the republic. There was no link between the foundation of Roman monarchy and its problems in their own time; they need not explain in detail how it displayed the weaknesses of the earthly city.

If there was no concept of a 'first Decline and Fall', was Decline and Fall on their minds in any sense? The sack of 410 was a portentous event, and Antichrist might be at hand; but the barbarian incursions through Gaul, Italy, Spain and Africa might be no more than regional disorders, such as had been known before. We have found two ways of denying the occurrence of anything equivalent to Decline and Fall as we understand it. One was to say with Orosius (or any eastern observer) that the empire founded on the new Rome still stood, and would outlast the sack of 410, itself far less devastating than those of Rome by the Gauls or of Carthage and Numantia by the Romans. This left room for Gibbon's 'decline and fall of the city', but not for his 'decline and fall of the empire'. The other was to say with Augustine that none of these events was finally of account, and that the tensions between the earthly and heavenly cities did not take place in historically narratable forms.[57]

It is the second perception which counts for more in our occidentally formed minds. We are accustomed to narrate the events leading to 410 as in sequence with those leading through 476 to the extinction of the empire in the west and the formation of barbarian kingdoms in the Latin former provinces. This sequence we call 'the Decline and Fall of the Roman Empire', and we look for ways of relating it as a chain of

---

[57] Brown, 1967, pp. 289–98, for the subtleties of Augustine's responses to the sack.

causes and effects in the history of state, church and society. We think of Augustine's *De civitate Dei*, certainly a great secession of the Christian intellect from history either secular or sacred, as a response to crisis in that history – as in several ways it is – and we call that crisis Decline and Fall, as if it were the end of the history of empire that called forth Augustine's response. A study of the texts has failed to confirm this traditional view of his work. The history whose end he describes in depth and detail is the history of the republic as bearer of pagan values, and he ends that history before Tacitus has begun to describe its after-effects. The history of the principate sees that of empire as increasingly bound up with that of church, and Augustine is not recording an end to the history of sacred empire so much as saying that it is not and never has been of the greatest spiritual significance. We may say that *De civitate Dei* is a response to the collapse of the western empire, but Augustine will not say it for us and there is not much evidence that he thought such an event had occurred. We have therefore to continue our search for the historical origins of our concept of Decline and Fall, before returning to the problem of a Tacitean 'first Decline and Fall' preceding the events of the fifth century and in some way now furnishing them with an explanation.

CHAPTER 6

# Otto of Freising and the two cities

(1)

Seven hundred years separate the histories of Orosius and Otto of
Freising, and the justification for treating this humanly gigantic interval as a simple lapse of time must be that Orosius' text is strongly present
in that of Otto, where it conveys many of the meanings we may suppose
it to have had in the original. This is of course a simplification; we might
focus on numerous moments during those centuries, at which Orosius'
text was being read and utilised, or at which Otto's text was taking
shape, and read the texts as responses to the complexities of experience
and discourse, so that these moments in their histories are no longer
moments in a simple continuity of transmission. Further even than this,
there is a sequence of historical events to be found in Otto, to which the
thought of Orosius may be applicable, but which modify that thought
in the act of application; and these determine the historical narrative
that concerns Otto, so that what he designed as an Augustinian history
*de duabus civitatibus* becomes in some measure a history *de translatione imperii*. We are obliged to discover what this *translatio* means, both because
it is a key concept in the structure of medieval Latin thinking, and because it dominates medieval understandings of the history of the Roman
empire until replaced by Decline and Fall as we know it; so that the latter
cannot be fully understood unless we understand its emergence from a
former matrix. Decline and Fall is both a product and a negation of the
medieval organisation of remembered experience, and the sequence of
events to be found in Otto are those around which that organisation took
shape.

Mainly though not wholly Latin in character, they may be presented
in the following sequence. From the end of the western succession of
emperors in 476 and the establishment of new kingdoms in the Latin
provinces, the canonical narrative proceeds to Justinian's destruction of

98

the Gothic kingdom of Italy and the consequent uneasy position of the bishop of Rome between the Roman exarchate in Ravenna and the Lombard power elsewhere in Italy. The locus now moves to the eastern succession and the Arab Muslim conquests of Syria, Persia, Egypt and Mediterranean Africa as far as Spain; an alteration of the geopolitics of human culture in many ways more momentous than the barbarian conquests in far western Europe, but intelligible to Latin culture only as lying outside the world-view the latter was constructing for itself. The western narrative proceeds to the collision between the popes of Rome and the iconoclast policies of the emperors in Constantinople, and to the papal role in the overthrow of the exarchate of Ravenna. The papacy having become – though this is not the language in which it declared itself – a major actor in history both spiritual and temporal, the narrative proceeds to the alliance it formed with the Frankish kingdom against the Lombards, and to that central act in a new universal history, the acclamation of Charlemagne as emperor in Rome on Christmas Day 800. This was the *translatio imperii*; Constantine having transferred the exercise of *imperium* from Rome to Byzantium – or as it increasingly appeared, from Romans to Greeks – the bishop of Rome, the *populus romanus* and the kingdom of the Franks were now combining to transfer it once more to Rome. The act did not, however, terminate or even restore Roman history, since Greeks and Franks could both be considered Romans; if there was a new actor (and perhaps only east Romans thought so) it was the pope and his claims to headship of the universal church as successor of Peter. His act of 800 was preceded and justified by a great but entirely fictitious event, the Donation of Constantine, by which that emperor, relocating his authority in his new city, had supposedly conferred *imperium* over Rome and perhaps all western provinces on Pope Sylvester. It was thus possible for Sylvester's successors to claim that the reconstitution of empire in the west had been achieved by their metropolitan or by their universal authority.

Each of these events is treated, as we shall see, as a turning point in Otto of Freising's *Historia de duabus civitatibus*, and in Edward Gibbon's *History of the Decline and Fall of the Roman Empire*. The latter, as we know, envisaged a first period of that history ending with 'the subversion of the Western Empire', a second beginning with the reign of Justinian and ending with 'the elevation of Charlemagne', after which 'the last and longest' would carry him to the fall of Constantinople in 1453.[1] It was

---

[1] For the words quoted see Womersley, 1994, I, pp. 1–2; *NCG*, pp. 372–4.

at the alliance between the popes and the Frankish kings that Gibbon placed the transition from ancient to modern history, from the supremacy of the civil power to that of the ecclesiastical; the advent of the modern in this sense being nearly co-terminous with 'the triumph of barbarism and religion'. The sequence of events by which the popes achieve the triumph of the modern are those that bring about the *translatio imperii*, and to this extent the narrative of the Enlightened historian is descended from that of the medieval.

There is a further series of events known both to Otto and to Gibbon, which carry us to the end of the former's lifetime, and point towards an era in which the problem of *translatio imperii* was to arrive at a climax and begin to change and disintegrate. The partition of Charlemagne's inheritance was a division between the kingdom of France and the Frankish Empire. The enmeshment of the popes in the local politics of the *populus romanus* reached a point where they had to be rescued by the Ottonian emperors from Germany, and threw off subjection to the latter by means of the struggle over Investitures, in which they claimed an imperial supremacy of the spiritual over the temporal power. The historian Otto was the contemporary and uncle of the emperor Frederick I, under whose family empire and papacy competed for universal supremacy and for control of the Lombard and Tuscan regions of Italy, where self-governing cities were to generate a politics – and a historiography – independent of either. It will be argued in subsequent chapters that between the Hohenstaufen and the Hapsburg supremacies the concept of *translatio imperii* began to change into, or be replaced by, that of Decline and Fall.

(11)

Otto, bishop of Freising or Frisingen, was, Gibbon once wrote in language characteristically ambiguous,

perhaps the noblest of historians: he was son of Leopold marquis of Austria, his mother, Agnes, was daughter of the emperor Henry IV, and he was the half-brother and uncle to Conrad III and Frederic I.[2]

This high birth of course equipped him for the classical role of the historian, that of recording events to which he had been witness and participant. Of a speech he puts in the mouth of the emperor Frederick I (Barbarossa), rebuking the disobedient Romans, Gibbon remarks:

---

[2] *DF*, vi, ch. 69; Womersley, 1994, iii, p. 998, n. 53.

Cicero or Livy would not have rejected these images, the eloquence of a Barbarian born and educated in the Hercynian forest.[3]

He thus places the bishop in the classical tradition, but it is equally apparent that Otto's history is in the tradition of Orosian and Augustinian anti-history, while no less so that Frederick at this point is informing the Romans that empire has been transferred from them to the Franks, a Teutonic people with whom he is identified.[4] The *translatio imperii*, an event brought about as much by religion as by barbarism, is at, or near, the centre of Otto's perception of history, but he saw the emperor's claim as at least precarious, while Gibbon knew that it had failed;[5] the alliance of the Roman pope and people, however unreal, had been too strong – or its weakness had.

It is in the convergence of Christian anti-history with imperial history that Otto situates his narrative, and the convergence of Frankish with ecclesiastical history in the *translatio imperii* that furnishes the medieval shaping of the concept of Decline and Fall. His major work, the *Chronica sive Historia de Duabus Civitatibus*, seems to have been written between 1143 and 1147, and revised some ten years later; the *Gesta Friderici Primi Imperatoris* was left unfinished when he died in 1158.[6] Dedicating the revised *Chronica* to Frederick I in 1157, Otto says that it was written in times of disorder before the emperor's reign, but that news of Frederick's planned expedition against the rebellious cities of Lombardy gives him hope of compiling a happier narrative; this was to be the unfinished *Gesta Friderici*, and the emperor's deeds were to be as uncompleted as the bishop's history. It would be an error, however, to explain the two works solely by reference to their immediate contexts. When Otto says, in the course of his dedication:

nobilitas vestra cognoscat, nos hanc historiam, nubilosi temporis quod ante vos fuit turbulentia inductos, et amaritudine animi scripsisse, ac ob hoc non tam rerum gestarum seriem, quam earundem miseriam in modum tragoediae texuisse: et sic unamquamque librorum distinctionem, usque ad septimum et octavum, per quos animarum quies resurrectionisque duplex stola significantur, in miserias terminasse[7]

[let Your Nobility know that I wrote this history in bitterness of spirit, led thereto by the turbulence of that unsettled time which preceded your reign, and therefore I did not merely give events in their chronological order, but rather wove together, in the manner of a tragedy, their sadder aspects, and so ended

---

[3] Womersley, 1994, III, p. 1000, n. 57.    [4] *Ibidem*, p. 1001, n. 58, for Gibbon's observation of this.
[5] *Ibidem*, pp. 1001–2.    [6] Mierow, 1928, pp. 18–20. For the *Gesta* itself, Mierow, 1953.
[7] *MGH*, xx, p. 116.

with a picture of unhappiness each and every division of the books down to the seventh and the eighth. In the latter books the rest of souls and the double garment of the resurrection are shadowed forth][8]

he is echoing Orosius, and indeed the language of others in the Latin Christian tradition.[9] The miseries of the 1140s are in the full sense typical, and the business of the historian is to recount the misery to which the earthly city, typified as Babylon, is by its nature condemned. This can only be done in the form of a universal history, since Babylon has been a condition of the human existence since at latest the fall of the Tower of Babel; we are in the presence of a Christian rhetoric which reiterates the Babylonish condition, and in a sense the Babylonish captivity, of humanity at each successive phase of its history. In this rhetoric, history is the register of the crimes, follies and misfortunes of mankind, and these miseries are moral and physical rather than historical, as we should use the latter word. Nevertheless, Otto's history, like that of all his predecessors since Eusebius, is historically and politically organised in at least one sense. It is a history of empires, from Ninus of Babylon down to Frederick himself, and the miseries of mankind are presented as those attending both the rise and the decline and fall of empires. The activity of making and unmaking empires is contrasted with the activity of God in making and sustaining his Church, both in and out of historical time; d'Alembert and Gibbon were to contrast it with the activities of social beings and philosophers.[10]

Otto has therefore organised past history into six books, recounting the miseries of empire in a scheme which owes a great deal to Daniel's four, as far as his own time and that of his nephew the emperor. At this moment, however, there occurs a very great change and a historical moment of profound and salutary uncertainty. The two concluding books look beyond the earthly city and its history to the heavenly city and the condition of redemption: *animarum quies resurrectionisque duplex stola.* This condition *significatur*, is 'shadowed forth'; it can be depicted only figuratively, never by means of narrative, and yet it is presented within a *chronica sive historia de duabus civitatibus*, as if there were a history in which narrative was transformed into figuration. Otto's metaphysics are fully capable of explaining this;[11] but the question remains whether the earthly history arrives at a climactic moment, at which one sees in its

---

[8]  Mierow, 1928, p. 89.     [9]  E.g. Rufinus, the translator of Eusebius' Greek history; *ibidem*, n. 13.
[10]  *EEG*, pp. 181 (d'Alembert), 209 (Gibbon).
[11]  Consider the detailed Aristotelian analysis in Book 1 of the *Gesta Friderici*, showing how it is that entities may be complex and therefore mutable; Mierow, 1953, pp. 31–40.

narrative something more than misery, namely some signification of the heavenly city to come. The history of empires ends with an eschaton; does it contain an eschatology?

This question subdivides, and gives rise to others. Frederick and Otto may possibly be situated at an apocalyptic moment, at which the emperor's expedition to Milan and Rome announces the imminence of the end of days or, short of that, signifies or typifies its character. Against this stands the stern Augustinian warning against supposing that any knowledge we have empowers us to predict the moment or the circumstances of the last coming. It remains possible that the history of empires contains more than miseries; it may typify the way in which it will itself end, and the replacement of Babylon by Rome may tell us how the earthly Rome which is Babylon will be replaced by the heavenly Rome which is Peter's. This too may not be; the signs given in advance may be too deep to be deciphered. In this case there can still be asked a question in secular historiography. Orosius, Augustine and Otto all made use of ancient histories narrating both human actions and processes of change. Are the miseries of the earthly city immediate and existential, the simple consequences of human sin? Or do they in some cases require complex narratives of the political and historical condition, as recounted by Tacitus or as implicit in the concept of Decline and Fall? These questions can be discussed as we explore Otto's history, and we may occasionally find them discussed by Otto himself.

Otto is a direct heir of Orosius, in the sense that he finds to his purposes meanings intended by the latter seven centuries before. In that vast interval, much has happened that was unknown to Orosius. As Otto sees history, it includes the transfer of empire from the Romans to the Greeks of Constantinople, from the Greeks to the Franks of Aachen, and the crisis in relations between that empire and the Church centred at Rome. To the extent that Orosius wrote a history of empire, Otto is required to enlarge it; and the extent to which Orosius wrote a history of the two cities is complicated by the emergence of the Church as an actor in imperial history, on which it may claim to impose a history which the heavenly city is beginning to enact on earth. The principal effect for Otto is that he must reiterate the scheme based on Daniel's four empires,[12] in the knowledge that the role of Rome as last of the four must be re-valued in the light of the *translatio imperii*, and that there is more than one way of regarding this event.

---

[12] Above, p. 72.

Otto's work *de duabus civitatibus* therefore displays a rich mixture of the dualities and conscious ambiguities of the Christian view of history. There are two fundamental senses in which he is writing an anti-history rather than a history at all. That of the earthly city is a register of the crimes, follies and misfortunes of mankind, which does not need a narrative of the complex process by which these have come about; that of the heavenly city does not proceed through processes that can be narrated in human terms. Against this scenario of double darkness – there is a darkness of the absence of light and a darkness occasioned by its excess – there nevertheless exist two counter-narratives. There is a narrative of successive empires, occasioned by the Augustinian decision that the *libido dominandi* exerts itself in empires and the further claim that Daniel had prophesied their sequence;[13] and there is a narrative of sacred and ecclesiastical history, set in train by God's actions in taking to himself the first Israel and later the second. The second narrative takes place in historic time and coincides at points with the first, and since its end is the redemption of humanity, it is a question whether the earthly city is at any of these points enlisted in its own redemption and given meaning by the history of the latter. If so, it is possible that Otto's history is a chronicle of the interactions between the two histories, and that Otto himself in writing it may find himself at one of the latter's climactic moments. As against this, there are the Augustinian warnings that this history of the earthly city is no more than a chronicle of sin, and that redemption from sin is an existential process not to be identified with any historical process. Otto applies a powerful and judgematic intelligence to asking whether these problems can be solved.

His *chronica sive historia* is therefore divided into eight books, of which six end at climactic moments in the linked histories of the two cities. These are: the fall of Babylon to the Medes, linked with the foundation of Rome by Romulus; the establishment of the principate by Augustus, linked with the birth of Christ in Judea; the victory of Constantine and his association of the empire with the Church; the deposition of the last western emperor by Odovacar; the re-foundation of empire by Charlemagne, followed by its division; and the collision of empire and papacy in the time of Henry IV and Gregory VII. Of each of these it can be asked how far the moment signifies a new age in the two histories. In the seventh book Otto reaches a time close to his own, and asks whether a new climax is approaching; and in the eighth he turns from history to eschatology, and prefigures

---

[13] Augustine himself had treated Daniel with some caution; Dyson, 1998, pp. 1021–4.

the coming of Antichrist and the general resurrection at the end of the history he has followed as far as the time present to him. In the first three of the six concerning the past, he is reiterating the narrative of Orosius and relying largely on him. In the second series, he has to do with a new theme, which to him is *translatio imperii* and to us Decline and Fall: the extinction of the western empire, the establishment of non-imperial kingdoms in the Latin provinces, their relations with the papacy, and the transference of empire from the Romans to the Greeks and from the Greeks to the Franks. Otto's history is occidental and Latin-centred; when he recounts the history of eastern empire, he does not organise his macronarrative around it, and he sees a divorce between Greek and Roman which neither Byzantine nor recent historians would accept. Sacred history has moved west with Peter, and its meanings are to be found in the relations of the Roman church with the consequences of the *translatio imperii*. The heavenly city is represented by – it is not identified with – the church centred at Rome, and this is why the history of the Frankish empire may, or may not, possess eschatological significance.

In the four empires of Daniel, whose history interacts with the narrative of Otto's eight books, an overwhelming predominance belongs to the first and the fourth. The history of Babylon, derived from the Tower of Babel – the attempt at empire being the original sin of post-diluvian mankind – typifies that of the earthly city in all the empires which are to succeed it, including that of Rome which is to be the last. Rome as earthly city is simply a second Babylon; a 'mystical' Babylon, reiterating the history of the first to the point where it contains, occasions, but does not generate, something which is to succeed it and the earthly city itself – the stone cut from the mountain without the work of hands, which overthrows the fourth empire in Daniel's vision.[4] It is because of this ambivalence of Rome in the history of the four empires and the two cities that Roman history has to be given precedence over that of the Medes and the Greeks, second and third in the Danielic sequence. Otto's first book ends with Darius the Mede's conquest of Babylon, but stresses the coincidence of that event with the foundation of the Latin (and Trojan) kingdom on the Aventine hill, and he opens his second book saying:

> Superiore libro promisisse me recolo de rerum mutatione ac miseriis scripturam. Quam quidem historiam usque ad defectum primae sequentisque initium, quam Romam dico, Babyloniae, Deo opitulante, utcumque complevi. Has enim germanas esse civitates, non solum ex historiographorum dictis, qui

---

[4] Daniel, 2, verses 34, 35.

huius illi regnum quasi patri filium, mediis ac brevibus Medorum seu Persarum ac Macedonum regnis, tanquam parvuli filii tutoribus, non iure hereditatis, sed et ex principis apostolum epistola, qui a Roma scribens, eam Babyloniam vocat: *Salutat vos*, inquiens, *ecclesia, quae est in Babylonia*, conici potest.[5]

[I recall that in the preceding book I promised that I would write about the instability and the sorrows of the world. And, by God's help, I have indeed brought down this history – in some fashion – as far as the fall of the first Babylon and the beginning of the second, I mean Rome. For that these are related empires may be inferred not only from the words of the writers of history – who have stated that the sovereignty of the latter city succeeded that of the former as a son succeeds his father; the short-lived empires of the Medes and the Persians and the Macedonians intervening (like the guardians of a little child) not by right of permanent inheritance but by mere temporary succession – but also from the epistle of the chief of the apostles, who, writing from Rome, calls that city Babylon, saying 'the church that is in Babylon saluteth you'.][6]

This is a classic case of the Christian appropriation of history by means of typology. It is unlikely that any but a Christian writer would have represented Rome as the lawful heir of Babylon, and we cannot understand why there is a direct inheritance from the former to the latter without invoking the sacred history of the heavenly city in the terrain dominated by the earthly. Interwoven with the narrative of empire in Otto's first book we find record of God's covenant with Abraham to create a people peculiarly God's, from which there follows – interestingly as much from Josephus as from the books of the Old Testament – the history of that people from Egypt to Canaan and through the judges to the kings, as far as the Babylonian captivity and the messages spoken by the prophets. Daniel is prominent among these because he exposes the history of empires; but the prophets preceding the Exile present Babylon as the unwitting instrument of God's punishment of his people, and those during it foretell the Messiahship of Christ which Israel will not accept. We are far advanced with the history of Jewish apostasy as Christians see it; but what is only foretold under the first Babylon will be manifest under the second, when the second Israel will replace the first. The relation of empire to redemption, of the earthly city to the heavenly, constitutes the inheritance to be taken up by Rome, but the exercise of empire in relation to redemption changes as the inheritance is taken up. For this reason the history that matters after the fall of the first Babylon is Roman. That of the Medes and the Greeks is a mere interval before the coming

---

[5] *Chronica*, II, prologue; *MGH*, xx, p. 144.
[6] Mierow, 1928, p. 153; the quotation in the text from 1 Peter, 5:13.

of the empire that may perhaps be sanctified by the Church, while that of Israel between the Exile and the Incarnation is an interval of another sort: a prophecy has been given to Israel, but Christian historians do not explore in depth the history of why Israel does not accept it. The period of the Second Temple and of Hellenised Judaism receives little attention; the history of empire runs only incidentally through the successors of Alexander.

Since the wars of the Medes and the Greeks are not of primary importance, Otto inserts the Persian and Peloponnesian wars and their sequels into a chronology organised around events from Roman history. No doubt this has to do with his limited access to the history narrated by Herodotus, Thucydides and Xenophon; but the sequence of empires imposed by Daniel does not leave room for central concern with the city-state period of Greek history to which we attach paramount importance. Classical Hellas, as we should call it, appears only when Otto's twelfth-century intellect makes him insert Plato, Aristotle and the history of philosophy in a history of the two cities to which it rather enigmatically belongs;[7] and the struggles for preponderance between Athens, Sparta and Thebes[8] interest him chiefly as preludes to the advent of the third empire of Macedon. This too is no more than a trustee for the future, and his second book is increasingly constructed around the history of Rome's rise to power. Here indeed the values we consider classical make their appearance. The fourth empire is the achievement of a Rome both heathen and republican, and Otto has entered on the territory in which Orosius and Augustine – both of whom he follows closely – were necessitated to argue that its virtues, while very real, arose from the *libido dominandi* and the lust for glory of the earthly city and were destined to bring it misery. Otto of course understands this position, which his sources dictate to him in any case; but there are no pagans for him to debate against in the twelfth century, and the great rediscovery of ancient virtue has not yet occurred. His problems as a historian will arise from the *translatio imperii*.

(III)

Otto's history is Orosian down to a point near that at which Orosius himself wrote. He makes it a principal crisis in the history of the fourth empire that the republic which had conquered it found it too great

---

[7] *Chronica*, II, 8; Mierow, 1928, pp. 161–3.     [8] *Chronica*, II, 19; Mierow, 1928, pp. 174–5.

to sustain without a transformation of its own institution. He gives an account of the Roman civil wars which relies on Cicero rather than Sallust for their origin in moral corruption,[19] and at their climax he says:

> Igitur ex omni parte mundi vires contractae, multoque Romanorum sanguine gentes devictae, ipsorum modo vacatione congredi coguntur. Iam enim in tantum rei publicae profecerat status, ut ulterius non posset. Et cum extrinsecus corrumpi non valeret, iuxta poetam, in se ipsum ruere debuit.[20]

[So then strong forces were assembled from every part of the world, and nations conquered at the cost of much Roman blood were now forced to fight each other merely at the call of the Romans. For by this time the growth of the republic had reached such a stage that it could go no further. And as it could not be destroyed from without it must needs collapse upon itself, as the poet says.][21]

Otto may well know a passage in which Augustine says as much,[22] adding that monarchical rule was now the only possibility. The poet here mentioned, however, is Lucan, a belated republican in opposition to Nero, and the occasion is Caesar's defeat of Pompey at Pharsalus.[23] The language of the two cities here enlists that of republican decay, but the latter is not continued into either an Augustan or a Tacitean[24] narrative. We are at the point where the earthly city prepares the way for its own opposite, and the function of Caesar and Augustus is to establish that ecumenical peace under which God condescends to be born as man. Like his predecessors, Otto explains that it was convenient to God's purposes that the world (he ignores the fact that the Parthians were still exercising the empire of the Persians) should come under the rule of a single city, since this furthers the expansion of the Church, which is the heavenly city peregrinant and militant in the fallen world. A further concession to pagan history occurs when he says that the philosophers had prepared the way for Christian truth.[25] It is a consequence rather implicit than explicit that the rule of a single city entails the rule of a single man; we do not read that monarchy is the natural form of government, or that it mirrors the rule of the universe by a single creator. Both Otto's philosophy and the new experience of his own times taught him that imperial rule was earthly, fragmentary and exposed to misery.

---

[19]　Mierow, 1928, pp. 206–7; it is doubtful how well he knew of Sallust's texts.
[20]　*Chronica*, II, 49; *MGH* xx, p. 168.　　　[21]　Mierow, 1928, pp. 213–14; see also pp. 215–16.
[22]　*De civitate Dei*, xviii, 45.　　　[23]　Lucan's words are *in se magna ruunt*; *Pharsalia*, I, 81.
[24]　Tacitus is cited occasionally, usually under the name of 'Cornelius' (Mierow, 1928, pp. 98, 232). Otto seems to know him through quotations by other authors, and has no access to a continuous text.
[25]　Mierow, 1928, p. 220.

The connection between the two cities, and as far as we can use the term their two histories, remained providential. Christ had promised that he would never leave the world, and the Church would remain in it to the end of time; a new chronology was necessary from the time of his birth; but empire had only been enlisted in the cause of universal redemption, and its history had not been sanctified as the vehicle of that process. The history of the earthly city therefore continued, no less trivial and miserable than it had been before; it did not change, even after there came to be points at which it was to be understood in the context of sacred history. Otto continued to labour the typological relations between the histories of Babylon and Rome, but for this reason his history of the fall of Nero is more Josephan than Tacitean; it is the fall of Jerusalem that matters, not the corruption of the principate. He indeed remarks that when Nero began to persecute the Christians and killed Peter and Paul, *secularis illius dignitas urbis minui coepit*,[26] but it is not certain that he has a long-term process of Decline and Fall in mind. The persecutions were a transitory phenomenon, brought to an end by Constantine, and the failures of the earthly city may always be understood as existential rather than historical. There is no First Decline and Fall to be found in Otto's text.

Writing seven centuries after Orosius, however, Otto was aware of a history extended over the first and second phases of Decline and Fall as Gibbon set them out six centuries after him: the end of the western empire, the rise of the barbarian kingdoms, the re-institution of empire by the Frankish kings and the Roman popes, and their subsequent contests for primacy. His fourth book ends with Odovacar and Romulus Augustulus, his sixth with Gregory VII and Henry IV. These processes, which to us include Decline and Fall, are known to Otto as *translatio imperii*, and he recounts their history within the scheme, metahistorical or antihistorical, of a *chronicon de duabus civitatibus*. At the outset of these two books, however, the acts of Constantine present him with a double problem in the understanding of *translatio imperii*, the concept of which must guide the remainder of his history. Constantine built a new Rome, and made it the capital of an empire so durable that Constantinople is still *urbs regia* in Otto's own time.[27] Does this mean that he transferred empire from the Romans to the Greeks, or is the Danielic scheme still valid? Is Roman empire to endure until the stone cut without hands is hurled against it, so that redistributions of empire can only occur within

---

[26] *MGH*, xx, p. 181; Mierow, 1928, p. 243.     [27] *Chronica*, IV, 5; Mierow, 1928, p. 283.

it? This problem is complicated for Otto by the later institution of a Frankish empire, and by the role of the Church in bringing about that *translatio*, if *translatio imperii* is what it was.

The problems of *translatio* pervade his later books, but are discussed in the context of the second problem, that of the Church. At the outset of Book IV, when Constantine is at hand, Otto begins to discuss the central question of political thought in the history of Christian Europe.

> Sed gravis hic oritur quaestio, magnaque de regni ac sacerdoti iustitia dissensio. Quidam enim religionis obtentu, alii vero secularis dignitatis, qua regni auctoritas imminuta cernitur, intuitu hanc gloriam honoremque temporalem sacerdotibus Christi, quibus coelestis regni gloria promittitur, non licere autumant, multaque huius rei argumenta monstrant.[28]

[But here a serious question arises, and a great argument regarding the justification of kingship and of priesthood. For some under colour of religion, others out of regard for secular dignity – since by such dignity the authority of the kingship is seen to have been diminished – claim that this temporal glory and honour are not permissible to priests of Christ, to whom the glory of the heavenly kingdom is promised, and they point out many arguments in support of this contention.][29]

Otto sets out the argument that there are two swords, spiritual and temporal, and that Peter was wrong to draw the latter in defence of Christ since it belongs only to the magistrate; he furthermore is the sole guarantor of property, so that even the Church possesses temporal goods by his permission.

> Quibus hoc modo respondetur, quod mundiali dignitate quae regalia dicuntur, Dominus ecclesiam suam honorare voluit, ex Dei enim ordinatione id factum, ratio quam supra reddidimus, declarat . . . His ergo aliisque modis, quos longum est exequi, probatur, et Constantinum ecclesiae iuste regalia contulisse et ecclesiam licite suscepisse.[30]

[To all this the reply is made that the Lord wished those powers which are called royal to honour His Church with earthly dignity. For the explanation that we have made above indicates that this was done by God's ordering . . . By these arguments, therefore, and by others which it would take too long to recount, it is shown that Constantine properly bestowed royal powers upon the Church, and that the Church legitimately accepted them.][31]

When Otto comes to state his own judgement, it is cautious to the point of equivocation. He was after all a member of an imperial family,

---

[28] *Chronica*, IV, prologue; *MGH*, xx, p. 193.     [29] Mierow, 1928, p. 272.
[30] *MGH*, xx, p. 194.     [31] Mierow, 1928, p. 273.

and knew that a negotiation between imperial and papal claims was the prime necessity. He writes:

Ego enim, ut de meo sensu loquar, utrum Deo magis placeat haec ecclesiae suae, quae nunc cernitur, exaltatio quam prior humilitatio, prorsus ignorare me profiteor. Videtur quidem status ille fuisse melior, iste felicior. Assentio tamen sanctae Romanae ecclesiae, quam supra firmam petram aedificatam non dubito, credendaque quae credit, licite possidenda quae possidet, credo . . . Haec de sacerdotii regnique iustitia dicta sufficiant. Caeterum si quis subtilius ac profundius inde ratiocinari vult, a nobis minime praeiudicium patietur.[32]

[For, to speak as I think myself, I admit that I am absolutely ignorant whether the exaltation of His Church which is so clearly visible today pleases God more than its former humiliation pleased Him. Indeed, that former state seems to have been better, this present condition more fortunate.[33] However, I agree with the holy Roman Church, which, I doubt not, was built upon a firm rock, and I believe that what she believes must be believed and that what she possesses can legitimately be possessed . . . let what has been said concerning the righteousness of the priesthood and of the kingship suffice. But if any one wishes to reason about it more subtly and profoundly, he will by no means submit to having the matter prejudged by me.][34]

Otto's subscription to the doctrines of clerical authority and property is less than whole-hearted, and three chapters later we encounter a historical position he is not about to endorse:

ut Romanorum habet historia . . . caput omnium in tantum Romanam exaltavit ecclesiam, ut beato Silvestro eiusdem urbis pontifici, insignibus regni traditis, ipse se Byzantium transferret, ibique sedem regni constitueret. Ex hinc Romana ecclesia occidentalia regna, sui iuris tanquam a Constantino sibi tradita affirmat, in argumentumque tributum, exceptis duobus Francorum regnis, usque hodie exigere non dubitat. Verum imperii fautores, Constantinum non regnum Romanis pontificibus hoc modo tradidisse . . . atque ad hoc probandum, quod ipse Constantinus, regno inter filios diviso, alii Occidentem, alii Orientem tradiderit . . . Quae omnia diffinire praesentis negocii non est.[35]

[And, as the history of the Romans has it, (Constantine) so greatly exalted the Roman Church that he handed over the imperial insignia to Saint Sylvester, pope of that city, and withdrew to Byzantium and there established the seat of his realm. This is why the Church of Rome claims that the western realms are under its jurisdiction, on the ground that they had been transferred to it

---

[32] *MGH*, xx, p. 194.
[33] Could the Latin of this passage have been in Gibbon's mind when he wrote that Gregory VII was 'a second Athanasius, in a more fortunate age of the Church' (*DF*, v, ch. 56, n. 83; Womersley, 1994, III, p. 504)?
[34] Mierow, 1928, p. 274.      [35] *Chronica*, IV, 3; *MGH*, xx, pp. 196–7.

by Constantine, and in evidence thereof does not hesitate to exact tribute to this day – except from the two kingdoms of the Franks. But the advocates of empire affirm that Constantine did not hand over his kingdom in this way to the Roman pontiffs . . . (a)nd to prove this they adduce the fact that Constantine himself, when he divided the kingdom among his sons, handed over the West to one, the East to the other . . . To settle definitely all these matters is not the purpose of the present work.][36]

This is the famous Donation of Constantine, in which Otto clearly does not believe. The documented facts are against it, and a *translatio imperii* – that is, a transfer of imperial powers; regal might be another matter – to the heir of the chief of the apostles is incompatible with either the two cities or the four empires as these exist in his thought. The autonomy of the two Frankish kingdoms, with their sacred centres at Rheims and Aachen, is necessary to that of the western empire at whose heart Otto lives, and this entails a *translatio imperii* to the Franks in which the Church may be an agent but cannot be a sovereign. From this point in his history Otto must perpetually look ahead from Constantine to Charlemagne, and even to his own nephew Frederick, and there is a tissue of consequences in which this involves him. Since the empire is now Christian, its history cannot be disentangled from that of the church militant, and the latter is exposed to infection by that of the earthly city.

Ac deinceps . . . videor mihi non de duabus civitatibus, sed pene de unum tantum, quam ecclesiam dico, hystoriam texuisse. Non enim, quamvis electi et reprobi in una sint domo, has civitates, ut supra, dixerim duas, sed proprie unam, sed permixtam tanquam grana cum paleis. Unde in sequentibus libellis . . . de civitate Christi . . . utpote sagena missa in mare, bonos et malos continente, coeptam hystoriam prosequamur.[37]

[But from that time on . . . I seem to myself to have composed a history not of two cities but virtually of one only, which I call the Church. For although the elect and the reprobate are in one household, yet I cannot call these cities two as I did above; I must call them properly but one – composite, however, as the grain is mixed with the chaff. Wherefore in the books that follow . . . our history is a history of the city of Christ, but that city . . . is 'like unto a net, that was cast into the sea',[38] containing the good and the bad.][39]

Otto can suggest at this point that the earthly city persists only where there are Jews and other actual unbelievers; but he has for some time been writing the history of heresies arising within the Church, and should the clergy claim imperial powers that do not belong to them, there is the

---

[36] Mierow, 1928, pp. 279–80.    [37] *Chronica*, v, prologue; *MGH*, xx, p. 214.
[38] Matthew 13:47.    [39] Mierow, 1928, pp. 323–4.

possibility that they may be entangled in the history of the earthly city as it persists in the exercise of all empire not excluding the Christian. The heavenly city does not intervene to redeem that history, and it remains true down to the moment in which Otto is writing – *ex amaritudine animi*[40] – that the history of empire is a history of miseries. But at this point the four empires re-assert themselves in harness with the two cities, and we find Otto committed to a dilemma from which he may not be able to extricate himself. The transfer of empire from the Romans to the Greeks and from the Greeks to the Franks must go on within an empire in which all are Romans – as indeed all claim to be – since otherwise the scheme of four must be given up. To sustain it, there must be continuing empire, its feet partly of iron and partly of clay, which will persist until the advent of the stone cut without hands marks the end of time. Otto does not need the history of this empire in order to predict, let alone explain or narrate, the coming of the Antichrist and the last days; but he does seem to need it in order to maintain the presumption of an eschatology at all. To suppose a new sequence of empires – even one which typologically repeated that set forth in Daniel – would be to postpone Christ's return too far. Perhaps we should evoke the voice of Augustine saying that this too may have to be endured; but it seems to be Otto's predicament that he must continue history until an eschaton it can neither predict nor prefigure.

Meanwhile, the history of *translatio* has to be written, and has both a western and an eastern aspect. Western history is Roman, barbaric, and increasingly papal, encompassing most of what is meant by Decline and Fall; eastern history is that of the *urbs regia*, to which Constantine transferred the exercise of empire while leaving the ancient city to act as its symbol. This is one reason why the patriarch of Rome ranks at least equal with those of Alexandria and Antioch – Constantinople and Jerusalem join them at a later date[41] – but there is of course the further reason that the chief of the apostles exercised their supremacy from Rome. How the heirs of Peter and Paul regarded their apostolic brethren further east is a question much overlaid by that of the *translatio imperii* to the west, but to deal with this a history of the barbarian peoples is of course necessary. The sack of 410 is noted as the occasion on which Orosius, Augustine and Jerome wrote their histories;[42] but they did not live to see

[40] *MGH*, xx, p. 116.
[41] For the origins of the patriarchates, see *Chronica*, iii, 2; Mierow, 1928, pp. 224–5.
[42] *Chronica*, iv, 21; Mierow, 1928, p. 306.

the far more symbolic events[43] of 476, when Odovacar deposed the last Roman to wear the purple in the western provinces. At this moment the narrative of Decline and Fall is in essence complete, and we look ahead with Gibbon to the triumph of barbarism and religion. Otto presents the sequence in the following, not wholly dissimilar, terms:

> Sed quia de rerum mutationibus regnorumque inminutionibus ad ostenden-dos mortalium casus mundique instabiles rotatus scribere proposui, sicut supra dixisse me memini, cum Roma parturiretur, Babylonia finem accepit, sic et modo dum regnum Francorum ut ita dixerim, seminaretur, Roma sub augus-tulo suo in ultima senectute, id est a conditione sua 1227 anno, barbaris tradita, occasum minatur.[44]

> [But inasmuch as I have undertaken to write about the vicissitudes of history and the fall of empires to illustrate human misfortunes and the fluctuations of our unstable world, I will note this: just as Babylonia came to an end while Rome was being born (as, I remember, I said above), so now, while the kingdom of the Franks was, so to speak, being planted, Rome in its extreme old age under Augustulus – that is, in the one thousand two hundred and twenty-seventh year from its founding – was given over to the barbarians and threatened to fall.][45]

Otto's purposes are still antihistorical – the history of the earthly city is being recounted to show its ultimate meaninglessness – but organisation into narratives keeps being reasserted. Because human misery consists in the pursuit of empire, a narrative of state-building is imposed; because prophecy has organised the history of empire into four and given it typo-logical and perhaps eschatological structure, there are ways of showing Babylon as repeated in Rome and the Romans repeated by the Franks. Here, however, the macronarrative is telescoped; the Franks play the role of Romans, not of Medes, and they are not post-Romans initiating a his-tory typologically successive to that of Rome, but a new kind of Roman acting within history still Roman. For this reason they need a history, and it should seem that this will be part of a history of barbarism. Otto goes on, however, to supply the Franks with a Trojan ancestry, like that of the Romans themselves, and to remark that, as Roman power declined,

> gentes quae Romanorum provincias non regna habitabant, reges creare, iam ex illorum potestate subduci ac in proprii arbitrii auctoritate stare discunt.[46]

> [the peoples that before had inhabited provinces of the Romans – not kingdoms – were learning to choose kings; now they were learning to break loose from

---

[43] *Chronica*, IV, 31; Mierow 1928, pp. 317–18.    [44] *Ibidem; MGH*, XX, p. 212.
[45] Mierow, 1928, p. 318.    [46] *MGH*, XX, *ibidem*.

the power of the Romans and to stand in the authority set up by their own discretion.][47]

Kingship, it is worth remembering, was more a barbarian construct than a Roman; here it is a device by which barbarians learn both to be independent of the Romans and to be Romans themselves. The Franks are of Trojan origin, not Gothic, Scythian or Japhetic, contrary to what early modern scholarship insisted; and it would seem that Otto is more interested in *translatio imperii* than in any general contrast between barbarism and either *Romanitas* or civility. The history of the Franks, even while the conspicuous actions are those of the Gothic Alaric or the Rugian Odovacar, is being given precedence over the histories of other peoples.

What, meanwhile, is taking place in the history centred on the *urbs regia*, where a measure of Roman empire has been transferred into the hands of Greeks? Here Otto's narrative seems thin, and it is hard to tell whether this is due to shortage of information or to an increasing identification of the two cities with their Latin manifestations. In east as well as west, the history of empire is inseparable from that of the church, and consists largely in the rise and repudiation of successive heresies. There is a sense in which the heresies are the successors of the persecutions, especially when emperors are rulers turned heresiarchs; but unlike the persecutions, they arise within the history of the city of Christ, that net in which some very strange fish are drawn up. There is a passage setting a *translatio studii* alongside the journeyings of empire, which may indicate that the history of philosophy figures in the story; wisdom, we are told, has moved like empire from east to west.[48] Otto, trained in philosophy at Paris, may be saying that Christian dialectics are better preserved there than among the Greeks; but such a conviction might attenuate his understanding of Orthodox history, and there is little indication that philosophy was itself a cause of the great debates on the divine nature. The history of eastern empire also loses salience, since it is not directly involved in the *translatio ad Francos*; there is an account of the wars of Justinian in Italy,[49] but little connected account of how his destruction of the Gothic kingdom led to the invasions of the Lombards and the papacy's appeal to the Franks. The Iconoclast emperor Leo is mentioned as the reason why Pope Gregory II led Italy to withdraw

[47] Mierow, 1928, *ibidem*; or 'to subsist by authority of their own government'.
[48] *Chronica*, v, prologue; Mierow, 1928, pp. 322–4.     [49] *Chronica*, v, 4; Mierow, 1928, pp. 328–30.

from his jurisdiction;[50] but this is not the turning point in history it is for Giannone and Gibbon.

Nor is there an alternative interpretation. Otto is assembling narratives from various sources, but not synthesizing them into a history of either city; neither a *translatio imperii* nor a fulfilment of typological sequences lends meaning at this stage to the essential insignificance and misery of the *civitas terrena*. This is particularly evident when he reaches the reign of Heraclius. His victories over the Persians and recovery of the Holy Cross are recorded, but it is mentioned only in passing that

Circa idem tempus Mahumet, quem Sarraceni hactenus colunt, ex stirpe Ismahelis, patre gentili et matre Iudaea fuisse dicitur.[51]

[About the same time Mahomet, whom the Saracens hold in reverence to this day, is said to have lived. He was of the stock of Ishmael by a Gentile father and a Jewish mother.][52]

Heraclius became a heretic and astrologer, and prevailed on the Frankish king Dagobert to join him in enforcing baptism on the Jews, since he had read in the stars that the circumcised would devastate his empire.

Non multo post tempore Agareni gens circumcisa imperium vastant . . . qua de causa dum apertis portis Caspiis, gentem saevissimam, quam Alexander Magnus ob immanitatem sui super mare Caspium incluserat, educeret, bellumque instauraret, nocte ab angelo quinquaginta duo milia de exercitu eius percussa feruntur.[53]

[Not long after [the circumcised race of Hagar[54]] laid waste his empire . . . When on this account he opened the Caspian Gates and led forth through them that most savage race which, on account of its cruelty, Alexander the Great had shut up north of the Caspian Sea, and so renewed the war, in one night fifty-two thousand men of his army, it is said, were smitten by an angel of the Lord.][55]

The emperor died of a dropsy soon after. Otto incites us to observe the just punishments of God and learn contempt for this world, but assigns to the episode no special role in sacred or imperial history. In calling in the Avars (who seem to be meant) Heraclius is performing an act in Gentile history; but if they are the sons of Magog son of Japhet (as Scythian peoples were generally said to be), the sons of Ishmael son of Hagar figure in the history of God's people, and the vast conquests of the

---

[50] *Chronica*, v, 18; Mierow, 1928, pp. 344–5.     [51] *Chronica*, v, 9; *MGH*, xx, p. 219.
[52] Mierow, 1928, p. 337; n. 51 remarks that the tale of the Jewish mother occurs in no known author earlier than Otto.
[53] *MGH*, xx, p. 220.     [54] Trans. JGAP; Mierow has 'the Saracens, a circumcised race'.
[55] Mierow, 1928, p. 338.

Moslem Arabs might be seen as of apocalyptic significance in the history of church and empire. That Otto does not so present them cannot be explained as the result of simple ignorance or unawareness, since at a later point in the *Chronica* – writing of the Crusades of his own time, when Islam could certainly be seen as the Antichristian Other – he goes out of his way to stress that, contrary to crusading legend, Moslems are not worshippers of idols:

quia constat universitatem Sarracenorum unius Dei cultricem esse, librosque legis necnon et circumcisionem recipere, Christum etiam et apostolos apostoli- cosque viros non improbare; in hoc tantum a salute longe esse, quod Iesum Christum humano generi salutem afferentem Deum vel Dei filium esse negant, Mahometque seductorem, de quo supra dictum est, tanquam prophetam mag- num summi Dei venerantur et colunt.[56]

[as is well known, the Saracens universally are worshippers of one God; they accept the Books of the Law and also the custom[57] of circumcision, and do not even reject Christ and the apostles and the apostolic men;[58] they are cut off from salvation by one thing only, the fact that they deny that Jesus Christ, who brings salvation to the human race, is God or the Son of God, and hold in reverence and worship as a great prophet of the supreme God Mahomet, a deceiver of whom mention was made above.][59]

Moslems are difficult to classify; they are neither heathens nor heretics, nor Jews apostate from their own Messiah, and the false prophet whom they follow cannot accurately be termed Antichrist since he lays no claim to Christ's mission or his person. Otto's precision of knowledge stands in the way of any type-casting of Islam, though in his account of the Crusades there is some indication that the war is directed against the King of the Babylonians, who holds the ground where Babylon once stood.[60] It may be that the first of the empires still mystically stands and will return in the last days, in describing which Otto enquires whether at the general resurrection Babylon will be reborn as the locus of damnation.[61] He does not suggest, however, that the armies of the Cross are seeking to reverse the disaster of Manzikert, and it is true that in his later books he is diminishingly in search of any master narratives of either imperial or apocalyptic history. It is tempting to attribute to this a gathering sense on his part that the tensions between Roman Church and Frankish empire are such that the historian's only recourse is to the

---

[56] *Chronica*, VII, 7; *MGH*, XX, p. 251.     [57] 'Custom' is Mierow's.
[58] Possibly the 'apostolic fathers', who had known the apostles themselves.
[59] Mierow, 1928, p. 412.     [60] *Chronica*, VII, 3; Mierow, 1928, pp. 407–8.
[61] *Chronica*, VIII, 20; Mierow, 1928, pp. 481–2.

instability and misery fundamental to the earthly city; the *amaritudo mentis* which he recollected when writing to Frederick ten years after concluding the *Chronica*. His fifth book concludes, not with the re-foundation of western empire by Charlemagne and Pope Stephen, which would be the culmination if this were primarily a history of *translatio imperii*, but with the partition and disintegration of Carolingian empire in the following century. But the end of history remains obstinately open. The mutability of human things serves as a constant reminder that the end is always at hand, but are there actions which rulers should perform – or alternatively, may be perceived as performing – which enable us to predict or sense the end, or know what actions we should perform in it? The more meaningless and miserable our actions, the less they have to tell us about their transfiguration.

The problematic relation between the two cities, the problematic relation between history and eschatology, reaches a peak of inscrutability at the end of the sixth book, where Otto finds himself recounting the deposition of the emperor Henry IV by the pope Gregory VII and the subsequent death of that pope in exile from Rome. There have been no events of this order before, Otto observes, so that:

Hic, quod supra distuli, solvendum puto, quod Romanum imperium ferro in Daniele comparatum, pedes ex parte ferreos, ex parte fictiles habuit, donec a lapide exciso de monte sine manibus percussum subrueretur. Quid enim aliud, sine melioris sententiae praeiudicio, lapidem sine manibus excisum quam ecclesiam, capitis sine corpus sine carnali commixtione ex Spiritu sancto conceptum et virgine natum, quam quoque sine humana operatione et ex spiritu et aqua regeneratam dixerim? . . . Hoc nimirum regnum . . . in ea parte quae infirmior fuit, percussit, dum regem urbis non tanquam orbis dominum vereri, sed tanquam de limo per humanam conditionem factum fictilem gladio anathematis ferire decuit. Ipsa vero quae antea parva fuit et humilis in quantum montem excreverit, ab omnibus iam videri potest. Quanta autem mala, quot bella bellorumque discrimina inde subsecuta sint, quotiens, misera Roma obsessa, capta, vastata, quod papa super papam sicut rex super regem positus fuerit, taedet memorare. Denique tot mala, tot scismata, tot tam animarum quam corporum pericula huius tempestatis turbo involvit, ut solus ex persecutionis immanitate ac temporis diuturnitate ad humanae miseriae infelicitatem insufficeret comprobandum.[62]

[At this point I think I ought to relate what above I postponed, the fact that the Roman Empire – compared in Daniel to iron – had feet 'part of iron and part of clay', till that it was struck and broken to pieces by a stone cut out of the

---

[62] *Chronica*, VI, 38; *MGH*, XX, pp. 246–7.

mountain without hands. For, without the prejudgment of a better interpretation, how can I interpret 'the stone cut out without hands' as anything other
than the Church, the body of its Head, a body that was conceived by the
Holy Spirit without carnal admixture, was born of a virgin and reborn of
the Spirit and of water – a rebirth in which mortal man had no part? . . . The
Church smote the kingdom in its weak spot when the Church decided not to
reverence the king of the City as lord of the earth, but to strike him with the
sword of excommunication as being by his human condition made of clay. All
can now see to what a mountainous height the Church, at one time small and
lowly, has grown. What great calamities, how many wars and perils of wars
followed in consequence of the weakness of the kingdom; how often unhappy
Rome was besieged, captured, laid waste; and how pope was placed over pope
even as king over king, it is a weariness to record. In a word, the turbulence of
this period carried with it so many disasters, so many schisms, so many dangers
of soul and of body that it alone would suffice to prove the unhappy lot of our
human wretchedness by reason of the cruelty of the persecution and its long
duration.][63]

The stone cut without hands has failed – if it ever attempted – to
terminate the condition made of clay by action in human history, and
there is no alternative in this world to the miseries and frustrations of
that condition. Otto continues through his seventh book to narrate the
unsuccessful and meaningless actions of Henry IV, Gregory VII and
their successors, and makes it clear that the history of the Church – that
is the church militant, the net cast into the sea – is in no way exempt
from the history, or antihistory, of the earthly city.

Porro ecclesiam ecclesiasticas personas, id est sacerdotes Christi eorumque sec-
tatores, tam ex usu locutionis quam consideratione potioris partis diximus, non
ignorantes, quod ex ipsi si reprobam vitam duxerint, ad civitatem Dei in aeter-
num non pertinebunt.[64]

[We have, then, designated as the Church certain ecclesiastical personages –
namely, the bishops[65] of Christ and their attendants – both in accordance with
the common usage of speech and out of regard for the finer element,[66] though
we are not ignorant of the fact that these ecclesiastical personages also, if they
have lived an evil life, will not belong to the City of God in eternity.[67]

The renewed Augustinian insistence that the Church does not act
redemptively upon earthly history, and that neither papal nor imperial
action prepares, or even prefigures, the processes which will take place
in the last days – in more technical language, that history contains no

---

[63] Mierow, 1928, pp. 400–1.    [64] *Chronica*, vii, prologue; *MGH*, xx, p. 248.
[65] Or 'priests' (*sacerdotes*)?    [66] Or 'the stronger part' (*potioris partis*)?    [67] Mierow, 1928, p. 405.

antetypes of the eschata – leaves Otto recounting, *in amaritudine mentis*, a history of human actions, down to the moment at which he is writing, that have no meaning other than that God's judgements admonish us to turn our thoughts towards heaven – a heaven, moreover, of which we may or may not be judged worthy. There is neither a sacred nor a secular history to enlarge their significance; and the modern mind, indifferent to the former, is peculiarly aware of the absence of the latter. Otto is not inscribing the actions he records in any larger process which carries us from one historical condition of things to another, and these volumes are devoted to the origins and operation of Gibbon's capacity to write in this mode. A postmodern intellect may, however, find much to applaud in Otto's implicit message that the history of an action is at best that and no more, and does not possess the means of enlarging its own significance. In subaltern studies, for example, we pay a proper attention to actions which were lost in human misery and played no part in the morphology of larger human systems; we may even find suspicious Otto's unstated premise that it is the actions of the rulers (*potioris partis*), rather than the sufferings of the ruled, which best display the miseries of the human condition. Otto, however, was a ruler by both birth and office, and this was the state of his understanding of history as he concluded his *Chronica* with a commentary on the *Apocalypse* in 1146. All that he had written gave no key to the end of days and the redemption of the elect; that, paradoxically, was its message and its value.

(IV)

The concept of Decline and Fall is proving both elusive and elastic. It has as much to do with religion as with barbarism, and is entangled with the rise and character of a Christian and anti-classical perception of history. The barbarian actions *circa* 410 led to a need to vindicate the Christian community *contra paganos*, and so to the work of Augustine and Orosius in which a history and anti-history of the two cities was set forth. This was in significant measure a repudiation of the Roman republic and its virtue, but did not continue the history already told of its decay past the victory of Augustus. It had no need of 'the Tacitean narrative' or 'the first Decline and Fall', less because Christians wished to vindicate the triumph of the monarchical principle (as they sometimes did) than because they thought universal empire providentially and provisionally legitimised – but not sanctified – by the birth of Christ and the advent of the Church, which did not exempt Rome from the fate of the earthly city. The scenario of the two cities could easily enough be extended from 410 through 476 and the extinction of direct imperial rule in most of the western provinces, but could less easily be extended eastwards, where the rulers of the imperial city still considered empire sanctified by the partnership of the Church. The Two Cities and the Decline and Fall were increasingly and perhaps exclusively western and Latin concepts, preoccupied by another partnership, that of the bishops of Rome and the recently founded kingdoms in Italy, Gaul and Germany.

It is a temptation to suppose that by 1146 the history *de duabus civitatibus* had reached the end of its capacities. Such language, however, presupposes what Otto implicitly denied, the ability to write histories of complex secular processes (which the Christian and the postmodern intellects may unite in denying). Since the history of Gibbon and his *Decline and Fall* is necessarily a history of the rise and exercise of that ability, we are further tempted to inscribe Otto in a history whose telos is its recovery, and if such a history can be written and seems to have taken place, we are justified in proceeding, cautiously and self-consciously, to write it. Otto's later, and last, historical writings can be used as a platform from which such a history may depart. Ten or more years after completing the *Chronica* – he says he considered and abandoned another work, whose nature he does not specify[68] – he committed himself to writing the *Gesta Friderici Primi Imperatoris*, a chronicle of the reign of his nephew Frederick Barbarossa. What we have of this work by Otto covers only the first four years of the emperor's rule; Otto himself died in 1158 and the *Gesta* was continued by another hand. We must be careful of reading into it meanings derived from our knowledge of Frederick's long reign, but it is hard, especially for a modern reader, not to find in it evidence of a changing history and new historical actors.

In dedicating to the emperor both this work and a revised text of the *Chronica*, Otto says that the times are happier than when he wrote his major work in bitterness of spirit.[69] The question must arise whether he has higher hopes that Frederick may act successfully in the history of the earthly city, or in anticipation of the last days. A reader fresh from the *Chronica* will be very cautious before attributing to Otto anything but the greatest caution on this subject, but the emperor's reign appeared to some in retrospect – a retrospect, of course, denied to his uncle the historian – to have had, or aspired to, apocalyptic significance; it was

---

[68] *Gesta*, 1, prologue; Mierow 1953, p. 25. It may have been a history centred on the Crusades.
[69] Mierow, 1928, p. 89; 1953, p. 27.

said he had meant to carry the Crusade to Jerusalem and lay down his crown at the Holy Sepulchre, indicating that the work of empire was done and the last days were at hand. Such visionary acts were still imaginable, but Otto knew what it was to despair of these hopes. All that can be said is that, in this fragment on the beginning of his reign, Frederick seems to have restored empire in Germany and to be at the point of extending it to Rome and beyond; a new scheme of relations with the papacy appears possible.

As the story unfolds – assuming that it is planned to do so – the action moves into the high politics of the world of scholastic philosophy. Bernard of Clairvaux, who is inciting the kings of Christendom to a new Crusade, is also instituting proceedings for heresy against Peter Abelard – whose condemnation Otto thinks justified[70] – and Gilbert de la Porrée, whose ultimate discharge Otto seems to consider deserved.[71] These proceedings are described at length.[72] Gibbon, reading the *Gesta* as we know he did, must have wondered whether Otto meant that an emperor's dealings with the Church and the papacy were now so close that he was obliged to pay attention to such disputes, as Constantine had been obliged at Nicaea; we may ask whether the *translatio studii* has gone so far in the west that the imminence of the heavenly city may be better understood in terms of scholastic precision. Otto, however, looks on both Bernard and Gilbert with a piercing eye, aware of human frailty in the most holy persons,[73] and the trials occur before Frederick has succeeded the emperor Conrad. Scholastic disputation is a new actor in his narrative, little present in the *Chronica*, but we do not know what its presence means.

There are three Italian theatres in this history, in each of which Frederick may expand his empire by overcoming powerful adversaries, so that Otto is impelled to descriptions of the Italian scene. There is Lombardy, where Frederick mounts an expedition to repress the disobedience of the Milanese. Here Otto attempts to explain to his feudal and monastic readers north of the Alps the turbulence, freedom and ferocious rivalries of independent and self-governing cities;[74] we know, as he does not, that these will defeat Frederick I and II in the end, and Gibbon knows that they will do so in alliance with the Popes. As a reader

---

[70] *Gesta*, I, xlix–li; Mierow, 1953, pp. 83, 87–8.     [71] *Gesta*, I, lxi; Mierow, 1953, pp. 83, 87–8.

[72] Chs. xlviii–lxi in their entirety.     [73] Mierow, 1953, p. 101; cf. Mierow, 1928, pp. 302–4.

[74] *Gesta*, II, xiii–xv, esp. Mierow, 1953, pp. 127–8. It was this passage which Quentin Skinner selected to open his presentation of 'the foundations of modern political thought, as laid in their modernity by the city republics of Italy' (Skinner, 1978, I, p. 3).

of Muratori, Gibbon had even before commencing the *Decline and Fall* taken a Guelfic view of the history of liberty and civility in Europe.[75] There is Rome itself, where the emperors' problems in receiving their crown from the Pope without acknowledging his sovereignty have been complicated by the rise of a populist republicanism led by the probably heretical Arnold of Brescia,[76] affirming that the ancient *senatus populusque* still live, may elect their bishop and are free to confer their powers upon the emperor. At the end of the *Decline and Fall*, Gibbon must still decide whether this self-assertion by the city where it all began was to be taken seriously, and if not why not. Lastly, there is Sicily,[77] a realm both insular and peninsular, perhaps subject to the papal *imperium*, perhaps enjoying the remnant of a Byzantine independence of it. Here the still formidable Norman kings are challenging the emperor to extend his empire from the Alps to the Mediterranean and the drama of Hohenstaufen history will be played out in the next century. All this has been stated in terms more proleptic than any available to the middle-aged bishop of Freising, which must raise the question what his intentions were in displaying all three theatres so prominently in the *Gesta Friderici*; what did he think they might mean?

In the second of these theatres there is set a rhetorical debate which proved of such interest to Gibbon that he paraphrased it at length in a late chapter of the *Decline and Fall*. Barbarossa, marching towards Rome, is met by a deputation claiming to speak for the republic of that city, which Otto makes them impersonate by employing the first person singular. They do so in order to greet the emperor as an equal, and their grammar is bold to the point of outrageousness. Reverting for a moment to the more stately 'we', they affirm the past greatness of republican empire.

Scis quod urbs Roma ex senatoriae dignitatis sapientia ac equestris ordinis virtute et disciplina a mari usque ad mare palmites extendens, non solum ad terminos Orbis imperium dilatavit, quin etiam insulas extra Orbem positas Orbi adiciens, principatus eo propagines propagavit . . . Sed exigentibus peccatis, longe positis a nobis principibus nostris,

(Gibbon's theme: the retreat of empire from city)

nobili illo antiquitatis insigni, senatum loquor, ex inerti quorundam desidia neglectui dato, dormitante prudentia, vires quoque minui necesse fuit.[78]

But ancient virtue is now reborn.

[75] *NCG*, pp. 384–6, 391.  [76] *Gesta*, I, xxviii; II, xxviii.
[77] *Gesta*, I, iii, xxiv. Cf. *NCG*, ch. 2.  [78] *Gesta*, II, xxix; *MGH*, xx, pp. 404–5.

Audi ergo, princeps, patienter et clementer pauca de tua ac de mea iusticia, prius tamen de tua quam de mea. Etenim: ab Iove principium. Hospes eras, civem feci. Advena fuisti ex Transalpinibus partibus, principem constitui. Quod meum iure fuit, hoc ubi dedi. Debes itaque primo ad observandas meas bonas consuetudines legesque antiquas, mihi ab antecessoribus tuis imperatoribus idoneis instrumentis firmatas, ne barbarorum violentur rabie, securitatem praebere, officialibus meis, a quibus tibi in Capitolio adclamandum erit, usque ad quinque milia librarum expensam dare . . .[79]

[Now you know that the city of Rome, by the wisdom of the senatorial dignity and the valour of the equestrian order,[80] sending out her boughs from sea to sea, has not only extended her empire to the ends of the earth, but has even added to her world the islands that lie beyond the world, and planted there the shoots of her dominion . . . But, for our sins, since our princes dwelt at a great distance from us, that noble token of our antiquity – I refer to the senate – was given over to neglect by the slothful carelessness of certain men. As wisdom slumbered, strength too was of necessity diminished . . .

Hear then, O Prince, with patience and with clemency a few matters that have to do with your justice and with mine. About yours, however, before I speak of mine. For 'the beginning is from Jove'. You were a stranger. I made you a citizen. You were a newcomer from the regions beyond the Alps. I have established you as prince. What was rightfully mine I gave to you. You ought therefore first to give security for the maintenance of my good customs and ancient laws, strengthened for me[81] by the emperors your predecessors, that they may not be violated by the fury of barbarians. To my officials, who must acclaim you on the Capitol, you should give as much as five thousand pounds as expense money . . .][82]

Frederick has been listening to this tissue of impertinences with mounting fury, and now interrupts with a reply of which Otto says that it was improvised, and that it was delivered with modesty and charm (*corporis modestia orisque venustate*) – a description scarcely borne out by the language with which Otto furnishes him and of which Gibbon says that the ancients would not have disdained it.[83] It runs in part:

Sensit Roma tua, imo et nostra, vicissitudines rerum. Sola evadere non potuit aeterna lege ab auctore omnium sancitam cunctis sub lunari globo degentibus sortem. Quid dicam? Clarum est, qualiter primo nobilitatis tuae robur ab hac nostra urbe translatum sit ad Orientis urbem regiam, et per quot annorum curricula ubera deliciarum tuarum Graeculus esuriens[84] suxerit. Supervenit

[79] *Ibidem*, p. 405.
[80] A feudal error about the Roman *equites*, shared by Otto and all speakers in his narrative.
[81] Or: 'confirmed to me in the proper documents'.       [82] Mierow, 1953, p. 145.
[83] Above, pp. 100–01. Gibbon paraphrases the whole exchange; Womersley, 1994, III, pp. 998–1001.
[84] An echo of Juvenal.

Francus, vere nomine et re nobilis, et eam quae adhuc in te residua fuit inge-
nuitatem fortiter eripuit . . . Nostram intuere rem publicam. Penes nos cuncta
haec sunt . . . Penes nos consules tui, penes nos senatus tuus, penes nos et miles
tuus. Proceres Francorum ipsi te consilio regere, equites Francorum ipsi tuum
ferro iniuriam propellere debebunt.[85]

[Your Rome – nay, ours also – has experienced the vicissitudes of time. She
could not be the only one to escape a fate ordained by the author of all things
for all that dwell beneath the orb of the moon. What shall I say? It is clear how
first the strength of your nobility was transferred from this city of ours to the
royal city of the East, and how for the course of many years the thirsty Greekling
sucked the breasts of your delight. Then came the Frank, truly noble in deed
as in name, and forcibly possessed himself of whatever freedom was still left to
you . . . Behold our state. All is to be found with us . . . With us are your consuls.
With us is your senate. With us is your soldiery. These very leaders of the Franks
must rule you by their counsel, these very knights of the Franks must avert harm
from you by the sword.][86]

And so on, in language insistent that there has been a *translatio virtutis* as
well as a *translatio imperii*. There is an element of comedy in this exchange –
Otto visibly does not think the pretensions of the Romans are to be taken
very seriously – but the language he gives to both sides is extraordinary
enough to indicate that something extraordinary is happening. We seem
to be at a proto-humanist and proto-republican moment. The Romans,
however absurdly, are challenging the whole concept of *translatio imperii* in
the name of civic virtue. Their claim that senatorial and legionary virtue
declined because the *principes* were relocated at a distance from the city
(*alibi quam Romae*) anticipates Gibbon's basic perception of the decline
of city and empire, and contains elements of both 'Tacitean narrative'
and 'first Decline and Fall'. They are not far from saying that republican
virtue declined because of the extent of the empire it had won, but their
counter-claim that it survives in their own persons hints at renaissance, at
Petrarch's *non è ancor morto* quoted by Machiavelli.[87] In inviting Frederick
to accept the status of their elected prince, they seem to be appealing to
a *lex regia* drawn from Roman law rather than Roman historians, but the
appeal to Roman virtue precedes it.

In his retort and rebuke of this insolence, Frederick must rehearse the
doctrine of the *translatio imperii*. The Frankish claim to Rome is based on
conquest and the sword – *fortiter eripuit* – and there is no mention of a
papal sanction of their empire; but the sword presupposes the virtue to

---

[85] *Gesta*, II, xxx; *MGH*, xx, p. 405.     [86] Mierow, 1953, pp. 146–7.
[87] *Il Principe*, ch. xxvi, the closing words; Petrarch, *Canzone* xvi, lines 13–16.

bear it, and in the assertion that Roman virtue is now possessed wholly by Frankish empire we seem to find the implication that barbarians are now Romans – 'the fierce giants of the north' have 'mended the puny breed'[88] – later central to neo-classical and romantic reconstructions of European history. The Pope is absent from this narrative, but the pontiff and the prince are in fact in collusion against the people[89] (it is the unreality of all three terms that will impress itself upon Gibbon)[90] and there is a triumph of religion as well as of barbarism to be discerned in the historical situation. The *translatio imperii* is not to be divorced from the antihistory of the two cities, and when Frederick reminds the Romans that they have not escaped the fate of all sublunary things, his own empire must be included in the warning. We are reading the text of Otto of Freising, who ten years before had believed that there was no way for empire to escape from the earthly city, and he is not telling us that he has changed his mind.

---

[88] *DF*, I, 2; Womersley, 1994, I, p. 84. Below, pp. 439–40.
[89] *Gesta*, II, xxxi; Mierow, 1953, p. 149. They were in fact collaborating to bring about the sentencing and death of the Roman leader Arnold of Brescia.
[90] *DF*, VI, 69–70.

# CHAPTER 7

# The historiography of the translatio imperii

## (1)

The discourse of *translatio imperii*, which Otto of Freising presents to us at a mid-point in its development, may be traced from the ninth, or even the fifth, century to the fourteenth, and may be carried on into the sixteenth century if not further. It occupies a central role in this volume precisely because *translatio imperii* is in several ways the antithesis of Decline and Fall, and there is a need to understand how the latter displaced, and possibly emerged from, the former. *Translatio* implied that the empire had been transferred from hand to hand and place to place, from Romans to Greeks and from Greeks to Franks (both remaining Romans), and had therefore survived. Survival might entail revival, a decline of the empire in one form preceding its reconstruction in another, but this is not cardinal to Latin Christian ways of thinking during the millennium confronting us. There is the further problem that empire was sacred, in the terms laid down by Eusebius and not demolished by Augustine. It was a metahistorical concept, whose existence entailed historical events but was not to be critically evaluated within the context that events provided; and the greatest if most fictitious of these events, the so-called Donation of Constantine, was not seen primarily as providing the historical sequences that followed it – the survival of Christian empire for a thousand years of east Roman history, paired with its failure to maintain control of the Latin west and the advent of historical conditions that obliged the popes to recognise the revival of empire by the Franks four centuries later. It was not that these sequences were unknown; Otto of Freising, a great historian, was able to locate Odovacar, Heraclius, Muhammad, Charlemagne, Otto I and Gregory VII at moments of historical significance; but he saw these moments as continuing the sequence of Danielic prophesied history, and his deepest misgivings arose from the fear that the city of God on earth was falling into the ways of the earthly city, which could only mean that Antichrist was at hand. The complexities of secular history, with which he was far from unacquainted, played a negative and secondary role in the metahistory that occupied his mind. Will this oblige us to treat the displacement of *translatio imperii* by Decline and Fall as an emancipation of secular history from sacred?

Certainly it appeared so to Gibbon, and in a history leading to his view of the world the narrative of such an emancipation must be given paradigmatic status. When in the opening paragraph of his first volume, however, he wrote of the Roman empire and its decline and fall, 'a revolution which will ever be remembered, and is still felt by the nations of the earth',[1] he was saying what was true enough in his own time – if we do not extend 'the nations of the earth' to include those who had not yet heard of Decline and Fall and had not felt its consequences – but was about to write the history of a thousand years, from the fifth century to the fifteenth, during which the Decline and Fall had not figured as an organising concept, whatever might have been its impact on European existence. We may read the history of the *translatio imperii* as meaning that medieval west Europeans 'felt' the fall of the Roman empire; but they were less concerned to 'remember' it than to deny it, and this they did very effectively.

The discourse of *translatio imperii* and the Donation of Constantine was metahistorical; that is to say, both church and empire were conceived as sacred entities transcending time and circumstance, modes of divine action upon, rather than in, secular history.[2] It followed that the great debates over the relative primacy of church and empire, and the extent to which the church's spiritual authority was itself an exercise of empire, were conducted in metahistorical terms: discourses of theology, jurisprudence and philosophy, in which we may discern the outlines of a philosophy of history but which did not oblige the disputants to recognise that they were constructing any such thing. We have come to call the history of these debates 'the history of medieval political thought',[3] and because the construction of historical narratives played a minor and uncanonical role in it, we are disposed to consider 'the history of historiography' a field distinct from 'the history of political thought'; either

---

[1] *DF*, 1, ch. 1; Womersley, 1994, 1, p. 31.

[2] The histories of the concept of empire on which I principally rely are: Folz, 1969; Muldoon, 1999; for its transition to early modern times (below, chs. 11–12), Pagden, 1995; Armitage, 1998. For the Donation of Constantine, Maffei, 1964.

[3] A bibliography of this great subject would be a history of its historiography. In English, see most recently Burns, 1988.

a fallout from it, or a phenomenon extraneous to it. If, however, we accept as paradigmatic a process whereby 'political thought' became, and was increasingly seen as being, pervaded by 'history', we are obliged to enquire how such a process occurred. We may look for a progressive invasion of both sacred history and metahistorical thinking by concepts of secular rule, and with it secular history; but such an invasion, and the ascendancy to which it gives rise, are so far ingrained in our minds by the very procedure of writing history, that we must beware of taking their triumph for granted, and so writing whiggishly.

The discourse of *translatio* implied a narrative involving at least two actors, and by extension more, who were varyingly dependent upon metahistory, sacred history, and secular history. The church as a primary actor claimed a direct but not a temporal derivation from the *civitas Dei*, and consequently tended to rely overwhelmingly on the first two of these three – 'metahistory' being here a term for the theological and philosophical arguments justifying the supremacy of the spiritual over the temporal: 'political thought' in its medieval form. The central event in sacred history on which the church relied was Christ's gift to Peter of a supremacy over other apostles and the power of the keys as the church's head. The nearest to a secular history which this claim entailed was provided by the proofs, part traditional and part documentable, of the apostolic succession of the bishops of Rome to Peter; and it is interesting to note that, from an early date, some part in this was played by the awesome presence of the ruins of Rome, once pagan and imperial but now sanctified by the church. In so far as there is a medieval sense of 'decline and fall', it is to be sought here. But we are dealing with ecclesiastical history in the Eusebian sense, the triumph of martyrs over persecutors and doctors over heretics, and though Roman history was strong in the former of these – both Peter and Paul being among its martyrs – the history of heresy and orthodoxy was largely Greek and eastern. It was in the relation of church to empire that the key to Roman and Latin ecclesiastical history was to be found, and in this the city of Rome itself played an elusive and somewhat enigmatic role.

The supposed Donation of Constantine was the central event here; it entailed both that emperor's removal to an eastern capital, and his bestowal of imperial authority on the Pope. If *imperium* had been simply his to give, the bishop might be no more than his officer; but the legend had Constantine recognising something sacred in Pope Sylvester's office. There arose juristic argument contending that the gift of *imperium* was irrevocable, and, more importantly, theological and ecclesiological argument contending that Sylvester derived *imperium* from the *sacerdotium* that was above it, so that Constantine's apparent Donation was really a recognition that Peter's successor enjoyed it already. These arguments, developed in the course of centuries, were plainly metahistorical in character, and it is important that the empire, as vehicle of the church, shared the latter's nature as an eternally existent mode of God's rule over men; the church, maintaining that it took part in empire while remaining above it, did not as a rule seek to reduce empire to a mere incident in secular time. The narrative of Donation, however, entailed problems in imperial history with which both church and empire must at times reckon.

There was the problem of the removal to Constantinople, from which empire continued to be exercised unaffected by the Donation, or by the *translatio* which re-established empire in the western provinces. There were hints of a secular argument: Constantine's heirs had abandoned Italy and Gaul, justifying Peter's heirs in the actions they took; but in proportion as the latter wished to assert the absolute primacy of *sacerdotium* over *imperium*, they had to decide whether the *imperium* exercised from Constantinople had never been separately legitimated, or whether it had been diminished to a mere kingship by the recognition of empire in Charlemagne. By the time of Frederick Barbarossa, the relation of western to eastern empire had been vastly exacerbated by the Crusades, and half a century later there occurred the Fourth Crusade and the establishment of the Latin Empire of Constantinople: a step doubtful as an extension of the universal claims of the papacy, which mistrusted it, and certainly no extension of the empire of the Hohenstaufen, with whom the popes were at odds. It might be left as an episode in a merely Constantinopolitan history, and thus separated from the great debates over the meaning of *translatio*, which popes and western emperors conducted in terms so much their own as to mean little to eastern theologians. The separation between the Catholic and Orthodox discursive universes, which faced Gibbon with so great a problem in historiography, was already far advanced; both ecclesiastical and secular history would be conducted in overwhelmingly Latin terms.

The papacy needed a narrative of *translatio*, and this might entail a separation from eastern church as schismatic and eastern empire as intrusive or irrelevant. The heresy of Heraclius and the inroads of Islam appear in Otto's history;[4] he has less to say about the iconoclasm of the

---

[4] Above, pp. 116–17.

seventh-century emperors and the subsequent downfall of their power in Italy, which had obliged the papacy to choose between the Lombards and Franks. It is here that we encounter the narrative produced by the empire, as the second principal actor in the history of *translatio*. From the Carolingians to the Hohenstaufen, it was necessary to explain that empire had been translated to the Franks, and that they enjoyed *imperium* by an authority which was their own rather than the pope's. This was to be done theologically, juristically and scholastically, by explaining that the *imperium* was the equal of the *sacerdotium* and the emperor a sacred officer; but it also entailed a history showing that Franks were Romans and had inherited their *imperium* rather than displaced them. Otto's Frederick, informing the Roman delegation that Franks exercise empire by right of conquest, declares that everything which was Roman is now in the possession of the Franks;[5] but he is not necessarily proclaiming a history of barbarian triumph. He may mean merely that the Franks are now Romans, having acquired *imperium* through lawful conquest, and the fact that they were once barbarians may not have assumed the importance which occasioned debate among early modern historians over the Roman or Germanic origins of western kingship. A Trojan rather than a Gothic ancestry permitted a claim to equality with the descendants of Virgil's Aeneas; and when Gibbon, in a famous passage, observed that the ark of Noah took the place previously occupied by the fall of Troy,[6] he may be read as reminding us that a biblical genealogy for barbarous peoples was a baroque rather than a medieval necessity. So too, it may be, was the image of the barbarian as a being culturally remote from the Roman but coming to share his history; the discourse of *translatio* did not essentially require it, once the barbarian had become a Christian.

If there had been a *translatio*, Rome was not dead; it survived as the type, even the form, of the *civitas Dei* militant on earth. But it survived as the *imperium* that Charlemagne and Pope Leo had revived, and here there arose the problem that Christian principalities not included in it nevertheless existed. As well as the empire of Constantinople – perhaps reduced to that of a *rex Graecorum* – there were western kingdoms over which Charlemagne had not ruled and Frederick did not rule as emperor. Since the partition of the Carolingian inheritance, the kingdom of France had been separate from the empire of the Franks, and the *rex Francorum* – equally descended from Charlemagne and anointed at Rheims in a ceremony as sacred and symbolically loaded as that of the

---

[5] Above, pp. 123–6.    [6] *DF*, I, ch. 9; Womersley, 1994, I, pp. 233–4.

imperial coronation – could claim to be *imperator in regno suo* or to enjoy an authority no less imperial than his cousin's. It was a corollary that there existed a kingdom, sometimes styled an empire, of the Germans, conferred by electors and distinguishable from the Roman empire, to which it gave a right that, paradoxically, only the Pope could confirm; if the popes preferred election because it was not hereditary, Germans might prefer it because it was not Roman. West of the Frankish, imperial and papal complex of rivalries, in the Spanish peninsula and the British archipelago, there reigned kings it was unsafe to call *reguli*, whose realms might have been provinces of Caesar's empire but had never acknowledged that of Charlemagne.[7] If these styled themselves *reges* and not emperors, it is noteworthy that they sometimes used the words *imperium* and *imperator* to denote something akin to our 'multiple monarchy', a rule over several realms conceptually independent of the discourse of *translatio*; and especially after 1500, both the Spanish and English monarchies were to begin developing concepts of 'empire' in senses more familiar to modern readers. Lastly, to the south of Rome there lay the kingdom of the Two Sicilies, reconquered from the Greeks and Arabs in ways which permitted the Pope to claim a suzerainty exercised through the Normans, but also encouraged the Hohenstaufen who acquired the kingdom to develop ideas of empire that had more to do with Constantine than with his Donation. Lying apart from the discourse of *translatio*, though never unaffected by it, any of these kingdoms might come to have their own perceptions of Roman, Trojan and barbaric history.

There was a third actor in the narrative of *translatio*, capable of a discourse of its own: the Roman people itself – if its 'self' could be held stable enough to be deserving the name. At intervals down to the fifteenth century, the miscellany of noble households, tradesmen and clerics inhabiting the ancient city recollected that they had elected their bishop until the popes had succeeded in vesting that process in the Curia, and recalled an even more distant past in which they had been a senate and people who chose a prince or might even rule without one. They made an appearance in the histories of Otto of Freising, voicing what seemed to be a nostalgia for the age before the exercise of empire had moved away from the city, and recalling to our minds Sallust's observation that empire had been the republic's before it was the emperor's. They did not seem, however, to be claiming more than that the *princeps* – like the bishop? – was

---

[7] Folz, 1969, pp. 40–1, 53–8. In the Spanish peninsula, these claims might be made by the kingdoms of Leon and Castile; those of Navarre and Aragon had belonged to Charlemagne's Spanish March.

of their making and owed them acknowledgement; in which case they were claiming agency in the process of *translatio imperii*, not seeking to terminate it. In pursuing the transition from *translatio* to Decline and Fall, we need to understand what role the image of the republic played in the former process, as well as how it became a revolt against it.

(11)

The history of the thirteenth through fifteenth centuries, as our understanding is shaped to see it, is not centrally treated in the later volumes of the *Decline and Fall*. Gibbon is concerned with Latin European history only as it affected that of the east Roman empire, and yet it is a difficulty for him that he can follow eastern history only as it is illustrated by Latin and Islamic impacts upon it. During this era the Hohenstaufen emperors took control of the kingdom of Sicily, hoping to consolidate an imperial position in the Italian peninsula, while facing the opposition of self-governing cities in what had once been the Lombard 'kingdom of Italy'. Otto of Freising had laid stress on what we see as the secular process by which these cities assumed independent power,[8] and it is of this that Gibbon used the phrase 'the Guelfs displayed the banner of liberty and the church',[9] meaning that the Lombard and Tuscan cities were the allies of the papacy in its attempts to undo imperial policy in Italy. We know from his abandoned Swiss history that it was from the failure of Frederick II that Gibbon dated the rise of municipal independence, which he had learned from Muratori to reckon among the keys to European political development.[10] The exact meaning of 'liberty' in his formula has yet to be established; but we also know, from Otto's account of the debate between Barbarossa and the Romans, that we have to do with the 'republican' language, and its use of ancient history, which is a contested theme in recent historiography. Its role in the history of *translatio* is now to be considered, but there are other settings in which that history proceeds.

The popes made use of the French house of Anjou to destroy Hohenstaufen power in both Sicily and Tuscany, and we see the establishment of the Angevin kingdom of Naples as beginning the history of regional resistance to papal suzerainty recounted by Giannone in the eighteenth century. There is a southern history intimately connected with that of *translatio*, but marginal to its centrally sub-alpine character.

---

[8] Above, p. 123.     [9] *DF*, v, ch. 49; Womersley, 1994, III, p. 144.     [10] *NCG*, pp. 384–6.

We see the Angevin victory as a climax in the latter's history; imperial power will never confront the papacy in Italy on the same terms as before it. From this moment, however, we proceed to the confrontation between Boniface VIII and Philip the Fair, and the effective humiliation of the former by agents of the French king and henchmen of the house of Colonna claiming to act in the name of the 'Roman people'. The last-named we know as a wild card in the history of *translatio*, but in 1302 it acts together with the French monarchy; and the latter employs the discourse of *imperium* against *sacerdotium* in terms rather Gallican than imperialist – the *imperium* it claims is that of the royal heirs of Charlemagne, effectively if not formally the equal of that inherited by his imperial heirs in Germany. The keyword *imperium* displays the diversity of its meanings, and the kingdoms west of the imperial succession have become visible; Philip's successors will fall into dynastic crisis, in which the Plantagenet kings of England intervene.

We connect the defeat of Boniface VIII with the subsequent removal of the papal residence to Avignon, where for decades the popes were French and the papacy's politics occurred in a French environment. Its return to Rome permitted Roman popular intervention and provoked a lasting schism; we seem to embark on a period in which empire and papacy were sharply reduced in power, the latter becoming little more than an actor in the peninsular politics of Italy, in which the former occasionally intervened. It is this state of things that is transformed after the end of the fifteenth century, by the massive interventions of the French and Spanish monarchies. While it lasted, there is held to have occurred a growth of new modes of political thought, in which the city republics of Italy and the transalpine territorial monarchies took part, and which are conventionally interpreted as entailing a transition to thought that can be called 'modern'.[11] A transition from the discourse of *translatio imperii* to that of 'decline and fall of the Roman empire' can be included in this pattern; but since the latter thesis entailed a confrontation between the images of 'republic' and 'imperial monarchy', we find ourselves concerned with relations between the thinking current in city republics and that current in territorial monarchies which took over some of the attributes of empire.

We date from a broadly defined thirteenth century a recrudescence – to say 'revival' would involve us in the question whether it had ever seemed to disappear – of thinking and imagery that extolled the virtues of civil society, thus intensifying the role of nature in its unending and

---

[11]  See further, below, pp. 154–5.

sometimes adversarial partnership with grace.[12] Since the Word had been made Flesh, grace had entered into nature, which it *non tollit sed perficit*; but the revival of nature we are considering was that of society as natural to man, rather than that of the body direct. A world increasingly populated by corporations, *communitates* and *universitates* was growing familiar with persons at once artificial and natural, and in the discourse that concerns us the *communitas* or *res publica* was as visible as its *imperium*; Caesar's relation to the *res publica* therefore needed re-definition. Among the various sources for thought emphasising the community we may distinguish the philosophy of Aristotle, the rhetoric of Cicero and the jurisprudence of Justinian. The first two had originated in ancient city-states before these were absorbed in the imperial monarchy of the last, and therefore depicted the political society ruled by its citizens without king or prince, to which the term *res publica* is attracted in taking on its modern meaning of 'republic'. In thirteenth-century Europe there were emerging self-governing communes and cities, especially in the regions of Italy north of Rome which found themselves a debatable land between empire north of the Alps and papacy south of the Apennines, and these took an understandable interest in the notion of the kingless 'republic'. It is a matter of some importance to the history of historiography that the city of Rome itself did not come to join this category; lacking (thought Gibbon) a sound mercantile base, the *senatus populusque*, all too easily reducible to the feuding Orsini and Colonna, remained overshadowed by the *sacerdotium et imperium*.

It is of more immediate consequence that thought concerned with the *res publica* was in no way inherently opposed to kingship. Italian cities, where the *vivere civile* or government by citizens assumed importance, had not to contend directly – at least after the fall of the Hohenstaufen – with the *imperator* or the *rex* who was *imperator in regno suo*; these were distant figures, intermittently if vividly present. Their problem was with the fierce instabilities of their own civic life, often leading to the assumption of single-person rule by a variety of *podestà*, *signori* and *principi*, whose authority was varyingly durable and legitimised variously if at all. The prince – the Machiavellian echo is deliberately proleptic – might use that title to assimilate himself to the condition of a king, sanctified if not anointed in an immeasurably monarchical universe where God was the king of kings (Machiavelli's *principe naturale*); or he might find himself a *principe nuovo* whose power was not legitimated at all. Italian cities had

---

[12] Skinner, 1978, 1, pp. 3–68.

practical knowledge of the tyrant – *tyrannus in exercitio* and *in defectu tituli* – who was much more than a term of rhetorical abuse employed in the contentions of pope and emperor. If the *principe* chose to style himself a *princeps* in the Roman sense, he could not well aspire to the imperial dignity of a Caesar; that name if used by him might suggest the triumvir who had taken over power in a collapsing republic, and must choose (if he could) between the roles of its reformer and its tyrant. As late Roman history became known in greater textual detail – particularly as there emerged the contrast between the philosophy and the active life of Cicero, who had perished in the struggle ending with Caesarian power – scholars in Italian cities had better reason to understand its contested nature and compare these contests with their own.

But this is to anticipate both the crises of republican ideology and the humanist expansion of textual and historical knowledge. We return to the point at which it must be seen that *res publica* was not incompatible with monarchy. Aristotle had conceded that the rule of a king might be the highest form of government, whether or not this was compatible with saying – as he also had – that the highest form was rule over one's equals who ruled over one in their turn. His eye may have been on Plato's image of the philosopher king, rather than the actual kings of Persia or Macedon; but he had certainly served the latter, and what he had to say about monarchy was included by Latin Europeans in the metahistorical justification of empire, which ideally placed the whole earth under the rule of a single and sacred monarch. Aristotle could be enlisted in the school of Eusebius, though at some strain to its confines; while the Roman Cicero, irrespective of what he thought of Caesar or Octavius, could be taken into the justification of empire on a greater and more Christian scale. As author of the *De officiis* and *De legibus*, he could appear the panegyrist of the just society, in which the function of rule became the maintenance of justice, and that of *imperium* the *patrocinium* of all the relations among men that made up society. From this point one looked towards Caesar the *princeps* of Roman law, whose empire was a universal jurisprudence and *libertas* the freedom one enjoyed under his protection; and the equality of rule exercised by citizens, who ruled in the act of being ruled by others, became incidental rather than essential, a detail in the enjoyment of equality and freedom of social action under a law which Caesar guaranteed in the exercise of ruling the social world the *res publica* had become. To modern or postmodern eyes, there begin to appear the distinctions between the social and the political, between negative and positive liberty, which account for the problematic character of self-determinant citizenship in both the historical record and contemporary political theory.

We have still not reached the full extent to which republic could be made compatible with empire and *translatio*, monarchy and kingship. It was essential to the Eusebian thesis that Augustus provided the world empire under which it was providentially appropriate that Christ should be born. There was the implication that rule and civil order were conditions necessary to the spread of his word, and if the Word had been made Flesh and the church was the extension of that person in unity, the metaphorising Christian mind could see rule and civil order as aspects of Christ's church and even his person. If, then, republic and monarchy (empire and kingdom) displayed the natural beauty of justice and the common good, the virtues of the republic could be extended to become the virtues of sacred empire. Certainly, they might be the peaceable virtues of obedience to law rather than the warrior sternness of active citizenship, but the latter was not excluded; not subjected, that is to say, to the Augustinian judgement that it had amounted to no more than the pursuit of glory and the *libido dominandi*. Augustus establishing the peace of the empire was Augustus restoring the virtues of the republic. There remained one half-hidden question. Included in the thesis was Sallust's judgement that Romans had become corrupt as their empire reached its height. Had this corruption been a consequence of empire, and had Augustus succeeded in reversing its course?

(iii)

The *trecento* and *quattrocento* writers with whom we have now to deal were predominantly Tuscan and French – though Thomas Aquinas is to be included among them – contemporary with the Angevin victories over the Hohenstaufen and the related Guelf victories over the Ghibellines in Tuscany, as well as with the catastrophe of Anagni and the papal removal to Avignon. We see them as living at a time when the papal–imperial struggle underwent transformation and perhaps an ending, but this may be misleading; the attempted interventions of the emperors Henry of Luxemburg and Louis of Bavaria produced several of the most remarkable works in all the literature of *translatio imperii*, those by Dante and Marsilius of Padua among them. In all these writers we find a very strong presence of the literature of *res publica* and the common good; there is a question whether it anticipates, or modifies, what may be thought a more radical republicanism emerging at a later date, subversive of the ideas of both empire and papacy. *Prima facie*, it would seem that this cannot be so, since the image of the Roman republic found in these works is wholly compatible with the Christian vision of Augustan empire as providentially appointed to prepare the way for the church of Christ. There is a drastic abandonment of the Augustinian proposition that Roman virtue was no more than an exercise of the *libido dominandi*; it is presented in Aristotelian and Ciceronian terms, as civil, sociable and even charitable, enlarged beyond nature into grace, and made to justify the republic's exercise of a benign empire foreshadowing the church. These writers are predominantly Guelf; they accept the *translatio imperii* as meaning that Charlemagne and Otto I held their empire in virtue of the Pope's consecration; but they do not wish to diminish or secularise empire, since its sacredness and universality enhance the supremacy of the same qualities in the *sacerdotium* and papal empire from which it is held. The Donation of Constantine persists. The great exception is of course Dante, a Guelf driven by the divisiveness of faction in post-Ghibelline Florence to an extreme of imperialism that no Ghibelline could exceed. He saw the Donation as an apocalyptic corruption of the Christian community,[13] and believed that his republic could enjoy peace only under the rule of an emperor who embodied Christ as fully as the pope did. He had if anything fewer doubts than his Guelf predecessors and contemporaries of the republic's compatibility with empire in its Augustan and Eusebian forms. As a twentieth-century scholar put it:

> For Augustine, Roman patriotism was ultimately based on the sin and folly of egoistic pride. For Dante [Alighieri, author of *De monarchia* and the *Divine Comedy*] it was holy, for Remigio [de' Girolami, a preacher at Santa Maria Novella] it was rational, and for Ptolemy [of Lucca, an assistant to St Thomas Aquinas] it was charitable.[14]

Dante passionately admired the virtues of the republic, to which he accorded a role in human redemption. He indeed placed Brutus and Cassius in hell beside Judas, since treason against Caesar was equivalent with treason against Christ;[15] but Marcus Cato, an enemy of Caesar and a suicide, enjoys second place among the virtuous heathen, as the doorkeeper of purgatory,[16] whereas Virgil, the all-but-prophetic poet of empire, rises as high as the Earthly Paradise before he must turn back.[17]

---

[13] Dante, *De monarchia*, III, 10, 1–130; *Inferno*, XIX, 115–17; *Purgatorio*, XXXII, 124–9; *Paradiso*, XX, 55–60.
[14] Davis, 1974, p. 33. Insertions by JGAP. Ptolemy's name, in Italian 'Tolomeo', probably indicates that he was baptised 'Bartolomeo'.
[15] *Inferno*, XXXIV, 55–67.        [16] *Purgatorio*, I, 31–9, 70–5.        [17] *Purgatorio*, XXX, 43–54.

The imperialist denies tension between republic and empire, and if by empire we mean rule of the world it was the republic that achieved it; but the figure of Cato reminds us that there is tension between the liberty of citizens and the rule of emperors, and that it was the former that achieved rule of the world. We cannot quite eliminate this tension by shifting our attention from the liberty of the citizen to the liberty of the subject.

It is therefore worth asking whether the Guelfic combination of papalism with republicanism – Gibbon's 'banner of liberty and the church' – led to a more critical view of the Caesars, or beyond it to a vision of Decline and Fall. The crucial text for this enquiry is that of Sallust, who had provided a narrative in which kings were ever jealous of the virtue of their subjects, but after their expulsion from Rome the liberated virtue of many – not necessarily a democratic 'the many' – raised the republic to heights of greatness, in which widespread or universal empire is certainly included. The capacity to rule others is certainly among the attributes of virtue, but in our anti-imperialist climate we have to beware of reducing all virtue to hegemony and thus dismissing it. From Virgil to Dante and Ptolemy of Lucca – the two latter are here in agreement – we read that the virtue of the Romans made them just and charitable towards each other, and thus acceptable to their subjects over whom their *patrocinium* was just and charitable also; a doctrine Augustine and Orosius did not share. Sallust saw this virtue, including its capacity for empire, as disintegrating in the time of the Jugurthan war and the conspiracy of Catiline; and he furnished an account of the last in which Cicero – who gave his own account of the matter – Cato and Julius Caesar played parts which made all three crucially significant actors in the drama of the republic's fall and its replacement by the line of the Caesars. With an image of the 'first decline and fall' established in our minds, we find ourselves looking for an extension of the Sallustian narrative in which the emperors display the same weaknesses as the kings, and the empire is lost with the republican virtue that achieved it.

Brunetto Latini, who returned to Florence with the Guelfs and whom Dante remembered with affection as a teacher, wrote a study in French of rhetoric as active civic virtue, containing a history which indicates how the narrative might be extended. He says:

> fu establis par les romains ke jamés n'i eust roi, mais fust la cité governee en tot son regne par les sinatours, par consoles, et patrices et tribuns et dicteours, et par autres officiaus, selonc ce ke les choses sont grans et dedens la vile et dehors.

Et cele signorie durra iiii et lxv. ans, jusk'a tant ke Catelline fist a Rome la conjurison encontre ciaus ki governoient Rome, por l'envie des signatours. Mais cele conjurison fu descoverte au tans ke li tres sages Marcus Tullius Cicero . . . fist destruire une grant partie par le conseil dou bon Caton ki les juga a mort, ja soit ce ke Julius Cesar ne consilla pas k'il en fussent jugié a mort, mais fusent mis en diverses prisons. Et pour ce disent li plusour k'il fu compains de cele conjuroison. Et a la verité dire il n'ama onques les signatours ne les autres officieus de Rome, ne il lui, car il estoit estraise de la lignie as fius Eneas. Après ce il estoid de si haut corage k'il ne baioit fors que a la signorie avoir dou tout, selonc ce ke ses anciestres avoient eu . . .

Après la mort Julle Cesar fu empereres Octeviens son nevou, ki regna xlii. ans et vi. mois avant la naissance Jhesucrist et xiiii. ans aprés, et tint la monarchie de trestot le monde . . . Mes ci se taist li mestres a parler de lui et des empereours de Rome, et retorne a sa matire.[18]

[The Romans decreed that they would never again have a king, but that the city and its territory should be governed by senators, consuls, patricians, tribunes, dictators and other officials in matters appropriate to their position, both inside the city and outside. This rule lasted 465 years, until Catiline conspired against the rulers of Rome because of his desire to acquire high rank. But this conspiracy was uncovered during the consulship of the very wise Marcus Tullius Cicero, who . . . had many of the guilty killed through the counsel of good Cato, who condemned them to death, even though Julius Caesar did not recommend death, but rather that they be put in various prisons, and for this reason many say that he was an accomplice in this conspiracy. The truth of the matter is that he had no love for the senators and other officials in Rome, nor they for him, for he was descended from Aeneas' sons. After this he was of such great courage that he took over the rule of all, as his ancestors had done . . .[19] and because the Romans could not have kings . . . he had himself named emperor . . . After the death of Julius Caesar, Octavian his nephew was emperor, and he ruled forty-two years and six months before the birth of Jesus Christ, and fourteen more years after that, and he was monarch of all the world . . . And now the narrative ceases speaking of the emperors of Rome and returns to its subject matter.][20]

Brunetto, not a sophisticated historian, sees the republic as brought to an end by Catiline's conspiracy and commands no narrative leading to the victory of Augustus. Julius Caesar is an enigmatic figure, but the context seems to connect both monarchy and empire with the coming of Christ; it may be worth recalling that this was a providential decision and that providence may choose unhallowed instruments. Brunetto is a Guelf and proceeds to a narrative of *translatio* featuring the Donation of Constantine, the loss of Persia to 'the evil preacher Mohammed, who was

[18] Carmody, 1948, pp. 44–6 (*Tresor*, chs. xxxvi–viii).    [19] Chapter xxxvii omitted.
[20] Barette and Baldwin, 1993, pp. 36–8.

a monk',[21] the expulsion of the iconoclast emperors from Italy, the papal appeal to the Franks, and the history of empire down to the extinction of the Hohenstaufen, after which it may or may not be finally at an end.[22] From history he turns to civil philosophy, which significantly focusses on the rule of a *podestà* over a city of free men.[23] There is not to be found any narrative of the ancient emperors and their empire, other than of the persecutors who precede Constantine.

It has been suggested[24] that this missing narrative is to be found in the *De regimine principum* attributed to Thomas Aquinas and Ptolemy of Lucca.[25] The former author recounts Sallust's version of the expulsion of the kings and quotes him on the marvellous growth of the city once liberty had been attained. The text agrees that citizens may be more diligent in their own service than in that of a master, and rather interestingly chooses to illustrate this by observing that the republic paid its soldiers out of both public funds and private contributions.

Sed cum dissensionibus fatigarentur continuis, quae usque ad bella civilia excreverunt, quibus bellis civilibus eis libertas, ad quam multum studuerant, de manibus erepta est, sub potestate imperatorum esse coeperunt, qui se reges a principio appellari noluerunt, quia romanis fuerat nomen regium odiosum. Horum autem quidam more regio bonum commune fideliter procuraverunt, per quorum studium romana respublica et aucta et conservata est. Plurimi vero eorum in subditos quidem tyranni, ad hostes vero effecti desides et imbecilles, romanam rempublicam ad nihilum redegerunt.[26]

[But when they were worn out by the continual dissensions which escalated into civil wars – during which liberty, for which they were very zealous, was ripped from their hands – they came under the power of the emperors. From the beginning the emperors were unwilling to be called kings, because this title was odious to the Romans. Some of them procured the common good faithfully, as is the true royal custom, and through their zeal the Roman Republic was increased and preserved. But most of them were tyrants to their subjects yet idle and feeble toward their enemies, and these led the Roman republic to naught.][27]

How far does this take us toward a republican thesis of decline and fall? The text is emphatic that tyranny is most likely to occur where there is the rule of many,[28] from which it would seem that the civil wars were the product of liberty rather than usurpation. There is a closer association between emperors and kings than we found in Brunetto, and it is clear

[21] *Ibidem*, p. 49.  [22] *Ibidem*, pp. 54, 60.  [23] *Ibidem*, pp. 351, 350–80.
[24] Blythe, in Hankins, 2000, pp. 39–40.  [25] Blythe, 1997.
[26] Busa, 1980, III, p. 596. (Capitalisation added.)  [27] Blythe, 1997, p. 71.
[28] Blythe, 1997, p. 73.

that emperors are liable to become tyrants and lose their states through weakness. But we have only the single word *aucta* ('increased') to tell us that the 'common good' is equivalent with empire, and there is not a strong statement that the 'republic' came to 'naught' and ceased to exist through losing provinces to barbarians. Nor, above all, does the author seem concerned to tell us whether he is speaking of the pagan emperors and persecutors, or of the Christian successors to Constantine. He does not seem to have reached a point where the Eusebian narrative, or that of the *translatio imperii*, have become crucial. What is to happen when the text of Aquinas, if this is his, is continued by his collaborator?

Ptolemy of Lucca situates Caesar in the history of the Four Empires.

Post hanc autem monarchiam romanus principatus vigere incepit. Tempore enim Iudae Machabaei, qui immediate quasi post mortem floruit Alexandri, cum Ptolomaeo Lagi concurrente, in lib. i mach., multa de romanis traduntur. In quibus ipsorum potentia ad omnes mundi plagas videbatur diffusa, sub consulibus tamen: quia superstitibus regibus cum finitimis sollicitabantur regionibus, et modicae adhuc erant virtutis, duravitque consulatus, immo monarchia, usque ad tempora Iulii Caesaris, qui primus usurpavit imperium; sed parum in ipso supervixit, a senatoribus quidem occisus propter abusum dominii. Post hunc Octavianus filius sororis suae successit, qui vindicta exercita contra occisores iulii, interfectoque Antonio, qui monarchiam tenebat in oriente, solus ipsam obtinuit. Et propter suam modestiam longo tempore in eo principatum habuit, ac in quadragesimo secundo anno sui regiminis completa septuagesima sexta hebdomada, secundum Danielem, sui dominii, cessante regno et sacerdotio in Iudaea, nascitur Christus, qui fuit verus rex et sacerdos, et verus monarcha.[29]

[After this monarchy [the Macedonian] Roman rule began to be strong. The book of 1 Maccabees tells us many things about the Romans in the time of Judas Maccabeus, who flourished almost immediately after the death of Alexander, at the same time as Ptolemy of Lagus. The might of the Romans seemed to be diffused through all the regions of the world under the consuls, but they were still vexed by kings who survived in adjoining regions,[30] and up to that time they demonstrated moderation and virtue. The consulate, or rather this monarchy, lasted up to the time of Julius Caesar, who first usurped command [or empire: *imperium*]. After this he survived only a short time; indeed, the senators killed him for his abuse of lordship. Afterwards Octavius, the son of Julius's sister, succeeded and took the monarchy for himself alone, after he exacted vengeance against the killers of Julius and slew Antony who held the monarchy in the east. As a result of his modesty Octavius maintained his rule for a long time, and in the forty-second year of his government, when the seventy-ninth period of seven days

---

[29] Busa, 1980, VII, pp. 558–9. Capitalisation added.
[30] Perhaps the Macedonian and other successors of Alexander.

foretold by Daniel was completed, when the kingdom and priesthood had come to an end in Judea, Christ, who was true king, priest and monarch, was born.]³¹

Ptolemy is leaving it in no doubt that the church of Christ is the Fifth Monarchy and the stone cut without hands; but it has been on earth for more than twelve centuries and empire has not ceased. Augustus 'stood in the place' of Christ as 'true lord and monarch of the world',

(cuius vices gerebat augustus,) licet non intelligens, sed nutu dei, sicut caiphas prophetavit. Unde hoc instinctu dictus caesar mandavit tunc temporis, ut narrant historiae, nequis de romano populo dominum ipsum vocaret.³²

[although he did this not through his understanding but through the motion of God, in the same way as Caiaphas prophesied.³³ Feeling this instinctively, Caesar Augustus issued a mandate, as the histories relate, that none of the Roman people should call him 'Lord'.]³⁴

If we read this, as Ptolemy might, as indicating Augustus' insistence that he was not other than a first citizen, it will follow that the republic and its legality were not extinct, and we shall be excused supposing that only the republic could terminate the sequence of empires.³⁵ The effect of Ptolemy's argument is to widen the distance, without breaking the link, between the *imperium* of the Caesars and the *sacerdotium* to which it is subject. There ensues a narrative running through the Donation of Constantine to the *translatio imperii*, effected because the empire at Constantinople could no longer defend the church against the barbarous Lombards, and the popes therefore saw fit to transfer empire from the Greeks to the Germans (here not distinguished from the Franks).³⁶ What the status of the eastern monarchy was thereafter we are not told, but after the Saxon emperors the Pope set up the system of German electors, and the empire so constituted endures. 'As long as it lasts, so long will last the Roman Church, which has the supreme rank in rule;'³⁷ the two are not equal but interdependent, and secular time cannot be imagined without both. The Sallustian narrative is firmly enclosed within that of *translatio*; the virtues of the republic, which foreshadow the coming of the church, are transferred to the empire as the church's subordinate.

---

³¹ Blythe, 1997, pp. 184–5.     ³² Busa, 1980, VII, p. 559.
³³ This allusion explained by Blythe, loc. cit. n. 228.     ³⁴ Blythe, 1997, pp. 186–7.
³⁵ Blythe (Hankins, 2000, p. 47) must be read with caution when he says that Ptolemy's Augustus 'served as a vicar for Christ [o]nly because declining Roman virtue had previously undermined the Republic'. A republic could represent Christ's person only in thinking of the most apocalyptic kind, which Aquinas and Ptolemy did not share; nor had Christ been on earth in republican times.
³⁶ Blythe, 1997, pp. 197–201.     ³⁷ Blythe, 1997, p. 202.

Only the apocalyptic impudence of Cola di Renzo could imagine that the republic still held *imperium* over pope and emperor alike, and he had to resort to a Joachite belief that the godhead could be directly embodied in a human society.

(IV)

So long as the revival of civic virtue found in writings of the *trecento* located the republic within the dialectic of church and empire, we cannot make the transition from *translatio imperii* to Decline and Fall; and the tribe of scholars who set themselves to deny that the Florentine humanism of the *quattrocento* and *cinquecento* contains anything not to be found at an earlier date[38] will have to decide whether a breach with *translatio* occurred, and if so when. As we shall see, this is not as simple a question as it may sound; the *translatio* died hard if it died at all, and persisted alongside many of the writings we shall consider as making a transition to Decline and Fall. Treatises *de translatione imperii* and *de ortu et fine imperii romani* – the 'end' in question being the Aristotelian 'purpose' and implying no historic termination – continued to be produced through the fourteenth century and at least the first two-thirds of the fifteenth.[39] They coincide in time with the first works by Florentine and other humanists in which we find a radically different and apparently republican ordering of Roman history, and they reach a point separated by no more than a generation from the renewal and transformation of empire in the age of Charles V. We may therefore need to resist the conditioning of our minds which enjoins us to consider them as 'medieval' survivals and the discourses of the fifteenth to sixteenth centuries as 'modern'. To us it seems evident that the empire was a mere ghost after the fall of the Hohenstaufen, and the imperial papacy of Innocent III and Boniface VIII little more than a ghost after the chain of disasters from Anagni to the Conciliar movement;[40] we see medieval universals being replaced by the secular

---

[38] Hankins, 2000, *passim*.

[39] See Izbicki and Nederman, 2000. This collection contains translations of Engelbert of Admont, *De ortu et fine imperii romani* (c. 1310), Aeneas Sylvius Piccolomini, *De ortu et auctoritate imperii romani* (1446), and Juan de Torquemada, *Opusculum ad honorem romani imperii et dominorum Romanorum* (1468). For Aeneas Sylvius and his connection with Flavio Biondo, see below, pp. 181, 184, 194, 199–200. Torquemada's work vindicates the authority of Roman law (and therefore empire) in the kingdom of Castile, where it was sometimes denied.

[40] Gibbon took this view of the empire (*DF*, v, ch. 49; Womersley, 1994, III, pp. 146–50) while emphasising the temporal sovereignty of the popes at Rome (VI, ch. 70; Womersley, 1994, III, pp. 1048–54).

histories of city republics and national monarchies. This perception may be not so much false as in need of re-ordering.

The myth of Roman empire, translated, universal and persisting to the end of time, was still a necessary component of Latin Christian discourse. It provided a framework within which to debate the relations between *sacerdotium* and *imperium*, and continued to play that role even when *imperium* was recognised as possessed by sovereigns other than the *imperator*. Kingdoms claiming that the *rex* was *imperator in regno suo*, cities claiming that the citizen body was *sibi princeps*,[41] were not necessitated to deny the emperor a formal supremacy as embodying the *imperium* they exercised, since he did not seek to exercise a practical sovereignty over them; it is possible to say that his weakness in practice enhanced his importance in theory. Those who needed to take account of the theoretical presence of kingdoms which might have been provinces of Trajan's empire, but never of Charlemagne's or Otto I's, sometimes found it convenient to resort to that aspect of the image of Roman empire as just and sacred, which suggested – as Cicero had – that the subjection of other peoples to the Romans had been legal and consensual, and the empire a commonwealth even when it was a monarchy (this term denoting the rule of a single people before that of a single person).

Papalists no less than imperialists maintained the image of the empire's universality; it was in the combat between universals that the scholastic mind preferred to debate principles; and the great disputes of the age – at their intellectual height after rather than before the fall of the Hohenstaufen – are therefore conducted in the metahistorical vocabularies of theology, philosophy and jurisprudence. The last-named may be said to have compressed all Roman history into the single formula of the *lex regia*, by which the Roman people were said to have transferred their sovereignty over *urbs* and *orbis* to the emperor; it was debated whether this transfer had been irrevocable, and what part the heirs of Peter had played in it. Only when there arose challenges to the universal authority of the pope was it conceivable that the empire might be similarly challenged; but such challenges usually came from the imperial party. Marsilius of Padua seems to have written his very radical *Defensor pacis* in Paris, and to have left France when his authorship became known. He entered the service of the emperor Ludwig of Bavaria, and accompanied him to Rome in 1323, where the imperial authority attempted a

---

[41] For the role at this period of Bartolist jurisprudence, see Skinner, 1978, 1, pp. 9–12. It may be seen as transferring attention to the *populus* or *communitas* as the repository of right, whereas the emphasis of this history lies on *libertas* as the precondition of *virtus*.

conjunction with that of the 'Roman people' under Colonna leadership, proclaiming a doctrine of clerical poverty which would have subjected the clergy to secular rule.

In the *Defensor pacis*[42] Marsilius had gone to the extreme of challenging St Peter's supremacy among the apostles, on the grounds that Christ could be manifest only in the church as a whole; it was the false claim of the bishops of Rome to reign as Christ's vicars which had made them the enemies of government and civil peace. The effect was to exile the church from 'coercive jurisdiction', vested only in the *legislator* or *pars principans* of every human society. But was there a plurality of such sovereigns, or was the emperor a universal legislator? The *Defensor* had been written in France, where it is possible to imagine it being taken up by a powerful king of the kind of Philip the Fair, and made to play a Gallican role as much later it was to play an Anglican; subjecting the clergy in all civil respects to the sovereign and denying that *sacerdotium* entailed any *imperium*. Marsilius, however, went to work for Ludwig of Bavaria (where he ended his days) and wrote a treatise *de translatione imperii*,[43] in answer to a work of the same name but Colonna authorship;[44] he was clearly not aiming to lodge any enduring sovereignty with the Roman people or republic.

Predictably, he insists that Constantine's *imperium* was his own, and that, if he was indeed unwise enough to make a Donation, he could not give away what was lodged in his person and could invest the bishop of Rome only with authority over the western churches that the latter could not claim on any other grounds. *Imperium* must have originated in the city; sometimes it meant simply the city's rule over itself, but at others:

significat Imperium Romanum universalem sive generalem totius mundi vel plurium saltem provinciarum monarchiam, qualis fuit Romae urbis et principatus, in eius processu; secundum quam etiam acceptionem de ipsius translatione tractare propositum magis est nobis.

A prioribus itaque secundum ordinem incipientes narrabimus primum Romanae urbis sive civitatis originem eiusque primordium exiguae monarchiae, deinde ipsius augmentum sive processum ad totius orbis monarchiam seu principatum supremum. Post haec autem, ipsius translationem ex sede in sedem, seu ex gente in gentem, secundum consequentia tempora describemus.[45]

['Roman empire' signifies a universal or general monarchy over the whole world, or at any rate over the majority of the provinces, such as was the government

---

[42] Gewirth, 1951.    [43] Nederman, 1993.

[44] Bernard Guenée, in his introduction to Jeudy and Quillet, 1979, deals with Landolfo Colonna's *De translatione imperii* in some detail.

[45] Jeudy and Quillet, 1979, p. 376.

and city of Rome as these emerged; it is in accordance with such a meaning that we propose to treat the matter of transfer. Therefore, beginning in correct order with the earliest events, we will first relate the origin of the city or civic body of Rome and the humble beginnings of its monarchy, then its growth or progress into monarchy over the whole world or the supreme government. Then we will relate its transfer from seat to seat, or from nation to nation in successive periods.][46]

This *monarchia* or *imperium* is universal, legitimate and transferable, but we suspect Marsilius of seeing it in secular, political and populist terms, rather than sacred. He insists on the difference between Augustus, whose authority was given legal form by the senate, and his uncle Julius, whose power was not.

Imperium Romanum a Iulio Caesare secundum quosdam, sed verius ab Octaviano Augusto, primo Romanorum imperatore, sumpsit initium. Nam secundum historiae veritatem, Iulius Caesar licet primus fuerit, qui sibi arripuit Romanorum monarchiam, non fuit imperator sed rei publicae violator et illius potius usurpator; et propterea non ponitur in catalogo principum Romanorum.[47]

[According to some, the Roman Empire took its beginnings from Julius Caesar, but more truly from Octavian Augustus, the first Emperor of the Romans. For, according to true history, although Julius Caesar was the first who seized for himself the monarchy of Rome, he was not an emperor but rather a violator and usurper of the republic; and therefore he does not have a place in the litany of the Roman Emperors.][48]

This is to push beyond Brunetto and Ptolemy in the legitimation of Augustus and the departure from the Sallustian moment. The republic is restored by the *princeps*, and Marsilius need not deny the Eusebian account of the Christian empire. Nevertheless, if authority originates in the secular community it has a secular history. Like others before him, Marsilius takes note of the Arab conquests, presumably as indicating the weakness of the eastern empire before the *translatio*, but in his own terms.

Conveniens iudicavi causam et modum describere, quo dicti Orientales se a Graecis et Latinis in dominio et cultu divinorum omnimode diviserunt. Causa siquidem, quare Orientales, videlicet Perses, Arabes, Caldei et aliae confines nationes a dominio Romani Imperii recesserunt, fuit tyrannicus principatus Heraclii.

Nam post magnam victoriam de Persis habitam, Heraclius Persas et alias Orientales nationes nimis crudeli dominatu premebat, propter quod rebellandi occasionem concorditer assumpserunt. Sed ut ab obedientie praedicta

[46] Trans. Watson, in Nederman, 1993, p. 66.    [47] Jeudy and Quillet, 1979, pp. 378–80.
[48] Watson, in Nederman, 1993, p. 67.

sic recederent firmiter, ut numquam ad eandem revocarentur amplius, consilio Mahometi tunc inter Persas divitis et potentis, diversum cultum assumunt, ut causa diversae credulitatis et fidei sive sectae, ad pristinum dominium de cetero non redirent; a Yeroboam forte sumentes exemplum, qui decem tribubus ipsum sequentibus diversum cultum tradidit, ut in pristinum et debitum dominium non redirent.

Quod etiam vel consimile Graeci fecerunt, volentes enim ab Ecclesiae Romanae obedientia separari, acceperunt diversum cultum seu ritum in ecclesia ministrandi, et sic in diversos errores scienter prolapsi sunt. Omnes enim eorum calogeri, qui conservant et nutriunt scismata, vel sunt Nestoriani aut Euticites, aut Ariani aut Iacobitae aut Hebionitae. Sic ergo factum est de illis populis et nationibus illarum regionum, in quibus iam dicta rebellio et inobedientia contigerunt.[49]

[I have judged it suitable to describe how and why the peoples of the East separated themselves altogether from the Greeks and Latins, in lordship and in worship. The reason why the Easterners, namely the Persians, Arabs, Chaldeans and other bordering nations, departed from the sway of the Roman Empire was the tyrannical government of Heraclius. For after his great victory over the Persians, Heraclius oppressed the Persians and the other Eastern nations with too savage a rule, because of which they unanimously seized on the opportunity for revolt. But so as to set aside their obedience to the Roman Empire irrevocably, following the advice of Mahomet, who at that time was allied with rich and powerful Persians,[50] they adopted a different religion, so that on account of different beliefs and faiths or sects they would not return to this first lordship from the other one. In this they followed the example of Jeroboam, who converted the ten tribes that followed him to a different religion, so that they might not return to their old and rightful allegiance.

The Greeks took the same or similar action, for wishing to be separated from obedience to the Roman church, they adopted a different religion or a different ceremony in their administration, and so fell knowingly into diverse errors. For all their splendid priests, who defend and foment schisms, are Nestorians or Eutichites or Arians or Jacobites or Ebionites. That, then, is what happened in regard to the peoples and nations of those regions in which the insurrection and disobedience already mentioned occurred.][51]

False religions are the work of statecraft, not of Antichrist; the Prophet is not an apocalyptic figure. The Greeks likewise are schismatic for reasons of state, and a Protestant or Enlightened reader would not take long to conclude that the bishop of Rome is himself not far from schism, having propounded a false doctrine to increase his power. His error, however, is confined to the Petrine claim to supremacy and by consequence *imperium*.

---

[49] Jeudy and Quillet, 1979, pp. 386–8.
[50] Or: 'who was then rich and powerful among the Persians'.
[51] Watson, in Nederman, 1993, pp. 68–9.

When Marsilius comes to Pope Gregory's breach with Leo the Isaurian, he does not defend the latter's iconoclasm and remarks merely:

propter quod dictus pontifex Gregorius tertius praefatum Leonem imperatorem anathematizare praesumpsit et totam Apuliam totamque Italiam et Hesperiam ab eius dominio et obedientia separari suasit et quantum in ipso fuit, hoc opere, quamvis minus debite, adimplevit eidemque vectigalia, nescio qua tamen auctoritate, sed bene qua temeritate, sollempniter interdixit Romaeque congregans synodum, venerationem sanctarum imaginum confirmavit et violatores huius anathemate condemnavit.

Demum Leo praedictus in hoc proposito moritur eique successit in imperio filius eius Constantinus quintus, eiusdem cum patre propositi. Et quoniam imperator hic in nullo Romanae favebat Ecclesiae, papa secundus Stephanus Imperium Romanum transferre de Graecis in Francos aliqualiter ordinavit.[52]

[Because of this, the pontiff Gregory III presumed to excommunicate the Emperor Leo, and urged the whole of Apulia and all of Italy and the West to secede from Leo's lordship and withdraw their obedience to him. In these dealings, he did for them all that he could and more than he should have. I know not by what authority, but certainly rashly, he solemnly remitted their taxes and, congregating a synod at Rome, confirmed as doctrine the veneration of sacred images and condemned violators of this creed to excommunication.

At last the said Leo died, still holding to these purposes, and was succeeded by his son, Constantine V, who had the same intentions as his father. Since this emperor gave no support to the Roman church, Pope Stephen II resolved to transfer the Roman Empire to some extent from the Greeks to the Franks.][53]

The censure falls on the remission of taxes and perhaps also on an excommunication extending as far as the emperor, but Gregory is not credited with deposing Leo or absolving his subjects of their obedience. As for the *translatio ad Francos*, it is performed *aliqualiter* – by some means or other? – and Marsilius does not positively affirm that the popes had no authority in the transaction, or tell us by what right it was carried out. Since Charlemagne was not an emperor, he had no power to make himself one; but neither the Franks by conquest, nor the Roman people by election, figure very convincingly in the role of Marsilian *legislator*. It is tempting to suppose that, in the last analysis, no actor at Rome can really make an emperor, so that – whatever Ludwig of Bavaria might have made of this – the German king owes his imperial power to his German subjects. The *De translatione* carries history as far as the establishment of the college of electors and concludes:

---

[52] Jeudy and Quillet, 1979, pp. 396–8.
[53] Watson, in Nederman, 1993, p. 72. Punctuation slightly altered.

Praemissa quidem igitur omnia per Romanos episcopos attemptata, et cum sibi assentientibus consummata, quantum robur habuerint aut habeant in presenti, ex nostro *Defensore pacis*, 1, 12 et 13, 2, finali capitulo, liquido patet rationabiliter intendenti.

Explicit tractatus de translatione Imperii.[54]

[These developments were all aims of the bishops of Rome and were accomplished with their assent. What force they had and have today is explained in our *defensor pacis*, Discourse 1, chapters 12 and 13, and in the final chapter of the second Discourse, for anyone with a serious interest in the subject.

Here ends the treatise 'On the Transfer of the Empire'.][55]

If we imagine Marsilius as the historian he was not, he would have been a student of *Staatsräson* and *Realpolitik*. The Roman people's monarchy over the world is perhaps more justified by fact than by law, but the transfer of *imperium* to Caesar is authorised and irreversible. It must have been – if we allow him knowledge of the distinction – both an *imperium domi* and an *imperium militiae*; the growth of empire was necessary to it; but there is no suggestion that the people lost their liberty or that the empire ended in the loss of provinces to the barbarians – except in the East, which is no part of the history of *translatio*. It is the conjunction of these two propositions which constitutes Decline and Fall as we know it; and there is reason to suppose that we must look for the origins of this concept outside the discourse of *translatio imperii*.

---

[54] Jeudy and Quillet, 1979, p. 432.     [55] Watson, in Nederman, 1993, p. 81.

# PART III

# The humanist construction of Decline and Fall

# CHAPTER 8

# *Leonardo Bruni: from* translatio *to* declinatio

(1)

Rather more than forty-five years ago, the late Hans Baron began publishing the series of studies of which the centrepiece is entitled *The Crisis of the Early Italian Renaissance: Civic Humanism and Republican Liberty in an Age of Classicism and Tyranny.*[1] He presented a complex thesis which it is necessary to summarise. Focusing on the writings of Florentine authors from Coluccio Salutati and Leonardo Bruni in the first half of the fifteenth century to Niccolò Machiavelli and Francesco Guicciardini in the first half of the sixteenth, Baron posited a 'crisis of liberty' occasioned by the war of 1400–02, in which Florence had confronted the danger that Giangaleazzo Visconti, the lord of Milan, was about to establish a hegemony over all the city republics of north and central Italy. This had produced a sudden and intense awareness of the values of liberty, specifically that liberty enjoyed by citizens in the government of their republic and themselves, as described by Athenian authors including Aristotle and Roman authors including Livy; and because the humanist rediscovery of Greek and Roman texts included so many in which *eleutheria*, *autonomia* and *libertas* in this sense were presented as among the highest values, Baron felt justified in describing as 'civic humanism' an ideology valuing classical antiquity in which the good life for man was held to be that of the citizen in a republic. There was of course an alternative set of values, derived from a slightly later antiquity, in which a high value was placed on the rule of Caesar as *princeps* or *imperator*, and this was exploited in the fifteenth century not only by the emperors who still acted in the affairs of Italy, but by such *signori* and *principi* as the Visconti of Milan. An ancient rhetoric in which the Caesars were denounced as tyrants was countered by one in which they were praised as princes.

[1] Baron, 1955a, 1955b, 1966, 1968, 1988; a bibliography of his writings to 1969 in Molho and Tedeschi, 1971, pp. lxxxi–vii.

Baron, positing a crisis of liberty in 1400–02, sought to establish a chronology in which texts written by Florentines responded to the Viscontian threat not merely by extolling the liberty of citizens, but by rewriting the history of both Florence and Rome. The Tuscan city had been founded when Rome was still a republic and had succeeded in retaining the liberty which Rome had lost. The history of the latter was presented in a deeply anti-Caesarian sense; the emperors had commonly been tyrants, and even when they were not their rule had stifled the freedom, the *libertas* and (a crucial term) the *virtus*, by which the republic had maintained itself and established a universal empire. It is here that we find in 'civic humanism' that association between *libertas* and *imperium* which has played a series of crucial roles in the present volume, from Polybius and Sallust through Orosius and Augustine to Dante Alighieri and Ptolemy of Lucca. To Baron this had a double significance. The freedom of the citizen implied the freedom of the city; the *libertas* of the former the *imperium* of the latter, both the *imperium domi* by which it maintained its independence and (perhaps) the *imperium militiae* which led to empire over others. Liberty implied the state; Baron was among the last great exponents of the German historical school, for whom history was the movement towards the freedom of the individual in the life of the state. He therefore saw the Florentine rewriting of Roman history as 'modern', entailing a decisive breach with 'medieval' thought – which he simplified as an unbroken assertion of the unbroken continuity of the translated Roman empire – and a move into history, itself defined as the self-determining existence of states and their citizens in secular time.

It may be debated whether this reconstruction is adequate as an account of the intellectual experience of reflective intelligences in fifteenth-century Italy, though a sudden departure into new ways of thinking is by no means to be ruled out. Criticism of Baron has focussed on his attempts to show that 'civic humanist' concepts of citizenship appeared suddenly in the crisis of 1400–02, but this has not led to a dethronement of the concept of the 'modern'. In *The Foundations of Modern Political Thought*[2] Quentin Skinner laid emphasis on the praise of the civic life to be found in Brunetto, Ptolemy, and other writers of thirteenth- and fourteenth-century Italy including Florence. He saw this as Ciceronian even more than Aristotelian in its intellectual foundations, and as massively anticipating the 'civic humanism' of Baron's Renaissance thinkers. It may be

---

[2] Skinner, 1978, I, chs. 1 and 4. For his criticisms of Baron, see pp. 69–71, 77, 79, 82. See further Skinner, 1990 and 1997.

noted that his work of the above title opened with an account of Otto of Freising's attempt to explain Italian civic liberties to his readers in imperial Germany,[3] as if the 'foundations of the modern' had been laid by forces akin to Baron's but operating centuries earlier. In the present work, which has pursued the history of *translatio imperii* and is about to pursue its replacement by 'decline and fall' – but is not so far committed to the view that this entails a replacement of 'medieval' by 'modern' – it has been argued that the 'republicanism' of the *trecento* was perfectly compatible with the *mythos* of Eusebian sacred monarchy and the *translatio imperii*. If it can be established that an abandonment of *translatio* for *declinatio* occurred within the same narrative as that recounted by Baron, we shall have evidence that a breach of some kind occurred and can proceed to enquire whether it was connected with a new understanding of republican liberty and citizenship – a return, perhaps, from *translatio imperii* to *libertas et imperium*. It would be paradoxical if this re-assertion of values so ancient as to be pre-Christian proved to be the foundation of the 'modern'.

Baron extended his narrative and thesis from Leonardo Bruni in the fifteenth century to Niccolò Machiavelli in the sixteenth, recognising that Machiavelli confronted different problems and advanced new and alarming arguments, but contending that these arose from a belief in free and republican citizenship which he shared with his predecessors. Rather more than twenty-five years ago, the present author published *The Machiavellian Moment: Florentine Political Thought in the Atlantic Republican Tradition*,[4] a work which does not rely upon Baron's account of the events and writings of 1400–02, but does share his thesis that a concern for active citizenship and its values operates in the Florentine understanding of politics and history from Bruni (if no earlier) to Machiavelli and Guicciardini. The title by which this work is known is designed to suggest that Machiavelli presented republican liberty – a *libertas* much caught up in the exercise of *imperium* – as historically precarious and morally ambiguous; this did not prevent him deeply believing in it and depicting history as the record of its attempts to maintain itself. This is clearly a 'historicist' reading of Machiavelli, not incompatible with that advanced by many interpreters including Isaiah Berlin,[5] but it is continued into an

---

3 Skinner, 1978, 1, pp. 3–5. For Otto, above, p. 124.
4 Pocock, 1975. This work has been coupled with Baron's as the subject of considerable controversy, both historical and philosophical. For a recent collection of criticisms see Hankins, 2000, and for a response see the Afterword to Pocock, 2003 (1975).
5 'The Originality of Machiavelli' (1979), reprinted in Berlin, 1997, pp. 269–325.

account of subsequent or 'early modern' history unlike that advanced by most writers of the German historical tradition.

Machiavelli was much concerned with the exercise of arms as a pre-requisite – even a form – of civic liberty, and with the changing historical circumstances in which arms were exercised and effective in the Italy of his times. By pursuing the history of the discourse of arms through seventeenth-century England into eighteenth-century Britain and America, *The Machiavellian Moment* claimed to have uncovered a history in which arms remained crucial to the analysis of both liberty and society – as they clearly were to Adam Smith, who spoke of his lectures as dealing with 'justice, police, revenue, and arms'[6] – but in which the moral ambivalence of *libertas* studied by Machiavelli was augmented, if not replaced, by a material ambivalence. In this, the exercise of arms did not cease to be essential to the *virtus* of the individual, but he was held to have alienated it to the state in order to pursue more complex freedoms which followed involvement in the more complex relationships of a commercial society. A concept of 'ancient liberty', in which the exercise of arms signified the individual's direct involvement in the government of his republic, therefore confronted a 'modern liberty', in which arms had been alienated and his involvement in government was exercised indirectly, through his membership in what came to be termed 'civil society'. In *The Machiavellian Moment* and subsequent writings,[7] it is argued that this debate continued through the eighteenth century; and in later chapters of this volume it will be argued that Gibbon held the decline of 'ancient liberty' to explain the decline of the empire, while by no means holding that this process would be repeated in the modern world.

(11)

The revival of republican historiography occurred at Florence, not at Rome. To Gibbon and most historians after him,[8] it seemed clear that the intermittent republics of medieval Rome were mere theatricality, a shadow play behind which the Colonna and Orsini fought out their household feuds, and that the city, caught between the semi-perpetual presence of the popes and the Curia, and the occasional visits of demanding if indigent emperors, lacked the base – Gibbon learned from Muratori to consider it a mercantile base – on which an autonomous commune, still less a *civitas sibi princeps*, could be constructed. Even a

---

[6] *NCG*, p. 321.    [7] Pocock, 1985.    [8] E.g., Gregorovius, 1871, ed. Morrison.

convinced and momentarily powerful leader, like Arnold of Brescia or Cola di Renzo, could turn republican myth into action with no higher aim than that of claiming for the *populus romanus* authority to confer office on the emperor or the pope, and Roman republicanism remained an occasional actor in the scenario of the *translatio imperii*. We are in search of a decisive breach with that scenario and a transition to that of Decline and Fall, and it is now proposed that we shall find this in the literature of a city which was not Rome and rewrote Roman history to suit its own needs.

The failure of the empire to extend itself south of the Alps, and the failure of the papacy to extend its temporal power west of the Romagna, left Lombardy and Tuscany powerfully but uneasily exposed in the space that might have been occupied by a *regnum italicum*. In this region arose a number of cities self-governing enough to consider themselves republics, of which the more powerful exercised lordship over territories they might consider their dominions but scarcely their empires. Their competition for space and power was energetic enough to constitute, together with the papal state and the kingdom of Naples, the states-system of the Italian peninsula, but none of them could aim higher than a hegemony or hope to do without allies. As their learned classes came to read more deeply in ancient history, they might see Italy as parallel to ancient Hellas; there might be a potential Macedon somewhere to the north; but none of them could aspire to the role of Rome. Their fascination by the history of a republic which had swallowed up all others, conquered the known world, and lost itself as a republic in the process, arose in large part from their knowledge that their own history was distanced from it by the Decline and Fall; but it was the decay of medieval empire that had left them in a republican role. There are a number of important senses in which they needed to study Roman history because they knew it was unlike their own and yet illuminated it.

This sense of distance is characteristic of humanism – using that word to denote the intensely active recovery of ancient texts and the intensely excited scrutiny of them. It brought to light a world which seemed intimately knowable and with which the reader could imaginatively identify, yet which was not his, being pagan, republican, imperial and classical. As he sought to model his style upon it, he became aware that he could not live in it; the better he knew its language, the less he could speak that language in a world of his own. Rhetorical and poetical techniques without number existed for overcoming this distance, and the speech they framed impacted powerfully on the world in which it was spoken; yet the sense of distance remained. Techniques of philology, chronology and rhetoric were developed with the purpose of seeing more deeply into the meanings of the texts, and operated independently of their rhetorical and narrative deployment. It is conceivable that a history of the idea of Decline and Fall could be constructed without reference to the ideologically based narratives we have been studying here, showing simply how the philologists and antiquarians built up a knowledge of the ancient world so detailed as to render inescapable the fact of its disappearance; one component would be a reconstruction of the Latinity deemed classical so meticulous as to dramatise its barbarisation. There is evidence of a backlash driving some humanists to study the *volgare*, the vernacular, the barbaric and even the non-romance.

This is a starting point from which to study the importance the concept of barbarism acquired in humanist thinking – an importance it did not have in the discourse of *translatio*, so great as to contribute to the discourse of Decline and Fall. On the one hand the detailed *peinture* of classical antiquity called for a counter-image of the 'other' which had replaced it; on the contrary, the humanists found themselves impelled to extend their skills to deal with the texts of a culture both barbaric and Roman. For the barbarians had learned Latin, if at the same time they had barbarised it. It was possible to speak of an 'empire' of the Latin tongue, replacing the lost *imperium* of the city and its emperors. If, as we shall see happening, there arose a narrative of Decline and Fall as the loss of *imperium*, there would have to be a companion narrative of the loss, barbarisation and recovery of Latin letters, and the two narratives must somehow be connected.

Classical Latin had been the speech of citizens, a rhetoric freely exercised. As the writings of Tacitus re-emerged, there arose the question whether it declined under the emperors, or whether Maecenas and Virgil might be evoked to the contrary. A cult of citizen speech, action, liberty and virtue could certainly be distilled from the writings of Cicero, Livy and Plutarch, and there is every evidence that it was; the question of 'civic humanism' is in part that of how far it was interwoven with the praise of the active life, led by the modern citizen, of which there is so much in the writings of Florentine and other humanists. Hans Baron made much of the threat to this 'liberty' from 'tyranny', meaning by the latter that Florence responded otherwise than other cities to the rise of *signori* and *principi* to illegitimate single-person rule. Some of these *principi* – of whom the Visconti of Milan were for a time the most menacing – claimed to be 'princes' in the imperial sense and invoked the figure of the emperor himself, with the result that the textual and rhetorical controversy Baron studied contrasted republican and Caesarian rule, and the replacement of the former by the tyranny of the latter; Baron's claim was that 'civic humanism' mobilised the rhetoric of civic liberty in support of this view of history in the struggle against Giangaleazzo Visconti. Neither Giangaleazzo nor any other *signore*, however, was an emperor who could claim to be Caesar in the Eusebian sense of the *translatio imperii*; if the figure of Caesar was invoked by such a ruler, it was likely to be that of the questionable triumvir with much blood on his hands, and the narrative showing how his rule had become that of the just Augustus and had been consecrated as that of the Christian Constantine was not at the disposal of one who was neither emperor nor anointed king. The rhetoric of *translatio*, we shall find, was anything but extinct in *quattrocento* Italy, but it was of limited effect. If, then, the rhetoric of the *vivere civile* – as the self-rule of citizens came to be known – suggested a society of virtuous pagans rather than Christians, that of the *principe* – here we may look ahead to Machiavelli – suggested a form of rule neither legitimated nor consecrated, and potentially tyrannical; that of a Caesar who could not become the Augustus of Virgil, but only that of Tacitus.

If princely tyranny was a visible threat to the ideal of civic life – supposing as we do such an ideal to have existed – another, no less dangerous and potentially a cause of tyranny, was violence and warfare between factions within the city. Florentines could go back to Dante, Giovanni Villani or Dino Compagni, and find their history narrated as that of feuds between noble families obliged to live within the walls but powerful enough to defy the laws of the commune – a piece of social and secular history well known to Florentine writers. Roman history had not been like this; the struggles between patricians and plebeians, *optimates* and *populares*, had been struggles between orders constituted by the city's laws. It was possible to ask whether the Florentine republic had reconstituted the feuds of noble families as a contest between *ottimati* and *popolani*, and whether this would prove fatal in its turn. As Florentines looked back to the twelfth and thirteenth centuries, however, they found their history to be a product of the contest between Guelfs and Ghibellines, papacy and empire; and if Florence had been a Guelf city, an effect of the Angevin destruction of the Hohenstaufen had been the intensification of strife between factions of Guelfs which had made Dante an exile and an imperialist. The former *regnum italicum* had become a theatre of contests between cities destabilised by faction and engaged in warfare for territorial dominion in which none could hope to achieve empire or be a

Rome. This is the context in which we may situate the history written by
Leonardo Bruni, which developed an account of the fall of the Roman
empire in consequence of the destruction of liberty by the Caesars, in a
volume serving as prelude to a history of the Italian cities in the era in
which the historian was writing.

(III)

Bruni came from Arezzo, and though he ended his days as a distinguished servant of the Florentine state – with a well-born wife and a tomb
in Santa Croce[9] – he must always be seen in a context formed by the
relationship between cities. Gibbon mentions him as 'the most famous'
of those who took cognomina from their Aretine origin – Pietro Aretino
the pornographer being 'the most worthless' – and observes that he was
both chancellor of Florence and 'secretary to four successive popes;' he
also thinks that the use Bruni made of the text of Procopius in his own
*De Bello Gothico* amounted to theft.[10] Bruni is not a central figure in the
*Decline and Fall*, but he is of signal importance in the history of the concept itself. He saw Roman history as a setting and context to that of the
Florentine republic. The historical narrative in which he situates this
vision, however, is anything but simple, and the history which he writes
is far from idealisation. Among his many works the crucial historical text
is the *Historiarum Populi Florentini Libri XII*, which he may have begun by
1415 and was still revising when he died in 1444. Considered as a whole,
this work occupies several contexts and has many resonances; we shall
be concerned chiefly with its first book and the place it has in the composition of the whole series. Bruni's opening sentence runs: *Florentiam urbem
Romani condidere a Lucio Sylla Fesulas deducti* [the founders of Florence were
Romans sent by Lucius Sulla to Fiesole].[11] We encounter here the complex and important question of the myth of Florentine origins. There
was an alternative account in which the original settlers were veterans
of Julius Caesar in his pursuit of the conspirator Catiline (a conspiracy, it
will be recalled, in which Caesar was suspected of complicity); another in
which the Roman city had been destroyed during Justinian's Gothic wars
and refounded by Charlemagne; and the narrative was further complicated by a tradition of the absorption of hilltop Fiesole by the city at the

---

[9] For a summary of Bruni's career, see Griffiths, Hankins and Thompson, 1987.
[10] *DF*, vi, ch. 40, n. 14 (Womersley, 1994, ii, p. 562); vi, ch. 66, n. 98 (Womersley, 1994, iii,
   p. 901).
[11] Santini, 1927, p. 5; Hankins, 2001, pp. 8–9.

crossings of the Arno. A myth of republican origins came to confront one of Caesarian origins and imperial loyalties, and this debate can be traced back to the Guelf and Ghibelline conflicts preceding the *trecento*.[12] For our purposes, however, we need to enlarge the context further. Catiline and Caesar are figures in the narrative of Sallust (opposed by Brunetto to the virtues of Cicero and Cato)[13] and Sallust was the ancient historian on whom Orosius, Augustine and their medieval successors had all relied for their account of the 'first decline and fall': the self-corruption of republican virtue by the luxury and empire which it had won. For Augustine in particular, this had meant that ancient virtue had amounted to no more than a thirst for glory and power, and had been doomed to the fate attending all earthly cities. We have been examining, however, a Ciceronian and Aristotelian (perhaps also a civilian) revival of the association between virtue and earthly justice, which had profoundly affected the role of the republic in Christian history, without eliminating a still Sallustian narrative of its corruption by Catiline and perhaps (or perhaps not) by Caesar. There can therefore be no question of a simple antithesis between Augustinian and humanist values; the problem is rather how it came about that Bruni paid no attention to the perfection of civic virtue in the history of sacred empire and its *translatio* by way of the papacy.

Nor can it be maintained that, in proposing a Sullan rather than a Caesarian foundation, Bruni was transferring the origins of Florence from an imperial aegis to a republican. It had indeed been held that the Sullan foundation was proof of an origin in republican virtue;[14] but the greater the variety of ancient histories that were republished, the clearer it became that Sulla no less than Caesar was a figure of the Roman civil wars and the subjection of the republic to competing military chiefs. Sallust had said so, and Bruni acknowledges as much in his second sentence, where he says that Sulla gave lands to his soldiers *ob egregiam cum in caeteris tum in civili bello navatam operam* [because they 'had given outstanding service in the civil war as well as in other ways'].[15] His account draws closer to that we remember from Appian as he goes on to explain that Sulla's grants formed an example of what the Romans called *coloniae*, and that the settlement of legionaries on conquered and

---

[12] The debate on origins was conducted from the thirteenth century on, and is central to the twentieth-century debate on Florentine humanism.

[13] Above, p. 140.

[14] Baron, 1966, pp. 71–3 and repeatedly, for the elaboration of this thesis by Coluccio Salutati. When he mentions a refutation by Lorenzo Valla, for whom Sulla was a tyrant, Baron says that Valla 'could only sneer'. There was more than that to what Valla was saying.

[15] Santini, loc. cit., and Hankins, loc. cit.

devastated lands had recently been intensified by the effects less of civil
war than of social.

Quae autem occasio fuerit novos colonos in haec loca deducendi, pro rei
notitia aperiendum est. Haud multos ante Syllae dictaturam annos, cuncti ferme
Italia populi unum sub tempus a Romanis defecere, indignatione commoti,
quod ipsi una cum Romanis per singulas expeditiones militantes, laboresque
et pericula pro augendo imperio subeuntes, praemiorum expertes angebantur.
Quare saepius inter se conquesti, tandem legatis communi de re Romam missis,
quasi civitatis membra, honores et magistratus concedi sibi postularunt . . . Sed
cum tandem eorum postulata reiicerentur, aperte quasi ab ingratis rebellarunt,
bellumque gesserunt: quod quia a sociis gestum est, sociale bellum nuncupatur.[16]

[Why new colonists were sent to this area, however, must be explained. Not many
years before Sulla's dictatorship, there was a general rebellion among the peoples
of Italy against the Romans. They had been allied with the Romans on every
campaign, had fought and laboured by their side and shared the perils which
attended their expansion, and yet, as they were distressed to find, they had not
shared in the rewards. Hence their indignation. After much complaining among
themselves, they finally sent a delegation to Rome to discuss their common
problem, and to demand a share in honours and offices for themselves, as
though they were themselves organic parts of the state. (The question came up
during the tribunate of Marcus Drusus, and for some time the petitioners were
left in suspense.) Their demands were ultimately rejected, however, and then
the peoples involved rebelled openly and declared war on their ungrateful allies.
Because the war was made by former allies of Rome, it is known as the Social
War.][17]

The translation emphasises the extent to which Bruni's Italians are
demanding a full share in the Roman empire they have helped create.
The Orosian tradition made little of the Social War, but had employed
Lucan in stating that in the Civil Wars, at Philippi and Pharsalus, the
empire of Rome turned inward against itself. In the ensuing Roman
victory, Bruni states, four cities, three of them Tuscan – Chiusi, Arezzo
and Fiesole – were depopulated and exposed to colonisation. In the last-
named case, the settlers moved down to the Arno valley and erected
splendid buildings in imitation of Rome; but their luxury left them poor
and insecure at the death of their protector Sulla.[18]

Itaque partim indigentia, partim consuetudine praemiorum adducti, novum
aliquem motum exoriri optabant. Viri militares et civili bello assueti, quietos
esse nullo pacto sciebant: rursus novas dictaturas, et nova belli premia mente

---

[16] Santini, 1927, p. 5.      [17] Hankins, 2001, pp. 8–10.
[18] Santini, 1927, p. 6: Sulla their *unica largitionum spes*.

volutabant. Et accedebat aes alienum, acer quidem stimulus et qui timidis etiam animos facere soleat ad otium perturbandum.

[So, partly because of their poverty and partly because they were accustomed to getting rewards, they looked forward eagerly to some new disturbance. Soldiers and men used to civil war, they had no idea how to live in peacetime. Their thoughts ran ever to new dictatorships and new booty. And debt was an added incentive to draw the sword, for debt is a spur that drives even timid persons to make trouble.][19]

Cicero and Sallust seem to be the sources here, but something like the Appianic or 'Gracchan' explanation is re-emerging to give material substance to the moralist narrative Augustine derived from Sallust. The Catilinarian conspiracy arises at Rome from not dissimilar causes – Caesar is suspected of complicity – and the settlers of Fiesole and Florence become involved. There is, however, no mention of a recolonisation by new veterans, and the citizens learn by experience to give up the hope of new disturbances and live by austerity and industry instead. At this point we look in vain for any account of the Augustan peace, the prosperity of the empire, the birth of the Saviour of Mankind, or, alternatively, the consequences traced by Tacitus, whose works were becoming known. Bruni embarks on an altogether new narrative, for which nothing has prepared us.

Surgebant aedificia; soboles augebatur: crescere tamen civitatis potentiam ac maiorem in modum attolli, romanae magnitudinis vicinitas prohibebat. Ut enim ingentes arbores novellis plantis iuxta surgentibus officere solent, nec ut altius crescant permittere, sic romanae urbis moles sua magnitudine vicinitatem premens, nullam Italiae civitatem maiorem in modum crescere patiebatur. Quin immo et quae ante fuerant magnae, ob eius urbis gravem nimium propinquitatem, exhaustae porro diminutaeque sunt. Quemadmodum enim tunc cresceret civitatis potentia? Neque sane fines augere bello poterat sub imperio constituta, nec omnino bella exercere: nec magistratus satis magnifici, quippe eorum iurisdictio intra breves limites claudebatur, et haec ipsa romanis magistratibus erat obnoxia. Mercaturae quoque si quis forte eam partem ad incrementum civitatis attinere quidquam existimet, non alibi per id tempus quam Romae commodius exercebantur. Ibi frequentia hominum et venundandi facultas, eorum portus; eorum insulae; eorum portoria; ibi gratia; ibi publicanorum favor; alibi neque gratia, neque potentia par. Itaque sicubi quispiam per propinqua loca nascebatur ingenio validus, is, quia domi has sibi difficultates obstare videbat, Romam continuo demigrabat. Ita quidquid egregium per Italiam nascebatur ad se trahens, alias civitates exhauriebat: quod antecedentia simul et sequuta

---

[19] Hankins, 2001, pp. 13–14.

tempora manifestissime ostendunt. Etenim priusquam Romani rerum potiren-
tur, multas per Italiam civitates gentesque magnifice floruisse, easdem omnes
stante romano imperio exinanitas constat. Rursus vero posteris temporibus, ut
dominatio romana cessavit, confestim reliquae civitates efferre capita et florere
coeperunt, adeo quod incrementum abstulerat, diminutio reddidit.[20]

[New buildings arose and the fertility of the populace increased. Only the near-
ness of Rome in her grandeur limited Florentia's rise to power. As mighty trees
overshadow young seedlings that grow nearby and keep them stunted, so did
Rome overwhelm her neighbours with her size, allowing no greater city to arise
in Italy. Other cities that had once been great were oppressed by their neighbour
Rome, ceased to grow, and even became smaller. How, then, might Florentia's
power increase? Being under imperial rule she could not augment her borders
by war, nor indeed wage war at all; nor could she boast splendid magistrates,
since their jurisdiction was narrowly circumscribed and subject to Roman officials. As to commerce – in case anyone thinks that this activity is somewhat
relevant to the growth of the city – in those days it could most profitably be
carried on in Rome. That was the place where men gathered and where there
were markets. Rome had ports, islands,[21] tolls, privileges, official protection.
Nowhere else was there so much privilege and power. If a man of solid worth
was occasionally born elsewhere within the general region, he would see the
difficulties that stood in his way at home and move invariably to Rome.[22] Thus
Rome drew to herself everything wonderful that was engendered in Italy and
drained all other cities. The proof lies in any comparison of pre-Roman and
Roman times. Before the Romans took over, many cities and peoples flourished
magnificently in Italy, and under the Roman empire all of them declined. After
the fall of Rome, on the other hand, the other cities immediately began to
raise their heads and flourish. What her growth had taken away, her decline
restored.][23]

This is a new departure. Not only are we at a great distance from the
self-exhaustion of the *civitas terrena*, or the *translatio imperii* as a decisive moment in sacred history; we are *alibi quam Romae*, distant enough from the
primacy of republican, imperial and Petrine Rome to consider it as one
city among many, to whom it denied the independent histories of which
they were capable. We are looking at a Guelf understanding of history
at the point where a plurality of Italian cities became visible in a context provided by neither empire nor church; and, approaching Bruni's

---

[20] Santini, 1927, p. 7.
[21] May not *insulae* refer to the great apartment buildings that increased the population and market
of Rome?
[22] The voice of the provincial from Arezzo, who had moved to the metropolis of Florence?
[23] Hankins, 2001, pp. 17–19.

text from a standpoint in the eighteenth century, we recall what Gibbon learned from Muratori concerning the emergence of those cities from the conflicts between empire and papacy. We may recall also William Robertson's dictum that Rome had profoundly affected European history in two ways, first by the spread of its empire and second by its decline and fall;[24] and we must also call to mind that vision of a Europe of independently contending commercial states, which has been presented as fundamental to what we call Enlightenment. If the concept of Enlightenment could not possibly have been in Bruni's mind, it is by no means certain that concepts later accompanying it could not. The capacity of ancient cities for commerce matters to him, alongside the capacity for independent warfare denied by Rome to a Florence which was exercising it in his own time; and an eighteenth-century reader would only have queried his apparent belief that European cities recovered such capacities rapidly (*confestim*) after the fall of Rome, instead of through painful centuries of recuperation from barbarism, feudalism and monasticism. Above all, however, Bruni has established an Italian history distinct from that of Rome: a context in which Roman virtue and glory, liberty and empire, can be viewed critically, as by no means as beneficial to others as they were – for a limited period – to the Romans themselves. Civic humanism – the praise of city life as the source of liberty, activity, prosperity and glory – is not the single-minded worship of Rome we tend to see in it; there is a persistence of the Sallustian and Augustinian vision that virtue was destroyed by the empire that it had made possible. Roman history is, as it has always been, problematical.

Bruni goes on to say that he is writing a Tuscan history, which he will present as it was *qualis ante romanum imperium, qualisque postea fuerit* (both before the Roman empire and after it). This is introduced by a history of the Etruscans, a great and civilised people more ancient than the Trojans (and therefore than Aeneas) who colonised Italy from Mantua in the north to Capua in the south and ruled their empire as a confederacy. The rise of Rome is presented as a counterpoint to Etruscan history; both before and after the expulsion of the Tarquinian kings (themselves Etruscan) the Romans owed much to their neighbours and fought them with terrifying energy and real respect. The Etruscans declined only when trapped between Roman power to the south and the barbarian Gauls to the north, and even after their defeat were treated as allies rather

[24] *NCG*, p. 279.

than subjects of Rome. We already know, however, that *socii* may find cause to rebel, and Bruni's city of Arezzo takes the lead in unsuccessful rebellions in the time of Hannibal and in the Social War.[25] The narrative thus returns to the point where the history of Florence began, as a colony of a Roman empire afflicted by civil and social war.

Roman rule over Tuscany – this is the aspect of Roman empire with which Bruni is concerned – ended five centuries later, with the invasions of the Goths, followed by the Huns, Vandals, Herulians and Lombards. At this point Bruni introduces a series of perceptions crucial ever afterwards to the convention of Decline and Fall as we know it. In the first place, his emphasis is on the barbarians, who have been marginal but not central actors in the history of *translatio imperii*. He finds it necessary to recount the histories of the Goths, Huns and Vandals from their origins in distant lands to their invasions of Italy, and something like a 'triumph of barbarism' is before us. He does not yet, however, recount the fall before the barbarians of the Roman empire as a whole; his book is a history of Florence, to which the history of Etruria and its domination by Rome is a necessary prelude. Had it been a history of *translatio imperii*, the Goths and Lombards would have been less prominent than the popes, barbarism than religion; but for Bruni the end of empire is a prelude to the recovery of the Italian cities from Roman domination, and the barbarians are a phenomenon of Italian rather than universal or Christian history. It may be a consequent paradox that they owe their prominence in history to the limited horizon of west European historians.

There is a further paradox. Bruni is a historian of Florence, committed to a perception of Rome as an external and imperial power. He has presented the values of Etruscan citizenship as central to his story and his theme is the recovery of the Italian cities from the stifling weight of Roman empire, not from the barbarism that followed its fall. On the other hand, Bruni is a humanist, and humanists are students of Rome, obsessed with its literature and its civic values – and its empire – to the point where, as Petrarch put it, they see all history as the praise of Rome.[26] Nevertheless, Rome fell; the intellectual excitement of recovering its literature must be weighed against the need to recount its decline, and this in turn against the certainty – at least in Bruni's mind – that Florence could not have been great (or an Aretine great at Florence) if Rome had not declined and fallen. This complex terrain lies behind a move which Bruni now makes, one which seems to us far more conventional than

---

[25] Santini, 1927, pp. 7–14; Hankins, 2001, pp. 19–49.          [26] Kelley, 1998, p. 131 and note.

it is. Having identified the barbarian invaders of Italy, he introduces a concept of the decline of the Roman empire.[27]

Declinationem autem romani imperii ab eo fere tempore ponendam reor quo, amissa libertate, imperatoribus servire Roma incepit. Etsi enim non nihil profuisse Augustus et Traianus, etsi qui fuerunt alii laude principes digni videantur, tamen, si quis excellentes viros primum a C. Iulio Caesare bello, deinde ab ipso Augusto triumviratu illo nefario crudelissime trucidatos; si postea Tiberii saevitiam, Caligulae furorem, Claudii dementiam, Neronis scelera et rabiem ferro igneque bacchantem; si postea Vitellios, Caracallas, Heliogabalos, Maximinos et alia huius modi monstra et orbis terrarum portenta reputare voluerit, negare non poterit tunc romanum imperium ruere caepisse, cum primo caesareum nomen, tanquam clades aliqua, civitati incubuit. Cessit enim libertas imperatoris nomini, et post libertatem virtus abivit. Prius namque per virtutem ad honores via fùit, iisque ad consulatus dictaturasque et caeteros amplissimos dignitatis gradus facillime patebat iter, qui magnitudine animi, virtute et industria caeteros anteibant. Mox vero ut respublica in potestatem unius devenit, virtus et magnitudo animi suspecta dominantibus esse coepit. Hique solum imperatoribus placebant, quibus non ea vis ingenii esset, quam libertatis cura stimulare posset. Ita pro fortibus ignavos, pro industriis adulatores imperatoria suscepit aula, et rerum gubernacula ad peiores delata ruinam imperii paulatim dedere. Quamquam quid virtutis repulsam quis deploret, ac non potius communem civitatis interitum?[28]

[The decline of the Roman empire, however, ought, in my opinion, to be dated almost from the moment that Rome gave up her liberty to serve a series of emperors. Even though Augustus and Trajan may have been useful to Rome, and although the other princes too may have merited praise, yet we should consider the excellent men cruelly cut down in the civil wars of Caesar and during the wicked triumvirate of Augustus. If one considers the savagery of Tiberius after that, the fury of Caligula, the insanity of Claudius, and the crimes of Nero with his mad delight in fire and sword; if one adds Vitellius, Caracalla, Heliogabalus, Maximinus and other monsters like them, who horrified the whole world, one cannot deny that the Roman empire began to decline once the disastrous name of Caesar had begun to brood over the city. For liberty gave way before the imperial name, and when liberty departed, so did virtue. Before the day of the Caesars, high character was the route to honour, and positions such as consul, dictator, or other high public offices were open to men who had excelled others with their magnanimous spirit, strength of character and energy. But as soon as the commonwealth fell into the power of one man, character and magnanimity became suspect in the eyes of the rulers. Only those were acceptable to

---

[27] For Baron's attempt to integrate the following passage into his general thesis of the expansion of the Florentine civic consciousness, see Baron, 1966, pp. 47–78, 412–30. For other approaches, see Mazzocco, 1984, pp. 249–54, esp. p. 249, n. 1.

[28] Santini, 1927, p. 14.

the emperors who lacked the mental vigour to care about liberty. The imperial court thus opened its gates to the lazy rather than the strong, to flatterers rather than the industrious, and as the administration of affairs fell to the worst of men, little by little the empire was brought to ruin. Can one deplore a single instance where virtue is cast off and not deplore still more the destruction of the whole state?][29]

Bruni – presenting a 'decline and fall of the Roman empire' for the first time in the series of authors we have considered – is reverting to Sallust's account of its growth and extending this to cover its fall. Sallust had said that kings were jealous of men of talent about them (*semper eis aliena virtus formidulosa est*) and that the city, *adempta libertate*, had increased in glory and empire through the release of the energies of its citizens.[30] Bruni is attributing the same jealousy to the emperors, and saying that the loss of empire began with their rule. It is a long-term process; there were able and upright emperors, and he does not have to deny that (as Aquinas had remarked) the empire had increased under some of them (Augustus and Trajan, whom he mentions, might, though with reservations, be cases in point). Nevertheless, *cessit libertas . . . et post libertatem virtus*. Empire is a consequence of *libertas et virtus*, and perishes when they perish. Does this mean that, as Augustine had insisted, *libertas* and *virtus* had no meaning or function other than the pursuit of glory and the extension of empire? Bruni does not appear to think so; he regards *imperium* as one manifestation of the human excellence which comes with the free exercise of *magnitudo animi*, and his assertion cannot be simply dispelled by a postcolonial denunciation of the original sin of imperialism. There is room for his consuls and magistrates, extending empire through the exercise of *imperium militiae*, to preserve *libertas* and *virtus* within the city by means of the *imperium domi*, and he may not even rule out a Ciceronian vision of empire as *patrocinium* rather than *dominium*. Those who argue, as some have and will, that Bruni is rejecting an 'ancient' philosophy of politics as rooted in the moral nature of man, and reverting to an agonistic and emulative vision of citizenship as the freedom to compete for power, which that philosophy was intended to replace,[31] should remember that the agonistic was as 'ancient' as the philosophic, if not more so, and that it was certainly not eliminated by the rise of the latter. Sallust had said that Roman virtue began to decay when Carthage was destroyed as its rival and *aemula*; *virtus* and *imperium* had need of another.

---

[29] Hankins, 2001, p. 51.    [30] Above, pp. 35–7.
[31] Rahe, 1992 and 2000; Mansfield, 1979, 1996 and 2000.

It was therefore a question whether Roman empire had not undermined itself in becoming universal. Our minds, if not Bruni's, may look back to Tacitus' dictum that the spread of empire made one-man rule a necessity; if this was so, Bruni would be telling us, the decline of empire began from a point which empire itself had necessitated. We might look further, to the Augustinian principle that the *virtus* of the *civitas terrena* was self-destructive, a mere pursuit of vain glory.

But Bruni has an alternative in mind. He has already developed his own critique of universal empire, and it is aimed at the empire of liberty: the *virtus* of a single city stifled and devoured the *virtus* of all others. This *virtus* remained emulative and warlike; what the subordinated cities lost included the capacity to make war independently and increase their territories (it would be possible to say their *imperium*). There was an alternative to the *imperium* won by Roman *virtus* and *libertas*, and lost with it: the Etruscan model of a confederacy of like-minded cities, emulative and even agonistic among themselves, but subject to restraints which inhibited the growth of any one of them to empire. It is impossible for students of Gibbon not to recall the Enlightened vision of post-Utrecht Europe, in which an identical model had been maintained, and a *jus gentium* had guaranteed not merely the municipal liberties of the subjects of an empire, but the *jus belli ac pacis* of *civitates* exercising equal *imperium*. To say that Bruni prefers the Etruscan model to the Roman would be to over-simplify; he knows that empire was achieved by *libertas* and *virtus*, and laments the disappearance of all three; but the Etruscan alternative is present.

After the fall of the Roman empire cities began a return to independence, and modern – or as we should say medieval – Tuscany had a prospect of repeating, with better success, the history of ancient Etruria. Here we may look for a Florentine Guelf view of history, one that 'displays the banner of liberty and the church'; the danger to republican liberties is Ghibelline and Hohenstaufen, their saviours papal and Angevin. Bruni is indeed staunchly anti-Ghibelline, as we shall see; but what is hard to find in his history is any serious presence, not only of the *translatio imperii*, in either papalist or imperialist form, but of its necessary prelude, the Eusebian account of sacred monarchy. We are simply not informed that the empire of Augustus achieved the universal peace under which Christ was born, and there is no narrative of the growth of the church to set beside that of the monopoly of virtue by a single city. *Virtus* and *libertas* have their own history, and Bruni is not attempting to reconcile them with either sacred empire or the church which is above it.

We should remind ourselves to avoid epic dramatisation; the medieval world-view does not suddenly disappear. As 'secretary to four successive popes', Bruni spent much of his life in an environment where sacred empire and its translation were still animatedly discussed;[32] all the more remarkable, therefore, that the history of Florence is presented solely in the context of republican *virtus* and its imperial malformations. He translated Aristotle's *Politics*, but it seems in vain to debate whether this made him a doctrinaire republican or a conventional monarchist.[33] Kingship was less the issue than empire, and the portrait of a just king who was not a jealous tyrant or a military adventurer had little to do with the history of the Caesars. Nor need we ask whether Bruni upheld or abandoned a philosophy rooted in the common good and the political nature of man. The breach we see him making is not with Aristotelian but with Eusebian and Augustinian values; he proceeds to a history of the *translatio imperii* which does not have Constantine's sacred empire as its precondition.

As we have seen, the wickedness of depraved emperors – the Julio-Claudians, the four emperors of AD 70–71, the post-Severan monsters of whom he learned from the *Historia Augusta* – is displayed in killing off the senatorial elite and replacing them with men of no virtue.[34] Rome is left without liberty or the capacity for empire, and this leads to both *declinatio* and *divisio*.

Itaque paulatim evanescere vires et prolapsa maiestas interire coepit, ac deficientibus civibus, ad externos deferri. Sed primis quidem temporibus magnitudo potentiae incommoda tolerabat. Roma autem, etsi intestinis quae modo retulimus affligeretur incommodis, ab externo tamen hoste tuta perstabat. Postquam vero Constantinus, amplificato Bizantio, ad orientem subsedit, Italia et caeterae occidentales imperii partes, quasi pro derelictis habitae, negligi coeperunt, ac tyrannorum barbarorumque invasionibus exponi; qui ceu in vacuam possessionem ruentes, variis temporibus, tanquam diluvia quaedam, has terras inundarunt; de quibus, quoniam illi multa per Etruriam gesserunt, et hanc ipsam de qua scribimus everterunt urbem, brevi discursu, quantum necessitas flagitat, referemus.[35]

---

[32] See below, p. 181.     [33] Hankins, 2000, pp. 12, 143–76.
[34] In his life of Petrarch, Bruni tells the same story, emphasising that, after the wars at the death of Nero, there were no more emperors of Roman birth, but all, following Nerva, were provincials and military men. As a result, Latin literary style deteriorated, the Goths and Lombards completed its destruction, and it did not recover until the recovery of the cities in recent times. Dante wrote better in the *volgare*, and Latin returned to life only when Petrarch rediscovered the works of Cicero and began to write like him. Translation in Griffiths, Hankins and Thompson, 1987, pp. 95–6.
[35] Santini, 1927, p. 15.

[Roman power began little by little to drain away and her grandeur to decline, eventually falling into foreign hands for lack of native citizens. Yet in earlier periods the vastness of Roman power withstood her misfortunes. Though badly afflicted with internal troubles, as we have shown, Rome still remained safe from external enemies. The Emperor Constantine, however, enlarged the city of Byzantium and moved the capital to the east. The emperors thereafter began to view Italy and the western part of the empire almost as the abandoned part, to be neglected and left exposed to the invasions of tyrants and barbarians. The latter rushed into the deserted property, as it were, at various times like the waters of a flood and inundated these lands altogether. I shall briefly describe the barbarians here, as necessity requires, since they were active in Tuscany and even devastated the city of which we are writing.][36]

Bruni proceeds to an account occupying many pages of the successive barbarian invaders, the lands in which they originated, and their incursions into various provinces of the empire. Though he has just told us that these invasions are a mainly western phenomenon – he will have nothing to say of the Arabs or the Avars – there is an account of the disaster of Adrianople in 371;[37] this is a history of Florence and Tuscany, but not a provincial one. Nevertheless, we go on past Alaric's sack of Rome to Totila's destruction of Florence – which the citizens probably survived, even before they were aided by Charlemagne[38] – and the narrative of barbarism reaches its climax with the Lombard occupation of large areas of Italy, against which the popes turn to alliance with the Franks. Their origin is not related – perhaps because they did not settle in Italy – and it is a question just what role barbarism plays in Bruni's understanding of history. There is an obvious relationship between barbarism and religion, since it was the papal appeal to the Franks against the Lombards which led to the *translatio imperii*; but Bruni has nothing to say here about the clash between the eighth-century popes and the iconoclast emperors, producing the expulsion of the east Romans from Italy and the exposure of the popes to Lombard power, which most of the medieval writers we have studied considered an essential prelude to the *translatio*.

Perhaps this is why his account of Constantine makes no reference to Pope Sylvester or the supposed Donation. A Guelf dimension is necessary to the history he proposes to write, since his account of the distinctive politics of Florence is to begin with the Angevin victories over the last Hohenstaufen, but a history of the Church and the monarchical claims

---

[36] Hankins, 2001, pp. 53–5.  [37] Santini, 1927, p. 17; Hankins, 2001, p. 59.
[38] Santini, 1927, p. 24; Hankins, 2001, p. 195.

of the Roman pontiffs is not central to his design. Charlemagne's ac-clamation – it is not called a coronation – as emperor by Pope Leo is described in the following terms.

Hinc nata est, quae hodie quoque perdurat, imperii romani divisio, aliis in Graecis, aliis in Gallia Germaniaque romani principis nomen usurpantibus. De quo non ab re fuerit, pro cognitione rei, pauca repetere.

Romanum imperium a populo romano institutum atque perfectum est. Nam reges quidem non ita late possederunt, ut imperium meruerit appellari. Sub con-sulibus ac dictatoribus tribunisque militaribus, qui fuerunt libero populo magis-tratus, et res et nomen emersit imperii, Africa pene tota magnaque Asiae parte ultra Armeniam et Caucasum montem armis subacta, Europae vero, Hispaniis, Galliis, Graecia, Macedonia, Thracia aliisque subinde partibus bello domitis, Rheno et Danubio imperium terminarunt. Maria insuper insulaeque et litora Bosphoro in Britanniam cuncta paruerunt. Haec omnia per quadringentas sex-aginta quinque annos ab unius urbis libero populo perfecta. Externis invictum bellis, intestinae civilesque discordiae oppressere. Imperatores hinc creari co-epti, quod ante armorum castrorumque nomen fuit, id tanquam intestino vi-gente bello, intra moenia inductum: verbo quidem legitima potestas, re autem vera dominatio erat. Stipati armorum caterva, metu servire compellebant cives. Ab his imperatoribus Germania et quibusdam provinciis ad imperium adiunc-tis, foris quidem potentia non nihil extensa est: domi autem vires imperabant: Nerva autem, qui duodecimus ab Augusto successit, primus sibi consortem delegit imperii: quo postea exemplo, duo interdum principes eodem tempore extiterunt. In partitione tamen rerum, usque ad Constantini tempora, praecipua Roma servabatur auctoritas: post Constantium vero sedemque imperii Bizan-tium translatam, maxime factitatum est, ut duobus imperatoribus institutis, alter Romam atque Italiam, alter Orientem susciperet gubernandum. Sed fere apud Constantinopolim summa rerum habebatur: qui illic imperabant, saepe alio sibi adiuncto Romam Italiamque solebant committere. Iamque ex con-suetudine sequestratum, illud orientale, hoc occidentale vocabatur imperium. Occupantibus deinde Italiam barbaris, occidentale cessavit imperium: nec post Augustulum illum, quem ab Odoacre deiectum ostendimus, quisquam ne tiran-nice quidem, per Italiam et Occidentem id nomen suscepit usque ad Carolum Magnum, quem a Leone pontifice imperatorem diximus appellatum.[39]

[Hence was born the division of the Roman empire which still exists today, with some arrogating to themselves the title of Roman emperor in Greece, others in Gaul and Germany. For a clearer picture of this subject, it will not be amiss to say a few words.

The Roman empire was founded and perfected by the Roman People. The early kings never attained such wide domains as to merit the name of empire. The reality and the name of empire emerged under the consuls and dictators and military tribunes, the magistrates of a free people. It was created by the

---

[39] Santini, 1927, pp. 22–3.

armed conquest of almost all Africa and a great part of Asia to beyond the mountains of Armenia and the Caucasus. The parts of Europe subdued in war included Spain, Gaul, Greece, Macedonia, Thrace, and later other regions, and the Rhine and the Danube became the borders of the empire. The seas with their islands and their shores all obeyed Rome, from the Bosphorus to Britain.

All this was accomplished in four hundred and sixty-five years[40] by the free people of a single city. Unconquered by external foes, this people was overwhelmed at last by internal discord and civil war. From that time forth, emperors began to be chosen, and the word *imperator*, which before had meant arms and forts, was brought, as it were, within the city walls as though to signal continuous civil war. The word still referred to a legitimate function, but in reality it signified lordship and domination. Surrounded by armed troops, the citizens were cowed into subservience. Germany and certain provinces were added to the empire by the emperors, so the empire's external power was somewhat extended, but the strength of the empire at home was diminished by almost continual assassinations and slaughter. When they began the emperors reigned alone, but Nerva, the twelfth emperor after Augustus, was the first to choose a co-ruler. Thereafter two emperors from time to time ruled simultaneously as colleagues on this model. Until the time of Constantine, however, the division of business did not alter the primary authority of the city of Rome. After Constantine moved the capital to Byzantium, it became the habitual practice to have two emperors, one to rule Italy and Rome, the other to rule the east. The highest power was soon felt to belong to Constantinople, as those who ruled there often entrusted Rome and Italy to their co-ruler. Once the empires were divided in practice, moreover, they came to be called the eastern and western empires. When the barbarians then took over Italy, the western empire ceased to exist. After Augustulus was overthrown by Odoacer, as we have shown, no one, not even as an act of tyrannous usurpation, took up the name of emperor in Italy and the West until Charlemagne, to whom, as we have said, Pope Leo gave the title.][41]

Bruni is emerging as a fairly consistent anti-imperialist (if the term be not used in its modern sense). Empire can be achieved only by a *populus* enjoying *libertas*. How far that becomes a claim of right is not clear; no doubt there were ways of justifying the empire of the Romans by appeal to just war, conquest and occupation, but Bruni is not here employing a juristic vocabulary. *Imperium* is the reward of *libertas*, but we have found him reminding us that it represses the *libertas* and the *virtus* of others, and indicating at least the possibility of admiring the Etruscans above the Romans, even perhaps commerce among cities rather than empire over them. It is unclear whether the empire of the Romans was

---

[40] Brunetto had used this figure, concluding at the conspiracy of Catiline (above, p. 140).
[41] Hankins, 2001, pp. 87–9.

the cause of the civil wars in which they lost their liberty, but quite clear that nothing – certainly not the capacity for empire – legitimises the rule of *imperatores* or *principes*. These tyrants extinguish the *libertas* by which empire is won and maintained, and as well as losing provinces they divide the *imperium* over them. The sequence of adoptive successions from Nerva to Marcus Aurelius, later presented as an interlude of unparalleled prosperity, is here made to anticipate – Diocletian and the tetrarchs being omitted – the division of the empire and the abandonment by Constantinople of a neglected west. There is no sacred dimension to this story, no Eusebian, Orosian, or Dantean account of how empire was justified and sanctified by the birth of Christ; a Christian reader might suspect that the values of *libertas* were replacing those of justice and redemption. The function of the western barbarians in the narrative is to impose a complete separation between east and west and a complete caesura on the history of empire in the latter. There is no emperor in the west between Romulus Augustulus and Charlemagne, and no Constantinopolitan presence in western history; nor does Bruni show interest in the loss of eastern or western provinces to Arabic Islam. It seems to be the case that his history is, in the last analysis, focussed on the relation between Rome and the cities of ancient Etruria, which is what he chiefly means by 'Italy'; and the recovery of the latter from the effects of Roman domination in antiquity is achieved through victory over the successors of Charlemagne, to whose empire he is not about to concede imperial legitimacy – itself a contradiction in terms, since *imperium* is derived from the rule of *libertas*, not of *imperatores*.

Post Carolum vero neque consortium ullum nec ulla penitus remansit communio: divisi animi, divisa autem signa. . . . Fuit praeterea disceptatio varia, cum alii veterem imperatorem seriem et antiquum succedendi morem servandum censerunt; alii, etsi alienum a iure, tamen quia expedient, novum electionis exemplum a pontifice introductum probarent. Nobis autem plurimum videtur referre, populus romanus hortatu pontificis an pontifex ipse iniussu populi creavit. Constat enim nullius magis quam populi romani id munus esse. Nam pontificatus per illa tempora magis ab imperatoria auctoritate pendebat, nec quisquam praesidebat, nisi quem post senatus, cleri et populi romani electionem, imperatoria comprobasset auctoritas. Verum haec censurae illorum, qui iuris pontificii peritiores habentur, subiicimus.[42]

[After Charlemagne there was no association at all, and nothing remained in common between the eastern and western empires; they were divided in spirit, divided even in their emblems. . . . There was also a complicated dispute

[42] Santini, 1927, p. 23.

about imperial elections. Some thought that the old series of emperors and the old customs of succession should be maintained while others approved, as an expedient procedure, a new form of election introduced by the pope, even though it lacked a legal basis. To us it seems highly debatable whether the Roman People creates the emperor on the urging of the pope, or the pope himself, without instruction from the Roman People, creates the emperor, since it is evident that this office most properly belongs to the Roman People. In those times, it was more the case that the papacy depended on the emperor, and no one presided over the Church unless, after election by the senate, the clergy, and the people of Rome, he had been approved by imperial authority. But we submit these questions to the judgement of those who are considered more learned in canon law.][43]

The last sentence is the sole occasion we have met on which Bruni alludes to juristic thinking as a way of settling problems. It may be doubted whether he would have written this way when serving as 'secretary to four successive popes', since while it seems clear that the emperor enjoys no legitimate authority inherited from the days before Constantine, there is no legal foundation for his election by papal recognition and there have been times when popes were chosen by the people and approved by the emperor. There remains the authority of the *populus romanus*, but Bruni does not seem to think that they are any longer what they were in antiquity. It is tempting to believe that he does not regard the issue between pope, emperor and people as of any great importance. What matters as the source of *imperium* is *libertas*, its loss by the ancient Roman people and its revival in the free cities of Tuscany. This would be the effect of addressing the appeal to the values of 'civic humanism' – the values of civic liberty – rather than civil law or scholastic disputation. But the new appeal necessitated a history of liberty which must still be narrated in Guelfic if not in papal terms.

After the re-establishment of the empire in German hands, he says, *civitates Italiae paulatim ad libertatem respicere, ac imperium verbo magis quam facto confiteri coeperunt* [the cities of Italy began to want liberty and to acknowledge the emperor's authority nominally rather than in practice].[44] They began to recover from the barbarism of the last five centuries; and Bruni lists those in Tuscany which now became powerful, his own Arezzo not really among them. This is a history of wars and rivalries rather than of peace and commerce, but there is an external explanation for this.

Attulerunt autem his bellorum et discordiarum abundantissimum fomitem crebrae inimicitiae inter pontifices romanos imperatoresque coortae. Nam

---

[43] Hankins, 2001, p. 91.     [44] Santini, 1927, p. 23; Hankins, 2001, p. 93.

imperium illud, quod in Carolo Magno maxime propter tutelam romanae ecclesiae fundatum ab initio fuit, in Germaniam ut supra ostendimus delatum,
tales plerumque habuit successores, ut ad nullam rem magis quam ad perse-
quendos evertendosque pontifices creati viderentur: adeo unde salus petita erat,
scelus emersit.

[The many disputes between the Roman pontiffs and emperors brought plen-
tiful tinder to our local wars and quarrels. For the empire which began with
Charlemagne and was founded mainly for the protection of the Roman church,
once it was, as we have explained, transferred to Germany, fell into the hands of
successors whose main purpose in life seemed to be the persecution and overthrow of the popes. What had once been a source of security became a vortex
of evil.][45]

Bruni's account is resolutely one-sided, yet it is localised by the context
in which he places it. The effect of the struggle between powers claiming
universal and sacred authority is the intensification of faction within the
Tuscan cities,

una fautrix pontificum, imperatoribus adversa; altera imperatorio nomini
omnino addicta. Sed ea, quam imperatoribus adversam supra ostendimus, ex iis
fere hominibus conflata erat, qui libertatem populorum magis complectebantur:
Germanos autem barbaros homines sub praetextu romani nominis dominari
Italis, perindignum censebant. Alia vero factio ex iis erat, qui imperatorio nomini addicti, libertatis et gloriae maiorum immemores, obsequi externis quam
suos dominari malebant. Hinc studia partium coorta, magnarum calamitatum
initia fuere. Nam et publicae res contentione et cupiditate magis quam bono
et honesto tractabantur; et privatim odia inimicitiaeque in dies crescebant. Ita
privatim et publice simul invaserat morbus, qui primo enutritus contentionibus,
tandem exacerbatus odio ac lethifer factus, ad arma et caedes ac vastitatem
urbium ad extremum prorupit.[46]

[one favoured the pope and was opposed to the emperors, the other was entirely
devoted to the imperial name. But the side which, as we said, opposed the emperors was essentially composed of those who were more inclined to embrace
the liberty of the peoples: they considered it degrading for Germans and barbarians to rule over Italians under the pretext of the Roman name. The other
faction consisted of men who had bound themselves to the imperial cause and
had forgotten the liberty and glory of their ancestors – men who preferred to
serve foreigners rather than be ruled by their own people. Hence partisanship
arose and this was the beginning of great calamities. For public affairs began to
be conducted more in accordance with greed and rivalry than with goodness
and honour, and in private life hatred and enmity increased daily. Thus the

[45] Hankins, 2001, p. 101.      [46] Santini, 1927, pp. 25–6.

disease took hold of private and public life at the same time. First it was nurtured by quarrels, then it worsened and became deadly hatred, finally it burst
out in arms and slaughter and the devastation of cities.][47]

Once more, Bruni's partisanship is not the issue. It may be true that
all patriots who love liberty and hate foreign barbarians are on the Guelf
side, but this does not prevent their being corrupted by faction and led to
crimes of hatred. Bruni, who at another time wrote a life of Dante,[48] was
well aware of the complex and violent history of his adopted city. The
real meaning of this passage is that the universal is being absorbed by the
particular, the history of *translatio imperii* by the history of *libertas* in those
cities capable of it. The first book of Bruni's *Historiarum Florentini populi
Libri XII* ends as the rise of faction reaches a climax with the career of the
emperor Frederick II. With his defeat the cause of empire in Italy is at
an end and Bruni can begin a history of Florence, in which the factions
inherited from partisanship may or may not be converted into citizens
capable of *libertas* if not *imperium*. At the outset of Book 11 Bruni tells us
that all that has gone before

uno in libro collegimus, ut neque civitatum Etruscarum initia atque progres-
sus, neque imperii romani declinatio atque divisio, neque haec ipsa, quae mox
omnia quassarunt, studia partium factionesque, unde ortum augmentumque
habuerint, ignota essent. Iam vero non cursu, sed incessu erit utendum.[49]

[has collected in one book whatever was necessary to understand what would
be said later. For this reason we treated the beginnings and progress of the
Etruscan cities, the decline and division of Roman power, and the origins and
growth of that partisanship and those factions which were afterwards to convulse
the world. But now we must walk, not run.][50]

The universal issues of decline and fall, *translatio imperii*, church and
empire, spiritual and secular, have been enclosed within a history of
*libertas* in the cities of Tuscany; even the history of how Roman empire
was achieved by liberty and disappeared with it becomes a narrative of
how the Romans denied to others a gift uniquely their own (not altogether
unlike the role of the Jews in the history of the Christian dispensation).
The universal history of Bruni's first book is only a prelude to the detailed
narrative of Florentine politics in the remaining eleven, a history of the
none too secure attainment of *libertas* within the walls of a single city

---

[47] Hankins, 2001, pp. 101–3.
[48] Translation in Griffiths, Hankins and Thompson, 1987, pp. 85–95.
[49] Santini, 1927, p. 27.      [50] Hankins, 2001, p. 109, slightly modified.

and *dominium* if not *imperium* outside them; for no one of the Italian states can achieve empire over the others, still less pursue it beyond the *regnum italicum* now dissolved into so many warring cities. For the first time, the history of Decline and Fall, with that of the *translatio imperii* which followed it, is being narrated as prelude to the history of a European states system, though one of limited extent. Even barbarism and religion – the latter significantly de-emphasised – are subjected to the history of *libertas et imperium*.

# CHAPTER 9

# Flavio Biondo and the decades of decline

## (1)

Leonardo Bruni gave life to the concept of Decline and Fall by equating the decline of the empire with the rule of the emperors, and the consequent loss of the *virtus* and *libertas* by which empire had been achieved and sustained. It was to be a problem attending this thesis that the rule of emperors had lasted three to four hundred years before the events at which an end of empire, confined to the western provinces, could be said to have occurred. There ensued a further series of events, involving bishops of Rome, Lombard and Frankish kings, eastern and western emperors, constituting a *translatio imperii* in our parlance, a 'triumph of barbarism and religion' in Gibbon's, and of central importance in medieval historiography. With these Bruni was not primarily concerned, because the theme of the first volume of his *Histories* was not the interactions of church and empire so much as the revival of civic liberties in central Italy; he displayed the banner of liberty more than that of the church.

We need to beware, however, of supposing that Bruni singlehandedly, or Florentine civic humanism collectively, dispelled the medieval paradigms of the *translatio imperii* or the two cities. There are moments – not of themselves fatal to his argument – where Hans Baron's language suggests a catastrophe of this sort: it is as if a manmade asteroid from outer time, loaded with non-compatible information, makes its impact and all the dinosaurs die. It is not impossible that the humanist recovery of Roman culture was sometimes obsessive enough to produce such an image, but we have to beware of a further thesis shaped as far back as the nineteenth century: that there has occurred a sudden birth or rebirth of the state, and an understanding of history peculiar to the state, of which the Italian republics and their vision of antiquity acted as the predecessor. This thesis, a central achievement of German historicism, entails a debate as to the meaning and moment of 'modernity' with which the present study is not intended to engage. There did indeed occur, over a lengthy period, a displacement of *translatio imperii* by Decline and Fall, and a displacement of the thirteenth-century empire and papacy by the states system of the sixteenth century; but it is important not to render these processes equivalent or to condense and dramatise the narrative of their occurring. In the narrative it is necessary to construct, the relation of the Italian republics to the monarchies and empires that replaced them will prove to have been far from simple, and the understandings of Roman history entailed by the process correspondingly complex. As a chapter in this narrative, we now pursue the invention of the Decline and Fall in a context other than Florentine.

Flavio Biondo from Forli (1392–1463, a younger contemporary of Leonardo Bruni)[1] spent his active life in the papal service, where he at various times encountered Bruni, that 'secretary to four successive popes', but was immersed without interruption in a climate which may be called that of papal as opposed to civic humanism. Papal humanists were students of Roman antiquities, both textual and monumental, and the central assertion in which they desired to interest both popes and the learned public was not only that the pontiffs were patrons of humane learning, but that it was possible for the glories of antiquity to be preserved, or even reborn, in a Christian form.[2] It was a proposition filled with doctrinal as well as scholarly problems and perils, and not all these humanists were as good Christians as they claimed to be; but it permitted the assertion that the Church was reversing the dilapidation of the city and even re-building it – whatever might be entailed by the reconstruction of temples as churches. Gibbon in 1763 had mixed feelings when he heard the bare-footed friars singing vespers in the temple of Jupiter, but the reconstruction of Rome by Renaissance and baroque popes was a process on which even *philosophe* historians looked with favour, and Gibbon was to end the *Decline and Fall* by exculpating even the early Christians from the charge of destroying the ancient city. The desertion of the city by its empire, the theme from which Gibbon set out, antedated even the foundation of Constantinople and the indifference of Christian emperors to the fate of the pagan capital, and it was possible for humanists in Biondo's time to aver that Peter and his heirs had preserved and restored the city when Caesar had abandoned it. Here was a theme of

---

[1] For biography, see Nogara, 1927.
[2] For papal humanism in Biondo's lifetime, see Brezzi and Lorch, 1984; for the transition to its last phase before the disaster of 1527, Ramsey, 1982 and Rowland, 1998.

Decline and Fall, with the eastward move of empire as its centre, and the popes of the fifteenth century – some of them humanists – were witnesses to the last years of the New Rome, ending in 1453.

The language of *translatio imperii*, however, was still far from extinct. A late development in the history of papal schism and its healing led the Emperor Frederick III to attempt an intervention, in the course of which the humanist and future pope, Aeneas Sylvius Piccolomini, composed a tract *De ortu et auctoritate imperii romani* (1446), rehearsing the imperialist themes of the emperor's supreme authority, even over those princes who denied receiving *imperium* from him.[3] The crisis of the eastern empire produced schemes for the reunion of the eastern and western churches, in which the authority of the latter would necessarily be paramount. Flavio Biondo was present at the Council of Florence, where such a reunion was attempted, and later addressed letters, in the humanist mode, to both the emperor and the king of Naples, inciting them to a crusade, which might in theory have led to an extension of western empire over a recovered east. This would have been the ultimate *translatio* – some Orthodox notoriously preferred life in a Muslim ecumene to a Latin – and the papal–humanist contention that Peter had restored sanctity to a fallen pagan Rome was not incompatible with the view that his heirs had restored sacred empire in the west at large. A post-Sallustian thesis of decline could at need be fitted into this picture.

A narrative of Decline and Fall, not free from Sallustian and therefore civic elements, consequently takes shape in the discourse of papal humanism. The empire built up by the virtue of citizens is exhausted by its own grandeur, and by contact with the luxury and corruption of the Hellenised east.[4] It is a question how far this extends to a criticism of the empire ruled from Constantinople, but the latter fails to protect its western provinces and the Latin empire, together with the metaphorical empire of the Latin tongue and letters, are submerged by a deluge of barbarism. Once again, we see barbarism as a humanist invention – sharpened by the perception that all who were not Italians were barbarians – but it is the function of humanism, here under papal protection, to restore the *studium* if not the *imperium*. Lorenzo Valla, who was and was not a humanist of this school, declared in his *Elegantiae* that the Latin tongue restored the empire of Rome, even though it was now spoken by former barbarians who had no further need of the *imperator*.[5] It was of

---

[3] Izbicki and Nederman, 2000, pp. 24–30, 95–112; Burns, 1992, pp. 114–17. These commentaries situate *De ortu* in the context of political theory rather than historiography.
[4] Mazzocco, 1982, p. 190.      [5] Valla, 1543, pp. 9–10.

course Valla who employed the new philological skills in launching the
most devastating attack yet made against the Donation of Constantine;[6]
he did this while under the protection not of the emperor but of the
Aragonese king of Naples – a dubious ally of the papacy – though Gibbon
read his *De falsa donatione* as a revolutionary pamphlet addressed to the
Roman people in one of their periodic rebellions against papal rule.[7]
It was clear to Gibbon that he was still looking at the world – though
the very last phase of that world – in which *imperator, pontifex* and *populus*
could compete for commanding roles in effecting the *translatio imperii*.
He remarked in a concluding chapter of the *Decline and Fall* – written at
least ten years later than the chapters composing the volume of 1776 –
that 'Eugenius the fourth was the *last* pope expelled by the tumults of the
Roman people' (an episode of 1434), 'and Nicholas the fifth the *last* who
was importuned by the presence of a Roman emperor' (in 1452, when
Frederick III came to be crowned at Rome).[8] But of the last incident he
says:

> So tame were the times, so feeble was the Austrian, that the pomp of his
> coronation was accomplished with order and harmony: but the superfluous
> honour was so disgraceful to an independent nation, that his successors have
> excused themselves from the toilsome pilgrimage to the Vatican; and rest their
> imperial title on the choice of the electors of Germany.[9]

It is better that political authority be national than universal, and even
the weakness of a state may bring it to a more autonomous title; Gibbon
is looking with satisfaction on the death of the medieval dinosaurs,
and their rebirth as a more harmless species. But great predators are
by no means extinct; he goes on to remark that the present settled
condition of Italy, in which Rome enjoys a peaceful servitude, is the
result of the domination of the peninsula by the Spanish and Austrian
(in competition with the French) monarchies, and that the history of this
domination has been written by Machiavelli, Guicciardini, Sarpi and
Davila,

---

[6] Coleman, 1993.
[7] *DF*, v, ch. 49, n. 72; Womersley, 1994, III, p. 116: 'I have read in the collection of Schardius . . . this
animated discourse, which was composed by the author, A.D. 1440, six years after the flight of
pope Eugenius IV. It is a most vehement party pamphlet: Valla justifies and animates the revolt
of the Romans, and would even approve the use of a dagger against their sacerdotal tyrant. Such
a critic might expect the persecution of the clergy; yet he made his peace, and is buried in the
Lateran.'
[8] *DF*, vi, ch. 70; Womersley, 1994, III, p. 1051. The emphases are Gibbon's.
[9] Womersley, 1994, III, p. 1052.

justly esteemed the first historians of modern languages, till, in the present age, Scotland arose to dispute the prize with Italy herself.[10]

We have to cover this terrain in the next few chapters; the immediate question is where Flavio Biondo stood in relation to the *translatio imperii*. Three years later than the date of composition of *De falsa donatione*, we find Biondo presenting to the same king of Naples and Aragon the introductory books of his ambitious *Historiarum ab inclinato Romano imperio decades III*,[11] a work known as the *Decades* from its division into three groups of ten books each. Gibbon knew some of the works of Biondo, and mentions him among others in the very last footnote to the *Decline and Fall*;[12] but he uses him chiefly as a source for Venetian history,[13] and may have had only second-hand knowledge of his writings on the topography of Rome,[14] which must outweigh the *Decades* in any assessment of his career. Biondo worked on the latter from 1438 to 1452, but its composition kept pace with a series of volumes of a different character: *Roma instaurata* (1440–46), *Italia illustrata* (1448–53), and *Roma triumphans* (1456–60).[15] These are surveys of the topography of the ancient city and of Roman Italy; they belong in the category of antiquarianism or archaeology rather than history, among those studies of the ancient world from non-narrative and non-documentary sources which – together with philology – were to supplement the writing of history until they had transformed its character. Given what we know of the progress of Gibbon's interests from the topography of the city and the geography of Italy to the history of the empire,[16] it is hard to believe that he would have ignored these works had he known them well. The three studies cited, however, are not confined to topography; they contain a programme of Christian and papal humanism in which we may perceive Biondo's vision of history. At the end of *Roma instaurata* he proclaims:

Viget certe, uiget adhuc, et quanquam minori diffusa orbis terrarum spacio, solidiori certe innixa fundamento, urbis Romae gloria maiestatis. Habetque Roma aliquod in regna et gentes imperium, cui tutando augendoque non legionibus, cohortibus, turmis et manipulis, non equitatu peditatuque opus, nullo

---

[10] *DF*, VI, ch. 70, n. 89; Womersley, 1994, III, p. 1057.

[11] Hay, 1959, p. 103; Nogara, 1927, pp. 147–53. The fullest study in English of Biondo as a historian appears to be that of Hay, 1959. It is focussed on the history of antiquarianism in Italy.

[12] *DF*, VI, ch. 71, n. 75; Womersley, 1994, III, p. 1084.

[13] *DF*, VI, ch. 60, nn. 54, 63; ch. 61, n. 2. Ch. 69, n. 30 cites him on Roman history.

[14] See ch. 71, n. 75: Montfaucon 'reviews the topographers of ancient Rome; the first efforts of Blondus', etc.

[15] For these see Mazzocco, 1982 and 1984. He presents the historical thought of Biondo's topographical volumes independently of that of the *Decades*.

[16] *EEG*, chs. 11 and 12.

nunc delectu militum, qui aut sponte dent nomina, aut militare cogantur, educ-
tae Roma et Italia copiae in hostem ducuntur, aut imperii limites custodiun-
tur. Non sanguis ad praesentem seruandam patriam effunditur, non mortalium
caedes committuntur. Sed per dei nostri et domini nostri Iesu Christi imperatoris uere summi, uere aeterni religionis sedem, arcem atque domicilium in
Roma constitutum, ductosque in illa ab annis mille et quadringentis martyrum
triumphos, per dispersas in omnibus aeternae et gloriosissimae Romae tem-
plis, aedibus, sacellisque sanctorum reliquias, magna nunc orbis terrarum pars
Romanum nomen dulci magis subjectione colit, quam olim fuit solita contrem-
iscere. Dictatorem nunc perpetuum non Caesaris, sed piscatoris Petri succes-
sorem . . .[7]

[The glory and majesty of Rome live certainly to this day, diffused it is true over
a lesser area of the earth, but based on a surer foundation. For Rome has a kind
of empire over kingdoms and nations, to protect and enlarge which requires no
legions or cohorts, squadrons or troops, horse or foot; no levying of soldiers, or
armies voluntarily enlisted or compelled to serve, sent out of Rome and Italy to
meet the foe or guard the frontiers of this empire. No blood is shed to preserve
this fatherland, no slaughter of men committed. But by the seat, citadel and
dwelling place of our God and Lord Jesus Christ, our true emperor, and his true
everlasting religion, now set up in Rome; by the triumphs of the martyrs there
these fourteen hundred years; by the relics of the saints distributed among the
temples, churches and sanctuaries of glorious and eternal Rome; a great part
of the world now owns the Roman name, by a subjection far sweeter than that
at which it once trembled. The perpetual dictator is now the successor not of
Caesar but of Peter the fisherman. . . .][18]

It is Gibbon's triumph of religion, though not of barbarism; the substitution of Peter for Caesar, of *evangelium* for *imperium*. If the church rules
a smaller region than the former empire, the reason is the Moslem conquests nearing their climax in 1453, and the frontiers may need guarding
after all; Biondo was to join Pius II in calling vainly for a crusade. But
there is nothing here of a *translatio* of empire to the church; we are a little
closer to Augustine's renunciation of worldly glory; not so close, however,
that the relation between church and empire, martyr and legionary, can
ever be free from ambivalence. Dedicating *Roma triumphans* to his patron
Pope Pius, Biondo wrote:

Idque immensum opus quinque partita distributione tractabimus: ut quae
ad religionem spectauere primum, quae reipublicae administrationis fuerunt
secundum, tertium militiae disciplina: mores uero ac uita instituta quartum,

---

[7]  *Roma instaurata*, p. 271, separately paginated in Biondo, 1559.
[18]  Trans. JGAP, as are all quotations from Biondo in this chapter. I am indebted to Matthew Roller
for checking my transcriptions and translations, all responsibility for which remains mine.

et triumphi ipsius ratio, quintum obtineant locum. Praefari tamen hoc initio libet: nos de Romanorum gentiliumque aliorum religione, ea ratione ac intentione dicturos: ut deorum appellationes, cum templorum, aedium, phanorum uocabulis edocentes, simul loca urbis Romae, in quibus ea fuere ostendamus: inde rituum quos dii gentium, sicut Propheta inquit, daemonia suis sacrificiis adhiberi iusserint, spurcitia, impietate atque etiam maxima leuitate ostensa, Christianae religionis sanctimoniam bonae uoluntatis hominibus gratiorem esse faciamus.[19]

[We shall treat this immense work according to a five-fold division: first as regards religion, secondly the government of the commonwealth, thirdly the discipline of the armies; the manners and customs of life shall have the fourth place, and the celebration of triumphs the fifth. Let us add this preface: we shall describe the religion of the Romans and other pagans with the intention that the names of their gods, with those of their temples, edifices and shrines, shall be connected with the places in the city of Rome to which they belonged. Thus when we have displayed the filthiness, impiety and utter levity of the rituals with which, as the prophet says, the gods of the heathens by demonic power ordered that their sacrifices be performed, we shall have made the holiness of the Christian religion even more pleasing to men of good will.]

In the first sentence of this passage, Biondo goes beyond the description of buildings to describe in detail the imperial culture that once inhabited them: its religion and laws, its arms and manners. A whole-hearted humanist would have included the severity of ancient religion in his systematic account of Rome's former virtue, before going on to enquire how this imposing structure had come by its decline and fall. But there is a tension within Christian humanism: the austere cults of the Capitol must become the tissue of idolatry and obscenity against which the martyrs took their stand, and Biondo does not here adopt the solution of saying that Roman religion was exposed to Oriental debasement. Perhaps this is one reason why the *Decades* recount history *ab inclinato imperio*, but do not attempt to explain that *inclinatio* or write its history.

Like Leonardo Bruni, whom he knew,[20] Biondo was a humanist who, when he turned to compiling a history – or a compendium of histories (*historiarum*) – approached the task with assumptions he took, often rightly, to be those of Greek and Roman antiquity. These included a strong presumption in favour of a present or recent scene, which a historian should aim to record for posterity; only a search for origins and causes, itself secondary to the task of narration, led him into a remoter past and a

[19] *De Roma triumphante* (*sic*, in Biondo, 1559), pp. 2–3.
[20] Letters between them are translated in Griffiths, Hankins and Thompson, 1987, pp. 161, 162, 164, 229–34.

quest for beginnings. Eleven of Bruni's twelve books are concerned with the history of Florence and the post-Roman and post-imperial world of city states, Tuscan and Lombard, in which that history was situated; he supplies a universal history of *libertas et imperium* only as a prelude. Biondo, similarly, began the *Decades* as a history of the fifteenth-century Italy in which the cities he knew and the papacy he served had their being. He wrote what became his third 'decade' – books XXI to XXX, covering the years 1410 to 1440 – before committing himself to the grand project of a survey of history *ab inclinato imperio*;[21] and the first and second decades, the first twenty books, never quite lost the character of a prelude, necessary but secondary, to the author's true work as a historian. But the thousand years they cover – Biondo for some reason took 412 rather than 410 as his starting point – were not easily summarised or relegated to irrelevance; they were those of the *translatio imperii*, contained within the history of the Two Cities and the Four Empires, which Otto of Freising had related in a full awareness of its complexity, and it was not more than a century since this history might have ceased to be of central importance. If, as we are constrained to assume, Bruno and Biondo were living at a time when history could no longer be written along Ottonian or Dantean lines, it is a question what exactly could be put in their place, and what humanist historians could make of the millennium since the end of the western empire or the six centuries since its revival. It is a possibility that they were operating without a predetermined scenario.

Bruni's solution we have seen: the revival of Tuscan and Italian city liberties under post-Roman and post-Hohenstaufen conditions, and the competitive inter-city politics of which he makes himself the historian. Though he acknowledges the necessary role of the Guelf and Angevin triumph of the later thirteenth century, he does not supply a history of the papal monarchy in its conflict with the emperor, still less in the vicissitudes of the fourteenth century (by no means ended in his own time). It is as if the humanists had not found a successor model to the history of *translatio imperii*, and were beginning to set the death and rebirth of ancient letters and liberty in the place it might have occupied. Bruni wrote as a Florentine, at least as he progressively entered that service and citizenship. Biondo, from a lesser city of the Romagna, moved from the Venetian service into the papal, which he never left (sharing Pope Eugenius' nine-year exile from Rome); we should not expect from him a primary commitment to civic values or their history.

[21] Hay, 1959, pp. 102–5.

We know of his decision to write the first and second *Decades* from the letter in which he presents the first of them to Alfonso king of Naples. In 1440, three years before the date of this letter, Lorenzo Valla had written the *De falsa donatione* while resident in Naples. If we follow Gibbon, however, in supposing that Valla's tract upholds the revolutionary doings of the Romans under Colonna leadership, we may suspect that the Neapolitan king did not want too close an alignment with them, and that Biondo in the papal service might seek his patronage. Since the narrative of the *Decades* begins *ab inclinatione*, meaning from the Gothic sack of 410 or 412, it does not include the actions of Constantine a century earlier, and we are inhibited from reading too much into its lack of any mention of the Donation. We have seen how a Christian and papal humanism might supply an account of the transformation of the city and empire of Rome, and was beginning to do so in Biondo's other authorial enterprises. In his letter to Alfonso, he offers first of all a strictly humanist justification of the first and second *Decades*: there has been no history on this scale since Orosius, and the revival of letters suggests that one be written now.[22] This of course is a humanist topos, a standard rhetorical exordium; but we have only to suppose that humanists were serious in setting the history of letters (and liberty?) before that of empire (and the church?) to see that Biondo might have expected this self-affirmation to be taken as an argument of weight. He addresses Alfonso as a king as well as a patron, and says that his history of Italy may serve as a proemium to Alfonso's achievements, but does not seem to offer a justification of any claims he might be making; and when he says that, as king of Aragon, Alfonso will wish to read of Charlemagne's conquests in Arabic Spain,[23] he is offering to enter on a history outside Italy he found himself unable to write. The letter concludes with a further advocacy of historiographical enterprise: the rescue from oblivion of the later Roman emperors, from the Antonines to the Illyrians (but not Constantine), whose names, good and ill, he gives in full,[24] but who play no part in the *Decades* though they do in the *Decline and Fall*. Biondo at this point is offering only literary justification of a literary enterprise.

We should be cautious before searching for much ideological or philosophical weight in Biondo's *Decades*; he may be no more than an honourable pedant, seeking to fill a gap in the literature. Alternatively, if letters should count for more than liberty – he mentions Maecenas in the time of Augustus[25] – he will not be concerned with the civic explanation

[22] Nogara, 1927, p. 148.    [23] *Ibidem*, p. 149.    [24] *Ibidem*, pp. 151–2.    [25] *Ibidem*, p. 151.

of the decline of empire. He opens his first book by saying that he must seek for a *culmen* at which Rome turned from the height of empire toward its *inclinatio*, and that this may be fixed at the moment of Alaric's sack of the city, after which it rapidly reverted *ad eum pene rerum statum . . . quem paruam et a pastoribus conditam in primordiis eam scribitur habuisse* [almost to that condition of a small settlement founded by shepherds in which it is recorded to have had its beginnings].[26] He very well knows, however, that from Orosius to Bruni there have been attempts to supply general causes of this peripeteia, and he must give his opinion of them.

He initially defines a period *ab diui Augusti initio imperii*, thus avoiding a 'Sallustian moment' with its emphasis on Catiline and Caesar, and continues:

> De ipsa igitur re paulo post dicturi primum, quod multis placuisse legimus, hanc de qua agimus Imperii inclinationem, in C. Caesaris dictatura coepisse, ea ratione non approbamus quia aucta potius quam imminuta fuit sub Caesarum multis Romana potentia. Pari ratione translationem sedis imperii facta a Constantino Byzantium, quemadmodum remotam inclinationis futurae causam fuisse non abnuerim, ita illius principium non concesserim appellandum, cum et ipse et alii decem in imperio successores, quos ea habuit translata Byzantium sedes, Imperii iura partim auxerint, partim in maiestate solita conseruauerint. Pariter de causis sicut et de principio quid sentiamus praefaturi, dicimus haudquaquam absurde sentire qui ea imperii quassationem ab Caesaris oppressione reipublicae, ideo causam habuisse opinantur, quod simul cum libertate interierint bene et sanctae uiuendi artes, et sublato per unius potentiam legum metu, principibusque uirtutem et animi magnitudinem ducentibus suspectam, ignaui fortibus, bonis perditi, grauibus et sanctis ganeones ac adulatores fuerunt in magistratibus honoribusque praelati. Nec eos asperandos sentimus, qui ab caduca et fluxa rerum mundi conditione sumpta ratione, dicunt Romanos eadem fatorum serie orbis imperium amisisse, qua nonnulli populi, et magnitudinis prope paris urbes ad opum tenuitatem maximam deuenerunt.

> [To speak first of that which we shall say later, we do not endorse the opinion we find pleasing to many, that the decline of empire with which we are concerned had its beginning from the dictatorship of Caius Caesar, for the reason that Roman power was increased rather than diminished under many of the Caesars who followed. For the same reason, the transference of the seat of empire to Byzantium by Constantine, which we do not deny was a remote cause of the future decline, cannot be accepted as its beginning, since both he and ten of his successors acknowledged by the new capital at Byzantium sometimes enlarged the imperial sway and sometimes maintained its established authority. To indicate what we hold concerning the question of causes and beginnings,

---

[26] *Decades* (in Biondo, 1559), p. 3.

let us say that it is by no means absurd to find the cause of the weakening of empire in Caesar's subversion of the republic, since the arts of living well and honourably were lost along with liberty, and when law lost its terror under the rule of one man, and virtue became suspect to princes and greatness of soul to those in power, in promotions to office and honour cowards were preferred to the brave, scoundrels to the good, and debauchees and flatterers to the sober and worthy. Nor are those to be despised who argue from the fallen and unstable condition of this world, and say that the Romans lost the empire of the world through the same fatal sequence which has brought many peoples and cities of equal greatness to the greatest insignificance . . .]

(He rehearses a sequence of four empires, Babylonian, Median, Carthaginian and Macedonian.)

Ut, quod scribit Orosius, nulla ratione sit mirandum, si quae serua sub regibus nata est Roma, libertatem sub consulibus partam amisit sub decemuiratu, et trecentesimo sexagesimo anno postquam fuerit conditam, a Gallis capta et incendiis latissimis foedata fuit: tandemque post mirandam instaurationem, cum potentia crescente superbia et uitiis diuitias superantibus, bellis est lacerata ciuilibus, ad extremumque circa septingesimum annum uni domino Caesari colla submisit.[27]

[So that, as Orosius has written, it is no wonder that Rome, born as a servant to kings, should have lost under the decemvirs the liberty begotten by the consuls, and in the three hundred and sixtieth year from its foundation should have been taken by the Gauls and devastated by extensive fires; and after a marvellous recovery, pride increasing with power and vices overcoming wealth, should have been torn by civil wars, and at last in about its seven hundredth year bowed to the lordship of a single Caesar.]

Biondo is distancing himself from both Bruni and Orosius, while retaining as much from both as he finds convenient to his limited purposes. He does this in two ways: first by establishing a distinction between the causes of decline and its starting point; second, by collapsing as far as he can the explanations of his predecessors into one another. His account of Roman moral decline moves from a civic anti-Caesarism like Bruni's to a Sallustian narrative compatible with Orosius', and with an Augustinian stress on the decay which worldly virtue and worldly empire bring to each other; but it is observable that the sequence of four empires is directed only by fortune and has no prophetic outcome. He does not employ the Virgilian and Christian image of the universal peace of Augustus, under which Christ consented to be born and bring the church into existence with the empire; it is as if *translatio* had yielded ground to *inclinatio*. Biondo

---

[27] Biondo, 1559, p. 4.

proceeds to offer a fourth cause of decline, which he considers superior
to the others.[28] It is that the guilt of the persecutions and the blood of the
martyrs weighed so heavily on the city that even the removal of the seat
of empire to Constantinople could not atone for it, and a hidden judgement of God decreed ruin as a necessary punishment. Here, however,
we have to do with a double vision like Gibbon's: the decline of the city
juxtaposed with that of the empire; and a papal humanism is in view,
wherein Caesar's city is redeemed by Peter and the edifices of empire
replaced by those of the Christian church. But Biondo was able to write
his trilogy on the topography of ancient and Christian Rome only after
the Curia he served could return to the city after a nine-year quasi-exile
(1434–43), and both church and empire in his time were, as he knew, far
from universal powers. The history of Christendom *ab inclinatione imperii*
was the prelude to two things: the disturbed state of Italy which he had
set out to chronicle, and – as is increasingly significant in his works –
the Turkish conquests leading to the fall of Constantinople. Biondo was
living and writing history at the moment where Gibbon, three and a half
centuries later, chose to terminate his. He was, however, far less than
Gibbon possessed of a universal narrative which might connect the beginning and end of his history, and this is one reason – there are certainly
others – why he was unable to separate the moment of *inclinatio* from its
remoter causes, or avoid the question whether these had continued to
operate after it.

> Ipsam itaque imperii inclinationem, siue ob praedictas omnes causas, siue ob
> earum aliquam sit facta, dicimus principium habuisse a Gothorum in urbem
> Romam irruptione.[29]

[And so we say that this decline of empire, whether produced by all the fore-
mentioned causes or by any one of them, had its beginning from the irruption
of the Goths into the city of Rome.]

### (III)

> Annus ergo quem a condita urbe sexagesimum quartum et centesimum supra
> millesimum numerabant, qui et salutis Christianae duodecimum et quadringen-
> tesimum fuit, nobis primus erit ab inclinatione imperii constitutus.[30]

[The year which was reckoned the 1164th from the foundation of the city, and
was the 412th year of Christian salvation, will be established here as the first of
the decline of the empire.]

---

[28] *Ibidem.*    [29] *Ibidem.*    [30] Biondo, 1559, p. 10.

Biondo was seeking to construct a chronology of his own, counting *ab imperio inclinato* alongside Livy's reckoning *ab urbe condita* (AUC) and Dionysius Exiguus' reckoning from the birth of Christ (*anno Domini* or AD). Readers of the *Decades*, however, have noted that he was unable to keep this up, and after about 1000 AD reverted to the Christian chronology, though the thousandth year from 412 would have brought him to his own times and the era at which the composition of his history had originally begun its narrative.[31] The reason for this, one suspects, is that he was unable to maintain a narrative sequence sufficiently coherent to be organised by a chronology of its own. Biondo recurrently admits that much takes place outside the history of empire in the west – in the French, English, Spanish and perhaps Neapolitan monarchies – which he can neither document nor narrate, and so cannot fit into his histories;[32] while in upper Italy – where empire and papacy have interacted and independent cities have risen to power – the history he does mean to narrate, which supplies the *Decades* with their original motive and most of their subject matter, is unintelligible without the internal political history of the several cities, confronting him with far too many narratives to be organised into one.[33] Bruni could override this problem, since he was writing a Florentine history and the affairs of Italy could be recounted from a Florentine point of view. The curialist Biondo had not that option; but it is a corollary that the papacy was no longer able to furnish him with an organising theme. It was more than one Italian state among many, but less than a universal presence, the city of God upon earth, which could narrate a history that was an Augustinian anti-history at the same time. As for the empire descending from Charlemagne, Otto or Frederick, the mere fact that Biondo was writing a history *ab imperio inclinato* showed that the medieval revival did not adequately continue the history of the ancient empire. Apart from its defeats at the hands of the papacy and the Guelfs, it had never controlled the policies or included the histories of the kingdoms of the Latin west, or – as we shall find Biondo increasingly aware – the alternative empire of the Greek east. We have reached the death of the dinosaurs, and Biondo's is a history in search not so much of a theme as of an organising narrative.

Because he lacks a unifying theme, however, he pursues a number of secondary but major themes which tell us much about the formation of historical concerns in his time; there is a sense in which it is the ordinariness of Biondo's intellect that makes him interesting. There are the

---

[31] Hay, 1959, p. 114.    [32] Hay, 1959, pp. 106, 110.    [33] Hay, 1959, pp. 108–9.

barbarians: he has plenty to say about the Goths and the Huns,[34] the Vandals and the Burgundians,[35] the Picts and the Scots[36] and even – a new departure among the historians we have been studying – the Slavs,[37] whom he knows to have settled in Istria and Dalmatia, provinces of the eastern empire, as well as in Bohemia and Poland at a later period. There is a reasonably coherent account of the barbarian movements out of Scythia, their invasions and settlements in Roman provinces, from the Gothic migration and the defeat of Valens, through the sack of Rome which marks the moment of *inclinatio*, to the end of the western emperors and the establishment of Theodoric's kingdom in Italy. This ruler restores the buildings of Rome and the ancient good customs (*excepta militari disciplina . . . quam primus reipublicae oppressor Caesar substulit*[38]), but his kingdom is destroyed by the wars of Justinian – described at length out of Procopius and no doubt Bruni[39] – and the way is open for the further invasion of the Lombards. But, we may ask, what is the function of the barbarians in Biondo's narrative? It may seem pointless to ask the question; we are so far programmed to think of 'the Decline and Fall' as a story of barbarian invasions, with which the sons of Theodosius are unable to cope, that we take them simply as given, present in the narrative because they cannot be omitted. The historians of *translatio*, however, were not primarily interested in the fact of barbarism, and in the earlier texts the Franks were of Trojan descent rather than Scythian or Gothic. In the move from *translatio* to *declinatio*, have not the barbarians a role to play in making the latter – the Decline and Fall – something other than the former?

It seems worth remembering that the barbarian tribes, enumerated by Biondo and Bruni alike, are the founders of the European kingdoms lying for the most part outside Italy and the empire as the latter exists in the fifteenth century. If Biondo were in a position to write a general history of western Europe – and he knows he is not – it would necessarily be a history of these kingdoms, including that of Germany as the effective substance of the existing empire; and the historiography beginning to take shape in each of them goes back to their barbaric origins, Gothic, Frankish, Burgundian, Anglian, Saxon, in search of the laws and rights that may be claimed from their foundation. Biondo lived at a time just before the rediscovery of Tacitus' *Germania* helped pull together the

---

[34] Biondo, 1559, pp. 4–6, 21–5.    [35] *Ibidem*, pp. 11–13, 20.    [36] *Ibidem*, pp. 18–19.
[37] *Ibidem*, pp. 11, 115–16.    [38] *Ibidem*, p. 34.
[39] This takes up most of Books IV–VIII of the first *Decade*.

myth of Germanic or Gothic liberties common to western Europe; but he had access to a wide range of barbarian histories – Jornandes for the Goths, Bede for the English, Gregory of Tours for the Franks, Paulus Diaconus for the Lombards.[40] These histories of barbaric peoples were written in Latin and recorded their evangelisation and civilisation; but it was an ecclesiastical Latin, towards which humanists had very mixed feelings. We touch here on two conjunctions of great importance to the development of western historiography: that between 'the triumph of barbarism' and 'of religion', and that between the barbaric and the Latin. It was central to the definition of 'the barbarians' that they did not know Latin; yet they had learned Latin. The Latin they had learned was in many respects barbaric, and humanists were trying to restore its classical purity; but the non-classical components in medieval Latin were derived in part from the experience of medieval history – Biondo was one who refused to seek classical equivalents for terms in medieval Latin – and in part from the vocabulary of Latin Christianity. A Christian humanist who saw the language of Peter as fulfilling the language of Cicero had problems before him which the rediscovery of ancient texts must intensify.

## (IV)

Biondo does not seem to enter on these matters. After recording his grief and shame over the disgraceful abdication of Romulus Augustulus in 476 – *imperii Romanorum non magis inclinationem quam occasum* [not so much the decline of the Roman empire as its fall] – he consoles himself with the thought that many Italian cities which he enumerates, not all lying to the north of Rome, have risen to fame and prosperity since that event. In a passage forcibly reminiscent of Leonardo Bruni, he remarks that the imperial predominance of a single city debarred all others from enlarging themselves by either war or commerce, and that all wealth and talent migrated to Rome, to the exhaustion of municipal *virtus*. The *imminutio* of one city was necessary to the *incrementum* of the remainder; Venice, of which Biondo began a separate history, being the principal example.[41] This is urban, not barbarian, history; it does not matter whether the reviving cities were of civilised Etruscan or of barbaric Lombard origin, and we may suspect once again that the concept of barbarism mattered

---

[40] Hay, 1959, pp. 111–12, 118. Biondo also consulted Geoffrey of Monmouth, but shared Polydore Vergil's judgement that he told no truths at all.
[41] Biondo, 1559, pp. 30–1. See his *De origine Venetorum*.

in the history of kingdoms, laws and letters, more than in that of urban republics. The revival of the Italian cities is for Biondo, just as it was for Bruni, a prelude to the history of peninsular affairs in the century in which both historians lived: the dominant theme of Bruni's *Historiarum Florentini populi*, and that which Biondo had undertaken before deciding to enlarge it into the *Decades ab inclinatione imperii*. Since his perspective was curial and not civic, however, there were limits to his will to see the recovery of republican liberty as the chief consequence of the Decline and Fall, or its loss as explaining the former process. Biondo never quite knew whether the fall of the empire was a great tragedy to be narrated, or the starting-point of a new chronology.

Lombard rather than Gothic history, nevertheless, was a component in a narrative Biondo could not avoid recounting; one, however, derived from the discourse of the *translatio imperii* rather than the *declinatio*. Whatever may have been his perception of the papacy as an actor in the history of his own times, he was writing in its service and must recount its history, or rather its place in the compendium of histories he was putting together. There was, as we know well, an established historiography in which the papacy's breach with the eastern empire, the establishment of the Frankish empire, and the destruction of the Hohenstaufen empire were necessary moments. It was a problem for Biondo that much of the empire's history lay outside that of the papacy, and much of the history of Latin Europe outside that of the empire; but though the great debate *de translatione* was effectively over, and no longer provided the framework that had given the narrative of empire and papacy its significance, Biondo was not freed from the necessity of recounting it. There was another framework, supplied by great and appalling contemporary events, which can be seen acting on his perception of a history which took its departure from the empire of Constantinople. Biondo had been active at the Council of Florence in 1439;[42] he lived beyond the fall of Constantinople in 1453, to Pius II's attempt at a crusade a decade later.[43] In 1452 he addressed an oration to both the Emperor Frederick and Alfonso of Aragon and Naples, inciting both to the crusade and reminding them of their common Christian and barbarian origins;[44] and in August of the next year – Constantinople having fallen in May – he again urged Alfonso to a crusade, and supplied him with a history of events since 1204, including both the Latin empire of Constantinople and the Greek

---

[42] Hay, 1959, pp. 100–1; Nogara, 1927, pp. lxxxii–iii.
[43] He died in 1463, Pius II in 1464.     [44] Nogara, 1927, pp. 107–14.

recovery under the Palaeologi.[45] We could look back as far as his earlier letter of 1440, and enquire whether the *Decades* were constructed in order to interest the Aragonese king in the history of empire. There is an eastern dimension to the history Biondo recounts.

We must continue to allow, however, for his somewhat pedantic search for moments of decline from which to date a chronology or chronologies. The ninth book of his first decade begins with Pope Gregory the Great's letter to the usurper Phocas, on which Enlightened comment was to be censorious.[46] Biondo merely has Gregory reminding Phocas that whereas barbarian kings rule over slaves, Roman emperors are princes over free men.[47] In the last year of Phocas' reign occurs the massive invasion of the Persians under Chosroes, and this leads to the extraordinary triumphs and defeats of the emperor Heraclius (previously noted by Marsilius of Padua).

Eodemque in anno Africam, Aegyptum et perditas de Asia prouincias Romano recuperauit imperio, Arabia dumtaxat excepta, a cuius rebellione ingentia in orbe terrarum mala initium habuerunt. Macometus quidam, ut alii Arabs, ut alii volunt Persa, fuit nobili ortus parente deos gentium adorante, sed matrem Hebraicae gentis Ismaelitam: is ex duabus huiusmodi omnino sibi in uicem aduersantibus superstitionum sectis originem trahens, nulli earum omnino adhaesit, sed homo acerrimi callidissimique ingenii inter Christianos conuersatus perniciosissimum humano genere ex duarum huiusmodi gentium legibus conflauit incendium . . . Subsequenter de lege Hebraeorum quam magna ex parte Arabes sectabantur, Christianorumque traditionibus ita disputabat, ut unam eandemque esse utramque affirmaret, licet magnis utraque gens abduceretur erroribus: quos quidem errores ita ipse moderabatur, ut Hebraeos reprenderet Iesum Christum ex uirgine natum negantes, quod sui maiores futurum expectandumque predixerant aduenisse: Christianos uero redargueret leuitatis, quibus persuasum sit Iesum dei amicissimum et ex uirgine natum, opprobria et demum crucis mortem a Iudaeis perpeti uoluisse; et suam ipse praedicans legem, quam superuacaneum duximus narrare, futurum affirmabat, ut si eam acciperent custodirent Saraceni, et sibi diuino ad id nuncio obsequerentur, sese in libertatem asserant, et principatu regnoque in finitimos potiantur.[48]

[In a single year he won back to the Roman empire Africa, Egypt and the provinces of Asia that had been lost; but with the exception of Arabia, whose rebellion was the beginning of gigantic evils for all the world. A certain Mahomet, whom some hold for an Arab and others for a Persian, was of a noble family worshipping the heathen gods, but had an Ishmaelite mother of Hebrew stock. Drawing his origin from these utterly opposed superstitions, he adhered

---

[45] Nogara, 1927, pp. 31–51.    [46] *DF*, v, ch. 46; Womersley, 1994, II, p. 903.
[47] Biondo, 1559, p. 117.    [48] Biondo, 1559, pp. 122–3.

to neither; but being a man of the keenest and most cunning wit, and acquainted with the Christians, he lit from both a fire most pernicious to the human race . . . At a later time he so disputed against the Jewish law, widely followed among the Arabs, and against the Christian traditions, that he affirmed them to be one and the same, though each people had fallen into several errors. These he so represented that he could rebuke the Hebrews for denying Jesus Christ was born of a virgin, though their own ancestors had taught that one such would come and must be awaited; while he accused the Christians of absurdity, in believing that Jesus, being beloved of God and born of a virgin, would have willingly suffered disgrace and death on a cross at the hands of the Jews. Preaching his own law which we have judged it superfluous to describe, he declared it a certainty that if the Saracens would adopt and maintain it, and follow him as their heavenly messenger, they should win their own liberty, and a rule and kingdom over their neighbours.]

This is a clear account of the Prophet as no demon but a human innovator, a religious syncretist from a marginal culture; but Biondo does not consider his teachings as the chief cause of the Arab victories over the Greeks and Persians. He reverts to the tale of Heraclius' fall into heresy and incest, and says that in spite of his triumphs he was the first emperor under whom the loss of provinces in Asia, already begun, proved irreversible.[49] Of a somewhat later date Biondo says

> Erat tunc quinquagesimus annus inclinationis Romanarum imperii orientalis, quam ostendimus anno Focae imperii extremo inchoasse. Saracenique per id tempus intantum hauserant opes, ut post subactas et quiete possessas quae Romanorum fuerant prouincias Asiae, Europam inuadere praesumerent.[50]

[It was now the fiftieth year of the decline of the eastern Roman empire, which we have shown to have begun in the last year of the reign of Phocas. During that time the Saracens had extended their powers so far that they had subdued and securely possessed what had been the Roman provinces of Asia and could now aspire to the invasion of Europe.]

And a little later still:

> Multa fuerant in Gallia, Hispanis, Anglia, Germania, et aliis Romanorum quondam prouinciis proximo gesta tempore, quibus libros implere, et res cum uarietate gratas, tum etiam magnas narrare potuimus: sed illae omnes prouinciae continuata diu possessione sui iuris factae erant: nihil autem a principio huius operis quaesitum magis quam Romanorum imperii inclinationem ostendere, quam nuper duplicem nacti sumus. Siquidem annos nunc septuagintaquinque supra ducentos Romanorum occidentale, et septuaginta

---

[49] Biondo, 1559, p. 126.
[50] Biondo, 1559, p. 127. 'Hauserant opes' should mean 'drained their resources', but the sense seems to demand the translation given here.

sex a Focae imperii inclinatione ostendere temporibus, orientale inclinat imperium.[51]

[Many things were done about this time in Gaul, the Spains, England, Germany, and other sometime provinces of the Romans, with which we could have filled books and recounted matters as interesting for their variety as they were great; but all these provinces had been made autonomous by long possession of their own laws and this book from the beginning has had no other purpose than to display the decline of the Roman empire, which we have now found to be a twofold story. The eastern empire was therefore in decline two hundred and seventy-five years after that of the western, and seventy-six after the reign of Phocas.]

If (following Biondo) we take 412 as the initial year of the western decline, we are in the year 687, and the eastern decline is to be dated from 611. Tiresome as we may find these calculations, Biondo is telling us something important to Gibbon when he discovered it as a schoolboy:[52] that the history of the empire of Constantinople is distinct from that of the provinces centred upon Rome, and does not fit well into the categories used to organise the latter. He is telling us something further, which does credit to his honesty: there are at least three histories before him, and he is competent to relate only one. There is the history of Byzantine empire, consisting after the Arab conquests of provinces in Asia Minor and wars with the Avars and Bulgars to retain those in the original Europe. There is the history of the far western kingdoms and of Germany as distinct from that of the empire; and there is the only history with which Biondo is equipped to deal, the history of Italy, whose past is that of the struggle between empire and papacy, and which is being continued now the latter is over. In addressing himself to Alfonso king of Naples, however, Biondo brings into focus an Italy which is not the *regnum italicum* in which the cities flourish, and whose history has in the past been that of eastern empire and papal scrutiny.

The last book of the first *Decade* is devoted to the overthrow of east Roman power in Italy, where it has been established since the days of Belisarius and Narses, and the subsequent exposure to Lombard aggression which leads the popes to turn to the Frankish kingdom taking shape in Gaul. This had been a central episode in the historiography of the *translatio imperii* from Greeks to Franks, and was to be as crucial to Giannone's *Istoria civile del regno di Napoli* and to Gibbon's 'triumph of barbarism and religion'. Biondo narrates it in terms that make the

[51] Biondo, 1559, p. 133. The last sentence is recalcitrant, and translated in summary.
[52] *EEG*, pp. 28–42.

emperor Leo, known as 'the Isaurian', unmistakably the villain and the campaign against images the motive that leads him to the loss of Italy. *Maiora in dies exaggerans scelera* [deepening his crimes with every day that passed], he enjoins the pope *ut . . . sanctorum imagines ubique in Italia, sicut ipse in suo fecerat Orientali imperio, aboleri, deponi, incendique curaret* [to see to it that the images of the saints should everywhere in Italy, as had already been done in his eastern empire, be forbidden, torn down and cast into the flames]. The Pope commands that *per uniuersum orbem Christianum* this impious command be not obeyed;

> tantamque autoritatem tunc habuerunt Romani pontificis decreta, ut Rauennates primi exinde Veneti populi atque milites, apertam in imperatorem exarchumque rebellionem prae se tulerint, impulerintque pontificem et caeteros Italiae populos, ut abrogata Constantinopolitano imperii maiestate, alter ex Italia Romaue imperator deligeretur. Eoque processit ipsa rebellio, ut depositis exarchi magistratibus singulae ei ciuitates, singula oppida tunc primum postquam Romanum inclinauit imperium, proprios magistratus quos appellarunt duces, sibi creare et praeficere inchoauerint.[53]

[and such authority then belonged to the decrees of the Roman pontiff that the townsmen and men at arms, first of Ravenna and then of Venice, took upon themselves an open rebellion against the emperor and his exarch, and urged the Pope and the other peoples of Italy to do away with the sovereignty of the empire at Constantinople and seek another emperor from Italy or Rome. And this rebellion reached such a height that the officers of the exarch were deposed, and each and every city and township, for the first time since the Roman empire began to decline, began themselves to choose and instal magistrates who were called *duces*.[54]]

The Pope is carefully excused from enjoining or even legitimising this rebellion; he continues to obey the emperor even to the point where he is required to install another; but there is a clear proto-Guelfic association between his spiritual authority and the rebirth of civic freedom and autonomy. The narrative continues through the papacy's delicate negotiations between the emperor, the rebels and the Lombards, to the successive steps towards an alliance with the Franks. As these proceed towards the climax of the year 800 (recounted in the opening books of the second *Decade*), when Charlemagne is acclaimed emperor by the pope and the people of Rome, and crowned by the former, Biondo does not seem to be saying more than that Pope Leo legitimised the event; but

---

53 Biondo, 1559, p. 144.
54 The Latin term retained; neither 'dukes' nor 'dogi' seems appropriate.

there is no need by the 1440s to rehearse the momentous history of dispute *de translatione imperii*. What is more to be noticed is the need to retain a Byzantine presence in the story, and this is surely to be explained by curial dismay at events in the years preceding the fall of Constantinople. It is interesting to consult the epitome of the *Decades* prepared by, or for, Pope Pius. At the outset of the account of Charlemagne's reign we read:

> Per hoc tempus Turci Asiam inuaserunt: Halanos primo, post Colchos et Armenios: inde Asiae minoris populos: ad extremum Persas Saracenos. Fueruntque Turci Scythae, ex his quos Alexandrum Macedonum inter Hyperboreos montes ferreis clausisse repagulis beatus Hieronymus affirmat. Conuenit autem inter Saracenos et Turcos, ut restituto Persarum regni nomine, quod Saraceni Focae et Eraclii temporibus in suum confuderant, Turci per se appellarentur.[55]

> [About this time the Turks invaded Asia: first the Alani, then the Colchians and Armenians; thence the peoples of Asia Minor; finally the Persians and Saracens. These Turks were Scythians, of those whom the blessed Jerome affirms that Alexander of Macedon had enclosed within the Hyperborean mountains by means of an iron barrier. It was agreed between the Turks and Saracens that the name of the Persian kingdom be restored, which in the days of Phocas and Heraclius the Saracens had confounded with their own, and that they should take the name of Turks.[56]]

This reads like a highly medieval attempt to telescope Abbasid history with Seljuk and even Ottoman, but informs us of a papal–humanist anxiety to keep alive an eastern perspective on Frankish–Latin history. Biondo and his epitomiser insist that the iconoclasm issue continued to figure in the negotiations between Charlemagne and the Empress Irene,[57] and it cannot have escaped Aragonese and Neapolitan attention that

> Inter Carolum et Hirenem facta est imperii diuisio. Italiae partem quae ad dexteram Neapoli, ad sinistram Manfredonia incipiens, supero inferoque mari clauditur, ac Sicilia, Constantinopolitana tenuit imperatrix. Beneuentanus autem gentis Longobardae dux, etsi graeco magis fauebat, neutri tamen imperatorem subditus erat. Pariter altera in Italiae parte Veneti, etsi graeco magis consentiebant quam romano, non tamen in illius omnimodo potestate erant. Carolus occidentale imperium instaurabat, et Hirenes orientale.[58]

> [A division of empire was arranged between Charles and Irene. The empress of Constantinople retained that part of Italy which with Naples on its right and Manfredonia on its left is enclosed by the upper and lower seas, together with Sicily. Likewise the duke of Benevento, a Lombard by race, though he leaned

---

[55] Pius II, 1533, p. 25.   [56] Trans. JGAP.
[57] Pius II, 1533, pp. 23b–27b.   [58] Pius II, 1533, p. 28.

towards the Greek, was subject to neither emperor. In the same way in another part of Italy, the Venetians, though they had more in common with the Greek than the Roman, were not wholly within the jurisdiction of the former. Charles upheld the empire of the west, Irene of the east.]

It might miss the point to ask whether *inclinatio* is over or entering a new phase. To emphasise that much of Italy had not been included in the Carolingian empire was to the advantage of a papacy remembering the Hohenstaufen threat, and the king of Aragon might be glad to hear that his Italian dominions had once been Greek and no part of a Frankish empire. He might know, however, that many papal claims over Naples dated from treaties with the Norman conquerors; alternatively, the memory of their exploits before and after the first crusade might incite him to war against the increasingly threatening Ottomans.[59] Biondo's last word may be that the amicable partition between Charles and Irene did not take effect.

Consideranti mihi nunc orbis olim Romanis subiecti statum, nulla uidetur inclinanti pridem imperio funditus euertendo causa efficacior fuisse, quam inchoata nuper Constantinopolitani cum Romano principe dissensio. Si namque Nicephorus Graecus ita in Asiam et Africam mentem cogitationesque intendisset, sicut Carolus Magnus domandis uel imperio uel fidei Christianae rebellibus Europeae populis incuberat, facile potuit instaurari Romanae rei dignitas quam uterque imperator titulo praeferebat.[60]

[When I consider the present state of the world formerly ruled by the Romans, I see no cause why the empire, long in decline, was altogether overturned, more efficacious than the distance which now began to grow between the Constantinopolitan ruler and the Roman. For if Nicephorus the Greek had turned his thoughts and plans upon Asia and Africa, in the same degree as Charles the Great had resolved upon the subjection of the rebellious peoples of Europe to the empire and the Christian faith, it would have been easy to restore the greatness of the Roman state, proclaimed in the title of each emperor.]

But this was not to be; Charlemagne's empire was beset by Northmen, Nicephorus' by Saracens (though a better antithesis might have been between the one's dealings with the Saxons and the other's with the Bulgarians), and *dissensio* seems to mean 'distraction' rather than 'disagreement'. Biondo at the Council of Florence would have heard all he needed to know about the long history of antagonisms between the Greek and Latin civilisations, and there is reason to suppose that, if one of the endpoints towards which the *Decades* look was the politics of

[59] King Alfonso died in 1458, the year of Pope Pius' election.    [60] Biondo, 1559, p. 166.

*quattrocento* Italy, another was the death of the eastern empire and the failure of the last crusades; this would account for the prominence of crusades in Biondo's later narrative.[61]

(v)

Flavio Biondo's was not a historical intelligence of the first order, and he lived at a time when it was far from clear what a history of post-Roman Europe should take as its subject-matter, or from what sources and with what structure it should be put together. But he was aware of his limitations, both of capacity and opportunity, and comments on them in ways that help us to see what he could and could not do. A full treatment of his work, as of Bruni's, would focus on the history of fifteenth-century Italy, which forms so large a part of both histories that *declinatio* and *inclinatio* are present only as a prelude; but we are in search of their roles in the slow formation of Decline and Fall as it presented itself to Gibbon. Biondo may be thought of as the archaeopteryx who comes after the dinosaurs; the mutation of *translatio* into *declinatio* has begun but is not complete. He is aware of Bruni's thesis that the narrative should focus on the decline, rebirth and problematic nature of urban civic liberty; it is one thread guiding him towards the history of northern Italy; but he is aware that this is only one history among many, and declines to adopt the republican explanation of the failure of empire. Indeed, he declines any explanation; he falls back on *inclinatio* as a moment from which its own chronology can be traced. He joins Bruni in a detailed narrative of the barbarian invasions from the Goths onward, but admits his inability to develop this into a history of the western kingdoms not included in the re-vived empire. Since the medieval struggle between papacy and empire – perhaps also that between the papacy and the Roman people – is at an end, there is no need of a history of *translatio imperii*; and this is not the place to enquire whether Biondo perceived any universal or governing themes in the history of contemporary Italy.

If by 'Decline and Fall' we mean a prelude to 'the triumph of barbarism and religion', we must see it as a strictly western concept: the starting point of a history of post-Roman Europe, in which Latin culture is re-created among barbarian peoples for whom the institutions of the Christian church enjoy exceptional dominance. Because it is a long way from Alaric to Charlemagne, the problem with a 'civic humanist' reading

---

[61] Hay, 1959, pp. 106–7.

of history is that of getting from the decline of *libertas* and *virtus* to the re-creation of empire by papacy; and we are beginning to see that this interval was filled, significantly if only in part, by episodes narrated by the historians of the *translatio*. In these the crucial sequence consisted of the reconquest of Italy by Justinian; the rejection of Byzantine authority by the papacy's opposition to iconoclasm; and the reason of state which led it to appeal to the Franks against the Lombards. In Biondo's day, it is clear, this story could no longer be set in that of the spiritual warfare between the Two Cities; but there remained a clear understanding that one of its themes, throughout the eighth century, had been the breach between the western church and the eastern church and empire. Earlier writers – Otto and Marsilius – had realised that the loss of Syria, Africa and Spain to Arabic Islam must be included in this narrative; but Biondo's need to fix a moment and trace a chronology of eastern *inclinatio*, as a process distinct from western, is clearly affected by the events taking place as he writes, conducive to the fall of Constantinople in 1453. Though he is less able even than Gibbon to write the history of both Declines as a single narrative, he is living at the moment where Gibbon chose to stop, and an end of one universal history is taking place before his eyes. When his attention is not fixed on the politics of an Italy in which the papacy is one actor among others, he turns towards the kingdom of Naples and the Ottoman conquests beyond it.

He does not organise his history around it, or around any guiding theme at all. It may well be that the history of post-Roman Latin Europe must be organised around its interior relationships, not those with an eastern world become strange to it; and we need not fall back on the fashionable tactic of denouncing any coherent history because it excludes some other. With Bruni and Biondo we have reached an experiment in narrating western history in terms of the decline and rebirth of civic liberty, and we have to trace how this generated a concept of Decline and Fall which was transmitted, in interaction with the historiography of the western monarchies, to become that which figures as part of 'the Enlightened narrative'. The scene is now transported back to Florence.

CHAPTER 10

# Niccolo Machiavelli and the imperial republic

## (I)

We now possess a series of layered concepts – deposited as it were by history in a sequence of surviving texts – which may be said to constitute a notion of 'the decline and fall of the Roman empire'. If we arrange them in historical sequences, these nearly anticipate the process they come to describe, beginning with a Sallustian (it could also be a Polybian) moment at which the *imperium* won by *libertas* is seen subverting the *virtus* on which the *libertas* depends. This account was preserved through the medieval centuries by the successors of Orosius and Augustine, for whom it signified that Roman *virtus* was no more than a worship of glory, doomed to share the fate of the *civitas terrena*. In the thirteenth century and after, however, this *virtus* was enlarged into a much fuller code of political and social living, and in the fifteenth we have seen it restored to something like its original meaning; the Caesars are denounced for destroying the citizen elites among whom *libertas* and *imperium* were possible, and so depriving Rome of the *virtus* which defended *imperium* against the barbarians.

Orosius and Augustine were not much interested in what we are terming Gibbon's 'first decline and fall', the Tacitean narrative of how the principate set up by Augustus failed to keep control of its succession problem and its armies; this was one reason why Julius rather than Augustus Caesar came to be imprecisely considered the first *princeps et imperator* who had destroyed the republic. Nor did they pay close attention to the larger narrative of civil war from the Gracchi to the victory of Actium, recounted by Plutarch, Appian and others. They looked on the more nefarious of the emperors as persecutors of the martyrs rather than tyrants over the free; this because they had begun to present the empire (though not the emperors) as the precondition for the incarnation of Christ and the growth of the church. The persecutions ended

203

with the conversion of Constantine; but it was possible for Christians to view his removal to a new capital in the east, and his supposed donation of imperial authority to the bishops of Rome, as preconditions for the loss of the Latin-speaking provinces to successive waves of barbarians. Those invasions, however, though they provided the context in which Orosius and Augustine wrote, were not of central importance in the construction of the narrative of *translatio imperii*, focussed rather on the process by which the heirs of St Peter at Rome had moved away from the eastern emperors and the churches that looked to other apostles. This history tended to emphasise a series of episodes beginning with the loss of most eastern provinces to Islam, and proceeding through the papal rejection of the authority of the iconoclast emperors, to the appeal from Lombard power to Frankish and the *translatio* of empire from the Greeks to the Franks. From that point could begin the long history of the contestation of authority between the emperors, the popes and the people of Rome, which was seen as encapsulating the cosmic history of the Two Cities and the Four Empires, so that universal history took place in the Latin west. Eurocentrism began as an exclusive concern with Latinity, and though Flavio Biondo knew that there were two histories of decline, one of which was ending before his eyes in 1453, the eastern *inclinatio* was necessary but marginal to the history he intended to write. Decline and Fall, we may say, had been absorbed by *translatio imperii*, with the result that Gibbon's 'triumph of barbarism' was still far from the equal partner of the 'triumph of religion', and the latter reflected the division of Christian history into two narratives which could not be told as one.

By the time Biondo wrote, however, the great debate over the *translatio* was at a standstill, with the exhaustion of the empire and temporarily of the papacy, and the advent of kingdoms and republics asserting imperial authority over themselves. The historians and political reasoners we choose to call 'civic humanists' were Italians, servants and citizens of independent republics, and precisely because their vision was limited to Italy were obliged to construct a new vision of post-Roman history. They telescoped this narrative to the point where they did not pay close attention to the history of the Julio-Claudians or the emperors between Nero and Constantine or even Theodosius, but proceeded at high speed to the barbarian invasions located in the fifth century. Of these they gave accounts so detailed that barbarism seems at the point of becoming a central force acting in history; they had their own reasons for emphasising the collapse of western empire, including the importance they attached to the ensuing collapse of Latin literature into a 'barbarism' from which they alone had rescued it. But they were not yet at the point where they could give barbarism a central role in the history of church, empire, the western kingdoms or their own Italian cities. It was of these last that Leonardo Bruni provided a new history of the greatest originality and importance in the history of historiography we are tracing. He proposed that the empire of one city, Rome, had stifled the liberty and virtue of many others, and that a major consequence of the Decline and Fall had been the re-emergence of Italian cities to the exercise of sovereignty over themselves; a process to which the victory of the thirteenth-century papacy over the Hohenstaufen had been necessary. Bruni did not present a general thesis regarding the relations, since Avignon and the Schism, between the diminished papacy and the cities liberated by its victory. The importance of his work in the history of historiography lies elsewhere. He had highlighted the tension between *libertas* and *imperium*, latent in Roman history since authors began to write it, by asking whether universal empire, the achievement of a single city, had not been fatal to liberty in that city and many others; whether an Etruscan society of cities were not preferable to a Roman empire of one; and whether the recovery of liberty, after both that empire and the conflict between the church and its successor, were not a history of the competition for power and commerce between many cities in upper Italy. These questions arose because, not in spite, of Bruni's awareness of the values of civic liberty, but the formula of *libertas et imperium* obliged him to regard those values as self-problematising. Humans needed liberty; but could liberty exist without destroying the world in which it was possible? It was the Augustinian question, re-posed without the *civitas Dei*, the church militant, or the imperial papacy, being present as immediate possibilities. As for 'civic humanism', we do not understand the thought-patterns designated by that term unless we understand that they regularly presented as a problem what they might have presented as an ideal.[1]

(11)

Between 1434, when Cosimo detto il Vecchio de' Medici returned from exile to establish his family in a kind of principate over the city of Florence, and 1537, when Cosimo di Giovanni delle Bande Nere completed its transformation into a grand duchy within the orbit of the Spanish

---

[1] A point recurrently made in Pocock, 1975.

monarchy, the affairs of both Florence and Italy may be studied though the eyes of a sequence of Florentine writers culminating in Machiavelli and Guicciardini. The remarkable quality of Florentine political analysis during this century may be attributed to many causes; one which concerns us here is the circumstance that the rule of the successive Medici, down to 1492 and even afterwards, differed in character from a pattern common among the *signori* and *principi* who had obtained rule over other cities. The Medici were neither nobles nor military men, but merchant bankers; they ruled not as lords or adventurers, but as leading citizens, *principes* in the Augustan sense, who held republican magistracies but monopolised and manipulated them through their friendships and connexions. This did not prevent their being perceived as princes or behaving like them; in an earlier volume we saw how Voltaire could equate Lorenzo de' Medici with Pericles and Augustus as patrons of the state and the arts;[2] but it meant that there was, until the coming of the *granducato*, a perpetual tension between their princely and their republican roles, which deprived them of complete legitimacy. Their enemies accused them of tyranny, but this was often the tyranny of an Augustus or a Tiberius, the product of an ambiguity inherent in their public position. We look for a revived analysis of the Julio-Claudian principate, as a means to the analysis of the principate of the Medici; but on the whole, the rediscovered texts of Tacitus made their impact during and after the transformation of Medicean rule into *granducato*.

There was a distance between Roman and Florentine realities, which sharpened and intensified the understanding of both. Machiavelli's *principe nuovo* is not a gloomily suspicious Tacitean psychopath and tyrant, but neither is he a Medici ruling as Medici normally did. He is a usurper, a daring adventurer and innovator, illustrating that one among a number of possible roles which Machiavelli desired to exhibit to the Medici brothers restored to power in 1513; that author's creative imagination enlarged him into a blend of *condottiere* and legislator, to find whom in the actual history of Europe we must await the coming of Napoleon Bonaparte. But if the Medici were more like Augustan *principes* than Machiavellian *principi* (*nuovi* or *naturali*), they differed altogether from the Roman model in that they were never *imperatores*. Their power did not rest on the massive armies of a republic, perverted by empire into an instrument of despotism in the hands of competing generals; and here we encounter a further radical distinction between Roman and Italian

---

[2] *NCG*, p. 85.

history, with which *quattrocento* and *cinquecento* historians came to be deeply concerned. The four or five competing states of the *cose d'Italia* were none of them empires, and none had any prospect of absorbing the others; they did not command armies like those of the late republic and the principate, or like those (unstable as these often were) of the great territorial monarchies which at the end of the Medicean century would conquer and absorb nearly all of them. Their military power – such as it was, Machiavelli scornfully interjected – rested upon hired mercenaries, and a common cause of republican failure was held to be the inability of magistrates to bridle the power of those who hired them. Leonardo Bruni admitted as much when he conceded that Florence was no longer defended by a militia of citizens, and had consequently become an oligarchy directed by the paymasters of mercenaries.[3] Machiavelli was to enlarge this theme till he returned to the image of Rome as a republic whose armies had made an empire of the world and had immediately ceased to be its armies; the root cause of Decline and Fall. We must remember, however, that this was an invention, the work of the historical imagination. There was no republic in Machiavelli's world capable of attaining continental empire and being corrupted by it, and was to be none until about the year 1800, when Napoleon's Consulate and Empire co-existed with but did not confront Thomas Jefferson's 'empire of liberty'. The Italian mind studied Rome and the Decline because they were necessary to its understanding of itself, at a distance it was necessary to bridge.

The Florentines, then, studied Rome because they knew that Rome and Florence were unlike one another. It was an exercise in comparative history; a model of the one served as benchmark for the understanding of the other. In the midst of this exercise, certainly, arose the problems of mimesis and *imitatio*, and Guicciardini had Machiavelli in mind when he observed that one could not use the actions of the past as *exempla* unless one were very sure that the circumstances in past and present were identical, as was hardly ever the case.[4] But Machiavelli, of all people, cannot reasonably be accused of not knowing this; Guicciardini probably meant that Machiavelli still hoped for a revival of Florence's civic and military *virtù*, whereas he himself was convinced that the *città* was irretrievably *disarmata* and had more need of *prudenza* (and oligarchic government) than of the *virtù* of Machiavelli's *fantasia*. It was this that ensured his ending his days as a disenchanted, but nevertheless committed, supporter

3 Baron, 1966, pp. 427–8.     4 Pocock, 1975, pp. 268–9.

of the Medici as they converted their rule into the *granducato* – a role in which it is hard to imagine Machiavelli had he lived a few years longer – but it also led him to examine the government of republican Rome, and question the thesis that its civil and military institutions had been framed to support one another.[5] The move from *imitatio* to *eruditio* was inherent in the Florentine critical intellect.

(III)

Decline and Fall was predicated of an empire, but an empire unusual in having been founded by a republic. The literature of Decline and Fall therefore began – and had begun before the decline occurred – with an account of how the republic disintegrated under the burden of its own empire. Augustine and Orosius adopted the narrative of Sallust, and his text had been transmitted to authors of the twelfth and thirteenth centuries. When the text of Polybius reappeared and a Latin translation became available to Machiavelli, it was seen as predicting the fall of the republic and providing explanations of greater sophistication. If we go in search of what Machiavelli has to say concerning a decline and fall, it is at this point that we must begin; and here, as is well known, we find him laying down a model which declares that Rome from its foundation chose a course which must lead to empire and its disintegration, and that this choice must be accepted and even applauded. Machiavelli's declaration is part of his understanding of what a republic is and should be; added to Leonardo Bruni's setting of Roman history in an Etruscan context, it makes with finality the point that republics were seen as dynamic and mortal even by those who idealised them, and that the humanists we call 'civic' could exhibit as problematic even that which they presented as exemplary.

The model occurs in those early chapters of the *Discorsi sopra la prima deca di Tito Livio* where Machiavelli contrasts the republic that aims only at its own preservation with that which is organised for expansion. The question is considered after Machiavelli has given his version of the Polybian theory of mixed government at Rome, emphasising that the balance of the orders enabled Rome to triumph, conquer and expand, but that (as Polybius had foreseen) it proved mortal in the long run. He goes on to ask whether it is possible to design a republic – he is not writing history so much as providing a theory of foundation – in which

5  Pocock, 1975, pp. 239–40, 247–8.

there will be no strife between the nobles and the people, and concedes that in the end the latter

cominciorono poi col tempo a adorare quelli uomini che vedevano atti a battere la nobilità; donde nacque la potenza di Mario e la rovina di Roma.[6]

[were in time ready to idolize men whom they saw qualified to beat down the nobility. From this sprang the power of Marius and the ruin of Rome.][7]

Similarly

le controversie intra il Popolo ed il Senato . . . seguitate infino al tempo de' Gracchi . . . furono cagione della rovina del vivere libero.[8]

[the controversies between the people and the senate . . . continued until the time of the Gracchi . . . caused the ruin of free government.][9]

Machiavelli envisages a continuous history of the civil wars from the Gracchi to the victory of the warlords; he understands 'free government' as a relation between senate and people, and thinks it was destroyed by the hatred between the two, arising from their differing understandings of liberty. Nobilities see liberty as the power to rule, peoples as the freedom from being ruled by others. It is hard to harmonise these perceptions, and the secret of Roman government is that by arming the people, it empowered them to defend their liberties as they understood them, but converted a passive and negative understanding of liberty into something positive and dynamic by endowing the city with an armed force and *virtù* capable of defeating its enemies. Because the people were armed, there was constant strife between the orders; but over and above this there was a political and religious discipline – perhaps arising from the very tension between rival understandings of liberty – that ensured that the strife would be conducted within limits and would be suspended at the approach of an enemy.[10] It is known that this tensile liberty collapsed in the end, and there will be need of a study of the causes of this; but at this point in the *Discorsi*, Machiavelli is concerned with the contrast between Rome, the republic organised for expansion, and Sparta or Venice, republics organised to preserve themselves. Here the people will not be armed – since the Spartans were the most militarised citizenry on record, the reference must be to the Helots excluded from citizenship – and the republic's warriors will be few in number or, in the Venetian case, mercenaries outside the citizen body. Government will be in the

---

[6] *Discorsi*, 1, v; Raimondi, 1967, p. 139.    [7] Trans. Gilbert, 1965, 1, p. 205.
[8] *Discorsi*, 1, vi; Raimondi, 1967, p. 140.    [9] Gilbert, 1965, 1, p. 207.    [10] *Discorsi*, 1, iv.

hands of a few, in the Venetian case those who hire and pay the mercenaries; and these will be more interested in preserving their power over
a disarmed people than in expanding it by arming them. We have come
upon ground where allusion to Medicean rule in Florence is possible;
Bruni had said that their rule was oligarchic because there was no citizen
militia, Machiavelli had hoped that such a militia might be revived, and
Guicciardini preferred the rule of a prudent few over a disarmed city.
The Florentines had isolated a political and historical problem which
was to teach the captain of the Hampshire grenadiers something about
the history of the Roman empire.

Machiavelli proceeds to say that in principle the republic aiming no
higher than preservation must last longer than that aiming at expansion;
Sparta and Venice came to grief only when they attempted a territorial
empire for which they were not organised. Here there clearly lies a
deeper problem; Rome was organised for empire yet came to grief after
acquiring it, and the jealousy between senate and people is the only
cause of decline so far offered us. Machiavelli appears to postpone this
problem; he says merely that though the republic for preservation will be
the more stable and long-lived, the republic for expansion is nevertheless
to be preferred.[11] In these early chapters he argues that all republics live
in a dangerous world of hostile neighbours from whom there can be
no isolation, and that a strategy of defensive self-preservation may be
more dangerous than one of dynamic expansion. But he also says that
the latter choice is *la parte più onorevole*,[12] and we may if we wish read into
this a tacit admission that Augustine was right in holding that the pre-
Christian citizen preferred glory to length of days, and even to *buon governo*
and the pursuit of justice and felicity. However this may be, the republic
is now committed to empire, and we await Machiavelli's treatment of
the problem of *imperium et libertas*. What will he have to say about the
Sallustian, Appianic and Tacitean sequence, the civil and social wars
and the rule of the Caesars?

The fall of the republic, and the transition to rule by emperors, once
it was conceded that it had something to do with the expansion of empire, must be considered a 'first decline and fall', even earlier than the
emergence of the Tacitean *arcanum* to which we previously gave that title.
Machiavelli has so far explained it as resulting from hatred between senate and people, while affirming that a creative tension between the two
was a necessary precondition of empire. If we look for a further account

---

[11] *Discorsi*, I, v–vi.    [12] Raimondi, 1967, p. 143.

of this hatred and the disruption it caused, we must keep in mind that Machiavelli is not a historian, but is commenting on history in order to make a diversity of points, and that in commenting on the first ten books of Livy, he is concerned more with the republic's heroic and virtuous beginnings than with its corruption and fall. Discussion of the latter therefore occurs within specific contexts to which it may be crucial or incidental, notably in the course of considering the differences between moments when the people of a republic are 'virtuous' and those when they are 'corrupt'. It is important to Machiavelli to show what these terms mean, and in the course of one such discourse we read:

> Non dava il popolo romano il consolato e gli altri primi gradi della città, se non a quelli che lo domandavano. Questo ordine fu nel principio buono, perché e' non gli domandavano se no quelli cittadini che se ne giudicavano degni, ed averne la repulsa era ignominioso; sì che per esserne giudicati degni ciascuno operava bene. Diventò questo modo poi nella città corrotta perniziosissimo; perché non quelli che avevano più virtù ma quelli che avevano più potenza, domandavano i magistrati; e gl'impotenti, come che virtuosi, se ne astenevano di domandarli per paura. Vennesi a questo inconveniente non a un tratto, ma per i mezzi, come si cade in tutti gli altri inconvenienti: perché avendo i Romani domata l'Africa e l'Asia e ridotta quasi tutta la Grecia a sua ubbidienza, erano divenuti sicuri della libertà loro, né pareva loro avere più nimici che dovessono fare loro paura. Questa sicurtà e questa debolezza de' nimici fece che il popolo romano nel dare il consolato non riguardava più la virtù, ma la grazia; tirando a quel grado quelli che meglio sapevano intrattenere gli uomini, non quelli che sapevano meglio vincere i nimici: dipoi da quelli che avevano più grazia, ei discesono a darlo a quegli che avevano più potenza; talché i buoni per difetto di tale ordine ne rimasero al tutto esclusi.

The liberty to propose a law and the liberty to vote upon it were good while the citizens were good.

> Ma diventati i cittadini cattivi, diventò tale ordine pessimo: perché solo i potenti proponevono leggi, non per la comune libertà, ma per la potenza loro; e contro a quelle non poteva parlare alcuno per paura di quelli: talché il popolo veniva o ingannato o sforzato a diliberare la sua rovina.[13]

[The Roman people did not give the consulate and the other chief officers of the city to any except those who asked for them. This habit was in the beginning good, because only those citizens asked for them who judged themselves worthy, and to be refused was ignominious, so that in order to be judged worthy everybody conducted himself well. Later, in the corrupt city, this method became very harmful, because not those who had most ability but those who

---

[13] *Discorsi*, I, xviii; Raimondi, 1967, pp. 167–8.

had most power asked for the magistracies; and those without power, however worthy, abstained from asking for them through fear. This bad condition came about not all at once but gradually, as happens for all other objectionable things. Because, after the Romans had conquered Africa and Asia and brought almost all Greece under their rule, they felt sure of their freedom, and believed they had no more enemies who could cause them fear. This security and this weakness of their enemies caused the Roman people, in awarding the consulate, no longer to consider ability, but favour, putting in that office those who best knew how to please men, not those who knew best how to conquer enemies. Then from those who had most favour, they descended to giving it to those who had most power, so that the good, because of the weakness of such a procedure, were wholly excluded from office.

But when the citizens became wicked, such a basic custom became very bad, because only the powerful proposed laws, not for the common liberty but for their own power, and for fear of such men no one dared to speak against those laws. Thus the people were either deceived or forced into decreeing their own ruin.][4]

We are at a Sallustian or a Polybian moment, when conquest has made Rome a superpower with no apparent enemies; there had been those who thought Carthage should be allowed to survive in order to furnish Rome with a challenge. It is not quite clear, however, exactly how the citizens fall into corruption; is it simply through overconfidence, sloth and flattery? We might ask whether such words as *intrattenere* and *grazia* imply not merely the ability to please men, but the power to maintain them as clients and followers; there is a point at which favour gives place to power and may have given it birth. The republican lexicon, for three centuries to come, was to contain many words describing how the independence and self-reliance of citizens could slide into the dependence of some upon others. But was the extension of empire a precondition of power in this sense, or an actual cause and source of it? Possible answers occur, as is common with Machiavelli, in the contexts provided by particular discourses.

An explanation of the republic's decline which has not come before us for many chapters occurs in the context furnished by the ancient adage that the city should be rich and the citizens poor. We hear again that the Roman order collapsed when the people desired equality with the nobles; but the meaning of this is that the *lex agraria*, which ordained that conquered lands be distributed among the people, was so regularly perverted by the nobility in their greed for land that the former

[4] Gilbert, 1965, i, pp. 241–2.

were compelled to demand expropriation of what the latter had come to possess.

Andò questo omore di questa legge così travagliandosi un tempo, tanto che gli Romani cominciarono a condurre le loro armi nelle estreme parti di Italia o fuori di Italia; dopo al quale tempo parve che la cessassi. Il che nacque perché i campi che possedevano i nimici di Roma essendo discosti agli occhi della plebe, ed in luogo dove non gli era facile il cultivargli, veniva a essere meno desiderosa di quegli: e ancora Romani erano meno punitori de' loro nimici in simil modo, e quando pure spogliavano alcuna terra del suo contado, vi distribuivano colonie. Tanto che per tali cagiono questa legge stette come addormentata infino ai Gracchi; da quali essendo poi svegliata, rovinò al tutto la libertà romana: perché la trovò raddoppiata la potenza de' suoi avversari e si accese per questo tanto odio intra la plebe ed il senato, che si venne nelle armi ed al sangue, fuori d'ogni modo e costume civile. Talché, non potendo i publici magistrati rimediarvi, né sperando più alcuna delle fazioni in quegli, si ricorse ai rimedi privati, e ciascuna delle parti pensò di farsi uno capo che 1a difendesse. Prevenne in questo scandolo e disordine la plebe, e volse la sua riputazione a Mario, tanto che la lo fece quattro volte consule; ed in tanto continuò con pochi intervalli il suo consolato, che si potette per se stesso far consulo tre altre volte. Contro alla quale peste non avendo la nobilità alcuno rimedio, si volse a favorire Silla; e fatto quello capo della parte sua, vennero alle guerre civili, e dopo molto sangue e variare di fortuna rimase superiore la nobilità. Risuscitarono poi questi omori a tempo di Cesare e di Pompeio; perché, fattosi Cesare capo della parte di Mario, e Pompeio di quella di Silla, venendo alle mani, rimase superiore Cesare: il quale fu primo tiranno in Roma; talché mai fu poi libera quella città.

Tale adunque principio e fine ebbe la legge agraria.[5]

[The dissension over this law kept on giving trouble for a while, until the age when the Romans took their armies to the remote parts of Italy and outside Italy; after that time it apparently stopped. This happened because the land owned by enemies of Rome, being distant from the eyes of the multitude and in a place where they could not easily cultivate it, became less desirable; and also the Romans did not much penalize their enemies in that way; and if they did despoil any city of its land, they placed a colony there. Hence, for such reasons, this law lay as though asleep until the Gracchi appeared; when they waked it up, it wholly ruined Roman liberty, because by that time the power of its adversaries was redoubled; as a result, it stirred up so much hatred between the multitude and the Senate that it led to arms and bloodshed, contrary to every lawful habit and custom. Since the public magistracy could not remedy it, the factions, placing no more hope in them, had recourse to private remedies, and each of the parties decided to get a leader to defend it. The multitude acted early in this turmoil and disorder by turning its support to Marius, so that four times it made

[5] *Discorsi*, I, xxxvii; Raimondi, 1967, p. 193.

him consul, and he continued his consulate so long with slight intervals that he was able to make himself consul three times more. Having no remedy against this plague, the nobility backed Sulla, and making him the head of their party, entered the civil wars; after much bloodshed and variety of fortune, the nobility were victors. These feuds came to life again in the time of Caesar and Pompey, when Caesar made himself head of Marius' party, and Pompey of Sulla's. In the war that followed, the victor was Caesar, the first tyrant in Rome; as a result, that city was never again free.

Such were the beginning and the end, then, of the Agrarian Law.][16]

(IV)

Here is Machiavelli's version of what we have called 'the Gracchan explanation', and linked with the 'Tacitean narrative'. We have been given the kernel of the explanation of the civil wars and the turn towards monarchy as arising from the agrarian crisis confronted by the Gracchi. Machiavelli's account, however, is truncated in two ways, of neither of which is there reason to suppose him unaware. In the first place, he does not tell us that *latifundia perdidere Italiam*; there is no suggestion that the spread of great estates was creating a landless soldiery, and that after the Gracchi failed to check it the party chiefs became warlords in search of lands for their soldiers. It is not clear why Tiberius Gracchus acted as he did; we are told only that the greed of the nobles had been held in check and that the attempt to remove its causes was misguided; and the ambition of the people takes second place to the ferocity of the nobles' reaction. Machiavelli seems to deny that there was an agrarian crisis in the second century BC, and he does not tell us that it was essential to the public virtue of the legions that the soldiers should have lands distributed by the republic. To this extent he does not give us a history rooted in the balance of property; that was to come later.

In the second place, apart from the ominous remark that Caesar 'fu primo tiranno in Roma', he does not carry his narrative into the wars of the second triumvirate, the *bellum Actiacum*, the establishment of the principate, or the crisis of AD 70–71. The *Discorsi* lack a Tacitean dimension; they do not explore the nature of post-republican history, the problems of the principate, or the *arcanum* of continued military intervention. We do not know – though we may easily guess – what Machiavelli thought of Augustus or Tiberius, Galba or Vespasian. Chapter 19 of *Il Principe*, however – self-described as a *discorso*, which has raised the question whether

---

[16]  Gilbert, 1965, I, p. 273.

it might once have belonged to the larger work[7] – surprises us by taking a long stride beyond the Julio-Claudians, the Flavians and even the Antonines, to study the emperors from the death of Marcus Aurelius to that of Maximin. Machiavelli has passed beyond Tacitus – whom he certainly knew – to examine figures he can have read of only in Dio Cassius and the *Historia Augusta*: the emperors of the Severan period and the military anarchy before and after it, who are furthermore, and strikingly, the figures with whom Gibbon's narrative begins. His purpose is to consider why some good rulers came by violent ends and some more criminal reigned successfully, and this chapter is the setting for the classic account of the fox and the lion, united in the person of Septimius Severus. But there is a further setting and context, more historically specific for the very reason that the Tacitean period is its unstated prelude.

Ed è prima da notare, che dove negli altri principati si ha solo a contendere con l'ambizione de' grandi ed insolenza de' popoli, gli imperadori romani avevano una terza difficoltà, d'avere a sopportare la crudeltà ed avarizia de' soldati; la qual cosa era si difficile, che fu la cagione della rovina di molti, sendo difficile satisfare a' soldati ed a' popoli, perchè i popoli amavano la quiete, e per questo amavano i principi modesti; e i soldati amavano il principe d'animo militare, e che fussi insolente, crudele e rapace. Le quali cose volevano che egli esercitasse nei popoli, per potere avere duplicato stipendio, e sfogare la loro avarizia e crudelta; donde ne nacque che quelli imperatori che per natura o per arte non avevano una grande riputazione, tale che con quella tenessero l'una e l'attro in freno, sempre rovinavano; e il più di loro, massime quelli che come uomini nuovi venivano al principato, conosciuta la difficultà di questi duoi diversi umori, si volgevano a satisfare ai soldati, stimando poco l'ingiuriare il popolo . . . il che tornava loro nondimeno utile o no, secondo che quel principe si sapeva mantenere riputato con loro.[18]

[First I observe that while in other princedoms a ruler struggles only against the ambition of the rich and the arrogance of the people, the Roman emperors had a third difficulty: to deal with the cruelty and greed of the soldiers. This difficulty was so great that it caused the ruin of many emperors, since they could not satisfy both soldiers and people. The people loved quiet and therefore loved modest princes; the soldiers loved a prince of military spirit who was arrogant, cruel and grasping; these qualities they wished him to practise on the people so the troops could have double pay and give vent to their greed and cruelty. As a result of this condition, those emperors who did not have by nature or acquirement so great a reputation that through it they could hold both parties in check, always fell. Most of them, especially those who came to the throne as upstarts, recognizing the problem of these two opposing factions, attempted to

---

[7] Gilbert, 1965, I, p. 75, n. II.    [18] *Il Principe*, c. 19; Raimondi, 1967, pp. 103–4.

please the soldiers, without hesitating to damage the people . . . This resulted, nevertheless, to their advantage or not, according as such princes managed to keep up their reputation in the armies.][19]

This is a historical situation. The emperors are trapped between the armies and what is left of civil authority – why does Machiavelli write *popolo* when we should expect *senato*? – as a consequence of a process reaching back through the principate to the triumvirates and the wars between Marius and Sulla. There is a Tacitean and Gracchan history to be recounted, and Machiavelli is certainly not unaware of it. He does not recount it, because his concern with history is to extract generalisations and maxims governing the behaviour of republics and princes living in history, where the republic is perpetually expanding and the prince perpetually new. We may speculate that he is not much interested in the Tacitean concept of a new kind of history, taking place no longer in public but in the secret hearts and councils of princes; and the discovery that princes could be made by armies enlarged this history into a space less public than imperial. We may also ask how well he knew, or how closely he had studied, the history of the Julio-Claudians and their successors. He was certainly acquainted with both Tacitus' name and his text, but few of his *exempla* are drawn from the latter. In his *Arte della Guerra* there is mention of what the first *principes* did to the structure of the Roman army, but the language here suggests a rhetorical rather than a textual origin.

. . . Ottaviano prima, e poi Tiberio, pensando più alla potenza propria, che all' utile pubblico, cominciarono a disarmare il popolo Romano, per poterlo facilmente comandare, ed a tenere continualmente quelli medesimi eserciti alle frontiere dell' imperio. E perchè ancora non giudicarono bastassero a tenere in freno il popolo e Senato Romano, ordinarono un esercito chiamato pretoriano, il quale stava propinqua alle mura di Roma, ed era come una rocca addosso a quella città. E perchè allora ei cominciarono liberamente a permettere che gli uomini deputati in quegli eserciti usassero la milizia per loro arte, ne nacque subito l'insolenze di quelli, e diventarono formidabili al Senato e dannosi all'imperadore. Donde ne risultò che molti furono morti dall'insolenza loro, perchè davano e toglievano l'imperio a chi pareva loro; e talvolta occorse che in un medesimo tempo erano molti imperadori creati da varii eserciti. Dalle quali cose procede prima la divisione dell'imperio, ed in ultimo la rovina di quello.[20]

[ . . . Octavian first and then Tiberius, thinking more about their own power than about the public advantage, began to disarm the Roman people in order to command them more easily, and to keep those same armies continually

---

[19]  Gilbert, 1965, I, p. 71.     [20]  Omitted by Raimondi. See Anselmo and Varotti, 1992, I, p. 169.

on the frontiers of the Empire. And because they still did not judge that they would be enough to hold in check the Roman people and the Senate, they set up an army called Praetorian, which remained near the walls of Rome and was like a castle over that city. Because they then freely began to allow men chosen for those armies to practise soldiering as their profession, these men soon became arrogant, so that they were dangerous to the Senate and harmful to the Emperor. The result was that many emperors were killed through the arrogance of the soldiers, who gave the Empire to whom they chose, and took it away; sometimes it happened that at the same time there were many emperors established by various armies. From these things resulted, first, division of the Empire, and finally its ruin.][21]

This passage reads as a generalisation, based on no single text but on humanist reading and conflation of several, permitting the writer to scan history from the establishment of the principate to the recurrent military anarchies of the third century. Tacitus' *arcanum* is seen as inherent in the structure of empire and as occasioning its ultimate collapse; the last sentence quoted seems to envisage Diocletian's tetrarchy, Constantine's foundation of New Rome and the sons of Theodosius. Here we have a pattern of explanation governing the whole Decline and Fall and finding its end in its beginning; a pattern which Gibbon will certainly use, based on the conversion of the legionaries from citizens into professionals – *arte* meaning both skill and trade – and their regrouping into garrisons permanently stationed on the frontiers of empire and at Rome itself. The Caesars are both emperors concerned with the government of what Hume calls an 'enormous monarchy' – the sheer extent of empire is enough to transform the republic and its armed citizenry – and *principi nuovi* concerned with the domination of a former republic. The use of the very Italian word *rocca* to denote the camp of the praetorian guard is enough to recall the Fortezza da Basso – unbuilt in Machiavelli's time – which Florentines recognised as marking the end of their liberty.[22]

The contemporary resonance of the passage does not end here. The *Arte della Guerra* is written to maintain the inferiority of soldiers who have no *arte* other than *guerra* to those who fight to protect their position in citizenship and civil society. Of the latter the armed citizens of a republic are held to be the highest type; but the *Arte della Guerra* goes on to affirm that prudent kings will recruit their officers from the gentry and their soldiers from those who have farms and trades to absorb them when their service is done. Machiavelli is thinking here of the monarchical states of his time, most of which were not taking his advice but employing

[21] Gilbert, 1965, 1, p. 578.    [22] Hale, 1968.

mercenaries, short-service *condottieri*, very different from the legionaries of the empire in their lifelong camps. It is for this reason that chapter 19 of *Il Principe* goes on to distinguish between the post-Antonine emperors and the rulers of modern Europe.

> . . . e dico che i principi de'nostri tempi hanno meno di questa difficultà di soddisfare straordinariamente a' soldati nei governi loro, perchè non ostante che si abbia ad avere a quelli qualche considerazione, pure si risolve questo, per non avere alcuno di questi principi eserciti insieme, che siano inveterati con i governi ed amministrazioni delle provincie, come erano gli eserciti dell'impero romano; e però se allora era necessario soddisfare più a' soldati che a' popoli, era perchè i soldati potevano più che i popoli; ora è più necessario a tutti i principi, eccetto che al Turco ed al Soldano, satisfare a' popoli, che a' soldati, perchè i popoli possono più di quelli. Di che io ne eccettuo il Turco, tenendo sempre quello intorno a sè dodicimila fanti e quindicimila cavalli, dai quali dipende la sicurtà e la fortezza del suo regno, ed è necessario che, posposto ogni altro rispetto de' popoli, se li mantenga amici. Simile è il regno del Soldano, quale essendo tutto in mano dei soldati, conviene che ancora lui, senza rispetto dei popoli, se li mantenga amici.[23]

> [And I say that the princes of our times do not have this difficulty of conducting themselves in a way to give the soldiers unmeasured satisfaction; though they do have to give some thought to the soldiers, yet they can decide that matter quickly, since these modern princes do not have standing armies that have grown old along with the governments and administrations of their territories, as had the armies of the Roman empire. Therefore, if then a ruler was forced to please the soldiers rather than the people, because the soldiers were stronger than the people, now all princes, except the Turk and the Soldan, are forced to please the people rather than the soldiers, because the people are the stronger. From this I except the Turk, who always keeps around him twelve thousand infantry and fifteen thousand cavalry, on whom depend the security and strength of his kingdom; hence, setting aside all other considerations, that lord must maintain the friendship of these troops. Likewise, since the Soldan's realm is entirely in the soldiers' hands, he too must maintain their friendship without regard for the people.][24]

We are looking again at Machiavelli's power of historical generalisation, his ability to extend the Tacitean *arcanum* over the centuries of post-Roman history. Whatever he may have meant by *i popoli* and their power in the Europe of his time – theories of feudal and post-feudal property were to supply an answer – this passage is a reflection on the history of armies and their role in government. His contempt for the mercenaries of contemporary Italy (other than the Swiss) knew no bounds, but

[23] *Il Principe*, c. 19; Raimondi, 1967, pp. 106–7.    [24] Gilbert, 1965, 1, pp. 75–6.

he was not to know that for the next century and a half the monarchies of Europe were to wage war by means of mercenary armies, enlarged by an inflationary economy, which would inflict enormous damage and suffering on civil society. The mercenaries of 1560–1648, however, were an essentially anarchic force; they made civil government even more difficult but did not act within it, since as masterless men employed on short-term contracts they played no part in the administration of the state. The only army of the period that intervened to bring about an alteration of the government was the English of 1647–49, and their claim that they were not mercenaries but bearers of public authority obliged them to act as legislators and even revolutionaries, which they proved unable to do; it might be asserted that *il popolo* – meaning the nobles, gentlemen and freeholders – proved stronger than they were. The case may remind us how hard it was to fit Oliver Cromwell into the patterns of ancient history; it could be done only by representing him as a Marius and George Monk as a Sulla – roles which each would have instantly rejected. Once more we must turn to Napoleon Bonaparte if we are to find a Caesar *redux*.

The Roman armies had been part of the structure of empire; but armies, and consequently empire, had been unassimilable by either the republic or the principate, so long as the latter sought to maintain the legitimacy of republic as well as empire, *princeps* as well as *imperator*. There was a history to be written of how the *imperator* had become other than a *princeps* in the Julio-Claudian sense, but it was entangled with the history of how the empire had become a Christian ecumene in which the emperor figured in a very different role. This helped to dramatise the contemporary figure of the Muslim *imperator* (a commander of the faithful) in whose empire the Roman pattern of frontier armies and palace guards seemed to be repeated – the praetorian role being played by janissaries at Istanbul and Mamluks at Cairo[25] – unchallenged by the legitimacy of either a remembered republic or an actual church. The Roman and the 'oriental' images interestingly interact; but if on the one hand the Roman ruler's legitimacy (unlike that of the Turkish) is never free from challenge, so that he remains something of a *principe nuovo*, the princes of early modern Europe do not re-enact the history of the Roman empire. They do not maintain great frontier armies, which are part of their state yet which they cannot wholly control. Feudal and

---

[25] The 'Soldano' of the above passage is the ruler of Egypt, not annexed to the Ottoman empire till 1517.

mercenary forces are imperfectly included within their reason of state. This last term comes to form part of the history and the discourse of a state which can maintain 'standing armies' – it is interesting to see this term employed in translating Machiavelli – together with a legitimacy they do not directly challenge. Gibbon lived in the world of these states and their armies, yet saw them criticised by means of both a Livian and Machiavellian republicanism and a Tacitean pessimism regarding palace government and reason of state. Tacitism and reason of state go together in the history of an early modern Europe which Machiavelli did not live to see.

(IV)

What, in conclusion, were Machiavelli's perceptions of the decline and fall of the empire, and the subsequent history of Europe? The plural is used because he was not writing a history of these processes, or constructing either a narrative or a general theory that must rest on an explanation of them; what he has to say of them occurs in a plurality of rhetorical contexts, and need not exhibit unity or even consistency. We must – but equally we may – trawl through his major works in what seems to have been their order, in search of what he has to say on these subjects – the calibre of his mind rendering it unlikely that this will be trivial, and the tensions of his age unlikely that it will be conventional.

*Il Principe* is concerned with acquiring and governing new states, either usurped or annexed; the *Discorsi* with the early history and victories of the Roman republic. There are errors to be avoided, but though these may lead to disasters they may not amount to long-term causes of decline. In chapter 13 of *Il Principe*, however, there occurs the explicit statement:

> Pertanto colui che in uno principato non conosce i mali se non quando nascono, non è veramente savio; e questo è dato a pochi. E se si considerassi la prima cagione della ruina dello imperio romano, si troverrà essere suto solo cominciare a soldare Goti; perché da quello principio cominciorno a enervare le forze dello imperio romano; e tutta quella virtù che si levava da lui, si dava a loro.[26]

> [So a prince who does not recognize the ills in his state when they spring up is not truly wise; but this power is given to very few. On considering the chief cause for the fall of the Roman Empire, we find it was solely that she took to hiring Gothic mercenaries. After that beginning, the Empire's forces steadily failed, for she stripped away all her own vigour to give it to the Goths.][27]

---

[26] *Il Principe*, c. 13; Raimondi, 1967, p. 91.   [27] Gilbert, 1965, I, p. 54.

No reader of Machiavelli would be surprised to find him giving other causes for decline in other places, since he often makes such general statements in particular contexts. There are two such operating here: the difficulty for a single ruler of recognising and adjusting to changing circumstances, and the necessity of being defended by military forces that are one's own – in both which respects a republic is probably better placed than any prince. In these contexts, the Goths – here singled out from barbarians in general – appear as mercenaries (*soldati*) rather than invaders; they penetrate the empire rather than assault its frontiers, and they take over its *virtù* from within. A further context is that which we have already seen laid out in chapter 19: the dependence of the emperors on armies they have used to subvert the republic, but cannot adequately control since they are obliged to reside in Rome as *principes* instead of personally commanding them as *imperatores*. This is the point at which Machiavelli comes closest to the analysis of Tacitus, with whom repeated textual allusions show that he was acquainted. We have found that he carries the narrative of the emperors' insecurity through the Julio-Claudians and Flavians studied by Tacitus, and on through the Severi and the successive rulers depicted in the *Historia Augusta*; there is even a passage in which we hear for the first time of the five 'good' emperors from Nerva to Marcus Aurelius, an age of universal happiness contrasted with the Tacitean horrors that came before and after it.[28]

The Caesars are blamed for this, essentially because they ruled through armies subject to no public discipline. Machiavelli's narrative is still more Sallustian or Plutarchan than Tacitean, in that he has the sequence of Caesars begin from Julius rather than Augustus; what is Tacitean is the deepening of the analysis beyond Leonardo Bruni's simple statement that they destroyed *virtù* by destroying the senatorial elites. Machiavelli is concerned with the corruption of the armies, and presents the Goths, not as invading barbarians whom the armies have no longer the *virtù* to resist, but as the last stage in the conversion of the armies into mercenary forces under no public discipline or loyalty. This led to the division of the empire as well as to its ruin, and these are distinguishable concepts. Emperors at the head of armies set themselves up in diverse capitals, and even the foundation of Constantinople might be seen in this light; Machiavelli has very little to say about Constantine, but in his *Istorie Fiorentine* he remarks that emperors seated in the eastern capital sometimes left power in the western provinces to be exercised by those who possessed it, including

---

[28] *Discorsi*, I, x; Raimondi, 1967, p. 151; Gilbert, 1965, I, pp. 221–2.

both successful usurpers and those chosen by the inhabitants to protect them.[29] This introduces an account of Odovacar's deposition of Romulus Augustulus, a climactic moment in the scenario of Decline and Fall; Machiavelli deals with this process in a number of ways.

Barbarians cannot appear solely in the role of Gothic mercenaries; they invaded the empire as armed peoples on the move, with whom the armies of the republic or the emperors found it difficult and ultimately impossible to cope. There is a chapter in the *Discorsi* which distinguishes wars between civilised peoples, *che cercano di propagare lo imperio*, from wars occasioned by *Volkerwänderungen*,

quando uno popolo intero con tutte le sue famiglie si lieva d'uno luogo, necessitato o dalla fame o dalla guerra, e va a cercare nuova sede e nuova provincia: non per comandarla, come quegli di sopra, ma per possederla tutta particularmente e cacciarne o ammazzare gli abitatori antichi di quella. Questa guerra è crudelissima e paventosissima.[30]

[when a whole people, forced by hunger or war, departs from its home to hunt for a new dwelling and a new country, not merely to rule it, like those mentioned above, but to occupy all of it as individuals, and to drive away or kill its ancient inhabitants. This kind of war is very cruel and very frightful.][31]

Sallust is Machiavelli's source for the saying that war against most peoples was war over power, but war against the Gauls was war for existence. The chapter enumerates Rome's Gallic wars – the Gauls are always called *Franciosi* – and the war with the Teutones and Cimbri fought by Marius. Machiavelli does not ask, as a modern might, whether civilised armies are not more likely to fight wars of extermination than hordes of migrating barbarians,

perché si vide poi come la virtù romana mancò e che quelle armi perderono il loro antico valore, fu quello imperio destrutto da simili popoli: i quali furono Gotti, Vandali e simili, che occuparono tutto lo Imperio occidentale.

[because later, when Roman ability[32] failed and her armies lost their ancient courage, her empire was destroyed by such peoples – the Goths, the Vandals and the like – who conquered the entire Western Empire.][33]

For the first time we are meeting 'the barbarians' as a sociological category – peoples who are as they are because of the way they live – and they are to conquer and settle the western empire, not the eastern;

---

[29] Below, p. 228.     [30] *Discorsi*, II, viii; Raimondi, 1967, p. 249.     [31] Gilbert, 1965, I, p. 344.
[32] Gilbert translated *virtù* by such synonyms as he thought the context called for.
[33] Gilbert, 1965, I, p. 345.

the Arabs are an imperial, not a migratory people. The category requires a further extension.

Escono i popoli grossi, e sono usciti quasi tutti, de'paesi di Scizia: luoghi freddi e poveri, dove, per essere assai uomini ed il paese di qualità da non gli potere nutrire, sono forzati uscirne, avendo molte cose che gli cacciono e nessuna che gli ritenga. E se da cinquecento anni in qua non è occorso che alcuni di questi popoli abbiano inondato alcuno paese, è nato per più cagioni. La prima, la grande evacuazione che fece quel paese nella declinazione dello Imperio; donde uscirono più de trenta popoli. La seconda è che la Magna e l'Ungheria, donde ancora uscivano di queste genti, hanno ora il lora paese bonificato in modo che vi possono vivere agiatamente: talché non sono necessitati di mutare luogo. Dall'altra parte, sendo loro uomini bellicosissimi, sono come uno bastione a tenere che gli Sciti, i quali con loro confinano, non presumino di potere vincergli o passarli. E spesse volte occorrono movimenti grandissimi de' Tartari, che sono dipoi dagli Ungheri e da quelli di Polonia sostenuti; e spesso si gloriano che, se non fussono l'armi loro, la Italia e la Chiesa arebbe molte volte sentito il peso degli eserciti tartari. E questo voglio basti quanto ai prefati popoli.[34]

[Such peoples in great numbers – indeed almost all of them – have come from the Scythian lands, regions cold and poor. Since their numbers are great and the country is such that it cannot feed them, they are forced to go out, for many things drive them and nothing keeps them. If for five hundred years now none of these peoples has flooded any country, the causes are many. The first is the great outpouring from that country, at the decline of the empire; from it more than thirty peoples came out. The second cause is that Germany and Hungary, from which also these peoples come, have now improved their land to such an extent that they can live there easily; hence they are not forced to change their abode. On the other hand, since their men are very warlike, they are like a fortress to keep the Scythians, who live on their borders, from supposing that they can defeat them or pass through their country. Oftentimes there are great movements among the Tartars, which the Hungarians and the Poles repel. The latter often boast that without their weapons Italy and the Church would many times have felt the weight of the Tartar armies. This I think enough on the aforesaid peoples.][35]

Machiavelli has not much more to say on the culture of the nomad steppe than he might have learned from Herodotus, but he has worked it into the history of the Decline and Fall and of Europe afterwards. Like Gibbon after him – but without the presumption that nomad history has reached its end – he is asking whether Europe has anything more to fear from these invaders, and is finding reassurance in the eastward extension of agricultural and feudal civilisation. Hungary as he writes

---

[34] *Discorsi*, II, 8; Raimondi, 1967, p. 251.    [35] Gilbert, 1965, I, pp. 346–7.

is only a few years from Mohacs field, but the Ottoman Turks are an imperial and religious people. When he says it is five hundred years since the last nomad invasion, he seems to have the Magyars in mind to the exclusion of the Mongols; but it is Tartar raids that the Poles are keeping out. Attila is not going to reappear at the gates of Rome, but there is more than a hint that 'Italy and the Church' are not of themselves in good shape to cope with his successors. Gothic and Scythian invaders of the Roman empire have to be worked into a more complex pattern of European history, which has begun to take shape in this chapter of the *Discorsi*.

It is in the second book of the *Discorsi*, before the chapter on the barbarians occurs, that we find Machiavelli's most macrohistorical reflections on the rise and fall of great empires. In the course of an enquiry into the appropriateness of admiring and following ancient models, he is moved to the following.

[G]iudico il mondo sempre essere stato ad uno medesimo modo ed in quello essere stato tanto di buono quanto di cattivo; ma variare questo cattivo e questo buono di provincia in provincia: come si vede per quello si ha notizia di quegli regni antichi, che variavano dall'uno all'altro per la variazione de' costumi; ma il mondo restava quel medesimo. Solo vi era questa differenza, che dove quello aveva prima allogata la sua virtù in Assiria, la collocò in Media, dipoi in Persia, tanto che la ne venne in Italia ed a Roma; e se dopo lo imperio romano non è seguito imperio che sia durato, né dove il mondo abbia ritenuta la sua virtù insieme, si vede nondimeno essere sparsa in di molte nazioni dove si viveva virtuosamente: come era il regno de' Franchi, il regno de' Turchi, quel del Soldano; ed oggi i popoli della Magna, e prima quella setta Saracina, che fece tante gran cose ed occupò tanto mondo, poiché la distrusse lo Imperio romano orientale.' In tutte queste provincie adunque, poiché i Romani rovinono, ed in tutte queste sette è stata quella virtù, ed è ancora in alcuna parte di esse, che si disidera e che con vera laude si lauda.[36]

[I judge that the world has always gone on in the same way and that there has been as much good as bad, but that this bad and this good have varied from land to land, as anyone understands who knows about those ancient kingdoms which differed from one another because of the difference in their customs, but the world remained the same. There was only this difference, that whereas the world first placed excellence[37] in Assyria, she later put it in Media, then in Persia, and finally it came to Italy and Rome. If the Roman Empire was not succeeded by any empire that lasted and kept together the world's excellence, that excellence nevertheless was scattered among many nations where men lived excellently, such as the kingdom of the French, the kingdom of the Turks, and

---

[36] *Discorsi*, II, *proemio*; Raimondi, 1967, p. 232.    [37] *Virtù*.

that of the Soldan, and today the people of Germany, and earlier that Saracen tribe[38] that did such great things and took so much of the world after it destroyed the Eastern Roman Empire. In all these regions, then, since the Romans fell, and in all these peoples,[39] has existed, and in some part of them still exists, this high ability[40] that is longed for and praised with true praise.][41]

It is scarcely a prophetic or a Christian vision. The sequence of Danielic empires is no more than a series of devices for the corporate monopolisation of *virtù*, and it is possible that they fall through their success in achieving this aim. A few chapters later, after an account of natural cataclysms which only a few mountain dwellers survive,[42] we find:

cosi interviene in questo corpo misto della umana generazione, che, quando tutte le provincie sono ripiene di abitatori, in modo che non possono vivervi né possono andare altrove, per essere occupati e ripieni tutti i luoghi; e quando la astuzia e la malignità umana è venuta dove la può venire, conviene di necessità che il mondo si purghi per uno de' tre modi; acciò che gli uomini, sendo divenuti pochi e battuti, vivino più comodamente e diventino migliori. Era dunque, come di sopra è detto, già la Toscana potente, piena di religione e di virtù; aveva i suoi costumi e la sua lingua patria: il che tutto è suto spento dalla potenza romana. Talché, come si è detto, di lei ne rimane solo la memoria del nome.[43]

[the same process appears in this mixed body of the human race. When all the lands are full of inhabitants, so that men cannot live where they are and cannot go elsewhere, since all places are settled and filled full, and when human craft and malice have gone as far as they can go, of necessity the world is purged in one of three ways mentioned, so that by becoming few and humble, men can live more comfortably and grow better. Thus as I said above, Tuscany was once powerful, religious and vigorous, having her own customs and her own native language. All this achievement, as I have mentioned, was wiped out by the Roman power, so that there remains only a record of the name.[44]

Machiavelli did not believe that only a few mountaineers survived the fall of the empire, any more than Gibbon believed that there survived only the bedrock of stubbornly improving peasants imagined in the *General Reflections*.[45] The analogy is not altogether clear; was Tuscany once an overcrowded empire purged by the Roman conquest, or is her former prosperity to be restored by the purgation of Rome? The latter seems the more likely, in view of the number of times we are told that Roman empire was achieved over peoples and princes who enjoyed freedom and fought bitterly to retain it;[46] the idea that Roman *virtù* cannibalised that

---

[38] *Setta*; a common meaning is 'sect'.   [39] *Sette*.   [40] *Virtù*.   [41] Gilbert, 1965, I, p. 322.
[42] Gilbert, 1965, I, pp. 340–1.   [43] *Discorsi*, II, 8; Raimondi, 1967, pp. 346–7.
[44] Gilbert, 1965, I, p. 341.   [45] Womersley, 1994, II, p. 516.   [46] *Discorsi*, II, ii.

of the world is as visible as it was in Bruni. Machiavelli reviews three ways of combining the *virtù* of many in a single system: a league of equally free partners, the universal empire of one sovereign power, and an alliance recognising the hegemony of a preponderant leader.[47] He prefers the last, and suggests that Rome adopted it; but as he well knows, there is strong historical evidence that the policy became perverted if it was ever undertaken. The problem of *libertas et imperium* knows no final resolution. The subjection of many cities to one cannot last – the example here is the empire of Athens; the league of free cities, Etruscan or Swiss, must be limited in size and fails if obliged to grow beyond it.[48] The association of cities under Roman hegemony combined liberty and empire while confined to Italy; when, outside the peninsula, Rome began to conquer peoples who had been ruled only by kings, the Italians found themselves threatened with reduction to subject status, and rebelled in the Social War too late to avoid it.[49] The extra-Italian empire was exercised – we have to infer this – primarily over Greeks and hellenised orientals living under post-Macedonian monarchies; but it was exercised also over barbarians, and the self-corrupting rule of the Caesars began to encounter barbarians in the form of peoples migrating in search of new lands. There is a Europe constituted by the revival of free cities, a Europe constituted by the kingdoms into which the barbarians transformed Roman provinces.

The *virtù* of this Europe is *sparsa in molte nazioni*, as we were told in the passage penultimately quoted. Of these two are western and barbarian – France and Germany, a kingdom and a confederacy – but the others cited are Moslem and not Christian, *sette* rather than *stati*.[50] A triumph of religion has occurred, as well as a triumph of barbarism. What Machiavelli thought of Islam and the Ottoman empire it might be hard to say; but these are the chapters of the *Discorsi* in which he enquires why the moderns are less assertive of their liberty than the ancients were, and returns the answer – both Augustinian and anti-Augustinian – that the Christian religion teaches them to despise the things of this world and submit to tyrants rather than resist them.[51] This is usually taken to indicate Machiavelli's preference for city-state paganism over Christianity; but it is hard to see what programme he could have for replacing the latter.[52] He has pointed to a real contradiction in values, and it is a

---

[47] *Discorsi*, II, iv.     [48] Raimondi, 1967, pp. 244–5.     [49] *Ibidem*, p. 243.
[50] Above, nn. 38, 39.     [51] *Discorsi*, II, ii; Raimondi 1967, pp. 238–9.
[52] There is of course the Straussian thesis that he entertained the satanic ambition of making himself the hidden philosopher of a transhistorical Nietzschean elite, ruling humans through their knowledge of the nullity of all values: Mansfield, 1996.

question how he understood the history of a Europe in which *virtù* was widely distributed and partly Christian.

He greatly admired the French monarchy,[53] and thought the free cities of Germany capable of association on the Swiss model.[54] The redistribution of *virtù* in post-Roman Europe is a fact, and he comments on the transformation of Gaul into France and Britain into England;[55] barbarian settlements have become states. For such comment as Machiavelli has on European history at large, however, we must turn to the first book of his *Istorie Fiorentine*, written for the Medicean Pope Clement VII. This resembles the first book of Bruni's *Historiarum populi Florentini* in that it serves as deep background to a detailed narration of *quattrocento* Italian history; Machiavelli thinks, however, that Bruni did not study the internal history of Florence in enough detail, and he plans an account of Florence under Medicean rule from 1434 to 1494, which Bruni did not live to see. His history is intended for Clement VII both as Medici and as pope, and concludes with the disasters for all Italy which followed Lorenzo de' Medici's death in 1492. The family's government of the city at its highest point of legitimacy – which Machiavelli does not overestimate – coincides with the equilibrium among the major Italian states that Lorenzo's diplomacy was held to have accomplished but the French invasion of 1494 destroyed along with the first phase of Medicean rule. The first book of the *Istorie Fiorentine* therefore deals with two long-term themes: the history of Florence since its growth as an independent city, designed to show why its republic never achieved complete stability or autonomy, and the history of the papacy since the end of the Western Empire, designed to show why its role in Italian affairs has generally been disastrous. Machiavelli's detestation of papal Rome can rise very high indeed, but as a humanist and historian he wrote as a counsellor, and it is possible to read him as offering Pope Clement unpalatable but wholesome advice on the mistakes of his predecessors, which may perhaps be avoided. What he may have hoped from Giulio de'Medici as Pope and head of his house does not concern us; the event was more disastrous than he lived to see.

Book I of the *Istorie* begins unequivocally with the barbarians, northern peoples living beyond the Rhine and the Danube, whose increase in numbers leads them to send out organised swarms – later writers would call them hordes – in search of new land.

---

[53] *Ritratto di Cose di Francia*; Raimondi, 1967, pp. 805–17.
[54] *Ritratto di Cose della Magna*; Raimondi, 1967, pp. 821–5.
[55] *Discorsi*, II, viii; Raimondi, 1967, p. 250.

Queste populazioni furono quelle che destrussono lo imperio romano; alle quali ne fu data occasione dagli imperadori, i quali, avendo abbandonata Roma, sedia antica dello imperio, e riduttisi ad abitare in Gostantinopoli, avevano fatta la parte dello imperio occidentale più debole, per essere meno osservata da loro e più esposta alle rapine de' ministri e de' nimici di quelli. E veramente a rovinare tanto imperio, fondato sopra il sangue di tanti uomini virtuosi, non conveniva che fusse meno ignavia ne' principi, né meno infedelità né ministri, né meno forza o minore ostinazione in quegli che lo assalirono; perché non una populazione, ma molte furono quelle che nella sua rovina congiurorono.[56]

[The groups which left home were the multitudes that destroyed the Roman empire. Opportunity to do so was given them by the emperors, who, by abandoning Rome, the ancient seat of the empire, and living in Constantinople, made the western part of the empire weaker, since by watching it less carefully, they left it exposed to plunder by their officials and their enemies. And certainly for the overthrow of so great an empire, founded on the blood of so many able men, the fitness of things demanded that the rulers should not be less sluggish than they were, or the officials less disloyal, or the attackers weaker and less persistent. Actually, not one multitude but many joined forces for her destruction.][57]

Monarchs have a way of surrounding themselves with the unworthy, but there is more here than the destruction of republican *virtù* by the Caesars. The emphasis falls on the removal of the capital to the east, and this has happened before the disasters of 410 with which Machiavelli's history begins. It may have been in some way a consequence of Constantine's becoming a Christian, or a mistaken strategic decision for dealing with the barbarians; but the narrative now becomes that of the invasions and settlements of various peoples, often at the instigation of imperial servants – Stilicho brings in the Goths, Vortigern the Angles, and later Narses the Lombards. These invasions have many consequences. On the one hand – a sentence later echoed by Robertson and adapted by Gibbon –

se alcuni tempi furono mai miserabili in Italia e in queste provincie corse da' barbari, furono quegli che da Arcadio e Onorio infino a lui erano corsi.[58]

[if any times were miserable in Italy and in these provinces overrun by the barbarians, they were those extending from Arcadius and Honorius up to Theodoric.][59]

On the other hand, the complex history of urban decline and renewal moves Machiavelli to list both those cities which were destroyed during this period and those which were founded and grew strong; Florence in

---

[56] *Istorie Fiorentine*, I, 1; Raimondi, 1967, p. 466.     [57] Gilbert, 1965, III, p. 1034.
[58] *Istorie Fiorentine*, I, 5; Raimondi, 1967, p. 470.     [59] Gilbert, 1965, III, p. 1039.

the latter category, Rome in both. The period is one of cultural transformation, in which customs, religion and language all change.

Intra queste rovine e questi nuovi popoli sussono nuove lingue, come apparisce nel parlare che in Francia, in Ispagna e in Italia si costume; il quale mescolato con la lingua patria di quelli nuovi popoli e con la antica romana fanno un nuovo ordine di parlare. Hanno, oltre di questo, variato il nome non solamente le provincie, ma i laghi, i fiumi, i mari e gli uomini; perché la Francia, l'Italia e la Spagna sono ripiene di nomi nuovi e al tutto dagli antichi alieni: come si vede lasciandone indrieto molti altri, che il Po, Garda, l'Arcipelago sono per nomi disformi agli antichi nominati; gli uomini ancora, di Cesari e Pompei, Pieri, Giovanni e Mattei diventorono.[60]

[Among these ruins and these new peoples originated new tongues, as appears in the languages now used in France, Spain and Italy; these are mixtures of the native languages of these new peoples and of the ancient Roman, that make a new sort of speech. Besides this, not merely have the provinces changed their names, but so have the lakes, the rivers, the seas and the men, for France, Italy and Spain are full of names that are new and wholly unlike the ancient ones; for example, omitting many others, the Po, Garda, the Archipelago are known by names unlike the ancient. The men, too, instead of Caesars and Pompeys, are now Pieri, Giovanni, and Mattei.][61]

The *volgare* was always of deep interest and concern to humanists, and Machiavelli is not considering those cases where it was not a romance language at all. The passage leads us to expect that the new personal names should be of Gothic or Lombard origin, but the fact that they are those of three apostles – two evangelists and the Rock of the Church himself – indicates that something else is going on. The rise of a Christian culture accompanies that of a semi-barbaric, and we have reached a point where Gibbon's two triumphs can be seen in conjunction.

The removal to Constantinople has left Italy open to invading barbarians, but also to the gathering authority of the bishops of Rome. In Spain and France – Machiavelli would have had no objection to adding England – barbarian settlements have given rise over time to powerful territorial monarchies, and the Gothic kingdom of Theodoric might have done the same for Italy. The destruction of this state was no work of the popes, but of the eastern emperor Justinian, whose generals left the peninsula divided between imperial authority exercised from Ravenna and the territories controlled by the Lombards. A succession of historians from Otto to Biondo have told us of the papacy's role in overthrowing the former and appealing to the Franks against the latter;

---

[60] *Istorie Fiorentine*, I, 5; Raimondi, 1967, p. 471.     [61] Gilbert, 1965, III, p. 1040.

but when Machiavelli narrates the process, he differs from his predecessors in making no mention of the great controversy over iconoclasm
dividing the popes from the emperors. It is not that he means to minimise
what was happening; we have come to a macrohistorical change in his
narrative. The successors of St Peter, he says, were venerated for their
holiness, and the Christian religion increased to the point where

> i principi furono necessitati, per levare via tanta confusione che era nel mondo,
> ubbidire a quella. Sendo adunque lo imperadore diventato cristiano, e partitosi
> di Roma e gitone in Gostantinopoli, ne seguì, come nel principio dicemmo, che
> lo imperio romano rovinò più presto e la chiesa romana più presto crebbe.[62]

[the princes were obliged, to get rid of the great disorder then existing in the
world, to adopt that religion. When the Emperor became a Christian and left
Rome for Constantinople . . . the Roman empire fell more quickly and the
Roman church grew more rapidly.][63]

It is hard to tell how far the Christian religion was a cause of disorder,
or of the empire's decline relative to the church; Machiavelli privileges
multicausality. The popes remained obedient subjects to the emperors
until the latter's power was weakened by the division of Italy with the
Lombards and the invasion of the eastern provinces by the Slavs and
more momentously by the forces of Islam. It was the popes' exposed
position which decided them to turn to the Franks.

> Di modo che tutte le guerre che dopo questi tempi furono dai barbari fatte
> in Italia furono in maggiore parte dai pontefici causate, e tutti e barbari che
> quella inondorono furono il più delle volte da quegli chiamati. Il qual modo di
> procedere dura ancora in questi nostri tempi: il che ha tenuto e tiene la Italia
> disunita e inferma. Pertanto, nel descrivere le cose seguite da questi tempi a'
> nostri, non si dimosterrà più la rovina dello imperio, che è tutto in terra, ma
> lo augumento de' pontefici e di quegli altri principati che di poi la Italia infino
> alla venuta di Carlo VIII governorono. E vedrassi come i papi, prima con le
> censure, di poi con quelle e con l'armi insieme, mescolate con le indulgenzie,
> erono terribili e venerandi; e come, per avere usato male l'uno e l'altro, l'uno
> hanno al tutto perduto, dell'altro stanno a discrezione d'altri.[64]

[Hence the many wars that were carried on by the barbarians in Italy after these
times were for the most part caused by the popes, and the many barbarians that
flooded her were usually summoned by them. This sort of thing has lasted
even to our times; it has kept and now keeps Italy disunited and weak. So, in
describing events from those times to ours, the fall of the Empire will no longer

[62] *Istorie Fiorentine*, I, 9; Raimondi, 1967, p. 475.
[63] Gilbert, 1965, III, p. 1045 (punctuation altered).
[64] *Istorie Fiorentine*, I, 9; Raimondi, 1967, p. 476.

be shown – since it has struck bottom – but the growth of the pontiffs and those other princedoms which have ruled Italy from that time to the coming of Charles VIII. It will be evident that the popes, first with censures, and then with censures and arms at the same time, mixed with indulgences, excited fear and awe, and that through bad use of censures and arms they have wholly lost awe, and as to fear they are in the power of others.][65]

Machiavelli is not writing antipapal polemic, but recounting history so as to give his patron Pope Clement a lesson in reason of state. It was not the Church, but the barbarians and the empire, that created the situation in which the popes brought in the Franks, but from that first step there has been no turning back. They have used the Hohenstaufen against the Saxons and the Angevins against the Hohenstaufen. The latter move, in combination with the rise of independent cities, created the Ghibelline and Guelf factions whose feuds have rendered Florence unstable and Medicean rule both necessary and insecure. Machiavelli's sights are set less on the imperial papacy of the twelfth and thirteenth centuries than on the post-Schismatic papacy, a loose cannon in the politics of Italy, which must bear much of the blame for the French and Spanish invasions – 'barbarian' by Italian standards – following Charles VIII's incursion in 1494. Why, however, has papal conduct been more fatal than that of other princes?

It is a temptation to say – following a later vocabulary – that Machiavelli is targeting the papacy's temporal power rather than its spiritual. He has nothing to say about iconoclasm or Investitures, or any of the great issues defining the spiritual power's independence of the secular, and the struggle between papacy and empire are only background to the former's role in impeding the emergence of a strong kingdom in central Italy. But Machiavelli is not a Ghibelline, and the alternative to a *regnum italicum* is the prudent conduct of a balance of power between the papal state and the kingdom of Naples. The *Istorie Fiorentine* end with the death of Lorenzo and the destruction of his diplomacy, the starting point of Guicciardini's *Storia d'Italia* a decade and a half later. How Machiavelli hoped that Clement VII might combine papal with Medicean authority to wiser purposes can only be conjectured, but it must be a question of state rather than of the Two Cities.

For all that, the temporal power is unstable because it rests on spiritual foundations, just as the spiritual power is rendered contemptible by its involvement with the temporal; by mingling arms with censures, the

---

[65] Gilbert, 1965, III, p. 1046.

popes have lost the use of both, and inhibited their fellow Italians from effectively using the former. This is the thought behind the devastating account of ecclesiastical principalities in *Il Principe*[66] – because they are neither governed nor defended they are somehow never lost – and the chapter in the *Discorsi* explaining that Italians have no religion because of the Church of Rome.[67] We must be careful, however, not to read Machiavelli as a prototype freethinker or *philosophe*; his unbelief is not of an Enlightened kind.[68] It was the Church of Rome, not the church universal, that waxed as the empire waned, and the cause was not that spiritual authority grew and replaced secular, but that the empire withdrew to Constantinople and left barbarism and religion face to face in the Italian peninsula. This is Machiavelli's Decline and Fall, the link between the events of 410 and those of 1494.

(v)

In reflecting upon the *Discorsi* a few years after Machiavelli's death, Francesco Guicciardini found little to say about the decline of the Roman republic, principate or even empire. His philosophy of history – it deserves the title – focussed always on the extreme difficulty of assessing either one's political circumstances, or one's moment in historical change, as a prelude to decision or action.[69] For this reason he preferred prudence to the audacity of *virtù*, and thought it might be necessary to submit to the tyranny of the Caesars or the rule of the Medici – as he found himself doing when it became a grand-ducal power after the final suppression of the Florentine republic, in historical circumstances he had not foreseen and did not welcome. His *Considerazioni intorno ai Discorsi del Machiavelli* – written at Rome during his exile from the last republican regime – are mostly aimed at asking whether the lamented Niccolò has not simplified Roman conditions in order to draw conclusions from them;[70] and his much greater *Storia d'Italia* – written in retirement after he ceased to serve the Medici ruling as *principi* rather than *principes* – aims at a remorselessly continuous account of the interaction between intention and circumstance in the generally disastrous conduct of Italian rulers in the four decades following 1494. As a history of *ragione di stato* – meaning the failures of reason in the affairs of state – the *Storia* was recognised as the greatest work of its kind since that of Tacitus. What this

---

[66] *Il Principe*, c. ii.    [67] *Discorsi*, i, xii.    [68] De Grazia, 1989; Parel, 1992.
[69] For references see Pocock, 1975, pp. 267–8, nn. 105–10.
[70] Translation in Grayson, 1965, pp. 61–124.

means we shall consider in another setting; its immediate significance is that Guicciardini had little occasion to engage in long-term narratives of change. He expanded his context spatially, recognising that the actions of the Spanish, the English or the Turks repeatedly affected or governed what happened in Italy; but he did not share Bruni's, Biondo's or Machiavelli's need to go back to the fall of the Roman empire to supply a background to Italian history.

There is one exception to this rule: the history of the church, or rather of the papacy. In his *Considerazioni* he concurs with Machiavelli that one can never speak too much ill of the Roman Curia or its effects on the politics of Italy, but asks just what is meant by saying that the papacy has impeded the emergence of a strong state in the peninsula. This must have been a monarchy, either in the sense of a kingdom or empire, or in that of the hegemony of a ruling city over all others; and any of these would have stifled the growth of that plurality of independent republics which gives liberty the meaning it has in Italy.[71] It is the Guelf thesis; but Guicciardini was writing in 1530, and by the time he composed the *Storia d'Italia* he knew he was recording the subjection of the cities to great territorial monarchies originating outside Italy. He did not examine the connexions between barbarian settlement and urban renewal, but inserted in his fourth book a history of the papacy since Peter and Constantine, in which he gave full expression to his loathing of papal conduct, but left its role in history less than fully explained.[72]

Guicciardini's Decline and Fall begins with the bishops of Rome living in holy poverty and as confessors under persecution, until the time of Constantine, whose conversion coincides with his removal to an eastern capital to bring them rich endowments and temporal power. Guicciardini dismisses the Donation – of which we have not heard for some time – and suggests that the foundation of Constantinople was a response to difficulties occurring in the east; but it left Italy open to Gothic invasions and the growth of papal authority, the latter for reasons originally innocent enough. Though beginning to succumb to the temptations of hypocrisy, the popes submitted to imperial authority as long as it was effectively exercised. Guicciardini passes over the wars of Justinian and the destruction of the Gothic kingdom, and has nothing to say about the iconoclast controversy or the downfall of the exarchate of Ravenna; the

---

[71] Grayson, 1965, pp. 81–2.
[72] *Storia d'Italia*, IV, xii; Seidel Menchi, 1971, I, pp. 417–28; trans. Alexander, 1969, pp. 140–50. This passage was omitted from many editions when the *Storia* came to be published; Gibbon owned one of 1775–76 in which it was included.

Lombards are simply another wave of barbarians. His history begins to display its own logic only after the institution of the Carolingian empire; it divides the empire and partitions Italy – Naples and Sicily remaining under Greek rule – and begins the process by which popes come to be chosen by neither the emperors nor the Roman people, and claim an authority extending even to the power of deposing the former.

The history of papacy and empire at the height of the former's pretensions is recounted down to the Angevin intervention and the destruction of the Hohenstaufen. The consequences usually ascribed to the last event – the feuds of Guelfs and Ghibellines and their effects upon the Italian cities – stand alongside the removal of the papacy to Avignon and the subsequent Great Schism; but, also as usual, there is no study of these events in the setting provided by the French monarchy. What seems to interest Guicciardini is the final extinction of the Roman people as a factor in the making of popes and the latter's establishment as *signori* of Rome. From that point he has little to recount except luxury, simony, nepotism, and hypocrisy; the latter arising from the knowledge that though respect for the papal office has never been lower, reverence for religion makes it hard to oppose the noxious policies of its holders. This enables the popes to stir up much trouble in Italy; however, Guicciardini does not seem to intend more than a ruthlessly severe analysis of papal statecraft whenever it falls in the way of his narrative. The popes are no better than other princes; but worse only because they claim to be better. Guicciardini is not offering an account of the sixteenth-century papacy as acting out of the necessities imposed by its own history; the triumph of barbarism and religion has ended only in the reduction of the church of Rome to a common human level.

In a later book of the *Storia d'Italia*, however, he encounters the figure of Martin Luther. Guicciardini once wrote that if he had not been compelled by fortune to seek a career in the papal service, he would probably have become a Lutheran, as the best way of giving vent to his detestation of popes and priests as political actors.[73] In the *Storia* he finds Luther's protest against indulgences defensible, but condemns him as a rebel and schismatic. This need not be dismissed as mere conformity; the point is rather that with Luther there began something beyond the scope of Guicciardini's history. The *Storia d'Italia* – indeed, the history of Italy – had reached a point where great multiple monarchies, Spanish, Austrian and French, could dominate the peninsula and bring to an end the system

---

[73] *Ricordi*, B 124, c. 28; Spongano, 1951, p. 33.

of independent republics, recovering their liberty after the Romans and again after the Hohenstaufen, which since Leonardo Bruni had been the central theme of Italian historiography. Guicciardini had witnessed, and was perhaps responding to, the end of Florentine history and the start of the 'forgotten centuries' when the Medici Pope and the Hapsburg Emperor joined forces to extinguish the republic and reduce the city to a *granducato* under their unequally shared control. But the era of the multiple monarchies was also to be an era of religious warfare, in which the papacy would paradoxically recover the universal significance it seemed to have lost altogether, precisely because its authority would be challenged on grounds first profoundly religious and later profoundly secular. The great Florentines did not live to see this happen; but as one detail of the history of the period there was already occurring a revival of Tacitist thinking, which by a strange parabola would lead historiography back to the 'first decline and fall' as inherited from Tacitus by Gibbon. This revival, furthermore, would occur in the context of an apparently triumphant rebirth of both monarchy and empire.

PART IV

*Extensive monarchy and Roman history*

# CHAPTER II

# Pedro Mexía: empire and monarchy

## (1)

The extinction of the Florentine republic after 1530 was the work of empire and papacy in an unexpected conjunction. As recently as 1527, the armies of Charles V had sacked Rome and nearly destroyed its papal-humanist culture; the event had given rise to neo-Ghibelline and even neo-Joachite speculations, in which the papacy lost significance in an apocalyptic vision of the Christian emperor.[1] Instead, however, the empire had allied itself with a recovering Medici pope to re-impose his family's rule upon Florence and replace the republic with a grand-duchy of Tuscany, one of a chain of princely states that maintained Habsburg control over Italy and would later maintain the ecclesiastical order of Tridentine Catholicism. The empire in this partnership was no longer that of a German prince leaving behind him an insecure power base which the popes could exploit. It was that of Charles V, combining the imperial dignity with Habsburg power in the Austrian lands and the Netherlands acquired through his grandfather's marriage, and with the power of the consolidated Spanish kingdoms that supplied the effective means of his control over Italy. In hindsight we know of his abdication, separating Spain from the empire and attaching the Netherlands to Spain; we know also of the persistent rivalry of the French monarchy, which was to enable William Robertson to present his reign as beginning the polyarchy and possible equilibrium of the modern European states system.[2] Like Robertson again,[3] we know of the Portuguese and Spanish voyages and conquests which transformed the meaning of 'empire' by representing it as oceanic rather than Eurasian and exercised over 'savages' rather than 'barbarians'. There is before us a transformation of our subject, in which *imperium* will be exercised by 'extensive' or

---

[1] Headley, 1997, pp. 93–127; Armitage, 1998, pp. 45–78.    [2] *NCG*, ch. 18.
[3] His *History of America* was published in 1778; Brown, 1997.

'enormous' monarchies – Spanish, French and Anglo-British – and the Dutch confederacy of commercial republics, lying west of the Italian–German theatre in which the rivalries of translated empire had been played out. The 'decline and fall of the Roman empire' will be rewritten in the perspectives this states system supplies.[4] We may go so far – and it is a long way – before we encounter the changes in the Christian perception of the earthly city and its history induced by the vast schism of the Protestant Reformation.

The reign of Charles V, however, was a period of some forty years during which visions of universal empire could still be sustained. A significant shift of emphasis may be detected within them. There was to arise a vision the reverse of Robertson's in which Charles and his successor Philip II threatened Europe not with a revived 'universal empire' of Rome, but with a 'universal monarchy' of Spain; the incomplete shift from 'empire' to 'monarchy', and the annexation of the former term to the latter, indicate a shift in historical emphasis. But humanists who were not Florentine republicans continued to operate within imperial and even papal frameworks, and the last work in the genre of *translatio imperii* we shall have occasion to study is the achievement of a Spaniard in the service of Charles V; we shall find in it some interesting tensions between the concepts of empire and monarchy.

(11)

There is no sign that Gibbon knew of Pedro Mexía's *Historia imperial y Cesarea*, first published in 1551 – though it was not unknown in England – and it is studied here as an indicator of things happening in the history of Latin European historiography. Its author was a *magnífico cavallero* from Seville,[5] who hoped to become the accredited historian of the reign of Charles V.[6] This ambition was frustrated by his own death in 1552, and he did not live to witness his sovereign's abdication in 1555 and the consequent dissociation of the Roman empire and the Spanish monarchy. The *acta* of Charles, had he lived to recount them, would have been those of both an emperor and a king in Spain, and we cannot tell how Mexía would have dealt with such a narrative, still less with its conclusion. It may be that the *Historia imperial*, which has been described as

---

[4] Pagden, 1995; Armitage, 1998; Muldoon, 1999, with their bibliographies.
[5] Mexía, 1578, with a *privilegio* authorising publication dated 1551, and a dedication to Prince Philip dated 1545. The account of Mexía as a *cavallero* occurs in the former.
[6] Kagan, 1999, pp. 42–3.

a 'potboiler',[7] was intended as a grand introduction, in the manner of the opening books of Bruni and Biondo, but it is, as we have it, the last and most ambitious essay in the genre of *translatio*. It starts with Julius Caesar and proceeds without interruption to the death of Maximilian and the election of Charles. We ask, therefore, what species of succession or translation Mexía saw as providing his history with continuity, and how he dealt with the dramatic caesurae associated with such names as Constantine and Romulus Augustulus, Charlemagne and Constantine Palaeologus. This is to ask what observations, digressions, generalisations and extraneous information made their way into a history rigorously and conventionally organised as a presentation of the life, deeds and character of each emperor in succession. We are not yet in the era analysed by Momigliano, when antiquarian learning and social philosophy combined to reinforce and transform classical narrative and medieval chronicle.

Mexía's initial narrative is Sallustian and Orosian. The end of Roman liberty begins when

> . . . entrando en esta republica, que tanta libertad y poder tenia, la discordia y ambicion, porque no bastauan las ajenas, con sus proprias fuerças y armas se hizo sujeta y cautiua.[8]

[. . . discord and ambition entering into that Common-wealth which was so free and puissant, seeing that sovraine forces were not sufficient, with their owne forces and armes they subdued and captiuated themselves;][9]

a process which culminated in the wars of Pompey and Caesar, though those between Marius and Sulla display the causes of the civil wars at their origin. Caesar declines the name of *rex*,

> contentose con se llamar Dictador perpetuo, y tambien Emperador: aunque no por nombre de dignidad y señorio, como sus succesores lo hizieron despues: sino como appellido que denotaua auer sido vencedor en las guerras y batallas, porque en este significado se daua à los capitanes Romanos, quando alcancauan alguna muy señalada vitoria. Pero despues de Iulio Cesar, todos que le sucedieron lo tomaron, y se preciaron de llamar Emperadores, y quedo consagrado por el mas alto titulo y dignidad del mundo.[10]

[. . . contenting himselfe to be called perpetuall Dictator and also Emperor; although not with a name of such dignitie as his successors have done since, but

---

[7] Kagan, 1999, p. 42. As such, it was not unsuccessful; it was enlarged and translated into Italian, and by the time of its English translation (Traheron, 1604) had been carried down to the Emperor Rudolf then reigning. Traheron dedicated his version to Horace Vere, commander of English troops combatting Spain in the Low Countries.
[8] Mexía, 1578, p. 2.    [9] Traheron, 1604, p. 4.    [10] Mexía, 1578, p. 12.

as by a name which signified that hee had been a conquerour in the warres, which in this sense was giuen to the Romane Captaines, when they had obtained any notable victorie; but after IULIUS CAESAR, al his successors tooke that name, and gloried to be called Emperours, which was sacred for the most high title and dignitie in the world.] [11]

It is not clear what weight should be assigned to the words *consagrado* and 'sacred'. [12] Octavian's rise to power as Augustus is not whitewashed; his war with Antony results from the unlimited nature of the thirst for supremacy, [13] and he has earlier betrayed Cicero to the proscriptions. [14] But 'God in his secret judgement had reserved the sole Monarchie' [15] and as we have earlier been told of Caesar's clemency so

I say that *Octavian* enjoying so much prosperitie and good fortune, was not altered in his naturall condition, as in other Princes it hath happened, but rather made more gentle, milde, iust and affable, more curteous, more liberall and more temperate. [16]

This observation comes, however, at the end of a passage in which we are told that Christ chose to be born in a time of 'quietness and general peace', but it is instantly added that his holy life and blessed death and resurrection ought not to be recounted in a history of profane matters. If we are not to have a Brunian account of the Caesars as fatal to both *libertas* and *imperium*, neither do we hear that their government of the world was sanctified by the growth of the church. The loss of liberty, for which peace is the reward, was resented by some proud barbarians, [17] while it was in a Rome where no man remembered liberty that the tyranny of Tiberius began. [18] Mexía begins to rely on Tacitus, [19] but never on his deeper levels of analysis; the disasters of 69–70 do not reduce the empire's strength and prosperity [20] – though the metropolis has begun to suck dry the wealth of the provinces. [21] Nero was

last of the Caesars, though the name continues, *Galba* the first that received the Empire from the hand of the Armie, *Otho* the first that by the cohorts (which were the Army lodged too neere the citie of *Rome*) was chosen and made Emperour . . . an accursed and most pernicious introduction for the Romane Empire. [22]

[11]  Traheron, 1604, pp. 19–20.
[12]  Professor Teofilo Ruiz suggests that Traheron should have used 'anointed'. Neither the accentuation nor the translation cited here will satisfy a modern eye.
[13]  Traheron, 1604, p. 41.     [14]  Traheron, 1604, p. 32.
[15]  Traheron, 1604, p. 34.        [16]  Traheron, 1604, pp. 49–50.
[17]  Traheron, 1604, pp. 47–8. The rebels are Spanish and German.
[18]  Traheron, 1604, p. 53.      [19]  Traheron, 1604, pp. 55, 84.     [20]  Traheron, 1604, p. 79.
[21]  Traheron, 1604, p. 94.      [22]  Traheron, 1604, pp. 101, 109.

This is the point at which Gibbon, having followed 'the Classics as low as Tacitus . . . insensibly plunged into the Ocean of the Augustan histories'.[23] Mexía, no intellectual giant and working two centuries earlier in the history of historiography, is nevertheless a product of humanism, reliant on the same authorities and sometimes dissatisfied with them. He begins to choose for comment details that also attracted the attention of Gibbon, and sometimes to make comments that Gibbon independently made later; we begin to wonder what was philosophical history and what humanist commonplace. Recounting the fall of Jerusalem and the Diaspora that followed it, both the Spanish Catholic and the English sceptic remark how strange it is that the Jews, stiff-necked and rebellious against their God when he ruled them directly by miracle and prophecy, were stiff-necked and literalist in observing what they took to be his law when he had manifestly cut them off.[24] Recounting the Gothic incursions of the third century, when fleets of light craft are said to have emerged from the Black Sea and ravaged the Aegean, both find this navigationally implausible; Mexía indeed goes further than Gibbon in remarking that the boats must have come down the Danube and the Goths were never a people great by sea.[25] At the time of the so-called Thirty Tyrants, both remark on the virile qualities – *varonil y valerosa* – of the two women, Zenobia and Victorina, who aimed at military power.[26] Gibbon was still living in Mexía's world when it came to the use of sources; both rely on the *Historia Augusta*.

Barbarism and religion have begun to keep step with each other in Mexía's compilations. He recounts each persecution of the church as it occurs in the order of his chronology – as we shall see, Gibbon does not do this – and from the time of Hadrian he begins developing a picture of northern barbarians, Scythian and German, recurrently pressing against the empire's frontiers; Hadrian polices them by setting up markers where there are no rivers to form natural boundaries.[27] Gibbon, we shall find, is inclined to defer the subject of barbarism until the disintegration of the principate is complete. For Mexía, in contrast with his predecessors,

---

[23] *NCG*, p. 399.
[24] Mexía, 1578, p. 93; Traheron, 1604, p. 161. Gibbon, *DF*, I, ch. 15 (Womersley, 1994, I, p. 449).
[25] Traheron, 1604, p. 268. Cf. Gibbon, *DF*, I, ch. 10 (Womersley, 1994, I, pp. 275–9).
[26] Mexía, 1578, pp. 145, 148; Traheron, 1604, pp. 260–1, 264. For Gibbon see below, p. 469 (he uses the name 'Victoria'). Mexía joins Gibbon in recounting Zenobia's sexual relations with her husband Odaenathus and her intellectual relations with the philosopher Longinus (Traheron, 1604, p. 275).
[27] Traheron, 1604, pp. 159–60.

the subject has a new importance; as a humanist, he is both reading later sources for the disasters of the third century, and preoccupied with the collapse before the barbarians of the world of ancient letters. The best thing Nerva ever did, he remarks, was to make Trajan his successor,[28] and the panegyric of universal peace under the 'five good emperors' is now in place.

Es cierto que en este lugar es cosa de considerar y notar, en lo que toca el poder y policia humana, quan grande y poderosa cosa era el imperio Romano, y que contento, y libertad tan grande era la de las gentes entonces, en el tiempo deste Emperador, y de Trajano y Adriano, y de otros buenos que vno: y que cosa seria ver la grandeza y riqueza de su corte, frequentada de la mas y mejor gente del mundo, y ver aquella populissima ciudad de Roma, sus grandezas, su riqueza sus edificios: considerar la libertad y seguridad que auia para andarse y caminarse el mundo todo, obedesciendo y siruiendo a vn señor, y esse bueno y justo, sin temores de guerra, de cossarios, de ladrones, sin hallar a cada passo nueuas leyes, nueuas monedas, nueuos señores y reyes y tyranos, como agora ay: sin necessidad de seguros, o saluocondutos, sin ser presos ni captiuos, o maltratados por enemigos y estrangeros o no conocidos: antes tratandose todos, y entendiendose como amigos y vezinos, en todo lo mas o mejor del mundo, de la manera a que agora los de un pequeno reyno pacifico y justamente gouernado, proueyendose las vnas tierras à las otras de lo que abundaua en estas, y saltaua en aquellas, corriendo las mercadurias y tratos por todo el mundo, sin tantos vedamientos y estoruos como agora ay, valiendo y obedecir endose vnas leyes en todo el: finalmente auiendo paz y vnidad en lo mas y mejor del mundo. De lo qual mucho mas perfetamente se gozo, despues que los Emperadores fueron Christianos, como adelante se dira. Pero como estos todos fueron humanos poderes, no pudieron durar mucho sin caerse y mudarse y trastocarse. Condicion es del mundo que ninguna cosa sabe se ostener en vn estado.[29]

[And truly in this place is to be noted and considered the power and gouernment of the Romane Empire, and how contentedly and at what libertie the people lived in the time of ANTONINUS, TRAIANE, ADRIAN, and other good Emperours, and to see the greatness and riches of that court frequented by the greatest and best men in the world, and to see the greatness and buildings of that most populous citie of *Rome*; and to consider of the libertie and securitie wherein men might trauaile throughout the world, obeying and serving one Lord, and he good and just, without feare of warres, robbers by sea or land, without finding euery where new lawes, new coynes, new Lords, Kings and tyrants, as there are now adayes, needing no securitie or safeconducts, without being taken prisoners, and made captiue or ill vsed by enemies, strangers and vnknowne persons, but using all men as friends and neighbours in the greatest and best parts of the world, which as a little Kingdome was quietly and iustly gouerned.[30]

---

[28] Traheron, 1604, p. 141.    [29] Mexía, 1578, p. 96.    [30] A somewhat condensed translation?

One country was furnished from another, with such things as in the one did abound, and the other wanted. Merchandize and traffick passing through the world without so many prohibitions, molestations and troubles, as we see now adayes, all liuing then vnder one lawe euerywhere, in the best and greatest parts of the earth in vnion and peace, which they more perfectlie enjoyed, after that the Emperours were Christians, as hereafter shall be declared. But as this was but humane power, so could it not continue long without fall, alteration or change: for it is the condition of the world, that nothing can continue long in one estate.][31]

This glowing account of a common market and European community has resonances beyond those it has for us. It harks back (as Mexía might know) to a passage in which Orosius celebrates the peace of the empire even in times as disturbed as his own.[32] At the end of the next century it caught the eye of the English publicist and proto-economist Charles Davenant, who took it to be propaganda for a universal monarchy exercised by Charles V and replied, in terms looking back to Bruni[33] and forward to David Hume, that commerce flourished better when cities and kingdoms were free to follow their own laws.[34] Lastly, Mexía's language cannot but remind us of the second chapter of the *Decline and Fall*, where Gibbon celebrates, and depicts in detail surpassing the rhetorical, 'the union and internal prosperity of the Roman empire in the time of the Antonines', but ends by finding in it the 'secret poison' of an *imperium* lacking *libertas*:[35] a conclusion owing more to Davenant and Hume than to Mexía's pagan or Augustinian conviction of the mutability of all earthly things. Mexía may have intended to make a utopia of the empire and monarchy of Charles V – the Emperor would entertain no such illusions – but he had come close to saying that prosperity compensated for the loss of liberty.

### (III)

This panegyric, however, is situated in the era of the adoptive emperors, and will form part of its image as a period of supreme happiness in human history. It comes to an end with the transformation of Antonine into Severan empire, and there ensue images of military rule, in which the senate is impotent or disregarded, and military anarchy, in which generals compete with each other under increasing barbarian pressure. There is a possibly significant correlation between Mexía's repeated observation

---

[31] Traheron, 1604, p. 167.   [32] Above, pp. 88–9.   [33] Above, pp. 164, 169.
[34] Pocock, 1975, pp. 436–45; Hont, 1990, pp. 57–101.   [35] Below, pp. 438–40.

that the disorders of the third century lack historians who have recounted them intelligibly[36] – he is so far dependent on his sources that he can complain when they are not to be depended on – and his insistence that the Christian religion spread in these times because disorder taught that only other-worldly values brought (and still bring) consolation.[37] By the time that Aurelian, Probus and Carus have overcome their rivals and expelled the barbarians, Mexía can observe that

la gente de guerra ya estrava en possession de elegir emperadores, y como en el proceso dela historia se ha mostrado, siempre tenian por odioso el Emperador que el Senado elegia, y aunque el imperio tenia en diuersas partes exercitos y legiones ordinarias, aquel exercito en que el Emperador se hallaua, quando acaecia su muerte, pretendio tener mejor derecho, y el elegido por el parescia tener mas justo titulo, y era auido por Emperador.[38]

[Now were the men of warre againe in possession of authoritie to chuse Emperours. For as it appeareth by the processe of this historie, they euer hated that Emperour which was chosen by the Senate. And although that in diuers parts of the Empire there were armies and ordinarie legions; yet that armie wherein the Emperour was at the time of his death, euer pretended to have greatest right; and hee that was chosen thereby, seemed to have the most iust title, and was held for right Emperour.][39]

Emperors are being chosen *alibi quam Romae*, and the city's supremacy is being disregarded. This is not only a consequence of the slide from senatorial towards military rule; Mexía is moving towards the generalisation that the empire has become too enormous to be governed either by one ruler or by several.[40] It is becoming a problem for us to determine how far such observations were to be found in the historian's sources or were generalised by him from them, and how necessary to the latter activity were political or philosophical principles such as abounded in the eighteenth century. Are we to ask how far Mexía was able to get without them? Meanwhile a change of another kind is at hand; for Diocletian, though his institution of the tetrarchate proved unstable, is said to have done so more in the manner of a king than an emperor. This significant distinction means that he insisted on being venerated 'after the manner of the kings of *Persia*'; his subjects were to kneel before him, and instead of his embracing them were to kiss his foot, shod with pearls and jewels.[41]

---

[36] Traheron, 1604, pp. 247, 283, 288–9, 308.    [37] Traheron, 1604, pp. 210–11, 251–2.
[38] Mexía, 1578, p. 162.    [39] Traheron, 1604, p. 291.
[40] Mexía, 1578, pp. 171, 181; Traheron, 1604, pp. 308, 321.
[41] Mexía, 1578, p. 167; Traheron, 1604, p. 300.

To Gibbon, as we shall see,[42] this indicated a move towards government of the Roman world from an oriental palace. Mexía, having singled out these facts, goes on – as Gibbon does not – to observe that at this point Diocletian was moved by the Devil to persecute the Christians. His history is governed by two sets of imperatives: the one to narrate it as the lives of successive Caesars, the other to follow the Eusebian scheme in which the persecutions were the prelude to the triumph of Constantine.

With that event vast changes occur, raising the question of what kind of history Mexía is writing. Persecutions, as trials of the Church and tests of its faith, are replaced by heresies, to which emperors sometimes succumb; but when he reaches the conflict between Arius and Athanasius, Mexía remarks with significant ambivalence 'I rather write the lives of the Emperours, than any Ecclesiasticall historie, whereof I must of necessitie make often mention hereafter.'[43] The text has already begun to do so; there are extended discussions of the date of Constantine's baptism,[44] of whether he made the Donation to Pope Sylvester – he probably did not[45] – and of whether he is to be blamed for endowing the Church with wealth (there is a fairly long repudiation of the ideal of clerical poverty).[46] The narrative proceeds, following both its linked genres, to the reign of Julian the Apostate, of whose anti-Christian actions we hear that it is a great pity that 'such accursed blindness' should have appeared in one 'que tantas habilidades y buenas inclinaciones tenia'.[47]

By this time, however, a new and momentous theme is making its appearance. The *Historia imperial y Cesarea* is by definition a history of *translatio imperii*; the line of Caesars is unbroken to the moment of writing and the Roman empire still exists. But from the time when the emperors became Christian, we begin to hear that, as all earthly things must perish in time, the secret judgements of God are preparing an utter destruction of the empire at the hands of the barbarians. As a prognostication of the 'general decay and diminution' on which he has resolved, it pleases God to permit great wars to break out 'in the Northerly parts of *Scythia*' between the Huns and the Goths, leading to the migration of the latter into the empire and the overthrow of Valens at Adrianople.

A qui suelen los historiadores todos alargarse mucho en escreuir el origen y patria destas gentes de los Godos, y como y en que tiempo salieron, y son tan

---

[42] Below, pp. 479–81.  [43] Traheron, 1604, p. 322.
[44] Mexía, 1578, pp. 173, 179; Traheron, 1604, pp. 310, 317.
[45] Mexía, 1578, p. 179; Traheron, 1604, p. 318.  [46] Traheron, 1604, pp. 318–20.
[47] Mexía, 1578, p. 188; Traheron, 1604, p. 332.

largo e tan varios en las opiniones, que yo determino de abhorrar deste trabajo, porque en ello va muy poco, y si va, no se puede acabar de auerigar. Pero la verdad es, que ellos fueron gentes que baxaron de la Scithia de Europa segun los mas, o fuessen de alli naturales, o venidos de otras partes como algunos dizen, no sie me da nada, ni de hazer diferencias de nombres de los llamar Ostrogothos, o Visigothos, porque en esto no ay mas diferencia, que ser los Ostrogothos mas Orientales, y los Visigothos mas Occidentales, y comunemente los vnos e los oltros se llaman Gothos, y assi los determino yo de llamar Godos en buen Castellano, cada vez que se ofreciere, que seran muchos. Porque en la verdad la mas notable y principal herida y danno que el Imperio Romano recibio, y principio de su cayda por ellos. Por lo qual estas gentes se puede tener y juzgar por las mas valientes en armas, de todas las del mundo, pues ellas, aunque con muchos trabajos y batallas, bastaron a domar y sojuzgar el pueblo y imperio domador de todas las otras gentes.[48]

[Here the historiographers at large describe the originall and countrie of these Gothes; and by what means and when they came forth of their countrie; wherein they are so tedious and so contrarie in opinions, the one to the other, that I purpose to eschew that labour, for that it little importeth; neither can the truth be fully explained. But it is true, that they were a people which came out of Scythia in *Europe*,[49] according to the most writers; but whether they were borne there or came from some other countrie (as some say they did) it importeth not much; neither the difference in their names in calling them Ostrogothes or Visigothes; for herein is no greater difference, but that the Ostrogothes were the more easterly, and the Visigothes more westerly; but generally both the one and the other were called Gothes, and so I purpose to call them, so often as I shall haue occasion to speake of them, which will be very often; for in truth the greatest wound, and chiefest hurt that the Romane Empire receiued, and the beginning of the fall thereof, was through their occasion. Wherefore these people may iustly be accounted and esteemed for the most valiant in armes of all other nations in the world, seeing that they (although with much labour, and by fighting many battailes) were able to tame and subdue that people and Empire, which was the tamer and subduer of all other nations.][50]

This is something we have not met before (there is no need to claim that Mexía originated it): a firm assertion, in the midst of a history of *translatio*, that the Roman empire came to a catastrophic end. When he reaches the disasters of the fifth century and the loss of control over Gaul and Spain, Mexía elaborates a point we have seen made by Flavio Biondo (who is among his authorities)[51] and adds one of his own.

---

[48] Mexía, 1578, p. 196.
[49] There may be a distinction between a 'European' and an 'Asian' Scythia, perhaps at the line of the Don.
[50] Traheron, 1604, p. 345.    [51] Traheron, 1604, p. 394 (for a history of Venice).

Grandes son las cosas y trances prosperos y aduersos por donde el Imperio
Romano ha passado, en los quatrocientos y setenta annos (poco mas y meno)
que del auemos contado, como facilmente el lector podido notar. Peco aunque
por algun tiempo se ha visto en grandes aprietos y trabajos, y estado a peligro
de se perder en todo o en parte, al cabo aunque aquellas aduersidades durasser
alguno tiempo visto tenemos comose libro dellas, venciendo las y remediandolas.
Y podemos dezir que sanaua de las enfermedades que padescia, recobraua
las perdidas que perdia, hasta el punto en que agora estamos. Lo qual por
secreto juyzio de Dios ya no es assi, en lo que adelante nos queda, antes se
van multiplicando las perdidas, y enflaqueciendo sus fuerças. Y aunque algunas
vezes por el valor de algunos excelentes Emperadores y Capitanes suyos, se
esforço el imperio a recobrar su antigua magestad, y estuuo honorado y temido,
nunca por esto pudo llegar a lo passado, y aun esto fue pocas vezes. De manera
que de aqui adelante [*marg.*: Declinacio del Imp. Rom.] en diuersos tiempos
y por diuersos acaecimientos fueron los Emperadores perdiendo prouincias
y regiones, y en ellas [*marg.*: Origen de los Reynos] commençaron Reynos y
señorios particulares, y de las fuerças que el imperio perdio se hizieron otros
reynos grandes y poderosos, y assi como se multiplicaron los principados y
thronos, assi fueron mas y mas diuersas las cosas que passanon. Las quales yo
no podere por ninguna manera contar, ni aun me tengo por obligado a ello,
porque mi proposito y intento no es, ni fue escreuir historia general, sino la de los
Emperadores, y aun esso breue y summeriamente. Por lo qual con la breuedad
possible, lo tratare y proseguire mi camino, escriuiendo lo mas importante de
la historia Imperial, dexando la de los otros Reyes y reynos que en el discurso
fueron naciendo, para otros, que auran tomado o tomaren este cuydado, pues
para mis pocas fuerças y caudal bastara esto, y plego a Dios que pueda salir con
ello medianamente, con cuyo fauor passemos pues adelante.[52]

[Great in truth are the accidents and wars, happie and infortunate, which haue
happened in the Romane Empire in the space of foure hundred and seauentie
yeeres (little more or lesse) that we haue written thereof, as the reader may
easily perceive. But notuithstanding that we haue sometimes seene it in distresse,
troubled, and in daunger to haue been lost in the whole, or in part; yet in the
end, although those aduersities continued for a space, we haue seene how it hath
been deliuered from those calamities, by ouercoming them and redressing them
by some meanes. So as we may say, that it hath beene cured of those infirmities
wherewith it was oppressed, and recouered the losses which it sustayned, untill
the time, whereto we are now come. But through the secret iudgement of God,
from henceforth matters succeeded not in any such manner, but the losses
multiplied and the forces diminished. And although that sometime through the
valour of some excellent Emperours and their captaines, the Empire enforced
it selfe to recouer the auncient maiestie thereof, and was both honoured and
feared; yet it could neuer attaine to the former; and this also was very seldom.
So as from henceforth, at sundrie times and by diuers accidents, the Emperours

---

[52] Mexía, 1578, pp. 214–15.

lost prouinces and countries, and in them began kingdomes and particular
dominions; and of those countries which the Empire lost, arose great and mightie
monarchies; and as principalities and kingdomes multiplied, so great and more
strange were the accidents which happened, which I cannot relate, neither am
I bound thereto; for my purpose and intent was, not to write a generall historie,
but only of the Emperours, and that briefly and in summe. Wherefore as briefly
as I shall be able, I will discouer the substance, and hold on my way, writing
such things as shall be of greatest importance in the historie of the Emperours,
leauing that of other Kings and kingdomes which in process of time shall present
themselves to others, which alreadie haue, or hereafter shall take that charge
vpon them. For this which I have alreadie taken in hand, will be enough for my
small abilitie, which I pray God, I may be able to bring to any reasonable good
end, and honest satisfaction of those which shall reade the same.][53]

The point that 410 or thereabouts marked the beginning of *inclinatio*,
because thereafter the empire could never recover provinces it had lost,
was made for us by Biondo,[54] whom Mexía may be following here. It
is not accompanied by any general thesis of Roman degeneracy, and in
this sense Fall is not preceded by Decline; the secret providence of God,
and the warlike prowess of the barbarians, furnish sufficient explanation.
What Mexía stresses more than Biondo is that the decline of empire was
accompanied by the growth of kingdoms and other principalities and
lordships, and that these have a history of their own which cannot be
recounted by following the sequence of emperors. This may indicate a
dilemma of his own; he is writing in Spain, whose monarch does not
use the title of emperor in his Spanish kingdoms, and Charles V has a
pedigree as king distinct from that he has as emperor. In a dedication,
dated 1545, of the *Historia imperial* to Charles's heir Philip (who was never
to be emperor), Mexía wrote of

las leyes destos reynos, que ordeno el Rey Don Alfonso, llamado por excelencia
el Sabio . . . que a los Reyes y Principes de Castilla les lean ordinariamente
historias . . .[55]

[the laws of these kingdoms, ordained by King Alfonso, called for his merits
the Wise . . . and generally attributed by historians to the kings and princes of
Castile].

There is a history here he is not writing. He falls back on genre, saying
that the history of emperors relates only indirectly and allusively to the
history of kings and kingdoms; what we notice is that he lacks a rhetorical
or philosophical vocabulary which might enable him to explain how the

[53] Traheron, 1604, p. 374.    [54] Above, pp. 186, 190, 196.    [55] Mexía, 1578, title page.

provinces of empire were transformed into the distinctive phenomenon
of kingdoms. Yet Mexía not only knows that there is such a problem,
but knows what the roots of such a problem might be. If we turn back
to the passage quoted earlier, exalting the Goths as the conquerors of
the world's conquerors, we find that we are looking at more than an
account *de inclinatione imperii*. There follows in the Spanish text, for some
reason not in the English translation, an eloquent account of the valour
and antiquity of the nobles and kings of Spain. These virtues are derived
from the Goths – Mexía does not invoke the heroically defeated Iberians
of Numantia – whose descendants took refuge in the mountains when
Spain was lost to the Moors and proceeded to its reconquest.[56] There
emerges a perception of history not to be expected of Italian humanists
writing of their cities: the kingdoms of the west are barbaric in origin,
and the barbarians, having overthrown empire, were the authors of new
political forms which the history of empire and its *translatio* does not
explain because it does not contain. The narrative of Decline and Fall
takes on a new dimension.

(IV)

The history of kingdoms, which Mexía is resolved not to write, confronts
him in consequence of his insistence on an absolute breach in the history
of western empire. The successive sacks of Rome are recorded as divine
judgements –

permitio Dios . . . que andando los tiempos gentes de todas las naciones que
ella auia sojuzgado, la hollassen y sojuzgassen, y de sus riquezas della todas
lleuassen pressa y despojo como si vinieran a cobrar y restituyrse en lo que les
auia tomado a sus passados.[57]

[through the diuine prouidence of God, in processe of time it was taken and
despoiled by the same people and nations which it had subdued and brought
under her yoke. And the people of all those nations came to *Rome*, tooke the
same, and made boote and spoyle thereof, as if they had come to set home,
and to haue that restored to them which in former time was taken from their
ancestors.][58]

– and in the year 476

assi acabo in este Augustulo el imperio y señorio de Roma, que non tuuo
Emperador por mas de trezientos y treynta annos. Y passo esto en los mil y

---

[56] Mexía, 1578, p. 196.    [57] Mexía, 1578, p. 231.    [58] Traheron, 1604, pp. 403–4.

dozientos y veynte y nueue annos que Roma fue fundada, y a los quinientos y veynte y nueue que Iulio Cesar se hizo señor o tyrano della, y a los quatrocientos y setenta y sieste que Christo nascio.[59]

[And so in this AUGUSTULUS ended the Empire and dominion of *Rome*, which afterwards had no Emperour for the space of three hundred and thirtie yeeres. This happened in the yeere one thousand, two hundred, nine and twentie after the building of *Rome*, and in the five hundred, nine and twentieth year after that IULIUS CAESAR made himself tyrant and Lord thereof, and in the yeere four hundred seauen and seauentie after the birth of our Sauiour Christ.][60]

But what is the effect of such absolute finality upon a *historia imperial y Cesarea*? If the Roman empire has ended for ever, what is the *imperium* that continues to be exercised by the emperors reigning at Constantinople, who though Greeks style themselves Romans for another thousand years?[61] And what is the nature of the empire of Charlemagne, to whom Charles of Ghent succeeds in an unbroken line? Since Mexía has rejected the Donation, he can hold neither that the Pope exercises empire in the western provinces, nor that he does so as lieutenant of Constantine's continuing authority. It is to the historian's credit that he has left himself with nothing to relate beyond the recorded facts, but his misfortune that he has no macronarrative in which to situate them. What is lacking after 476 is an interpretative narrative of east Roman history, and the reason for this lack is that such narratives are constructed out of Latin and western preoccupations. Emperors before Constantine and Theodosius had to deal with the legions and the barbarians, with the decline of ancient virtue an implied presence; emperors after Charlemagne had to deal with the Popes, the Romans, the princes of Germany and the cities of Italy. Like Gibbon, the historians were driven to return to the city of old Rome; they did not have a scenario with the new Rome as its epicentre. They concluded, as Gibbon did, that the history of this city was empty of meaning.

De manera que no parecer ya las vidas y Emperadores que agora vamos contando, en comparacion de los passados, sin o como en los vasos grandes que han tenido vino o orio licor muy bueno, quando ya aquel seva acabando, siempre se hallan assientos y hezes dessabidos y malos, assi acontece agora en el imperio oriental donde auia grandes y poderosos Principes, que fu assiento y cabo era qual se vee, cuyo fin y remate podemos dezir que se acerca, pues desde a tan pocos annos fue passado a los Franceses y Alemanes el verdadero

---

[59] Mexía, 1578, p. 234.   [60] Traheron, 1604, p. 409.
[61] Mexía, 1578, p. 269; Traheron, 1604, p. 469.

titulo y dignitad del Imperio, pues que en Grecia quedaron grande tempo Emperadores.[62]

[So that these seeme not to be the liues of Emperors which we now relate, in comparison with those which are past; but like as in great vessels wherein wine or some other good liquor hath bin kept, as it consumeth, so it becometh a worse tast, and in the bottom there remaine some lees and dregs: so befell it in the East Empire, wherein had been verie great and mightie princes, whose head and beginning was such as you have seene, and whose end we may say drew neere, seeing that within few yeeres the title and dignitie of the Empire was translated from them to the Frenchmen and the Germanes; notuithstanding that in Graecia there remained Emperours a long time after.][63]

The dregs are the successors of Justinian, in whom, like the historians the young Gibbon read at Stourhead,[64] Mexía is unable to find much of interest; but the reason is that they lack antitheses in a dialectic which can only be Latin. It can come as no surprise that the *Historia imperial* perceives the eastern emperors mainly as they act upon the west. The wars of Justinian establish the exarchate of Ravenna.[65] Heraclius – an apparent exception – defeats the Persians, but prepares their final destruction by the Muslims, who take Jerusalem from him and proceed to the conquest of Africa, the domination of the Mediterranean and the invasion of Spain;[66] these events are given due weight, but never perceived as altering the character of the Christian world. A narrative with which we are by now familiar is retold as successive emperors take up iconoclastic policies,[67] to which the papal resistance explains the destruction of the exarchate, the rise of the Frankish kingdom, and

las causas y caminos por donde la yglesia passo el imperio a las partes Occidentales, primeramente en la casa de Francia: para lo qual ha fido menester lo dicho, y lo que adelante se dira, porque aunque no es derechamente de los presentes Emperadores, es necessario para la historia dellos y para la perspicuydad y buena disposicion de las cosas de adelante.[68]

[the course and reason why the Pope [cf. the original] transported the Empire into the Westerne parts, first into the house of *France*: for which cause it was requisite to declare what is said, and shall be said hereafter: for although it be not directly of the Emperours, yet it is very expedient for the historie of them, and the cleerenes and order of what we shall write hereafter.][69]

---

[62] Mexía, 1578, p. 290.    [63] Traheron, 1604, p. 507.    [64] *EEG*, pp. 28–42, esp. 37.
[65] Traheron, 1604, pp. 421–40.    [66] Traheron, 1604, pp. 471–2, 476, 493–94.
[67] Traheron, 1604, pp. 497, 500, 505 (Leo III and Gregory II), 508–9, 518 (moderate policy of Irene).
[68] Mexía, 1578, p. 292.    [69] Traheron, 1604, p. 510.

The successive lives of eastern emperors are intelligible only as their impact upon the Roman church and its response; but it is none too clear by what authority the Popes effected the *translatio*, or exactly what they were doing. For if the Roman empire was extinguished, what was the *imperium* by which the heirs of Constantine ruled in the east, and how did it survive after the investiture of Charlemagne? To these questions answers could be given, but it is a problem in Pedro Mexía's historiography that he is not sure how to answer them. He confronts it as a problem in narrative arrangement.

Digo esto porque como la yglesia passase en este tiempo el imperio en Carlos Magno, y despues aya perseuerado en Alemania, y en Grecia tambien quedassen principes que se llamauan Emperadores, y pretendieron que ellos lo eran con buen derecho, de manera que el imperio y titulo podemos dezir se diuidio y vino a auer dos imperios y Emperadores, veo me agora yo en muy grande confusion y duda, sobre acordar de que manera trate este negocio, porque querer escriuir una ves los vnos y despues boluer a tratar de los otros, como hizo Baptista Ignacio en la Epitoma breuissima que de emperadores escriuio, parece grande inconueniente, llegar con los vnos al cabo, y despues hazer boluer al lector setecientos annos otros en la historia. Pues querer escreuir vno o dos vidas de los vnos, y luego otras tantas de los otros, como hizo Iuan Cuspiniano,[70] tan poco me paresce buen consejo, porque se confunde mucho la historia, y casi no se estender las vnas ni las otras, y tan poco me paresce que se pueden contar bien todos juntos ygual y complidamente, por lo mucho que se ofresce, y por la diuersidad de los tiempos y lugares. Tomar pues los vnos solos, como hizieron algunos, oluidando los otros del todo, tambien lo juzgo por iniusticia y crudelidad, dexar assi hundir y desparecer una cosa tan grande como el señorio de los Emperadores de Grecia, y que tanto tiempo duraron despues, si los queremos dexar, pues dexar los successores de Carlos Magno, donde oy permanece el imperio, seria dexar el camino verdadero, que va la parar a donde yo camino, y tomar otro, por el qual nunca llagasse donde queria. Por lo qual ya que por ambos yo no puede caminar, despues de algunas consideraciones acuendo tomar por principal cuentosa historia del imperio, que la santa yglesia Romana aprobo y aprueua, que es el de Italia y Alemania, en Carlos sus successores, contando las vidas y hechos dellos, con la orden que hasta a qui he hecho las de todos, y incidente y breuamente haziendo siempre memoria de los Griegos que occurrieren, y assi se terra manera, con que el que esta historia leyere, entiendo el successo de entrambos imperios, debaxo del titulo y nombre de solo el uno.[71]

---

[70] Johannes Cuspinianus (Johann Spiessheimer), 1473–1529; Breisach, 1994, p. 162. My thanks to Guido Abbatista for this reference.

[71] Mexía, 1578, p. 302.

[I say this much, for that the Pope in this time passed the Empire to CHARLES the great and it hath euer since continued in *Germanie*: And in *Graecia* also remained princes, which in like manner were called Emperors, and pretended good right to be so; so as we may say that the Empire and the title thereof was diuided, and came to be two Empires and to haue two Emperors. But I finde myselfe in a great confusion, to think how this matter may be handled; for first to write of one, and then to returne to write of the other, as did BAPTISTA IGNATIVS, in the short epitome which he wrote of the Emperors; it seemeth to be inconuenient to bring one of them to an end, and then to make the reader turne backe againe seauen or eight hundred yeares in the historie. And to write one or two liues of the one Empire, and then as many of the other, as did IOHN CVSPINIAN, that liketh me as ill: for it greatly confoundeth the historie, and so in a manner neither the one nor the other can be understood; and well to discouer all together at large (for the many occasions which are offered, and the diuersitie of the times and places) I see not how it can be. To treat only of the one (as some haue done) and wholy to leaue out and forget the other, I also hold it for an iniurie and crueltie: to let sincke and die in obliuion a matter of so great importance as is the dominion of the Greek Emperours, which continued so long afterwards, and to leaue the successors of CHARLES the Great, in which at this day the Empire remaineth, were to leaue the right way which leadeth to the place whither I am bound, and to take another whereby I should neuer attaine to my iournies end whither I am to trauaile. Wherefore seeing that I cannot go both waies, after some considerations, I have resolued to take for my principall subiect and historie of the Empire, that which the Church of *Rome* approued and then established, which is that of *Italie* and *Germanie*, in the person of CHARLES and his successours, recounting their liues and actes with such order as I haue obserued in those which are alreadie past; and by the way of discourse euer to make some mention of the Greeke Emperors, as occasion shall be offered, whereby he that shall reade this historie, may understand the successe of both Empires, vnder the name and title of one only.][72]

This partial solution of an insoluble problem has historicising implications. Mexía knows – even within the confines of a convention that obliges him to recount lives in serial order – that human beings act in contexts: that is, in the times and places peculiar to them and in the conditions which they partly shape. It follows that the histories of two sets of actors in distinct though not separate contexts cannot be recounted as a single history. Mexía is better equipped to recount the history of the western emperors, and ill placed to consider the conditions – even to generalise them – under which the eastern rulers acted; he therefore adopts a solution which gives the former a central place and assigns the

---

[72] Traheron, 1604, p. 525.

latter to the margins. He does this, however, with his eyes open; he knows that there is more to eastern history than he is recounting and hopes that it can be indirectly illuminated by the narrative of western (though in saying this of him, we must avoid overstating his capacity for historical generalisation in either context). He is aware that eastern history exists and that he is not telling the whole of it; and as a consequence, he knows that in some sense – it is significant that he is not sure in what – the eastern empire continued a legitimate existence even after the popes restored empire in the west. It is a further consequence – especially after his insistence that the ancient Roman empire ceased to exist – that he leaves unexplained in what sense the Carolingians, Salians and Hohenstaufen exercised empire with the approval of the western church. The unbroken succession of Caesars therefore bridges some signal discontinuities, as this historian knows well according to the conventions he is using. In the passage just quoted, Mexía confronts the problems of relating the history of medieval Constantinople to that of medieval Rome, which Gibbon first encountered in his schoolboy reading at Stourhead. It is unlikely to recur in the present series of studies until we reach Gibbon's attempt to solve it in the last volumes of the *Decline and Fall*.

It further follows that the history of the western empire, even though sanctified by the approval of the Church, cannot be the history of a sacred and universal rule over all mankind, so that we must ask just what the *Historia imperial y Cesarea* offered when presented to Charles V. Here we may single out Mexía's express statement that the 'historia del imperio que la santa yglesia Romana aprobo . . . es el de Italia y Alemania', and therefore excludes other histories which he is not committed to write. To Bruni and perhaps Biondo, these were primarily the histories of the revived cities of Lombardy and Tuscany; but to Mexía and perhaps Biondo, they were the histories of the kingdoms of the further west, founded by barbarians in what had been Roman provinces. One of these was Spain, where Charles as king and monarch could be provided with a lineage not subordinate to that he enjoyed as Caesar. It followed that the *monarchia universalis* which could be ascribed to Spain – globally and perhaps apocalyptically powerful in the Mediterranean, the New World and the Indies beyond it – could not be the result of a simple *translatio imperii*, but rather of a *renovatio*; a new Virgil would be required to sing it. The story of this imagination has been told,[73] but we know how Spanish jurists and theologians preferred to ground universal monarchy

---

[73] Pagden, 1995, ch. 2, pp. 29–62.

in natural law and the civil obedience of peoples, rather than in conquest and prophecy. As monarchy came to enjoy a natural history, it became important that – as Mexía in his way had foreseen – the origins of the kingdoms west of the medieval empire were barbaric, and compelled a new approach to Decline and Fall, redefined as the loss of Roman provinces to migrating barbarians. These kingdoms furthermore were several in number, and the image of a *monarchia universalis* was one to which there arose sustained French, Dutch and English resistance. As these principalities defined their several histories, their barbarian origins came to play a new part in the narratives of kingship, law and civil society which they constructed for themselves. The barbarians became significant actors in the history of civil society, and barbarism – to say nothing for the present of religion – became integral to the construction of the 'Enlightened narrative'. As it did so it encountered a persistent republican counter-thesis: the thesis, that is to say, of *libertas, imperium* and the complex relations between them, which we have watched descending from Sallust, Tacitus, Bruni and Machiavelli. Our attention has now to turn to the component of Decline and Fall in the historiography constructed for the western kingdoms.

# CHAPTER 12

# History in the western monarchies: barbarism, law and republican survivals

(I)

From this point the locus of our attention must shift, away from the German–Italian region in which the history of *translatio* has been re-counted and that of *libertas et imperium* revived, into regions and kingdoms which had once belonged to the empire of Constantine, but not always to that of Charlemagne and never to that of Otto I or Frederick I. Mexía has shown us the distinction between Charles V's Roman empire and his Spanish monarchy; and by Gibbon's time, two centuries later, we have to do with an 'Enlightened narrative' shaped very largely in the French and Anglo-British territorial monarchies. His Italian sources – the Neapolitan Giannone and the Lombards Muratori and Maffei[1] – serve to illustrate a history which is continuingly that of medieval papacy but diminishingly that of medieval western empire, and its perspectives are increasingly those shaped by Enlightenments taking place in and among the western monarchies. From this narrative the Spanish monarchy seems to have dropped out; that is to say, if there is an Enlightened history of Europe written from a Spanish perspective, it has escaped Gibbon's attention[2] (and that of the present writer), and a task before us is that of seeing what historical narratives of the end of Roman empire were shaped in France and Britain. This is a further shift westward, emphasising the extent to which European constructions of history were shaped in the Latin-speaking provinces lost to Roman empire in the fifth century, and were not a history of the *translatio imperii* so much as of Decline and Fall. They were, however, histories of barbarism and religion; the former necessary to the understanding of feudal power, the latter to that of the western

---

[1] *NCG*, chs. 1–4 (Giannone), pp. 384–6, 399 (Muratori and Maffei).

[2] He admired the history written by Juan de Mariana, but thought of it as what we should call baroque: a Jesuit history which almost became the work of a modern Livy. For references, see Womersley, 1994, III, p. 1239. Historians of Spanish America seem not to have gone deeply into the history of the Iberian Peninsula, which remained marginal to that of 'Europe'.

monarchs' dealings with the Christian church and papacy. And we are to find that Italian, especially Florentine, historiography ensured that Livy, Tacitus and Machiavelli continued to play disturbing roles at the heart of a western thought otherwise monarchical. It is a thesis of the present study that something in the nature of a 'Machiavellian moment' is necessary to the understanding of the first volume of the *Decline and Fall*.[3]

### (II)

The western monarchies – in this we may include the Spanish and more ambiguously the Habsburg-German – had histories and origins lying outside the narrative of translated empire. The French kingdom could be situated in that narrative; it was no less the heir of Charlemagne than was the empire of the German nation, and in the legends of the dove and the *ampoule* of Rheims could claim a sacrality equal to any conferred by papal coronation. But though French publicists might assert that their king exercised an *imperium* as absolute as the emperor's, they did not situate that claim in the narrative of *translatio*. Western kings wore closed crowns, to show that they shared *imperium* with no competitor – not even an *imperator* little disposed to claim it of them – but did not attempt to write histories of how it had descended to them from Rome. Better to rely on jurisprudence or scholastic philosophy to prove it necessary; the historiography would follow. Even so drastic a claim as that of the English king in 1533, that 'old authentic histories and chronicles' showed his realm to be an empire and himself its ruler in spirituals as well as temporals, did not supply the narrative the histories contained.[4] The history the kingdoms constructed of their descent from the Roman provinces they had once been took shape indirectly, as a product of many statements they found it desirable to make about their pasts. Their *imperium* was manifest in many histories, but there was no history of *imperium* itself.

The provinces that became kingdoms had been lost by the Roman empire in the fifth century through processes conspicuously involving barbarian invasions: Goths and Vandals in Spain, Franks and Burgundians

---

[3] This theme is among those pursued in the Afterword to *The Machiavellian Moment*, second edition (Princeton: Princeton University Press, 2003 (1975)).

[4] The Act in Restraint of Appeals (1533). For the rejection of any thesis that the Crown had inherited Constantine's *imperium* through Arthur, see Hay, 1952, Koebner, 1961, pp. 53–4, 314–15, Williamson, 1979.

in Gaul, Angles and Saxons in southeast Britain, Picts and Scots further north and west. The province that became France (*Francogallia*) could look back over a history immensely violent but continuous with that of a Roman Gaul in which Roman institutions existed beside those imported by barbarians, whereas in Britain it was believed – once the legends of Brutus and Arthur were discarded – that Celtic barbarians had destroyed Roman civility, after which Angles and Saxons had driven the Britons into Britanny, Cornwall, Wales and Galloway. The kingdom of Scotland came to rely on a history of invasions from Ireland, and both British kingdoms believed themselves to possess a barbarian frontier with a maritime Gaeldom originating west of the Roman *limites*. In all these kingdoms there was need of a history of barbarism, which – with Britain as a partial exception – became one in which the supposedly Germanic peoples who had broken the frontiers in the fifth century predominated to the point where the history of 'Europe' became one of Roman–Germanic interactions west of the Rhine. Whether the revival of formerly Etruscan free cities could be fitted into a history of Lombard Italy was a question overshadowed by that of *translatio imperii*.

The history of *Decline and Fall* thus became a history of barbarian presence. In the long run, it may be suggested, the moving force was the establishment of territorial kingdoms. Kings were creations partly barbaric and partly Christian; the king was a war chief consecrated by the Church, and it took time to make him a Roman *princeps*. The Church with its Constantinean and Eusebian roots conferred on him some of the attributes of a Christian emperor, and coronation and anointment brought him an *imperium* which might not require a *translatio*; the baptism of barbarians might be a sufficient precondition. With time, however, his authority became territorial and jurisdictional, based on the control of disputes arising from the local and regional tenure of land, and this is the point from which the concepts and discourses of law and property acquire the enormous importance they have possessed in Euro-American social, political and historical thought – which, however, the history of *libertas et imperium* has not so far had much occasion to consider. We have now to enquire how these patterns of discourse became part of a history of the termination and transformation of Roman empire in the west of Europe.

As kings expanded their jurisdiction and authority, they had need of systems of law and professional jurists. There presented itself the Roman civil law as codified by Justinian and augmented by subsequent emperors, with its imprecisely but vividly perceived history looking back as far as the Roman republic. From the moment when he presented himself as its head or source, the *rex* or *cyning* could begin to become a *princeps* and situate himself in a history of empire more Eusebian than Tacitean (though for this reason it might be a history more sacred than civil). This system existed in a complex relation with the canon law of the Church, part of the complex relationship between *imperium* and *sacerdotium*; we must keep in mind the probability that dispute between them would produce theology rather than historiography. At the same time, the civil law and its *princeps* must come into contact with a diversity of other systems, feudal or customary in character, barbaric in origin or self-image, presented in the practices of courts or codified in their encounter with the *jus scriptum*. Here is the principal, if limited and partial, means by which the barbaric component of culture, and the image of the barbarians as historical actors, entered the memory and literature of Latin European historiography. It did so – as should be needless to say – not through the medium of classically written history, but through the steady accumulation and interpretation of past states of culture, which we attribute to scholars rather than historians and denote by using such terms as humanism and antiquarianism. It has been rightly emphasised how much the huge change in our historical understanding owes to the humanist and philological re-interpretation of legal systems, for the reason that legal practice conserves by controlling the enormous variety of human social practices.[5] By the middle of the sixteenth century, what we describe as legal humanism was not only accumulating much of the antiquarian knowledge that was to be unified with historical narrative of the classical kind, but was developing a debate, and a new kind of narrative, around the question of the Roman and barbaric origins of western European law and kingship.

This debate occurred largely in the kingdom of France, where we have seen that the co-existence of Roman and Frankish institutions was documented from the beginning – by the eighteenth century it could be disputed how far the first kings had been Frankish war-chiefs and how far Roman provincial governors – and where systems of Roman and customary law co-existed in the structure of the kingdom. It has been documented how there arose scholarly debate among humanist jurists over the origins of the *feudum*, as a practice of late Roman estate management or as a species of gift among barbarian warbands; and how this became a debate over metahistory, disputing whether systems of law could be understood only in linguistic and historical context, or whether

5 Kelley, 1990.

the philosophy of law on the one hand, or the practices of custom on the other, were capable of preserving the authority of laws through the vicissitudes of historical change.[6] This is a development of cardinal importance in the history of historical thought, and its political implications were far-reaching. Of more immediate concern to this enquiry, we may see it as a moment in the history of the topos of Decline and Fall: this became a massive but partial replacement of Roman by barbaric culture, and there arose the question of what the latter was and how it had displaced the former.

We are at a point where the barbaric has become a component of the concept of liberty, giving that term meanings somewhat if not altogether removed from those borne by the Roman word *libertas*. The barbaric, the feudal and the customary became associated with the notions of right and property as drawn direct from the soil and possession of it, and pleadable by nobles, estates, townships and parliaments in systems of law originating in the same way and therefore distinct from those *leges scriptae* from which the *princeps* was *solutus* and which existed only *quod principi placuerant*. That the Roman law was absolutist and the barbaric constitutionalist was a simplification so enormous that it does not explain even its own history; but there is a road running from it which leads back to the contention that the Caesars failed because their rule was despotic and undermined both the *libertas* of the people and the *virtus* by which empire was maintained. There remained, of course, the question whether a *libertas* founded in right and property was the same as a *libertas* founded in citizenship and *virtus*. The freeman whose land gave him arms was supposed to know the answer.

At this point we may inject a text into the story, returning to the author from whose importance to Gibbon this volume set out. Tacitus' *Germania* or *De moribus Germanorum* is a work standing apart from his *Histories* and *Annals* but rediscovered and published not long after them.[7] It is not a narrative of the corruption and loss of liberty, or of the actions of humans when liberty has been lost, but rather a utopia – so at least it has been read – depicting liberty in a universe where such a narrative is not possible. It purports to describe the manners and customs of the tribes collectively known as Germans, existing beyond the Rhine and Danube *limites* in an endemic condition of intermittent war with Rome (which Domitian is at the time of writing conducting none too successfully[8]).

---

[6] Pocock, 1987b, chs. 1, 4; Kelley, 1970.    [7] Warmington, 1970; Kelley, 1993.
[8] *Germania*, 37; Warmington, 1970, pp. 182–3.

They extend as far as the dimly glimpsed Fenni, a people of hunter-gatherers inhabiting a region rather Scythia than Germania,[9] but are in essence forest-dwelling pastoralists of considerable warrior capacity. It is this character, and those accompanying it, which the rediscovery of Tacitus was about to impose indelibly on the category of 'barbarians' as it appeared in the historiography of *Decline and Fall*.

The peoples he describes are allowed many virtues: they are free and valiant, they consult with one another, they obey law and custom, they speak truthfully, they respect women.[10] At the same time they are uncouth and drunken, they lack the military discipline which would enable them to fight wars as well as engaging in heroic combat,[11] and they lack both the civic discipline which would make them citizens and the civil manners which would make them artists and philosophers. Lacking these qualities, however, they are incapable of the corruption that comes of losing them after they have had them; Tacitus is providing a primitive utopia in which the history of Rome cannot take place. The *Germania* is an important source for the early modern concepts of the state of nature, barbarism and (a later development) savagery. In providing a collective portrait of a number of peoples, already formidable in war, from whom subsequent invaders of the empire could be derived, he was contributing to a later practice – though it entailed a name he did not use[12] – of collectively describing all these invaders as 'Goths', and rendering the terms 'Gothic' and 'barbaric' interchangeable as opposed to 'Roman' and 'classical'. The peoples who invaded the western provinces, laying the foundation of the millennium of barbarism and religion from which Enlightenment was the escape, were 'Gothic' in the sense that they were both primitive and free, whereas those whom they overcame – perhaps also those who were to succeed them – were both civilised and corrupt (the pairing is a favourite with Gibbon). Tacitus, whether he intended it or not, is an author of the paradox that liberty may be barbaric and the progress of history a regression to servility; and a great deal of post-Roman history consists of a series of elaborations on these themes.

His Germans partition and re-partition the land among themselves,[13] and are obedient to the customs which regulate these procedures. In the eyes of later jurists and political philosophers, they could appear

---

[9] *Germania*, 46; Warmington, 1970, pp. 212–15.
[10] *Germania*, 7–9, 18–19, 23; Warmington, 1970, pp. 142–5, 156–61, 166–7.
[11] *Germania*, 30; Warmington, 1970, pp. 178–9.
[12] A people called 'Gotones' is mentioned in *Germania*, 43; Warmington, 1970, pp. 204–5.
[13] *Germania*, 26; Warmington, 1970, pp. 174–7.

archetypical of the free man who establishes the law of property in the act of appropriating it – though we shall find Gibbon asking whether these forest pastoralists practising a slash-and-burn clearance of land are engaged in the appropriation that entails agriculture and out of which a system of law can develop.[4] These doubts, however – traceable to the sixteenth-century debate over the origins of the *feudum* – did not displace Tacitus' Germans from that central myth of our civilisation whereby only in western Europe did the 'Goths', free if barbaric invaders of a civilised but servile agricultural and urban economy, succeed in establishing land tenures which, perhaps after a feudal and serf-based interlude, would be guaranteed by systems of law and lay the foundations of freedom. This freedom would be liberty in the modern sense that it set property and exchange above citizenship and virtue; yet it would enable admirers of 'Gothic' Europe to claim that it had re-established that freedom of the warrior, proprietor and citizen whose corruption, perceived by Tiberius Gracchus, had been the fatal moment of Roman and ancient history. At this point history might seem to have completed a cycle; but tensions between 'ancient' and 'modern' understandings of liberty remain cardinal in determining the architecture of Gibbon's *Decline and Fall*.

(III)

As the western kings consolidated their jurisdictions (or dealt with problems attending the attempt to do so) they engaged also – the process has been intensively studied in the case of England[5] – in an enterprise of intellectual and pictorial internal colonisation of the landscapes of their realms. It has been shown how cartography, topography, chorography and geography joined with descriptive literature and poetic imagination to depict kingdoms, counties and even new-found lands as the property and dominion of their rulers and principal inhabitants. This enterprise could not fail to disclose a historical dimension to landscape and territory, by no means monolithic or capable of inclusion within any one narrative. Monuments, inscriptions, patterns of cultivation, laws, folkways, languages and legends would all disclose a bewilderingly rich archaeology, with which the historical categories of sixteenth-century thought would have to wrestle. The pre-Roman, Roman, barbaric, Christian

---

[4] *DF*, I, ch. 9; Womersley, 1994, I, pp. 235–51.
[5] See the extensive bibliography in Mayhew, 2000. I have been greatly helped at various times by Kendrick, 1950; Ferguson, 1979; Helgerson, 1992; Baker, 1997.

and 'Gothic' would all raise their heads and demand attention, and what travellers, scholars, humanists and antiquarians found to say of all these would form part of a kingdom or region's historiography, including its existence as a Roman province and subsequent mutations into what it was now. This intellectual endeavour, however serendipitous, would acquire a history of its own, and its great figures – Camden, Peiresc, Muratori – would be praised and remembered. In writing a history of Gibbon's *Decline and Fall* in terms of the grand historical narratives preceding it, one must remember that there is a history of scholarship that equals that being constructed.

The term 'antiquarian' has been used advisedly. Studies by this name were a product of the programme of regional description, and aided the historical discovery of landscape. They were, however, only one aspect of the enterprise of antiquarian study, supposing it to have aimed at intellectual unity. This, however, almost by definition, it did not. The term came to be used of one devoted to the study of ancient materials to the point where his enquiries became marginal to, or lay outside, any of the disciplines of enquiry or the liberal arts. It could be used of jurists who became interested in the past meanings of terms whether or not they were employable in contemporary practice; of grammarians interested in the past state of language to the point where it became unusable by the rhetorician or the poet. On the one hand, we can see how such undisciplined enquiry – developing its own disciplines of philology and criticism – played a huge part in the transformation of historiography into the archaeology of documented culture; on the other, how widely it was attacked as useless, even as the sin of curiosity, and was obliged over time to develop arguments presenting 'curiosity' and 'amusement' as culturally positive goods. In tracing Gibbon's earlier studies in a previous volume, we saw how humanist studies of Roman roads and buildings and the topography of the ancient city – he seems not to have recognised Flavio Biondo as a pioneer in this regard[16] – contributed to build up the enterprise which he transformed by rendering it a narrative of imperial decline.[17] In the fields of territorial and topographic study, 'antiquarians' of this kind played a major role in providing western states with a visible and narratable past, Roman, barbaric and religious.

The term last used indicates another way in which the western kingdoms – and not they alone – became involved in the history of the replacement of Rome. From the first half of the sixteenth century to the

[16] Above, p. 183.   [17] *EEG*, chs. 11, 12.

second half of the seventeenth, Latin Christendom was caught up in the intense controversies that ensued from the Protestant Reformation, and for a long period resulted in religious warfare: in France and the Netherlands from 1560 to 1598, in Germany from 1618 to 1648, in the three Stuart kingdoms from 1637 to 1652. These conflicts involved intense debate, much of it conducted in theological and ecclesiological terms that came no nearer to historiography than the field of sacred history, debating the nature of the Church founded by Christ and therefore – a theme to which we shall constantly return – the nature of Christ himself. It was possible, however, to move debate, at least in some degree, into the narrative of history after Constantine: was that emperor the apostle of imperial power or its betrayer? Was the alliance between the papacy and the Frankish kingdom that brought about the *translatio imperii* a proof of Christ's gift to Peter or an episode in the papal usurpation? The decision to debate the matter in these terms was itself of ecclesiological import; it implied that the pope was not an agent of Antichrist operating in an apocalyptic perversion of sacred history, but an actor in a history of secular power – some said of reason of state[18] – akin to that we have seen related by Guicciardini. The errors of his church might therefore be understood as historical, rather than condemned as diabolical. The age we call Enlightened was to employ historical process as an intellectual tool in bringing to an end the disasters wrought by religious belief operating in sacred history, as well as by unpaid armies operating in secular.

(IV)

In this intellectual enterprise – which came to involve 'the first Decline and Fall' as well as the histories of barbarism and religion – antiquarian history was to play its part alongside the narrative and philosophical modes designated by Momigliano. To understand this pattern it is necessary – following flags planted by some important recent studies – to recommence the historical narrative from a new point. This chapter has been concerned with the shapings of Roman history in kingdoms lying west of the regions contested in the debates between papacy and empire, but its predecessors focussed upon the rewritings of history that went on in Italian and above all Tuscan republics momentarily liberated from either; and it has been here that the republican restatement of the decline of empire as a consequence of Caesarian rule has forcibly emerged. It is

---

[18]  *EEG*, p. 35.

conventional among historians to treat Florentine political and historical thinking as a first movement of modernity, but that is not the convention adopted here. The values of citizenship on which it rested were Sallustian, pre-juristic and pre-Christian in Roman terms, pre-Socratic and pre-Platonic if translated into Greek. They were in short radically 'ancient', and if we are to think of the territorial monarchies as 'modern' – especially as they emerged from the Wars of Religion into Enlightenment – we must see the 'ancient' as accompanying the 'modern', sometimes reinforcing it but as often furnishing the means by which it could be criticised. This is the history of the 'Machiavellian moment', and we have now to look at the ways in which Roman and republican thought was woven into that of the monarchies in the era succeeding the defeat of the Florentine republic.

Sallustian and Tacitean narratives of the decline of *libertas* were necessary to imperial history, even in its most Eusebian and Ghibelline forms; but no western monarch owed his crown to the supersession of a republic, or had to cope with the resentments of a former senatorial elite. It is therefore surprising to find, as we certainly do, images of Roman and republican liberty in the historiography of the western monarchies, and one of the most penetrating of political philosophers blaming its literature for the civil wars in England.[19] To understand its presence, we need to look beyond the sheer weight of humanist literature – a preponderance of the texts now made authoritative dealt with the crises of the republic and the principate – and consider the structure typical of a territorial monarchy and the location of its politically involved readerships. Any one of these entities would be a 'multiple' monarchy, made up of a diversity of provinces, estates, principalities and subordinate kingdoms – this marginalises, but does not eliminate, the formation of what we censoriously call 'nation states' – but in so far as its monarchy was effective, there would be at its centre a court: the more or less stationary locus, situated in one or more palaces, where the monarch resided in personal contact with those who executed his authority and sought access to his favour. These would include ministries, counsellors, courtiers and courtesans, as well as those magnates powerful enough to negotiate with him.[20] A complex culture grew up around the concept of service in return for favour, and drew on Roman sources, including Cicero's account of the social exchanges between patrons, their clients and their fellow patrons,

[19] Hobbes, *Behemoth* (c. 1668); Holmes, 1990, pp. 3, 23, 56.
[20] For what might happen when the prince was female, and the roles as well as the pronouns altered, see McLaren, 1999.

and Seneca's account of the relations between the *princeps* and his friends at a time when it might be said that the former was the only patron and all others his clients. These relationships might be managed, but were prone to deterioration. Tacitus' histories had been written in an interval between princes who could not be counselled and princes to whom their friends might again speak freely; and the former situation was what was meant by tyranny. Seneca himself had perished in a Tacitean narrative, and there survived the wildly subversive, because no longer effective, republican poetry of his nephew Lucan. The humanists, counsellors and ambitious courtiers of the European monarchies all knew how dangerous it could be to approach a prince and offer him service in return for favour; and they were not far removed from the Ottoman palace – 'this is the English, not the Turkish court' – where the isolation of the prince assumed the lineaments of oriental despotism.

It is therefore no surprise that Tacitean images of tyranny came to form part of the literature of European humanism, centred as it so often was upon courts; but it was to be a very long time, and a very circuitous journey, before the problems of kingship came to be connected with the suppression of republican liberty, or with that second Tacitean theme, the state's control of its armies. In one way, however, that journey may be represented as a return to a starting point; we may represent 'Tacitism' – a term of high significance, not quite identical with the many ways in which Tacitus was read[21] – as originating with the approaching end of republican government in Florence; a development which may be dated, for interpretive if not for narrative purposes, from Francesco Guicciardini's dictum that Tacitus was a most instructive historian because he both taught the tyrant how to exercise his rule and advised the prudent man how to live under a tyrant if he had to.[22] This startling observation sweeps the republic out of sight, presupposing its replacement by a species of one-man rule which will probably be tyrannous but may be tempered by prudent conduct on the part of either the ruler or a subject obliged to live on terms of some personal intimacy with him; for it is the prince's susceptibility to jealousy and suspicion that will make him a tyrant if not counteracted. We seem to be looking at the classical usurper, Tacitus' Tiberius or Machiavelli's new prince; he has obtained power over men formerly free, and he and they will never be able to trust one another. There is, however, a further startling development at hand,

---

[21] For introductions to Tacitism, see Dorey, 1969; Schellhase, 1976; Burke, Peter, in Burns and Goldie, 1991, IV, ch. 16; Tuck, 1993; Luce and Woodman, 1993; Mellor, 1995.

[22] *Ricordi*, C 18; Spongano, 1951, p. 22.

which Guicciardini may or may not have foreseen: the process by which this image of the city-state usurper ceased to be simply a portrait of the Italian *signore* or *principe*, and became part of an ideology that both criticised and upheld European kingship during the whole of the baroque period.

There arose a Tacitism which was part of the ideology and literature of courts; it was concerned with the possible degeneration of palace monarchy into tyranny, or with the substituted tyranny of over-powerful favourites like Tacitus' Sejanus. These consequences might occur if the prince failed to accept counsel, or if counsel were denied him by manoeuvre in the intimate world of antechambers and bedchambers. It was agreed by the most devoted of monarchists, in cultures where alternatives to monarchy were hardly thinkable, that kings were exposed to the temptation of tyranny, that its chief source was jealousy among the prince and his advisers and courtiers, and that its necessary remedy was the free giving and receiving of counsel, which kept the prince in mind of moral (and political) reality.[23] Here the chief role of Tacitus was to supply the contrast between Tiberius or Nero, denied counsel or unable to accept it, and Nerva or Trajan, to whom one might speak the truth without fear of resentment or suspicion. But the *amici principis* in Tacitus' world were still senators, living in the shadow of a republic in which power had been exercised by those who exchanged information and counsel among themselves; and the underlying problem of the *Annals* and *Histories* is whether the freedom of counsel can survive the republic's suspension, in a world where it persists as memory though it has ceased to be reality. European kings, west of Italy, did not rule by the supersession of republics, but they were surrounded by ministers, magnates and courtiers, who might as discontented counsellors imagine themselves as senators, whose counsel might almost do without the prince. Behind Tacitus' account of the world after the republic lay the image of the republic itself, and this image took on significance in political cultures otherwise wholly committed to monarchy. Only in England was a point reached where a parliament of estates claimed to be the sole source of the counsel by which a king should govern, and as a result found itself committed to the abolition of monarchy, which it did not in fact desire.

But there was a *realpolitik*, a disenchanted account of the politics of counsel, favour and access, viewed at quarters too close for the mechanisms of moral legitimation to be seen as operating effectively. In this

[23] For the philosophy of counsel see the unpublished dissertation of Conrad, 1988.

perspective the king's shadow was always that of the tyrant, the counsellor's that of the flatterer; and Tacitus could be read either as warning each of the need to escape his shadow, or as advising either on the conduct appropriate when this escape was cut off. There arose an *aulica ratio* or advisory for the court, merging with a *ratio status, ragione di stato*, or *raison d'état*;[24] though use of the latter terminology entailed the always incomplete shift from 'state' meaning the personal status of the ruler, magnate or minister to 'state' in the impersonal sense where 'reason of state' could mean the techniques whereby the monarch controlled his realms, and 'states' as governed entities could have interests and pursue a *ragione* of their own.[25] To understand 'Tacitism', however, we must begin with the politics of intimacy – which could be depicted as the point where princely rule had replaced the republic – and see them as projecting, across the entire spectrum of meanings, the image of a society where politics were not perfectly legitimated and could not always be practised according to the laws of morality. The most austere of Christian moralists did not attempt to escape the problem of casuistry; the *civitas terrena* was a fact.

If we suppose the climate of 'Tacitism' to be one in which the possibility of tyranny, servility and villainy was ever present to the point of near-actuality, we can understand why its moral precepts were multivalent and even ambivalent. Giuseppe Toffanin long ago[26] distinguished between a *tacitismo nero*, which taught that a prudent submission to the will of the prince might after all be the best way of forestalling his descent into tyranny, and a *tacitismo rosso*, which encouraged criticism of his rule and the thought that there might be – even had been – alternatives to it. The 'red' variety carried scepticism to the point of subversion; it contrasted the prince with the liberty he denied to his intimates and subjects, and reached so far as to remind both that, at least in the Roman past, there had existed a republic ruled by free men who were one another's equals. But this was a republicanism of the court; it arose when discontented counsellors, whether ministers or magnates, began to picture themselves as senators and employ a Tacitean scenario to denounce the tyranny, less often of the prince himself than of the favourite, their own successful competitor.[27] Buckingham might be Sejanus, and it was hard

[24] The literature of reason of state is large; see initially Meinecke, 1957, Church, 1972, and the bibliography in Burns and Goldie, 1991, pp. 760–4. For *aulica ratio* (Annibale Scotti, 1589), see Tuck, 1993, p. 44.
[25] For the increasing impersonality of 'state', see Skinner, 1978, 'Conclusion', and his 'The State', in Ball et al., 1987, pp. 90–131.
[26] Toffanin, 1921.
[27] Peltonen, 1995; Worden, Blair, in Burns and Goldie, 1991, p. 445; Elliott and Brockliss, 1999.

to say so without implying that Charles I was Tiberius or in danger of resembling him.[28] But identifications of Sejanus and Tiberius themselves implied that there was no way back to rule by a senate, even had such a state of things ever existed in the western kingdoms. *Tacitismo nero* and *rosso* might easily merge into one another, and at the point of merger there might well arise a moral scepticism as to the meaning of acts and decisions, and a practical scepticism as to their predictability. We may now venture two generalisations: first, that the literature of *tacitismo nero* greatly outweighs in quantity that of *tacitismo rosso*; second, that the literary form it predominantly took was that of the collection of aphorisms. In the century beginning about 1580, there have been counted more than a hundred published works in the genre of *discorsi* or *commentarii sopra Cornelio Tacito*,[29] which we are bound to see as in some way antithetical to Machiavelli's *discorsi sopra Tito Livio*; as dealing with the Julio-Claudian principate where the latter had dealt with the heroic early republic, and therefore as concerned with an anti-heroic politics and history.

The Tacitist *discorsi* are not, in an immediate sense, histories at all. In our pursuit of the role of Tacitus in the *Decline and Fall*, we are concerned with narrative: that of how the principate failed to deal with the consequences of its suppression of the republic and became prone to tyranny, crises of succession and the interference of armies acting *alibi quam Romae*. The *discorsi* of the baroque century are so far from being concerned with this narrative that they avoid narrative altogether, mining the texts of Tacitus for aphorisms and 'maxims of state', precepts and general laws instructing the prince or the courtier how to avoid tyranny and servility where possible, how to recognise them when they inescapably occur, how to comport oneself where they cannot be avoided, and how – reason of state coming into action – to avoid the more disastrous consequences of one's own actions or those of others. At this point the aphorism takes on moral significance; it is advice, at once serious and sceptical, often but not necessarily cynical, on how to act, live and behave in a world where actions are not fully under moral or political control. In Tacitus this results from the loss of *libertas et imperium*; it would not have surprised any author studied in this volume to learn from Machiavelli that under republican liberty and its empire action might be more glorious but not necessarily more ethical.

The exclusion of narrative by aphorism now requires scrutiny. When humans exercise *imperium* – the rule of self and others – under conditions of *libertas* – one's actions shared with those of others, but not dominated by any of the latter – they can claim to be enacting a history intelligible as the consequence of such actions, even when the consequences have proved unexpected, unfortunate or tragic. But when *imperium* is not exercised *in libertate*, it does not follow that history can be narrated as intelligible, and the injunction to live under Tacitist conditions may entail the injunction to cease acting as if one understood the sequence of events in which one is living and acting or attempting to control. This injunction may be prudential; at the point where Guicciardini was noting the importance of Tacitus as an adviser on how to live under tyranny and mitigate it, he was penning *ricordi* in which he advised himself and his descendants against believing that one understood the political situations in which one found oneself, or even that one had calculated with finality the difficulties in the way of understanding them.[30] He wished to warn, less against simple-mindedness than against over-cleverness. A century after Guicciardini, we have Virgilio Malvezzi,[31] a Bolognese nobleman in the Spanish service, asking in his *discorsi sopra Cornelio Tacito* both how far it was safe or justifiable to write history in the climate of the court, and how far it was possible to write it in a political universe where even the wisest of maxims of state turned inwards and counselled against believing them. The aphoristic genre converted history into secular mystery: mystery of state, perhaps even the mystery that there was no mystery.[32] Gibbon's conception of irony, even of 'the fine philosophy of Mr. Hume',[33] becomes distinctly visible.

It was of Malvezzi that John Milton irritably remarked that he had 'cut Tacitus into slivers and steaks', and it has been said of Milton that 'aphorism' was for him a term of abuse.[34] He wrote the words quoted in 1641, at a time when neither regicide nor republic had become thinkable, and he did not mean that Malvezzi ought to have been writing a Tacitean history of the degeneration of monarchy into tyranny. He was attacking the reduction of politics to paradoxes and gnomic maxims for exactly the same reason that moved Hobbes to praise it, both in the style of Tacitus and in that of Thucydides: that it discouraged the sententious and periodic eloquence that enabled subjects to believe that they could shape

---

[30] *Ricordi*, C 23 (Spongano, 1951, p. 28), C 79 (p. 61), C 114 (p. 125), C 182 (p. 194); Pocock, 1975, pp. 266–70.
[31] Malvezzi, 1622; Bulletta, 1995, ch. 6; see also Belligni, 1999. The most *rosso* of Italian Tacitists was not Malvezzi but Traiano Boccalini.
[32] Donaldson, 1988.      [33] *NCG*, p. 177.
[34] Dzelzainis, Martin, in Armitage, Himy and Skinner, 1995, pp. 193–4.

the world and understand their own actions through rhetoric.[35] The maxim, glancing outwards from a narrative increasingly thick, knotty and intricate, reminded men that they lived in such a narrative, that the decisions of sovereigns alone could determine its values, but that there were severe limits on even the sovereign's capacity to guide its course.

This would not mean that there was no such thing as a Tacitean historiography, though the thrust of Tacitist thinking might lie in another direction. It might mean only that the texture of the narrative would be thick and knotty, filled with reason of state and *arcana imperii*, and designed to convey the message that the springs of action were hard to penetrate and the outcomes of actions usually other than the agents had intended. The baroque era is rich in histories of this kind, dealing with the conflicts of great monarchies with each other, with increasingly divided churches and with civil and religious war: Guicciardini's *Storia d'Italia*, Paolo Sarpi's *Istoria del Concilio Tridentino*, Jacques-Auguste de Thou's *Historiarum sui Temporis*, and – a late example – Clarendon's *History of the Rebellion*.[36] Whether or not 'Tacitist' in their political message, these may be termed (as they have been) 'Tacitean' in their portrayal of human struggles with a political, religious and circumstantial world which they have not made and in which they can command neither their actions nor – importantly – their passions. Tacitus was a 'philosophical' – Adam Smith was to add a 'sentimental' – historian inasmuch as he presented the historical world in this way before 'philosophy' took on the meanings it had in the eighteenth century.

'Tacitism', resolving narrative into aphorisms, also contributed to the shaping of a 'philosophy' that had little to do with history. From 1530 through the rest of the century and beyond, the states of Europe were increasingly plagued by religious division and religious wars. This conflict of values was more radical than any before it, since it entailed incompatible visions of how the soul was to be saved; and a monarch might find his rule radically desanctified, since he might be obliged to hold his realms together regardless of what he or his subjects thought about God. In these circumstances Tacitus became a significant author, since his thoughts on how the individual might preserve his integrity of mind under tyranny portrayed the life and death of senators and counsellors who were also Stoic philosophers: Thrasea Paetus, Seneca and Helvidius Priscus. Stoic

---

[35] Rossini, Gigliola, in Pagden, 1987, pp. 303–24; Skinner, 1996, ch. 7; Rogers and Sorell, 2001.
[36] It might be possible to add the Dutch Tacitist, Pieter Corneliszoon Hooft, whose works, now as then, remain only in Dutch. For what is available about him in English, see Haitsma Mulier, Eco, in Duke and Tamse, 1985, pp. 55–72.

philosophy, entailing a quietness of mind, a private moral integrity, and a certain scepticism towards ultimate metaphysical conclusions, came to be a dominant component in what we see as Tacitism, and joined with the political advice that offered both rulers and subjects a means of remaining sane[37] to give a new meaning to the term 'philosophy'; there are now histories of political philosophy in the baroque period which see it as developing from these foundations.[38] It had proto-deist and proto-Enlightened implications, in so far as it tended to substitute the philosopher's knowledge concerning God for the believer's communion with the body and blood of Christ, but the 'philosophy' of the eighteenth century was of a sharply different character.

The persona thus sketched had passed some way beyond that of a denizen of a court, concerned for his relationship with a potentially tyrannical prince – though the presence of such a role is never to be forgotten. He had become a philosopher, which is to say a moral individual concerned to control his passions and avoid capture by a world of furious conflict.[39] His thought, discourse and life-style therefore contributed to the history of philosophy, rather than (as we have seen) that of historiography. At the same time, however, he lived beyond the court, in a life of retirement, privacy and contemplation, but also of civil society, friendship, neighbourliness, duty and office. He was not beyond the reach of law, government or antiquity, and in his world there was room to collect and reflect upon historical information of a non-narrative kind. In this cultural landscape moved the figure of the antiquary as brilliantly described in a recent study of Fabri de Peiresc:[40] Tacitist and neo-Stoic in his withdrawal from court and conflict into a world philosophical in the sense that it was contemplative, sceptical and opposed to dogma and disputation, but philological in its deep commitment to language, curiosity and history – a history, however, bent on the *peinture* of what had been, rather than on the *récit* of how men had acted, and therefore on civil society rather than on the republic in which *libertas* pursued *imperium*. This antiquarianism was to come under bitter attack by a philosophy sceptical of all knowledge except the ideal, and was to retort by reorganising itself as a philosophical history of manners, modifying the meaning of the term philosophy as it did so. In this regrouping of philosophy, philology and history the images of republic and empire, barbarism and religion, were to play parts that must be traced.

[37] Conrad, 1988, on the therapeutic function of counsel.    [38] Especially Tuck, 1993.
[39] Keohane, 1980.    [40] Miller, 2000.

(v)

The history of Tacitism, then, had taken a long course more *nero* than *rosso*, though shot with enigmatic gleams. Where, all this while – one might wonder – was the Tacitus who knew what liberty had been and wrote the history of what men were like without it? One might ask the same question regarding Machiavelli, like him easily denounced as an apologist for tyranny but presenting an even richer history of the republican liberty that had preceded it. At what point – to put the question in other terms – might the Tacitean narrative re-assert itself at the expense of the aphorisms that had long fragmented and obscured it? In the chapters to come it will be argued that this did not happen (as far as the history of historiography is concerned) because the Tacitism of the court revealed what befell counsellors under autocracy, but in consequence of a larger problem afflicting the European monarchies: the problem of armies, no longer feudal but rather mercenary than maintained by the state, which had many resonances with the history of both the republic and the principate. The Tacitean narrative returned, in short, when it was once more enriched by the Gracchan explanation; when it became again Appianic. The image of the barbarian, and the relation between arms, property and liberty, returned with it as features of the narrative of the First Decline and Fall.

# CHAPTER 13

# Lipsius and Harrington: the problem of arms in ancient and modern monarchy

## (I)

Appian's history of the Roman civil wars, which explained the disintegration of the republic as the result of the failure of its military colonisation of Italy, became known in Greek to humanist scholars from about the year 1551.[1] As we have seen, it could be linked with Tacitus' intimation that the Julio-Claudian principate had been only partly successful in bringing the armies of the *imperium* under its control; and Gibbon's use of this thesis in explaining the failure of the Antonine principate at the death of Commodus furnished him with a narrative of the 'first decline and fall' which looked back towards the failure of the republic itself. We have now to consider how it was that Appianic arguments became established in both erudite scholarship and civil philosophy, and pointed the way towards a restatement of Tacitism in the eighteenth century.

A major source of the revival of Appian may be found in the writings of the Modenese scholar Carlo Sigonio (1522/3–1584).[2] He was not a historian of the wars or an analyst of military power – though we shall find him playing some part in shaping the thought of James Harrington[3] – and his importance for our purposes lies at a distance from these themes. It is that he shows us the sixteenth-century intellect critically examining an association of ideas basic to the notion of Decline and Fall since we first encountered it in Sallust: that between *libertas* and *imperium*. Sallust had proposed that the *libertas* of citizens freed from kings had produced an increase in civic energy, or *virtus*, and a consequent expansion of *imperium*, meaning empire; but had like others displayed doubts whether this *virtus* would survive uncorrupted by the empire it had acquired. Tacitus – writing after the end of the Appianic process – had considered how the extension of empire had led to the concentration of *imperium*,

---

[1] White, 1912–13, I, p. ix; McCuaig, 1989, pp. 10, 16.
[2] McCuaig, 1989, is a full study of Sigonio in English.     [3] Below, p. 297.

now meaning the republic's authority, in a single person, and so to a loss of *libertas*, meaning both the freedom from fear and the freedom to employ one's *virtus* in a public cause.[4] After a long interlude dominated by Augustine's assertion that *libertas* and *virtus* amounted to no more than a sterile pursuit of glory, the revival of civic life in Italian cities had produced an ideal of citizenship both just and sociable, but still entailing a pursuit of glory and the conviction that *imperium* was a precondition of *libertas*. Bruni had returned to the Tacitean account of Roman history, and had stressed the loss under Caesarian rule of the *libertas* necessary to *virtus* and *imperium*, so that the rule of emperors was co-terminous with the decline of empire. Machiavelli had rehearsed these themes, emphasising the extent to which liberty had been a conquering virtue, pagan rather than Christian.

It was acknowledged that liberty was a humane and social force, characteristic of men in cities; but the *imperium* necessary to it meant both the free government of the individual and collective self, and the extension of that self's empire over others. It was difficult to see how humans could be free without depriving other humans of their freedom, and the problem has not disappeared from modern or postmodern political theory. In the sixteenth century, the association of *libertas* and *imperium* meant that those who enjoyed the beauties of liberty naturally sought empire over others and might – it was the lesson of Roman history – find their liberty threatened by the empire it acquired. This lies behind the remarkable researches of Carlo Sigonio into the exact meanings of the *libertas* Roman citizens had claimed to enjoy.[5] The presumption thus far has been that *libertas* was the precondition of *virtus* and therefore of *imperium* – *ex libertate imperium*; but there has survived a disquieting aphorism attributed to no less a figure than Scipio Africanus the second, ending with the formula *ex imperio libertas*.[6] This may mean that it was Rome's empire over others that assured its freedom as a city, but what Sigonio brought to light was that such a formula – he may not have known the Scipionic reference – applied to the citizen as well as to the city, and that the Roman's *libertas* was a consequence of the *imperium* he enjoyed, either as exercising magistracy or military command by authority of the city – in which case it might mean his freedom to take decisions and interpret his commission – or

---

[4] Roller, 2001, ch. 14, argues against Wirszubski for a 'negative' interpretation of *libertas*.
[5] McCuaig, 1989, pp. 81–3, 125–8, 136–7, 218–19.
[6] Wirszubski, 1950, p. 40: 'ex innocentia nascitur dignitas, ex dignitate honor, ex honore imperium, ex imperio libertas'. I am indebted to both Jotham Parsons and Patricia Springborg for bringing this to my attention.

as participant in one or another of the city's voting assemblies. There did not disappear the Athenian ideal of a community of citizens taking decisions in which each both ruled and was ruled – this remained an important constituent of the ideal of *virtus* – but it was reinforced, and at times replaced, by the image of Rome as an oligarchy of seekers after authority, competing for the many kinds of *imperium* which the city granted and existed in order to grant. The breakdown of the republic was the breakdown of its capacity to control and authorise this competition.

Sigonio was led into deeply technical researches into the archaic roots of Roman society, entailing the conclusion that the citizen had pursued authority as a member of a *gens* or kindred before he did so primarily as a member of an *ordo* or estate. By 1560 he had begun to publish, and revise, two linked works, *De antiquo iure civium Romanorum* and *De antiquo iure Italiae*.[7] The term *jus* should not be taken as indicating that Sigonio was a student of systematic jurisprudence; it denoted rather the legal status of the active individual, his immunities as well as his authority, what might not be done to him as well as what he might do, with the emphasis in so deeply competitive a culture always falling on the latter. It is the double character of his work, on *jus* both Roman and Italic, that shows us Sigonio as a student of empire as well as *imperium*, and an Appianic student though he did not follow the course of Appian's narrative history. He knew that the diversity of *jus* – *jus Romanum*, *jus Latinum*, *jus Italicum* – was the product of Roman techniques for incorporating Italy into the body of the conquering state, by means of direct colonisation and the grant of colonial or municipal status; and he followed Appian's Gracchan thesis that this method of state-building had begun to break down when the military smallholder began to be replaced by the large slave-worked estate. He echoes Appian's strictures on this deflection of policy, and he regards Sulla, Caesar and Augustus as the destroyers of the republic;[8] but he does not join him in tracing how the armies degenerated into the followers of warlords in search of confiscated lands. Sigonio in all probability accepts this thesis, but he is not the kind of historian to relate it as a narrative. He is a student of institutions, displaying the intricate workings of a *jus* he well knows is to break down at no distant time; a student of norms, rather than their deformation. As a result, he does not study the norms of the principate, nor ask whether Augustus or Trajan succeeded in restoring anything of a working system. His later works, on the empire from Diocletian to Justinian and the *regnum italicum* of the

---

[7] McCuaig, 1989, chs. 2 and 3, for a close study of these works.        [8] McCuaig, 1989, p. 171.

Middle Ages,⁹ are discontinuous with his earlier, which he continued to elaborate. He did not become a historian of the Augustan principate, the Antonine monarchy, or the breakdown of either; the themes of Gibbon's first volume.

(11)

The republic had ended in the civil wars of the triumvirates; the *arcanum* of the principate had been revealed when the armies found they could impose emperors on Rome. These catastrophes could be explained by means of a history of arms, their social basis in the resources of the Roman state, and the failure of that state to keep them under its control. The basis of such a history was provided by the unknown historian who is Appian's source; and we have now to discover how a history of arms in antiquity was developed by early modern scholars and ideologues to the point where it became fundamental to the idea of Decline and Fall. A key actor in this story is the acknowledged leader of European Tacitism, the Netherlander Justus Lipsius. He may be considered in the first place as a 'Tacitist' of the kind already examined: a 'philosopher' who taught both detachment from the state and obedience to it, an *ataraxia* and *apatheia* tending to the reduction of Christianity to a philosophical religion. There is a literature which exhibits the dignity and nobility of this ideal, and its very broad appeal to the literati of all Europe.¹⁰ However, this philosophic Tacitism was not solely an ethos of acceptance and withdrawal. Lipsius saw himself as a Roman Stoic, not a Cynic; he was prepared to employ philosophy as a practical tool in the service of the state, and his Tacitism took the form of a certain freedom of choice as to which state he would serve, and even which religious confession he would profess and acknowledge. His practical writings in more than one political and religious service were to make him important as a military theorist and a shaper of the European sense of history.

Lipsius' writings on Roman military practice, coupled with his Tacitist and neo-stoic philosophy, may be divided at the year 1591. For twelve years before that date he taught at the Protestant university of Leiden, but in 1591 removed to the Catholic university of Louvain/Leuven in the Spanish Netherlands, apparently on the grounds that a single state religion was to be preferred to the tensions among several. This was

---

⁹ For the notions of civic liberty contained in these, McCuaig, 1989, pp. 81–3; for Sigonio's troubles with the Vatican censors, ibid., ch. 4.

¹⁰ Morford, 1991, and bibliography.

a thoroughly philosophical decision, and it was in the logic of his *De constantia* (1584) that his philosophy should have been little affected by his change of confession, as his modern students generally presume. In the exposition of military practice, however, the change is of some significance. In the Leiden years, his writings on Roman tactics were intended to be, and were, read by the princes of Nassau and Orange, stadholders and captains-general of the armies of the Dutch confederate republic. Lipsius claimed that he was not a useless pedant, and did not lay claim to mastery of the art of war; as a student of antiquity, he possessed knowledge of value to modern military captains.

Tunc haec audebis, homo umbraticus?, inquiunt, qui serio *numquam hostem, numquam castra videris, numquam denique partem ullius bellici muneris attigeris* [Cic. 11 De Orat.]?

Ego vero audebo, nec mei tamen ingenii aut virium fiducia, sed eorum a quibus jamdiu mutuor et sumo. Quid enim hic meum? ordo aliquis et contextus fortasse: at verba sensusque; mihi praeeunt illi, quos in hoc ipsa re (fidenter dicam) Annibal aliquis audire nihil abnuat, aut ipse Caesar. Namquid sapientes inclutosque illos viros fugit? cur non hic quoque rectum eorum et purum judicium? qui partim interfuerunt, imo et praefuerunt, bellis: partim in Senatu et populo illo versati sunt, ubi assidua materies et agitatio harum rerum. Viderunt igitur, audierunt: et quod caput est cum iudicio observarunt caussas ipsas originesque rerum, nec solum προφάσεις eventuum sed αἴτια ipsa.[11]

[But some will say unto me, darest thou enterprise these things, who art but a scholeman? who in earnest, *diddest neuer see the enemie in the face, no not so much as their tents, and to bee short, diddest neuer execute the least part of any warlike office?* Yea surely, euen I dare undertake it, yet not in the trust I repose in mine own capacitie or strength, but in their wisdome, from whome all this while I have borrowed and taken. For what is there heere of mine? It may be a certaine order, and composition of the discourse: but they do furnish me with words, and with sence, whom (I dare confidently say) *Haniball*, or *Cesar* himselfe, would not refuse to heare in the same matter. For what is it that these wise and worthy men were ignorant of? And why is not their iudgement herein good and sound? who partly were present, and did command in warre? partly were conuersant with the Senate, and with the people, where the like matters were ordinarily handled and discoursed of? They haue then seene the causes, and grounds of these matters, which were done there: and not onely the apparences of the successe of affairs, but euen the causes of them.][12]

In a marginal note Lipsius added:

---

[11]  Lipsius, 1634, pp. 241–3. This work, the *Politicorum libri sex*, was originally published in Leiden in 1589.
[12]  Trans. Jones, 1594, pp. 124–5.

Historici magistri ad militiam [Historiographers are the masters of military discipline][13]

and reiterated the points made above. This is primarily a vindication of rhetoric; ancient writings preserve not only the information, but the reflections made upon it in ancient political assemblies, and he is able to construct his own writings aphoristically, weaving together a tissue of sayings – like that of Cicero quoted above, but heavily dominated, as we would expect, by extracts from Tacitus – forming a repository of wisdom transmitted and elucidated by Lipsius himself. He is therefore philosophising; military technology is constantly enlarged into political and moral reflections; but Roman battlefield practice has much to say to commanders in sixteenth-century Europe. There exist documents in which the princes of Nassau, to whom Lipsius addressed himself, show real interest in the legionary drill which permitted each rank to throw its javelins in turn, and find it applicable to the musket tactics of their own soldiers.[14] There is not so great a difference between a missile weapon thrown by muscle power and the powder-driven shot from a musket worked by hand; if gunpowder worked a military revolution, it was through cannon mounted in star redoubts.[15] We are in the world where the captain of the Hampshire grenadiers, the student of Guichardt's *Mémoires militaires sur les Grecs et les Romains*, and the historian of the Roman empire could be useful to one another.[16]

Lipsius employed the masters of antiquity to teach not only tactics, but discipline in a moral sense. Gerhard Oestreich, his twentieth-century expositor in such matters, showed how he used Tacitist and neo-Stoic philosophy to formulate an ethos of service for the officers, at least, of the masterless men and mercenaries who made up the sixteenth- and seventeenth-century armies.[17] It is the ethos of Shakespeare's Captain Jamy, 'who will do good service though he lie in the ground for it',[18] or at a level of greater complexity that officer in William III's army of 1688 who, being asked how he reconciled his Catholic faith with standing guard over the captive James II, replied that his sword was his prince's and his religion was his own.[19] Oestreich saw in Lipsius' advice to the

---

[13] Lipsius, 1634, p. 243; Jones, 1594, p. 125.    [14] Parker, 1988, pp. 16–24.
[15] Parker, 1988, ch. 1 generally.
[16] *EEG*, p. 117. Two centuries after Lipsius, the Duke of Wellington recalled learning much from Caesar's *Commentaries* when campaigning in India, and believed he had made some improvements on the Roman method of building floating bridges.
[17] Oestreich, 1982, chs. 5–6.    [18] *Henry V*, act III, scene 2.
[19] I should be glad to recover the source of this anecdote.

princes of Orange-Nassau the philosophical foundations of the modern state, absolutist, military and bureaucratic; and indeed it seems that German princes interested in erecting their dominions into states of this kind were diligent students of the tactics, organisation and discipline of the Dutch army.[20] But the princes of Orange – other than William III of England – were not the sovereigns of any state which they could organise as a military machine. The mercenaries of Europe repaired to them as the highly independent captains-general of a confederation of trading cities, whose mercantile wealth supplied the funds that enabled them to hold their armies together through long sieges and campaigns and make them a model to others. Oestreich was a historian very much in the German tradition.

At this point our perspective expands to take in the historiography of Rome. In the House of Orange the republic of the Netherlands possessed a principate, and in the States General and the States of Holland a senate, who found themselves often bitterly and sometimes violently opposed, but never reached the Tacitean condition of mutual corruption, tyranny and servility, for the very good reason that, if the princes commanded the armies and therefore the *imperium militiae*, the States commanded the treasury and therefore the *imperium domi*. We therefore look for some major interpretations of Roman history founded on the Dutch experience; and if – as seems to be the present state of knowledge – these are not to be found, we may return to Lipsius in search of what he thought about the basis on which the armies of the Roman republic and empire were paid, maintained and induced to accept demobilisation.

Here the 'Gracchan thesis', transmitted by Appian, was of central importance. If one was to look further than a mere idealisation of the smallholding warriors of the legendary early republic, it must be accepted that Rome had expanded by planting colonies and granting rights of association throughout central and southern Italy; but that this system had been undermined by the growth of *latifundia*, with the resultant growth of landless armies seeking grants of settlement from the commanders they followed in the civil wars occasioned by the Gracchan experiments. Appian had continued this narrative down to the victory of Augustus over Antony, but it was less clear what had happened next. Had Augustus tamed the armies by establishing them in permanent encampments along a stabilised frontier, with the right to colonise in those distant regions when their service expired? Had he employed the wealth of Egypt

---

[20] Oestreich, 1982, chs. 6–7.

to establish a treasury, out of which the soldiers might be paid in cash instead of land? In that case, what was to be said of Tacitus' *arcanum imperii*? Had the armies of 69–70 and after marched on Rome to instal their *imperatores* in search of ready cash, since they did not seem to have seized on the lands of Italy? These questions could be asked in the sixteenth century, but no authoritative answer was ready to hand. They must be asked, furthermore, in an environment where mercenary armies were increasingly employed in wars civil, religious and between kings, but there was little chance of settling them on the land and not much more of paying them on a regular basis. Lipsius was well aware what this might lead to; in the *Politicorum libri*, he writes feelingly of armies that

are burdensome to the husbandman, and their fashion is, *to burne, to waste, to make boote of all things*, as if they were among strangers, or in *the enemies Citties. They are the destruction of the countrey, which they should preserve from spoyle.* Yea, they will robbe the Prince himselfe, being *the verie horseleaches* (as it were) *of his treasurie*: whose principall exploits at this day, *is ever to suck the marrowe out of the Kings bones.*[21]

It is the recurrent complaint of the Wars of Religion. The words italicised, however, are all translations from classical sources inserted aphoristically to bring ancient language to bear on modern problems. The *Politicorum libri* go on to outline an ideal situation in which the prince's armies are composed mainly of his own subjects, with a leavening of foreign mercenaries (advice of limited use to the princes of Orange, who had few subjects of their own); mainly of trained bands summoned from their civil occupations, with a leavening of long-service professionals (distrusted as over-expensive and liable to seek political change); and predominantly of countrymen, as citizens garrisoning their own walls are prone to rebel.[22] The emphasis is always on the least costly method, and there is little to tell us where the prince is to find the revenue he is to expend. It is hard to say, therefore, what lessons of antiquity Lipsius here thinks relevant to the problem of soldiers' pay.

All the more is it relevant that Lipsius' two major works on Roman greatness and empire – *De militia Romana* and *Admiranda sive de magnitudine Romana*, both employed by Gibbon[23] – appeared after his removal to Louvain in 1591. Whatever his role in founding the modern state through popularisation of the Dutch model, almost any commentator of the following century would have agreed that, in leaving the Dutch service for

[21] Trans. Jones, 1594, p. 142; Lipsius, 1634, p. 271. The words italicised are from Tacitus, Cicero and Juvenal; Lipsius gives references.
[22] Lipsius, 1634, pp. 274–5.  [23] Womersley, 1994, III, p. 1235.

the Spanish, he was quitting the exemplary success story of early modern military finance and attaching himself to the equally exemplary failure. It became a commonplace that Spain imported bullion from the New World and beggared itself by spending it on armies, after which it was seen no more and the armies dissolved in mutiny and free quarter till the next silver fleet arrived; whereas the Dutch invested thriftily in their gigantic merchant capital, providing themselves with a steady income that maintained the armies year after year while the country grew rich. Whatever the shortcomings and simplifications of this account, it was itself the product of a culture hard put to it to provide either the theory or the practice of military finance. In Lipsius' defence it may be said that he left the Princes of Orange and attached himself to the Archdukes of Flanders at a time when the Spanish armies were at their most formidable and the monarchy's power to finance them at its height. We have to ask what account of Roman history he was moved to construct in these historic circumstances.

(III)

Lipsius began publishing the *De militia Romana* at Antwerp in 1595, and the *De magnitudine* – to give its short title – followed in 1598. The former work was intended to form a tripartite study entitled *Fax historica*, but this does not seem to have been completed. What we have is the *De militia*, a study of the raising and training of the Roman armies, and the *Poliorceticon*, a study of the engines and methods of siege warfare;[24] it is no doubt relevant that the wars in the Netherlands were becoming increasingly dominated by siege and manoeuvre. The missing third volume was to have been a study of Roman triumphs; Gibbon, it will be recalled, had drafted a work on the same subject.[25] It is immediately noticeable that the *De militia* is self-described as a *commentarius in Polybium*. That author's detailed study of the Roman armies became an *exemplum* for modern authors to follow; Gibbon has such a set piece in chapter 1 of the *Decline and Fall*.[26] Polybius had intended it as part of a portrayal of the republic's rise to supreme empire in the Mediterranean world, but we have seen that his history contained what posterity must read as foretellings of that empire's decline. Gibbon is conscious that he is using a portrait of the republic's armies as if it were applicable to the armies of the Antonine

---

[24] The *De militia* was published in 1595, the *Poliorceticon* in 1596.
[25] *EEG*, p. 286.     [26] *DF*, 1, ch. 1; Womersley, 1994, 1, pp. 38–47.

emperors; but between the second century BC and the second century AD a great deal of history had intervened, in which the armies had changed profoundly and played a critical role. What was Lipsius' position? At what point in ancient history did he situate his commentary upon Polybius, and how did he expect it to play an exemplary role in modern?

Dilectum vide; nihil accuratius. Ordinem; nihil aptius. Disciplinam; nihil severius sanctiusque. Itaque per annos septingentos, tot triumphos paene quot annos numerant, et imperio suo subiecerunt quidquid validum aut bonum in orbe terrarum. Nam alios quosdam latius imperasse fortasse dixeris, aut nunc imperare (certe magnum nostrum Regem): sed in tam selectis gentibus aut terris, non dices. Poenos, Macedonas, Assyrios vicerunt, et imperium in eos usurparunt qui ante imperarant. Quid Hispanos, aut Gallos? quos vincere non gloriae fortassis maioris, sed operae fuit.[27]

[Consider their choice of soldiers; nothing could be more careful. Their formation; nothing could be better chosen. Their discipline; nothing more severely or faithfully observed. And so for seven centuries they counted almost as many triumphs as years, and subjected to their empire almost all that was strong and virtuous in the known world. You may perhaps claim that others have exercised empire more widely, or do so now (as certainly does our great King); but not over lands or peoples of such distinction. They conquered the Carthaginians, the Macedonians, the Assyrians, and seized empire over those who had exercised empire before them. What of the Spaniards or the Gauls? To conquer them could bring no greater glory, though it might bring greater toil.][28]

Gibbon was to observe that the Mongol and Russian (but not the Spanish) empires exceeded the Roman in extent;[29] but his language does not hint either that the Roman was the last of the Four Empires, or that to subject all the virtue in the world might not be an absolute good. Lipsius goes on to concede that the *militia* and the *magnitudo* of Rome were both mortal, but it is less than clear what he wishes his readers to make of this.

Atque haec ita olim fuerunt, quamdiu disciplina et sanctitas quaedam, ut ita dicam, armorum viguit: postquam sanguine civili infecta ea et corrupta sunt, postquam rapere et lancinare, atque etiam lascivire, in morem vertit; resedit illa virtus, et quod sequitur, fortuna, nec aliud quam umbra et nomen fuit militiae Romanae. Ideo si vis me illustrare hanc et explicare: de veteri modo promitto, nec inferiorem istam, nisi parce, tangam.[30]

[And so it once was, as long as the discipline and religion of arms (if I may so call them) flourished. But after they were infected and corrupted by civil wars,

---

[27] Lipsius, 1596, pp. 2–3.  [28] Trans. JGAP.  [29] *DF*, 1, 2; Womersley, 1994, 1, p. 56.
[30] Lipsius, 1596, p. 3 (continuous with last quoted passage).

after theft, loot and even luxury became customary, virtue declined and with it fortune, and nothing remained but the name and shadow of the Roman armies. If you wish me to illustrate and explain this, I will undertake to speak only of the ancient practice, and will not touch upon the later, except sparingly.][31]

Lipsius is concerned with the *exemplum*, not the narrative; the *peinture* of what Rome once was, not the *récit* of how it ceased to be. Yet he cannot avoid the imagery of Decline and Fall, the questions of what caused decline and when these causes began to operate. If we reckon the seven centuries mentioned above from 753 BC, the accredited date of Rome's foundation, with any precision, we come to the wars of the triumvirates and the victories of Caesar and Augustus. Were these the civil wars with which the armies began to decline into the *umbra et nomen* of their former self, or are we to think of the wars of 69–70, the victory of Septimius Severus, the anarchy of the third century, the tetrarchate, Constantine at the Milvian bridge? It was the perpetual problem of Decline and Fall that any explanation operated over a period of three or four hundred years. Lipsius is not going to confront this problem, but he cannot quite escape the question whether his *exemplum* contained the seeds of its own decline. Appian and the Gracchan explanation confront him with it, by insisting that the basis of Roman power was once the sending out (*deductio*) of military colonies. We turn to the *De magnitudine*, where we find:

Ista igitur deductio Coloniarum, et causae: in quibus tamen tyranni aut violenti aliquot cives fraudem et iniuriam miscuerunt, ut Corn. Sulla, qui non, ut olim, agros ex hoste captos distribuit, sed in ipsa Italia, quod sciebat milites appetere, sedes iis dedit. Quod fieri non potuit, nisi pacatis fidisque populis, per summam iniuriam et scelus, expulsis. Appianus auctor est *vigintitres* legiones ab eo sic deductos, quae facerent (si probe commemini) *centum viginti millia*, cum iis qui adiuncti. Simile et Caesar Iulius, in pace et Consulatu fecit, qui agrum Campanum et Stellatem *viginti millibus* civium, colonia Capuam deducta, diuisit. Idem iam Dictator, *in transmarinas colonias octoginta millia ciuium distribuit*, Suetonio auctore: id est, in Carthaginem maxime et Corinthum. Quod noto, ut numerus videatur deductorum: qui sane grandis fuit, siue e ciuibus togatis, siue e militibus veteranis. Augustum *centum viginti millia* deduxisse sub *quintum Consulatum* suum (bellis Ciuilibus iam finitis) lapis Ancyranus ostendit: et postea multa millia adiunxit. In sola Italia *duodetriginta colonias* collocasse, Suetonius notauit. Itaque huius Principis plurimae, et in toto orbe terrarum fuerunt: quod ipsa agnomina earum ostendunt. Denique paulatim tanta frequentia, ut negem regionem, imo vix regiunculam fuisse, in qua Coloniae aut Colonia non esset. Tot illis vinclis

---

[31] Trans. JGAP.

miramur orbem compeditum et adstrictum, in Romana ditione et imperio mansisse? Non ego: sed nec Velleii iudicium valde probo, *inter perniciosissima Gracchi habentis, quod extra Italiam colonias posuerit*. Equidem planissime contra sentio: et [aut?] ad hunc coercendi finem, aliter oportuit: aut nec imperium extra Italiam proferre. Timor[em] quem timet, ne qua Colonia potentior matre sua fiat, sic longinqua: nullus est, et certe locum in romano aliquo imperio non habet. Sed nec Hispano: et prudentissime eos censeo Nouum orbem coloniis implesse. Quarum alia atque alia genera tamen erant, et quaedam *Romani*, aliae *Latini*, quaedam et *Italici* iuris . . .[32]

[Such was the plantation of colonies, and such its causes. Tyrannous and violent citizens, however, introduced corruption and injustice into this system; as did Cornelius Sulla, who no longer distributed lands taken from the enemy, as had been the practice, but gave his soldiers land in Italy itself, as he knew they desired. This could not be done without the unjust and criminal expulsion of peaceful and faithful citizens. Appian tells us that he so settled twenty-three legions, making a total (if I am not mistaken) of one hundred and twenty thousand men, with their dependants. The like was done by Julius Caesar, in time of peace and during his consulate, when he divided the lands of Campania and Stellas among twenty thousand citizens, planting a colony at Capua. Then, when he was dictator, he settled eighty thousand citizens in overseas colonies, according to Suetonius, for the most part at Carthage and Corinth. I mention this so that the number of colonists may appear; it was assuredly large, whether composed of civilians or veterans. The inscription of Ancyra shows that Augustus sent out a hundred and twenty thousand under his fifth consulate, when the civil wars were long finished, and many more thousands after that. In Italy alone, Suetonius observes, he established twenty-eight colonies; there were many more set up by this prince in all parts of the world, as their names testify. In time these grew to be so common that I may say there was no region, scarcely even any petty district, in which a '*Colonia*' or 'Coloniae' were not to be found. Will anyone wonder that a world bound and shackled by so many of these chains remained subject to the Roman domination and empire? Not I; yet I do not endorse the judgement of Velleius that it was among the most pernicious actions of Gracchus that he established colonies outside Italy. I am altogether of the contrary opinion; this control would have had to be achieved otherwise, or there would have been no empire outside Italy. The fear some have that a colony may grow stronger than its mother city, being at a distance, is of no weight; certainly it did not happen in the Roman empire. Nor will it in the Spanish; I judge it altogether prudent that they have filled the New World with colonies. However, there were many kinds of these: some with Roman, some with Latin, some with Italian rights . . .][33]

and the analysis of colonies in terms of the *jus* they conferred is resumed from the point at which Sigonio had left it. A great deal has happened, however, in the course of the passage cited. Lipsius is clear from Appian

[32] Lipsius, 1599, p. 35.  [33] Trans. JGAP.

that Roman empire, like recruitment (*dilectum*) to the Roman armies, depended upon the establishment of colonies; but that this process was open to misuse by the violent and self-seeking – not excluding the rank and file, whose land-hunger drove their generals on – and could lead not only to the dispossession of the lawful occupants of the soil, but to the disruption of lawful authority itself. Sulla and Caesar were the gravediggers of the republic, and Augustus carried on their work under pretence of controlling it. Once the process of colonisation is extended beyond Italy, however, the meaning of the story changes. Civilians as well as discharged soldiers are involved, and the process is seen as essential to the maintenance of empire. It becomes possible to see colonisation as a cultural as well as a military phenomenon; this is how the Latin tongue became dominant, at least in the west, and the world became a single city. Lipsius quotes Rutilius Namatianus, that author significant to Gibbon:[34]

> Fecisti patriam diversis gentibus unam,
> Profuit iniustis te dominante capi;
> Dumque offers victis proprii consortia iuris
> Urbem fecisti quod prius orbis erat.[35]

But it is explicitly a method of domination and control; and if the pre-Gracchan colonist was a citizen whose *jus Romanum* (if he had it) entitled him to go to Rome and vote in the assemblies, the Augustan colonist, living outside Italy, was the subject of a monarch whose law protected him. The empire had replaced the republic, and to the extent that colonisation was still a military phenomenon, the *imperium* was dependent on the *imperator*. But what, meanwhile, had become of the land-hunger of the soldiers? The armies of the civil wars had conquered provinces for their commanders, meaning to increase their power to give them confiscated lands in Italy. Augustus had transformed this process, setting limits to further conquests and offering soldiers lands wherever they might be found in the empire. This implied longer terms of service, and disciplined behaviour while the legions remained under arms. Clearly, this could not be achieved without pay, and the emphasis shifted from the prospect of lands at discharge to the immediate assurance of pay on active service. The comparison between the Roman and the Spanish empires indicates

---

[34] *EEG*, pp. 272–4.
[35] Lipsius, 1599, p. 37. 'You made one fatherland out of many peoples. It profited the unjust to fall under your rule. While you offered the conquered the fellowship of your laws, you made a city where once there was a world.'

that this problem had a modern face. The colonists of Spanish America might be conquistadores, but they were not the massively resettled veterans of the *tercios*; what then was the method of pay, in antiquity as well as modernity?

*Admiranda sive de magnitudine Romana* – it seems always to have been known by the latter part of its title – is in the form of a dialogue between Lipsius, in the role of master, and a younger Auditor who is clearly a student. Auditor has a personality, and his exchanges with his mentor have a certain liveliness; he has a way of exclaiming 'Hem, Lipsi' when faced with something hard to accept which does something to reconcile us to this always irritating literary form. Lipsius seems, furthermore, to have used both Auditor's persona and his own to convey the strangeness of the Roman world he finds himself introducing. From the study of colonies he goes on to consider the massive growth of the slave population, accompanied by correspondingly massive manumissions by rich men aiming to increase their *clientelae*; this has the effect of filling Rome with a still servile population of freedmen and converting the *Romana olim plebs* into a *cloaca ac sentina vitiorum*.[36] Meanwhile, in the colonised provinces there is an increasing practice of recruiting newly conquered populations into the armies, as well as Roman or Italian colonists; this supplies Lipsius with one of his few projections of ultimate decline:

peccatumque a secutis Imperatoribus (maxime post Constantinum) qui Barbaris receptis, imperium et urbem prodiderunt.[37]

[and it was ill done by later emperors, particularly after Constantine, who by accepting barbarians betrayed both the empire and the city.][38]

This may be the first case we have encountered of the idea of Decline and Fall as produced by the barbarisation of the armies, resulting from the problem of balancing the military against the civil in the management of provincial society. There follows a meditation on rulers both ancient and modern – Louis XI, the Incas – who have experimented with the transfer of whole populations; an expedient dangerously attractive to great kings

qui se exhauriunt semper (ut sit in militibus aut colonis emittendis) nec addunt: quid nisi fontem ipsum exhaurient et siccabunt? Serio, serio prouidendum est.[39]

[who are forever exhausting themselves, by sending out armies and colonies, without adding to their resources; how can this fail to drain the spring and run it dry? This is a problem to be most seriously provided against.][40]

---

[36] Lipsius, 1599, p. 36.   [37] Lipsius, 1599, p. 40.   [38] Trans. JGAP.
[39] Lipsius, 1599, pp. 40–1.   [40] Trans. JGAP.

Is this the portrait of an empire, Roman or Spanish, which must exhaust its population resources yet cannot go on expanding them for ever? The problem was to appear that of ensuring population growth by industry and prosperity, rather than by conquest, enslavement and brute appropriation. Book I of *De magnitudine* ends at this point. From the outset of Book II, Lipsius and Auditor are engaged in the study of Roman techniques of tribute and taxation, and though they begin with the tithes of produce imposed upon pre-Gracchan colonies and municipalities, it is clear that they are concerned with the world after the civil wars. Augustus, while continuing intensive colonisation in Italy and beyond, faces the problem of maintaining a standing army by regular payments in cash, and Lipsius transcribes a passage from Suetonius:

Quidquid ubique militum esset, ad certam STIPENDIORUM PRAEMIO-RUMQUE formulem adstrinxit: definitis, pro gradu cuiusque, et temporibus militiae, et commodis missionum, ne aut aetate, aut inopia, solicitare ad res nouas possent. Utque perpetuo, ac sine difficultate, sumptus ad TUENDOS et PROSEQUENDOS suppeteret, Aerarium militare cum VECTIGALIBUS NOVIS instituit.[41]

The emphatic capitals are Lipsius'. A modern translation of Suetonius runs:

Augustus also standardised the pay and allowances of the entire Army – at the same time fixing the period of service and the bounty due on its completion – according to military rank; this would discourage them from revolting, when back in civil life, on the excuse that they were either too old or had insufficient capital to earn an honest living. In order to have sufficient funds always in hand for the upkeep of his military establishment and for pensioning off veterans, he formed an Army Treasury maintained by additional taxation.[42]

There are repeated passages in *De magnitudine* which stress the need to keep up payments to discharged veterans (*emeriti*) as well as to serving soldiers. We are passing – though the transition will never be complete – from a military economy based on land grants to one dependent on a continuous cash flow. Hence the *aerarium militare* and the *vectigalia nova*, and it is going to be a problem whether the Roman empire – or the Spanish? – can bear the weight of taxation imposed on it. As persona and author, Lipsius sets out to explore this question, and has difficulty understanding the world he is entering. To begin with, his sources are deficient.

---

[41] Lipsius, 1599, p. 53. For Suetonius' original, see Rolfe, 1979, I, p. 202.
[42] Trans. Graves, 1979, p. 83; cf. Rolfe, 1979, I, p. 203.

Utinam Appiani liber existaret, qui haec omnia fuit complexus! Ita enim ipse, initio operis, ubi id diuidit et disponit. *Ultimus liber*, inquit, *habebit* COPIAM MILITAREM, *quam et quantum Romani habeant, tum et* PROVENTUS PECUNIASQUE, *quas per singulas gentes capiunt*: *item quid in* CLASSES *impendant, et si quid erit huiusmodi*. O pulchrum, o desiderabilem illum librum! sed periit: scire tamen Appianus illa potuit, tum quia et ipse in Republica fuit, tum quia moris rationes illas imperio in publico edi[dit].[43]

[If only we had Appian's book which covers all this! At the beginning of his work, where he sets out its divisions, he says that the last book will contain the entire military force which the Romans commanded, and the resources in money which they drew from the several peoples; also what they spent upon the fleets, and other matters of that kind. How valuable such a book would be, and how much to be desired! But it has perished. Yet Appian was in a position to know, since he had held office in the empire and had practised the exercise of its principles.][44]

Lacking a systematic account of how Roman military revenue was collected and expended, Lipsius is forced back on an attempt to understand the economy of empire in general, and one can see that he was sometimes bewildered and sometimes dazzled by what he read. He notices the readiness with which tribute was collected from the expanding colonies and subject provinces, and takes account of the twenty-second chapter of *Matthew*,[45] where Jesus points out that the coin handed him is not a Temple shekel but a Roman *solidus*, circulated as a medium of exchange for the purpose of paying tribute to Caesar; this euro of the ancient world furnishes its common market with a government and an army. There is some understanding of the ease with which wealth can be concentrated in a money economy; when Auditor has trouble with Benjamin of Tudela's account of the prosperity of Constantinople at a time when its empire was much reduced, Lipsius explains the advantages to an empire of a single emporium.[46] But such cases are rare in modern times, and we are told why. Auditor enquires whether there is now any prince who can maintain so great a treasury.

Non est, fateor; et caussae aliae etiam sunt, sed et illa quam, pro mea nunc mente, dicam. Non uni Regi aut Principi, quisque in sua prouincia, damus, ut olim: sed varie magis et diuisim, ita ut summa magna ad unum non redeant, magna tamen contribuantur. Quomodo? in exemplo nostro vide. Conferimus hodie Principi quaedam, post eum Ordinibus, post hos Magistratibus opidanis,

---

[43] Lipsius, 1599, p. 54. For Appian's text here cited, and a translation, see White, 1912–13, I, pp. 22–3.
[44] Trans. JGAP.    [45] Lipsius, 1599, p. 49.    [46] Lipsius, 1599, pp. 59–60.

post eos Toparchis municipiorum aut pagorum. Denique Ecclesiae etiam et Ecclesiastici, quam multa a nobis habent? et iustissime quidem, atque ex lege diuina, sed tamen habent. Haec igitur omnia si conferas, et in aceruum iungas: affirmo tibi nos paria aut plura dare. Quid, quod concussiones et raptus militares omitto? quae maxima ratio est, et misera nostra Belgica satis sentit. Negabis in unam caenam militarem, rusticum aliquem plus imputasse, quam in annuum tributum? Atque haec non semel eueniunt, o quando tollenda? quando securitas et pax erit, aut saltem disciplina militaris? quando oeconomia et ordo in acceptis expensisque? Ista sint, fortiter et audacter dicam: tondeant accidantque nostri Principes, renascemur.[47]

[There is none, I confess it; the causes are several, but especially that which I will now relate, in accordance with my current thinking. We do not give to a single king or prince, each in his own province, as was once the case; but variously and dividedly, so that though much is given, it does not accrue to a single receiver. Why? consider our own case. We today give money to the prince, but after him to the Estates, and after them to the city magistrates, and after them to the lords of the towns and villages. And finally the church and the churchmen; how much do they have of us? very justly, no doubt, and by divine law, but still they have it. Add all these together in a single reckoning, and I assure you we pay as much or more.[48] And why do I leave out the muggings and lootings of the soldiers? a major grievance, as our unhappy Belgium knows too well. Will you deny that a feast for a troop of soldiers may cost a peasant as much as a year's taxation? And this goes on all the time; when will it stop? When will there be any peace or security, or any military discipline? any order or economy in the state's income or expenditure? This is how things are, I say it boldly and without compunction; if our princes can reduce these evils or cut them out, we may be born again.][49]

This is a criticism of modern and post-feudal extensive monarchy, forced to bargain with a host of regional lordships and the competing authority of the Church, and unable to control its armies by the monopoly of their effective maintenance. It is contrasted with a sometimes idealised portrait of ancient empire, in which a central imperial treasury could directly command the inflow of money, raised by tribute and taxation from all parts of a colonised empire of provinces. There is something unreal about Lipsius' portrayal of this system (of which he has acknowledged his information to be imperfect); Gibbon noticed this when he observed:

Lipsius de magnitudine Romana (L.ii.c.3) computes the revenue at one hundred and fifty millions of gold crowns; but his whole book, though learned and ingenious, betrays a very heated imagination;[50]

---

[47] Lipsius, 1599, p. 61.    [48] As the Romans paid, or as reaches the prince?    [49] Trans. JGAP.
[50] *DF*, 1, 6, n. 96; Womersley, 1994, 1, p. 181 n. The allusion may be to Lipsius, 1599, p. 53.

and indeed there is a kind of mystification about his account of the massive extraction of precious metals from the earth by slave labour, and the vast quantities of spoil and booty – often in metallic form – regularly brought to Rome by triumphs, to be distributed by imperial munificence. Perhaps because he lacked a detailed account of how taxes were levied and collected, or a detailed understanding of the ancient economy on which they were imposed, he was left with an exotic vision of a world in which huge quantities of moveable wealth were regularly placed in the emperor's hands, to be instantly paid out again in the salaries of soldiers, obligatory public display and the maintenance of a huge population of paupers. He seems amazed that such a system should have worked at all; a chapter headed *Impensae publicae in Militem, Magistratus, Populum; et de Frumentatione* begins:

Oceanus si Aerarium fuisset, dixisses dessiccandum. Impendia igitur sub Principibus (ulteriora omittam) Duplicia fuere, *Necessaria* et *Arbitraria*: ex quibus sane colligas immensas et vere ADMIRANDAS quasdam opes.[51]

[If the treasury had been the ocean, you would have said it must dry up. Under the emperors (I omit those who came later) public expenditures were of two kinds, the necessary and the arbitrary; from which you may easily gather how immense and indeed wonderful must have been their resources.][52]

*Admiranda*, we must recall, was the title of Lipsius' whole book; he is using it here to tell us that the resources and the expenditures of the emperors were so great as to be prodigious and hardly believable. Military expenditure he has already described; the need to stipendiate the regulars and pension the veterans was perpetual.[53] The maintenance of magistrates and their expenses provides the rational structure of the state. The provision of free corn for the swelling population of the *urbs Roma*, however, though among the *necessaria*, is so strange as almost to defy understanding. Faced with an estimate of the numbers receiving this support, Auditor exclaims: 'Good lord, Lipsius, that's a very high figure; were there that many poor at Rome?', and Lipsius replies: 'All poor, or very glad of some relief; mostly freedmen and people like that.'

AUD. Mehercules Lipsi, grandis hic numerus: et tot illi Romae pauperes?
LIPS. Pauperes, aut saltem qui subleuari gauderent: inter quos liberti, et id genus, maxime fuere.[54]

It is the shock of the historically strange, not merely the lack of solid information, which is compelling Lipsius to write with 'heated imagination'. These utterly dependent masses, without crafts or masters – so at

---

[51] Lipsius, 1599, pp. 70–1.    [52] Trans. JGAP.    [53] See n. 50.    [54] Lipsius, 1599, p. 72.

least he saw them – are hard to relate to the normal scenes of Brussels or Antwerp, and he is as amazed that the emperors were able to sustain their needs as he is by the fact of their existence. It was a bad, but not a catastrophic decision when Constantine created a second dole-fed population at New Rome;[55] and the corn-supply as one of the *necessaria* is juxtaposed with the *arbitraria* without becoming one of them. They are classified as *ludi, opera* and *dona*.[56] The two first, public games and public buildings, are part of the antique world in which the prince ruled by display and munificence; not unknown to a modern ruler who must include 'liberality' among his virtues, and in Rome shared by wealthy private citizens who maintained their eminence by the same public display,[57] but rendered extraordinary in antiquity by the ready wealth that maintained it. But *dona* are another matter, consisting as they did mainly of donations to the soldiery; extravagant scatterings of wealth wherever an emperor succeeded to power or otherwise obtained it. The light-hearted Auditor declares that if he'd been born in those times, he'd certainly have been a soldier, since all wealth came their way in the end; *si eo saeclo ego viuam, quid nisi miles sum? ita omnes ad eos opes adfluunt et concurrunt*.[58] Lipsius in his own persona more grimly remarks:

Certe Spartianus in Seuero tradit, *Milites per seditionem dena millia poposcisse a Senatu, exemplo eorum qui Augustum Octauianum Romam deduxerant, tantumque acceperant*. O peritos historicos vel antiquarios, et in rem suam lecta aptantes![59]

And elsewhere:

Ne milites nostri audite, et exempla haec cupite aut sperate. Unde enim Iulius, unde Romanae opes?[60]

[Certainly Spartianus in his life of Severus reports that mutinous soldiers demanded ten thousand sesterces each from the senate, on the model of those who established Octavianus at Rome, and received as much. Learned historians and antiquaries indeed, adapting what they've read to their own history!

May our soldiers never hear of this, or demand or hope for the like. Whence came Julius Caesar; whence the wealth of Rome?][61]

The historiographer who is the master of military discipline is bringing to light some disturbing information. All Lipsius' admiration for Augustus' military and fiscal policies has not quite explained to him the emperors' instant access to unlimited wealth, or their obligation to

---

[55] Lipsius, 1599, pp. 74–5.   [56] Lipsius, 1599, p. 76.
[57] *De magnitudine*, 11, xv: 'De privatorum aliquot opibus'.   [58] Lipsius, 1599, p. 85.
[59] Lipsius, 1599, p. 86.   [60] Lipsius, 1599, p. 82.   [61] Trans. JGAP.

expend it as instantly on government by conspicuous expenditure. And when he turns his eyes from ancient to modern monarchy, he sees clearly that no prince in his day could hope to collect wealth as instantly and successfully, and that the problem of soldiers' pay in modernity has not even reached the point where it could not be solved in antiquity. A critic in his own century might have observed that this was where the abandonment of Dutch service for Spanish had led the great humanist, and that paying armies by the instant coinage of American silver might soon face the kings of Spain with a starving and dependent population like that of imperial Rome. For Lipsius the problem is that of a widening gap between the exemplary and the historical. As a Stoic he must continue to isolate the Roman virtues as the only ones worth imitating. The *De magnitudine* closes with a chapter on the *diuturnitas Romani imperii* – it may be significant that there is a digression on the question whether Constantine was born in Britain – and a *conclusio et laudatio magni imperii*, in which universal monarchy is held up as an ideal for the modern world.[62] But it is not to be concealed that these virtues decayed in the course of history, and that the decline may have begun as early as the civil wars. After Augustus – *flaccescante iam Romana indole* – there is no exemplary figure, except perhaps Germanicus and more certainly Trajan.[63] The military-fiscal problem, as ancient as Tiberius Gracchus, continues to gnaw at the roots of virtue, and malignantly bridges the gap between ancient and modern monarchy. A crisis in one of the European monarchies was to lead to a revaluation of the Gracchan thesis as a scheme explaining both the Decline and Fall and the subsequent history of Europe.

(IV)

The concept of 'Europe' has too often been allowed to degenerate into a verbal device for denying that English or British history possess any autonomy, or may be explained in terms they have set for themselves. If this tendency can be reversed, we shall be able to see the crisis of the English monarchy, the Wars of the Three Kingdoms (1637–51) and within them the English Civil Wars (1642–48), as episodes extraordinary within both British and European history, productive of a rich intellectual literature – Hobbes, Harrington, Milton, Clarendon – which sought to explain their causes and meaning. To the present enquiry into the processes whereby an image of the Decline and Fall of the Roman empire was generated in

---

[62] *De magnitudine*, IV, xi–xii.   [63] Lipsius, 1599, p. 176.

western European historical consciousness, an important place belongs
to the military intervention in English politics of 1647–49, which led
to regicide and republic, commonwealth and protectorate. The army
that intervened was like other European armies of the period in being
not fully under the control of the state, but had a composition distinc-
tively its own: not fully mercenary but including small proprietors and
tradesmen, tenants and pressed men. It intervened in a disordered political process of unusual complexity, by which it was itself partly (and
temporarily) politicised and even radicalised; it attempted, but did not
succeed in, a transformation of the state, which might have resulted
in its becoming a permanent part of that state's governing structure.[64]
The problem which initiated its intervention was one common to most
European states of the time: the state's inability to meet the arrears of
payment due to the soldiers; but the English army's behaviour differed
from the organised but unpolitical mutinies and the resorts to free quarter
which had characterised the Spanish *tercios* a generation earlier.[65] The
English state, riven by civil war, could not raise funds, by taxation or
borrowing, equal to the provision of a functioning military treasury; it is
noteworthy, however, that it possessed, within severe limits, the resource
of military colonisation which had become crucial to the understanding
of Roman history. Soldiers were invited to take part in the conquest of
Ireland, and promised a share in confiscated lands if they did so; most
of them, however, demanded to be paid, indemnified for illegal acts in
time of civil war, and restored to the civilian lives they had left. They
were in search of a government capable of paying them off, and would
intervene in a revolutionary process in order to secure it.

Some years after this crisis had been at its height, an independent
observer of original mind, James Harrington, neither parliamentarian
nor soldier, wrote between 1654 and 1656 an analysis of this situation,
presented within a semi-fictional history of a country, Oceana, easily
recognisable as England.[66] His *Commonwealth of Oceana* is significant in
the history and historiography of Decline and Fall because Harrington
had determined that the predicament of regicide England was intelligible
only in a history of arms and property reaching back to the Roman republic and extended to the collapse of its empire, the barbarian invasions, and

---

[64] For recent interpretations of this army's politics and history, see Kishlansky, 1979; Woolrych, 1987; Gentles, 1992; Mendle, 2001.

[65] Parker, 1972.

[66] For editions and interpretations of his work, see Pocock, 1975, ch. 11; 1977; 1987b, ch. 6; 1992; also Fukuda, 1997. Gibbon owned the edition of 1771 (*Library*, p. 144).

the rise and fall of feudal tenures. He therefore enlarged the 'Gracchan thesis' beyond the fall of the republic which it had been constructed to explain, into an outline of the history of ancient Rome and modern (we should prefer 'medieval') Europe, and based it on a history of the land tenures by which arms and freedom had been supported; the duality of *libertas* and *imperium* is clearly to be seen in his writings.

Harrington divided history into 'ancient prudence' and 'modern prudence'; the fall of the former, at a time when the latter did not even exist, he placed at

the execrable reign of the Roman emperors, taking rise from that *felix scelus*, the arms of Caesar, in which storm the ship of the Roman commonwealth was forced to disburthen herself of that precious freight, which never since could emerge or raise the head but in the Gulf of Venice.[67]

The precious freight is the capacity for liberty and empire, recovered by the maritime state of Venice on terms altogether unlike those on which it flourished in the central Italy of primitive Rome. Here too it had failed; the Romans

through a negligence committed in their agrarian laws, let in the sink of luxury, and forfeited the inestimable treasure of liberty for themselves and posterity.[68]

Harrington was a close reader of Machiavelli, but the author he cites for the succeeding paragraphs is Sigonio, and therefore Appian.[69] How well he knew this historian may be debated – his direct allusions to him are few and on a distant matter[70] – but there can be no doubt that he makes Roman history turn upon the failure of republican colonisation.

Their agrarian laws were such whereby their lands ought to have been divided among the people, either without mention of a colony, in which case they were not obliged to change their abode; or with mention and upon condition of a colony, in which case they were to change their abode and, leaving the city, to plant themselves upon the lands so assigned. The lands assigned, or that ought to have been assigned, in either of these ways were of three kinds. Such as were taken from the enemy and distributed unto the people; or such as were taken from the enemy and, under colour of being reserved unto the public use, were by stealth possessed by the nobility; or such as were bought with the public money to be distributed. Of the laws offered in these cases, those which divided the lands taken from the enemy, or purchased with the public money, never occasioned any dispute; but such as drove at dispossessing the nobility of their usurpations, and dividing the common purchase of the sword among the people, were never

[67] Pocock, 1992, p. 43; 1977, p. 188.   [68] *Ibidem.*   [69] Pocock, 1992, p. 43 n.
[70] Pocock, 1977, pp. 519, 555. These refer to voting practices in ancient city assemblies.

touched but they caused earthquakes, nor could ever be obtained by the people or, being obtained, be observed by the nobility, who not only preserved their prey but, growing vastly rich upon it, bought the people by degrees quite out of those shares that had been conferred upon them . . . For (quite contrary unto what hath happened in Oceana, where the balance falling unto the people, they have overthrown the nobility) the nobility of Rome, under the conduct of Sulla, overthrew the people and the commonwealth; seeing Sulla first introduced that new balance, which was the foundation of the succeeding monarchy, in the plantation of military colonies, instituted by his distribution of the conquered lands – not now of enemies, but of citizens – unto forty-seven legions of soldiers; so that how he came to be *dictator perpetuus*, or other magistrates to succeed him in like power, is no miracle.[71]

Sulla rather than Caesar institutes the execrable reign of the emperors, and its foundations lie in a single person's control of military colonisation. If we are to follow Bruni from this point, we need an account of how imperial colonisation led to the loss of empire. Harrington supplies one, but his emphasis is not on Tacitus' *arcanum*, the intervention of provincial armies in dynastic conflicts at Rome; it is placed more selectively.

These military colonies, in which manner succeeding emperors continued (as Augustus by the distribution of the veterans, whereby he had overcome Brutus and Cassius) to plant their soldiery, consisted of such as I conceive were they that are called *milites beneficiarii*; in regard that the tenure of their lands was by way of benefices, that is for life and upon condition of duty or service in the war, upon their own charge. These benefices Alexander Severus granted unto the heirs of the incumbents, but upon the same conditions; and such was the dominion by which the Roman emperors gave their balance.

Alexander Severus was a figure of exemplary and unreal virtue, but his policy here is part of the execrable reign of the emperors. Harrington is paying no attention to the *aerarium militare*, the *tributa*, the *vectigalia*, the payments made to the *emeriti*, or any aspect of the maintenance of the armies by cash and donatives. His attention has shifted altogether to the growth of dependent military tenures, for the reason that his historical schema is about to be grounded on two antitheses: that between the Roman *beneficium* and the Gothic *feudum*, and that between both and the Turkish *timar*. The last precedes the two former, which in history come before it.

But to the beneficiaries, as was no less than necessary for the safety of the prince, a matter of eight thousand, by the example of Augustus, were added, which departed not from his sides, but were his perpetual guard, called praetorian bands; though these, according to the incurable flaw already observed in this

---

[71] Pocock, 1992, pp. 43–4; 1977, pp. 188–9. Cf. 1992, pp. 15–16; 1977, p. 167.

kind of government,[72] became the most frequent butchers of their lords that are to be found in story. Thus far the Roman monarchy is so much the same with that at this day in Turkey – consisting of a camp and an horse-quarter; a camp in regard of her spahis and janissaries, the perpetual guard of the prince, except they also chance to be liquorish after his blood; and an horse-quarter in regard to the distribution of his whole land unto tenants for life, upon condition of continual service or as often as they shall be commanded, at their own charge, by *timars* (being a word which they say signifies benefices) – that it shall save me a labour of opening the government.[73]

But the Roman monarchy was not a pure oriental despotism. Senate and people remained in possession of some land and liberty, alongside the empire of the prince and his military colonists. This may be explained by contrasting the freedom of westerners with the servility of orientals, other than the Israelites, who had an agrarian of their own;[74] but here there is danger of a circular argument – are Europeans free because they have tenure, or have they tenure because they are free by nature? And a sign of this freedom is the movement from life tenure at will to hereditary tenure, begun by Alexander Severus; the first hint of the feudal order which will replace the imperial. The latter, mixed rather than despotic in nature, was the cause of its own decline.

Whence this empire, being neither hawk nor buzzard, made a flight accordingly; and having the avarice of the soldiery on this hand to satisfy upon the people, and the senate and the people on the other to be defended from the soldiery, the prince, being perpetually tossed, seldom died any other death than by one horn of this dilemma, as is noted more at large by Machiavel,[75]

in a passage we have already considered.[76] Here Harrington introduces a new perception, of some importance in the punctuation of Decline and Fall. In 1576 there had been published an incomplete history by one Zosimus, a sixth-century Greek pagan bitterly critical of Constantine, who had made that emperor into an architect of Roman military decline. An English translation rather later than Harrington runs:

but besides this *Constantine* did another thing too, that gave the *Barbarians* a free passage into the *Roman* Dominions. For whereas the *Roman* Empire, by the care of *Diocletian* was fortified (as I told you) in the most remote parts of it with Towns and Castles and Forts, where the Soldiers lived, and consequently it was impossible for the Barbarians to pass, because there was always a sufficient number of

---

[72] Pocock, 1992, p. 31; 1977, p. 179.
[73] For this and the preceding quotation, Pocock, 1992, pp. 44–5; 1977, p. 189.
[74] *Ibidem*, 1992 and 1977. There are many invocations of the division of lands in Old Testament Israel in Harrington's writings; e.g. 1977, pp. 631–4.
[75] Pocock, 1992, pp. 45–6; 1977, p. 190.    [76] Above, pp. 215–16.

Enemies to withstand 'em; *Constantine* destroy'd that Security, by removing the greater part of the Soldiers out of those Frontier Places, and putting them in Towns that wanted no assistance, For he Strip'd them whom the *Barbarians* oppressed of all defence, and plagu'd the Towns that were quiet with a multitude of Soldiers, in so much that some were quite forsaken of their Inhabitants. He likewise caused his Soldiers to grow effeminate by giving themselves to publick Shows and Pleasures. And to tell you plainly, he was the first cause, why things were brought to that miserable state they now are in.[77]

Zosimus has achieved a certain immortality; debate among historians as to the effects of Constantine's regrouping of the armies continued in the late twentieth century.[78] His thesis recurs in Gibbon.[79] Harrington makes a different use of it, linked much more aggressively with the growth of dependent military tenure.

But the praetorian bands, those bestial executioners of their captain's tyranny upon others, and of their own upon him, having continued from the time of Augustus, were by Constantine the Great (incensed against them for taking part with his adversary Maxentius) removed from their strong garrison which they held in Rome, and distributed into divers provinces. The benefices of the soldiers, that were hitherto held for life and upon duty, were by the prince made hereditary, so that the whole foundation whereupon this empire was first built, being now removed, showeth plainly that the emperors must long before this have found out some other way of support, and this was by stipendiating the Goths, a people that, deriving their roots from the northern parts of Germany, or out of Sweden, had (through their victories obtained against Domitian) long since spread their branches unto so near neighborhood with the Roman territories, that they began to overshade them; for the emperors, making use of them in their arms (as the French do at this day of the Switz), gave them that, under the notion of stipend, which they received as tribute, coming (if there were any default in the payments) so often to distrain for it, that in the time of Honorius they sacked Rome and possessed themselves of Italy. And such was the transition of ancient into modern prudence, or that breach which, being followed in every part of the Roman empire with inundations of Vandals, Huns, Lombards, Franks, Saxons, overwhelmed ancient languages, learning, prudence, manners, cities, changing the names of rivers, countries, seas, mountains and men; Camillus, Caesar and Pompey being come to Edmund, Richard, and Geoffrey,[80]

names more 'Gothic' than those in the parallel passage from Machiavelli.[81] Here for the first time we have a connected explanatory

[77] Trans. Anon., in Zosimus, 1684, pp. 116–17. For the Greek original, Zosimus 11, 34, Paschoud, 1971, p. 107.
[78] Ferrill, 1986.      [79] *DF*, 11 (1781), 17; Womersley, 1994, 1, pp. 619–20.
[80] Pocock, 1992, p. 46; 1977, p. 190.      [81] Above, p. 229.

narrative connecting the fall of the republic with the fall of the empire, the barbarian invasions and the establishment of feudal tenures. Its structure is Gracchan, not Tacitean (though the reference to Gothic victories against Domitian recalls the *Germania*). Constantine's resettlement of the frontier legions is transformed into the removal of the praetorians and a grant of hereditary tenure to the *milites beneficiarii*, so that the barbarians may be shown first entering the empire as mercenaries, and only afterwards as invaders; it is the final development of that transformation of soldiers from citizens into beneficiaries that began with Sulla (and the foundation of Florence). The emperors, as was the case with Bruni and Machiavelli, have no other role than that of gravediggers of their own empire; but instead of undermining the *virtus* of a Sallustian citizenry of wielders of *imperium*, they subvert the armed (and landholding) *popolo* imagined by Machiavelli, and placed by Appian at the start of the process in which Tiberius Gracchus sought to restore the republic's control of the colonising process. The Goths complete what the latifundists began.

Harrington constructed his history of Rome in terms of the rise and fall of military colonisation in order to construct a history of Europe in terms of the rise and fall of military tenures. 'Modern prudence', which the Goths established, is co-terminous with a feudal structure in which the many hold their lands from the few on condition of military service (he does not say very much about the processes by which this system was established, beyond John Selden's discussion of the relation between Anglo-Saxon thegnage and Norman knight-service).[82] The system was, however, imperfect (especially when judged by Turkish standards) in the same way that the Roman had been; the domains and vassals of a feudal king were counterbalanced by those of his greater barons, and the history of modern prudence was, like that of the Roman emperors, one of incessant war between kings and nobilities in which neither could finally triumph.[83] (Harrington, though militantly anti-clerical as well as anti-papal,[84] does not supply a history of empire and papacy.) This history has now reached its end, and here we encounter the principal ideological purpose with which he wrote *Oceana*: that of explaining and rectifying the supremacy of the army in an English republic. He could account for its highly politicised intervention only by supposing that it was made up of men capable of civic action, and he accounted for their presence by

---

[82] Pocock, 1992, p. 48; 1977, p. 192.　　[83] Pocock, 1992, p. 53; 1977, p. 196.
[84] Goldie, 1987, 1993; Champion, 1992.

supposing that they had recently been emancipated from the control of their lords. Here he took part in the establishment of a paradigm which controlled English historiography down to the time of the Scotsmen Hume and Smith.[85] Following Francis Bacon's *History of Henry VII*,[86] he proposed that this king's Statute of Retainers had abolished the nobility's control over the military services of their tenants – there was a need here to telescope the vassals of a great honour with the retainers of a great household – and had created a class of independent proprietors who bore arms only in their own interest, and saw their freedom as the greatest interest they had. This had been the death of modern prudence, since the armed people served neither king nor nobility; he saw the civil wars as the moment of their revolutionary emergence, leaving them in control of a republic as at present constituted, with neither a king nor a House of Lords.[87] So much for the history of England/Oceana; Harrington wrote as if the collapse of feudal monarchy were a phenomenon common to contemporary Europe, but did not describe the process by which it had happened elsewhere.

This is the end, the telos as well as the termination, of Harrington's history of empire and liberty as the seating of arms in the tenure of lands; having set it forth in the 'Second Part of the Preliminaries', he devotes the rest of *The Commonwealth of Oceana* to imagining a republic in which arms and citizenship shall be the same thing.[88] In the course of doing so, however, he makes remarks about the seating of liberty in the land which tell us much about the ways in which Roman history would be imagined in the age following his. The premises are still Gracchan; the only way to maintain an army is to settle it in the land, and it is through the anchorage of liberty in property that men become as gods, anchoring spirit in matter.[89] If you have on your hands an army of men without property, you must find lands for them, and here there arises the possibility that the English may cleanse Ireland of its native inhabitants and make it a colony in which 'every citizen will have his villa'.[90] The utopian, or rather euhistorical, premise, however, is that this is no longer necessary; the growth of hereditary feudal tenures, completed by the Tudor abolition of service to lords, has perfected the process of Gothic colonisation and created an army and citizenry of proprietors. Harrington insists, however, that there is no alternative to land. An army cannot

---

[85] *NCG*, pp. 202–4.     [86] Vickers, 1998.     [87] Pocock, 1992, pp. 54–6; 1977, pp. 197–8.
[88] The question whether Harrington's conception of citizenship was classical with Platonic overtones, or an eccentric gloss upon Hobbes, is distinct from the character of his historiography.
[89] Pocock, 1992, p. xxii.     [90] Pocock, 1992, pp. 6, 113; 1997, pp. 159, 241.

be supported by taxation, since taxes are a perpetual violence committed by governments upon proprietors.[91] A critic of *Oceana* pointed out that there was less objection to paying taxes on moveable goods, and that the English armies were quite satisfactorily supported by an excise rather than a land-tax.[92] To this Harrington returned a double answer. In the first place, he said, in a community controlled by personal wealth, property would always be passing from hand to hand and it would never be known for certain who the citizens were. A republic of expanding commerce should expand its land to keep pace with it, or be governed by money and not by men; this had happened to Genoa, but might not happen to Amsterdam, while the shires were a guarantee that London would not impose it on England. In the second place:

A bank, where money takes not wing but to come home seized, or like a coy-duck may well be great; but the treasure of the Indies, going out and not upon return, makes no bank. Whence a bank never paid an army or, paying an army, soon became no bank. But where a prince or a nobility hath an estate in land, the revenue whereof will defray this charge, there their men are planted, have toes that are roots, and arms that bring forth what fruit you please.[93]

With these words we reach the end, not so much of 'modern prudence' as of Harrington's perception of it. The Gracchan thesis, extended into feudal history, proposed that there was no foundation for arms and liberty other than colonisation, the settlement of armed freemen upon land. The Roman empire and the feudal kingdoms had been deformations of this principle, and since both had destroyed themselves, there was room for a return to 'ancient prudence'. The massive expropriation of American silver had failed to monetarise the maintenance of mercenary armies,[94] and Harrington could claim that he was living in a world where neither taxation nor capital could leave the freeholder any alternative but despotism to the freedom, and the obligation, to bear his own arms and appear in his own cause. Under these conditions, the Gracchan reading of Roman history remained immediately relevant. With half a century of 1656 (the date of *Oceana*), however, all this would be changed. Means would have been found by which banks could pay armies, and become part of the structure of states capable of maintaining both banks and armies on a permanent basis. With this there emerged a

---

[91] Pocock, 1992, pp. 58–60.    [92] Wren, 1657–58; Pocock, 1977, pp. 82–3, 88–9.
[93] Pocock, 1977, p. 404.    [94] Pocock, 1977, pp. 408–9; note the reference to Wren.

new 'modernity',[95] neither ancient nor medieval, in which the history of the Roman republic and empire, and their decline and fall, were viewed at a remove, by an age which had solved their problems, yet found their values an effective criticism of the world which had replaced them. It was in this intellectual climate that the writings of Tacitus took on renewed significances.

[95] As in the heading of *EEG*, ch. 4: 'The Hampshire militia and the problems of modernity'.

# PART V

# Republic and empire: the Enlightened narrative

# CHAPTER 14

# European Enlightenment and the Machiavellian moment

In the fifty to seventy years following Harrington's writings (1656–60), the political structure and culture of western and especially Atlantic Europe underwent great changes and entered a condition to which the term 'Enlightenment' can in various senses be usefully applied. In the preceding volumes of this series the condition so termed was characterised as a plurality of states composing a system, each strong enough to guarantee civil society under government – a common term for this was *les états bien policés* – and to conduct a 'reason of state', that is a system of wars and treaties rationally controlled. It was further shown that this condition was contrasted with a previous condition of regional revolts and wars of religion, itself supposed the product of centuries of feudal power and ecclesiastical supremacy; Gibbon's 'triumph of barbarism and religion'. There came to be formulated what an earlier volume termed 'the Enlightened narrative', a history beginning sometimes with Constantine and sometimes with Charlemagne and pursued through what we termed 'the Christian millennium' until it reached the 'modern' or 'enlightened' moment when there emerged the Europe of contending yet co-existing states. These were connected with each other, and formed a system, not only by their power to conduct relations of war and peace – John Locke's 'federative power' – but by powerful economic and cultural forces: the 'commerce' by which they exchanged goods and money, ideas and values, with each other, and the *moeurs* or 'polite manners' which they were supposed to possess in common and derive from a past history that was in process of being written. It is no accident that the first and most ambitious of these 'Enlightened narratives' was termed by its author an *Essai sur les Moeurs*, though the history of manners was often organised as a natural and civil history of jurisprudence, and Voltaire's *Essai* was rivalled, even as a history of manners, by Montesquieu's *De l'Esprit des*

*Lois.* All these forces in combination were supposed to constitute a civil society and civil sovereignty proof against even the destructive forces of contending religious convictions; and there began to appear a history of the Church, of Christianity and even of religion in the abstract, which traced the rise and fall of its power to disrupt government and society.

It was the need to explain and wind up the history of religious war and ecclesiastical supremacy which caused the 'Enlightened narrative' to begin from one or other moment of the foundation of Christian empire; that of Constantine or that of Charlemagne. Yet Gibbon's first volume begins with Commodus and ends with Constantine, stopping short of his establishment of the Christian religion; and it will be argued that this religion plays no significant part in his history of the 'first Decline and Fall' before that date. A problem which confronts us now is whether the establishment of Enlightenment necessitated any re-valuation of the history of republic and principate; whether there was an 'Enlightened narrative' of the history of the Roman empire before it was Christian, extending as far as a 'first decline and fall'.

Although the European states order of the 'Enlightened narrative' was contrasted with a preceding feudal and religious disorder, it was perceived as having been achieved by a struggle against the 'universal monarchy' of Louis XIV's France, and in particular against his attempt to incorporate in it the preceding 'universal monarchy' of Spain.[1] The plurality of trading and treaty-making states, competing with each other within a universal commerce and a European culture of manners, was set against 'universal monarchy' in this sense, and Dutch and English theorists[2] joined in arguing that commerce – and with it civil society and civil liberty – flourished best where there existed a number of territorial sovereignties, each strong enough to unite trading cities and agricultural countrysides in an internal market that could develop external commerce with its neighbours. Free trade went on between sovereign states; it had not reached the point of seeking to abolish them.

In these circumstances there could not fail to arise the perception that the Roman empire had been the first and perhaps the greatest 'universal monarchy' in the history of the world as Europeans conceived it, and that this empire had been achieved by a republic obliged to transform itself into a monarchy by the extent of its success. Universal history – a

---

[1] For recent treatments of this concept, see Bosbach, 1988; Robertson, 1993; Pincus, 1995, 1996; Pagden, 1995; Armitage, 2000; Weil and Courtney, 2000, pp. 325–33.

[2] E.g., in the Netherlands, Pieter de la Court (Haitsma Mulier, 1980), in England, Charles Davenant (Pocock, 1975, pp. 437–6; Hont, 1990; Robertson, 1993, pp. 357–62).

term increasingly civil rather than sacred – returned to the point at which Polybius and Tacitus had left it, and the Enlightened belief in commerce and plurality might develop a critique of the otherwise exemplary culture of antiquity. We may recall the Florentine contention that an Etruscan confederacy of cities was preferable to a Roman empire of one,[3] and that a people whose *virtus* subjugated and destroyed the *virtus* of all others might end by losing its own.[4] The problem of *imperium et libertas* could now become a critique of *libertas* as the ancients understood it, and Augustine's Christian contention that it had been no more than a *libido dominandi* could be reinforced by an Enlightened contention that it had aimed at conquering others when it should have traded with them. There arose – though by no means instantly – a critique of Rome as an economy of conquest and enslavement, rather than of commerce and industry, into which could be fitted a post-Gracchan critique of a state that could survive only by the incessant colonisation of conquered lands and had fallen into civil war and despotism when colonisation ceased to be economically viable. Out of this could develop a contrast between an ancient liberty founded on citizenship and conquest, and a modern liberty founded on civility and commerce;[5] but the Enlightened perception of ancient history was shaped less by this direct contrast than by the inexhaustible ambiguities of sentiment towards it.

(11)

'The Machiavellian moment' is a term coined a quarter-century ago with the intention of conveying a double meaning: that of a moment in history when the possibility of a republic of equal citizens, enjoying the ancient liberty of ruling and being ruled, is perhaps briefly discerned; and that of a moment, possibly but not necessarily the same, at which such a republic is perceived as precarious, threatened either by internal contradictions or by contingent historical circumstances.[6] From the moment of perception we may pass cautiously to the moment perceived. It may be said that, throughout the history of the concept of Decline and Fall, we have been dealing with the most enduring and inherent 'moment' of this kind:

---

[3] Above, pp. 165–6.     [4] Machiavelli, *Discorsi*, 11, 2; Pocock, 1975, pp. 216–17.

[5] The first contrast between the two may be that in Lord Hervey's *Ancient and Modern Liberty Stated and Compared* (1734). The climate of Walpolean Britain in which this appeared was very unlike that of post-revolutionary France in which Benjamin Constant wrote on the same topic (Holmes, 1984; Fontana, 1991). It would be interesting to study the similarities and dissimilarities between the two treatments.

[6] Pocock, 1975, pp. vii–viii; see now 2003.

that constituted by the problem of *libertas et imperium*, in which liberty is perceived as accumulating an empire by which it is itself threatened; the history of Roman historiography is the history of this problem. We have now reached the point of considering a 'Machiavellian moment' of the second kind: one at which ancient *libertas* was itself challenged by a new conception of liberty, but the latter was perceived as containing its own tendency towards self-corruption, which the confrontation with ancient liberty helped bring to light. This dilemma, which did much to heighten the Enlightened sense of history, is inherent in the debate between virtue and commerce, about which so much has been written; but we need at this point to return to its origin – one origin, it may be, among several – in the concept of arms and their relation to property, around which Harrington had constructed his historical theory.

Early in the seventeenth century, Francis Bacon had proposed that three technological inventions had transformed human history about the year 1500: the compass, the printing press, and gunpowder.[7] About 1700, it began to be perceived that history was being again transformed by a new series of inventions, of which the two that here concern us were social rather than technological in character; the third, the new philosophy of Locke and Newton, was a separate if more universally important phenomenon. The two were the standing army and public credit.[8] The first – the acquisition by the state of the means of paying and maintaining an army year after year – transformed not only the nature of warfare but the nature of the state itself, giving it an effective monopoly of the means of violence. The standing army, regularly paid out of the state's fiscal resources, was professional, an arm of the state proper, whereas its immediate predecessor, raised by short-term contracts on which the state regularly defaulted, was mercenary; the former was unlikely to intervene in the government of the state, but gave the state new and alarming power over its citizens. It had been the strength of Harrington's politico-historical perception that he saw that a state lacking such fiscal resources was dependent on an army that could live of its own, but his weakness that he greatly underestimated the state's ability to acquire such resources. Premising that a bank could never pay an army, he had imagined the New Model as a body of armed proprietors – which it was not – and had constructed a Gracchan history of Europe, in which the free military colonists of the republic had become the stipendiated

---

[7] Bacon made this statement on a number of occasions; references in Peltonen, 1996, pp. 5, 37; Zagorin, 1998, p. 35.

[8] Pocock, 1975, ch. 12; 1996.

but unreliable legions of the principate, and had been replaced by the feudal colonies of the Goths, out of whose unbalanced system a free people in arms had emerged in England, as an unintended consequence of Tudor legislation. His scheme could be modified, but not replaced, by the supposition that the Gothic model had included freemen in arms, living by tenures rather allodial than feudal.

It was the invention of public credit that destroyed the Harringtonian account of history. Many banks, both national and diasporic, took part in it; but a major effect upon Britain of the Dutch invasion of 1688 and the enlistment of England and Scotland in the Dutch resistance to France was the erection of the Bank of England to which the Revolution regime pledged its credit, and the consequent growth of the 'military-fiscal state' that enabled the Kingdom of Great Britain to challenge both the French and the Dutch for hegemony in both Europe and Europe's oceanic empires.[9] The Enlightened vision of a European republic of states was the expression of a temporary equilibrium in this contest for *imperium*; it came to an end a century later, when the burden of public debt to pay for the wars of empire grew too great for some of the contending states to bear. Meanwhile, however, what were the effects of the new military-fiscal order upon the individual as proprietor, subject and freeman? The state's possession of a standing army went far towards eliminating any possibility of a civil or religious war in which he might have to draw the sword himself. Notably in England, where such a war was a nightmare not far from recurring, this assurance was heartily welcome; and it freed the individual to take part in all the rich diversity of commerce, manners and civil society offered him by what we are calling Enlightenment. But in laying aside the sword, as Hobbes had adjured him to do, he was laying aside the *ultima ratio* he had once possessed for determining what the state might or might not do, in peace or war. Machiavelli had located this freedom in the Roman *plebs*, so long as they retained the arms which made them necessary to the republic's armies; and this is why Roman history remained of importance to Europe in the age of Enlightenment and the standing army. The new state of Great Britain, where civil war was a vivid and highly politicised memory but military strength in the state a new experience, furnished an ideological theatre in which these issues were contended for in detail.

The Scotsman Andrew Fletcher, whose importance as a post-Harringtonian theorist has long been recognised, took part in 1698 in a

---

[9] Dickson, 1967; Brewer, 1989.

crucially timed debate on the character and future of standing armies, together with the Anglo-Irishman John Trenchard and the Londoner Daniel Defoe.[10] Fletcher argued that since 1500, and the advent of Bacon's transforming technologies, the individual's prospect of wealth, enlightenment and security had vastly increased – Fletcher, a proponent of the Darien scheme, was never an adversary to commerce – but he had paid the price of a diminishing reliance on his own arms and an increasing dependence on those of the state. He and his neighbours no longer met on horseback to decide public issues, and there was danger that they were losing the capacity to defend by their own efforts the freedom they enjoyed. Though Fletcher's language may point to some myth of Gothic or Gaelic warrior liberty, it was Roman history that indicated the danger he feared. It was a commonplace that as Romans ceased to be soldiers of the republic, they lost the moral as well as material capacity to defend themselves against the mercenaries, warlords, despots and barbarians who took their place. Known frequently as 'effeminacy' but more illuminatingly as 'corruption', this degeneration of the personality under conditions of unfreedom was a commonplace to readers of Sallust, Tacitus, Zosimus or Machiavelli. Only arms could guarantee *virtus*, and there was no reason to suppose that commerce and politeness could restore it.

This was a bedrock point at which ancient liberty had something to say for itself that the rhetoric of modern liberty found hard to reason away. Defoe, arguing against Trenchard rather than Fletcher, maintained forcibly that the society where the individual owned his own arms was impoverished, barbaric and feudal, whereas commercial man, freer, richer and happier, could command through his representatives in parliament the purse-strings that paid the armies who conducted its wars more effectively and threatened neither its prosperity nor its liberties. To this it was retorted – less in 1698 than in the far more savage debates of a decade later, when Swift and Bolingbroke set out to ruin the Duke of Marlborough and Defoe was obliged to compromise[11] – that it was not clear where power in the military-fiscal state ultimately lay. There was a new kind of property, consisting in the ownership not of lands and arms, moveable goods or even personal wealth, but of the tokens of public confidence in the state's future. These paper tokens had been created to maximise the state's credit in paying for its wars, and there was now

---

[10]  Fletcher, 1697–98; Trenchard, 1698; Defoe, 1698. Robbins, 1959, pp. 115–17, 180–4; Schwoerer, 1974, pp. 163–4, 183–7; Pocock, 1975, pp. 427–35; Robertson, 1985, 1997.

[11]  Foot, 1957, is still worth reading on this.

a 'monied interest' allegedly anxious to maximise those wars and their power with it. Precisely because this situation had grown so far beyond that of Rome and the later republic, the history of the latter could be used to great effect in metaphorising and dramatising it; Marlborough could be made to seem the Marius or Caesar of a crisis driven not by latifundists but by stock-jobbers. And the historical benchmark from which both situations departed was the same: the Roman virtue still taken as an ideal by an age whose interest in modern liberty did nothing to diminish its classicism.

(III)

There has been energetic scholarly debate as to whether Georgian England can be described – as once was general among historians of English literature – as passing through an 'Augustan age', or used the epithet in describing itself.[12] What has emerged is the portrait of a deeply divided culture and society, in which to idealise the image of Augustus was to make the claim that its divisions had been brought to an end. In first-century Roman literature, the emperor himself, and those who endorsed the image he sought to present, had depicted the principate as terminating the civil wars, establishing a regime in which the ascendancy of a first citizen rested on the legitimacy of still republican institutions, restoring the traditional Roman virtues, enjoying the support of great poets, and maintaining that Virgilian empire of peace and justice which was to become the Eusebian empire under which Christ was born and the Church became universal on earth. To adopt any part of this rhetoric in Georgian England was to claim that the Hanoverian succession of 1714 – George I had been George Augustus of Hanover – had ended the danger of dynastic civil war (the rebellions of 1715 and 1745 did not become wars among the English); that it had reconciled monarchy with the mixed and balanced constitution of king, lords and commons; that – here unlike Rome – Britain had become a guarantor of a balance of power in Europe; that – unlike Rome again – it stood at the head of an empire of commerce rather than conquest; that England – Augustan claims were less often made for Scotland – had achieved a peaceable order which was also a peace of the Church. Such claims were compatible both with the recognition of profound historical differences between Rome and Britain – Augustus was a metaphor and an analogy – and

---

[12] Weinbrot, 1978, 1993a, 1993b; Erskine-Hill, 1983.

with a realistic approach to Roman history; Octavian the bloody-handed triumvir could be recognised before becoming Augustus the father of his country. We have found this in earlier writings – the emperor Julian had called him a chameleon – and it occurs in Gibbon.[13] 'Augustan' claims need not be historically naive or bland, though they were sometimes both.

What has emerged in recent research and writing, however, is a massive perception of the extreme precariousness of the Hanoverian succession, and the bitterness with which every one of the claims that could underwrite the 'Augustan' ideology was contested. To present Georgian England as an Augustan order was to adopt the discourse of those Whig factions that had succeeded in effecting the succession and – as Gibbon's Tory antecedents made him well aware – had been obliged to secure it by such 'strong' (and oligarchic) 'measures' as the Septennial Act.[14] It could well be doubted that Hanoverian monarchy had left the balance of the constitution intact, and those who had such doubts could conflate the image of an executive enjoying too much patronage and controlling parliament through corrupting its members with that of Augustus claiming to perpetuate the republic while concentrating all its authority in his own person. The image of corruption was central to eighteenth-century British political rhetoric, and the fact that it was regularly abandoned by oppositions that had professed it as soon as they got into office confirmed the belief that corruption was universal. It was projected back into Roman history; a satirist of the *Decline and Fall* wrote, 'His book well describes how corruption and bribes o'erthrew the great empire of Rome,'[15] though in fact this was not how Gibbon had stated the matter. He had, however, traced the corruption of Rome from the servility of the senate, and this from its loss of both *imperium* and *libertas* once control of the armies had passed into the hands of the *imperatores*. The Hanoverian kings did not rule as commanders of the frontier legions of a territorial empire – this indeed was part of their claim to the more benign aspects of the 'Augustan' image – but it could be alleged that their rule was reinforced by a standing army paid out of funds not wholly controlled by parliamentary grants, and that these funds extended the crown's influence over parliament. Once again we see how the analogy of Roman history could be effective in historical conditions recognised as different.

---

[13] *DF*, 1, 3; Womersley, 1994, 1, p. 96.　　[14] *EEG*, p. 19.
[15] For the view that the satirist in question was Charles Fox, see *EGLH*, pp. 135–6.

The Hanoverian dynasty was disliked for many reasons: because it was there at all; because its relation to the Church of England was uncertain and rendered that church uncertain of itself; because the conditions under which it had been established had not been adequately stated; because social critics were appalled by the metropolitan, military-fiscal and mercantile society that Britain was becoming in the historical process that had brought it to power. It could be defended on 'Augustan' grounds – those prepared to break with the Roman paradigm altogether were few – but those (and they were many) who disliked it on any, or any combination, of the grounds above-mentioned commonly adopted some anti-Augustan account of Roman history as metaphor and analogy. This is the moment, in English history but not confined to it, at which Tacitus ceases to be a source of aphorisms supporting neo-Stoic resignation to monarchy as the alternative to disorder, and becomes a critic of the ways in which monarchy claims to have substituted itself for disorder. The critique is historically sophisticated; it is understood that the modern world differs from the ancient, and while ancient analogies may reveal weaknesses and dangers in the modern world they may also indicate reasons why the ancient order came to corruption and collapse. There may remain the primeval image of the free society of warrior freemen – Livian Rome or Gothic liberty – but this order was not simply overthrown by Caesars or absolute monarchies in the role of usurpers; it contained in each case the seeds of its own failure. The confrontation between ancient and modern rendered all history problematic; the ancient world appeared both exemplary and self-destructive because it was studied by a modern order very doubtful of the grounds on which it claimed to have replaced the ancient. This is why readings of history hostile or critical towards both the Augustan and the Hanoverian order can easily be presented as outweighing in number those which defended the latter on the analogy of the former. Augustan Court Whigs were an embattled minority claiming that all disputes had been settled in a culture where they were furiously alive and increasing in number.[16] The Tacitean narrative, framed to deal with consequences of the transition from republic to principate, was becoming a critique of the transition from ancient to modern – from, among other things, a world of republic and empire to a plurality of trading states – and was aided in so becoming by the circumstance that it could easily be extended into a narrative of Decline and Fall. In England before Gibbon there seem to be no master narratives of

---

[16] Browning, 1982, remains an excellent study of their arguments.

Decline and Fall or of ancient and modern; we may have to look for them
in France and Scotland; but Georgian England is a rich field in which to
study the ideological situation that made such narratives necessary. We
learn more of this by examining the only Tacitean historian of note in
that culture; one who rather surprisingly had a European impact and
reputation.

## (IV)

Thomas Gordon was a London Scot seeking his fortune in that city. He
attached himself to the commonwealthman John Trenchard, and with
him wrote and published *Cato's Letters* (1720–23), calling loudly for the trial
and execution of the directors of the South Sea Company (who included
the grandfather of Edward Gibbon).[7] At a later date he edited the *London
Magazine* for Walpole, to the fury of Alexander Pope, who considered
Walpole a figure no less corrupt than the South Sea directors.[8] He
was a ribald anti-clerical, and probably the kind of religious sceptic we
imprecisely term deist. Trenchard and Gordon also edited a journal
called *The Independent Whig*, given over largely to abuse of the higher
clergy; it was widely read in the American colonies – where William
Livingstone edited a New York imitation called *The Independent Reflector*[19] –
and caused a scholarly stir some years ago, when it seemed to have
been more widely read there than Locke's *Treatises of Government*[20] (that
philosopher's advocates have been at pains to show that there is nothing
incompatible with his doctrines in *Cato's Letters*).[21] Gordon also produced
a version of Jean Barbeyrac's *Traité de la Morale des Pères*.[22] Its contents
were so violently derisive towards the Fathers of the Church that it caught
the eye of Holbach, who arranged for a French translation.[23]

   Gordon's European rather than American reputation rests, however,
on his translation into English of the works of Tacitus, which appeared
in 1728 and 1731. Gibbon owned a copy; it was noticed by Voltaire,
translated into French and consulted by Montesquieu and d'Alembert.[24]

[7]  For this detail, see *EEG*, p. 19. For Gordon's career, Robbins, 1959, pp. 115–17; Hamowy, 1995,
    pp. xxv–xxvi.
[8]  Elwin and Courthope, 1967, III, p. 459.      [19]  Klein, 1963.
[20]  Dunn, 1969; Bailyn, 1967.      [21]  Hamowy, 1990, and 1995, p. xxxi.
[22]  Barbeyrac, 1728 (the edition owned by Gibbon); Gordon, 1722.
[23]  Hamowy, 1995, p. xxiii, n. 6.
[24]  For Gordon's career in France in the eighteenth and twentieth centuries, see Volpilhac-Auger,
    1985, pp. 25, 159–66 (Voltaire, Montesquieu, the *Encyclopédie*; facts inserted in a negative judg-
    ment). For d'Alembert, see Ranum, 1980. Gibbon's copy is listed in *Library*, p. 261.

This attention must have been paid, not to Gordon's English version of Tacitus' writings, but to the 'political discourses upon that author' prefixed to the translation of the *Annals* in Gordon's first volume (which we must not omit to notice was published at the sign of Locke's Head). Since Gordon was not a scholar of weight or authority, the reception of his work in Britain and Europe suggests that it must have caught a moment at which it gave readers something they wanted; the restitution of Tacitus, perhaps, to the role of author of a post-republican narrative. Gordon's *Discourses*, certainly, are concerned with the loss of liberty as leading to universal corruption, decline and fall. Liberty is lost when the armies fall under Caesarian control, and universal corruption is the consequence.

I cannot omit observing here, that by the same means that CESAR and AUGUSTUS acquired the Empire, they destroyed its force. In the Civil Wars great part of the people perished, and the rest they debauched: they had ut-terly drained or corrupted that source of men which furnished soldiers who conquered the earth: henceforth the *plebs ingenua* became a mere mob, addicted to idleness and their bellies, void of courage, void of ambition, and careless of renown: armies were with difficulty raised amongst them; when raised not good, or apt to corrupt the rest: it was such who excited the sedition in the German Legions, after the death of AUGUSTUS: *vernacula multitudo, nuper acto in urbe delectu, lasciviae sueta, laborum intolerans, implere ceterorum rudes animos; venisse tempus, etc., An. I. c. 31*: 'the recruits lately raised in Rome, men accustomed to the softness and gayeties of the City, and impatient of military labour and discipline, inflamed the simple minds of all the rest by seditions, infusions and harangues, etc.' Indeed the Roman Armies (so chiefly in name) were mostly composed of foreigners.[25]

Provincials? Non-Italians? Barbarians? Gordon – though the term *plebs ingenua* should carry the connotation of independence and sub-stance – seems to be without any Gracchan or Harringtonian dimension to his thinking. He does not see the uncorrupted armies as composed of free colonists, but of the plebeian townsmen before they became a mob, and does not enquire who they were or how they were paid under the empire. The cause of their demoralisation is the loss of virtue, the dependence on a despot in disguise.

AUGUSTUS was become the center and measure of all things; he was the Senate, Magistracy and Laws: the arms of the Republick he had wrested out of her hands; those who had wielded them for her, he had slain; *Bruto et Cassio caesis, nulla jam publica arma*. The armies of the State were now the armies of AUGUSTUS, and every Province where Legions were kept or necessary, he reserved to himself;

[25] Gordon, 1728, 1, pp. 47–8.

such as were unarmed he left to the Senate and people . . . Italy, the original
soil of Liberty and Freemen, he utterly disarmed, agreeably to the Maxims of
absolute Monarchy: the Roman people and the Roman Senate he had reduced
to cyphers and carcasses: *patres et plebem, invalida et inermia.*[26]

The soldiers retain energy, but it is violent and lawless.

These Emperors of Rome, who had sacrificed their Country and all things
to their supreme power, found little ease and security from its being supreme.
From CESAR the Dictator, who had sacrificed publick Liberty, and was himself
sacrificed to her *manes*, till CHARLEMAIN, above thirty of them were murdered,
and four of them murdered themselves: the soldiery were their masters, and upon
every pique put them to death. If the Prince were chosen by the Senate, this was
reason enough for shedding his blood by the Armies; or if the Armies chose him,
this choice of their own never proved an obstacle against shedding it: 'twas the
soldiers that despatched the Emperor PERTINAX, after he had been forced to
accept the Empire. These lofty Sovereigns, having trod under foot the Senate,
People, and Laws, the best supporters of legitimate Power, held their Scepter
and their lives upon the courtesy of their masters the soldiers: he who swayed
the Universe, was a slave to his own mercenaries.[27]

The fates of Galba and Vitellius in the *Histories* are implicit here,
but Gordon does not make use of the *arcanum* of *alibi quam Romae*. It is
unusual to carry the story as far as Charlemagne, and should have obliged
Gordon to know something about the eastern emperors between AD 500
and 800. It is doubtful if he does, however; he is going past Tacitus to Dio
Cassius and the *Historia Augusta* with his eye on a western Decline and
Fall. Its cause remains despotism, a force which operates independently
of personality and must master it in the end.

It is allowed that amongst the Roman Emperors, there were some excellent ones.
But was not all this chance? They might have proved like the rest, who were
incredibly mischievous and vile. They had nothing but their own Inclinations to
restrain them; and is human Society to depend for security and happiness upon
uncertain Inclination and Will? They were good by conformity to the Laws, as
Laws are the only defence against such as are bad. The bad ones had almost sunk
the Empire to a chaos, before there appeared one Prince of tolerable capacity
and virtue to retrieve it. Insomuch that VESPASIAN declared it to be absolutely
necessary to raise a fund of above three millions of money (of our money) purely
to save the state from absolute ruine and dissolution, *ut Respublica stare possit.*
After DOMITIAN there succeeded five good Reigns, during which Law and
Righteousness prevailed. and the Emperors took nothing, neither power nor
money, but what Laws long established gave them, and professed to derive
everything from the Law, and to occupy nothing in their own Name. But as

---

[26] Gordon, 1728, I, pp. 48–9.      [27] Gordon, 1728, I, pp. 60–I.

the Emperor might still be a Tyrant if he would, that wild Prince COMMODUS resumed the measures of violence, and becoming a second CALIGULA, dispatched and overturned in a few years all the treasure, wise provisions and establishments, contrived and gathered by his Predecessors during the best part of a Century.[28]

The good reigns to which Tacitus had looked forward were no more than an accident; personal virtue is no substitute for the rule of law, and there is nothing to prevent the Tacitean scenario repeating itself indefinitely. There might come a time – it had seemed so to Mexía[29] – when military rule had dispensed with senatorial legitimacy even as a shadow, but Gordon is willing to postpone that to a very distant date.

As the Popes pretend to derive all power from the Gospel, which they pervert and suppress, so did the other Roman Tyrants theirs from the Senate; as if the ancient free State had still subsisted, *tanquam vetere Republica*; and to have destroyed the Senate, would have been to have abrogated their own title to Sovereignty. They must likewise have destroyed the Consulship, which was still reckoned *summum Imperium*, the supreme Magistracy; with the Office of the Pretor, and every Office great or small in the State, with the title or stile of every Law of Rome, and every Tribunal of Justice there: for, every Law and every Office depended upon the Senate, or upon the Senate and People. They must have abolished Learning, History, Records, all Process and Memory; nay the very Military Titles, and Laws of War and Negotiation; those about the Colonies and Provinces, Customs and Trade; and have introduced absolute Oblivion, a new Language and a new Creation.[30]

The intractability of language, and the impossibility of inventing a new one, furnish a better explanation than the conventional cynicism of saying that men are governed by names and shadows. Gordon lived before the French initiated the modern revolutionary practice of seeking to change language and consciousness at a blow, and thought that only a historical process was capable of it.

TIME, however, with the continuance of Tyranny, and Barbarity its inseparable companion, cancelled by degrees the old names and forms, after the essence had been long cancelled; and introduced a cloud of offices and words, of rumbling sounds and swelling titles, suitable to the genius of absolute Rule, and as different from the purity of the old Republican Language, as are Liberty and Politeness from grossness and bondage.[31]

This seems to allude to the palace magniloquence of the later, possibly the eastern, empire; but Gordon does not explore the transformations of

[28] Gordon, 1728, I, p. 67.   [29] Above, p. 246.
[30] Gordon, 1728, I, p. 89.   [31] Gordon, 1728, I, p. 90.

monarchy by Diocletian or Constantine. He does however wish that he
had better things to say of the latter,

> the first Emperor who embraced Christianity, the same stiled CONSTANTINE
> THE GREAT. All the Princes, even the persecuting Princes who went before him,
> hurt not Religion as much as he did; by blending it unnaturally with Politicks and
> Power, by laying the foundation of a spiritual Tyranny, and enabling the Bishops
> of Rome, and other great Prelates, to exert the domineering spirit, which before
> they had but ill concealed: a spirit which has almost extinguished that of the
> Gospel.[32]

Here is the poison poured out on Christendom, the unqualified repudiation of Christian empire. What Gordon thought to be the true gospel
he does not tell us; probably a simple and pious morality. The Enlightened narratives which began to appear after him (he died in 1750) were
to spend much time exploring the foundations of the strange idea of
spiritual authority; Gordon, much as he hates it, treats it only as an ad-
junct to his central image of imperial rule as an endemic reign of terror,
maintained by incessant accusations and incessant confiscations under
Constantius and Valentinian no less than under Tiberius and Domitian.

> The Emperors to gratify their own cruelty, were continually wasting the
> publick Strength by sacrifices noble and many; and, to satiate their avarice
> or that of their creatures, encouraged endless seizures and confiscations. This
> crying Oppression was by the Emperor CONSTANTINE, before mentioned,
> carried higher than any of the Pagan Emperors before him.[33]
>
> These depredations were restrained during the Reign of JULIAN, who . . . was
> superstitious even to weakness, and had conceived an aversion to the Christians
> altogether unsuitable to his remarkable candour and equity: an aversion which
> they themselves improved too much, by a behaviour unworthy of so great a
> Prince, much more unworthy of so meek a Religion . . . The truth is, the Chris-
> tians were then strangely degenerated from the primitive peaceableness and
> purity, become licentious and turbulent to the last degree, and perpetually insti-
> gated by the arrogance and ambition of the Bishops, who were come to contend
> with arms as well as curses, for the possession of opulent Churches. . . . More-
> over, a great part of the wealth and revenue, which used to go towards the
> publick Charge, particularly to defend the Frontiers against the Barbarians, was
> diverted and appropriated to maintain the grandeur and pomp of the great
> Prelates: *Sacerdotes specie religionis fortunas omnes effundebant*, as TACITUS says upon
> another occasion.[34]

For the priests of all religions behave like this. Last of all,

> the Reign of JOVIAN, whose intention seems to have been honest and good, was
> followed by those of VALENTINIAN and VALENS; Princes exceeding furious,

---

[32] Gordon, 1728, 1, p. 80.    [33] Gordon, 1728, 1, p. 90.    [34] Gordon, 1728, 1, p. 91.

suspicious and sanguinary: under them the old Accusations, Confiscations and Carnage were revived without mercy, and continued thenceforth with few intervals, until the Roman Empire was quite overthrown. The people in every part of it being quite harrassed and consumed, finding no relaxation from Oppressors and Accusations, no protection from Law, no refuge in the Clemency of the Emperors, grew desperate, and revolted to the Goths, Huns, Vandals, and other Invaders.[35]

The narrative is not much continued past this point. Here we have a radically Enlightened account of Decline and Fall in a fairly crude condition. It has been constructed by taking some dramatic scenes from Tacitus –

transactions of another sort [from Livy] and other sorts of men; (for by Governments men are changed); the crooked arts of policy, the false smiles of power, the jealousy, fury and wantonness of Princes uncontrolled; the flattery of the Grandees; the havock made by the accusers, and universal debasement of all men: matter this chiefly for reflection, complaints and rebuke![36]

– and extending them through 'the ocean of the Augustan histories' to become an uninterrupted sequence of tyranny and decay. Gordon contrasts this chiaroscuro with the steadily flowing narrative of Livy, who had thought, speech and actions to recount; we are close to Adam Smith's perception that Tacitus is concerned with the emotions, sentiments and sufferings of men without power and of ourselves who read about them.[37] It is possible that Gordon's European reputation was a *succès d'estime* of sentiment; his Tacitus in translation may have afforded his readers the emotions they desired to feel. We have travelled a great distance from the *tacitismo nero* which taught a disenchanted submission to absolute rulers contending with disorder.[38] The prince is now seen as a source of dehumanisation, likely not only to be a despot in himself but to form an alliance with priestcraft. Gordon's True Whig libertarianism finds easy targets for Tacitean denunciations, admires the ancient republic having neither kings nor priests, but must sooner or later enquire into the costs of living in the mercantile and polite monarchies which offer to replace both religious tyranny and royal absolutism. The *Discourses* that trace Decline and Fall are followed by others which describe the corruption of courts and the dangers of standing armies.[39]

---

[35] Gordon, 1728, I, p. 92.     [36] Gordon, 1728, I, p. 16.

[37] *NCG*, p. 326, n. 45; for a detailed study of sentiment in eighteenth-century British historiography, see Phillips, 2000.

[38] Not so far in time. The earlier tradition may have lasted until the recent writings of Amelot de la Houssaye; Soll, 1997, 2000.

[39] Gordon, 1728, I, *Discourses* VIII, IX.

This narrative of Decline and Fall is a narrative of exclusively moral decay, lacking a material base. It is the Caesars who destroy virtue when soldiers cease to be citizens; Gordon does not enquire into how this came to happen. His *Discourses* contain no Gracchan or Harringtonian explanation of the decay of the *plebs ingenua*; there is no Tacitean moment when the armies discover the *arcanum* of making princes far from Rome, no Zosiman moment when they become incapable of resisting barbarians or become barbarised themselves. All these perceptions were available to scholars by Gordon's time, but we have to look elsewhere for them. What there is of a 'modern' as opposed to an 'ancient' understanding of Roman history is contained in the last section of the *Discourses*, entitled 'Of Armies and Conquests'. Here it is remarked:

> The Gothick Governments were military in their first settlement: the General was King, the Officers were the Nobles, and the Soldiers their Tenants: but by the nature of the settlement, out of an Army a Country Militia was produced.[40]

It was a colonisation; the soldiers were settled on the land, and not even feudal tenures could reduce them to subordination. There were no standing armies, and medieval kings could not rule, as the Turk does, through janissaries (in which term Harrington's spahis and timariots are perhaps included).[41] Gothic government has not ended in empire and decay; nor has it engaged in conquest, at which point we return to the problem of the conquering republic, and would be the better for what Gordon does not give us, a Sigonian account of Roman colonisation. He does indeed show that Rome was corrupted by engaging in conquest, but does so in the following terms.

> The State of Carthage after many Countries conquered, but not bettered by her Arms, was almost destroyed by her own barbarous Mercenaries, and at last conquered and destroyed by the Romans; who were in truth the most generous conquerors that the world has known; and most Countries found the Roman Government better than their own. This continued for some time, till their Provincial Magistrates grew rapacious, and turned the Provinces into spoil.[42]

The more adventurous intellect of Daniel Defoe, whom Gordon must have known, had a year or two earlier singled out Carthage as a trading republic, and lamented its conquest by the land-grabbing and slave-hauling Romans.[43] Gordon, however, has a point which could be made against this. Why did a trading republic engage in huge wars for the

---

[40] Gordon, 1728, I, p. 120.    [41] Above, p. 299.    [42] Gordon, 1728, I, p. 122.
[43] Defoe, 1726–27, pp. 95–8; Weinbrot, 1993a, pp. 255–6.

control of Spain, Gaul and Italy, if not because it had employed an army larger than it could control? As far back as Machiavelli, there had been criticism of the Venetians for seeking an empire on the *terra firma*;[44] the Dutch had employed their landward army in a prudently defensive strategy; and the British were debating whether they should use their credit-based army in European power politics, or confine themselves to the pursuit of trade and an empire on blue water.[45] But Gordon seems to have no theory of the commercial state and the problem of empire; he does not have a counterpoint to the history of Rome as conquering by land. This continues from the sentence last quoted, in good set terms.

Rome itself perished by her conquests, which being made by great Armies, occasioned such power and insolence in their Commanders, and set some Citizens so high above the rest, an inequality pernicious to free States, that she was enslaved by ingrates whom she had employed to defend her. Rome vanquished foreign nations; foreign luxury debauched Rome, and traiterous Citizens seized upon their mother with all her acquisitions. All her great blaze and grandeur, served only to make her wretchedness more conspicuous and her chains more intensely felt. Upon her thraldom there ensued such a series of Tyranny and misery, treachery, oppression, cruelty, death and affliction, in all shapes; that her agonies were scarce ever suspended till she finally expired. When her own Tyrants, become through Tyranny impotent, could no longer afflict her, for protection was none of their business; a host of Barbarians, only known for ravages and acts of inhumanity, finished the work of desolation, and closed her civil doom. She has been since racked under a Tyranny more painful, as 'tis more slow; and more base, as 'tis scarce a domination of men: I mean her vassalage to a sort of beings of all others the most merciless and contemptible, Monks and Spectres.[46]

These hags rule at Rome and in the lands of popery; Gordon's anticlericalism does not make him say that the despotism of barbarism and religion is universal, only that it may be. The question is what alternative he has in mind for it, and in ancient history he clearly knows of none. It is probably no accident that he has some reflections on Spain and the superiority of trade over gold,[47] before bringing the *Discourses on Tacitus* to an end with this passage.

The Roman State owed her greatness in a good measure to a misfortune: it was founded in War and nourished by it: the same may be said of the Turkish Monarchy. But States formed for peace, tho' they do not arrive to such immensity

---

[44] *Discorsi*, I, 6; Gilbert, 1965, I, p. 210. For the debate at large, Bouwsma, 1968.
[45] Armitage, 2000; Gould, 2000, for recent full discussion of this question.
[46] Gordon, 1728, I, p. 122.     [47] Gordon, 1728, I, p. 123.

and grandeur, are more lasting and secure: witness Sparta and Venice. The former lasted eight hundred years, and the latter has lasted twelve hundred, without any Revolution: what errors they both committed, were owing to their attempts to conquer, for which they were not formed; tho' the Spartans were exceeding brave and victorious: but they wanted the *Plebs ingenua*, which formed the strength of the Roman Armies; as the Janizaries, a militia formerly excellently trained and disciplined, formed those of the Turk. With the latter, fighting and extending their dominions, is an article of their Religion, as false and barbarous in this as in many of its other principles, and as little calculated for the good of man.[48]

*Finis*. If Venice was a trading republic, Sparta was none. Gordon is merely reiterating Machiavelli's characterisation of both as commonwealths for preservation, not expansion,[49] and ignoring his point that both were oligarchies – only very marginally does he notice that the landed oligarchy of Sparta formed itself into an infantry as terrifying as the janissaries, whereas the merchant oligarchy of Venice employed mercenaries. What is on his mind is the danger presented by armies in states formed for expansion, and the standing armies of his own time, deeply as he mistrusts them, are the property of states aiming at plurality and commerce. The heroic republic of Rome was a commonwealth of soldiers colonising lands in a process of perpetual expansion, and something like the Gracchan explanation is emerging in the sentences that close Gordon's treatise on Tacitus. What is more startling is the equation between the janissaries and the *plebs ingenua*. This adjective cannot but connote civic independence and property, and one wonders whether Gordon is telescoping the slave-infantry of the janissaries with the precariously tenured spahis and timariots. The *plebs ingenua*, till dispossessed by rapacious ranchers and squatters,[50] held their lands by the complex series of *jura* described in Sigonio; but if Gordon knows this, it does not prevent his equating them with the fanatical warriors of a despotic empire. The exemplary republic of Rome and the alien and recently menacing Sultanate of Rūm[51] have in common a commitment to conquest based less on religion – which did not motivate the Romans – than on a system of property in nothing but land.

---

[48] Gordon, 1728, 1, p. 124.    [49] *Discorsi*, 1, 2; 5,6, Gilbert, 1965, 1, pp. 195–6, 204–5, 207–8.
[50] I am using the last term in its Australian sense.
[51] An Ottoman term for the Asian provinces of the former east Roman empire.

# CHAPTER 15

# *The French narrative*

## PART I: BOSSUET AND TILLEMONT

### (1)

We are now entering the intellectual climate – classical and neo-classical, clerical and anti-clerical, ancient and modern, *philosophe* and *érudit* – in which has been situated Gibbon's undertaking to write the *Decline and Fall*. We are doing so in search of minds who viewed the history of the principate as an extension of that of the republic, and both as predictive of the ultimate loss of imperial control over the Latin provinces and Rome itself. The search will lead us to two master works published fifty years apart – Montesquieu's *Considérations sur la Grandeur des Romains et de leur Décadence* (1734, revised 1748) and Adam Ferguson's *History of the Rise, Progress and Termination of the Roman Republic* (1783, revised 1799) – which precede, accompany and succeed the first volume of the *Decline and Fall* (1776). This intellectual climate (the 'Enlightenments of Edward Gibbon') was as we have seen cosmopolitan – English, francophone Protestant, Parisian, latterly Scottish – and consisted of discourses highly distinct from, though interacting with, one another. The English setting of the early Hanoverian period, reviewed in the last chapter down to the publication of Gordon's *Tacitus* in 1728, is chiefly of ideological interest, revealing a context in which values were deeply divided and Roman history was studied both because its lessons illustrated contemporary problems and because they revealed how deeply these differed from those of antiquity. The scene in France, we shall find, was different; not only because the problems of historical self-perception differed from those in England, but because the higher level at which scholarship, like other intellectual pursuits, was organised into the *académies* of Ludovican monarchy encouraged a more systematic pursuit of the philosophical and methodological issues of the age. As we already know from Gibbon's encounter

325

with the *Encyclopédie*, it is in francophone debate that we can pursue the collision and reconciliation of philosophical with erudite historiography that is one of the keys to Gibbon's achievement.

It is not that such issues went unnoticed in England, or that they were not discussed in relation to Roman and ancient history. Paralleling both the *querelle des anciens et modernes* and the philosophical debate over the pyrrhonist assault on the reliability of ancient history, there was in England a Battle of the Books in which the struggle between mimesis and criticism was fought out in a setting not remote from that between parties in church and state.[1] This went on in both the clerical universities and the ungovernable world of London print journalism (not a *république des lettres* because it made few claims to rise above partisanship). The Moderns in this Battle were the advocates of philosophical criticism, and this could take the form of that archaeology or *peinture* of past states of language and culture which was the object of erudition but could be condemned as antiquarianism. It did not preclude the construction of narrative histories. William Wotton, a young and aggressive Modern who had made the outrageous claim that the critic might arrive at knowledge concerning an ancient text which had not been accessible to its ancient author,[2] published in 1701 a *History of Rome from the Death of Antoninus Pius to the Death of Severus Alexander*,[3] which commands our attention for two reasons: because it focusses on the moment, ending in the golden age of the post-Tacitean principate, at which Gibbon began the narrative of the *Decline and Fall*; and because it has this if little else in common with Bossuet's *Discours sur l'Histoire Universelle*, that it was originally written to edify an heir to the throne – in this case the young Duke of Gloucester, whose death in 1700 led to the long dynastic crisis of his mother Anne's reign and the Hanoverian succession. Forty years later, Conyers Middleton, whose doubts on the miracles of the early Church brought about Gibbon's juvenile crisis and expulsion from Oxford,[4] published a life of Cicero[5] – dedicated to Lord Hervey, the author of *Ancient and Modern Liberty Stated and Compared*[6] – which concealed neither the orator's faults of character nor the fact that he was betrayed and murdered in the dirty negotiations between the triumvirs Mark Antony and Octavius Caesar. From Augustine to Pedro Mexía we have found this noted;[7] there is no moment in the history of historiography when Augustus is not an ambiguous figure.

[1] Levine, 1987, 1991, 1999a, 1999b; *EEG*, pp. 48–50.    [2] Levine, 1991, *passim*, esp. p. 41.
[3] Wotton, 1701; Levine, 1991, pp. 343–51; below, pp. 448–51.    [4] *EEG*, pp. 43–9.
[5] Middleton, 1741.    [6] Hervey, 1734. Above, p. 309, n. 5.    [7] Above, pp. 92–3, 242.

There are then English works on Roman history which address themselves to moments of change in the history of government and seem to elude the censures which English critics were fond of passing on the practice of history in their own culture. These censures were often based on a comparison with what was thought to be forward in France, and we may now turn to the history of Rome as studied and written there. Here, it must be our first discovery, we have to do with a Catholic monarchy, in which the perspectives of secular history necessary to both church and state looked back to the Roman empire, and the former at least included the empire in the perspectives of sacred and ecclesiastical history, while looking on these as providing both empire and monarchy with much if not all of their legitimacy. Among the great histories written late in the reign of Louis XIV and after, we find works of sacred and ecclesiastical history, whose understandings of the Roman empire and the French monarchy contribute to the historiography of the Decline and Fall.

Gibbon owned two French editions and two English translations of Bossuet's *Discours sur l'Histoire Universelle*, as well as of his works on Catholic authority and Protestant anarchy.[8] The latter may have been in Gibbon's possession since the years of his undergraduate crisis,[9] and since he emerged from this a sceptic who subordinated religion to history, it is not to be expected that he should ascribe authority to the *Discours*, which we have seen Voltaire erecting into the antithesis of the 'Enlightened narrative' itself.[10] Bossuet's work, composed in 1681, is in fact one of several late flowerings of Christian history in the grand Eusebian manner, in which secular history is subordinate to the history of the Church in the world, and organised into the history of empires of which sacred history makes use to the point where the two can hardly be separated; we find ourselves returning to the themes of Orosius and Otto of Freising. There are four empires, of which Rome is the last and most crucial, rendered so by the divine decree that chooses the Virgilian peace of Augustus as the moment for Christ to be born and his Church to spread on earth.[11] It is therefore a question how far the Church sanctifies the empire and the emperor's sanctified authority becomes necessary to the Church; and in confronting this far from simple question, the secular history of empire becomes relevant. Initially, the emperors are pagans and persecutors; they do not automatically become sacred Christian kings at the conversion of Constantine – heresy sees to that – and there is room for the

---

[8] *Library*, pp. 75–6.  [9] *Memoirs*, pp. 59–60.  [10] *NCG*, pp. 105–8.
[11] Bossuet, 1788, part III, chs. I–VI, pp. 328–534; Ranum, 1976, pp. 299–361.

implication that Davidic kingship is reborn at the subsequent conversion of the barbarians. Emperors who are persecutors may also be tyrants – it is a problem when, like Marcus Aurelius, they are the one but not the other – and there exists by Bossuet's time a mass of literature recovered by the humanists which exhibits their power as rooted in the supersession of Roman liberty by Augustus, and the latter as an ambiguous figure creating a monarchy often, and potentially always, tyrannical.

Precisely because Bossuet was a Christian classicist who regarded ancient literature, its imagery and its values, as part of the armoury of Christian kingship – if not of the message of the Church – he came face to face with the problem of Roman *libertas*, its relation to *imperium*, and the nature of rule by *imperatores*. The decline and fall of the republic was necessary to his story, and since he must carry on at least to the *translatio imperii*, his Eusebian acceptance of a sacred monarchy did not deliver him from narratives of tyranny and weakness in the decline and fall of empire. If it was not his primary aim to recount these matters, they could not, and cannot, be invisible to his readers. We therefore note his praise of Roman liberty, virtue, frugality and the wise rule of the senate.[12] It is hinted that the people had too much power, and that only kingship could have resolved the tension between them and the senate; but the latter are credited both with expanding the republic's empire and with rendering it just, so that the subject peoples not only accepted it but – aided by processes of colonisation – became Romans themselves.[13] There are elements here of the Dantean and Ptolemaic idea that the civic virtues of the Romans made them worthy of both republic and empire, but this is at the service of the Eusebian vision of Augustus closing the gates of Janus and giving the world peace in preparation for the birth of Christ; and how Augustus came to be emperor is a story already told, by many authors and with much ambivalence. We therefore need to know how Bossuet dealt with the decline of the republic, and whether he saw elements in it that weakened or corrupted the principate and prepared the decline of the empire. If he is not the kind of historian primarily committed to asking such questions, this does not mean that answers to them will be excluded from his discourse.

The decline of the republic is ascribed to the people's jealousy of the senate. They are given credit for resisting senatorial arrogance when this goes too far,[14] but in general it is their demands which are excessive

---

[12] Bossuet, 1788, III, ch. VI.    [13] Bossuet, 1788, pp. 530–1; Ranum, 1976, pp. 358–9.
[14] Bossuet, 1788, p. 534; Ranum, 1976, p. 361.

and the senate which is the source of all wisdom; and when there is the question of the division of lands – the central theme of Gracchan history inasmuch as Bossuet cannot exclude it from his narrative – he has the assurance to declare that, whereas the tribunes (the Gracchi are only mentioned) wished to distribute conquered lands among the people, the senate wished them sold to the benefit of the public treasury.[5] This is unusual; one asks whether anything other than a conviction that the higher authority must always be right as against the lower could have impelled Bossuet to ignore the well-documented portrait of the senate as a gang of corrupt oligarchs that appears in nearly all the literature. There was no pressing need to take either side in recounting how Augustus came to make the peace between them, and Bossuet does not conceal that Julius Caesar, if not his grand-nephew, was a military adventurer like Marius who offered lands to the soldiers and the people.[6]

Of Augustus we are told that he reduced the world to servitude, that his power was founded on the armies who would suffer no return to senatorial rule, that though his system entailed a renunciation of unlimited expansion the soldiers regularly and bloodily intervened in the choice of emperors, and that this led to divisions of the empire, wars between rival emperors, and an inability to resist either Persian or German barbarians.[7] This sufficiently explains the fall of the empire; there is in Bossuet the outline of a Decline and Fall going back to the conquests of the republic. The Augustan peace necessary to the Eusebian mythos and the birth of the Church seems achieved by the wisdom and justice of the senate in expanding the republican empire; it is a secondary though an enormous theme that this expansion produced huge and dissatisfied armies whose turbulence rendered the principate necessary but whom the principate failed to control. The junction between the empire of Augustus and the birth of Christ is providentially arranged, and providence is God's mode of action in Bossuet's theodicy of history. Providence, however, is a divine ordering of what would otherwise be accidental, and it is not necessary for the accidents to display a historical logic or narrative of their own. If they do, it commands our interest and our awe, but to insist on it or enquire too far may be to fall into the sin of curiosity.

The fall of empires is a necessary theme in the education of princes – Bossuet wrote his *Discours* for the Dauphin – but since princes are commanded to serve a Church to which their service is important without

---

[5] Bossuet, 1788, p. 539; Ranum, 1976, p. 364.    [6] Bossuet, 1788, p. 543; Ranum, 1976, p. 367.
[7] Bossuet, 1788, pp. 547–8, 552–4; Ranum, 1976, pp. 369–70, 372–3.

being necessary, we must turn back from the study of Decline and Fall that concludes the *Discours* to the earlier chapters, which exhibit emperors from Constantine to Charlemagne in the course of ecclesiastical history.[18] It is the duty of emperors to maintain a space within which the Church can flourish on earth, and therefore the loss of western provinces by the successors of Theodosius, or of eastern provinces by Heraclius and his successors, are important moments in history both ecclesiastical and civil. They are also obliged to uphold the Church in its spiritual mission, however, and therefore the history, not always creditable, of their dealings with heresy is, as it was to Eusebius, more important still. The eastern emperors lose provinces to the Arabs as a punishment for the heresies of Heraclius, and the iconoclastic heresy, favoured by rulers from Leo to Irene, is an important theme in the narrative of how Charlemagne came to be emperor in the west.[19] Here, however, we encounter a lacuna – he may have intended no more than a postponement – in Bossuet's scheme. There is little account of how the popes acquired the territorial authority in Italy that left them exposed to the barbarian threat of the Lombards and the iconoclastic threat of the Roman power at Ravenna, and less of how they were obliged to profit from the Italian rebellion that destroyed the latter. When they turn to the Frankish kingdom and establish Charlemagne as emperor, they are not dealing with a dangerous imbalance of power so much as withstanding the persistent heresy of the Greeks. This is how Charlemagne,

élu Empereur par les Romains sans qu'il y pensât, et couronné par le Pape Léon III, qui avoit porté le Peuple Romain à ce choix, devint le fondateur du nouvel Empire et de la grandeur temporelle du saint Siege.[20]

[elected emperor by the Romans without having sought that honour, and . . . crowned by Pope Leo, who had persuaded the Roman people to make that choice . . . became the founder of the new empire and of the temporal greatness of the Holy See.][21]

Bossuet has reached the moment of *translatio imperii*, but has not become its historian. He informs the Dauphin that the latter has arrived at his own moment in the last age of the world, and at that of his own great ancestor, of whose deeds and those of his descendants a history remains to be written; this will be presented in a further volume, if the prince does not deign to write it himself.[22] Bossuet did not write it, and does not seem

---

[18] *Discours*, I, XI–XII.    [19] Bossuet, 1788, pp. 142–9; Ranum, 1976, pp. 102–6.
[20] Bossuet, 1788, p. 152.    [21] Trans. Forster, in Ranum, 1976, pp. 108–9.
[22] Bossuet, 1788, pp. 5–6, 557–8; Ranum, 1976, pp. 5–6, 375–6.

to have commissioned anyone else to do so;[23] and the result is that in the *Discours sur l'Histoire Universelle* we have Bossuet's account of ancient history – that of the Four Empires down to the coming of what may or may not be the stone cut without hands – but no account of modern history, as Gibbon and all others of the age understood the term: no account of the 'Christian millennium' recounted in 'the Enlightened narrative'. It seems a further consequence that, while Voltaire and Emilie du Chatelet were outraged by an ancient history which exalted the Jews above the Chinese, what they set out to provide was not a counter-narrative of ancient history, but an account of the modern history which Bossuet had not given.[24] Since Giannone, Hume and Robertson joined them in writing the 'Enlightened narrative', we are only now in search of the Enlightened account of the history of ancient Rome.

Bossuet completed the *Discours* in 1681, at a time of acute crisis between the papacy and the French king: that of the dispute over the *régale*, which Voltaire was to judge a moment of missed opportunity, the failure to establish an independent Gallican Church with its own Patriarch.[25] It is imaginable that Bossuet judged the time not ripe for what extreme courses might have made necessary: a full ecclesiastical history of the French kingdom and its Church, in the setting of a modern history which would still have been that of the last age of the world. It would have displaced that of the *translatio imperii ad Germanos* in favour of one in which Charlemagne's Frankish heirs, of the *troisième race* as well as the *deuxième*, were the equals, as actors in history both sacred and civil, of the Saxons and Suabians to whom the imperial title had descended. It would have looked towards a *siècle de Louis XIV* other than that of which Voltaire wrote the history, and the *Essai sur les Moeurs* and the Enlightened narrative might not have existed as we know them. In the event, there was no Gallican schism; Bossuet ended his authorial career as a historian of Protestant divagations;[26] and Gibbon was obliged to look elsewhere for the Gallican synthesis of history which he came to need.

---

[23] The *Tableau de l'histoire moderne*, in three volumes, by Guillaume-Alexandre Méhégan (Paris, 1766), is identified as an intended completion of the *Discours* by Ricuperati (1999, p. 37, n. 41). Further editions appeared (1772, 1778, 1782) after the author's death in 1766, the year of first publication. There was an English translation in 1779. Méhégan was an abbé who did time in the Bastille for an injudicious life of the prophet Zoroaster, and did not write like Bossuet in the grand Eusebian manner. The 1788 Rouen edition of the *Discours*, cited in this chapter, has a second volume covering the centuries from AD 800 to 1700. It is a chronicle of principal events, betraying no evident scheme of history, either theological or philosophical.

[24] See n. 10, above.    [25] *NCG*, pp. 92–3.

[26] '[P]erhaps his greatest work' (Ranum, 1976, p. xli); Gibbon, who read it at Oxford, might have agreed.

(11)

He did not find it in the much greater scholar if lesser historian on whom he came to rely: Louis-Sebastien Le Nain de Tillemont,[27] whose *Histoire des empereurs et des autres princes qui ont regné durant les six premiers siècles de l'église* was licensed (at least in part) for publication in 1688.[28] Tillemont was a Jansenist, and what he and Bossuet thought of one another need not concern us; both in their ways were ecclesiastical historians in the fullest sense. He tells us that the history of the emperors, and the empire, is ancillary but necessary to the history of the Church; he has learned from experience – does he mean study? – that

> il y a une telle liaison entre l'histoire sainte et la profane, qu'il faut necessaire-ment s'instruire avec soin de la derniere pour pouvoir posseder l'autre, et pour en resoudre solidement les difficultez. Il est difficile aussi qu'on ne souhaite pas de savoir qui estoient ces princes, ces magistrats, et ces grands du siecle, qu'on voit si souvent meslez dans les affaires de l'Eglise, soit pour les sanctifier par leurs persecutions, soit pour la soutenir par leur puissance, et luy donner cet éclat exterieur qui luy a servi à renfermer dans son sein les foibles avec les forts, les imparfaits avec les parfaits. Voila ce qui a obligé l'auteur à joindre l'une et l'autre histoire ensemble, et à étudier la profane pour mieux savoir celle de l'Eglise.[29]

[there is so close a connection between history sacred and profane, that it is necessary to inform oneself diligently of the latter if one is to master the former and adequately resolve its difficulties. It is also hard not to wish that one knew who were these princes, magistrates and other notables of the age, whom one sees so often active in the affairs of the Church; whether to sanctify her by their persecutions, or to protect her by their power, bringing her to that outward glory which has enabled her to enfold in her bosom the weak as well as the strong, the imperfect together with the perfect. This is what has obliged the author to bring the one and the other history together, and to study the profane the better to understand that of the Church.][30]

Tillemont – as Gibbon never ceases to remind us – was superlatively literal-minded, and may mean no more than that the facts of sacred history as recorded are unintelligible without those of profane history that are mingled with them. We should not hasten to suppose that he means that the one history has a logic which affects that of the other. Nevertheless, there is something in the above passage which recalls Otto

---

[27] Neveu, 1968, for his career as a whole. *Library*, pp. 267–8, for Gibbon's holdings of his works.
[28] Tillemont, 1732–40, 1, p. xx. The work was published in 1690–1739, in part posthumously.
[29] Tillemont, 1732–40, 1, p. iii.
[30] Trans. JGAP, as are all quotations from Tillemont in this section.

of Freising's net cast into the sea;[31] Tillemont may have something
Jansenist to say about the Church in this world. He has other introductory remarks to make about the interactions of profane with sacred
history. Emperors perform acts in the history of the Church:

Auguste y en a aussi quelqu'une par l'édit qui fit aller la Sainte Vierge à Bethléem;
et c'est luy d'ailleurs qui a établi la monarchie Romaine en l'état qu'elle entre
dans l'histoire de l'Eglise. Il a donc falu parler de ce changement, et marquer
autant qu'on a pû l'origine des choses qui se doivent voir dans la suite.[32]

[Augustus has one to his name in the edict which caused the Holy Virgin to go
up to Bethlehem; and he too it was who established the Roman monarchy in
the state it was in when it entered into the history of the Church. It has been
necessary to speak of this change, and to observe as best one can the origin of
those things which must be seen as its consequence.]

The second of Augustus' acts need be no more than the establishment
of that general peace in which Christ was born; but 'changement' –
*innovatio? res novae?* – is a term loaded with the dangers and ambiguities
of secular history, and in that history it would seem to have consequences
of its own. Secular history has consequences in the sacred also, of a kind
not comfortable to read about in this century.

L'histoire des guerres et de la ruine des Juifs doit necessairement entrer dans
celle de l'Eglise, et elle est visiblement liée à celle de Neron et de Vespasien.
On n'a donc pû se dispenser de la mettre: et quoyque ce ne soit presque qu'un
abregé de Joseph, on y verra peut estre avec plaisir l'accomplissement de tant de
predictions des anciens Prophetes et de JESUS-CHRIST mesme, la vengeance
du sang du Sauveur et des autres justes, et la preuve que le Messie estoit venu,
puisque le sceptre estoit absolument osté de la maison de Juda, et l'observation
de la loy impossible.[33]

[The history of the wars of the Jews and their downfall must necessarily form
part of the history of the Church, and it is visibly linked with that of Nero and
Vespasian. It cannot be omitted; and though what follows is little more than
an abbreviation of Josephus, one may read with pleasure of the fulfilment of so
many predictions of the ancient prophets and Jesus Christ himself, the avenging
of the blood of the Saviour and others of the just, and the proof that the Messiah
is indeed come, since the sceptre is altogether taken from the house of Judah
and the observation of the Law made impossible.]

Vespasian and Titus act in the history revealed by Josephus, as well as
in that recorded by Tacitus. With this addition, however – Gibbon excises
it[34] – Tillemont's division of his history into volumes accords well enough

---

[31] Above, p. 112.   [32] Tillemont, 1732–40, I, p. v.   [33] Tillemont, 1732–40, I, p. vi.
[34] Below, p. 427, for Gibbon's partial silencing of Jewish history.

with the punctuation of secular history in volume I of the *Decline and Fall*.
His first volume runs from Augustus to Vitellius and the first Tacitean
crisis; his second from Vespasian to Pertinax, who perished after the death
of Commodus, where Gibbon begins; his third from Septimius Severus
to Diocletian, the founder of a new style of monarchy; his fourth from
Diocletian to Jovian, when the frontiers begin to retreat.[35] Constantine is
not a turning point, and the organisation is one of secular history rather
than sacred. Tillemont remains for ever an *érudit*, concerned with getting
his facts straight; but he seems to know that the history of emperors runs
a course of its own.

His account of Augustus begins from the victory of Actium, before
which he could be called *imperator* only in the republican sense of a
victorious general, not in the imperial sense of one who monopolised
military authority. This late commencement means that there will be
no Sallustian or Appianic history of the civil wars and triumvirates, no
'Gracchan' thesis as to their origin. Augustus confers with Agrippa and
Maecenas, and resolves to rule 'comme un veritable Roy', not taking
this or any other title, but engrossing all republican authority in his own
person.[36] There is a Tacitean account of the exhaustion of the senatorial
elites which made this possible, and Tacitus is regularly cited among the
authors Tillemont is following. The chapter headings tell us clearly that
Augustus is ruling through military power:

Auguste se fait contraindre à conserver l'autorité souveraine; se charge des
provinces où étoient les troupes, laisse les autres au peuple et au Senat.
  Des troupes Romaines; Auguste fait un fond pour les payer.[37]

[Augustus commits himself to preserving sovereign power; takes control of the
provinces where troops are quartered, and leaves the others to the people and
the senate.
  The Roman legions; Augustus sets up a fund for their payment.]

Under the latter heading occurs a significantly post-Gracchan observation.

On donnoit d'abord les terres aux vieux soldats: ce qui produisit de grands
maux, comme les Eglogues de Virgile l'ont appris à tout le monde. Auguste
en la 19. année de son regne ordonna qu'au lieu de terres, on leur donneroit

---

[35] The contents in full run: '1. Depuis Auguste jusqu'à Vitellius, et la ruine de Jerusalem. 11. Depuis
Vespasien jusques à Pertinax. 111. Depuis Severe jusqu'à l'election de Diocletian. 1v. Depuis
Diocletian jusqu'à Jovien. v. Depuis Valentinien I jusqu'à Honoré. v1. Depuis Theodose II
jusqu'à Anastase.'
[36] Tillemont, 1732–40, 1, p. 2.     [37] Tillemont, 1732–40, 1, pp. 2, 15.

une certaine somme d'argent . . . Cette recompense s'appelloit par les Latins
*Emeritum*.[38]

[Veterans were originally rewarded with lands; this gave rise to great evils, as
the Eclogues of Virgil have taught all posterity. In the 19th year of his reign,
Augustus ordained that instead of land, they should be given a fixed sum of
money . . . called *emeritum* in Latin.]

He goes on to describe the *thesaurus militum* and the taxation necessary
to maintain it, but cannot be said to have reached the generalisations,
either that the legions' demands for ready cash were a cause of dynastic
civil wars, or that the empire was ultimately worn down by over-taxation.
Historical hypotheses of this kind are simply not Tillemont's business,
but it cannot be said that he idealised the Augustan empire or underestimated the costs of its peace. When he comes to Augustus' carefully-
staged deathbed, he remarks that 'la foi' (surely *la bonne foi* rather than *la
sainte foi*)

nous fait voir des suites horribles de cette mort si heureuse en apparence

[shows us the hideous consequences of this death so happy in appearance],

a thoroughly Tacitean comment; and continues:

Nous n'entrions point ici dans le jugement qu'on a fait, ou qu'on doit faire, de
l'esprit, des actions, et de la conduite d'Auguste, dont nous n'avons parlé que
pour éclaircir la suite de l'histoire. Il suffit de remarquer ce qu'on a dit, qu'il
ne devoit jamais naître à cause des maux qu'il a faits pour se rendre maître
de la Republique; ou qu'il ne devoit jamais mourir, à cause de la sagesse et
de la moderation avec laquelle il la conduisit lorsqu'il fut venu à bout de ses
desseins. Cependant on assure que peu de personnes le plurerent d'abord: mais
la conduite de son successeur le fit ensuite regretter de tout le monde.[39]

[We shall not enter here upon the judgement which has been, or should be,
made concerning the character, actions or behaviour of Augustus, which we
have described only in order to clarify the historical sequence. It is enough to
remark what was said: that he should never have been born, on account of
the evils which he wrought to make himself master of the republic; or that he
should never have died, on account of the wisdom and moderation with which
he governed it when he had reached the goal of his designs. It may certainly be
added that few mourned him to begin with, but that the conduct of his successor
soon made him regretted by all.]

It was likewise said of Septimius Severus that it were better that he
had never been born, but that, since he had been, that he should never

---

[38] Tillemont, 1732–40, I, p. 16.    [39] Tillemont, 1732–40, I, pp. 18–19.

have died; and of Augustus that he was rare among emperors in having become a better man in that office. Pedro Mexía had noted this, and taken it as a sign that God had inscrutably willed his ascent from triumvir to *princeps*;[40] Tillemont is expressing the same judgement, and giving us a little more of the portrait of Augustus as chameleon – the expression of Julian the Apostate – or hypocrite, the verdict of Gibbon.[41] It is a providentialist judgement; God chooses unworthy instruments for his purposes, and may shape them in more worthy form when he does so. But Tillemont looks a stage further. The system founded by Augustus will not last; Tiberius, Caligula and Nero will succeed him, and – though the weakness of a regime founded on the armies is less heavily underlined than it is by Bossuet – the reign of the last will end in civil war. At the opening of the second volume of the *Histoire des Empereurs*, the mystery of God's judgements reappears.

On a vu dans le premier Tome de cette Histoire, que Dieu après avoir formé la Monarchie Romaine par Auguste, l'a aussi-tost rabaissée de la maniere du monde la plus humiliante, en la soumettant à des princes ou sans jugement et sans capacité, ou les plus cruels, les plus furieux, et les plus detestables que l'histoire nous ait peut-estre jamais fait connoistre: Et tout cela finit par de sanglantes guerres civiles, qui ravagèrent une grande partie de ce que l'avarice des Empereurs et leurs ministres avoit epargné.

Domitien et Commode nous representeront encore dans ce second volume, quelques traits de cette idée si triste et si affreuse. Mais à la reserve de ces deux princes, et peut-estre d'Adrien qui a esté assez meslé de bien et de mal, nous y verrons le temps le plus heureux de l'Empire Romain, et presque tout ce que le paganisme y a pû produire de plus excellent; n'y ayant guere qu'Auguste dans ce qui precede, et Alexandre avec Probe dans ce qui suit, qu'on puisse comparer à ceux dont on va voir ici l'histoire.[42]

[In the first volume of this history we saw that God, having formed the Roman Empire by means of Augustus, thereupon cast it down in the most humiliating manner possible, subjecting it to princes who either lacked all judgement and capacity, or were the most cruel, savage and detestable perhaps ever recorded in history; and all this ended in bloody civil wars which devastated most of what the rapacity of the emperors and their ministers had left untouched.

Domitian and Commodus in this second volume will present some features of this dark and terrifying image. But with the exception of these two princes, and perhaps of Hadrian who was a mixture of good and evil, we shall now behold the happiest age of the Roman empire, and almost every good which paganism is able to produce; there being none but Augustus in the age preceding it, and Alexander and Probus in that which will follow, whom we can set beside those whose history is now to appear.]

---

[40] Above, p. 242.    [41] Below, pp. 442–3, 478–81.    [42] Tillemont, 1732–40, II, p. I.

The Jansenist Tillemont is perhaps a shade less assured than Bossuet that monarchy is a form of government enjoying a special divine approval. God selects Augustus, a thoroughly sinful man, to bring about the peace in which his Son will be born, but permits it to fall under a succession of tyrants for whose succession Augustus is answerable, and into civil wars which may – Tillemont is not explicit – result from the weakness of his military system. These wars are ended by Vespasian and Titus, God's instruments in accomplishing the ruin of the Jews; but Tillemont looks ahead to Domitian, under whom Tacitus began to write, and Commodus, who will bring about the downfall of the empire's golden age. That age may receive every encomium – Hadrian as an ambivalent figure will reappear in Gibbon[43] – but it is mortal; if only Augustus (a more than doubtful paragon) is the equal of Trajan and the Antonines in the age before them, we can look past them, and past Commodus and Pertinax, and find only the exemplary Alexander Severus and the military worthy Probus to act as their moral equivalents. God's purposes are not accomplished through the provision of virtuous successors or ages of imperial peace; the ways of providence are too inscrutable to have their history written.

Tillemont's second volume, and his third, will be histories of pagan emperors; Constantine will appear halfway through the fourth, and we must postpone consideration of how Eusebian the account of him will be. Tillemont is nevertheless writing ecclesiastical history; he has told us already that the emperors act in sacred history and the history of the Church. Vespasian acts in the narrative of Josephus before that of Tacitus, and as well as a whole group of chapters recounting *la ruine des Juifs*, there is a digression on the life of Apollonius of Tyana, a significant if fraudulent figure.[44] The *Histoire des Empereurs*, in short, will lead Tillemont into his far more ambitious *Mémoires pour servir à l'histoire ecclésiastique* (1693–1712), both confined to the first six centuries of the Church. Tillemont's *oeuvre* will have to be considered as we come to Gibbon's writing of ecclesiastical history. What may be stated now is that he read Tillemont *en érudit*, not *en philosophe*. The Jansenist's histories are not driven by any theological or ecclesiological scheme; Gibbon could find nothing in them on the interpretative level but a painstaking and painful orthodoxy of which he never ceased making fun. But he never thought Tillemont ridiculous as an authority; he saw in him an infinite capacity for taking pains, an inexhaustible and nearly always successful pursuit of accuracy

---

43 *DF* I, ch. 1 (Womersley, 1994, I, p. 37), ch. 3 (pp. 100–1).
44 For Gibbon on Apollonius, see below, p. 472.

and verification, for which he had nothing but respect and on which he came to depend (*sine Tillemontio duce, saepius noster titubat*).[45] It is a question how far back to trace the roots of Gibbon's discovery that he must write a history of church as well as empire; but the distinctions between sacred and profane, ecclesiastical and imperial history, given by Tillemont at the outset of the *Empereurs*, are one starting point from which he proceeded to write an Enlightened history of the Church which is more than the sum of Enlightened ideas about it. And this, furthermore, is a pivotal moment in Gibbon's synthesis of philosophy and erudition.

Tillemont, however, can only marginally be related to a history of Tacitean or Appianic explanation. If he thought there were flaws in the structure of the empire, over and above the alienation between virtue and tyranny in the personalities of the emperors, he allowed these to become absorbed into his providentialist theodicy; and though God may make use of processes within secular history, the narrative of his hidden judgements is inscrutable and cannot be written. Tillemont is not an analyst of the Augustan institution, or its evolution into the empire that shared power with the Church; confining himself to the first six centuries, he does not venture far into the history of the eastern empire or the prehistory of the *translatio*. When Gibbon needed a detailed Gallican treatment of modern history, he sought it in a third great ecclesiastical historian of the age of Louis XIV, Claude Fleury.[46] The history of *libertas et imperium* was not a theme extended through Christian history, and to account for its treatment in post-Ludovican France we must revert to historians for whom the secular asserted its primacy.

## PART II: MONTESQUIEU AND BEAUFORT

### (III)

There are senses in which Enlightened historiography may be seen as a continuation, in other terms, of a rather elusive Gallican reading. In a chapter of the previous volume,[47] Voltaire was seen to present the monarchy of Louis XIV as a principal agent of European Enlightenment: a territorial superpower which had replaced religious civil strife by wars for glory, and had employed courtly and aristocratic politeness,

---

[45] 'Without Tillemont to guide him, our author too often stumbles;' the German critic quoted, not without agreement, by Gibbon himself; *Memoirs*, pp. 193–4. For bibliographic detail, Craddock, 1987, p. 57, item 7.
[46] For his works as held and used by Gibbon, see *Library*, p. 125; Womersley, 1994, III, pp. 1216–17.
[47] *NCG*, ch. 6.

neo-classical literary and plastic art-forms, and philosophy both ancient and modern, in the establishment of a civil society that might have rendered the monarch and his subjects proof against any ecclesiastical challenge based on extra-civil spiritual authority. Voltaire organised the whole sweep of history so that it had the *beau siècle de Louis XIV* at its centre.[48] The ensuing struggle against that king's 'universal monarchy' (questioned by Voltaire) had important consequences. It rendered Enlightenment polycentric, substituting for a single hegemony a system of regulated competition between independent powers, and laid increased emphasis on the commerce between the national markets which these controlled; a companion piece to Montesquieu's work on Roman history is his unpublished *Réflexions sur la monarchie universelle en Europe*,[49] in which he argued that the growth of commerce had rendered empires of conquest impracticable – as, by implication, was not the case with the archaic economies of antiquity. But this contention did not alter the history of Enlightenment related by Voltaire beyond admitting a greater diversity of actors and agencies to the narrative of its making.

If the underlying theme, dominant even where it was implicit, was the re-creation of a civil society able to resist both papal monarchy and confessional anarchy, the monarchy of France – especially for those who lived under it and wrote history around it – possessed a history reaching back to the Decline and Fall itself. Unlike that of England – where Roman culture was held to have been destroyed by Picts and Scots before Angles and Saxons drove the Britons into Wales – the monarchy was Francogallic, rooted in the processes by which invading barbarians had settled in a Gaul still Roman. In the sixteenth century this had led the great historical jurists to debate whether feudal tenures had been Roman or German in origin; in the eighteenth there was a *thèse nobiliaire* which located the foundations of monarchy in the relations between barbaric chiefs and the companions of their war-bands, a *thèse royale* which located them in a surviving Roman and imperial authority.[50] The interplay between these theses produced highly sophisticated scholarship, though it did not of itself require historians to look further back than the late empire. This empire, however, must be seen as in decline, and the origins of that decline might be questioned.

---

[48] *NCG*, pp. 118, 149–50.
[49] The two are published together in the critical edition of Weil and Courtney, 2000.
[50] Ford, 1953; Ellis, 1988; Wright, 1997. Gibbon owned works on this subject by Boulainvilliers, Dubos and Mably; *Library*, pp. 77, 114, 186. The closing books of the *Esprit des Lois* show Montesquieu's involvement in it.

In a Francocentric historiography, the tales of Clovis, the *sainte-ampoule* and the dove of Rheims, antedating those of Charlemagne, the papal alliance and the *translatio imperii ad Francos*, could be used to supply the monarchy with its own spiritual foundations, independent of Rome though never opposed to it; a Carolingian historical myth required descent from Charlemagne as much as it demanded equality with his heirs the German emperors. It is here that we look for the fully 'Gallican' history of medieval Christendom that seems so far to have eluded us; it is enigmatic that Bossuet's *Discours* was composed at a time when the possibilities of a Gallican patriarchate, or alternatively of the French king's election as Emperor, could be thought about even if rejected as practice.[51] We need to see, however, what forces, ideological or philosophical, impelled French historical speculation towards the history of the Roman republic and principate; and here there may arise the question of the relations between *philosophie* and *érudition*.

Voltaire had seen the *siècle de Louis XIV* as including a history of great opportunities created and then missed. He regretted the failure to proclaim a Gallican patriarch in 1681, and linked it with the two disastrous intolerances of the latter part of the reign: the Revocation of the Edict of Nantes and the demolition of Port-Royal, which had left behind them a Huguenot external diaspora and a Jansenist internal emigration, and had culminated in the grand betrayal of the monarchy's acceptance of the papal bull *Unigenitus*. There is a case for regarding the social and intellectual philosophy of Parisian Enlightenment as a campaign to remedy these failures; where Gallicanism had failed to hold the fort, Enlightenment must take its place; and by 'Enlightenment' here would be meant the provision of a complete intellectual account of civil society, owing nothing to the Church and decreasingly less to Christianity. Where English or Scottish Enlightenment eroded Christian philosophy and history, French Enlightenment assailed and meant to replace them.

The received account of Enlightenment accurately presents the *philosophes* as concerned with the construction of a science of society, and of nature, which would furnish a coherent account of phenomena and their causes. When Gibbon, as will be remembered, remarked of Montesquieu (probably referring to the *Esprit des Lois*) that his 'energy of style, and boldness of hypothesis, were powerful to awaken and stimulate the Genius of the Age',[52] he may have meant that he offered a way of supplying historical phenomena with their causes, or more generally that he offered a science of human nature that rendered these phenomena

[51] Ranum, 1976, pp. xiv–xvi, xxxii–xxxiii.    [52] *Memoirs*, p. 78; *EEG*, pp. 83–9.

open to explanation, whether the explanations were causal or not. The words 'boldness of hypothesis' are not free from doubleness of edge, and there are occasions on which Gibbon finds that Montesquieu's hypotheses are too bold, and pressed far enough to disregard the evidence. These were points at which erudition had something to say; but this is not the issue that concerns us as we seek to fit the *Considérations sur la Grandeur des Romains et leur Décadence* into a history of the topos of Decline and Fall. The question is whether this remarkable work must be treated exclusively as an episode in Montesquieu's progress towards the *Esprit des Lois*; whether all the *considérations* of which it consists are products of his endeavours to construct a *science humaine* and must be returned to that context if we are to understand what he is doing in the work. The alternative to be considered here is that of treating the *Considérations* as one of a series of treatments of Roman *grandeur* and *décadence*, *magnitudo* and *inclinatio*, and its content as shaped, in some degree to be determined, by what others had said in their attempts to confront problems encountered by previous writers on the subject.

There is a danger of isolating Montesquieu to the point where he can be explained only by his own enterprise, and a concomitant danger of over-simplifying the enterprises of those not engaged in it. Two authors in a recent symposium devoted to introducing and explicating the *Considérations* have assured us that it is not a history[53] – as indeed it is not by neo-classical standards; it is an assemblage of considerations, discourses and essays upon history – but seem to have based this assertion on two premises which appear fallacious. One is that histories in the classical sense presented the sequence of events as exclusively the work of fortune;[54] the other is that they were exclusively concerned to narrate the works and deeds of eminent men, displaying as it were the *virtù* that confronted *fortuna*.[55] But, all the way back to Polybius, we have had to do with historians affirming that the greatness of the Romans was not due to chance or fortune, but to an extraordinary combination of characteristics which made them the admirable but terrible people they were; and from Sallust if not Polybius onwards, historians have been telling us that the empire of the Romans was the result of their liberty and – prospectively or retrospectively – was lost when it grew greater than that liberty could sustain, and so led to the loss of the liberty which sustained it. By the time of Montesquieu, the complex and tragic relationship between

---

[53] Weil and Courtney, 2000, pp. 14–15, 17 (Volpilhac-Auger), 26 (Andrivet). The former rightly stresses the absence of either providentialism or erudition.
[54] Andrivet, in Weil and Courtney, loc. cit.
[55] Volpilhac-Auger, in Weil and Courtney, 2000, pp. 20–2.

*imperium* and *libertas* was an established topos, and there were narratives of its course and causes ranging from the simply moral – the Romans were destroyed by the luxury attained through empire – to the historical materialism of the Appianic narrative. There had taken shape a narrative, not of exemplary actions – though this remained present and highly important – but of systemic change: the journey from one set of conditions, which might indeed be termed 'virtuous', to another which might be termed 'corrupt'; and the actions of individuals could be evaluated according to their moment in this process.

Montesquieu may therefore be situated in two histories: that of the historiography of Roman republic and empire, decline and fall; and that of an 'Enlightened enterprise' of constructing a science of human nature capable of explaining the phenomena of history. The two may converge, and it is probable that the latter will have brought about lasting changes in the former; but the former may prove to have supplied Montesquieu with information and assumptions, method and intention. In the latter setting we expect to meet Montesquieu the jurist as well as the *philosophe*, since the science of human nature was derived in massive degree from the jurisprudence of natural law; in the former we may look for Montesquieu the humanist and also the ideologue (Montesquieu *érudit* is yet another question). We are not long in finding that he was interested in the problems of corruption and despotism, and therefore looked on Tacitus as narrating how these phenomena arose, rather than as providing aphoristic guidance on how to contend with them.[56] He was closer to Thomas Gordon in this respect than to Amelot de la Houssaye;[57] but no more than Gordon did he expect to find himself living under a Tiberius or a Nero, and the English and French Taciteans of the early eighteenth century were concerned with corruption leading to despotism in the ancient world because they feared the corruption inherent in the processes that were replacing that world by the modern. In England the spectre was that of the management of parliament by the monarchy allied with the monied interest; in France it was that of a court menacing the independence of the two *noblesses* – Montesquieu of the *robe* was not unsympathetic to the arguments of Boulainvilliers of the *épée* – and allied with the church to a degree the *philosophes* found insufferable. He

---

[56]  On Tacitus, see Volpilhac-Auger, 1985, 1993. In 1985, pp. 159–66, she dismisses, without denying, the presence of Gordon's *Tacitus* in Montesquieu's reading, arguing that he did not need Gordon to tell him that Tiberius was a tyrant, and that Gordon was anyway a mediocre writer. These contentions are true, but may miss the point. Did Montesquieu read Gordon, and did he find him interesting?

[57]  For Amelot's place in the history of Tacitism, see Mellor, 1995, pp. 142–7; Soll, 1997, 2000.

therefore came to depict a *monarchie* whose *principe* was *honneur*, and opposite to it a *despotisme* whose *principe* was *crainte*;[58] when he depicted the climate of suspicion and denunciation under the emperors he doubtless had the censors and the Bastille in mind, but at the beginning of the twenty-first century we need to remind ourselves how little reason he had to expect a climate of terror. The *ancien régime*, in so many respects modern, was promoting a new world of commerce in which ancient ideas of both tyranny and freedom were beginning to seem obsolete, and Montesquieu – a witness of the scandal of the Mississippi Company – had to ask himself whether this world was corrupting the personality as well as the government. The answer could not be simple. 'Le commerce', he famously wrote, 'corrompt les moeurs pures . . . il adoucit les moeurs barbares',[59] and there was an implication that ancient virtue might itself be barbaric. All these ambivalences must be kept in mind when we consider how Montesquieu came to establish as the first term of his triad the *république* whose *principe* was *vertu*. The topos was so deeply grounded in humanist thought that it might seem to need no explanation for its presence; but the historical sequence, in which the virtue of the republic was succeeded by the despotism of the Caesars, the latter after many centuries by the Christian-feudal monarchy of *honneur*, and this in turn, after another thousand years, by modern commercial society still monarchic, called for some very complex narration and explanation. Montesquieu did not furnish an 'Enlightened narrative' of the 'Christian millennium', but when we read the *Considérations* in conjunction with the *Réflexions sur la monarchie universelle*, one of the possibilities must be that we are looking at the rise and fall of an ancient world in which neither the feudal nor the commercial *principes* were yet known (and what of the Christian and the philosophical?).

## (IV)

The *Considérations* open with a statement which might have startled Machiavelli: the unequivocal comparison of the city of Romulus to a Tartar camp.

> Il ne faut pas prendre de la Ville de Rome, dans ses Commencemens, l'idée que nous donnent les Villes que nous voyons aujourd'hui, à moins que ce ne soit de celles de la Crimée, faites pour renfermer le butin, les bestiaux, et les fruits

---

[58] *Esprit des Lois*, I, II, i–v; I, III, ix. Though he thought the government of Louis XIV verged on despotism, he did not accuse it of terror.

[59] *Esprit des Lois*, IV, XX, i.

de la Campagne. Les noms anciens des principaux lieux de Rome, ont tous du rapport à cet usage.[60]

[We should not form the same impression of the city of Rome in its beginnings as we get from the cities we see today, except perhaps for those of the Crimea, which were built to hold booty, cattle and the fruits of the field. The early names of the main places in Rome are all related to this practice.][61]

Montesquieu continued:

Rome étant une Ville sans Commerce et presque sans Arts, le pillage étoit le seul moyen que les particuliers eussent pour s'enrichir.

On avoit donc mis de la discipline dans la maniere de piller; et on y observoit à peu près le même ordre qui se pratique aujourd'hui chez les petits Tartares.

Le butin étoit mis en commun, et on le distribuoit aux Soldats; rien n'étoit perdu, parce qu'avant de partir, chacun avoit juré qu'il ne détourneroit rien à son profit. Or les Romains étoient le Peuple du monde le plus religieux sur le serment, qui fut toujours le nerf de leur discipline militaire.

Enfin les Citoyens qui restoient dans la Ville, jouissoient aussi des fruits de la Victoire. On confisquoit une partie des terres du Peuple vaincu, dont on faisoit deux parts: l'une se vendoit au profit du Public; l'autre étoit distribuée aux pauvres Citoyens, sous la charge d'une rente en faveur de la République.[62]

[Since Rome was a city without commerce, and almost without arts, pillage was the only means individuals had of enriching themselves.

The manner of pillaging was therefore brought under control, and it was done with much the same discipline as is now practised among the inhabitants of Little Tartary.

The booty was assembled and then distributed to the soldiers. None was ever lost, for prior to setting out each man had sworn not to take any for himself. And the Romans were the most religious people in the world when it came to an oath – which always formed the nerve of their military discipline.

Finally, the citizens who remained in the city also enjoyed the fruits of victory. Part of the land of the conquered people was confiscated and divided into two parts. One was sold for public profit, the other distributed to poor citizens subject to a rent paid to the republic.][63]

Montesquieu has returned to the origin of Rome, and instead of involving himself in the erudite dispute over the reliability of the traditional account, is giving a philosophical explanation of it. To oppose barbarism

---

[60] Weil and Courtney, 2000, p. 89.

[61] Trans. Lowenthal, 1965, p. 23. This is the only complete translation of the *Considérations* into modern English. The excerpts translated by Richter, 1977, will also be cited on occasion, as more easily available. Gibbon owned the *Considérations* in the Paris edition of 1755 and several sets of Montesquieu's collected *oeuvres* (*Library*, p. 201).

[62] Weil and Courtney, 2000, pp. 93–4.    [63] Lowenthal, 1965, pp. 27–8.

to commerce was intentionally to suggest that there was something barbaric about virtue itself; and yet virtue was so intensely admired that after Romulus was reduced to the stature of a petty khan, it had to be explained how this khan and his people had somehow invented religion, discipline and above all a sense of 'le Public'. In comparing the Romans to the Tartars, Montesquieu was looking back to Machiavelli's account of nomadic peoples on the move, and forward to Adam Smith's account of how social institutions began at the shepherd stage, when *sauvages* were replaced by *barbares*. Because Rome was not a commercial society, and scarcely even one where proprietors farmed for a market, the only means of acquiring wealth was forcible appropriation by the sword, which could be effectively wielded only by *le Public*. Rome was therefore a city condemned to live by conquest, and all her institutions and virtues were modes of organisation for war.

Rome était donc dans une guerre éternelle et toujours violente: Or une Nation toujours en guerre et par principe du Gouvernement, devoit nécessairement périr, ou venir à bout de toutes les autres, qui tantôt en guerre, tantôt en paix, n'étoient jamais si propres à attaquer, ni si preparées à se deffendre.

Toujours exposés aux plux affreuses vengeances, la Constance et la Valeur leur devinrent des vertus nécessaires; et ne purent être distinguées chez eux de l'amour de soi-même, de sa famille, de sa patrie, et de tout ce qu'il y a de plus cher, parmi les hommes.[64]

[Rome was therefore in an endless and constantly violent war. Now a nation forever at war, and by the very principle of its government, must necessarily do one of two things. Either it must perish, or it must overcome all the others which were only at war intermittently and were therefore never as ready to attack or as prepared to defend themselves as it was . . .

Since they were always exposed to the most frightful acts of vengeance, constancy and valour became necessary to them. And among them these virtues could not be distinguished from the love of oneself, of one's family, of one's country, and of all that is most dear to men.][65]

In words once ludicrously familiar:

> How can man die better
> Than facing fearful odds
> For the ashes of his fathers
> And the temples of his gods?[66]

---

[64] Weil and Courtney, 2000, p. 94.    [65] Lowenthal, 1965, pp. 27–8.
[66] The author of these lines would not long ago have been right in saying that every schoolboy knew where they were to be found.

There were answers to brave Horatius' question. Montesquieu was not only concerned with the character of a patriotism which consisted in an exclusive dedication to one warring stronghold among many; he was also pointing out that the 'virtue' of the ancient Roman made him simply the man he was and nothing more. In the Christian universe the individual had tried to transcend his social being; in the commercial, he might try to extend (and perhaps dilute) it. But the secret of ancient Rome was the way in which the Roman's fiercely narrow self-limitation, his ultimately tribal identity, had been converted into a sense of the *res publica* more durable and selfless than that attained by any of his not dissimilar competitors. This was the particular version of the problem which later engrossed the mind of Adam Ferguson: how it was that virtue was essentially a primitive achievement, the reinforcement of self-awareness by the idols of the tribe. Rome, however, had somehow legislated its virtue into a means of universal conquest; all that could be said for the moment was that virtue and conquest, *libertas* and *imperium*, were inseparable, and that this was a consequence of the crudity of the ancient economy and its military technology.

Les Peuples d'Italie n'avoient aucun usage des machines propres à faire les sieges; et de plus les Soldats n'ayant point de paye, on ne pouvoit pas les retenir long-tems devant une place: ainsi peu de leurs guerres étoient décisives: on se battoit pour avoir le pillage du Camp Ennemi, ou de ses Terres; après quoi le Vainqueur et la Vaincu se retiroient chacun dans sa Ville. C'est ce qui fit la résistance des Peuples d'Italie, et en même temps l'opiniâtrete des Romains à les subjuguer; c'est ce qui donna à ceux-ci des victoires qui ne les corrompirent point, et qui leur laisserent toute leur pauvreté.

S'ils avoient rapidement conquis toutes les Villes voisines, il se seroient trouvés dans la décadence à l'arrivée de Pyrrhus, des Gaulois, et d'Annibal; et par la destinée de presque tous les Etats du Monde, ils auroient passé trop vite de la pauvreté aux richesses, et des richesses à la corruption.

Mais Rome faisant toujours des efforts, et trouvant toujours des obstacles, faisoit sentir sa puissance, sans pouvoir l'étendre; et dans une circonférence très-petite, elle s'exerçoit à des vertus qui devoient être si fatales à l'Univers.[67]

[The peoples of Italy made no use of machines for carrying on sieges. In addition, since the soldiers fought without pay, they could not be retained for long before any one place. Thus, few of their wars were decisive. They fought to pillage the enemy's camp or his lands – after which the victor and vanquished each withdrew to his own city. This is what produced the resistance of the peoples of Italy, and, at the same time, the obstinacy of the Romans in subjugating them.

[67] Weil and Courtney, 2000, pp. 96–7.

This is what gave the Romans victories which did not corrupt them, and which let them remain poor.

If they had rapidly conquered all the neighbouring cities, they would have been in decline at the arrival of Pyrrhus, the Gauls, and Hannibal. And following the fate of nearly all the states in the world, they would have passed too quickly from poverty to riches, and from riches to corruption.

But, always striving and always meeting obstacles, Rome made its power felt without being able to extend it, and, within a very small orbit, practised the virtues which were to be so fatal to the world.][68]

Urged on to conquest by the lack of a market, which left no means to increase its wealth but crude appropriation, the conquering city advanced to world empire by long strides. The first, early in the history of the primitive republic, is connected with the problem of debt slavery, to which Rome was condemned by the shortage of coin and the inadequacies of its circulation.

Il n'y eut plus dans la Ville que deux sortes de gens, ceux qui souffroient la servitude, et ceux qui pour leurs interêts particuliers cherchoient à la faire souffrir. Les Sénateurs se retirerent de Rome comme d'une ville étrangere; et les Peuples voisins ne trouverent de résistance nulle part.

Le Sénat ayant eu le moyen de donner une paye aux Soldats, le siege de Veïes fut entrepris; il dura dix ans. On vit un nouvel Art chez le Romains, et une autre maniere de faire la guerre; leurs succès furent plus éclatans, ils profiterent mieux de leurs victoires, il firent de plus grandes Conquêts, ils envoyerent plus de Colonies; enfin la prise de Veïes fut une espece de révolution. . . .[69]

Depuis l'etablissement de la paye, le Sénat ne distribua plus aux Soldats les Terres des Peuples vaincus: il imposa d'autres conditions; il les obligea, par example, de fournir à l'Armée une solde pendant un certain temps, de lui donner du bled et des habits.[70]

[There were then only two sorts of men in the city: those who endured servitude, and those who sought to impose it for their own interests. The senators withdrew from Rome as from a foreign city, and the neighbouring peoples met with no resistance anywhere.

When the senate had the means of paying the soldiers, the siege of Veii was undertaken. It lasted ten years. The Romans employed a new art of waging war. Their successes were more brilliant; they profited more from their victories; they made larger conquests; they sent out more colonies. In short, the taking of Veii was a kind of revolution . . .

With the establishment of military pay, the senate no longer distributed the lands of conquered peoples to the soldiers. It imposed other conditions on these

---

[68] Lowenthal, 1965, pp. 28–9.   [69] Weil and Courtney, 2000, p. 98.
[70] *Ibidem*, n. 157; a later addition.

peoples; it required them, for example, to furnish the army with its pay for a certain time, and to give it grain and clothing.][71]

The introduction of soldiers' pay (of which the growth of siege tactics was a consequence) visibly does something to cure the disease of debt slavery, but marks an ominous moment in Roman history. It does not immediately reduce the legionaries to mercenary status; they remain a militia rather than a standing army, and Montesquieu anticipates, or perhaps ignores, the Appianic thesis that the armies of the civil wars still expected to be rewarded by land and colonies. But it is a revolutionary step because it makes possible the extension of Roman tributary empire, with its repressive treaties, colonies and subject allies; while at the same time the cessation of the distribution of conquered lands foreshadows the social crisis which is to bring the republic to its end. Tribute and soldiers' pay will not cure the land hunger of the legionaries in an undeveloped economy, and the empire is to expand in such a way that the hunger will remain unsatisfied.

Montesquieu is arriving at a 'Gracchan' explanation of republican decline, but we must follow his steps by way of isolating the narrative component in the structure of the *Considérations*. This work, we were reminded, is not *une histoire* but a series of *discours sur l'histoire*; in a way no longer aphoristic, he is selecting a series of topics to which he devotes short chapters. These occur in a chronological order corresponding to the course of history, and the *réflexions* to which they give rise are not to be separated from their historical context and elevated into scientific laws; not even when they suggest *considérations* relevant to Montesquieu's historical present.

Les Fondateurs des anciennes Républiques avoient également partagé les Terres; cela seul faisoit un Peuple puissant, c'est-à-dire, une Societé bien reglée; cela faisoit aussi une bonne Armée, chacun ayant un égal interêt et très grand à deffendre sa patrie.

Quand les Loix n'étoient plus rigidement observées, les choses revenoient au point où elles sont à présent parmi nous: l'avarice de quelques particuliers, et la prodigalité des autres faisoient passer les fonds de terre dans peu de mains; et d'abord les Arts s'introduisoient, pour les besoins mutuels des riches et des pauvres: cela faisoit qu'il n'y avoit presque plus de Citoyens ni de Soldats; car les fonds de terre, auparavant à l'entretien de ces derniers, étoient employés à celui des Esclaves et des Artisans, instrumens de luxe des nouveaux possesseurs: sans quoi l'Etat, qui malgré son dérèglement doit subsister, auroit péri. [Avant la corruption, les revenus primitifs de l'Etat étoient partagés entre les Soldats,

[71] Lowenthal, 1965, pp. 29–30.

c'est-à-dire, les Laboureurs: lorsque la République étoit corrompue, ils passoient d'abord à des hommes riches, qui les rendoient aux Esclaves et aux Artisans; d'où on en retiroit, par le moyen des Tributs, une partie pour l'entretien des Soldats:][72] or ces sortes de gens ne pouvoient être de bons Soldats: ils étoient lâches, et déja corrompus par le luxe des Villes, et souvent par leur Art même; outre que, comme ils n'avoient point proprement de patrie, et qu'ils jouissoient de leur industrie partout, ils avoient peu à perdre ou à conserver.[73]

[The founders of the ancient republics had made an equal partition of the lands. This alone produced a powerful people, that is, a well-regulated society. It also produced a good army, everyone having an equal, and very great, interest in defending his country.

When the laws were no longer stringently observed, a situation just like the one we are in came about. The avarice of some individuals and the prodigality of others caused landed property to pass into the hands of a few, and the arts were at once introduced for the mutual needs of rich and poor. As a result, almost no citizens or soldiers were left. Landed properties previously destined for their support were employed for the support of slaves and artisans – instruments of the luxury of the new owners. And without this the state, which had to endure in spite of its disorder, would have perished. Before the corruption set in, the primary incomes of the state were divided among the soldiers, that is, the farmers. When the republic was corrupt, they passed at once to rich men, who gave them back to the slaves and artisans. And by means of taxes a part was taken away for the support of the soldiers.

Now men like these were scarcely fit for war. They were cowardly, and already corrupted by the luxury of the cities, and often by their craft itself. Besides, since they had no country in the proper sense of the term, and could pursue their trade anywhere, they had little to lose or to preserve.][74]

If Montesquieu's Europe is becoming an acquisitive society, this will not ruin its primitive virtue, for the reason that there is none to ruin; it is no longer a republic of yeoman citizen-warriors, and the unsuitedness of artisans for warfare does not matter if they are no longer tied to a slave economy and can support an economy that pays for professional soldiers. The fact remains, however, that in such a society there are neither citizens nor soldiers, and the artisanate, like Marx's proletariat, has no fatherland. Montesquieu could not know that he was living less than a century away from democratic revolutions that would re-create the huge conscript armies of patriotic citizen-soldiers; his problem, as it might be ours after their wars have ended, was to decide what sustained a culture no longer sustained by public virtue. The function of ancient history was to problematise modernity.

---

[72] The passage bracketed is a textual variation; n. 27 in the following citation.
[73] Weil and Courtney, 2000, p. 106, incl. n. 27.     [74] Lowenthal, 1965, pp. 39–40.

Meanwhile, the ancient narrative remained to be completed. As the legions spent more time outside Italy, it became harder for the soldiers to claim lands on their return home; they received pay in the field, but on demobilisation found the lands of Italy in the hands of great proprietors employing slave labour. This of itself tended to make them economically superfluous; they drifted into the landless crowds of the urban tribes, or placed themselves – whether as stormtroopers in civil strife, or as legions in the field in time of civil war – at the disposal of their politically ambitious commanders. One might emphasise that this was an agrarian problem, and tell the story of the successive failures of Tiberius and Gaius Gracchus to solve it by imposing, probably too late, a repartition of lands. Montesquieu, however, mentions Tiberius only in order to quote his speech,[75] and does not attempt to follow the narrative found in Appian (whom he knew and cited). Its essence is nevertheless there, and whether we are learning it from humanist *discorsi* or Enlightened *réflexions* does not seem to matter.

Mais lorsque les Légions passerent les Alpes et la mer, les gens de guerre, qu'on étoit obligé de laisser pendant plusieurs Campagnes dans les pays que l'on soumettoit, perdirent peu à peu l'esprit de Citoyens; et les Géneraux, qui disposerent des Armées et des Royaumes, sentirent leur force, et ne purent plus obeir.

Les Soldats commencerent donc à ne reconnôitre que leur Général, à fonder sur lui toutes leurs espérances, et à voir de plus loin la Ville. Ce ne furent plus le Soldats de la République, mais de SYLLA, de MARIUS, de POMPÉE, de CÉSAR. Rome ne put plus savoir si celui qui étoit à la tête d'une Armée dans une Province, étoit son Général ou son ennemi.[76]

[But when the legions crossed the Alps and the sea, the warriors, who had to be left in the countries they were subjugating for the duration of several campaigns, gradually lost their citizen spirit. And the generals, who disposed of armies and kingdoms, sensed their own strength and could obey no longer.

The soldiers then began to recognize no one but their general, to base all their hopes on him, and to feel more remote from the city. They were no longer the soldiers of the republic, but those of Sulla, Marius, Pompey, and Caesar. Rome could no longer know if the man at the head of an army in a province was its general or its enemy.][77]

In this process, Marius came to play a fatal part; he began the enrolment in the legions of landless men who had no property to which to return. Sulla is a somewhat more complex figure; he plays the role of

---

[75] Weil and Courtney, 2000, p. 108; Lowenthal, 1965, p. 41.
[76] Weil and Courtney, 2000, pp. 153–4.          [77] Lowenthal, 1965, p. 91; cf. Richter, 1977, p. 159.

the Machiavellian reformer who finds *la materia già corrotta*, has the ruthlessness necessary to adopt the terrible and unheard-of means called for if the city is to be restored, but cannot escape, at the same time, from employing the methods which have corrupted it.[78]

There is a third process which enters into the history: the effects of the Social War, when the subject allies of Italy rebelled against Rome in search of full citizenship and, though defeated in the field, were appeased by the grant of their political demands. The result was less the corruption of the *populus Romanus* than its annihilation by a flood of new citizens who were not patriots.

Pour lors Rome ne fut plus cette Ville dont le Peuple n'avoit eu qu'un même esprit, un même amour pour la liberté, une même haine pour la tyrannie; où cette jalousie du pouvoir du Sénat et des prérogatives des Grands, toujours mêlée de respect, n'étoit qu'un amour de l'égalité. Les Peuples d'Italie étant devenus ses Citoyens, chaque Ville y apporta son génie, ses intérêts particuliers, et sa dépendance de quelque grand protecteur. La Ville déchirée ne forma plus un tout ensemble; et comme on n'en étoit Citoyen que par une espece de fiction, qu'on n'avoit plus les mêmes Magistrats, les mêmes murailles, les mêmes Dieux, les mêmes Temples, les mêmes sépultures; on ne vit plus Rome des mêmes yeux, on n'eut plus le même amour pour la patrie, et les sentimens Romains ne furent plus.[79]

[After this, Rome was no longer a city whose people had but a single spirit, a single love of liberty, a single hatred of tyranny – a city where the jealousy of the senate's power and the prerogatives of the great, always mixed with respect, was only a love of equality. Once the peoples of Italy became its citizens, each city brought to Rome its genius, its particular interests, and its dependence on some great protector. The distracted city no longer formed a complete whole. And since citizens were such only by a kind of fiction, since they no longer had the same magistrates, the same walls, the same gods, the same temples, and the same graves, they no longer saw Rome with the same eyes, no longer had the same love of country, and Roman sentiments were no more.][80]

This is a development of Bruni's thesis; the subject citizens lost their *virtù* in bringing it to Rome and destroyed the *virtù* which they found there. It is worth emphasising, however, the Enlightened stress on sentiment; virtue is a product of the emotions which proclaim identity. But the Social War did not spell the end of 'virtue', regarded as the organisation of energy for conquest; only its persistence in malignant and destructive forms. Not only was there the terrifying genius of Sulla and Caesar – the

---

[78] Weil and Courtney, 2000, pp. 164–6; Lowenthal, 1965, pp. 101–2. See further Montesquieu's *Dialogue de Sylla et d'Eucrate*.
[79] Weil and Courtney, 2000, pp. 155–6.    [80] Lowenthal, 1965, pp. 92–3; Richter, 1977, p. 160.

latter probably inspired by a species of nihilist Epicureanism – but all that had made Rome formidable as a military organisation persisted, and led to new conquests in Gaul and Syria, even when the power of the legions was turned against the city itself.

Cette épouvantable Tyrannie des Empereurs venoit de l'esprit général des Romains: Comme ils tomberent tout-à-coup sous un Gouvernement arbitraire, et qu'il n'y eût presque point d'intervalle chez eux entre commander et servir, ils ne furent point préparés à ce passage par des moeurs douces; l'humeur féroce resta; les Citoyens furent traités comme ils avoient traité eux-mêmes les Ennemis vaincus, et furent gouvernés sur le même plan. SYLLA entrant dans Rome, ne fut pas un autre homme que SYLLA entrant dans Athenes; il exerça le même droit des gens. Pour nous qui n'avons été soumis qu'insensiblement, lorsque les loix nous manquent, nous sommes encore gouvernés par les moeurs.[81]

[This frightful tyranny of the emperors derived from the general spirit of the Romans. Since the Romans fell under an arbitrary government suddenly, with almost no interval between their commanding and their serving, they were not at all prepared for the change by a moderation of their manners. Their fierce humour remained; the citizens were treated as they themselves had treated conquered enemies, and were governed according to the same plan. The Sulla who entered Rome was no different from the Sulla who entered Athens: he applied the same law of nations. As for states that have been brought under subjection only by imperceptible degrees, when the laws fail them they are still governed by their manners.][82]

The text followed by the translator speaks of *états* which have lost their *lois* and are governed only by *moeurs*; that preferred by the most recent editors identifies them as *nous*, i.e. moderns. The *moeurs féroces* of the ancient Romans could be governed only by *lois*, and these were conducive to a *vertu politique* consisting largely in equal obedience to the same laws; when this failed it was replaced by despotism and terror. There is a plain relationship between *vertu* (not only *libertas*) and *moeurs féroces*, not yet *adoucis par le commerce*. What then is it that permits the *moeurs adoucis* of modernity to operate of themselves, unaided by laws, and prevent the growth of despotism – assuming that they do not yet subject us (*nous*) to despotism in a gentle form? It was a question facing Enlightened minds, still being asked at the outset of the twenty-first century. And what – the historian may ask of Montesquieu – is the role in this of the Christian religion? It seems probable that he did not believe in the supernatural virtues, and thought such a belief irreconcilable with the practice of the

---

[81] Weil and Courtney, 2000, pp. 199–200, and note giving an alternative text.
[82] Lowenthal, 1965, pp. 135–6.

natural virtues. The Enlightened insistence on the primacy of nature and commerce, presupposing modernity, is proving hostile to antiquity, both in its Christian and its heroically civic pagan form.

There is not much indication in the *Considérations* that the Augustan principate united the western world under civilising influence or prepared the way for Christ. The problem of the principate is the character of a monarchy disguised as the continuation of a republic; since the animating principle of the latter is conquering virtue, the former must present itself as the government of peace; but since the power of the *imperator* rests on military virtue separated from civic, his relationship to civil and military, peace and war, must be profoundly ambivalent.

Tous les gens qui avoient eu des projets ambitieux, avoient travaillé à mettre une espece d'Anarchie dans la Republique[83] . . . mais lorsque'AUGUSTE fut une fois le maître, la politique le fit travailler à rétablir l'ordre, pour faire sentir le bonheur du gouvernement d'un seul.

Lorsqu' AUGUSTE avoit les armes à la main, il craignoit les revoltes des Soldats, et non pas les conjurations des Citoyens; c'est pour cela qu'il ménagea les premiers, et fut si cruel aux autres: lorsqu'il fut en paix, il craignit les conjurations, et ayant toujours devant les yeux le destin de CÉSAR, pour éviter son sort, il songea à s'éloigner de sa conduite. Voilà le clef de toute la vie d' AUGUSTE. Il porta dans le Sénat une cuirasse sous sa robe; il refusa le nom de Dictateur; et au lieu que CÉSAR disoit insolemment, que la République n'etoit rien, et que ses paroles étoient des loix, AUGUSTE ne parla que de la dignité du Sénat, et de son respect pour la République. Il songea donc à établir le gouvernement le plus capable de plaire qui fût possible sans choquer ses intérêts; et il en fit une Aristocratique par rapport au civil, et Monarchique par rapport au militaire: gouvernement ambigu, qui, n'étant pas soutenu par ses propres forces, ne pouvoit subsister que tandis qu'il plairoit au Monarque; et étoit entierement Monarchique par conséquent.[84]

[All the men with ambitious projects had laboured to inject a kind of anarchy into the republic . . . But once Augustus was master, policy required his working to reestablish order so that everyone would experience the blessings of one-man government.

When Augustus was armed for war, he feared the revolts of soldiers and not the conspiracies of citizens; that is why he treated the soldiers with care and was so cruel to others. When he was at peace, he feared conspiracies; and always having Caesar's destiny before his eyes, he meant to follow a different line of conduct in order to avoid the same fate. This is the key to Augustus' whole life. He wore a breastplate under his robe in the senate; he refused the title of dictator. Whereas Caesar insolently stated that the republic was nothing

[83] Weil and Courtney, 2000, p. 186.    [84] Weil and Courtney, 2000, p. 187.

and that his own word was law, Augustus spoke only of the senate's dignity and of his respect for the republic. His intention, therefore, was to establish that government which was most capable of pleasing without damaging his interests; and he made it aristocratic with respect to civil affairs, and monarchical with respect to military affairs. But since it was not supported by his [sic] own strength, this ambiguous government could subsist only so long as it pleased the monarch, and consequently was entirely monarchical.][85]

*Gouvernement ambigu.* We read in James Harrington the perception that the principate, like the feudal monarchy long afterwards, was 'neither hawk nor buzzard',[86] but an unstable distribution of civil and military power; Montesquieu's point here is that Augustus was driven both to a profound hypocrisy in his own personality, and to the foundation of a government which was one thing pretending to be another, by the fundamental contradiction of Roman history, the separation of civic from military capacity, itself the consequence of the fact that virtue had been organised for conquest in obedience to the laws of a world without commerce. The principate did no more than stabilise, or rather freeze, the situation which had produced the civil wars of Sulla and Marius, or the two Triumvirates; looked at in the context of Roman history, it was altogether uncreative. Outside the City, however, lay the Empire, and sooner or later it must be recognised that the history of 'the Roman empire' was the history of the provincials as well as of the *populus Romanus*. We might suppose that the design of writing *Considérations sur la Grandeur des Romains et de leur Décadence* had blinkered Montesquieu's perceptions, were it not for his insistence that the *populus Romanus* lived on for centuries in its military capacity, after it had disappeared in its civic.

It was not perfectly precise to say that the *gouvernement ambigu*, 'n'étant pas soutenu par ses propres forces, ne pouvoit subsister que tandis qu'il plairoit au Monarque'. The forces, civic and military, which should have sustained it, were divided and therefore not fully its own; and this meant that the voice of the *imperator* in his military capacity must always drown out that of the *princeps* in his senatorial. But it did not mean that the *imperator* enjoyed a secure monarchic authority over the army. The legions *alibi quam Romae* were as responsive as ever to the voices of their immediate chiefs, and all Augustus could do was discourage further wars of conquest, in the hope that no new Marius or Caesar would arise. If the legions were as disciplined as ever in making camp or giving battle, the peaceable citizens (*bourgeois*) of Rome and other towns were no longer warriors and

---

[85] Lowenthal, 1965, pp. 121, 122. 'Its own strength' appears the better translation.
[86] Above, p. 299.

useless as a shield against the legions; the history of the praetorians was well known, though Montesquieu has not much to say about it; military virtue was not extinct, but it was unchecked by its civic counterpart. After the disasters of Nero's reign and Domitian's, an unaccountable renaissance of Stoicism – 'comme ces plantes que la terre fait naître dans des lieux que le Ciel n'a jamais vus'[87] – blessed Rome with the sequence of virtuous emperors whom it was now customary to celebrate; but the further disaster of Commodus returned the empire to military anarchy.

Ce qu'on appelloit l'Empire Romain dans ce siècle-là étoit une espèce de Republique irreguliere, telle à peu près que l'Aristocratie d'Alger, où la Milice qui a la puissance Souveraine, fait et défait un Magistrat qu'on appelle le Dey: et peut-être est-ce une Regle assez générale, que le Gouvernement militaire est plutot Républicain que Monarchique à certains égards.

Et qu'on ne dise pas que le Soldats ne prenoient de part au Gouvernement que par leur désobéissant et leurs revoltes; les Harangues que les Empereurs leur faisoient, ne furent-elles pas à la fin du genre de celles que les Consuls et les Tribuns avoient faites autrefois au Peuple? Et quoique les Armées n'eussent pas un lieu particulier pour s'assembler, qu'elles ne se conduisissent point par de certaines formes, qu'elles ne fussent pas ordinairement de sang froid, déliberant peu et agissant beaucoup, ne disposoient-elles pas en Souveraines de la Fortune publique? Et qu'étoit-ce qu'un Empereur; que le Ministre d'un Gouvernement violent, élu pour l'utilité particuliere des Soldats?[88]

[What was called the Roman empire, in this century, was a kind of irregular republic, much like the aristocracy of Algeria, where the army, which has sovereign power, makes and unmakes a magistrate called the Dey. And perhaps it is a rather general rule that military government is, in certain respects, republican rather than monarchical.

And let it not be said that the soldiers took part in the government only by their disobedience and revolts. Did not the harangues of the emperors delivered to them belong, in the last analysis, to the genre of those the consuls and tribunes had formerly delivered to the people? And although the armies did not have one particular place in which to assemble, although they did not conduct themselves according to certain forms, although they were not usually coolheaded – being given to little deliberation and much action – did they not as sovereigns dispose of the public estate? And what was an emperor except the minister of a violent government, elected for the special benefit of the soldiers?][89]

The history of the principate was not more than a continuation of that of the republic; the ghost of the deceased Senate and People, standing

---

[87] Weil and Courtney, 2000, p. 211: 'like plants that grow in earth that has never seen the sky'.
[88] Weil and Courtney, 2000, pp. 219–20. For Gibbon's use of this passage, see below, pp. 452–3.
[89] Lowenthal, 1965, pp. 152–3.

armed upon the grave thereof. Augustus had achieved no more than a treaty of peace between the two; the empire of the world meant that the provinces must be governed by a force at war with the politically atrophied heartland. Constantine – Montesquieu continued, following Zosimus – remodelling the principate as a palace-centred despotism, had found no better solution than the removal of the legions from the frontiers, where their military discipline was at least maintained, and their dispersal through the cities; and this had ensured the final decay of that military virtue which was all that had survived of the republic's achievement. The barbarians were moving from the wings to the stage.

We have arrived at the end of the humanist, and particularly of the Gracchan, explanation of Decline and Fall. The separation of military from civic capacity was, as we have seen, a specialisation of function and a division of personality. It could be ascribed to strictly administrative causes, the simple effects of the increasing size of empire; but it could also be explained as the decay of the soldiers as an Italian smallholding class, brought about by the steady growth of a consumer aristocracy exploiting slave labour and creating a world in which the peasant warrior had no place. In such an economy soldiers must be professionals and their virtue must decay; but there was a further problem. Given that slaves and artisans were equally useless as legionaries, only peasants would make soldiers; but in a world of slaves and townsmen, where were peasants to be found? We shall find Gibbon saying that, as Italians and colonists ceased to supply the armies, Illyrians from the Danube took their place; Montesquieu's far shorter and swifter-moving *Considérations* moves directly – as had Harrington before him – to the recruitment of barbarians, followed by the employment of barbarian nations as auxiliaries. The only unspecialised warriors were now to be found beyond the frontiers; they were invited into the empire in such numbers that they took it over. Hume might have called it the euthanasia of virtue.

This was an explanation in ancient terms, a conversation with the ghost of Tiberius Gracchus; a more modern one could be added. All this came about – Montesquieu mercantilistically proceeds – because of a shortage of bullion and an inadequacy in the means of circulating it. It had led to an over-taxation disastrous in its effects upon civilians, yet (like the silver of Spanish America) unable to keep the soldiers paid.

Toutes ces Nations qui entouroient l'Empire en Europe et en Asie, absorberent peu à peu les richesses des Romains; et comme il s'étoient aggrandis parce que l'or et l'argent de tous les Rois étoit porté chez eux, ils s'affoiblirent parce que leur or et leur argent fut porté chez les autres . . .

La milice, comme on a déjà vu, étoit devenue très à charge à l'Etat: les Soldats avoient trois sortes d'avantage, la paye ordinaire, la récompense après le service, et les libéralités d'accident, qui devenoient très-souvent des droits pour des gens qui avoient le Peuple et le Prince entre leurs mains.

L'impuissance où l'on se trouva de payer ces charges, fut que l'on prit une Milice moins chere. On fit des traités avec des Nations Barbares qui n'avoient ni le luxe des Soldats Romains, ni le même esprit, ni les mêmes prétentions.

Il y avoit une autre commodité à cela: comme les Barbares tomboient tout à coup sur un Pays, n'y ayant point chez eux de préparatif après la résolution de partir, il étoit difficile de faire des levées à temps dans les Provinces. On prenoit donc un autre corps de Barbares, toujours prêt à recevoir de l'argent, à piller et à se battre. On étoit servi pour le moment: mais dans la suite, on avoit autant de peine à réduire les Auxiliaires que les Ennemis.

Les premiers Romains ne mettoient point dans leurs Armées un plus grand nombre de troupes auxiliaires que de Romaines; et quoique leurs Alliés fussent proprement des sujets, il ne vouloient point avoir pour sujets des Peuples plus belliqueux qu'eux-mêmes.

Mais dans les derniers temps, non-seulement ils n'observerent pas cette proportion des troupes auxiliaires; mais même ils remplirent de Soldats barbares les corps de troupes nationales.

Ainsi ils établissoient des usages tout contraires à ceux qui les avoient rendus maîtres de tout: et comme autrefois leur politique constante fut de se réserver l'Art militaire, et d'en priver tous leurs voisins, ils la détruisoient pour lors chez eux, et l'établissoient chez les autres.

Voici en un mot l'Histoire des Romains: Ils vainquirent tous les Peuples par leurs maximes: mais lorsqu'ils y furent parvenus, leur République ne put subsister; il fallut changer de gouvernement: et des maximes contraires aux premieres, employées dans ce gouvernement nouveau, firent tomber leur grandeur.[90]

[All these nations surrounding the empire in Europe and Asia absorbed the riches of the Romans little by little. And as the Romans had grown great because the gold and silver of all kings had been carried to them, they grew weak because their gold and silver were carried to others . . .

The military, as we have seen, had become very burdensome to the state. Soldiers received three kinds of benefits: their ordinary pay, some compensation once their service was over, and occasional gifts which quite often became rights for men who held the people and the prince in their hands.

The lack of funds to pay these expenses made it necessary to find a cheaper army. Treaties were made with barbarian nations, who had neither the luxury of the Roman soldiers, nor the same spirit, nor the same pretensions.

There was another advantage in this. Since barbarians fell on a country swiftly, needing no preparation once they resolved to move, it was difficult to

---

[90] Weil and Courtney, 2000, pp. 233–5.

levy troops in the provinces in time. The Romans therefore used for their defence another body of barbarians, always ready to receive money, to pillage and to fight. They were served for the moment, but later there was as much trouble reducing their auxiliaries as their enemies.

The early Romans did not put a greater number of auxiliary troops than Roman troops in their armies. And although their allies were really subjects, they did not want to have for subjects peoples who were more warlike than themselves.

In this later period, however, not only did they fail to observe this proportion of auxiliary troops, but they even filled the corps of national troops with barbarian soldiers.

Thus, they established practices wholly contrary to those that had made them universal masters. And, as formerly their constant policy was to keep the military art for themselves and deprive all their neighbours of it, they were now destroying it among themselves and establishing it among others.

Here, in a word, is the history of the Romans. By means of their maxims they conquered all peoples, but when they had succeeded in doing so, their republic could not endure. It was necessary to change the government, and contrary maxims employed by the new government made their greatness collapse.][91]

The *gouvernement nouveau* is probably the monarchy of Constantine rather than the *gouvernement ambigu* of Augustus. It would be whiggish to say that this passage exhibits dawning political economy in an undeveloped because pre-Smithian form; the point is rather that it displays the intimate connexions between political economy and the history of military organisation and virtue, which existed in the minds of the Scottish theorists and (as it happens) Adam Smith in particular. This will be our theme as we pursue the fall of the republic, and its sequel the fall of the empire, through the shapes which they assumed in eighteenth-century minds.

## (v)

At this point Montesquieu has completed an account of *grandeur et décadence*, Decline and Fall, connecting the original republic with the decay of the principate and the barbarian invasions. There are three chapters to come, starting from the dispute in which Christians and pagans reproach one another for the disasters befalling the empire; Symmachus' claim that the ancient gods upheld the society that worshipped them is met by Augustine's claim that there are two cities and that Roman virtue

---

[91] Lowenthal, 1965, pp. 167–9; Richter, 1977, pp. 163–4.

is an earthly vanity.[92] We go on to an account of the greatness of Attila and the inability of Constantine's New Rome to defend the old:

> Le Peuple Romain presque toujours abandonné de ses Souverains, commença à le devenir, et à faire des Traités pour sa conservation; ce qui est le moyen le plus legitime d'acquérir la Souveraine puissance: [c'est ainsi que l'Armorique et la Bretagne commencerent à vivre sous leur propres loix.] Telle fut la fin de l'Empire d'Occident.[93]

> [Almost always abandoned by their sovereigns, the Roman people began to become their own sovereign and make treaties for their preservation, which is the most legitimate means of acquiring sovereign power. (This is the way Armorica and Brittany came to live under their own laws.)[94] Such was the end of the Western empire.][95]

Here we might expect to hear something of the Roman bishop at the head of his people. Montesquieu proceeds, however, to summarise the reign of Justinian and the subsequent course of east Roman history. This is seen as an empire of 'sectes' – the term denotes heresies rather than congregations – in which the emperor is seen as the head of the theological faction he happens to favour;[96] it is the *variations des églises chrétiennes.* These Romans cannot confront the fanaticised armies of the Arabs (who are compared to Cromwell's New Model, in terms less than fair to the Scottish Army of the Covenant),[97] and the narrative of Roman military weakness proceeds through the centuries to 1453; we are duly informed that all these evils proceed from the separation between ecclesiastical and civil authority.[98] What is remarkable, however, is that Montesquieu is giving us a dense summary of the history of medieval Constantinople without that of medieval Rome or the western Church; there is nothing here of either *translatio imperii* or Enlightened narrative. We know that the *Considérations* are not a connected history but a work of *philosophie*; the author selects historical episodes and uses them as the base for philosophical generalisations that explain the course of history better. But ancient history has been organised on these bases into a narrative connected from a beginning to an end. Montesquieu attempts no such organisation of modern history, though the Enlightened narrative would soon be supplying one for the history of the Latin west. It is noteworthy that he turns his attention to the history of Constantinople, but unclear

[92] Weil and Courtney, 2000, pp. 240–1.
[93] Weil and Courtney, 2000, p. 248. For the passage in brackets, see note at foot.
[94] Trans. JGAP. Omitted by typographic error in Lowenthal.    [95] Lowenthal, 1965, p. 181.
[96] Weil and Courtney, 2000, p. 257; 'Ces Sectes étoient des Nations entiers.'
[97] Weil and Courtney, 2000, p. 268, and n. 18.    [98] Weil and Courtney, 2000, p. 277.

what *principes* and *ressorts* he thought could be extracted from it or shown to drive it; and it had no Enlightened sequel, except in Russia.[99]

The *Considérations*, therefore point towards the development of Montesquieu's enterprise in the *Esprit des Lois*, by which Enlightened historiography was to be greatly enriched. They do not point directly towards the construction of what is termed the 'Enlightened narrative' – as Voltaire, its architect as author of the *Essai sur les Moeurs*, would have been the first to point out – and while they similarly enrich the other grand narrative, that of Roman and ancient history, they leave its essential structure in a shape it had already assumed. A discernible narrative in which the defects of the republic led to those of the principate, and so of the empire, had emerged from the writings of many historians over the centuries, until it was something of a consensus; while the proposition that modern history was differentiated from ancient by commerce as well as Christianity was taking shape in a number of minds during the half-century in which Montesquieu lived. To say this is to define, not to diminish, the originality and impact of his 'awakening the genius of the age'; but it sets the *Considérations* somewhat apart from both the formation of the Enlightened narrative and the convergence of narrative, philosophy and erudition to which Momigliano's formula guides the student of Gibbon. Montesquieu was a *philosophe* who was also a humanist, and, very importantly a jurist; he was not primarily concerned with the reconstruction of narrative history; and despite the vast breadth and depth of his reading and researches, he was not what the age termed an *érudit*. To observe the entry of the last component into the Momiglianan synthesis as occasioned by Roman history, we turn to another set of *considérations* of the ancient republic of which Gibbon made use.

Louis de Beaufort, on whom the young Gibbon called at Maastricht when returning to England in 1758, had been born in the Netherlands of a Huguenot family whose Dutch and German Protestant connexions antedated the Revocation. His long life (1703–95) seems to have been that of a retiring scholar and antiquarian, not active in seeking publicity or controversy; but his two major works – one before and one after his encounter with Gibbon – place him at the centre of some of the learned controversies of the age.[100] Gibbon was drawn to him by his *Dissertation sur l'incertitude des cinq premiers siècles de l'histoire romaine* (1738), which seemed to be a sequel to the more famous debate on the same

---

[99]  For a pointer to Peter the Great, see p. 269 of Weil and Courtney, 2000.
[100]  A full-length study of Beaufort may be found in Raskolnikoff, 1992, chs. 5–6, pp. 389–624.

subject between Levesque de Pouilly, Sallier and Freret in the *Académie des Inscriptions* some years earlier.[101] He refers to Beaufort as an author who knew how to doubt and how to decide;[102] a reminder that the debate on the uncertainty of Roman history was never a simple collision between humanists and pyrrhonists, and that the uncertainty was often presented as a problem to which there might be solutions.[103] Those like Beaufort who doubted the reliability of Livy's sources for the foundation of the city, the expulsion of the kings, and everything down to the occupation of Rome by the Gauls, were not pyrrhonist philosophers who held that nothing could be known of history, but critical scholars and antiquarians who thought they knew a great deal that was incompatible with the traditional accounts. They enter into Gibbon's early formation as contributors to his philosophy of history, in which erudition joined with the search for causes and turned it towards irony.[104] It has been noted that Beaufort was little regarded by Dutch scholars of his day and paid little attention to them.[105] The explanation has been suggested that the latter were 'ancients' rather than 'moderns', belonging to a German scholarly world that used Latin as a medium of communication and upheld the authority of classical texts, mistrusting the intrusive *république des lettres* which employed French to challenge and re-interpret them on grounds either critical or philosophical.[106] Beaufort and Gibbon employed that language to express the 'modern' enterprise of reinforcing their authority by interpreting them in new ways; and it is a further irony that it was German scholars using Latin who, over the next century, developed critical techniques till they became an instrument of historicism. Gibbon in his last years was to become aware that this was going on.

In 1766, eight years after their dinner in Maastricht, Beaufort published *La République Romaine*,[107] a work which may well have come into Gibbon's hands as he was turning from writing Swiss history in French to writing Roman history in English.[108] This study is marked by a profound admiration for Montesquieu[109] – as author of the *Esprit des Lois* as well as

---

[101] *EEG*, ch. 7.　　[102] *EEG*, p. 226.

[103] This is made clear by Raskolnikoff, whose book should be recognised as an important addition to the bibliography of this subject, and by Erasmus, 1962.

[104] *EEG*, ch. 9.　　[105] Raskolnikoff, 1992, p. 445.

[106] Raskolnikoff, 1992, pp. 432–535, where this world is described at length.

[107] Beaufort, 1766.

[108] *Library*, p. 65. He had known the *Dissertation sur l'incertitude* since his early years in Lausanne and it is discussed at length in the *Essai sur l'Etude de la Littérature*.

[109] Beaufort, 1766, p. ii.

of the *Considérations* – but differs from his in being very deeply the work of an *érudit*; one, however, who wishes to advance beyond erudition to something more like *philosophie*. In language that may recall d'Alembert – whose *Discours Préliminaire* there is no reason why he should not have read[110] – Beaufort prefaces his book by saying:

> A la renaissance des lettres on ne songea qu'à mettre au jour les monumens, qui avoient échappé à l'injure des tems. On s'oublia, pour ainsi dire, soi-même, pour ne songer qu'à bien connoître les Grecs et les Romains, et pendant tout le seizième siècle, ils furent presque les seuls objets des recherches des Savants. Quoique cette étude soit moins générale aujourd'hui, elle ne peut manquer de partisans . . . Car quoique nous ne vivions pas dans le siècle d'érudition, on aime à s'entretenir des Romains; on aime à voir éclaircir quelque point de leur histoire, de leurs loix, de leur gouvernement, et de leurs usages.[111]

[At the rebirth of letters, one thought only of bringing to light the materials which had escaped the ruin of times. One forgot oneself, so to speak, and thought of nothing but knowing the Greeks and the Romans, and for all the sixteenth century they were almost the only object of scholarly research. This branch of study is not so universal today, but can never lack its partisans . . . Though we no longer live in the age of erudition, we love to converse with the Romans; we love to throw light on some point of their history, their laws, government and customs.][112]

We are in the Enlightenment that succeeds Renaissance; when we converse with the ancients, we remember who we are, we know why we want to understand them, and their *usages* have taken on the meaning of their *moeurs*. We have advanced beyond erudition to philosophy, but there remains the fascination of direct knowledge of antiquity and the *érudit s'entretient avec le philosophe*. Even Beaufort's historical scepticism is at the service of this knowledge.

> Cependant on pourra trouver étrange, qu'après avoir ébranlé les fondemens de cette Histoire, et avoir prouvé que beaucoup d'évènemens, qu'on place dans les cinq premiers siècles de Rome, étoient absolument faux, et d'autres très douteux, j'entreprenne un ouvrage de la nature de celui-ci, où souvent je remonte jusqu'à l'origine de Rome, pour y chercher celle de divers usages, qui avoient lieu sous la République . . .
> Il m'importe peu, et je crois qu'il importe peu aux lecteurs, que leur antiquité soit plus ou moins reculée, pourvu qu'ils sachent ce qui a eu lieu dans les beau

---

[110] Raskolnikoff, 1992, pp. 532–3, notes that there is no work by d'Alembert in the catalogue of Beaufort's library, and no set of the *Encyclopédie*, though there is one work commenting on the latter.
[111] Beaufort, 1766, p. i.     [112] All translations of Beaufort here are by JGAP.

siècles de la République, et quelles en étoient les maximes fondamentales. C'est
à quoi je me borne . . .[113]

J'entreprens donc ici de fixer nos doutes sur l'Histoire Romaine, et de marquer
en abrégé quelques faits, de la vérité desquels nous ne pouvons raisonnablement
douter. Je suis le premier qui entre dans cette route . . .[114]

[It may indeed seem strange that after having undermined the foundations of
this history, and shown that many events ascribed to the first five centuries of
Rome are altogether false and others very doubtful, I should undertake a work
of the present character, in which I often go back to the origins of Rome, in
search of various usages which were found under the Republic . . .

It matters little to me, or I should think to my readers, whether their antiquity
was more or less remote, so long as we know how things were in the great days
of the Republic and what were its fundamental principles. It is to this that I limit
myself . . .

I therefore undertake to settle our doubts concerning Roman history, and to
give a brief account of certain facts of whose veracity there can be no reasonable
doubt. I am the first to have followed this path . . .]

Beaufort does not mean that no one before him has done research
on Roman history, but that he is the first to have done so in search of
Montesquieu's *principes*. It is a corollary that critical enquiry can give
us an account differing very much from the traditional of what these
*principes* were. Beaufort proceeds to tell us that the traditional histories
are often anachronistic, reading later conditions into earlier times, and
that the historians were often prey to aristocratic bias.[115] This is why we
have not realised that Rome under the kings was a large city, warlike and
expansive, and that the tyrant Tarquinius Superbus was a demagogue
who overthrew Servius Tullius when the latter was aiming at exclusively
aristocratic support. It follows that the expulsion of the kings was an aristocratic coup, carried through by the kinsmen of the dead Servius, and
the foundation of senatorial rule.[116] Beaufort is throughout his work an
ardent partisan of the Roman people – often the *menu peuple* or even the
*petit peuple* – in which he seems to have been preceded only by the English
historian Nathaniel Hooke.[117] It is easier to imagine Hooke inhabiting
some climate of London radicalism than to believe the same of the rather
solitary if vigorously independent scholar of Maastricht, and we may have
to do here simply with Beaufort's exercise of his own judgement. Archaeological research into the foundations of archaic Rome could lead – as

[113] Beaufort, 1766, p. iv.　　[114] Beaufort, 1766, p. vii.
[115] Beaufort, 1766, pp. xiv–xv, xxxvi.　　[116] Beaufort, 1766, p. xxxii.
[117] Hooke, 1738; Raskolnikoff, 1992, p. 454. She also discusses Hooke's response to the *Dissertation
sur l'incertitude*.

had happened with Carlo Sigonio – to conclusions startling to the historian or the philosopher. Beaufort was arriving at a position remote from the admired Montesquieu's, and knew it.

He proceeds to an account of Roman fundamental institutions based on religon, and the ethnicity of religion. Following Simon Pelloutier's *Histoire des Celtes* (1741),[118] he declares:

> Toutes les nations, qui peuplèrent l'Europe, venoient, selon lui, de la Scythe, et étoient Celtes d'origine.[119]

[All the nations who peopled Europe came, he says, from Scythia and were Celts by origin.]

This looks back to the *Remains of Japhet* and forward to Smith's settlement of Europe by successive waves of Scythian shepherds.[120] The exception was the Greeks, whom Beaufort – like most pre-modern historians a predecessor of Martin Bernal[121] – held to have been Phoenician and Egyptian colonists. Just as the sons of Japhet had preserved the true religion when it was otherwise lost to idolatry, the primeval Celts (including the Sabines and Latins who settled at Rome) had practised a simple religion of worship of a single God, and this with its attendant morality had been established by Numa Pompilius[122] (the Sarastro of ancient Italy). With the coming of the republic, however, the junta of aristocrats who founded it had turned to the oriental cults of the Etruscans and the Greeks, and had peopled Rome with a legion of godlings, intended – with much success – to control the people through multiplied superstition.[123] If every priest had been a citizen – a point much insisted on by anti-clerical admirers of antiquity – he had also been an oligarch, and Rome had been ruled by senatorial priestcraft. At the same time, however, the new religion had usurped, but had not displaced, the simple morality of Celtic monotheism, and, as the gods of Rome increased beyond number, there came to be a deity impersonating every point of public morality, legal, political or military practice.[124] The religion of the republic had been the superstition of virtue. It had given the Romans their scrupulous legalism and their ferocious military discipline. In the end they had worshipped themselves,[125] and what kind of city Numa would have founded remained an open question; would there have been the religion of conquest practised by the republic?

[118] Pelloutier, 1741.   [119] Beaufort, 1766, p. 2.
[120] *NCG*, pp. 323–5 (Smith), 334 (Ferguson), 360–1 (*Remains*).   [121] Bernal, 1987.
[122] Beaufort, 1766, pp. 8–9.   [123] Beaufort, 1766, pp. 10–15, 31–2, 68–71, 89.
[124] Beaufort, 1766, pp. 81–3.   [125] Beaufort, 1766, p. 31.

If this Greco-Etruscan polytheism was no more than an instrument of political control – and Beaufort is insistent that this is what it was – it might still have been an instrument of political justice. The people piously observed the domestic morality and the political virtue that the multitude of gods enjoined; and all would have been well if the senatorial aristocracy who introduced the gods had observed morality and justice themselves. That they did not was more than a matter of their unbelief in the gods whose priests they were, or of their immorality and luxury in their personal lives. We move at a single step into the Appianic narrative and the Gracchan explanation, and the luxury which moralists had been denouncing since the time of Sallust takes on the specific meaning of their usurpation of the public lands and their populating them with slaves.

Tous les travaux du peuple, toutes les conquêtes de la République, n'aboutissoient qu'à enrichir quelques familles puissantes, qui usurpoient tous les domaines de l'Etat, et se formoient des possessions immenses. Il s'agissoit encore de prévenir la dépopulation de l'Italie, et d'entretenir cette pepinière de braves soldats, dont on s'étoit servi si utilement. Car les Grands, dont l'avidité croissoit avec les richesses, faisant tous les jours de nouvelles acquisitions, s'emparoient de presque toutes les terres, et les faisoient cultiver par des esclaves; de sorte que GRACCHUS prévit ce qui arriva depuis, que bientôt l'Italie ne seroit peuplée que d'esclaves.[126]

[All the exertions of the people, all the conquests of the republic, ended only in the enrichment of a few powerful families, who usurped the domains of the state and formed for themselves estates of enormous size. It became a question whether the depopulation of Italy could be prevented, or that reservoir be maintained of brave soldiers who had valuably served the state. For the grandees, whose greed increased with their wealth, made new acquisitions every day, until they possessed themselves of nearly all the lands and cultivated them with slaves, until Gracchus foresaw what came about later, that Italy would soon support only a slave population.]

It was at this point that the compromise implicit in Roman religion broke down. Beaufort is emphatic that the people desired to keep their side of the bargain and maintain the public virtue, if the aristocrats would maintain it by keeping theirs. He sets himself firmly against the long line of moralists and historians, ancient and modern, culminating most recently with Montesquieu, who had held that the republic broke down when the people demanded more than was theirs by right. In his view the people, moderate and manageable by instinct, had been involved in an unsuccessful struggle against their own degradation.

[126] Beaufort, 1766, pp. 373–4.

Tant que le peuple conserva beaucoup de déférence pour le Sénat, qu'il lui laissa la principale direction des affaires; tant que dans ses Comices il détermina ses suffrages conformément aux vues du Sénat, la République s'éleva au plus haut dégré de gloire et de puissance. Mais tandis que ce peuple, assemblé en Comices, disposoit souverainement des provinces, adonnoit du sort des Rois et des nations entières, ce même peuple languissoit dans la plus extrême pauvreté. L'accroissement de la puissance de l'Etat tournoit toute entière à l'avantage de quelques particuliers, sans que le menu peuple y trouvât du soulagement.[127]

[So long as the people retained their deference for the senate and left it in the supreme control of affairs; so long as it shaped its votes in the *comitia* according to the wishes of the senate, the republic rose to the pinnacle of glory and power. But even as this people, assembled in *comitia*, made sovereign disposition of provinces and gave law to kings and whole nations, it was itself languishing in the most extreme poverty. The increase in the power of the state worked only to the advantage of a few, and the lesser people found in it no relief for their condition.]

Under this impoverishment, the very meaning of the word 'people' began to change.

Quand je parle ici du Peuple Romain, et des soldats qui avoient servi l'Etat, il ne faut pas confondre les idées, et croire que je comprens là-dessous toute cette foule d'artisans, cette populace toujours à charge à tout gouvernement dès qu'elle est en droit d'y prendre part, et qu'on trouvoit moyen d'en exclure, en la renfermant dans les quatre Tribus de la ville. Le service militaire, du tems des GRAQUES, n'étoit pas encore avili jusqu'au point d'admettre de pareilles gens dans les légions. Ce n'étoit point de ceux-ci qu'il s'agissoit, et il leur suffisoit d'avoir part à quelques distributions de blé, que leur faisoit la République; ou même on savoit en décharger la ville de tems à l'autre, en les envoyant dans les colonies, et en leur donnant quelques arpens de terre. Il s'agissoit de ces braves soldats, qu'on ne prenoit que dans les Tribus rustiques, et qui après avoir servi l'Etat pendant vingt-cinq ou trente ans, chargés d'armes et de blessures, revenoient chercher leur subsistence en cultivant le petit héritage de leurs pères, sans autre récompense que l'avoir bien servi la République. C'était eux que TIBERIUS songeoit tirer de la misère.[128]

[When I speak of the Roman People and the soldiers who had served the state, it is important not to confuse our ideas and suppose that I include in this phrase that crowd of craftsmen, that populace which was a burden on every government because it had some right to a part in it, and which was excluded therefrom by being enrolled in the four urban tribes. Military service in the time of the Gracchi had not sunk so low that such people were enrolled in the legions. They were not the issue; it was enough to admit them to the occasional distribution of

---

[127] Beaufort, 1766, p. 236.  [128] Beaufort, 1766, pp. 237–8.

grain, as the republic began to do, or to free the city of them from time to time, by sending them out in colonies and granting them a few yards of ground. The question was that of the brave soldiers listed in the rustic tribes, who after serving the state for twenty-five or thirty years returned, loaded with arms and wounds, to seek a living on the little plots inherited from their fathers, with no reward except the memory of good service. It was these whom Tiberius dreamed of rescuing from their poverty.]

But Tiberius and Gaius Gracchus failed in their enterprise, partly because the division between urban and rustic plebeians weakened their political base,[129] but more – as others had agreed – because they came too late to check the expropriation of the smallholder class. One might say of their initiative, as de Retz said of the Fronde, that 'le peuple entra dans le sanctuaire'; they revealed to the people that the aristocracy were altogether false to the religion of virtue they inculcated, and Romans would not believe in their government again. The way was open for an increasingly desperate military proletariat to expect lands and pay only from the military adventurers who appeared to lead them. In addition, it was Gaius Gracchus who laid it open to Italian allies, involved in the same process of impoverishment, to expect Roman citizenship, and thus filled the city with a throng of aliens who had never known the religion of virtue and would never care for the citizenship they acquired. Their 'indifférence . . . se communiqua bientôt aux anciens citoyens',[130] and 'la République n'étoit, dans le fond, qu'un fantôme'.[131]

On a pû voir dans le Chapitre précédent les causes de cette aversion, que le Peuple Romain et leurs soldats avoient conçue, contre le Sénat, et qui entraina enfin la ruine de la République. Cet éloignement avoit sa source dans la certitude, où le soldat étoit, qu'il n'avoit rien à attendre du Sénat, lequel ne récompenseroit jamais ses services, et servoit toujours attentif à maintenir la discipline militaire, au lieu qu'en tournant ses vues du côté de ses Généraux, il n'y avoit point de récompense qu'il n'en pût espérer . . .[132] Les armées suivirent la même maxime sous les Empereurs, et tournèrent toutes leurs vues du côté de ces Généraux-nés de l'Etat: qui de leur côté se les attachèrent par leurs libéralités, sachant bien que tant qu'ils pourroient compter sur elles, ils seroient maîtres de tout, et que le Sénat ne pourroit former d'opposition à leurs volontés.[133]

[The previous chapter has made clear the causes of the hostility which the Roman people and the soldiers conceived against the senate, and which ended by ruining the republic. This alienation arose from the soldier's assurance that

---

[129] Beaufort, 1766, p. 416.     [130] Beaufort, 1766, p. 244.     [131] Beaufort, 1766, p. 248.
[132] A view of Roman history recalled when an English army held a rendezvous at Newmarket, or American officers formed a conspiracy at Newburgh.
[133] Beaufort, 1766, pp. 271–2.

he had nothing to hope from the senate, which would never reward his services and would always take care to subject him to military discipline; to the point where, if he threw in his lot with his generals, there was no reward he might not hope for . . . The armies acted on the same principle under the emperors and gave all their support to these captains-general by birth; while these attached them to themselves by rewards and donatives, knowing well that as long as these were assured, they would be the masters of all and the senate could do nothing in opposition to their wills.]

Beaufort does not trouble to analyse either the magistracy or the treasury of Augustus, but looks directly ahead to the maxim of Severus, that the soldier was everything and the rest nowhere. He is anxious to dispel the fallacy that the principate was founded on a *lex regia* or had any constitutional legitimacy at all.

Je crois qu'il est facile à présent de se faire une idée juste de ce qu'étoit le pouvoir des Empereurs dans son origine. Bornés à divers égards, dans le pouvoir civil, l'autorité souveraine, qu'ils exerçoient sur les armées, les mettoit en état d'exercer le despotisme le plus entier toutes les fois qu'ils vouloient abuser du pouvoir qui leur étoit confié. Ils avoient laissé au Sénat une autorité assez étendue sur le civil; mais qui n'étoit que precaire, puisqu'il n'en pouvoit faire usage que selon leur bon plaisir. Les soldats, qui nourissoient une haine invéterée contre cette compagnie, ne respectèrent jamais ses ordres, s'opposèrent toujours à l'exercise de ses droits, et la firent enfin tomber tout à fait dans le mépris. Les Empereurs, pour exercer le pouvoir le plus arbitraire, n'eurent pas besoin de se faire autoriser par une Loi Royale. Les armées, dont ils étoient apuyés, leur repondoient de la soumission du Sénat, et le Sénat lui même, après quelques tentatives inutiles pour recouvrir son ancienne autorité, fut convaincu que le parti le plus sûr pour lui, étoit celui de la soumission. Après le règne des ANTONINS, ce ne fut que désordre et que confusion; les armées disposèrent toujours de l'Empire, et la discipline militaire fut entièrement ruinée . . . Ce ne fut plus qu'un désordre et un pillage continuel, et l'on vit les Empereurs, sacrifiés au moindre mécontentement des armées, ne paroitre sur la scène, que pour perdre la vie peu après.[134]

[It seems to me easy at this point to give a clear account of what the emperor's power was in its origin. Limited in some ways as a civil power, the sovereign authority which they exercised over the armies put them in a capacity to exercise complete despotism whenever they wished to abuse the power entrusted to them. They left in the hands of the senate an apparently extensive civil authority; but this was no more than precarious, since it could only be exercised at the emperors' pleasure. The soldiers, who nursed an inveterate hatred towards that body, never respected its orders, invariably opposed it in the exercise of its rights,

---

[134]  Beaufort, 1766, pp. 272–3.

and ended by making it an object of contempt. The emperors, exercising an altogether arbitrary power, had no need to authorise themselves by a *lex regia*. The armies who supported them rewarded them with the submission of the senate; and the senate itself, after a few vain attempts to recover its ancient authority, was persuaded that the safest path was that of submission. After the reign of the Antonines, there was nothing but disorder and confusion; the armies disposed of the empire, and military discipline went to ruin . . . Nothing but continual disorder and pillage, in which one sees the emperors sacrificed to the slightest discontent of the armies, and appearing on the scene only to lose their lives soon after.]

This narrative – well on the way to being established by the time Beaufort wrote – located the violences of AD 98, 180 and the third century at large, in the context of a continued struggle between imperial-military and civil-senatorial authority, in which the latter, a mere ghost since it had lost control of the armies, nevertheless possessed a legitimacy as indispensable as it was despised, and intermittently tried to re-assert itself. Its failure was assured less by the authority of the Caesars, perpetually insecure, than by the ineradicable and ultimately self-destructive hatred of the soldiers for the senatorial class, which – for anything Beaufort says to the contrary – was a simple continuation of the landless soldier's hatred of the slave-owning latifundists who denied him the soil. The rule of the Severi and the anarchy that followed it were spectral triumphs of the ghosts of the Gracchi, witnessing the fulfilment of their darkest prophecies; no further explanation was needed. Whether any historian, including Gibbon, reached the point of asking if there had been any change in the political economy of the Roman armies and the Roman empire in the two centuries after Augustus is a question it is now fair for us to ask. If the armies of the Severi were differently supported from those of the triumvirates, they might have had different reasons for intervening in disputed successions, or at least have been searching for different rewards; and the recovery of the empire at the end of the third century, the establishment of the systems of Diocletian and Constantine, might find corresponding explanations. These are not questions that Beaufort goes into; the Appianic and Tacitean narratives carry him as far as he has need to go.

There are a few hints of what would become an alternative explanation of the Decline and Fall, causally linked with that now familiar to us but distinct from it; one that besides focussing on the disorder of the armies, focusses attention on the exhaustion of provincial society. In his later chapters, Beaufort goes over ground earlier covered by Sigonio, and distinguishes *jus Romanum* from *Latinum* and *Italicum*.[135] His purpose is of course to look once more at the displacement and degradation of the free military colonists, and he finds occasion also to study the condition of the Italian *socii*, whose involvement in that process led them to the disastrous measure of seeking direct Roman citizenship. He turns aside to one more defence of the *populus Romanus* against the charges of mutiny and luxury; they were a frugal and industrious race, and the vices that ultimately destroyed them, materially and morally, were those of their betters.[136] The *socii* too were capable of a confederate polity; the Roman destruction of this system, and the absorption of the Italians into an increasingly meaningless Roman citizenship, were at best mixed blessings.[137] Beyond Italy and the *socii* lay the empire and the provinces. Beaufort sees through Flamininus' much-praised proclamation of the liberty of the Greek cities; it was in fact the proclamation of a protectorate,[138] and the precarious freedom of the Greeks was often a form of clientage to powerful men at Rome (it is on this that he has occasion to quote Catiline, not otherwise a significant actor in his story).[139] The exploitation of the provinces under the republic points the way to a new subject: that of their peaceable government, but increasing overtaxation, under the emperors.

Vers le declin de la République, les provinces furent pillées et saccagées impunément, et les gouverneurs exercèrent le pouvoir le plus tirannique sur les sujets, sans que ceux-ci pussent espérer de remède à leurs maux.

(In a passage elsewhere, Beaufort explains that this was the worse because provincial governors enjoyed the immunities of free citizens at Rome;[140] a theme as old as Cicero upon Verres.)

Leur condition devint un peu plus tolérable sous les Empereurs, dont l'autorité mit des bornes à celle des Gouverneurs, et contribua à les tenir en bride. Il est vrai que quelques Empereurs surchargèrent les provinces de nouveaux impôts, mais d'autres diminuoient les taxes, que leurs prédécesseurs avoient imposées, et même leur en quittoient tous les arrérages. Cependant vers la décadence de l'Empire, toutes les provinces étoient tellement surchargées d'impôts, qu'à peine y pouvoient-elles fournir; et elles étoient du moins autant foulées, qu'elles l'avoient été dans les derniers tems de la République.[141]

[Towards the decline of the republic, the provinces were looted and laid waste with impunity, and the governors exercised the most tyrannical powers over

[135] Beaufort, 1766, t. II, pp. 119–20.   [136] Beaufort, 1766, t. II, p. 137.
[137] Beaufort, 1766, t. II, pp. 214, 220.   [138] Beaufort, 1766, t. II, p. 276.
[139] Beaufort, 1766, t. II, p. 299.   [140] Beaufort, 1766, t. II, p. 369.
[141] Beaufort, 1766, t. II, pp. 334–5.

their subjects, who had no hope of remedy for their sufferings. Their condition became a little more tolerable under the emperors, whose authority set limits to that of the governors and helped to keep them under control. It is true that some emperors loaded the provinces with new taxation, but others lessened the impositions of their predecessors and even remitted arrears of payment. However, towards the decay of the empire, all provinces were over-taxed to the point where they could scarcely meet the demand; and at best they were as heavily burdened as they had been in the last years of the republic.]

There is here the beginnings of a new approach to the question of *libertas et imperium*: the history of a great territorial monarchy, whose taxation and over-taxation of the provinces may or may not have been the consequence simply of the demands of its ungovernable armies. We come in sight of a history of empire which is not limited to that of a republic destroyed by its empire; a theme further explored by Scottish philosophers in the next chapter. It is not Beaufort's subject. He returns to examining the structure of the republic, to enquiring how far it is illuminated by Montesquieu's theory of the separation of powers,[42] and to narrating for a second time how the virtue and frugality of the people were destroyed, at the death of Tiberius Gracchus, by the discovery that the senators were a class of exploiters to whom the despotism of the Caesars was to be preferred. These are the last words of Beaufort's treatise,[43] whose democratic sympathies may be less the result of any ideological context in which he can be placed than of a combination of erudition and philosophy, unlike Montesquieu's or that of any author so far studied.

---

[42] Beaufort, 1766, t. 11, pp. 400–5.
[43] Beaufort, 1766, t. 11, pp. 432–4. I am indebted to Eric Nelson for bringing to my attention (unfortunately too late for consideration in this chapter) the essay by Luciano Guerci, 'La République Romaine di Louis de Beaufort e la discussione con Montesquieu', in *Storia e ragione: le* 'Considérations sur les causes de la grandeur des Romains et de leur décadence' *di Montesquieu nel anno 250° della pubblicazione: atti del Convegno internazionale organnizato dall'Istituto Universitario Orientale e dalla Società italiano di studi sul secolo XVIII* (Naples: Liguori, 1987), pp. 421–53.

CHAPTER 16

# The Scottish narrative

## PART I: DAVID HUME AND ADAM SMITH

(1)

The Scottish philosophers who studied natural and civil history, and whom we have studied as authors of the four-stage theory and the Enlightened narrative,[1] were drawn to the history of the Roman republic and empire, but their writings on this subject rather accompany than precede the first volume of Gibbon's *Decline and Fall*. William Robertson did not go far into Roman history. David Hume had indeed completed his *Essays*, which were in part a vindication of 'modern' liberty after taking account of its 'ancient' criticisms, by the end of the 1760s, and Gibbon was reading them while he composed the *Essai sur l'Etude de la Littérature*.[2] Hume read and approved his first volume in the last months of the philosopher's life in 1776.[3] As for Adam Smith, Gibbon owned a copy of the 1767 edition of the *Theory of Moral Sentiments*,[4] but could have had no direct access to the content of his Glasgow lectures; and the *Wealth of Nations* appeared some months later than the first volume of the *Decline and Fall*. It is true that Smith and Gibbon were both members of the Literary Club, and possible to imagine that conversation between them on the history of society may have played its part in the development of the *Decline and Fall*; but the occasions on which they both dined at the Club seem concentrated in the years 1776 and 1777, too late for the composition of the first volume.[5] They corresponded, considered themselves friends,[6] and may have met on other occasions. Gibbon also corresponded with Adam Ferguson, who was not a visitor to London; he knew of the preparation of Ferguson's *History of the Rise, Progress, and*

---

[1] *NCG*, sections III–VI.  [2] *EEG*, p. 221.  [3] *Memoirs*, pp. 168–70; *NCG*, p. 175, n. 31.
[4] *Library*, p. 252–3; he also acquired the revised edition of 1790.  [5] Rogers, 1997.
[6] Gibbon to Smith, *Letters*, II, p. 166; Smith to Gibbon, Mossner and Ross, 1987, pp. 316–17.

*Termination of the Roman Republic*, and bought it when it was published in 1783,[7] but did not live to read its revised version in 1799. Hume may therefore be considered as a shaping agent in Gibbon's account of the Antonine monarchy and its place in Roman history, while Smith and Ferguson operate at greater distances. Gibbon came to know well what was going on in Edinburgh and Glasgow, and to understand its relation to the writings of Montesquieu and Hume. There is therefore a case for viewing the Scottish understanding of Roman history as a complex pattern and as part of the intellectual climate in which the *Decline and Fall* began to take shape. It may supply the last chapter in the long story of the journey through the centuries of the Tacitean and Appianic accounts of the formation of the principate and its weaknesses.

The Scots were concerned, even more specifically than Montesquieu and perhaps to greater narrative effect, with Roman history as an antithesis to that of modern Europe. They did not think it necessary, when writing about the ancient republic and empire, to envisage them as leading to the Christian millennium or the Enlightened narrative; these they treated in other contexts; but they were concerned with the age-old problem of *libertas et imperium* as leading to the Roman attempt to construct a universal order, the antithesis of the Enlightened plurality of *états bien policés* linked by commerce and a community of manners. Contemplating the conquest of the ancient world by a single republic, they took their departure from Montesquieu's post-Machiavellian dictum that though a small republic might be destroyed by its neighbours, a republic that grew into an empire must corrupt and destroy itself,[8] whether through the competitive wars of its proconsuls (the lesson of the Roman civil wars) or the loss of citizenship when it was extended beyond the city (the lesson of the Social War), until the republic was transformed into a military dictatorship. We know, as we read them, that this was the problem the founders of the United States set themselves to solve, in creating a federal republic that could be an empire of liberty; and it is striking to observe Hume's and Smith's emphasis on the solution Madison was to adopt, that of replacing the direct self-rule of citizens by self-rule exercised through representatives.[9] In eighteenth-century Europe, however, a universe of republics could be envisaged only by utopians[10] (of whom there were not a few); the plurality of states must consist predominantly, though not exclusively, of more or less enlightened monarchies, under

[7] Gibbon to Ferguson, *Letters*, 11, pp. 100–1.    [8] *Esprit des Lois*, XI, I.
[9] *Federalist Papers*, no. 10; the subject of an enormous secondary literature.
[10] E.g., Andrew Fletcher of Saltoun; Robertson, 1997.

whose rule internal and external commerce could flourish and there could be a dissemination of polite manners as much courtly as they were commercial. The most recent threat to this vision – it was to be repeated in a Napoleonic future – was that of universal monarchy, which might disseminate manners but would stifle the liberty on which commerce depended; and Hume and Smith set themselves to study the Antonine and Constantinean empire as an object-lesson in how universal monarchy might destroy itself through over-extending its military resources to the point where it could no longer control them. The history of both republic and principate displayed the dangers from which Europe after the wars against Louis XIV had perhaps escaped.

Whether a contrast or a transformation, the turn direct from ancient to enlightened values – 'modern' in the modern sense of the term – entailed a narrative unlike that studied in the previous volume, when it was ecclesiastical values that Enlightenment was to displace. The ancient world had been ruled by virtue, meaning the direct involvement of the arms-bearing citizen in the politics and wars of his city, and before Christian values had been heard of, there had been a narrative of *imperium et libertas* which recounted (and had even predicted) how virtue achieved an extension of power that must destroy it. Humanism and Enlightenment carried on the Christian indictment of Roman liberty as the virtue of a war-making society condemned to conquest, corruption and the loss of freedom itself; and just as Enlightenment hoped to employ commerce and manners as means to a civility proof against religious authority and religious anarchy, so it hoped to use them to achieve a society, even a confederacy, of polite states proof against the self-destruction of virtue. There was need of a history of manners, such as Montesquieu and Voltaire had in their different ways attempted and Hume and Robertson had carried on in continuing the Enlightened narrative; and this must also be a history of how the ancient world had failed through a lack of commerce and a reliance on virtue in the place of manners. It would be a history in which the *peinture* of what humans had been in past states of society and culture counted for more than the *récit* of what they had done in politics and war; but it would also be a narrative of how history in the former sense had come to replace history in the latter. This history, cultural as well as political, must be written in accord with the centrally Enlightened discovery that the progress of human society was inseparable from the progress of the human mind; perhaps there was nothing else in human history to record; and it would have to be both a philosophical history and, in important measure, a history of philosophy itself.

What this would mean for the relations between philosophy, erudition and narrative will concern us at another time.

The history of the Roman republic and empire, written in direct confrontation with the supposed state of Europe after the *siècle de Louis XIV*, displays much of the extraordinary efflorescence of interpretative skills that we associate with the concept of Enlightenment; but it also displays, and indeed brings to light, the deep sense in which that age was problematic and insecure in its own eyes. The individual was being asked to pay a heavy price for the security and prosperity of civil society: the loss of the capacity to bear arms in his own cause, the loss of direct action as a political being, the loss of any immediate apprehension of reality; and in all these ways and many associated with them, he (she is another story) was exposed to the sensation that he was being governed by agencies hard to recognise, which might well prove despotic and render him servile. The received name for this state of things was corruption, and there was no greater account of corruption available to west Europeans than that given by Tacitus of the condition of the Roman elites under the principate. The ancient image of corruption was repeatedly applicable to all the doubts and fears which Europeans in the era of Enlightenment might entertain about themselves, and despite all the demonstrations that ancient virtue had been the ethos of half-barbarous slaveowners and conquerors, the antithesis of corruption continued to be virtue: the self-possession of ancient man which moderns were in danger of losing. Adam Ferguson continued to stress this point where Hume and Smith thought it might be accommodated; and to all the rich rhetoric which presented the modern condition as preferable to the ancient, and virtue itself as historically contingent, a rhetoric of antiquity presented criticisms that could not altogether be ignored. It may be that Enlightened history of antiquity is more concerned to confront this tension than to overcome it.

(11)

The growth of representative institutions and the post-Utrecht *Europe des patries* both figure in David Hume's *Essays Moral, Political and Literary*, which contain much matter on the decline of Rome and were extensively cited by Gibbon. They consist of two collections, a shorter published in 1743 and an enlarged edition dated 1752. They therefore stand in a relation to Montesquieu's *Considérations* and *Esprit des Lois* (published in 1739 and 1748) which permits these works to be present in Hume's pages;

but Hume's concerns are Scottish and British, as well as European. In the 1742 collection, the essay, 'That Politics May Be Reduced to a Science' attempts a synthesis of ancient and modern knowledge, and in it we find the following:

> The constitution of the ROMAN republic gave the whole legislative power to the people, without allowing a negative voice either to the nobility or consuls. This unbounded power they possessed in a collective, not in a representative body. The consequences were: When the people, by success and conquest, had become very numerous, and had spread themselves to a great distance from the capital, the city-tribes, though the most contemptible, carried almost every vote: They were, therefore, most cajoled by every one that affected popularity: They were supported in idleness by the general distribution of corn, and by particular bribes, which they received from almost every candidate. By this means, they became every day more licentious, and the CAMPUS MARTIUS was a perpetual scene of tumult and sedition: Armed slaves were introduced among these rascally citizens; so that the whole government fell into anarchy, and the greatest happiness, which the ROMANS could look for, was the despotic power of the CAESARS. Such are the effects of democracy without a representative.[11]

There is more here than an ancient or modern contempt for the mob. The effect of representative government is that it obliges one to act mediately, sharing both passion and action with another, to whom one stands in a very complex relationship. It is not necessary for the representative to be wiser or more virtuous than his electors; by his existence he obliges either the few or the many to act considerately, to delay action over a longer time and to extend it over a greater distance. To Rousseau, it was a fatal objection that the represented ceased to act in his own person, and therefore gave up every pretension to virtue; but we shall find Hume's friend Adam Smith both pointing out that the institution of representation would have solved the problem of Italian citizenship, and considering why it could not be expected to take shape in the economic conditions of antiquity. Hume continues with a comparison of elective and hereditary chief magistrates and concludes with this passage:

> It may therefore be pronounced as an universal axiom in politics, *That an hereditary prince, a nobility without vassals, and a people voting by their representatives, form the best* MONARCHY, ARISTOCRACY, *and* DEMOCRACY.[12]

Whatever force is possessed by this statement of a 'universal axiom', its effect here is to pronounce that the Roman 'constitution' as described

---

[11] Miller, 1985, pp. 16–17.    [12] Miller, 1985, p. 18.

by Polybius was far from being a 'mixed constitution' as that term was used by Hume's contemporaries. The latter is a modern and post-feudal phenomenon, and is probably dependent on modern conditions for its realisation, since in feudal society the 'people' would be the 'vassals' of the nobility, and in Roman society very often their clients. In the 1752 essay 'Of Some Remarkable Customs', Hume wrote:

> A wheel within a wheel, such as we observe in the GERMAN empire, is considered by Lord SHAFTESBURY as an absurdity in politics. But what must we say to two equal wheels, which govern the same political machine, without any mutual check, control, or subordination; and yet preserve the greatest harmony and concord? To establish two distinct legislatures, each of which possesses full and absolute authority within itself, and stands in no need of the other's assistance, in order to give validity to its acts; this may appear, before-hand, altogether impracticable, as long as men are actuated by the passions of ambition, emulation, and avarice, which have hitherto been their chief governing principles. And should I assert, that the state I have in my eye was divided into two distinct factions, each of which predominated in a distinct legislature, and yet produced no clashing in these independent powers; the supposition may appear incredible. And if, to augment the paradox, I should affirm that this disjointed, irregular government, was the most active, triumphant, and illustrious commonwealth, that ever yet appeared; I should certainly be told, that such a political chimera was as absurd as any vision of priests or poets. But there is no need of searching long, in order to prove the reality of the foregoing suppositions: For this was actually the case with the ROMAN republic.[13]

Hume examines how the *comitia centuriata*, weighted in favour of the wealthy and therefore controlled by senatorial influence, exercised authority side by side with the more egalitarian and plebeian *comitia tributa* established by the tribunes. A chief reason is that the people, constantly victorious in foreign conquests, asserted their power in legislation, but did not cease to defer to aristocratic leadership exercised 'by intrigue, by influence, by money, by combination, and by the respect paid to their character';[14] so that it paid the nobles not to risk the position they held in the *centuriata* by openly opposing measures adopted in the *tributa*. The point is in a way Machiavellian; because Rome was a conquering city, the open dissensions between the orders could be kept moderate and fuel the fires for further conquests. In another way it is a continuation of an argument Guicciardini had urged against Machiavelli:[15] the Roman political structure was not a balance or even a *concordia discors*, but an incoherent

---

[13] Miller, 1985, pp. 370–1.  [14] Miller, 1985, p. 372.
[15] In the *Dialogo del Reggimento di Firenze*; Brown, 1994, pp. 143–53; see Pocock, 1975, pp. 245–8.

and unregulated series of tensions – like the 'wrestling ground' which Harrington had detected in feudal government[16] – held together only by the military and religious disciplines imposed by the kings, which alone supplied Rome with its energy and solidarity. The two Florentines had disagreed more in emphasis than in essence; but Guicciardini's partial rejection of the Polybian component in Machiavelli was being reiterated by Hume in the context of the antithesis between conquest and commerce, and this entailed the insistence that there was something barbaric about ancient virtue itself.

Examined by the criterion of Montesquieu's principle of the three powers – legislative, executive and judicial – the Roman republic was unlikely to emerge as a carefully constructed equilibrium; and this was peculiarly so when the principle was applied to the powers of provincial governors. In the *Esprit des Lois* Montesquieu importantly argued that the Romans had failed to observe the separation of powers when assigning *imperium* to these governors, so that their power became despotic.[17] In Hume's essay entitled 'That Politics May Be Reduced to a Science' (which antedated the *Esprit des Lois* by six years) the point becomes:

It may easily be observed that, though free governments have been commonly the most happy for those who partake of their freedom; yet are they the most ruinous and oppressive to their provinces: And this observation may, I believe, be fixed as a maxim of the kind we are here speaking of. When a monarch extends his dominions by conquest, he soon learns to consider his old and his new subjects as on the same footing, because, in reality, all his subjects are to him the same, except the few friends and favourites, with whom he is personally acquainted. He does not, therefore, make any distinction between them in his *general* laws; and, at the same time, is careful to prevent all *particular* acts of oppression on the one as well as on the other. But a free state necessarily makes a great distinction, and must always do so, till men learn to love their neighbours as well as themselves. The conquerors, in such a government, are all legislators, and will be sure to continue matters, by restrictions on trade, and by taxes, so as to draw some private, as well as public, advantage from their conquests. Provincial governors have also a better chance, in a republic, to escape with their plunder, by means of bribery or intrigue; and their fellow-citizens, who find their own state to be enriched by the spoils of the subject provinces, will be the more inclined to tolerate such abuses. Not to mention, that it is a necessary precaution in a free state to change the governors frequently; which obliges these temporary tyrants to be more expeditious and rapacious, that they may accumulate sufficient wealth before they give place to their successors. What cruel tyrants were the ROMANS over the world during the time of their commonwealth![18]

---

[16] Pocock, 1977, p. 196, 1992, p. 53.    [17] *Esprit des Lois*, XI, xix.    [18] Miller, 1985, pp. 18–19.

That the tyranny of a free people is the worst was one of the few charges that Paine and Jefferson neglected to hurl at the British nation. After rehearsing the topos of Verres, Hume continued:

After the dissolution of the commonwealth, the ROMAN yoke became easier upon the provinces, as TACITUS informs us; and it may be observed, that many of the worst emperors, DOMITIAN for instance, were careful to prevent all oppression on the provinces. In TIBERIUS' time, GAUL was esteemed richer than ITALY itself. Nor do I find, during the whole time of the ROMAN monarchy, that the empire became less rich or populous in any of its provinces, though indeed its valour and military discipline were always upon the decline.[19]

Republics governed empires badly, monarchies rather better; empire transformed republics into monarchies. Hume would not have objected to the proposition that even absolute monarchy might rule benignly over territories of wide extent. But the problem coming into view – it is part of the problem of Gibbon's 'Antonine moment' – was how to write the history of principate and empire, given that the political system under inspection was no longer a republic but had not become the centralised judicial and administrative system that 'absolute monarchy' denoted. Here the spectre of universal monarchy arose and blocked the path. In a 1752 essay entitled 'Of the Balance of Power', we find:

Enormous monarchies are, probably, destructive to human nature; in their progress, in their continuance [*note*: If the ROMAN empire was of advantage, it could only proceed from the fact that mankind were generally in a very disorderly, uncivilized condition, before its establishment.] and even in their downfall, which never can be very distant from their establishment. The military genius, which aggrandized the monarchy, soon leaves the court, the capital, and the centre of such a government; while the wars are carried on at so great a distance, and interest so small a part of the state. The ancient nobility, whose affections attach them to their sovereign, live all at court; and never will accept of military employments, which would carry them to remote and barbarous frontiers, where they are distant both from their pleasures and their fortune. The arms of the state must, therefore, be entrusted to mercenary strangers, without zeal, without attachment, without honour; ready on every occasion to turn them against the prince, and join each desperate malcontent, who offers pay and plunder. This is the necessary process of human affairs: Thus human nature checks itself in its airy elevation: Thus ambition blindly labours for the destruction of the conqueror, of his family, and of every thing near and dear to him. The BOURBONS, trusting to the support of their brave, faithful, and affectionate nobility, would push their advantage, without reserve or limitation.

---

[19] Miller, 1985, pp. 20–1.

These, while fired with glory and emulation, can bear the fatigues and dangers of war, but never would submit to languish in the garrisons of HUNGARY or LITHUANIA, forgot at court, and sacrificed to the intrigues of every minion or mistress, who approaches the prince. The troops are filled with CRAVATES and TARTARS, HUSSARS and COSSACS; intermingled, perhaps, with a few soldiers of fortune from the better provinces: And the melancholy fate of the ROMAN emperors, from the same cause, is renewed over and over, till the final dissolution of the monarchy.[20]

The use made of 'human nature' in this passage is interesting; contrary to Hume's usual practice, it suggests a self-destructive Machiavellian *virtù*. This is an oddly oblique attempt to prophesy the fate of Rome for the states of modern Europe, published after the Peace of Aix-la-Chapelle and before the outbreak of the Seven Years War. If Hume meant that Croats and Cossacks would play the part of barbarian *federati* in the Habsburg and Romanov empires, it was not among his better predictions; and he had switched in mid-sentence to the eastern empires from the monarchy of France, for which he felt far deeper concern and about whose future he avoided any prophecy. The Prussian and British monarchies make no appearance, and altogether it is not clear what message Hume was trying to send. The reference to 'ancient nobilities', however, informs us that we are in the modern world, and the foundations for saying so have been laid in an earlier passage.

After the fall of the ROMAN empire, the form of government, established by the northern conquerors, incapacitated them, in a great measure, for farther conquests, and long maintained each state in its proper boundaries. But when vassalage and the feudal militia were abolished, mankind were anew alarmed by the danger of universal monarchy, from the union of so many kingdoms and principalities in the person of the emperor CHARLES. But the power of the house of AUSTRIA, founded on extensive but divided dominions, and their riches, derived chiefly from mines of gold and silver, were more likely to decay, of themselves, from internal defects, than to overthrow all the bulwarks raised against them. In less than a century, the force of that violent and haughty race was shattered, their opulence dissipated, their splendour eclipsed. A new power succeeded, more formidable to the liberties of Europe, possessing all the advantages of the former and labouring under none of its defects; except a share of that spirit of bigotry and persecution, with which the house of AUSTRIA was so long, and still is so much infatuated.
In the general wars, maintained against this ambitious power, GREAT BRITAIN has stood foremost; and she still maintains her station.[21]

---

[20] Miller, 1985, pp. 340–1.    [21] Miller, 1985, p. 338.

But Hume proceeds to warn his countrymen against excess of zeal in opposing France everywhere, and entering into systematic alliances against her.[22] 'The balance of power' meant a plurality of states, including some territorial monarchies, and its function in the maintenance of civilisation was the preservation and development of commerce and culture. The ancient republics, other than conquering Rome, had done something to this end, but it could be properly pursued only where a diversified mankind organised an intertraffic between states. In the 1742 essay 'Of the Rise and Progress of the Arts and Sciences', Hume wrote that the Roman laws of the Twelve Tables were

sufficient, together with the forms of a free government, to secure the lives and properties of the citizens, to exempt one man from the dominion of another; and to protect every one against the violence and tyranny of his fellow-citizens. In such a situation the sciences may raise their heads and flourish. . . . [23]

The next observation, which I shall make on this head, is *That nothing is more favourable to the rise of politeness and learning, than a number of neighbouring and independent states, connected together by commerce and policy.* The emulation, which naturally arises among those neighbouring states, is an obvious source of improvement: But what I would chiefly insist on is the stop, which such limited territories give both to *power* and to *authority*.[24]

GREECE was a cluster of little principalities, which soon became republics; and being united both by their near neighbourhood, and by the ties of the same language and interest, they entered into the closest intercourse of commerce and learning. There concurred a happy climate, a soil not unfertile, and a most harmonious and comprehensive language; so that every circumstance among that people seemed to favour the rise of the arts and sciences. Each city produced its several artists and philosophers, who refused to yield the preference to those of the neighbouring republics: Their contentions and debates sharpened the wits of men: A variety of objects was presented to the judgment, while each challenged the preference to the rest; and the sciences not being dwarfed by the restraint of authority, were enabled to make such considerable shoots, as are, even at this time, the objects of our admiration. After the ROMAN *christian* or *catholic* church had spread itself over the civilized world, and had engrossed all the learning of the times; being really one large state within itself, and united under one head; this variety of sects immediately disappeared, and the PERIPATETIC philosophy was alone admitted into the schools, to the utter depravation of every kind of learning. But mankind, having at length thrown off this yoke, affairs are now returned nearly to the same situation as before, and EUROPE is at present a copy at large, of what GREECE was formerly a pattern in miniature. We have seen the advantage of this situation in several instances. What checked the progress of the CARTESIAN philosophy, to which the FRENCH nation shewed

---

[22] On this see Robertson, 1993.    [23] Miller, 1985, p. 118.    [24] Miller, 1985, p. 119.

such a strong propensity towards the end of the last century, but the opposition made to it by the other nations of EUROPE, who soon discovered the weak sides of that philosophy? The severest scrutiny, which NEWTON's theory has undergone, proceeded not from his own countrymen, but from foreigners; and if it can overcome the obstacles, which it meets with at present in all parts of EUROPE, it will probably go down triumphant to the latest posterity.[25]

There was a plurality of states in antiquity – Greek rather than Roman, though not unlike the Etruscan plurality supposed by Bruni – and the exchange between them stimulated the growth of the arts. It is not clear, however, that they were 'connected by commerce and policy', and perhaps this is why Rome was able to canalise virtue into a torrent of universal conquest. Under the empire the arts declined; but Hume passes over this Tacitean phenomenon, to arrive immediately at the ghost which came to be seated on the empire's grave, and does not summarise – as Robertson did – the long historical process which has restored Europe to plurality, commerce and cultural exchange. He has hinted at it, however, when mentioning the rise and fall of Habsburg universal monarchy.

The history of philosophy becomes relevant here, though it is not a subject on which Hume is at his best. He cannot maintain that the Roman emperors brought about a unification of philosophy during the Second Sophistic, and must fall back on the ghost of the empire; the church imposes a universal dictatorship of Aristotelian metaphysics, though a less accurate account of the first millennium of Christian intellectual history could hardly be found. Even in modern times, the relation of philosophy to monarchy is less than clear; does Hume see Cartesianism as the ideology of a French universal monarchy, and is there no possibility that Newtonian science may become the ideology of some other? The central message, however, is specific. The function of philosophy is to promote politeness and manners; for this there must be commerce and arts; for this there must be a plurality of states. China is a universal empire, in which commerce and politeness flourish, but are held to a threshold by the universal dictatorship of Confucianism over the intellect.[26]

We are now in a position to appreciate the characteristic ambivalence of Hume's historical judgements, when these are applied to the transition from ancient to modern history, as elsewhere they were applied to the history of England. He warned his readers of this in 'Of the Populousness of Ancient Nations', part of the 1752 collection and the longest of the *Essays*.

[25] Miller, 1985, pp. 120–2.    [26] Miller, 1985, p. 122.

There are commonly compensations in every human condition; and though these compensations be not always perfectly equal, yet they serve, at least, to restrain the prevailing principle.[27] To compare them and estimate their influence, is indeed difficult, even where they take place in the same age, and in neighbouring countries: But where several ages have intervened, and only scattered lights are afforded us by ancient authors; what can we do but amuse ourselves by talking *pro* and *contra*, on an interesting subject, and thereby correcting all hasty and violent determinations?[28]

*Pro* and *contra* then; 'Of the Populousness of Ancient Nations' is an inspection of the thesis that civilised and barbarous nations in antiquity must have been populous because they were able to field enormous armies. Apart from the unreliability of ancient historians – who, Hume remarks, lacked printed books and were therefore not compelled to check their sources[29] – there is the argument that in unspecialised pre-commercial societies the whole adult male population could and must take the field, which conditions our power to infer the population from the army. Hume employs this argument, but he also enquires, *pro* and *contra*, into the likely populousness of an unspecialised society of landholding warriors. On the one hand:

Enormous cities are, besides, destructive to society, beget vice and disorder of all kinds, starve the remoter provinces, and even starve themselves, by the prices to which they raise all provisions. Where each man had his little house and field to himself, and each county had its capital, free and independent; what a happy situation of mankind! How favourable to industry and agriculture; to marriage and population! The prolific virtue of man, were it to act in its full extent, without that restraint which poverty and necessity imposes on it, would double the number every generation: And nothing surely can give it more liberty, than such small commonwealths, and such an equality of fortune among the citizens.[30]

But there were pre-Malthusian checks on this bucolic idyll. Where the only wealth was land, over-population must produce war; the Romans would march out against Veii, the Cimbri and Teutones would go on trek with their herds; and ancient war, in which the whole male population was engaged, was necessarily genocidal. It followed that ancient virtue was the willingness to exterminate and enslave another nation, as well as to die for one's own; and since ancient politics was the display of virtue, violence within the city was as slaughterous as war without it.

---

[27] A comment on Montesquieu?    [28] Miller, 1985, p. 404.
[29] Miller, 1985, p. 422, n. 123.    [30] Miller, 1985, p. 401.

Corcyraean seditions and Sullan proscriptions pass before our eyes, and Hume casually dismisses a famous Machiavellian counter-example.

> It is to be remarked that AGATHOCLES was a man of great sense and courage, and is not to be suspected of wanton cruelty, contrary to the maxims of his age.[31]

Nor were exile and emigration available to refugee populations, given the laws of the ancient economy.

> The barbarity of the ancient tyrants, together with the extreme love of liberty, which animated those ages, must have banished every merchant and manufacturer, and have quite depopulated the state, had it subsisted upon industry and commerce. While the cruel and suspicious DIONYSIUS was carrying on his butcheries, who, that was not detained by his landed property, and could have carried with him any art or skill to procure a subsistence in other countries, would have remained exposed to such implacable barbarity? The persecutions of PHILIP II and LEWIS XIV filled all EUROPE with the manufacturers of FRANCE and FLANDERS.[32]

Ancient virtue therefore rested on an economic base conducive to depopulation by means of massacre and enslavement on a genocidal scale. On the other hand:

> It must be owned, that the situation of affairs in modern times with regard to civil liberty, as well as equality of fortune, is not near so favourable, either to the propagation or happiness of mankind. EUROPE is shared out mostly into great monarchies; and such parts of it as are divided into small territories, are commonly governed by absolute princes, who ruin their people by a mimicry of the greater monarchs, in the splendour of their court and the number of their forces. SWITZERLAND alone and HOLLAND resemble the ancient republics; and though the former is far from possessing any advantage either of soil, climate, or commerce, yet the numbers of people, with which it abounds, notwithstanding their enlisting themselves into every service in EUROPE, prove sufficiently the advantages of their political institutions.[33]

However, it is on the monarchies and their courts, cities and armies, that attention must be fixed if we are to understand modern Europe; and Hume is able to argue, *contra*, that the negative population checks of antiquity are lacking.

> The maxims of ancient war were much more destructive than those of modern; chiefly by that distribution of plunder, in which the soldiers were indulged. The private men in our armies are such a low set of people, that we find any abundance, beyond their simple pay, breeds confusion and disorder among

---

[31] Miller, 1985, p. 410, n. 91.    [32] Miller, 1985, p. 419.    [33] Miller, 1985, pp. 402–3.

them, and a total dissolution of discipline. The very wretchedness and mean-ness of those, who fill the modern armies, render them less destructive to the countries which they invade: One instance, among many of the deceitfulness of first appearances in all political reasonings.[34]

The specialisation of labour has reduced modern war to a few semi-skilled evolutions to be performed by drilled military proletarians. In a society where unskilled drifters can be spared from the workforce to join the army, the loss of a battle cannot decimate the male population, any more than the loutish handlers of the musket can exterminate the people of whole cities. It was the dream of the *ancien régime* that in commercial society war would not disappear, but be reduced by specialisation to its proper place on the margins of civilisation; the achievement of the democratic revolutions was to involve the people in war once more, and inaugurate the age of Clausewitz. Hume's eye now leaves the impact of war upon society; he concedes that camps, courts and capitals are unproductive and do little to encourage population, but proceeds:

All our later improvements and refinements, have they done nothing toward the easy subsistence of men, and consequently towards their propagation and encrease? Our superior skill in mechanics; the discovery of new worlds, by which commerce has been so much enlarged; the establishment of posts; and the use of bills of exchange: These seem all extremely useful to the encouragement of art, industry and populousness. Were we to strike off these, what a check should we give to every kind of business and labour, and what multitudes of families would immediately perish from want and hunger? And it seems not probable, that we could supply the place of these new inventions by any other regulation of institution.[35]

Security of property and ease of communication – the formula for commerce – furnish the conditions of population growth, rather than the concentration of virtue in agrarian strongholds. But this is to re-open the question whether such communication is better facilitated by a plurality of states trading with one another, or by the unification of the world in the peace imposed by the universal monarchy; and this in his-torical retrospect became the problem of how to treat the Augustan and Antonine principate. Here we find Hume characteristically modifying his earlier pronouncement that enormous monarchies were 'probably' destructive to human nature. This protean entity, it turns out, introduces self-corrective tendencies into universal monarchy itself.

[34] Miller, 1985, pp. 404–5.   [35] Miller, 1985, p. 420.

Whether the grandeur of a city be founded on commerce or on empire, there seem to be invincible obstacles, which prevent its farther progress. The seats of vast monarchies, by introducing extravagant luxury, irregular expence, idleness, dependence, and false ideas of rank and superiority, are improper for commerce. Extensive commerce checks itself, by raising the price of all labour and commodities. When a great court engages the attendance of a numerous nobility, possessed of overgrown fortunes, the middling gentry remain in their provincial towns, where they can make a figure on a moderate income. And if the dominions of a state arrive at an enormous size, there necessarily arise many capitals, in the remoter provinces, whither all the inhabitants, except a few courtiers, repair for education, fortune and amusement. LONDON, by uniting extensive commerce and middling empire, has, perhaps, arrived at a greatness, which no city will ever be able to exceed.

Chuse DOVER or CALAIS for a centre: Draw a circle of two hundred miles radius: You comprehend LONDON, PARIS, the NETHERLANDS, the UNITED PROVINCES, and some of the best cultivated parts of FRANCE and ENGLAND. It may safely, I think, be affirmed, that no spot of ground can be found, in antiquity, of equal extent, which contained near so many great and populous cities, and was so stocked with riches and inhabitants. To balance, in both periods, the states which possessed most art, knowledge, civility, and the best police, seems the truest method of comparison.[36]

In the second paragraph, Hume is of course circumscribing his own Europe, though Edinburgh seems to be excluded, and Gibbon would have pressed for the inclusion of the Pays de Vaud: the Europe of a plurality of states, where *le doux commerce* disseminated prosperity and enlightenment. There remained the problem of monarchy's proper extent, and later in the same essay Hume returned to it with a sentence that ranks him as a successor to Mexía and Lipsius, and a precursor of Robertson and Gibbon.

Were I to assign a period, when I imagine this part of the world might possibly contain more inhabitants than at present, I should pitch upon the age of TRAJAN and the ANTONINES; the great extent of the ROMAN empire being then civilized and cultivated, settled almost in a profound peace both foreign and domestic, and living under the same regular police and government. But we are told, that all extensive governments, especially absolute monarchies, are pernicious to population, and contain a secret vice and poison, which destroy the effect of all these promising appearances.[37]

Gibbon speaks of a 'secret poison' at the Antonine moment in history,[38] and we shall have to consider what he meant. Hume is citing the *Esprit des*

---

[36] Miller, 1985, p. 448.      [37] Miller, 1985, pp. 457–60.      [38] Below, p. 438.

*Lois*, XXIII, 19, 'Dépopulation de l'Univers', where Montesquieu cites Plutarch's work on the cessation of the oracles.

> I must confess, that this passage contains so many difficulties, that I know not what to make of it. You may observe, that PLUTARCH assigns, for a cause of the decay of mankind, not the extensive dominion of the ROMANS, but the former wars and factions of the same states; all which were quieted by the ROMAN arms. PLUTARCH's reasoning, therefore, is directly contrary to the inference, which is drawn from the fact he advances.
>
> POLYBIUS supposes, that GREECE had become more prosperous and flourishing after the establishment of the ROMAN yoke; and though that historian wrote before these conquerors had degenerated, from being the patrons, to be the plunderers of mankind; yet as we find from TACITUS, that the severity of the emperors afterwards corrected the licence of the governors, we have no reason to think that extensive monarchy so destructive as it is often represented.[39]

Hume never retreats from the balance of a judgement so delicately expressed as it is in the antithesis formed by his two passages on extensive monarchy; but if we compare his 'Antonine moment' with Gibbon's, we shall be reminded that the history of the principate remains problematic. If it was not a devastating universal despotism, if it brought law and prosperity where the republics had brought conquest and slave-hauling, it was not an age of fertilising commerce and enlightenment. Its peace was to be followed by the triumph of barbarism, its philosophy by the triumph of religion; and if the former were to be explained – as in Hume there is no hint that it should not – by the corruption of the legions followed by the employment of the barbarians, the fact would remain that the decline and fall of the empire was a consequence of the decline and fall of the conquering republic, and both an effect of the limitations of the ancient economy.

### (III)

Adam Smith was no less concerned than his friend David with presenting Roman history as an illuminating antithesis to that of contemporary Europe; but where Hume was by inclination a civil historian, interested in the European states system and its political culture, Smith was by preference a philosophical and at times a conjectural historian, concerned to discover general patterns of development and scrutinise their workings in the world of passion and contingency. In his Glasgow lectures of the

---

[39] Miller, 1985, pp. 460–1.

1760s – delivered while Hume was completing and revising his *History of England* – Smith presented to his students a historicised moral philosophy, founded in natural jurisprudence and contained within the progress of the mind and of society. What he has to say of Roman history exhibits familiar patterns, but it is no surprise to find them operating within the context of stadial theory, the settlement of Europe by shepherd peoples, and the foundation of cities as a distant prelude to the growth of political economy; a scheme Gibbon does not use directly, but which furnishes a deep background to his historical thought.

The sections of the *Lectures on Jurisprudence* which deal with Roman history are a small but highly informative proportion of the whole collection. They show us Smith pursuing two themes: the politics of a slave economy, and the origins of the *polis* and *res publica* in pastoral nomadism, at a point where it has just become stationary and begun to engage in agriculture and commerce. We encounter Smith rapidly developing the four-stages thesis, which seems to have been crucial to his Glasgow teaching and which he disseminated among his colleagues and students. Montesquieu had done something with it,[40] but it had not been of importance to Beaufort or Hume; in Smith, however, we find the shepherd stage becoming crucial to his entire theory of history and taking on more and more of the characteristics of steppe nomadism. As all students of Smith know, it is when human groups learn to domesticate wide-ranging hoofed mammals that chiefs appear, who can found lineages, claim a species of property in their herds and households, exercise authority over subordinate humans and lead them in pasture-seeking and war; their power over warriors is that of a chief, over captive humans that of a slavemaster (not very different from that of a herdmaster over his quadrupeds). Differentiation has begun, and with it class antagonisms, the state, and culture; songs are sung and epics chanted. In Smith this is the crucial stride away from 'savage' food-gathering and hunting; it may still be termed 'barbarism', but is followed by agriculture and commerce arising concurrently, since stationary cultivation necessitates spatial exchange and its media. The ancient Mediterranean city arises at exactly this point, when the shepherd camp has begun to be a storehouse for grains; its transitional character is one reason for its reliance on slave labour. Montesquieu's comparison of Romulus' Capitol to a Crimean *serai* may have been rhetoric; in Smith it becomes sociology.

[40]  *Esprit des Lois*, III, xviii, II.

If we should suppose that a nation of this sort was settled in country naturally defended against invasions, capable of maintaining themselves against their enemies, in such a country a regular form of government would soon take place. But this can never be the case in Tartary, as the country is unfit by its dryness and cold for agriculture, and has no fastnesses nor materials for constructing them; nor can it be in Arabia, where agriculture is debarred by the ruggedness and steepness of the country, which is a combination of hills without any intermediate valleys, or if there are any they are all filled with sand. But we see that this happened in other more fertile and secure countries pretty early. The first inhabitants of Greece, as we find by the accounts of the historians, were much of the same sort with the Tartars. Thus renowned warriors of antiquity, as Hercules, Theseus, etc. are celebrated for just such actions and expeditions as make up the history of a Tartar chief. We see also that they resembled them in this also that they made frequent demigrations. The Heraclidae, who were the followers or clan of Hercules, settled first of all in the great island of Euboea, and from there went out and settled at Mycenae and Sparta. These severall countries, being continually exposed to the inroads of their enemies, did not soon alter their way of life. . . . . Attica was the country which first began to be civilised and put into a regular form of government. The sea surrounded on two sides of the triangle and a ridge of high mountains on the third. It had therefore little to fear from enemies by land; the sea was the only means by which they could easily be attacked. They therefore at first built none of their villages near the sea. As the country was so much securer than the others, people flocked into it from all hands, tho it was rather the poorest of all the Grecian countries. But the rovers from the sea might still invade them in the night. The only method they had to secure themselves was to have some place of strength to drive their cattle and other goods into, upon an invasion. This was the advice given by Theseus; he advised them to live together in one place that they might be at hand to assist one another and might have a place to protect their cattle in. The city of Athens was therefore built and fortified under the acropolis or citadell.[41]

Theseus then abolished the separate jurisdictions of the chiefs – this is a Scottish reading of history – and obliged the inhabitants to live mainly in the city, thus confronting his monarchy with an aristocracy and a democracy; this, says Smith, is the origin of all ancient republics. We should note, however, that this theory of Hellenic and Italic history presupposes almost immediate contact between the steppe and the sea; the Horse People have arrived and begun to rule the Shore People, passing through the Thracian and Macedonian mountains, but never through the river valleys of Asia or Africa. The great cities of Egypt and the Fertile Crescent are excluded from this history and left to the

[41] Meek, Raphael and Stein, 1982, pp. 221–2. This is the edition cited as '*LJ*' in *NCG*.

domain of orientalism. The historic landscape is very like that visible where Smith was lecturing in Glasgow, and the rock of Dumbarton separated the upland black-cattle country from the lochs, sounds and islands of Argyll, Arran and Antrim (the Scottish Euboea). No Lowlander, however, believed that Glasgow, or any Scottish city, had been founded by the wild transhumants north of the escarpment; Dumbarton (the '*dun* of the Britons') was held to mark the point where emigrant agriculturalists from the south had wisely stopped at the first encounter with Highland barbarism. In such an archipelagic setting, however, agriculture and industry could develop.

We may easily conceive that a people of this sort, settled in a country where they lived in pretty great ease and security and in a soil capable of yielding them good returns for cultivation, would not only improve the earth but also make considerable advances in the severall arts and sciences and manufactures, providing they had an opportunity of exporting their sumptuous[42] produce and fruits of their labour. Both these circumstances are absolutely necessary to bring about this improvement in the arts of life amongst a people in this state. The soil must be improveable, otherwise there can be nothing from whence they might draw that which they should work up and improve. That must be the foundation of their labour and industry. It is no less necessary that they should have an easy method of transporting their sumptuous produce into foreign countries and neighbouring states. When they have an opportunity of this, then they will exert their utmost industry in their severall businesses; but if there be no such opportunity of commerce, and consequently no opportunity of increasing their wealth by industry in any considerable degree, there is little likelihood that they should ever cultivate arts in any great degree, or produce more sumptuous produce than will be consumed within the country itself; and this will never be wrought up to such perfection as when there are greater spurs to industry. Tartary and Araby labour under both these difficulties. For in the first place their soil is very poor and such as will hardly admit of culture of any sort, the one on account of its dryness and hardness, the other on account of its steep and uneven surface. So that in them there is no room for culture; the soil itself debarrs them. Neither have they any opportunity of commerce, if it should happen that they should make any advances in arts and sciences. They are deprived in most places of the benefit of water carriage, more than any other nation in the world; and in some places where they would have an opportunity of it, the land carriage which would be necessary before it, debarrs them no less than the other. In these countries therefore little or no advances can be expected, nor have any yet been made. But in Greece all the necessary circumstances for the improvement of the arts concurred.[43]

---

[42] This adjective conveys the idea of luxury; in Smith, however, it may indicate any product which improves the quality of life and acts as the object of taste.

[43] Meek, Raphael and Stein, 1982, p. 223.

This Clydeside view of world history is exclusively focussed on nomads and blue water. Caravan routes play no positive part in it, and if the Jordan and the Yenisei lead nowhere in particular, what of the Nile and the Euphrates? The romanticism of the desert has already begun to play its part in confusing Western understanding of Arab history, but there must be other reasons for the extraordinary importance which nomadism assumed in Scottish theory. However, we are now in a Mediterranean and archipelagic setting, and the history of the *polis* and *res publica* has begun, in a scarcely mediated emergence from heroic barbarism. Rome, Smith informed his students, was the best-known instance of the evolution of monarchy, aristocracy and democracy necessitated by the synoecisms of Theseus and Romulus;[44] but he did not need to remind them that at Rome this process entailed a very special set of circumstances, namely the conquest of a Mediterranean, Afro-Asian and European empire. The history of both republic and empire was in turn governed by a single set of circumstances, namely those attending the reliance of polity and economy on slave labour.

Smith did not point out – though it was in the logic of his argument – that a city founded by shepherd chiefs might well remain addicted to the *razzia*. He lectured rather as if a slave economy were the normal condition of mankind, and exceptions from its rule chiefly in need of explanation. Certainly both republican and democratic politics were in his view inseparable from slavery.

In a republican government it will scarcely ever happen that it should be abolished. The persons who make all the laws in that country are persons who have slaves themselves. These will never make any laws mitigating their usage; whatever laws are made with regard to slaves are indeed to strengthen the authority of the masters and reduce the slaves to a more absolute subjection. The profit of the masters was increased when they got greater power over their slaves. The authority of the masters over the slaves is therefore unbounded in all republican governments.[45]

In a monarchicall government there is some greater probability of the hardships being taken off. The king cannot be injured by this; the subjects are his slaves whatever happens; on the contrary it may tend to strengthen his authority by weakening that of his nobles. He is as it were somewhat more of an impartiall judge, and by this means his compassion may move him to slacken the rigour of the authority of the masters. We see accordingly that no absolute monarchy was ever in danger from the [slaves], neither the Mogulls country, Persia modern or ancient, nor Turkey, etc. ever were.[46]

---

[44] *Ibidem*, p. 227.    [45] *Ibidem*, p. 181.    [46] *Ibidem*, p. 182.

Notwithstanding of these superior advantages [i.e., those of free labour] it is not likely that slavery should ever be abolished, and it was owing to some peculiar circumstances that it has been abolished in the small corner of the world in which it now is. In a democraticall government it is hardly possible that it ever should, as the legislators are here persons who are each master of slaves; they therefore will never incline to part with so valuable a part of their property; and tho as I have here shewn their real interest would lead them to set free their slaves and cultivate their lands by free servants or tenants, yet the love of domination and authority and the pleasure men take in having every thing done by their express orders, rather than to condescend to bargain and treat with those whom they look upon as their inferiors and are inclined to use in a haughty way; this love of domination and tyrannizing, I say, will make it impossible for the slaves in a free country ever to recover their liberty. – In a monarchicall and absolute government their condition will probably be a good deal better; the monarch here being the sole judge and ruler, and not being affected by the easing the condition of the slaves, may probably incline to mitigate their condition; and this we see has been done in all arbitrary governments in a considerable degree. The condition of the slaves under the absolute government of the emperors was much more tollerable than under the free one of the Republick.[47]

Smith in 1762–63 did not envisage that a sovereign legislature would embark on the path to abolition. There were modern republics in which slavery had disappeared, but this had not been achieved by legislative means and these commonwealths were not democracies.

But of these we have none at this time in Europe. They were such as Genoa, Milan, Venice, etc. were formerly. The people of all these countries voluntarily resigned the power into the hands of the nobles, and they alone have since had the direction of affairs. We find nothing similar to this in any of the ancient republicks. In the modern republicks every person is free, and the poorer sort are all employed in some necessary occupation. They would therefore find it a very great inconvenience to be obliged to assemble together and debate concerning publick affairs or tryalls of causes. Their loss would be much greater than could possibly be made up to them by any means, as they could have but little prospect of advancing to offices. But in the ancient states the mechanick arts were exercised only by the slaves. The freemen were mostly rich, or if they were not rich they were at least idle-men, as they would have no business to apply themselves to. They therefore would find no inconvenience in being called to the public affairs. . . . But in the modern commonwealths this was a burden on the common people, without any hopes of rewards. They therefore have all given it up.[48]

Smith might never have heard of the bourgeoisie, or if he used the word it would have been in its proper sense of an urban patriciate; commerce

___

[47] *Ibidem*, pp. 186–7.     [48] *Ibidem*, p. 226.

in his mind bred a specialisation of activity, and therefore aristocracy. Nor did he draw his hearers' attention to the artifice of representation, whereby the specialised individual in a commercial society might exercise democratic control at one remove; there was not much in the Scotland of 1762 to suggest the possibility. 'Democracy', in his vocabulary here, meant the direct engagement of the individual, and his virtue, in civic and (needless to say) military activity; and not only had this been made possible only by slave labour, but it was actually incompatible with the engagement of the plebeians in free industrious crafts and trades. Civic and military virtue, it must follow, was the property of a society recently emerged from barbarism and still active in the appropriation of land and labour by the sword. The alternative was an industrious and polite society, with a free market ruled by a cultured patriciate or aristocracy.

Nor was it any too clear that the plebeian of antiquity had exercised the virtue which slave labour made possible to him.

We are told by Aristotle and Cicero that the two sources of all seditions at Athens and at Rome were the demands of the people for an agrarian law or an abolition of debts. This was no doubt a demand of the taking away so much of ones property and giving it to those to whom it did not belong. We never hear of any such demands as these at this time. What is the reason of this? Are the people of our country at this time more honestly inclined than they were formerly? We can not pretend that they are. But their circumstances are very different. The poor now never owe anything as no one will trust them. But at Rome the whole business was engrossed by the slaves, and the poor citizens who had neither an estate in land nor a fortune in money were in a very miserable condition; there was no business to which they could apply themselves with any hopes of success. The only means of support they had was either from the generall largesses which were made to them, or by the money they got from their votes at elections. But as the candidates would have been ruined by the purchasing the votes of the whole people at every election, they fell upon an expedient to prevent this. They lent them a considerable summ, a good deal more than what they gave for a vote, at a very high interest, ordinarily about 12 p cent and often higher, even up to 30 or 40 p cent. This soon ran up to a very great amount such as they had no hopes of being able to pay. The creditors were in this manner sure of their votes without any new largess, as they had already a debt upon them which they could not pay, and no other could outbid them, as to gain their vote he must pay off their debt, and as this had by interest come to a great amount there was no one who would be able to pay it off. By this means the poorer citizens were deprived of their only means of subsistence. It is a rule generally observed that no one can be obliged to sell his goods when he is not willing. But in time of necessity the people will break thro all laws. In a famine it often happens that they will break open granaries and force the owners to sell at what they think a reasonable price. In the same manner it is generally observed as a rule of justice that the property of any thing can not be wrested out of the proprietors hands, nor can debts be taken away against the creditors inclination. But when the Roman people found the whole property taken from them by a few citizens, and the whole of the money in the empire ingrossed also, it need not be wondered at that they desired laws which prevented these inconveniencies. – We may see from this that slavery among its inconveniencies has this bad consequence, that it renders rich and wealthy men of large properties of great and real detriment, which otherwise are rather of service as they promote trade and commerce.[49]

The right of the starving man to break through normal property restrictions was a key problem in Adam Smith's moral and economic theory.[50] Here, however, it is a tool of historical interpretation, the phenomenon of an underdeveloped exchange economy in which the poor lack the means to virtue and independence that comes of the opportunity to sell their skills and labour at a fair price. Hence the corn-hungry crowds of post-Gracchan Rome; and hence, it was needless to add, the land-hungry crowds of demobilised, or still embodied, legionaries. Debt, the product of slavery, destroyed the virtue which slavery made possible. The modern invention of a free market for labour made the whole syndrome unnecessary, since warfare was left to small forces of military proletarians who were no threat to anybody.

The *Lectures on Jurisprudence* conclude their analysis of ancient history with a demonstration of how republics thus constituted necessarily lose their liberty. Smith adopts Machiavelli's classification into commonwealths for preservation and for increase. The former are more likely to engage in commerce, and can afford to employ relatively small forces of mercenaries; this postpones the military consequences of the growth of productive trades, which renders a progressively smaller proportion of the population fit or available for army service. It is a paradox that the prevalence of slavery further delays this effect, by keeping freemen poor and willing to fight. But a time must come when only foreigners, barbarians, or the dregs of society can be found to bear arms, and the military technicians who command them – the growth of siege warfare is important here – become the real masters of the city and its policies. The commonwealth for increase commits great armies to the pursuit of conquest, but is probably more deeply committed to the maintenance of a slave economy, and the lands it conquers may be engrossed by a few slave-owners. The army of plebeian citizens therefore disappears; the

[49] *Ibidem*, pp. 197–8.     [50] Hont and Ignatieff, 1983, pp. 22–44.

legions become the dependents of their generals; and the familiar consequences ensue. At this point, however, Smith employs Machiavelli's
concept of the 'new prince' to evaluate the chances that empire will
become something like monarchy in the modern sense.

> The government of Rome after this was entirely a government of soldiers. The
> army made the emperor, the army supported him in his authority and executed
> his orders. The private affairs of individuals continued to be decided in the
> same manner and in the same courts as before. The emperor had no interest he
> could obtain by altering these forms, and on the other hand the people would
> more readily submit to his authority when they were allowed to continue. But
> the whole of the executive and the far greater part of the legislative power he
> took into his own hands. The Senate, the praetors, and all the other magistrates
> came to have no authority of their own but were intirely his creatures. War
> and peace, taxes, tributes, etc. he determined without comptroll by the power
> of his army; but right and wrong were as equally determin'd as they ever had
> been before. In the same way we see that Cromwell by an army of 10,000 men
> kept the whole country in awe and disposed of every thing as he pleased, more
> arbitrarily than they had ever been before, but left the course of justice between
> man and man as before, and indeed made severall improvements. Both these
> here mentioned were military governments, but very different from those of
> Turkey and the east. A system of laws had been introduced beforehand. This
> it was not his interest to alter. He therefore left the disputes concerning private
> property to be decided by the old rules, and even made severall improvements.
> He 1st changed feudall holdings into sockage lands, took away the *Navigation Act*;
> and we see accordingly that the first thing done after the Restoration of Ch. 2d
> was to make a statute in the 12th or 1st year confirming many of the regulations
> made by Cromwell. A new government always makes good laws, as it is their
> interest that the state should in its private affairs be under salutary regulations.
> Julius Caesar we are told had the same project of amending, not of altering the
> laws.[51]

That a 'new prince' should find it to his advantage to extend his jurisdiction, privatise his subjects, and move from being a despot to something
more like an absolute monarch, was a possibility which Machiavelli – no
jurisconsult – had not done much to explore; but it went well enough
with the concept that men under commercial rule became increasingly
concerned with their private affairs. Empire was exercised over private
subjects, not public citizens, and achieved at a price a vast expansion of
the jurisprudence that protected the privacy and prosperity of the former.
Smith made the customary point that provincial government improved
under the worst of emperors, and observed:

[51]  Meek, Raphael and Stein, 1982, pp. 237–8.

Thus a military government admitts of regulations, admitts of laws, tho the proceedings are very violent and arbitrary with regard to the election of emperors and in the punishment of all offenders against his dignity. . . . But in every other thing it was his interest that justice should be well administered. And this was the case in the Roman Empire from the time of Julius Caesar to that of the ruin of the Empire. But this government, as all others, seems to have a certain and fixed end which concludes it. – For the improvement of arts necessarily takes place here; this, tho it has many great advantages, renders the people unwilling to go to war.[52]

And so barbarians are employed, and in the end take control of provinces. 'The generallity of writers mistake the account of this story.'[53] Machiavelli had written that the empire of the world exhausted the virtue of the world; in Smith's less magical and more economically centred reading, this meant that the empire of the civilised world exhausted its reserve supply of unspecialised warriors and forced itself to recruit its armies from an 'external proletariat'; strictly speaking, the opposite of a proletariat, since it would probably consist of nomad herdsmen. But if a plurality of states were preserved instead of a universal empire, the reserves might not be exhausted and standing armies drawn from the internal proletariat might maintain the balance.

In the lecture notes dated at 1766, the account just given of Roman history is reiterated; but in the *Wealth of Nations*, ten years later, the differences between ancient and modern society are underlined. There is the following observation on the Social War of antiquity and that of Smith's own time:

The idea of representation was unknown in ancient times. When the people of one state were admitted to the right of citizenship in another, they had no other means of exercising that right but by coming in a body to vote and deliberate with the people of that other state. The admission of the greater part of the inhabitants of Italy to the privileges of Roman citizens, completely ruined the Roman republick. It was no longer possible to distinguish between who was and who was not a Roman citizen. No tribe could know its own members. A rabble of any kind could be introduced into the assemblies of the people, could drive out the real citizens, and decide upon the affairs of the republick as if they themselves had been such. But though America was to send fifty or sixty new representatives to parliament, the door-keeper of the house of commons could not find any great difficulty in distinguishing between who was and who was not a member. Though the Roman constitution, therefore, was necessarily ruined by the union of Rome with the allied states of Italy, there is not the least probability that the British constitution would be hurt by the union of Great Britain with

---

[52] *Ibidem*, p. 238.    [53] *Ibidem*, p. 239.

her colonies. That constitution, on the contrary, would be completed by it, and seems to be imperfect without it.[54]

The capacity to be represented, however, was no part of the virtue of antiquity; classical man could be no other than himself. In some paragraphs which may conclude our analysis of this part of his general theory, Smith concedes that warfare is not an art like any other, that it responds differently to the processes of specialisation, and that its organisation presents some keys to both ancient and modern history.

The art of war, however, as it is certainly the noblest of all arts, so in the progress of improvement it necessarily becomes one of the most complicated among them. The state of the mechanical, as well as some other arts, with which it is necessarily connected, determines the degree of perfection to which it is capable of being carried at any particular time. But in order to carry it to this degree of perfection, it is necessary that it should become the sole or principal occupation of a particular class of citizens, and the division of labour is as necessary for the improvement of this, as of every other art. Into other arts the division of labour is naturally introduced by the prudence of individuals, who find that they promote their private interest better by confining themselves to a particular trade, than by exercising a great number. But it is the wisdom of the state only which can render the trade of a soldier a particular trade separate and distinct from all others. A private citizen who, in time of profound peace, and without any particular encouragement from the publick, should spend the greater part of his time in military exercises, might, no doubt, both improve himself very much in them, and amuse himself very well; but he certainly would not improve his own interest. It is the wisdom of the state only which can render it for his own interest to give up the greater part of his time to this particular occupation; and states have not always had this wisdom, even when their circumstances have become such, that the preservation of their existence required that they should have it.[55]

Because war is not a productive activity, it is noble but neither private nor rational; it must be practised in the *res publica*, not in the *commercium*. It may remain the *ultima ratio* of states, but the wisdom of the state, when practised in the absence of either virtue or interest in the citizens, must certainly be one of the *arcana imperii*. In a commercial society, Smith says, where in principle every man has a specialised trade, the state must either institute a militia, obliging every citizen 'to join in some measure the trade of a soldier to whatever other trade or profession they may happen to carry on'; or it must institute a standing army, inducing or obliging a few to practise the 'trade' of a soldier to the exclusion of any

---

[54] Campbell and Skinner, 1981, II, p. 624.   [55] *Ibidem*, p. 697.

other.[56] But 'trade' is here a metaphor; no tradesman would willingly be a soldier, and only the state can designate the individuals who will practise skills they can sell to no other buyer. If its wisdom fails, they will sell to adventurers, becoming mercenaries. Living in a world of increasingly specialised craftsmanship, Smith may have discovered the private soldier as the original proletarian. This, however, was not the problem in antiquity, when military skill was developed at the expense of the unspecialised virtue of the citizen. Specialisation increased the soldier's skill to a level with which no citizen could compete, but the two competed in a public realm; major changes in their relationship were in consequence political revolutions, and the history of antiquity could be written in terms of soldier and citizen, standing army and militia.

> The fall of the Greek republick and the Persian empire [to Philip and Alexander of Macedon], was the effect of the irresistible superiority which a standing army has over every sort of militia. It is the first great revolution in the affairs of mankind of which history has preserved any distinct or circumstantial account.
> The fall of Carthage, and the subsequent elevation of Rome, is the second. All the varieties in the fortune of those two famous republicks may very well be accounted for from the same cause.[57]

We expect to read that the professionalisation of the legions, and the substitution of principate for republic, was the third revolution; but Smith passes over the age of the *imperatores* to reach the moment when Diocletian, or Constantine, brought the intervention of the legions in politics to an end by removing them from the frontiers and stationing them in provincial towns.

> Small bodies of troops quartered in trading and manufacturing towns, and seldom removed from those quarters, became themselves tradesmen, artificers, and manufacturers. The civil came to predominate over the military character; and the standing armies of Rome gradually degenerated into a corrupt, neglected, and undisciplined militia, incapable of resisting the attack of the German and Scythian militias, which soon afterwards invaded the western empire. It was only by hiring the militia of some of those nations, to oppose to that of others, that the emperors were for some time able to defend themselves. The fall of the western empire is the third great revolution in the affairs of mankind, of which ancient history has preserved any distinct or circumstantial account. It was brought about by the irresistible superiority which the militia of a barbarous, has over that of a civilized nation: which the militia of a nation of shepherds, has over that of a nation of husbandmen, artificers and manufacturers. The victories which have been gained by militias have generally been, not

---

[56] *Ibidem*, p. 698.   [57] *Ibidem*, p. 702.

over standing armies, but over other militias in exercise and discipline inferior to themselves. Such were the victories which the Greek militia gained over that of the Persian empire, and such too were those which in later times the Swiss militia gained over that of the Austrians and Burgundians.[58]

There were other such revolutions to come, probably culminating for Smith in the standing armies of the eighteenth-century states, one of which had defeated a barbarous militia at Culloden; but the *levée en masse* was to be decreed a few years after his death. With regard to antiquity, however, one thing is clear. The primitive citizen was as unspecialised as the shepherd, and an age of militias was to that extent an age of barbarism; for the barbarian is the unspecialised man. The victory of the barbarians over the empire was a result of the imperfect but effective civilisation of the latter; but how far the growth of specialised trades in the empire was an effect of commerce and enlightened monarchy, and how far of slavery and military rule, remained an open question.

## PART II: ADAM FERGUSON'S HISTORY OF THE REPUBLIC

### (IV)

Adam Ferguson's *Essay on the History of Civil Society* (1767), examined in chapters of the preceding volume,[59] is not a balanced work, but an agonistic one; it confronts, and does not seek to reconcile, the propositions that virtue is archaic – not to say barbarous – and that it is irreplaceable. To quote from Ferguson's later writings,

The virtuous who resign their freedom, at the same time resign their virtue, or at least yield up that condition which is required to preserve it.[60]

The sentiment is unexceptionally patriotic – though 'patriotism' to Ferguson's generation was still a term with seditious connotations; but the Highland chaplain defined both virtue and freedom as the almost explosive enhancement of the energies of the self which was brought by solidarity with the primeval tribal group, and insisted that it found expression in warlike collisions with groups of enemies. To the generation which remembered Culloden, and was anxious to distinguish civil

---

[58] *Ibidem*, pp. 704–5.   [59] *NCG*, chs. 22, 23.
[60] Ferguson, 1799, v, p. 76. All quotations are from this final and revised edition of the work. The aim here is not to study interactions between Ferguson and Gibbon, so much as to exhibit Ferguson's historiography at the furthest point of its development.

'liberty' from savage 'independence', this was all too challenging, and of course it lay at the heart of the problem of Roman history: virtue led to conquest, and conquest to corruption. Ferguson's treatment of Rome does not differ from those we have read in point of content or even moral, but the tone is very different; he recounts neither a progress nor a decline so much as an agony, and with more pathos than irony. He is stimulated rather than saddened by the thought that virtue is barbaric. In the *Essay* he had written:

> The term *barbarian*, in this state of manners, could not be employed by the Greeks or the Romans in that sense in which we use it; to characterise a people regardless of commercial arts; profuse of their own lives, and of those of others; vehement in their attachment to one society, and implacable in their antipathy to another. This, in a great and shining part of their history, was their own character, as well as that of some other nations, whom, upon this very account, we distinguish by the appellations of *barbarous* or *rude*.[61]

But Ferguson, like Machiavelli, was a Napoleon of Notting Hill.[62] Little furious wars among neighbouring communities did not end with the day of battle; somebody had to win, and the loser would be incorporated in his empire; conquest was the tragedy of heroic virtue.

> In proportion as territory is extended, its parts lose their relative importance to the whole. Its inhabitants cease to perceive their connection with the state, and are seldom united in the execution of any national, or even of any factious, designs. Distance from the seats of administration, and indifference to the persons who contend for preferment, teach the majority to consider themselves as the subjects of a sovereignty, not as the members of a political body. It is even more remarkable, that enlargement of territory, by rendering the individual of less consequence to the public, and less able to intrude with his counsel, actually tends to reduce national affairs within a narrower compass, as well as to diminish the numbers who are consulted in legislation, or in other matters of government.
> The disorders to which a great empire is exposed, require speedy prevention, vigilance, and quick execution. Distant provinces must be kept in subjection by military force; and the dictatorial powers, which, in free states, are sometimes raised to quell insurrections, or to oppose other occasional evils, appear, under a certain extent of dominion, at all times equally necessary to suspend the dissolution of a body, whose parts were assembled, and must be cemented, by

---

[61] Oz-Salzberger, 1995, pp. 184–5.
[62] The allusion is to G. K. Chesterton, *The Napoleon of Notting Hill* (London: John Lane, 1904), a fantasy of modern London divided into warring city states. It is an interesting case of the innocent love of bloodshed which possessed many literary men before 1914. 'Then the battle roared on; every man of Notting Hill was slain before night.'

means forcible, decisive and secret. Among the circumstances, therefore, which in the event of national prosperity, and in the result of commercial arts, lead to the establishment of despotism, there is none, perhaps, that arrives at this termination, with so sure an aim, as the perpetual enlargement of territory. In every state, the freedom of its members depends on the balance and adjustment of its interior parts; and the existence of any such freedom among mankind depends on the balance of nations. In the progress of conquest, those who are subdued are said to have lost their liberties; but from the history of mankind, to conquer, or to be conquered, has appeared, in effect, the same.[63]

It is not the vast size of territory that ruins the republic, but the fact that the vast territory was won by the sword. Conquest is what republics do, in the exercise of their heroic virtue; but 'the balance of nations' depends upon a number of 'commonwealths for preservation', which were probably not heroic in the first place. Peoples living in vast empires lose their civic virtue, and become passive, anomic and content, the subjects of a despotism produced by their inertia rather than imposed on their activity. The Romans and their subjects arrived at this condition under the emperors, and it is a secondary question whether we are to think of the latter as the despots which they were to those retaining active virtue, or as the benign autocrats which they were to those sunk in provincial passivity. Ferguson, like Montesquieu, was interested in the revival of Stoicism under the empire, but saw that it was problematical in both the victims of bad emperors and the personalities of good.

But are the evils of despotism confined to the cruel and sanguinary methods by which a recent dominion over a refractory and a turbulent people is established or maintained? And is death the greatest calamity which can afflict mankind under an establishment by which they are divested of all their rights? They are, indeed, frequently suffered to live; but distrust and jealousy, the sense of personal meanness, and the anxieties which arise from the care of a wretched interest, are made to possess the soul; every citizen is reduced to a slave; and every charm by which the community engaged its members, has ceased to exist. Obedience is the only duty that remains, and this is exacted by force. If under such an establishment it be necessary to witness scenes of debasement and horror, at the hazard of catching the infection, death becomes a relief; and the libation which Thrasea was made to pour from his arteries, is to be considered as a proper sacrifice of gratitude to Jove the Deliverer.[64]

But there are limits to an active virtue which can be displayed only in the form of martyrdom, just as there are limits to a ruling virtue which is exercised in the absence of equals.

---

[63] Oz-Salzberger, 1995, pp. 256–7.     [64] *Ibidem*, pp. 259–60.

Was it in vain, that Antonius [i.e., Marcus Aurelius] became acquainted with the characters of Thrasea, Helvidius, Cato, Dion, and Brutus? Was it in vain, that he learned to understand the form of a free commonwealth, raised on the basis of equality and justice; or of a monarchy, under which the liberties of the subject were held the most sacred object of administration? Did he mistake the means of procuring to mankind what he points out as a blessing? Or did the absolute power with which he was furnished, in a mighty empire, only disable him from executing what his mind had perceived as a national good? In such a case, it were vain to flatter the monarch or his people.[65]

Thomas Gordon had made the point that the goodness of the Antonines was accidental and owed nothing to the laws;[66] we shall find Gibbon arguing similarly, with the same hint that Marcus Aurelius was saddened by the thought of his own arbitrary power.[67] Ferguson is show-ing us the erosion of virtue in a world in which, in the end, there was nothing else to live by. It was not that other values could not be imagined or expounded, but that the ancient world had failed to realise them while destroying those it had. The legions had destroyed the republic, and the emperors had enfeebled the legions; the peace of universal monarchy had divided the world into haves and have-nots. Ferguson proceeds from this point to the apocalyptic vision of renewal we studied earlier:[68] the drama in which men have nothing left but their naked selves, and return to the desert to renew virtue in its most primitive form. The original Romans had been little different; where Montesquieu had compared Romulus' hold to a Crimean *serai*, Ferguson likened it to a Polynesian *pa*, like those in

some of the lately discovered islands in the Southern or Pacific Ocean, where every height is represented as a fortress, and every little township, that can maintain its possessions, as a separate state.[69]

Virtue was barbaric, but barbarism was the beginning of civil society. *The History of the Progress and Termination of the Roman Republic*, published in 1783 and revised in 1799, seems to have been regarded in Edinburgh circles as the Scottish complement to Gibbon's *Decline and Fall*. It is in five volumes, totalling near two thousand pages, and could obviously be ex-amined at much greater length than is possible here. Ferguson informs us that the original Romans were a 'horde' of cattle-raiding warriors; this term, part of the vocabulary with which nomad history was studied and the theory of the pastoral stage developed, is applied to Aetolian

---

[65] *Ibidem*, p. 251.  [66] Above, pp. 318–19.  [67] Below, pp. 445–6.
[68] *NCG*, pp. 350–4.  [69] Ferguson, 1799, I, p. 2.

Greeks as well as to the Cisalpine Gauls and the Cimbri and Teutones, Usepetes and Tencteri, who from time to time invaded Roman territory from beyond the Rhine and Danube.[70] Rome was one of the 'hordes' which became a stationary but warlike city; and Ferguson, like Montesquieu, faces the problem of showing what distinguished its institutions from those of other like cases. This may have been the work of creative individuals, Romulus, Numa and Servius Tullius; or it may have been the result of unintended social processes. Like Machiavelli, Ferguson is inclined towards the latter thesis by his conviction that tension and conflict pushed the Romans towards liberty and empire. The simultaneous existence of assemblies and magistracies which competed for power in the name of the patrician and plebeian orders had many disturbing and confusing effects, but it opened widespread opportunities to hold office; and as this was a society in which office was valued as a means to emulate competitors in the performance of military actions, competition and tension became motor forces in the expansion of public power.

Hitherto we have considered the Roman Republic as a scene of mere political deliberations and councils, divided at home, and seemingly unable to unite their forces abroad. The State, however, presented itself to the nations around it under a very different aspect. To them it appeared to be a mere horde of warriors, which made and preserved its acquisitions by force, and which never betrayed any signs of hesitation or weakness in the measures that were required for its safety.[71]

It may be difficult to determine, whether we are to consider the Roman establishment as civil or military; it certainly united, in a very high degree, the advantages of both, and continued longer to blend the professions of state and war together, than we are apt to think consistent with that propriety of character which we require in each: but to this very circumstance, probably, among others, we may safely ascribe, in this distinguished republic, the great ability of her councils, and the irresistible force with which they were executed [*note*: Polybius lib. VI c. 17].[72]

The union of forces was cemented by the tactical discipline of the legions, the enormous superiority of the trained veteran which distinguished an age of unspecialised warfare, and the singular intensity of Roman civil religion (which Ferguson considered superstition and Gibbon enthusiasm). The story proceeds through the Carthaginian wars, to the acquisition of empire in Spain, Africa and Greece; and the encounter with Macedon has more analytical significance than that with

---

[70] Ferguson, 1799, I, pp. 65–6, 87, 112–13, 114, 148, 323; II, 43; III, 95.
[71] Ferguson, 1799, I, pp. 65–6.    [72] *Ibidem*, p. 102.

Hannibal. The structure of Carthage itself made Hannibal little more than a *condottiere* of genius, but in the Macedonian kingdom the Romans

were engaged with an enemy renowned for discipline, who had made war a trade, and the use of arms a profession; while they themselves, it appears, for a considerable period both before and after the present war, even during the most rapid progress of their arms, had no military establishment besides that of their civil and political constitution, no soldiers besides their citizens, and no officers but the ordinary magistrates of the commonwealth.

If this establishment had its advantages, it may have appeared, on particular occasions, likewise to have had its defects. The citizen may have been too much a master in his civil capacity to subject himself fully to the bondage of a soldier, and too absolute in his capacity of military officer to bear with the control of political regulations. As the obligation to serve in the legions was general and without exception, many a citizen, at least in the case of any distant or uncompromising service, would endeavour to shun his task. And the officer would not always dare to enforce a disagreeable duty on those by whom he himself was elected, or on whom he in part depended for further advancement in the State.[73]

It is Smith's distinction; but at Cynoscephalae and Pydna the militia defeats the standing army. There are hints of future decay in this passage, but it will arise from the reversal of the conditions here suggested. The soldier is about to become too little of a citizen, not too much. The overthrow of Macedon ushers in the dynamic age of senatorial statecraft, but the empire thus acquired has the results by now familiar.

The wealth of provinces began to flow into the city, and filled the coffers of private citizens, as well as those of the commonwealth. The offices of State and the command of armies were become lucrative as well as honourable, and were coveted on the former account. In the State itself the governing and the governed felt separate interests, and were at variance, from motives of avarice, as well as ambition; and, instead of the parties who formerly strove for distinction, and for the palm or merit in the service of the commonwealth, factions arose, who continued for the greatest share of its spoils, or who sacrificed the public to their party-attachments or feuds.[74]

The number of great landed estates, and the multiplication of slaves kept pace together. This manner of stocking their country possessions was necessary or expedient in the circumstances of this people; for if the Roman citizen, who, even though poor, possessed so much consequence in his military and political capacity, had been willing to become a hireling and a servant, yet it was not the interest of masters to intrust their affairs to persons who were liable to be pressed into the legions, or who were so often called away to the comitia and assemblies of the People.[75]

---

[73] *Ibidem*, p. 300.    [74] *Ibidem*, pp. 379–80.    [75] *Ibidem*, p. 382.

Ancient freedom was the begetter of the slavery that undermined it. By the end of Ferguson's first volume we have reached the Gracchan crisis, though it is insisted that it was too late for agrarian equality, and that under conditions of extensive government a division into rich and poor is not only inevitable, but generates its own justice. It may now be perceived that if conquered lands are to be distributed among the poor, they should be given back to the conquered. The story proceeds through the conflict between Marius and Sulla – the former corrupting the legions by enlisting the indigent, the latter playing the terrible and ambiguous Machiavellian role we noticed in Montesquieu – to the crowning disaster of the Social War and the extension of citizenship to Italians. This spelt the end of the Roman People, and even of the conduct of Roman politics as a struggle between classes; nothing now remained except factions, and their leaders could only have private and irresponsible ambitions. There was one great exception, however, but even this drove the republic into wilder disorder; the military institutions and even their virtue remained intact and expansive, but were corrupted by the decay of the civil structure which they exacerbated.

War, in the detail of its operations, if not even in the formation of its plans, is more likely to succeed under single men than under numerous councils. The Roman constitution, though far from an arrangement proper to preserve domestic peace and tranquillity, was an excellent nursery of statesmen and warriors. To individuals trained in this school, all foreign affairs were committed with little responsibility and less controul. The ruling passion, even of the least virtuous citizens, during some ages, was the ambition of being considerable, and of rising to the highest dignities of the State at home. In the provinces they enjoyed the condition of monarchs; but they valued this condition only as it furnished them with the occasion of triumphs, and contributed to their importance at Rome. They were factious and turbulent in their competition for preferment and honours in the capital; but, in order the better to support that very contest at home, were faithful and inflexible in maintaining all the pretentions of the State abroad. . . . Contrary to the fate of other nations, where the State is weak, while the conduct of individuals is regular; here the State was in vigour, while the conduct of individuals was in the highest degree irregular and wild.[76]

In these circumstances human genius passed out of control, and the highest of military and political talents were devoted to the mere advancement of personality. The third and half the fourth volumes are taken up with the career of Julius Caesar, but it is evident that Ferguson

---

[76] Ferguson, 1799, II, pp. 232–3.

would have both understood and dismissed the nineteenth-century portrait of Caesar as superman – largely because he did not look on him as
the founder of a new historical order. Sulla possessed the magnanimity
to resign his office; he knew there was such a thing as the *res publica*; but
of Caesar Ferguson's final word is:

> Though in respect to the ability with which he rendered men subservient to
> his purpose; in respect to the choice of means for the attainment of his end; in
> respect to the plan and execution of his designs, he was far above even those
> who are eminent in the history of mankind; yet in respect to the end which
> he pursued, in respect to the passion he had to gratify, he was one merely of
> the vulgar, and condescended to be vain of titles and honours which he himself
> had extorted by force, and which he had shared with persons of the meanest
> capacity. Insensible to the honour of being deemed the equal in rank to Cato
> and Catulus, to Hortensius and Cicero, and the equal in reputation to Sylla, to
> Fabius, and to the Scipios, he preferred being a superior among profligate men,
> the leader among soldiers of fortune, and to procure by force from his fellow
> citizens a deference which his wonderful abilities must of themselves have made
> unavoidable, and still more if he had possessed the magnanimity to despise it.[77]

Sulla possessed that magnanimity; his ruthlessness arose from contempt for the good opinion of others, and for himself as evaluated by
them; but Caesar's clemency was the effect of unlimited and illimitable
self-love.

> In this speech was conveyed, not the indignant and menacing spirit of Sylla,
> who despised the very power of which he was himself possessed; but the conscious
> state and reflecting condescension of a prince who admired and wished to
> recommend his own greatness.[78]

'For always I am Caesar.' More analytically than Shakespeare – who
had certainly sensed this dimension – Ferguson explored the ideological aspects of a politics of unrestrained personality, and found them in
Epicurean and Stoic philosophy.

> In such a situation there were many temptations to be wicked; and in such
> a situation likewise, minds that were turned to integrity and honour had a
> proportionate spring and scope to their exertions and pursuits. The range of the
> human character was great and extensive, and men were not likely to trifle within
> narrow bounds; they were destined to be good or to be wicked in the highest
> measure, and, by their struggles, to exhibit a scene interesting and instructive
> beyond any other in the history of mankind.
> Among the causes that helped to carry the characters of men in this age to
> such distant extremes, may be reckoned the philosophy of the Greeks, which was

---

[77] Ferguson, 1799, IV, p. 101.    [78] *Ibidem*, p. 104.

lately come into fashion, and which was much affected by the higher ranks of men in the State. Literature, by the difficulty and expence of multiplying copies of books, being confined to persons having wealth and power, it was considered as a distinction of rank, and had its vogue not only as an useful, but as a fashionable accomplishment. The lessons of the school were admitted as the elements of every liberal and active profession, and they were quoted at the bar, in the field, in the Senate, and every where in the conduct of real affairs. Philosophy was considered as an ornament, as well as a real foundation of strength, ability, and wisdom, in the practice of life. Men of the world, instead of being ashamed of their sect, affected to employ its language on every important occasion, and to be governed by its rules so much as to assume, in compliance with particular systems, distinction of manners, and even of dress. They embraced their forms in philosophy, as the sectaries in modern times have embraced theirs in religion; and probably in the one case honoured their choice by the sincerity of their faith and the regularity of their practice, much in the same degree as they have done in the other.[79]

Caesar becomes the representative Epicurean, Cato the Stoic. The former was a philosophy for men 'glutted with national prosperity; they thought that they were born to enjoy what their fathers had won, and saw not the use of those austere and arduous virtues'[80] which had won it. Even those, like Caesar, who could practise the hard virtues, did so for show and to an end, which was pleasure. 'All good was private. The public was a mere imposture,'[81] as were the doctrine of a future state of rewards and punishments, and the belief that the world was governed by anything beyond the chance fall of atoms. The Stoics taught belief in providence, duty and the public good; they also held that the moral virtues were goods of the mind, not goods of fortune,

and that whoever does possess them has nothing to hope, and nothing to fear, and can have but one sort of emotion, that of satisfaction and joy; that his affections, and the maxims of his station, as a creature of God, and as a member of society, lead him to act for the good of mankind; and that for himself he has nothing more to desire, than the happiness of acting this part.[82]

Both philosophies taught the acting of a part; but the Epicurean theatre was provided by the ego, the Stoic by the republic. Ferguson was an ordained minister, though he no longer practised as one, and must have been aware that he was comparing two codes of ethics for the unredeemed self, two modes of pure self-possession. He later supplies one of the chillier accounts ever written of the advent of Christianity:

---

[79] Ferguson, 1799, II, pp. 360–1.     [80] *Ibidem*, p. 362.
[81] *Ibidem*.     [82] *Ibidem*, p. 365.

In one of the years of this period, or about the year of Rome seven hundred and fifty-one, is fixed, by the vulgar computation, the commencement of our aera at the birth of Christ; an event, not calculated to have an immediate influence on the transactions of State, or to make a part in the materials of political history, though destined, in the wisdom and goodness of Providence, to produce, in a few ages, a great change in the institutions, manners, and general character of nations.

At this date, from the imperfect records which remain, we have scarcely any materials of history, besides the occurrences of the court, and the city of Rome; the public entertainments that were given, the occasions on which they were exhibited, and the provision that was made in the capital for the subsistence and pleasure of an idle and profligate populace.[83]

The ordinary administration of Augustus, in pursuing the political, civil, and military forms, which he had established, no doubt was able and successful; but being once described, does not admit of repetition. The more interesting subjects of history, transactions that rouse the passions, and keep in suspense the expectations, the hopes, and the fears of men, were in this reign most carefully avoided.[84]

Ferguson knew that the subject of classical history was the performance of memorable deeds, for which the republic provided the highest ancient setting, and that he was recounting a history at the end of which there were no more such deeds to perform, and consequently no such history to write. It had been the *raison d'être* of the Romans of the republic to enact and inhabit that kind of history, but with the corruption of the republic the self, performer of the deeds, had run riot; philosophy had become a mode of self-exhibition, and there had been two philosophies, one for the disciplined self and one for the undisciplined. The cause of all this had been the separation of the military and civic principles, the hypertrophy of the one and the atrophy of the other; the self-destruction of virtue in a world in which there was nothing beyond the active self. Hence the closing scene, in which the self was condemned to be either the best or the worst: Cato or Caesar, Marcus Aurelius or Caligula. The second pair of names is the measure of Augustus' success in moving the world beyond the dilemma posed by the first.

Augustus was the product of an eliminating contest among warlords, trying to put an end to the conditions which had produced his own power, and to the titanism which men were required to exhibit. He therefore tried to revive the civil power by concentrating it in his own person, leaving the senate and the republican magistracies intact while himself

[83] Ferguson, 1799, V, p. 233.     [84] *Ibidem*, pp. 238–9.

becoming consul, tribune, censor, pontifex and so forth, and holding all offices simultaneously. This attempt to restore the republic was doubly ambiguous.

> There were meetings of the Senate, and assemblies of the People; there were laws enacted, and assemblies made; affairs proceeded, as usual, in the name of the Consul, the Censor, the Augur, and Tribune of the People. The only change which had happened, and that which the Emperor endeavoured to disguise, was, that he himself acted in all these capacities, and dictated every resolution in the Senate, and pointed out every candidate who was to succeed in the pretended elections.
>
> In these appearances of a head and members of government, which were preserved by Octavius [i.e., Augustus], we are not to suppose that there was any image of that mixed constitution of monarchy, which subsists with so much advantage in some of the kingdoms of modern Europe.[85]

In the republic, many magistracies preserve liberty; in the mixed monarchy, checks and balances preserve it in a very different form. But if the principate is not the image of a modern monarchy, it was the image of the republic: Gibbon's 'image of a free constitution . . . preserved with decent reverence'.[86] But ambiguity and unreality did not end there; the emperors as *principes* abated nothing of their power as *imperatores*, and the embodiment of the army as a force which the citizenry did not control remained precisely where it was. There was a sense in which Augustus did his best:

> this semblance of the ancient republic . . . vested the Emperor himself with a species of civil character, and with a political consideration which he could employ in support of his military power, and which, in some measure, secured him against the caprice of troops, who might think themselves entitled, at pleasure, to subvert what they alone had established. It enabled him to treat their mutinies as acts of treason, and as crimes of State. He was no longer obliged to court their favour, or to affect condescension, in order to obtain their obedience. He accordingly, in consequence of the late votes of the Senate, changed the style of his address to the legions, calling them *Milites*, not *Commilitones*; *Soldiers*, not *Fellow-Soldiers*, as formerly.[87]

But all this was only verbal, the compensatory rhetoric of a *gouvernement ambigu*. The soldiers were not citizens and their commanders were not magistrates; military anarchy could still recur, as it did at the deaths of Caligula, Nero and Commodus. Augustus was obliged to discourage further wars of conquest, and other means to the performance of deeds

---

[85] *Ibidem*, p. 138.     [86] Below, p. 423.     [87] Ferguson, 1799, v, p. 140.

by the undisciplined self; to try to bring about the end of a history in which men acted; but it would be three centuries before the emperors could emasculate the legions, at the price of bringing in the barbarians. Meanwhile the principate could not rid itself of the character of a military monarchy, or escape from a political culture in which it was necessary for leading actors to be either the best or the worst of men. The principate could not become a modern courtly monarchy; the empire could not become a modern polite or commercial society.

The history of the republic finally reaches an end with the accession of Caligula, who succeeds to the principate as next of kin by a kind of hereditary right.[88] But this does not make the office of emperor a hereditary kingship, or indeed give it an unambiguous title; neither does it make the palace of the Julio-Claudians a court. There have been some moves in this direction; Marcus Agrippa exhibits the self-respect of one who can serve his prince without sycophancy;[89] and indeed, modern historians might say that such an ethos had struck far deeper roots in Hellenistic monarchy and great Roman houses than Ferguson allows. In his mind, the court exists to provide politeness and manners, and is therefore modern; the ancient world was obliged to choose between freedom and despotism, the city and the army, the best and the worst.

The manners of the imperial court, and the conduct of succeeding Emperors, will scarcely gain credit with those who estimate probabilities from the standard of modern times. But the Romans were capable of much greater extremes than we are acquainted with. They retained, through all the steps of the revolution which they had undergone, their ferocity entire, without possessing, along with it, any of those better qualities, which, under the republic, had directed their courage to noble, at least to great and national purposes.

The state itself was just emerged from democracy, in which the pretensions to equality checked the ordinary rules which, under monarchies, are made of fortune and superior conditions. The distinctions of royalty, and with these the proprieties of behaviour which pertain to high rank, were unknown. An attempt at elegant magnificence and courtly reserve, which, in established monarchies, makes a part of the royal estate, and a considerable support of its dignity, were avoided in this fallen republic, as more likely to excite envy and hatred, than deference or respect.

The Roman Emperors, perhaps, in point of profusion, whether public or private, exceeded every other Sovereign of the world; but their public expences consisted in the exhibition of shows and entertainments, in which they admitted the meanest of the people to partake with themselves. Their personal expences consisted not so much in the ostentation of elegance or refined pleasure, as in a

---

[88]  *Ibidem*, p. 398.        [89]  Ferguson, 1799, IV, p. 433.

serious attempt to improve sensuality into a continual source of enjoyment; and their pleasures consisted, of consequence, in the excesses of a brutal and retired debauch.

The manners of imperial Rome are thus described in the remains of a satire [*Note*: That of Petronius], as elegant in the style as it is gross and disgusting in matter, and which we may suppose to be just in the general representation, whatever we may think of its application to any of the Princes whose names and successions have been mentioned. [*Note*: Mr. Voltaire has with contempt rejected its supposed application to the manners of a court.][90]

Although it would be absurd to imagine such a satire levelled at the corruptions of a modern court, whose principal weakness is vanity, and whose luxury consists in ostentation, we must not therefore reject every supposed application of it to the pollutions of a Roman barrack, or, what nearly resembled a barrack, the recesses of a Roman palace, where the human blood that was shed in sport, was sometimes mingled with the wine that was spilt in debauch. [*Note*: The Romans had combats of gladiators exhibited while they were at table.][91]

There is not much left of Ferguson's earlier claim that the historical function of the Christian religion was to transform the manners of nations; this is a work of Enlightenment, after all. Manners are the product of courts, or they are the product of commerce. If the principate failed in the former respect, it may have had more success in the latter; and there are passages in Ferguson's fifth volume – published, we must recall, in 1783, when he had had ample opportunity to read the opening chapters of the *Decline and Fall* – which depict the unity and peace of the empire, the improvement of provincial administration, the growth of jurisprudence, and the prosperity of commerce. It is perhaps hinted that too much of the consumption of luxury goods was concentrated in the capital; this was not an international market maintained by a plurality of trading states. Yet the growth of manners and arts is allowed for;

even Romans themselves were taught to become artists and mechanics, and, by following a multiplicity of inferior pursuits and occupations, were taught to let down the haughty spirit of the conquerors of the world to the level of the nations it had conquered.[92]

Primitive virtue, the spirit of conquest, must be itself or die; it hardly matters whether Ferguson is obsessed with its value or with its historicity. As it vanished among the citizens, decayed in the legions, and became

---

[90] The allusion may be to a note appended by Voltaire to his *Discours de Réception à l'Académie Française*; Van den Heuvel, 1961, p. 1431. He suggests that the *plaisirs* of Nero must have been more refined than the *débauches* of Trimalchio. Ferguson is less sure, but thinks it true of a modern court.
[91] Ferguson, 1799, v, pp. 404–7.     [92] *Ibidem*, p. 479.

brutalised in the imperial household, it lost all relationship to the spread of manners, and civilisation became morally as well as materially incapable of self-defence. A consequence was that the ancient personality was not transformed. Reverting to the history of philosophy, Ferguson comments on the paradox that:

While men had rights to preserve, and hazardous duties to perform, on the public scene, they had affected to believe, with Epicurus, that pleasure was the standard of good and of evil. But now, when the public occupations of State were withheld from them, and when personal safety was the highest object in their view, they returned to the idea, which seemed to have inspired the virtue of ancient times, that men were made happy by the qualities which they themselves possessed, and by the good they performed, not by the mere gifts of fortune.[93]

A Christian might have queried the ancient ethos after that, but Ferguson was content with Stoicism in the antique world, and perhaps in his own. He continued:

From these materials, the law was sometimes furnished with practitioners, the Senate, with its members, the army with commanders, and the empire itself with its head; and the throne of Caesar, in the vicissitudes to which it was exposed, presented examples as honourable to human nature in some respects, as they were degrading and shameful in others. In these varieties, however, it is no disparagement to the good, to suppose that they were not able to compensate the bad, or to produce effects, to which the greatest abilities in a few individuals cannot extend.

Then there is a sentence which places Ferguson in a line running from Gordon, if not Mexía, through Hume, Robertson and Gibbon:

The wisdom of Nerva gave rise to a succession, which, in the persons of Trajan and the Antonines, formed a counterpart to the race of Tiberius, Caligula, Claudius, and Nero; and it must be admitted, that if a people could be happy by any other virtue than their own, there was a period in the history of this empire, during which the happiness of mankind may have been supposed complete. This however is but a fond and mistaken apprehension. A People may receive protection from the justice and humanity of single men; but can receive independence, vigour and peace of mind only from their own. Even the virtues of this happy succession could do no more than discontinue, for a while, the former abuses of power, administrate justice, restrain the guilty, and protect the innocent. Many of the evils under which human nature was labouring, still remained without a cure; and the empire, after having in the highest degree

---

[93] *Ibidem*, p. 416.

experienced the effects of wisdom and goodness in such hands, was assailed anew with all the vices of the opposite extreme.[94]

At this point in the 1799 edition, Ferguson inserted a note which carries on his history of human nature in terms borrowed from Edmund Burke.

These extremes scarcely gain credit with the modern reader, as they are so much beyond what his own experience or observation can parallel. Nero seems to have been a brute of some mischievous kind; Aurelius, of an order superior to man; and these prodigies, whether in the extreme of good or of evil, exhibited amidst the ruins of the Roman republic, are no longer to be found. Individuals were then formed on their specific dispositions to wisdom or folly. In latter times, they are more cast in a general mould, which gives a certain form independent of the materials. Religion, fashion, and manners, prescribe more of the actions of men, or mark a deeper track in which men are constrained to move.

The maxims of a Christian and a Gentleman, the remains of what men were taught by these maxims in the days of chivalry, pervade every rank, have some effect in places of the least restraint; and if they do not inspire decency of character, at least awe the profligate with the fear of contempt, from which even the most powerful are not secure. In so much, that if human nature wants the force to produce an Aurelius or a Trajan, it is not so much exposed to the infamies of a Domitian or a Nero.[95]

Aristotle had written that, without the city, man must be either a god or a beast; and Ferguson is saying the same of Roman emperors, exerting absolute power in the decay of civic virtue. But virtue is the characteristic of antique and even primitive men; they generate it in themselves by the act of associating with their fellows; and the solidarity of their clan, or the discipline of the city, only release in men that which they are in themselves. Under the conditions of the ancient republic, the extremes of human nature are let loose; the Romans, or any free people, may be godlike to each other and beasts to those they rule; and the gods they worship are, in the last analysis, themselves. When civic virtue disintegrates men are not checked from being themselves, and the self-worshipping religion of Stoicism can only make them gods of a very fragile kind. After Marcus Aurelius comes Commodus, who is a lesser Nero or Caligula. Men are only what they are, and in the fall of empire naked human virtue must go back to the desert, to associate again.

But under modern conditions, there are manners, which make men both less and more than they are 'on their specific disposition'. Manners were complex social moulds or forms, generated in human society by

---

94 *Ibidem*, pp. 417–18.     95 *Ibidem*, p. 418 n.

forces originating in association but distinct from the sheer activity of virtue; they were disseminated through society by the forces making for communication, such as empire and commerce, which might disseminate them on an international scale. Their 'softer influence', in Gibbon's phrase, made them for Burke 'of more importance than laws',[96] and Ferguson is telling us here that they operate upon human nature, conditioning and conventionalising it and preventing it from rising as high or falling as low as it is in itself capable of doing. This is why the moderns find the ancients hard to believe in; they were more themselves than we are.

Commerce, to the *philosophes*, had been the great engine substituting *moeurs* and *manières* for the barbaric virtue of antiquity and the unreasoning spirituality of the Christian centuries. But the second paragraph of Ferguson's note signals an important change in perspective. In a famous passage of the *Reflections on the Revolution in France* (1790), to which Ferguson seems to be alluding, Burke had lamented the decline of the age of chivalry, 'in which vice lost half its evil by losing all its grossness', and had proceeded:

> This mixed system of opinion and sentiment had its origin in the antient chivalry; and the principle, though varied in its appearance by the varying state of human affairs, subsisted and influenced through a long succession of generations, even to the time we live in. If it should ever be totally extinguished, the loss I fear will be great. It is this which has given its character to modern Europe. It is this which distinguished it under all its forms of government, and distinguished it to its advantage, from the states of Asia, and possibly from those states which flourished in the most brilliant periods of the antique world.[97]
>
> Nothing is more certain than that our manners, our civilisation, and all the good things which are connected with manners and with civilisation, have in this European world of ours depended for ages upon two principles, and were indeed the result of both combined. I mean the spirit of a gentleman, and the spirit of religion.[98]

Burke had rebuked 'our economical politicians' for too readily supposing that modern manners owed their being to nothing but the growth of commerce, and in the face of the French Revolution had proclaimed that their roots in medieval chivalry and clerisy must not be torn up.[99] It was a great re-assertion of what the Scottish Enlightenment had known all along: that eighteenth-century commercial society was aristocratically governed and shared aristocratic values. Ferguson had no objection to endorsing Burke's proclamation, though in emphasising that modern

---

[96] *Letters on a Regicide Peace*, 1; Canavan, 1999, III, p. 126.    [97] Pocock, 1987a, p. 67.
[98] *Ibidem*, p. 69.    [99] *Ibidem*, pp. 69–70.

manners prevent the re-appearance of Nero, he does not mention Burke's
addendum that the Jacobins are far worse than Nero, since they intend
the universal subversion of manners by revolution. Yet it seems to have
been Burke and the French Revolution that obliged Ferguson to re-inject
the Christian religion into the historical process. As far back as his friend
Robertson's *View of the Progress of Society in Europe*, thirty years before
1799, he could find chivalry and clerical learning identified as the medieval contribution to modern manners and connected with the revival
of European commerce after the Crusades. But this was whiggish history,
the pursuit of the origins of modernity as far back as they might be found,
and entailed the convention that medieval was part of modern history.
Once Christianity was acknowledged, there existed the problem of late
antiquity: of the impact of Christian belief and practice on ancient virtue
and – as far as these existed – ancient manners. Ferguson had observed
in passing that the historical function of Christianity was to transform
the manners of nations; but if 'manners' were modern and succeeded to
'virtue', it must be considered how the transformation of religion – and
that was what Christianity had achieved – had impacted upon virtue
in its decay. It is not just the accident that Gibbon wrote the *Decline and
Fall of the Empire* and Ferguson the *Progress and Termination of the Republic*
which ensures that this theme is treated by the probably Epicurean
gentleman scholar and not by the Stoic professor and former minister.

There remained the problem of how the Roman empire had failed to
become a stable civilisation based on commerce and manners. By way of
conclusion, Ferguson wrote a coda making it clear that this was a period
in which men declined from being titans of good and evil, under a republic whose principle had been virtue, to become mediocrities of moral
indifference, under a despotism which failed to make its principle either
manners or commerce. The failure remained that of the military institution, acting separately from the civil. In all of this, Ferguson's portrayal
of the Decline and Fall is close to that which had been foreshadowed in
Gibbon's opening chapters; but perhaps it is because he does not confront the impact of religion upon personality, bridging the gap between
high and late antiquity, that Ferguson ends by stressing that the men of
the former age – whatever the prestige of ancient virtue in his own time –
are now a very remote historical species.

For some of the first ages, nevertheless, the frontier continued to be defended,
and the internal peace of the empire to be tolerably secure. Commerce flourished, and the land was cultivated; but these were but poor compensations for

the want of that vigour, elevation, and freedom of mind, which perished with the Roman republic itself, or with the political character of the other nations which had been absorbed in the depth of this ruinous abyss.

The military and other political virtues, which had been exerted in forming this empire, having finished their course, a general relaxation ensued, under which, the very forms that were necessary for its preservation were in process of time neglected. As the spirit which gave rise to these forms was gradually spent, human nature fell into a retrograde motion, which the virtues of individuals could not suspend; and men, in the application of their faculties even to the most ordinary purposes of life, suffered a slow and insensible, but almost continual, decline.

In this great empire, the fortunes of nations over the most cultivated parts of the earth, being embarked on a single bottom, were exposed to one common and general wreck. Human nature languished for some time under a suspension of national exertions, and the monuments of former times were, at least, overwhelmed by one general irruption of barbarism, superstition, and ignorance. The effects of this irruption constitute a mighty chasm in the transition from ancient to modern history, and make it difficult to state the transactions and manners from the one, in a way to be read and understood by those whose habits and ideas are taken entirely from the other.

FINIS.

Such are the final sentences of Adam Ferguson's *History of the Progress and Termination of the Roman Republic*.[100] It is not the superstitious and ignorant barbarians whom moderns find difficult to understand; they are closer to us than the paragons of republican virtue and the monsters of corruption and despotism, whom we have studied closely enough to understand why we do not know them at all.

---

[100] Ferguson, 1799, v, pp. 418–19.

# Gibbon and the structure of decline

CHAPTER 17

# *The Antonine moment*

(1)

We at last approach the text of the *Decline and Fall*, after a sesquimillennial journey from the construction of the Tacitean narrative which is one of the explanatory foundations of Gibbon's first volume. The history of that narrative, traceable as far back before Tacitus as Polybius, is that of a possibly insoluble problem in the relations between *libertas* and *imperium*. Liberty achieves empire, but is corrupted by it, and empire cannot be retained once it has destroyed the liberty that once conquered and no longer defends it; yet this self-destructive *libertas* remains intensely admired, under the name of *virtus*, as one of the highest achievements of human nature. It is possible to see Athenian philosophy, perhaps as Latinised by Cicero, as a criticism of virtue in this warrior and combative form; but the Athenian 'empire' was transitory in comparison with the Roman, and never became a transformation of provinces into a shared ecumenical culture. The problem of *libertas et imperium* is therefore carried on in the history of Latin historiography rather than Greek philosophy, and the criticism of both *virtus* and history is achieved by Augustine, who presents both as the work of the *libido dominandi*, and the *civitas dei* as the alternative to history. The criticism of *virtus*, *libertas* and *imperium* as having no foundation but the conquering sword is conducted in Christian and otherworldly terms, where one Roman at least had developed it in the materialist form found in Appian; but there is a process by which republic, empire and church are replaced by secular, commercial and Enlightened language critical of both the pagan and the Christian worlds.

The texts of Roman historiography including Tacitus – as they survive and are rediscovered during the 'Christian millennium' and are then written into the 'Enlightened narrative' – are with little exception composed from a senatorial point of view. It is common ground among them that the Caesars destroyed *libertas* – even when it is recognised that *libertas* had already destroyed itself – and it is hardly at all claimed that they provided *libertas* or its equivalent in some new form. Against them, however, Eusebian ecclesiastical history affirms that Augustan empire provided a universal peace conducive to the birth of Christ and the spread of his Church; and there is the question of what happened when the empire became Christian, either the partner of the Church or its temporal aspect. This is a complex narrative, on the one hand spiritual – the *civitas dei* has come to earth – on the other, secular – there is now a *civitas terrena* capable of acting as vehicle of the Church. Empire acquires a history, in which its peace, prosperity and even commerce become the means of spiritual blessedness, and it is in principle possible to write their history as a secular process; but this is enormously slow in becoming a theme of the histories written in the Latin west during and after the Christian millennium. There is instead a history of how empire failed in the western provinces, due in Roman terms to the loss of *libertas* and civic virtue, in Christian terms to the sins of persecutors and heretics; and there is a fragmentary perception of the empire removed by Constantine as persisting in the Greek east, but repudiated by a Latin church claiming a supremacy derived from the apostle Peter. Constantine, the founder of an empire which permits the Church's presence in empire and above it, is also the architect of its failure in the west and its paradoxical translation from east to west in a divided form.

Decline and Fall has emerged as a complex and perhaps not a coherent narrative, in which the republic's loss of *libertas*, and its transformation into a principate capable of governing the *imperium* that *libertas* has acquired, is made the long-term cause of the loss of Rome and the western provinces four centuries later, so that the empire is the cause of its own decline. This linkage has appeared in the works of two Florentines, Bruni and Machiavelli, and may be connectable with 'the Machiavellian moment', meaning a peculiarly sharp Florentine perception of the high value and the historical fragility of civic virtue (the *libertas* that attained *imperium*), which is transmitted to other regions involved in the spread of western humanism. The history of the Latin provinces, however, does not end with the extinction of empire in 476. There is a further history, involving Justinian's re-establishment of Roman control in Italy, the advent of the Lombards, the iconoclastic controversy, the papal alliance with the Frankish kingdom in Gaul, and the *translatio imperii* to Charlemagne, which supplies a beginning for both the Christian millennium and the Enlightened narrative. This is Gibbon's 'triumph of barbarism and religion', into which we see his 'history of the decline and fall' becoming transformed.

Volume I of the *Decline and Fall* is concerned with the empire before Constantine, and is therefore a history of pre-Christian culture, in which the problem of *libertas* and *imperium* may be worked out in ancient terms. It is true that chapters 8 and 9 offer a portrait of barbarism, and chapters 15 and 16 one of religion – that is to say, of Christian culture before Constantine – but it is possible to see these as deeply significant digressions from the theme that the loss of *libertas* has to do with the failure of *imperium*. Before pursuing that theme through the chapters of Gibbon's first volume, it is vital to consider some apparent changes in his intention since his history had first been conceived. The original idea, he has told us, had been that of a history of the city of Rome, declining as it was abandoned by its emperors; only by stages, of which we know little directly, had this been replaced by the idea of a history of the decline of empire itself. The foundation of Constantinople, and the replacement of imperial by papal Rome, were late moments in both imagined processes; but the first moment in either could very well be supplied by Tacitus, as the armies' fatal discovery that emperors could be made elsewhere than at Rome. This *arcanum* could very well be backdated to the era of the Civil Wars themselves, thus deepening its involvement in the history of *libertas et imperium*, and awareness of this plays some part in Gibbon's consciousness, and ours, that this exploration of Decline and Fall is almost indefinitely retrospective. If the principate found itself dependent on armies it could not be sure of controlling, this was no more than a continuation of the problem confronting the republic once the Gracchan decay had set in.

But since the papal–imperial victory over the Florentine republic, and the liquidation of the imperial–papal competition for control of the *regnum italicum*, there had entered into political theory and historiography a new concept of territorial monarchy as the theatre of civil society. During the *siècle de Louis XIV*, this had offered enlightenment and the end of religious warfare at the price of a universal hegemony, which had been resisted by means involving a criticism that could be extended to the ancient Roman empire itself. Since that empire had destroyed the republic that had achieved it, the language of *libertas et imperium* could be directed against any monarchy that seemed too enormous; but the criticism must apply to the conquering republic itself. As far back as the fifteenth century, Bruni had called up the image of the Etruscan league of equal republics. Since then, Polybius had been scrutinised to see why the Aetolian and

Achaean leagues had failed against Rome, and Montesquieu's interest in *républiques confédératives* had been part of his criticism that single republics could avoid neither growth nor the corruption it must bring. During and after the wars against Louis XIV, monarchies and republics had joined in presenting the Enlightened utopia of an informal confederacy of equal states, held together by sovereignty and international law, commerce and a community of manners; and this presented territorial monarchy, ancient as well as modern, in an altogether new light. In the extensive territories it ruled, law, commerce and manners could develop and it could trade with its neighbours; if republics remained necessary to liberty, thought Hume, monarchies were necessary to politeness, and the universe of commerce was open to both. The attraction of ancient empire, above all the Roman, to historians was now that here could be studied monarchy's power to extend civilisation, carried as far as could be without either ancient liberty or a modern plurality of states; and could it be that there was something defective about ancient political economy, founded as it was on slavery rather than industry?

For these reasons Gibbon's first volume is built around a double paradox. He begins his account of the failure of empire in the Latin provinces two centuries before it occurred, and bases it on a Tacitean explanation that looks back to Augustus and even beyond. This is a narrative, a *récit* of events displaying the principate's inability to control its armies, with the barbarians as a gathering presence on the frontiers of an *imperium* decreasingly energised by *libertas*. It is, however, a *peinture* of Roman imperial culture at the height of its prosperity and politeness. That the era from Nerva to Commodus was something of a golden age was already a commonplace among historians, but not even Lipsius' *De magnitudine Romana* was a *peinture* of quite this order. Chapters 1–3 of the *Decline and Fall* are a portrait of *moeurs* which places Gibbon at once in the grand company of the Enlightened historians; and these chapters supply keys to the organisation of the *Decline and Fall* which extend beyond the thematic. Gibbon has solved the problem which confined even Robertson to a series of appendices set aside from his narrative; from beginning to end, his six volumes will alternate between chapters of narrative and chapters of digression and rumination describing the manners of peoples, or historical situations from time to time existing. These chapters will balance philosophy against narrative, resting upon the infrastructure of erudition. On another scale, manners exist within the purview of monarchy, and he has found a Humean way of exhibiting the empire of the Antonines as a monarchy, something other than a despotism. But what is the relation of manners to virtue? The enemies of this world of culture are the armies, who interfere with its workings and in the end fail to defend it; the *imperium sine libertate* lacks *virtus*. But will it decline simply because the armies exploit and betray it, or is there some moral or material weakness at the heart of provincial or metropolitan culture itself? This problem appears by the end of Gibbon's second chapter.

(II)

In the second century of the Christian Aera, the empire of Rome comprehended the fairest part of the earth, and the most civilised portion of mankind. The frontiers of that extensive monarchy were guarded by ancient renown and disciplined valour. The gentle, but powerful influence of laws and manners had gradually cemented the union of the provinces. Their peaceful inhabitants enjoyed and abused the advantages of wealth and luxury. The image of a free constitution was preserved with decent reverence. The Roman senate appeared to possess the sovereign authority, and devolved on the emperors all the executive powers of government. During a happy period of more than fourscore years, the public administration was conducted by the virtue and abilities of Nerva, Trajan, Hadrian and the two Antonines. It is the design of this, and of the two succeeding chapters, to describe the prosperous condition of their empire; and afterwards, from the death of Marcus Antoninus, to deduce the most important circumstances of its decline and fall; a revolution which will ever be remembered, and is still felt by the nations of the earth.[1]

The opening paragraph of the *Decline and Fall* requires as close study as do the three chapters it introduces. It was written – we do not know how many times it was rewritten – when Gibbon was still in search of mastery over both his thesis and his style; but it is a highly wrought and complex piece of prose, conveying a diversity of messages which outline a problem. It clearly states that Rome has become both an 'empire' and an 'extensive monarchy'; two terms which have not an identical history. The 'extensive monarchy' – Hume's adjective had been 'enormous' – was held together by 'laws and manners', which had 'cemented the union of the provinces', a term we have not met before and a concept yet to be explained. 'Laws and manners' exercised a 'gentle but powerful influence', language which suggests that it was exercised, if not surreptitiously, at least without the full understanding of those whose perceptions it altered. We are looking at the Arendtian sequence in which behaviour matters more than action and the self is determined by forces other than its own. Whether there is

---

[1] *DF*, I, I; Womersley, 1994, I, p. 31.

anywhere a politics in which ancient Mediterranean humans can enact themselves, exercising what could be called their own *virtus*, may depend upon the extent to which the republic survives under the rule of emperors; and Christian and Enlightened thought had long agreed that *virtus* was too much a warlike and competitive ethos – a *libido dominandi* or a 'spirit of conquest' – which built up *imperium* and was destroyed by it. The question Gibbon is beginning to consider – in this he has had predecessors – is whether empire decayed because the *virtus* and *libertas* it had subordinated went on to disappear. He is, however, situating this by now familiar problem within the strongest 'modern' case that can be made for the ancient empire: that laws and manners, under extensive monarchy, made it a self-supportive civilisation, or civil society.

The Augustan principate, Montesquieu had said, was a *gouvernement ambigu*, and the attitude of Enlightened historians toward it was itself ambiguous. These ambiguities begin to be stated in Gibbon's opening paragraph. 'The frontiers of that extensive monarchy were guarded by ancient renown and disciplined valour'; by the military virtue which the republic had exported until it now survived in a condition separate from a civic virtue that no longer existed. Behind the frontiers it guarded, something had taken the place of virtue: the reign of manners, guaranteed by legal protection and encouraged by the growth of commerce, which in Ferguson's mind differentiated modern man from ancient. But this was still antiquity, and since the end of the story was known it must follow that there was something amiss with ancient politeness; being separated in its virtue, it was exposed to corruption. There was a 'union of the provinces', but 'their peaceful inhabitants enjoyed and abused the advantages of wealth and luxury'. The paired verbs form the first in a long series of Gibbonian counterweights, and tell us that there is something the matter with luxury: as it encourages manners, so it brings about corruption, just as Montesquieu had said of commerce; and perhaps the key is to be found in the word 'peaceful'. The provincials are defended; they are prosperous, happy and united by manners; but they do not defend themselves, and without the union of civil and military virtue they may lack the unity of moral self in the only form which ancient society brings. It is unstated whether there exists any alternative to virtue in the antique sense; meanwhile, the language Gibbon is using points towards the classic explanation of the decay of classical culture.

It is the design of this, and of the two succeeding chapters, to describe the prosperous condition of their empire; and afterwards, from the death of Marcus Antoninus, to deduce the most important circumstances of its decline and fall . . .

The crucial link is that between 'prosperous' and 'decline'. Something about the former leads towards the latter. Is this the classical moral critique of luxury, or the extravagance of an economy not yet modern or truly political?

In the paragraphs that follow we are introduced to the self-limitation of the empire, and in the same breath to our first encounter with the barbarians. We have to remember that republican virtue was incessantly expansive, but as it moved away from the city it turned inwards in civil war. Augustus, the last of the warlords, resolved to put an end to this process; in Gibbon's words, 'to relinquish the ambitious design of subduing the whole earth, and to introduce a spirit of moderation into the public councils'.[2] The Roman empire was an enormous, but not literally a universal monarchy. It now embarked on a policy of both limiting and monopolising virtue; 'military merit, as it is admirably expressed by Tacitus, was, in the strictest sense of the word, *imperatoria virtus*'.[3] But to set limits was, in the strictest sense of another Latin word, to establish *limites*, militarily defended frontiers; and to do so was to divide mankind into three categories. Beyond the *limites* were the barbarians, who now make their first appearance in the text; on the frontiers were the soldiers, who must be paid if their ambitions were to be moderated, and within the frontiers were the peaceful provincials.

Gibbon proceeds to a series of case studies in limitation and barbarism. Augustus holds back from 'the arrows of the Parthians', the tropical heat of Ethiopia and the Yemen (which 'protected the unwarlike natives of those sequestered regions'), and 'the forests and morasses of Germany'. The inhabitants of the last display what we will come to know as the characteristics of barbarism: they 'despised life when it was separated from freedom; and . . . by a signal act of despair, regained their independence[4] . . . by the slaughter of Varus and his three legions'.[5] Gibbon does not here consider the consolidation of Rhaetia, Noricum and Pannonia – the Danubian and Illyrian frontier offering protection to the Alpine passes, to be important in the empire's subsequent history. The next case is that of Britain, whose conquest was 'undertaken by the most stupid, maintained by the most dissolute, and terminated by the most timid of all the emperors', language which may suggest that this conquest was less than necessary.[6] These vices are set in contrast with the virtue of Tacitus' father-in-law Agricola, who would have proceeded

---

[2] *Ibidem.*    [3] *Ibidem*, p. 33, n. 5.
[4] *Ibidem*, p. 32. 'Despair' seems to mean 'desperation' rather than 'despondency'.
[5] *Ibidem*, n. 3.    [6] *Ibidem*, p. 33.

to the conquest of Ireland if the jealousy of *imperatoria virtus* had not forbidden him. It is still the end of virtue to conquer others and destroy their freedom; but

the various tribes of Britons possessed valour without conduct, and the love of freedom without the spirit of union. They took up arms with savage fierceness; they laid them down, or turned them against each other, with wild inconstancy; and while they fought singly, they were successively subdued.[7]

Nothing preserves the 'wild independence' of the Caledonians except their poverty.

The masters of the fairest and most wealthy climates of the globe turned with contempt from gloomy hills assailed by the winter tempest, from lakes concealed in a blue mist, and from cold and lonely heaths, over which the deer of the forest were chased by a troop of naked barbarians.[8]

A footnote directs the reader to 'the uniform imagery of Ossian's Poems, which, according to every hypothesis, were composed by a native Caledonian'.[9] Gibbon is, somewhat ironically, inclined to accept the authenticity of the poems in the controversy then raging, but his language here is obviously anti-Ossianic. There is in fact no literary evidence that Romans held the north of Britain in such Johnsonian contempt. The loss of savage freedom may be justified by the imposition of the discipline necessary to Roman virtue; but it is a question whether the legions of Agricola are not too far from home to preserve their own virtue and freedom. What would have happened if their general's 'rational, though extensive scheme of conquest' had taken them to Ireland is a counterfactual speculation never pursued. The confrontation with barbarism, foreshadowed by the death of Varus, does not take place in the outer islands. No 'signal act of despair' is recorded of the Caledonians.

The final case in this series is that of Trajan, last of the Roman conquerors. He subdues 'the new province of Dacia', whose king is permitted a constancy above the level of his barbarism; 'nor did he despair of his own and the public fortune, till . . . he had exhausted every resource both of valour and policy',[10] and these are Roman words. Trajan conquers the Tigris basin and marches to the Persian Gulf on a scale recalling Alexander; but he dies soon after, and his successor Hadrian resolves to resign his conquests. The god Terminus (a primitive black stone found on the Capitol), who once signified that the *limites* would never be withdrawn, now indicates that they will be no further extended; and we encounter

[7] *Ibidem.*   [8] *Ibidem*, p. 34.   [9] *Ibidem*, n. 13.   [10] *Ibidem*, p. 35.

the first of many anti-patristic jokes in a jeer at Augustine for jeering at Terminus.[11] But it is not clear whether Hadrian was moved by prudence or by envy. He is the most ambiguous figure among the last of the *principes*.

Nevertheless, we are now at midpoint in the series of 'five good emperors' which makes this the happiest age in the history of western mankind; and their 'goodness' consists (at this point) in possessing military virtue, but not practising it expansively. Expansion is still in its nature; the virtue of Agricola was frustrated by jealousy, that of Trajan by death (and geography); but prudence and moderation are also virtues, and senates or emperors can display them by checking the *imperatoria virtus*. It is this – indeed, this is all – which keeps mankind happy; but there are two words in the following passage which indicate that there is something unreal about it.

> By every honourable expedient they invited the friendship of the barbarians; and endeavoured to convince mankind that the Roman power, raised above the temptation of conquest, was actuated only by the love of order and justice.[12]

A barbarian in Tacitus had observed of this endeavour that 'they make a solitude and call it peace'.[13] But in his day there had been incessant wars on the frontiers, and these are supposed to have ceased.

> During a long period of forty-three years their virtuous labours were crowned with success; and if we except a few slight hostilities that served to exercise the legions of the frontier, the reigns of Hadrian and Antoninus Pius offer the fair prospect of universal peace.

A footnote indicates that all is not quite so simple:

> We must, however, remember that, in the time of Hadrian, a rebellion of the Jews raged with religious fury, though only in a single province.[14]

This is the war raised by Akiba and Bar-Kochba, and its ferocity was not confined to Judaea. That it was religious, however, and that it was Jewish, serve to set it aside from the course of Gibbon's narrative. The time when the inhabitants of the empire were moved to action by religious conviction has not yet arrived or begun to require attention; and we are going to discover ominous signs that, in Gibbon's mind, the Jews are self-excluded from the history of other peoples. But what he

---

[11] *Ibidem*, p. 36, n. 23: 'St. Augustin is highly delighted with the proof of the weakness of Terminus, and the vanity of the Augurs. See *De civitate Dei*, iv. 29.'
[12] Womersley, 1994, I, p. 37.    [13] *Agricola*, ch. 30.
[14] Womersley, 1994, I, pp. 37–8 and n. 27.

says in the next paragraph in apparent minimisation of the very massive Marcomannic war in the next reign is enough to show that this picture of the peace of the empire is of the nature of panegyric, and serves a rhetorical – in the end, an ironic – purpose.

The military strength, which it had been sufficient for Hadrian and the elder Antoninus to display, was exerted against the Parthians and the Germans by the emperor Marcus. The hostilities of the barbarians provoked the resentment of that philosophic monarch, and, in the prosecution of a just defence, Marcus and his generals obtained many signal victories, both on the Euphrates and on the Danube. The military establishment of the Roman empire, which thus assured either its tranquillity or success, will now become the proper and important object of our attention.[5]

Following the ancients from Polybius to Josephus, and the moderns from Lipsius to Guichardt,[16] Gibbon now sets about what seems almost a ritual account of the arms, training, discipline, tactics and fortification of the Roman legions.[7] This, however, is situated in a context of historical change,[18] in which the change from expansion to defence is a major but not the only item.

In the purer ages of the commonwealth, the use of arms was reserved for those ranks of citizens who had a country to love, a property to defend, and some share in enacting those laws, which it was their interest, as well as duty, to maintain. But in proportion as the public freedom was lost in extent of conquest, war was gradually improved into an art, and degraded into a trade.[19]

It is the voice of Machiavelli – Gibbon is exploiting the double meaning of *arte della guerra*[20] – and the voice of Montesquieu. But it is also the voice of the Hampshire captain, who had served in a militia no longer limited to proprietors taking time off from their lands, but based on extended periods of service and beginning to form a home-defence army maintained by the state. 'The populace,' remarks Gibbon in a footnote, 'excluded by the ancient constitution, was indiscriminately admitted by Marius,'[21] and under the principate the legions were recruited from landless peasants whose citizenship was only nominal, and

---

[5]  *Ibidem*, p. 38.
[16]  Above, pp. 284–5 (Lipsius); for Guichardt, *DF*, 1, n. 47, and *Library*, p. 141.
[7]  Womersley, 1994, 1, pp. 39–45.
[18]  He notes that the legion in the time of Vegetius differed from that in the time of Polybius. Womersley, 1994, 1, p. 41, and nn. 42, 43.
[19]  Womersley, 1994, 1, p. 38.      [20]  Pocock, 1975, pp. 199–200.
[21]  Womersley, 1994, 1, p. 38, n. 30. Gibbon does not often employ a phrase which may have resonance for others besides the present author.

like the mercenary troops of modern Europe, were drawn from the meanest, and very frequently from the most prodigal, of mankind.

That public virtue which among the ancients was denominated patriotism, is derived from a strong sense of our own interest in the preservation and prosperity of the free government of which we are members. Such a sentiment, which had rendered the legions of the republic almost invincible, could make but a very feeble impression on the mercenary servants of a despotic prince, and it became necessary to supply that defect by other motives, of a different, but not less forcible nature: honour and religion.[22]

Gibbon proceeds in this Montesquieuan vein to recount how a new set of *principes* – honour and religion – transformed the manners of the legions in the absence of virtue. We may recall his youthful account of how Virgil's *Georgics* had taught soldiers to be farmers;[23] but here he is depicting the formation of an ethos for long-service professionals. The legionaries took oaths of fidelity, which retained the religious force they had possessed for the primeval citizens and were reinforced by the worship of the eagles as 'gods of war'[24] (the phrase is from Tacitus). Together with regular pay and inflexible discipline,

from such laudable arts did the valour of the imperial troops receive a degree of firmness and docility, unattainable by the impetuous and irregular passions of barbarians.[25]

The classic description of weapons, training, tactics and fortification now takes up several pages, but there is a hint or two that all is not as it seems. To an account of the catapults and *ballistae* of pre-explosive artillery is appended this Machiavellian footnote:

We may observe, that the use of them in the field gradually became more prevalent, in proportion as personal valour and military skill declined with the Roman empire. When men were no longer found, their place was supplied by machines.[26]

And at a turning point in the text, we find the following:

Such were the arts of war by which the Roman emperors defended their extensive conquests, and preserved a military spirit, at a time when every other virtue was oppressed by luxury and despotism.[27]

These arts are not merely tactics; they entail an inculcation of manners, as soldiering becomes a trade. Virtue has turned from expansion to defence; but it was expansion which has separated military virtue from

[22] Womersley, 1994, I, p. 39.    [23] *EEG*, pp. 223–4.    [24] Womersley, 1994, I, pp. 39–40, n. 34.
[25] *Ibidem*, p. 40.    [26] *Ibidem*, p. 44, n. 59.    [27] *Ibidem*, p. 45.

every other – the eagles of the legion from the palladium of the city –
and left civic virtue (itself no longer expansive) to lie under oppression.
Despotism is both the cause and the consequence of this, and the role
of luxury is as yet none too clear. Gibbon soon after reverts to the study
of the provinces, living at peace and united by manners; but it is open
to us to wonder how long military virtue and civil manners can survive
when separated from each other. The latter are a poor defence against
luxury and despotism; they can rely on nothing but the former for defence against the barbarians or against civil war and anarchy originating
within.

(III)

Gibbon now proceeds, with clarity but in the form of a challenging
contrast, to depict the Roman empire as a single civilisation, and at the
same time to confront it with the modern culture of plural sovereignties
that has replaced it on the same ground.

> We have attempted to explain the spirit which moderated, and the strength
> which supported, the power of Hadrian and the Antonines. We shall now en-
> deavour, with clearness and precision, to describe the provinces once united
> under their sway, but, at present, divided into so many independent and hostile
> states.[28]

If the *Decline and Fall* can be thought of as possessing an epic structure –
as some contend it can – the catalogue of provinces which follows
occupies the place of Homer's Catalogue of the Ships. The provinces
of the empire are described in order, and in each case there is identified
the modern political structure which occupies the ancient territory. The
effect is twofold. In the first place, the description often furnishes a bridge
between pre-Roman, Roman and modern history.

> The Tiber rolled at the foot of the seven hills of Rome, and the country of the
> Sabines, the Latins, and the Volsci, from that river to the frontiers of Naples,
> was the theatre of her infant victories. On that celebrated ground the first
> consuls deserved triumphs; their successors adorned villas, and *their* posterity
> have erected convents.[29]
>
> The appellation of Roumelia, which is still bestowed by the Turks on the
> extensive countries of Thrace, Macedonia, and Greece, preserves the memory
> of their ancient state under the Roman empire . . . When we reflect on the fame
> of Thebes and Argos, of Sparta and Athens, we can scarcely persuade ourselves

---

[28] *Ibidem*, p. 47.   [29] *Ibidem*, pp. 49–50, and n. 76. Gibbon's emphasis.

that so many immortal republics of ancient Greece were lost in a single province of the Roman empire, which, from the superior influence of the Achaean league, was usually denominated the province of Achaia.[30]

Phoenicia and Palestine were sometimes annexed to, and sometimes separated from, the jurisdiction of Syria. The former of these was a narrow and rocky coast; the latter was a territory scarcely superior to Wales, either in fertility or extent. Yet Phoenicia and Palestine will for ever live in the memory of mankind; since America, as well as Europe, has received letters from the one, and religion from the other.[31]

Notwithstanding the change of masters and of religion, the new city of Rome, founded by Constantine on the banks of the Bosphorus, has ever since remained the capital of a great monarchy.[32]

Each ship is shown on its voyage through history, but at the same time the catalogue has a spatial configuration. The provinces of the former empire are regrouped in modernity as two great interlocking chains, the one Christian and European, extending from Spain to Dalmatia and from Britain to Transylvania. The former Noricum and Pannonia

now contain the residence of a German prince, who styles himself Emperor of the Romans, and form the centre, as well as strength, of the Austrian power.[33]

The language seems notably cool; Gibbon's Europe has little need of its Habsburg and Danubian frontier. The other chain is Muslim and Ottoman, extending from Moldavia and Wallachia south through Asia Minor to Egypt, and west to the Atlantic coast of the Maghrib and 'the residence of the barbarian whom we condescend to style the Emperor of Morocco',[34] a second *roi fainéant* to match the civilised Austrian? There is to be more to the Decline and Fall than the Germanisation of the western provinces. Perhaps it is this great partition between Enlightenment and Islam which accounts for Gibbon's otherwise rather unexpected reference to 'independent and hostile states'. The kingdoms and republics of the Enlightened west were supposed to be united by commerce rather than divided by war. If the Turkish system is slavish and despotic, and parts of it – Bosnia, Circassia – marked by conditions which may be called 'savage',[35] it might seem that barbarism has not vanished from the lands it formerly invaded; but Gibbon does not here use that term of the Ottoman extensive monarchy. By the time the Catalogue of the Provinces is complete, he has begun to direct his little shafts against

---

[30] *Ibidem*, pp. 51, 52.   [31] *Ibidem*, p. 53.   [32] *Ibidem*, pp. 51–2.
[33] *Ibidem*, p. 51.   [34] *Ibidem*, p. 54.
[35] *Ibidem*, p. 51. Gibbon does not differentiate between the terms 'savage' and 'barbarian', and seems to use them interchangeably.

authorities he considers unreliable – 'M. de Voltaire, unsupported by either fact or probability, has generously bestowed the Canary Islands on the Roman empire;'[36] 'Templeman's Survey of the Globe; but I distrust both the doctor's learning and his maps'[37] – and can conclude his first chapter with estimates of the empire's less than universal extent.

By now we know Gibbon's central strategy for displaying and analysing the Antonine moment. Behind a carapace of military virtue, already undergoing the consequences of its separation from the civic, a culture of manners becomes visible as an effect of the historiographic move from Rome to the provinces. Chapter 2 of the *Decline and Fall* – 'Of the Union and Internal Prosperity of the Roman Empire in the Age of the Antonines' – is an encomium, which becomes a criticism, of the extent of an ancient Enlightenment.

There have been, says Gibbon, empires of greater extent, more rapidly established. The Mongol power spread 'within less than a century . . . from the sea of China to the confines of Egypt and Germany', and 'the sovereign of the Russian deserts commands a larger portion of the globe' than did the Romans;[38] we remember that the Romanov conquest of the Eurasian steppe marks a turning point in the history of civilisation and barbarism.[39] The immediate point, however, is to display the Antonine empire as founded, in reality rather than appearance, on something more than conquest.

But the firm edifice of Roman power was raised and preserved by the wisdom of ages. The obedient provinces of Trajan and the Antonines were united by laws and adorned by arts. They might occasionally suffer from the partial abuse of delegated authority; but the general principle of government was wise, simple, and beneficent. They enjoyed the religion of their ancestors, whilst in civil honours and advantages they were exalted, by just degrees, to an equality with their conquerors.[40]

Gibbon is here at the height of a rhetoric which presents the Roman empire as more like an absolute monarchy than a despotism. It was a cardinal point with Hume and all admirers of Enlightened France that legal security and polite manners could flourish under an enormous monarchy, since (as Smith had shown his students) it was in the monarch's

---

[36] Womersley, 1994, I, p. 54, n. 87. The allusion seems to be to chapter CXLI of the *Essai sur les Moeurs*, where, however, Voltaire says only that the islands 'furent fréquentées par les Romains' before the disruption of the empire. In n. 86, Gibbon mentions the possibility (derived from Buffon) that Tenerife may be the Mount Atlas of the ancients.

[37] *Ibidem*, p. 55, n. 89. The allusion is to Thomas Templeman's *A New Survey of the Globe* (London, 1729); see *Library*, p. 263.

[38] Womersley, 1994, I, p. 56.   [39] *NCG*, p. 118.   [40] Womersley, 1994, I, p. 56.

interest to see that they did. Trajan was a lawgiver, and the great Roman jurists Papinian and Ulpian were to appear (and perish) when the Antonine system was actually collapsing.[41] 'The wisdom of ages', however – the phrase is calculated to make the imperial structure seem more ancient and durable than it actually was – recognised 'laws and arts', like 'laws and manners', as powerful principles of government: modes of social control which were most effective when left to operate freely, in a kind of negative, and indeed modern, liberty. This is what is meant by saying that Roman government was 'simple'.

There is a third principle. The words 'they enjoyed the religion of their ancestors' inform us that imperial rule was not only 'wise' and 'beneficent', but that it was tolerant. We are at a point of the greatest moment, since for the first time there is to be careful scrutiny of a social and political system of religion, and religion is one of two key principles in the organisation of the *Decline and Fall*, and of this series of studies. It has been premised so far that chapter 2 studies the Antonine empire as an empire of manners, and so as a species of Enlightenment; and it was the thrust of many forms of Enlightened thinking to reduce religion to an aspect of civil manners, and to stress that it was compatible with civil government only when it regarded itself as that and no more. It is part of the pathos of the Antonine moment that, for the last time in western history, its religion could be wholly contained within such a structure. Gibbon proceeds to investigate the terms on which ancient Enlightenment was possible, and to ask whether it is possible on any other.

The policy of the emperors and the senate, as far as it concerned religion, was happily seconded by the reflections of the enlightened, and by the habits of the superstitious, part of their subjects. The various modes of worship, which prevailed in the Roman world, were all considered by the people, as equally true; by the philosopher, as equally false; and by the magistrate, as equally useful. And thus toleration produced not only mutual indulgence, but even religious concord.[42]

The second sentence of this passage is well known, and is often abstracted from its context for use as an index to the extent of Gibbon's scepticism. It is possible to treat the passage and the pages that follow as a whole, and this may be done in at least two ways. One, which will be pursued here, is to continue the study of ancient religion as a system of

[41] *Ibidem*, pp. 147, 156, 171, 175.
[42] *Ibidem*, p. 56. Note Gibbon's use of the word 'enlightened', not so common in eighteenth-century usage as we lead ourselves to believe.

manners, and see how it fitted into the pattern of statecraft that converted the Roman empire into a civilisation. The other, more ambitious and far-reaching, is to consider Gibbon's account of polytheism as part of a philosophical and historical system, derived in large part from Hume's *Natural History of Religion*, here mentioned for the first time in the *Decline and Fall*.[43] Chapter 2 can be no more than the first stage in that system, and the imminence of later stages must be held to be implied; polytheism is to give way to monotheism, and the Ciceronian and Stoic philosophies that criticised the former are to be replaced by the neo-Platonist philosophies of the late empire, interacting with monotheism to furnish late-antique culture with the new invention of theology – a convergence of religion and philosophy that for the first time renders intolerance possible and tolerance necessary. This theme is to be of enormous importance in the *Decline and Fall*, and chapter 2 is one of several in the volume of 1776 that must be read as introducing it; but these will be reserved for separate treatment, while we pursue the Tacitean narrative of 'the first Decline and Fall'. For the duration of the Antonine moment, however long that may be, Gibbon has the relationships between the three forms of ancient theology – poetic, political, and philosophical – well under control, and can proceed to show how unlikely it was that a government of poly-theists by philosophers should ever resort to persecution. There was no separate order of priests seeking to reinforce their authority by enforcing dogma or ritual, since priests and magistrates were identical; and it can be shown that the age succeeding that of virtue was a golden age in the history of religion, since it was nothing other than an aspect of the edifice of manners. In their role as pontiffs, the emperors and senators

knew and valued the advantages of religion, as it is connected with civil gov-ernment. They encouraged the public festivals which humanise the manners of the people. They managed the arts of divination, as a convenient instrument of policy; and they respected as the firmest bond of society, the useful persuasion that, either in this or in a future life, the crime of perjury is most assuredly punished by the avenging gods. But whilst they acknowledged the general ad-vantages of religion, they were convinced that the various modes of worship contributed alike to the same salutary purposes; and that, in every country, the form of superstition, which had received the sanction of time and experience, was the best adapted to the climate and its inhabitants.[44]

Gibbon is beginning to use the word 'superstition' almost in a benign, or at least in a neutral, sense (we have seen the same tendency in Hume's

---

[43] *Ibidem*, p. 57, n. 3.    [44] *Ibidem*, p. 59.

*History of England*).[45] Under the Jewish law or the Christian sacraments, the case against superstition was that it made possible the rule of priests; but there was little danger of that under a plurality of ethnic cults, where the priests and the magistrates of the cities were the same men. And the tolerance of the empire was part of its commerce as well as its manners. He proceeds to depict the Roman statecraft, the policy by which 'the freedom of the city was bestowed on all the gods of mankind',[46] as part of the policy which encouraged the free movement of citizens, languages, letters, and goods as well as gods from one end of the empire to another. This was never a civic freedom:

> The provinces of the empire (as they have been described in the previous chapter) were destitute of any public force, or constitutional freedom. . . . The public authority was everywhere exercised by the ministers of the senate and of the emperors, and that authority was absolute, and without control. But the same salutary maxims of government, which had secured the peace and obedience of Italy, were extended to the most distant conquests. A nation of Romans was gradually formed in the provinces, by the double expedient of introducing colonies, and of admitting the most faithful and deserving of the provincials to the freedom of Rome.[47]

An extensive monarchy will be absolute, but under it the term 'freedom' can be used in the two senses of positive (lost) and negative (retained). Such a monarchy can flourish by the extension to all its subjects of languages, manners and arts; of civil peace, legal security and that fabric of rights under jurisprudence for which the French term in Gibbon's day was *bourgeoisie*. The Roman empire was what German theorists had begun to call a *bürgerlich Gesellschaft*. The spread of colonies and citizenship led to the spread of laws and languages; the western provinces were Latinised in their speech – to an extent which Gibbon possibly exaggerates – while the east ('civilised and corrupted')[48] remained Greek; and the empire became bilingual, using Latin as the speech of administration and Greek as that of culture. The only major exception was formed by

> the body of the natives in Syria, and especially in Egypt. The use of their ancient dialects, by secluding them from the commerce of mankind, checked the improvement of those barbarians. The slothful effeminacy of the former, exposed them to the contempt; the sullen ferociousness of the latter, excited the aversion of the conquerors. Those nations had submitted to the Roman power, but they seldom desired or deserved the freedom of the city . . .[49]

---

[45] *NCG*, pp. 210, 236.
[46] Womersley, 1994, I, p. 61. Cf. the 'republic of gods' appearing on p. 57.
[47] *Ibidem*, pp. 62–3.  [48] *Ibidem*, p. 65.  [49] *Ibidem*, p. 66.

It is worth remarking that the word 'barbarians' is being used here only in its linguistic sense, and that the 'commerce' from which language excludes the Syrians and Egyptians is that of culture rather than of trade. Greek and Latin culture formed the 'institutions' by which 'the nations of the empire insensibly melted away into the Roman name and people'.[50] There remains one gigantic though partial exception, that of the slaves. Gibbon explains that the empire was passing from an age of conquest, in which slaves were captives and frequently rebelled, to one of peace and commerce, in which they were bred as a species of property[51] and might hope for emancipation. He does not follow Adam Smith in emphasising that slavery was the foundation and condition of ancient virtue, or that the absence of free labour inhibited the growth of a market economy in antiquity;[52] unless the latter point is hinted at when he writes

we may venture to pronounce, that the proportion of slaves, who were valued as property, was more considerable than that of servants, who can be computed only as an expense. The youths of a promising genius were instructed in the arts and sciences, and their price was ascertained by the degree of their skill and talents. Almost every profession, either liberal or mechanical, might be found in the household of an opulent senator. The ministers of pomp and sensuality were multiplied beyond the conception of modern luxury. It was more for the interest of the merchant or manufacturer to purchase than to hire his workmen; and in the country, slaves were employed as the cheapest and most laborious instruments of agriculture.[53]

The Roman economy seems to have been one in which conspicuous expenditure counted for more than the surplus profits of industry; but Gibbon – possibly pursuing a familiar artifice of rhetoric – seems intent on admitting that it was a system of luxury and then giving the most favourable account of it that can be imagined. The population of the empire, slave and free, rose to one hundred and twenty million, a figure

which possibly exceeds that of modern Europe, and forms the most numerous society that has ever been united under the same system of government.[54]

The empire of civil peace has its own form of civic virtue. Gibbon now devotes several pages[55] to an account of the wealthy citizens' discharge of the duty of voluntarily erecting great public buildings at private expense,

---

[50] *Ibidem*, p. 67.
[51] *Ibidem*, '. . . the Romans were reduced to the milder but more tedious method of procreation'.
[52] For a reminder that this can be enlarged into an account of the Decline and Fall itself, see Schiavone, 2000.
[53] Womersley, 1994, I, pp. 68–9.     [54] *Ibidem*, p. 70.     [55] *Ibidem*, pp. 70–4.

and shows how this helped to fill the provinces with cities which have often vanished from the modern scene ('Turkish barbarism' has played its part here).[56] These cities were connected by the great military roads, and

> whatever evils either reason or declamation have imputed to extensive empire the power of Rome was attended with some beneficial consequences to mankind; and the same freedom of intercourse which extended the vices, diffused likewise the improvements of social life.[57]

These words once more illustrate Gibbon's capacity for holding an ironic balance between civilisation and corruption, and how the supersession of republic by empire was the supersession of virtue by manners. It needs further to be emphasised how far what Gibbon had in mind was the dissemination of material culture by the commerce of an extensive empire; he goes on to consider how the vine and the olive, grasses and the beasts that fed on them, minerals and the human populations thus employed, were distributed and exchanged among the provinces. The climax of chapter 2 is formed by Gibbon's first extended venture into the field of political economy.

> Agriculture is the foundation of manufactures; since the productions of nature are the materials of art. Under the Roman empire, the labour of an industrious and ingenious people was variously, but incessantly employed in the service of the rich. In their dress, their table, their houses, and their furniture, the favourites of fortune united every refinement of conveniency, of elegance and splendour, whatever could soothe their pride or gratify their sensuality. Such refinements, under the odious name of luxury, have been severely arraigned by the moralists of every age; and it might perhaps be more conducive to the virtue, as well as happiness, of mankind, if all possessed the necessaries, and none the superfluities of life. But in the present imperfect condition of society, luxury, though it may proceed from vice or folly, seems to be the only means that can correct the unequal distribution of property. The diligent mechanic, and the skilful artist, who have obtained no share in the division of the earth, receive a voluntary tax from the possessors of land; and the latter are prompted, by a sense of interest, to improve those estates, with whose produce they may purchase additional pleasures. This operation, the particular effects of which are felt in every society, acted with much more diffusive energy in the Roman world. The provinces would soon have been exhausted of their wealth, if the manufacturers and commerce of luxury had not insensibly restored to the industrious subjects the sums which were exacted from them by the arms and authority of Rome. As long as the circulation was confined within the bounds of the empire, it impressed the political machine with a new degree of activity, and its consequences, sometimes beneficial, could never become pernicious.[58]

---

[56] *Ibidem*, p. 76.    [57] *Ibidem*, p. 78.    [58] *Ibidem*, pp. 80–1.

Gibbon seems almost to have forgotten about slave labour, perhaps because he has by no means forgotten that in vindicating the luxury economy of antiquity he is also defending the consumer economy of the *ancien régime*. This somewhat physiocratic digression reminds us that the culture of politeness and manners idealised commerce from the point of view of the consumer and rentier, even before that of the investor or entrepreneur. But Gibbon is also well aware that the Roman economy drew money from the provinces in the form of tribute and taxation, and must return it to them, once the armies were paid and maintained, through conspicuous expenditure on personal luxury or public benefaction. Only Lipsius, among the pre-Enlightened scholars we have studied, seems to have dwelt on these matters. Whether the tax burden was absolutely heavy, or heavy only in relation to the limited circulation of coinage, Gibbon does not make clear; but the latter is suggested by the detailed enquiry that follows into the question whether the empire was being drained of silver by its export to India and Ceylon.[59] But if the climax of this chapter does indeed consist of this portrait of consumer economy at its height – the countryside acting as a garden to a chain of increasingly splendid cities – the anti-climax very soon follows.

It was scarcely possible that the eyes of contemporaries should discover in the public felicity the latent causes of decay and corruption. This long peace, and the uniform government of the Romans, introduced a slow and secret poison into the vitals of the empire. The minds of men were gradually reduced to the same level, the fire of genius was extinguished, and even the military spirit evaporated. The natives of Europe were brave and robust; Spain, Gaul, Britain, and Illyricum supplied the legions with excellent soldiers, and constituted the real strength of the monarchy. Their personal valour remained, but they no longer possessed that public courage which is nourished by the love of independence, the sense of national honour, the presence of danger, and the habit of command. They received laws and governors from the will of their sovereign, and trusted for their defence to a mercenary army. The posterity of their boldest leaders was contented with the rank of citizens and subjects. The most aspiring spirits resorted to the court or standard of the emperors; and the deserted provinces, deprived of political strength or union, insensibly sunk into the languid indifference of private life.[60]

We have returned with some abruptness to a Tacitean and Montesquieuan mode of explanation. The soldiers' loss of civic virtue is at the heart of the passage just quoted, but it entails a loss of both military and civic virtue by the citizens and provincials; and without virtue in both

---

[59] *Ibidem*, pp. 81–2.     [60] *Ibidem*, p. 83.

senses, Tacitus had insisted, the arts could never flourish. The paragraph that follows reviews with pungency the decline of letters, science, rhetoric and philosophy; and the cultural union of extensive monarchy, which has hitherto been the cause of the consolidation of manners, now appears the cause of their decline – or at least the separation of manners from genius.

> On the revival of letters, the youthful vigour of the imagination, after a long repose, national emulation, a new religion, new languages, and a new world, called forth the genius of Europe. But the provincials of Rome, trained by a uniform artificial foreign education, were engaged in a very unequal competition with those bold ancients, who, by expressing their genuine feelings in their native tongue, had already occupied every place of honour. The name of Poet was almost forgotten; that of Orator was usurped by the sophists. A cloud of critics, of compilers, of commentators, darkened the face of learning, and the decline of genius was soon followed by the corruption of taste.[61]

Where there is political diversity, there can be virtue; but under universal monarchy, the arts must decay, since their foundation is in liberty and rhetoric, and once virtue ceases to be expressed in speech, the splendid and seducing commerce of manners, and of material goods, must cease to have any meaning. The Enlightened cult of manners was rooted in the Renaissance cult of ancient letters; the controversies between philosophy and erudition, Ancients and Moderns, had been controversies over ways of maintaining this heritage; and here we see a pattern of thought, Tacitean rather than Virgilian, which insisted that letters must be rooted in liberty. Silver-age rhetoric decays, and late-antique manners with it, because speech is no longer connected with action. Gibbon is displaying a genius for historical images on a scale exceeding the neo-classical norms, and this chapter ends with one of the greatest and most famous of them. He quotes Longinus, who says that under 'a just servitude', his contemporaries are pygmies compared with

> the ancients, who, living under a popular government, wrote with the same freedom as they acted. This diminutive stature of mankind, if we pursue the metaphor, was daily sinking below the old standard, and the Roman world was indeed peopled by a race of pygmies; when the fierce giants of the north broke in, and mended the puny breed. They restored a manly spirit of freedom; and after the revolution of ten centuries, freedom became the happy parent of taste and science.[62]

There is something odd about the adjective 'manly', whose connotations are so much those of Victorian strenuousness that we are surprised

---

[61] *Ibidem*, p. 84.   [62] *Ibidem*.

to find it a recurrent favourite with the Whig and classical Gibbon.[63] Its stress upon masculinity implies a feminisation of culture going on somewhere, and though the 'fierce giants' are indubitably male, we are left wondering a little whether the 'happy parent' is father or mother, and 'taste and science' sons or daughters. Taken as a whole, however, the sentence completes the great cycle of Enlightened historical imagination. The fierce giants are the reverse of Ferguson's herd animals escaped to desert freedom, or Wordsworth's Arab riding ahead of the pursuing flood; but they come at a point where only barbarism can renew virtue, and, after a millennium in which barbarism is subdued by religion, freedom will renew manners at the revival of letters (we seem to be reckoning from the fifth century to the fifteenth). What will happen then, what will be the role of 'taste and science', those key terms of Enlightenment, and meanwhile what makes these particular barbarians capable of the discipline of liberty, are questions which must receive a political answer; for none of the wealth of ideas contained in chapter 2 furnish the political explanation of the decline of the empire of manners, which Gibbon proceeds to expound in the next chapter. Nor do they tell us something else with which we shall be concerned: why the fierce giants must spring only from the north, and must be *selvaggi* from the forests rather than shepherds from the steppe or orientals from the non-Greek east.

(IV)

Chapter 3, 'Of the Constitution of the Roman Empire in the Age of the Antonines', is transitional and in some ways incomplete in character. As its title tells us, it is the last of the three chapters which display the 'Antonine moment', and it contains at least one of the great panegyric sentences on the happiness of mankind while that moment lasted. But we shall find that statement subverted as soon as it is made, and there is a sense in which this chapter is both the last of the three which 'describe the prosperous condition of their empire' and the first of five which 'deduce the most important circumstances of its decline and fall'; we move in its course a considerable distance towards narrative. Because its subject is politics, we are concerned with the actions of men; because it recounts the growth of an absolute monarchy and a series of attempts to hold it back from degenerating, the personal characters of princes are of great but

---

[63] *Ibidem*, p. 84. Cf. n. III, where Longinus (just quoted) falls short 'of proposing his sentiments with a manly boldness'.

precarious significance. Gibbon's narrative therefore moves towards one of the classical modes of historiography, the literature of princely conduct; but there are, for whatever reasons, some unexpected gaps in its structure.

A Montesquieuan meditation opens the chapter, and leads without further preparation not *in medias res*, but to a narrative of the foundation of the principate by Augustus.

The obvious definition of a monarchy seems to be that of a state, in which a single person, by whatsoever name he may be distinguished, is entrusted with the execution of the laws, the management of the revenue, and the command of the army. But, unless public liberty is protected by intrepid and vigilant guardians, the authority of so formidable a magistrate will soon degenerate into despotism. The influence of the clergy, in an age of superstition, might be usefully employed to assert the rights of mankind; but so intimate is the connection between the throne and the altar, that the banner of the church has very seldom been seen on the side of the people. A martial nobility and stubborn commons, possessed of arms, tenacious of property, and collected into constitutional assemblies, form the only balance capable of preserving a free constitution against the enterprises of an aspiring prince.[64]

These (like Hume's 'universal axiom in politics', which draws a similar conclusion)[65] are reflections on modern history; church, nobility and estates are not phenomena to be looked for in the ancient world. Gibbon may be telling us that Roman society lacked the resources to protect itself against despotism, but he proceeds without explanation to display its condition at the end of the civil wars which destroyed the republic.

Every barrier of the Roman constitution had been levelled by the vast ambition of the dictator; every fence had been extirpated by the cruel hand of the Triumvir.[66]

The dictator may be Julius; the Triumvir is certainly Augustus. Here is Harrington's 'execrable reign of the Roman emperors',[67] the foundation of Montesquieu's *gouvernement ambigu*. Gibbon proceeds to a lengthy account of the personality of Augustus, the system of government which he established, and the conditions under which he founded it. The last are partly the result of wars which had destroyed the republican elite and its virtue, partly of the conditions which had corrupted virtue and led to social and civil war.

The people of Rome, viewing, with a secret pleasure, the humiliation of the aristocracy, demanded only bread and public shows; and were supplied with

---

[64] Womersley, 1994, 1, p. 85.    [65] Miller, 1985, p. 18.
[66] Womersley, 1994, 1, p. 85.    [67] Pocock, 1977, p. 188.

both by the liberal hand of Augustus. The rich and polite Italians, who had almost universally embraced the philosophy of Epicurus, enjoyed the present blessings of ease and tranquillity, and suffered not the pleasing dream to be interrupted by the memory of their old tumultuous freedom.[68]

These are effects, not causes, of the processes of republican decay, which Gibbon rather presupposes than describes in detail; but it leaves Augustus in a position where the principate he founds and the personality he displays are mirrors of one another. The master of Rome and its empire by monopoly of military force, he ostentatiously allows a packed and corrupted senate to legitimise his authority by investing the chief republican magistracies in his person for life, and we look beyond the separation of civil and military power to a consolidation of civil authority which would be constitutionally dangerous in itself. The system is dangerous, however, for a much deeper reason: it constantly pretends to be that which it is not, and obliges its master to a hypocrisy which is the instrument of his power. So long as he maintains his role, his authority is absolute and borders on the despotic; but he pays enormous psychic costs in maintaining it.

To resume, in a few words, the system of the Imperial government, as it was instituted by Augustus, and maintained by those princes who understood their own interest and that of the people, it may be defined as an absolute monarchy disguised by the forms of a commonwealth. The masters of the Roman world surrounded their throne with darkness, concealed their irresistible strength, and humbly professed themselves the accountable ministers of the senate, whose supreme decrees they dictated and obeyed.[69]

The tender respect of Augustus for a free constitution which he had destroyed, can only be explained by an attentive consideration of the character of that subtle tyrant. A cool head, an unfeeling heart, and a cowardly disposition, prompted him, at the age of nineteen, to assume the mask of hypocrisy, which he never afterwards laid aside. With the same hand, and probably with the same temper, he signed the proscription of Cicero, and the pardon of Cinna. His virtues, and even his vices, were artificial; and according to the various dictates of his interest, he was at first the enemy, and at last the father, of the Roman world. When he framed the artful system of the Imperial authority, his moderation was inspired by his fears. He wished to deceive the people by an image of civil liberty, and the armies by an image of civil government.[70]

Julian the Apostate, who is to be important in the pathos of the *Decline and Fall* as the last emperor with a human face, compared Augustus to

---

[68] Womersley, 1994, I, pp. 85–6.   [69] *Ibidem*, p. 93.   [70] *Ibidem*, p. 96.

a chameleon;[71] but the strain of constant shape-changing is very great, and Tacitus' portrait of Tiberius can be read as that of a man unable to bear the climate of hypocrisy by which he is enveloped. The *princeps* is destroyed by the failure of senatorial virtue; but it is also possible to interpret Tiberius, and still more vividly his immediate successors, as that familiar if lesser type of tyrant, the prince bred in the palace and corrupted by its flatteries and treacheries. There existed by Gibbon's time an extensive literature on the prevention and remedy of this kind of tyranny, but it was part of the literature of monarchy rather than republics. If the Hellenistic or European king was not to become an Oriental despot, surrounded by eunuchs, menaced by satraps, and perpetually jealous of his friends, he must learn to accept counsel and his counsellors must be faithful to him. As we have seen, there had grown up a literature of counsel which idealised this relationship, and a Tacitist literature which unmasked it. It could be argued, however, that once the relation of *princeps* to *senatus* had been as thoroughly falsified as it was by Augustus, Roman political culture contained nothing that could prevent the corruption of the prince by the palace. Gibbon had access to a literature which showed how the emperors might have become kings, but we shall find him more frequently concerned with their failure to act as magistrates. It was in the senate, not in the *consilium* and *amici principis*, that they might have found moral equals; but the Augustan foundation had made that impossible.

A prince bred in the palace might turn out delinquent to the point of monstrosity – Commodus, son of the best of emperors, was the first prince since Nero born in the purple, and no amount of counsel could save him – but the palace was capable of assassinating its own monsters, and the effects of their psychoses were seldom felt beyond the city itself. The deaths of monsters were more dangerous to the empire than their lives, since only the authority of the *imperator* kept the armies under civil discipline. When a monster perished, the palace guards – which was disastrous – or the frontier legions – which could be devastating – might be tempted to intervene in the succession. Their motives might not be all bad, but once the legions began marching on Rome, fighting one another, and murdering their own commanders, the whole system might begin to disintegrate. The guarantees that this would not happen were extremely fragile; but at this point the rhetorical structure of the *Decline and Fall* begins to turn around the paradox that nevertheless the system lasted a long time.

---

[71] *Ibidem*, n. 26; Gibbon strengthens Julian's language.

The insolence of the armies inspired Augustus with fears of a still more alarming nature. The despair of the citizens could only attempt what the power of the soldiers was, at any time, able to execute. How precarious was his own authority over men whom he had taught to violate every social duty! He had heard their seditious clamours; he dreaded their calmer moments of reflection. One revolution had been purchased by immense rewards; but a second revolution might double those rewards. The troops professed the fondest attachment to the house of Caesar; but the attachments of the multitude are capricious and inconstant. Augustus summoned to his aid whatever remained in those fierce minds of Roman prejudices; enforced the rigour of discipline by the sanction of law; and interposing the majesty of the senate between the emperor and the army,

(we should pause to observe that this majesty is an actor's or an ancestor's mask and nothing more)

boldly claimed their allegiance, as the first magistrate of the republic.

During a long period of two hundred and twenty years, from the establishment of this artful system to the death of Commodus, the dangers inherent to a military government were, in a great measure, suspended. The soldiers were seldom roused to that fatal sense of their own strength, and of the weakness of the civil authority, which was, before and afterwards, productive of such dreadful calamities. Caligula and Domitian were assassinated in their palaces by their own domestics; the convulsions which agitated Rome on the death of the former, were confined to the walls of the city. But Nero involved the whole empire in his ruin. In the space of eighteen months, four princes perished by the sword; and the Roman world was shaken by the fury of the contending armies. Excepting only this short, though violent, eruption of military licence, the two centuries from Augustus to Commodus passed away unstained with civil blood, and undisturbed by revolutions. The emperor was elected by *the authority of the senate*, and *the consent of the soldiers*. The legions respected their oath of fidelity; and it requires a minute inspection of the Roman annals to discover three inconsiderable rebellions, which were all suppressed in a few months, and without even the hazard of a battle.[72]

We become aware that at this stage the *Decline and Fall* is rhetoric rather than explanation, and that these two paragraphs form an antithesis rather than a sequence. There is no particular reason why the principate lasted so long, and the remarkable thing is that it did; in due course Gibbon will say the same thing of the empire itself. Vespasian might not have been able to restore the principate after the year of the four emperors, and his bold experiment of associating his son Titus with

---

[72] Womersley, 1994, I, pp. 97–8. The figure of 'two hundred and twenty years' seems to carry us back to 22 BC and it is not clear what is the significance of this date.

him in the empire might not have worked. Titus' 'more splendid and amiable character' was not transmitted to his brother Domitian, but his memory induced the Roman world to endure the latter for 'above fifteen years'.[73] What is more remarkable still, Gibbon gives no account whatever of how Domitian came to be murdered, of why there was no civil war at his death, or of how Nerva succeeded him. We are told only that he 'accepted the purple from the assassins of Domitian',[74] and that he adopted Trajan and declared him his colleague and successor. With that 'the golden age of Trajan and the Antonines'[75] begins; there follows a series of encomia upon the characters of these emperors – with serious reservations in the case of Hadrian – and after admiring the ideal personality of Marcus Aurelius we are left with one of Gibbon's most famous paragraphs, followed by another which immediately undermines it. The *gouvernement ambigu* is producing antitheses still.

If a man were called to fix the period in the history of the world, during which the condition of the human race was most happy and prosperous, he would, without hesitation, name that which elapsed from the death of Domitian to the accession of Commodus. The vast extent of the Roman empire was governed by absolute power, under the guidance of virtue and wisdom. The armies were restrained by the firm but gentle hand of four successive emperors, whose characters and authority commanded involuntary respect. The forms of the civil administration were carefully preserved by Nerva, Trajan, Hadrian and the Antonines, who delighted in the image of liberty, and were pleased with considering themselves the accountable ministers of the laws. Such princes deserved the honour of restoring the republic, had the Romans of their days been capable of enjoying a rational freedom.[76]

It has been noticed previously that the first sentence above is an exact echo of one from Robertson, dealing with a subsequent period 'during which the condition of the human race was most calamitous and afflicted'.[77] It needs also to be stressed that during the Antonine moment nothing maintains human happiness except forms and an image; these excellent rulers pretend to be accountable to the laws when they are accountable only to themselves. Gibbon has become enough of a whig to repudiate monarchy responsible only to the conscience of the king. He proceeds to emphasise the fragility of a philosopher kingship.

The labours of these monarchs were overpaid by the immense reward that inseparably waited on their success; by the honest pride of virtue, and by the

[73] *Ibidem*, p. 99.    [74] *Ibidem*.    [75] The phrase occurs at p. 104.
[76] Womersley, 1994, I, p. 103.    [77] *NCG*, p. 279.

exquisite delight of beholding the general happiness of which they were the
authors. A just, but melancholy reflection embittered, however, the noblest
of human enjoyments. They must often have recollected the instability of a
happiness which depended on the character of a single man. The fatal moment
was perhaps approaching, when some licentious youth, or some jealous tyrant,
would abuse, to the destruction, that absolute power which they had exerted for
the benefit of their people. The ideal restraints of the senate and the laws might
serve to display the virtues, but could never correct the vices, of the emperor.
The military force was a blind and irresistible instrument of oppression; and the
corruption of Roman manners would always supply flatterers eager to applaud,
and ministers prepared to serve the fear or the avarice, the lust or the cruelty,
of their masters.[78]

*Ubi virtus, ibi fortuna.* As soon as the philosopher Marcus Aurelius is
succeeded by his son Commodus, the pattern of AD 70 and 96 will be
repeated on a more disastrous scale, and there will be no Vespasian or
Trajan this time. Gibbon prefers hereditary to elective monarchy, when
it can be balanced and controlled by hereditary estates and inheritable
property, but under Roman conditions adoptive monarchy is the only
but inadequate solution; Commodus is a second Nero because he is
not a second Titus. The accidents of personality are uncontrollable by
anything in this system. In language which, we have already seen, was
to be developed by Adam Ferguson, Gibbon observes:

> The annals of the emperors exhibit a strong and various picture of human
> nature, which we should vainly seek among the mixed and doubtful characters
> of modern history. In the conduct of these monarchs we may trace the utmost
> lines of vice and virtue; the most exalted perfection, and the meanest degeneracy
> of our own species.[79]

From the comparison with Ferguson, we also know that the splendid
fabric of manners, the shared commerce and culture of the provinces,
which we saw holding the empire together in the preceding chapter,
does nothing whatever to remedy the problems of the principate in its
relationship with the armies; and of course it is the lack of military virtue
which will reduce provincial culture to impotence in the end. Roman
manners, unlike those of modern Europe, are not communicated to the
court, and in consequence the empire is ruled by an alternation of beasts
and gods. The eighty years (98–180) of the good emperors are exactly
balanced by the 'fourscore years (excepting only the short and doubtful
respite of Vespasian's reign)' when Rome is ruled by

---

[78] Womersley, 1994, I, pp. 103–4.    [79] *Ibidem*, p. 104.

the dark unrelenting Tiberius, the furious Caligula, the feeble Claudius, the profligate and cruel Nero, the beastly Vitellius, and the timid inhuman Domitian.[80]

And after Commodus will come Caracalla, Elagabalus and Maximin. There were two conditions, Gibbon remarks in concluding these three chapters, which rendered life under such 'monsters' peculiarly intolerable. One was the Stoic philosophy which kept alive the memory of republican virtue and reminded the Romans that they had once been free;[81] the other was that from a universal empire there was no possibility of escape. In the former respect the Romans are contrasted with the subjects of an Oriental despot, who do not miss freedom because they have never known what it is;[82] in the latter, the contrast is with the empire of manners in its modern form.

The division of Europe into a number of independent states, connected, however, with each other, by the general resemblance of religion, language, and manners, is productive of the most beneficial consequences to the liberty of mankind. A modern tyrant, who should find no resistance either in his own breast, or in his people, would soon experience a gentle restraint from the example of his equals, the dread of present censure, the advice of his allies, and the apprehension of his enemies. The object of his displeasure, escaping from the narrow limits of his dominions, would easily obtain, in a happier climate, a secure refuge, a new fortune adequate to his merit, the freedom of complaint, and perhaps the means of revenge. But the empire of the Romans filled the world, and when that empire fell into the hands of a single person, the world became a safe and dreary prison for his enemies.[83]

It might be the voice of Metternich or Talleyrand, conducting opposition to Napoleon in the name of the *douceur de vivre*, or of any Russian exile denouncing Nicholas or Stalin from the farther shore. More immediately, it informs us that manners could not last without virtue, the *imperium* without the *libertas* that had achieved it. The door is open to the fierce giants, but the role they will play for the next millennium is a complex one.

---

[80] *Ibidem.* Titus has not been mentioned.    [81] *Ibidem*, pp. 105–6.
[82] *Ibidem*, p. 107.    [83] *Ibidem*, pp. 106–7.

# CHAPTER 18

# The Severi and the disintegration of the principate

## (1)

The ensuing chapters (4–7) of the *Decline and Fall* possess a narrative structure; they recount the fall of a succession of princes in a manner as much exemplary as explanatory, and rhetorical and panegyric models are much in evidence among the not very impressive authorities Gibbon is obliged to follow. In his memoirs he alludes to 'the concise and super-ficial narrative of the first reigns from Commodus to Alexander', and contrasts these chapters with the fifteenth and sixteenth, which 'have been reduced by three successive revisals from a large volume to their present size [and] might still be compressed without any loss of facts or sentiments'.[1] Gibbon was still searching for the proper relationship between the narrative and the discursive, and it is in the latter mode that his understanding of barbarism and religion may be expected to unfold itself.

As we follow his narrative from Commodus to Alexander Severus, and from Maximin of Thrace to Philip the Arab, we are not only watching his first essays in the narrative mode; we are watching him expose the final disintegration of the Augustan principate and the Antonine mo-ment, and in the inferior rhetoric of his authorities we are witnessing the emperors pass out of a world in which rhetorically emphasised virtue has possessed much meaning. This is one reason – though another is that his sources forced it upon him – why the unreal exemplary figure of Alexander Severus occupies a central place in these chapters, and it lends significance to the fact that he had before him a modern narrative of this part of Roman history, written in a classically exemplary mode. William Wotton's *The History of Rome from the Death of Antoninus Pius to the*

---

[1] *Memoirs*, p. 156.

*Death of Severus Alexander*, published in 1701, was, as we have seen,[2] written by the tutor of Queen Anne's heir, the child Duke of Gloucester, and was published only after the death of 'a Prince of too great Hopes for such a wicked People'.[3] It is thus perhaps the last example in English of the 'mirror of princes', a history actually written to edify a future ruler and train him in the ways he should go; and the ability to receive and follow good counsel was among the cardinal virtues of a prince. Alexander Severus, the last of his line and the last *princeps* to reign before an onset of military and barbarian anarchy, was a minor and ineffectual figure – almost a Romulus Augustulus – but had since the fourth century been selected as the subject of panegyric,[4] and Wotton had been well aware both that he was writing panegyric and that he was writing it for the benefit of a prince far less able to disregard good counsel than Alexander had been, had he not been virtuous.

In *mixt Governments*, where Kings are supposed to do nothing without the Advice of their *Privy-Council*, and where Ministers are often called to Account by the States of a Kingdom for the Advice they give, it will scarce be thought a Commendation in *Alexander*, that he, a Youth of xvi, should leave all Business to a *Committee* of Wise Men, since it will hardly be imagined how he could have done otherwise. But in Absolute Elective Monarchies, such as the *Roman* Empire was in *Alexander's* time, the Case is different. The Prince in possession was bound by no Law, ty'd to no Rule, his Will, and that onely, was his Guide.[5]

The good Actions therefore which were done by *Alexander's* Ministers in his Youth, ought in justice to be ascribed to him: And those things, which would not enter into a limited Prince's Character, do truly make up a part of his deserved Panegyric. Such indeed, rather than a History, the greatest part of what is related of him by the Ancients, will seem to be. But if several things hereafter mentioned concerning him, shall look odd and little at this distance, allowance must be made for difference of Customs in different Ages and different Nations. And agen, if on the other hand it shall be thought incredible, that so many Excellency's should all dwell in the same Man, who after a Reign of xiii Years was not xxx Years old when he was killed, let us not measure every thing by what we ourselves have seen; but since even those who have labour'd to lessen the Reputation of *Alexander's* Reign, have yet spoken extremely well of his Person, we ought in justice to suppose that his Friends have spoken the Truth of him likewise, where we cannot at this distance of time disprove them.[6]

---

[2] Above, p. 326. Wotton is studied, and his *History* displayed in its proper setting, in Levine, 1987, chs. 6 and 7. Gibbon possessed a copy, and two editions of Wotton's *Reflection upon Ancient and Modern Learning* (*Library*, p. 285).

[3] Wotton, 1701, epistle dedicatory.

[4] '. . . when a century later the writers of the Augustan History wished to present a picture of the perfect emperor to Constantine . . .' Jones, 1986, vol. 1, p. 19.

[5] Wotton, 1701, p. 443.  [6] *Ibidem*, p. 444.

Wotton is writing a *miroir des princes*; his narrative begins with one ideal emperor, Marcus Aurelius, and ends with another, Alexander Severus, and for the purposes of panegyric it does not matter much if the latter is something of a fiction. This by no means makes Wotton's *History* a mere literary exercise; he was a modern and a critic, and can make acute historical observations as he goes along. He gives a fuller account than Gibbon does of the episode of Avidius Cassius, descended from the tyrannicide, who rebelled against Marcus Aurelius (of all emperors) in the name of republican liberty, but could do so only by appealing to his own soldiers, who understandably lost no time in killing him.[7] Wotton explains Marcus' indifference to Christianity on the grounds that he was a Stoic and the Stoics already held so close to Christian values that the wisdom of God appeared foolish to the pride of intellect;[8] it could well be intended as comment on not a few (deists especially) of Wotton's contemporaries. We can even see, in the extracts just quoted, a foretaste of Gibbon's and Ferguson's perception that under the conditions of ancient despotism, where the prince might do as he liked, there was little to protect his virtue or prevent his personality from oscillating between the divine and the bestial. But where the Enlightenment historians could place some faith in the complex integument of modern manners, and explore the presence, but insufficiency, of such a fabric in Antonine culture, Wotton, writing in a medieval and Renaissance tradition, must depict the friendship and advice of counsellors as the only agency that could stabilise the prince's personality. What makes the difference between Marcus and Commodus, or between Caracalla and Alexander, is simply the ability to receive good counsel; this will not only keep the prince prudent, but is all that can keep him sane.[9]

Gibbon did not intend a *miroir des princes*, but a history of decline and fall. He made no advance over Wotton's account of the main structural change in this period; the earlier historian's words

> For the Maxims of *Severus*, which were carefully preserved by his Son *Caracalla*, had in truth quite alter'd the whole *Roman* Government, and by making it entirely Military, had subjected every Emperor to the Humours of those Soldiers that at first set him up; which fatal Mistake in the Politics of *Severus* being the Ruine of *Alexander* . . .[10]

might well have been Gibbon's own. All that happens in his narrative is that Commodus is a second Nero, and that at his assassination the

---

[7] *Ibidem*, pp. 73–83.     [8] *Ibidem*, pp. 137–8.     [9] See, once more, Conrad, 1988.
[10] Wotton, 1701, Preface; see also p. 330. Cf. Mexía, above, p. 246.

pattern of AD 81 is repeated; the armies of Britain, Pannonia and Illyria intervene and there is war among their generals. But the pathetic figure is that of Pertinax, elected *princeps* by the senate but unable to repeat the performance of Nerva,[11] with the result that the praetorian guards kill him; and Septimius Severus, the governor of Pannonia who defeats his rivals, is not a Vespasian and does not trouble to re-erect the masking of military by civil powers which made the Augustan principate a simulacrum of Roman virtue. It is the end of the *gouvernement ambigu*, which vanishes once the adoptive succession is abandoned and the philosopher leaves power to his son.[12] Gibbon does not anticipate the suggestion that the armies insisted on hereditary succession and the senate on elective, and that only the accident of childlessness from Nerva to Antoninus Pius permitted the two to be reconciled by the fiction of adoption;[13] like Wotton, he was an eighteenth-century Englishman and preferred hereditary monarchy when an heir could be found.[14] Writing in dynastic security under George III, with the Jacobite leanings of his family well behind him, he knew no prince who need look into the mirror of Roman history, and could conduct the analysis of the Augustan monarchy as a continuation of the failure of republican virtue. Once the Antonine adoptive line had failed, the military wolves were loosed. The palace could continue to exhibit monsters – Commodus, Caracalla, Elagabalus – but the true shift in power was away from the image of the senate and towards the anarchic reality of the sword. The true successors of Severus were the half-barbarous military men, Maximin and Philip, who had fought their way into the capital and would hold it as long as they could, and the centre of power might remove to points *alibi quam Romae*. In telling this tale, the panegyric of Alexander was less a climax than a nuisance, and Gibbon is visibly impatient under the obligation to follow his authorities and recount it, returning his history to the exemplary mode.[15] He does not anticipate more modern historians in pointing out that the military men had commonly been co-opted into the senatorial aristocracy.

Under such stresses, Gibbon turns when he can from rhetorically based narrative to reflective discourse.

[11] It will be remembered that Gibbon has not told us much of how Nerva managed it.
[12] Plato's *Republic* might make this a topos for rhetoricians trained in philosophy.
[13] Jones, 1986, 1, p. 7.
[14] Womersley, 1994, 1, pp. 187–3; the opening paragraphs of chapter 7, a lengthy disquisition introducing the post-Severan disorder.
[15] Womersley, 1994, 1, pp. 172–8 (and n. 80), 190–1.

This internal change, which undermined the foundations of the empire, we have endeavoured to explain with some degree of order and perspicuity. The personal characters of the emperors, their victories, laws, follies and fortunes, can interest us no further than as they are connected with the general history of the Decline and Fall of the monarchy.[16]

These sentences introduce an important digression on the Edict of Caracalla, and as the succeeding princes pass through Gibbon's mirror, there are other digressions which are worth noting – though his verdict that these chapters are 'concise and superficial' is there to remind us that he was dissatisfied with his own performance in connecting princely history with general. Commodus, we learn, was a scandalous failure less because he conducted a reign of terror against the senate – though this is not understated[17] – than because he exhibited himself as a *venator* and *gladiator* in the arena. In playing the role of Hercules and other mighty hunters of primitive antiquity, he parodied the savage virtues, and it was a poor use of the great roads along which the Antonine peace had disseminated culture when rare and harmless ostriches and giraffes were transported to Rome to be butchered in public by the emperor.[18] Under a despotic government and a consumer economy, luxury parodied and distorted manners, and Commodus' reign was both a tyranny and a failure of decorum. The hypocritical gravity of Augustus and the philosophic melancholy of Marcus Aurelius were disgustingly undermined by a series of palace-bred successors, clowns in public and tyrants in the palace. When Commodus was murdered by a concubine, a chamberlain and the commander of the praetorian guard, there was not enough authority left in the senate to control the soldiers; though at the moment when the praetorians reached the climax of degeneracy by murdering Pertinax and putting the empire up to auction, Gibbon permits them an ideology and at least a simulacrum of virtue.

The advocates of the guards endeavoured to justify by arguments the power which they asserted by arms; and to maintain that, according to the purest principles of the constitution, their consent was essentially necessary in the appointment of an emperor. The election of consuls, of generals, and of magistrates, however it had been recently usurped by the senate, was the ancient and undoubted right of the Roman people. But where was the Roman people to be found? Not surely among the mixed multitude of slaves and strangers that filled the streets of Rome; a servile populace, as devoid of spirit as destitute of property. The defenders of the state, selected from the flower of the Italian youth, and trained in the exercise of arms and virtue, were the genuine representatives of

---

[16] *Ibidem*, p. 178.    [17] *Ibidem*, p. 112.    [18] *Ibidem*, pp. 117–18.

the people, and the best entitled to elect the military chief of the republic. These assertions, however defective in reason, became unanswerable when the fierce Praetorians increased their weight, by throwing, like the barbarian conquerors of Rome, their swords into the scale.[19]

This is the thesis put forward by Montesquieu,[20] that once military and civic virtue had been divorced, the soldiers had as good a claim as the citizens to be considered the Roman people; but the praetorians were as degenerate as the plebeians when the scale once used to weigh ransom became that of an auctioneer. The frontier legions refused to register the purchase, and swept aside the praetorians by using their swords in battle; but Septimius Severus, whom they installed in power, though a superbly cunning deceiver, lacked either the hypocrisy of Augustus or the decorum of Vespasian and Trajan. The government ceased to be ambiguous.

Till the reign of Severus, the virtue and even the good sense of the emperors had been distinguished by their zeal or affected reverence for the senate, and by a tender regard to the nice frame of civil policy instituted by Augustus. But the youth of Severus had been trained in the implicit obedience of camps, and his riper years spent in the despotism of military command. His haughty and inflexible spirit could not discover, or would not acknowledge, the advantage of preserving an intermediate power, however imaginary, between the emperor and the army. He disdained to profess himself the servant of an assembly that detested his person and trembled at his frown . . . whilst the senate, neither elected by the people, nor guarded by the military force, nor animated by public spirit, rested its declining authority on the frail and crumbling basis of ancient opinion. The fine theory of a republic insensibly vanished, and made way for the more natural and substantial feelings of monarchy. As the freedom and honours of Rome were successively communicated to the provinces, in which the old government had been either unknown, or was remembered with abhorrence, the tradition of republican maxims was gradually obliterated.

There could be gain here to the human mind's capacity to confront reality. At least the nature of imperial rule was perceived for what it really was; and we are being reminded that absolute monarchy was preferable to a republic as a government of the provinces. But at the point where a modern historian remarks that under Severus Greeks increased and Egyptians appeared in the senate for the first time,[21] Gibbon embarks on one of his few ventures into vulgar whiggism.

---

[19] *Ibidem*, p. 129.     [20] *Considérations*, ch. XVI. Weil and Courtney, 2000, pp. 219–20.
[21] Jones, 1986, I, p. 22.

In the reign of Severus, the senate was filled with polished and eloquent slaves from the eastern provinces, who justified personal flattery by speculative principles of servitude. These new advocates of prerogative were heard with pleasure by the court, and with patience by the people, when they inculcated the duty of passive obedience and descanted on the inevitable mischiefs of freedom. The lawyers and the historians concurred in teaching, that the imperial authority was held, not by the delegated commission, but by the irrevocable resignation of the senate; that the emperor was freed from the restraint of civil laws, could command by his arbitrary will the lives and fortunes of his subjects, and might dispose of the empire as of his private patrimony. The most eminent of the civil lawyers, and particularly Papinian, Paulus, and Ulpian, flourished under the house of Severus; and the Roman jurisprudence, having closely united itself with the system of monarchy, was supposed to have attained its full maturity and perfection.[22]

Gibbon is seldom so unequivocally libertarian; these orators and jurists sound like Laudian or non-juring bishops in the rhetoric of the Commonwealthmen; it is more remarkable still that the growth of Roman law, far from transforming an insecure *gouvernement ambigu* into the absolute monarchy of a *lex loquens* – a form of government not unadmired by Hume – is unequivocally associated with a purely military regime which can spell only decay. If law has failed to replace citizenship, manners have failed also. The civil wars of modern Europe are fought in the name of loyalty or religion, but the Romans whose republic is no more fight for nothing but pay and loot;[23] nor does Severus expect anything else from them. What seems to be Gibbon's final judgement on this emperor runs:

The contemporaries of Severus, in the enjoyment of the peace and glory of his reign, forgave the cruelties by which it had been introduced. Posterity, who experienced the fatal effects of his maxims and example, justly considered him as the principal author of the decline of the Roman empire,[24]

now dated from the end of the *gouvernement ambigu* rather than from its beginning. At the outset of the following chapter, we learn that the realistic Severus, seeing nothing around him that was legitimate – 'I've been everything', he once said, 'and nothing's any good'[25] – turned naturally to superstition, and for astrological reasons married a Syrian lady, who brought oriental religion into the imperial succession. He died at York, leaving two fratricidal sons, of whom the successful murderer, Caracalla, would not long detain us, if it were not for two digressions in which he

[22] For both the passages quoted, see Womersley, 1994, I, pp. 147–8.
[23] *Ibidem*, pp. 141–2.    [24] *Ibidem*, p. 148.
[25] 'Omnia fui et nihil expedit.' For Gibbon's rendering, see Womersley, 1994, I, p. 149.

is confronted first with barbarism and afterwards with commerce. The Caledonian war, remarks Gibbon,

would ill deserve our attention; but it is supposed, not without a considerable degree of probability, that the invasion of Severus is connected with the most shining period of the British history or fable. Fingal, whose fame, with that of his heroes and bards, has been revived in our language by a recent publication, is said to have commanded the Caledonians in that memorable juncture, to have eluded the power of Severus, and to have obtained a signal victory on the banks of the Carun, in which the son of *the King of the World*, Caracul, fled from his arms along the fields of his pride. Something of a doubtful mist still hangs over these Highland traditions; nor can it be entirely dispelled by the most ingenious researches of modern criticism.

Do these researches tend to undermine Ossian's authenticity or to affirm it? Gibbon inserts a footnote in which he points out the unlikelihood of Caracalla – who ruled under the name of Antoninus and scarcely acquired his cognomen until after his death – being the Caracul of Ossian. He continues:

but if we could, with safety, indulge the pleasing supposition, that Fingal lived, and that Ossian sung, the striking contrast of the situation and manners of the contending nations might amuse a philosophic mind. The parallel would be little to the advantage of the more civilised people, if we compared the unrelenting revenge of Severus with the generous clemency of Fingal; the timid and brutal cruelty of Caracalla, with the bravery, the tenderness, the elegant genius of Ossian; the mercenary chiefs who, from motives of fear or interest, served under the Imperial standard, with the freeborn warriors who started to arms at the voice of the king of Morven; if, in a word, we contemplated the untutored Caledonians, glowing with the warm virtues of nature, and the degenerate Romans, polluted with the mean vices of wealth and slavery.[26]

The mists are not dispelled, but we have come some way from the gloomy hills and naked barbarians of our last encounter with the Highlands. Gibbon was a closet Ossianist; he would have liked to believe in the authenticity of the epic, but with David Hume looking on in the last months of his life, knew better than to say so.[27] On the other hand, he had an alternative and less sentimental vision of what heroic barbarism and its poetry had really been like, and would develop it in his

[26] *Ibidem*, p. 152 and n. 14.
[27] For Gibbon's citation of Hume's letter dated 18 March 1776, see *Memoirs*, pp. 167–8; Hume died at Edinburgh on 25 August, and Gibbon had met him on his way through London. Their conversation is mentioned at p. 156; Hume thought the chapters now under review could have been expanded.

ninth chapter.[28] There is much that is rhetorical about the passage just quoted; but if the virtues of the Caledonians are ideal, there is nothing intended to be unreal about the degeneracy of the Romans. Manners were truly falling apart in the separation of military from civic virtue.

Caracalla makes his second appearance in civil as distinct from princely history in the context of an extended discussion[29] of the empire's fiscal structure. The occasion is his memorable edict (also known as the *Constitutio Antoniniana*)[30] which extended Roman citizenship to all the free inhabitants of the empire. This was to render them all liable to certain taxes, and that is the setting for a disquisition on the extension and exhaustion of citizenship as the ancients had known it. We are familiar by now with the thesis that civic virtue was the instrument of conquest; and Gibbon, mentioning Lipsius and more glancingly Montesquieu[31] among other authorities, proceeds to explain that by annexing treasuries and exacting tributes, the Romans amassed such a quantity of bullion in the capital that they delivered themselves from paying taxes. It is true that

> in a great empire like that of Rome, a natural balance of money must have gradually established itself. . . . as the wealth of the provinces was attracted to the capital by the strong hand of conquest and power, so a considerable part of it was restored to the industrious provinces by the gentle influence of commerce and arts.[32]

But this was an economy of high consumption, with the brute facts of conquest and enslavement never very far in the background, and when Augustus resolved to place limits on the expansion of empire, he saw at once that Rome and Italy must assume some share of the public burden. It was hardly the case, however, that there went forth a decree from Caesar Augustus that all the world should be taxed; the *princeps* had to proceed cautiously and indirectly towards taxing the Italians, first by imposing a variety of excise duties on the movement mainly of luxury goods, second by the institution of a tax on legacies and inheritances. It was public knowledge that the support of the armies relied chiefly on these two forms of taxation; and Gibbon observes that in the absence of 'any restraint from the modern fetters of entails and settlements'[33] – originally

---

[28] Womersley, 1994, I, pp. 246–7.  [29] *Ibidem*, pp. 178–86.  [30] Jones, 1986, I, pp. 16–18.
[31] Womersley, 1994, I, pp. 181, n. 96, 184, n. 110. Other moderns mentioned are Bouchard, 1772, and Burmann, 1734; for them see *Library*, pp. 76, 83.
[32] Womersley, 1994, I, pp. 181–2.
[33] *Ibidem*, p. 183. As the heir of an improvident father, Gibbon knew whereof he spoke.

produced by the existence of feudal ties between landownership and public service – the devising of lands by testament became so prevalent in the senatorial class, who used it to establish ties of benefice and alliance among themselves, that as a social phenomenon it threatened to pass out of control. The Severi, or later Antonines (they continued to use the name), governed by disregarding senatorial restraints on the demands of the armies; and the motive behind Caracalla's edict was simply to render all provincials liable to the legacy duties which had previously been exacted only from Italians. At the same time, tribute was not effectively reduced:

> the noxious weed, which had not been totally eradicated, again sprang up with the most luxuriant growth, and in the succeeding age darkened the Roman world with its deadly shade. In the course of this history, we shall be too often summoned to explain the land-tax, the capitation, and the heavy contributions of corn, wine, oil, and meat, which were exacted from the provinces for the use of the court, the army, and the capital.[34]

Gibbon's Tory forebears had been accustomed to prophecies of the same fate for the England of Queen Anne; it was because such foretellings had not been fulfilled that Gibbon could consider himself a Whig. But in the pre-feudal world it had been another matter. Citizenship had meant the pursuit of office, the endowment of public buildings, and the display of virtue; it was the contest for citizenship in this sense which had lent meaning to the exchange of legacies within the senatorial classes. When Caracalla made citizenship universal, he deprived it of any meaning except that of an obligation to pay taxes to support the army, and thus contributed one impulse more to the decay of virtue.

> As long as Rome and Italy were respected as the centre of government, a national spirit was preserved by the ancient, and insensibly imbibed by the adopted, citizens. The principal commands of the army were filled by men who had received a liberal education, were well instructed in the advantages of laws and letters, and who had risen, by equal steps, through the regular succession of civil and military honours. To their influence and example we may partly ascribe the modest obedience of the legions during the first two centuries of the Imperial history.
> But when the last enclosure of the Roman constitution was trampled down by Caracalla, the separation of professions gradually succeeded to the distinction of ranks. The more polished citizens of the internal provinces were alone qualified to act as lawyers and magistrates. The rougher trade of arms was abandoned to the peasants and barbarians of the frontiers, who knew no country

34 *Ibidem*, pp. 185–6.

but their camp, no science but that of war, no civil laws, and scarcely those of military discipline. With bloody hands, savage manners, and desperate resolutions, they sometimes guarded, but much oftener subverted, the throne of the emperors.[35]

The subversion of the Italian elites removed the only natural aristocracy which could have civilised the armies. Rank is the organising principle of a virtuous society, profession that of a specialised one. The post-Antonine order was one in which rank survived for a time, but could no longer rule the military profession. The cosmopolitan nation into which manners were forming the Roman world began to fall apart; Italy was no longer its centre, which began to migrate *alibi quam Romae* as the state ceased to be under the command of civil society.

(11)

The discussion of Caracalla's Edict closes chapter 6, but comes after the narrative of the reigns succeeding his. He was murdered by a conspiracy of his own guards while on 'pilgrimage' to the temple of the moon at Carrhae;[36] the location betrays both his Syrian extraction and his superstition. His killer Macrinus (who was not even a senator) was rapidly if rather fortuitously overthrown by a conspiracy involving the formidable matriarchs from the city of Emesa[37] who had entered imperial politics with the marriage of Severus to Julia Domna, and the son of one of these became emperor and took the name of Elagabalus from the god of a phallic stone of which he was priest. The young man has become a type-figure in the literature of orientalism, thanks both to the worship of his god which he established at Rome and to the diversity of his sexual tastes. As 'the first emperor of Asiatic extraction'[38] he marks a break with the grim sequence of palace-bred tyrants from Caligula to Caracalla; orientalisation and barbarisation are the themes which he introduces. The oriental was by definition effeminate, and Elagabalus is not here said to have numbered homicide among his faults; Wotton credits him with murdering his first political manager with his own hand,[39]

---

[35] See the concluding paragraphs of chapter 6; Womersley, 1994, 1, p. 186.

[36] Womersley, 1994, 1, p. 159–60.

[37] For Gibbon on matriarchy, see *ibidem*, pp. 170–1; nothing but chivalry has made it acceptable to 'the wiser, or at least the stronger of the two sexes'. The administration of Alexander's mother 'was equally for the benefit of her son and of the empire', and women rule successfully in 'modern' Europe.

[38] *Ibidem*, p. 165.     [39] Wotton, 1701, pp. 388–89.

but Gibbon says nothing of the incident. As for his bisexuality, the offence of Elagabalus was not that he liked boys as much as girls – most of his predecessors had been similarly disposed, and Gibbon has earlier observed, 'we may remark that of the first fifteen emperors, Claudius was the only one whose taste in love was entirely correct'[40] – but that he preferred the passive role, and adopted it publicly. In the midst of the purple prose which his antics necessarily evoke, Gibbon makes two remarks which show that the difference between ancient and modern manners is part of what is at issue.

A rational voluptuary adheres with invariable respect to the temperate dictates of nature, and improves the gratifications of sense by social intercourse, endearing connections, and the soft colouring of taste and the imagination. But Elagabalus . . . corrupted by his youth, his country, and his fortune, abandoned himself to the grossest pleasures with ungoverned fury, and soon found disgust and satiety in the midst of his enjoyments. The inflammatory powers of art were summoned to his aid: the confused multitude of women, of wines, and of dishes, and the studied variety of attitudes and sauces, served to revive his languid appetites.[41]

Gibbon is not sure how much of all this to believe, but observes that imperial Rome was not a place where the appetites of the powerful were subject to much social control.

The licence of an eastern monarch is secluded from the eye of curiosity by the inaccessible walls of his seraglio. The sentiments of honour and gallantry have introduced a refinement of pleasure, a regard for decency, and a respect for public opinion, into the modern courts of Europe; but the corrupt and opulent nobles of Rome gratified every vice that could be collected from the mighty conflux of nations and manners. Secure of impunity, careless of censure, they lived without restraint in the patient and humble society of their slaves and parasites. The emperor, in his turn, viewing every rank of his subjects with the same contemptuous indifference, asserted without control the sovereign privilege of lust and luxury.[42]

The rational voluptuary appears to be an Enlightened, rather than an ancient, Epicurean; his manners are polite, and he occurs in the order of history after the transformation of barbarism by chivalry and courtly love. Gibbon, like Ferguson after him, is saying that the Romans had

---

[40] Womersley, 1994, I, p. 101, n. 40. Much good had this correctness done the husband of Messalina.
[41] *Ibidem*, p. 167. It would be a mistake to denounce Gibbon for reducing women to consumer objects served up at table; he is saying that Elagabalus did this. A feminist's quarrel is with his preferred system of modern manners.
[42] *Ibidem*, p. 168.

no code and were *capables de tout*, because their culture was corrupted by slavery and despotism into one of conspicuous consumption; and in the second passage he is saying once again that imperial manners were corrupted by the absence of virtue. As for Elagabalus' establishment of the sun-god at Rome, Gibbon calls him 'the Imperial fanatic',[43] but perhaps displays less insight than Wotton, when the latter observes:

> The Gentile *Romans*, who had been educated with Sentiments of Reverence towards their other Gods, were extremely grieved to see, that whatsoever they held dear or sacred in their Idolatrous Worship, must all now be sacrificed to this new Image. They could have been contented to have worshipt it as the Tutelar Deity of the *Emeseni*, and as such to have erected a Temple to it; but to prostrate all their other Idols to this single one, that they thought was abominable.[44]

Gibbon must have understood this, but does not repeat it. The fact is that the episode of Elagabalus possesses more shock value than significance. The three years for which he reigned are merely the prelude to the thirteen years of Alexander Severus, and there is no intelligible account of that period. The rule of the Emesan women and their sons is a late stage in the decline of the senate's ability to control events, but what requires explaining is the persistent loyalty of the soldiers to the Antonine and Severan lines. When they are driven to kill Elagabalus and his mother Soaemias, it is to instal his cousin Alexander (and his mother Julia Mamaea). Gibbon is visibly irritated by the fact that Alexander's reign has been narrated only in the unreliable panegyric of the *Historia Augusta*; but he is still enough of a neoclassical historian to feel constrained to follow this in his text, expressing occasional doubts which are reinforced in the critical footnotes now appearing at the foot of the page.[45] Probably this is why the digression on the Edict of Caracalla occurs at a point where the reign of Alexander cannot be studied in depth.

With the death of Alexander and the end of the Severan–Emesan household, there is left no legitimate dynasty around which military action can be unified; in a real sense, Alexander is the last of the Antonines. He is overthrown, in circumstances obscurely recounted, by the troops of Maximin, a peasant soldier from Thrace, of mixed Gothic and Alanic descent. The fact of a barbarian emperor should be, and indirectly is, the occasion of weighty reflections; but there is again the problem that his character is variously and inconsistently described. On the one hand:

---

[43] *Ibidem*, p. 166.    [44] Wotton, 1701, pp. 395–6.
[45] Womersley, 1994, 1, pp. 170–8; nn. 62, 67, 69, 74, 80; 190–1, n. 5.

From the prudent conduct of Maximin, we may learn that the savage features of his character have been exaggerated by the pencil of party, that his passions, however impetuous, submitted to the force of reason, and that the barbarian possessed something of the generous spirit of Sylla, who subdued the enemies of Rome before he suffered himself to revenge his private injuries.[46]

On the other:

Such was the deserved fate of a brutal savage, destitute, as he has generally been represented, of every sentiment that distinguishes a civilised, or even a human being. The body was suited to the soul. The stature of Maximin exceeded the measure of eight feet, and circumstances almost incredible are related of his matchless strength and appetite. Had he lived in a less enlightened age, tradition and poetry might well have described him as one of those monstrous giants, whose supernatural power was constantly exerted for the destruction of mankind.[47]

Gibbon is still caught in the mirror of princes, and finding it hard to get out. However, when Maximin slew Alexander, he encountered a defensive and reforming stand of the senate, who tried to render the principate collegial and civilian, by setting up first the Gordians[48] and afterwards Maximus and Balbinus.[49] In the ensuing power scramble, six emperors perished by the sword, and Gibbon cites, in one of his rare quotations at length from a modern, that passage from Montesquieu which describes third-century Rome as an irregular republic;[50] he improves it by suggesting that the military republic was less an aristocracy than a democracy, and Mameluke Egypt a better comparison than Algiers.[51] The point is that both halves of the *gouvernement ambigu*, the hawk as well as the buzzard, have disintegrated: the senate cannot control the armies, the armies cannot control their own choice of an *imperator*, and there is no *princeps* who can control the one by invoking the image of the other. The Augustan system is at an end.

The victor for the moment was Philip, 'an Arab by birth, and consequently, in the earlier part of his life, a robber by profession'.[52] He is no longer, as medieval historians remembered him, a Christian in private. In order to legitimate his position, he resolved in AD 248 to celebrate the *ludi saeculares* or secular games, a solemn ritual of the civil religion

---

[46] *Ibidem*, p. 202.    [47] *Ibidem*, p. 204.    [48] *Ibidem*, pp. 194–8.
[49] *Ibidem*, pp. 199–207. For the role of the senate, see pp. 196, 197–8, 198–9, 200, 206.
[50] *Ibidem*, p. 210; cf. p. 355 above.
[51] *Ibidem*, nn. 69, 70. Gibbon characterises Montesquieu's parallel as 'ingenious, though somewhat fanciful'; language he several times uses of that author.
[52] *Ibidem*, p. 209.

of Rome, which were supposedly held only once in a century – though
they had been revived by Severus in 204 – and were considered by
Enlightened historians the true source of the papal jubilees.[53] In them
the gods were petitioned 'to maintain the virtue, the felicity and the empire of the Roman people', and the occasion gives Gibbon opportunity
for an especially sonorous *elogium*.

> The magnificence of Philip's shows and entertainments dazzled the eyes of
> the multitude. The devout were employed in the rites of superstition, whilst the
> reflecting few revolved in their anxious minds the past history and the future
> fate of the empire.
>
> Since Romulus, with a small band of shepherds and outlaws, fortified himself
> on the hills near the Tiber, ten centuries had already elapsed. During the first
> four ages, the Romans, in the laborious school of poverty, had acquired the
> virtues of war and government; by the vigorous exertion of those virtues, and by
> the assistance of fortune, they had obtained, in the course of the three succeeding
> centuries, an absolute empire over many countries of Europe, Asia and Africa.
> The last three hundred years had been consumed in apparent prosperity and
> internal decline. The nation of soldiers, magistrates, and legislators, who com-
> posed the thirty-five tribes of the Roman people, was dissolved into the common
> mass of mankind and confounded with the millions of servile provincials, who
> had received the name without adopting the spirit of Romans.

The cosmopolitan nation of manners is no more.

> A mercenary army, levied among the subjects and barbarians of the frontier,
> was the only order of men who preserved and abused their independence. By
> their tumultuary election, a Syrian, a Goth, or an Arab, was exalted to the
> throne of Rome, and invested with despotic power over the conquests and over
> the country of the Scipios.
>
> The limits of the Roman empire still extended from the Western Ocean
> to the Tigris, and from Mount Atlas to the Rhine and the Danube. To the
> undiscerning eye of the vulgar, Philip appeared a monarch no less powerful
> than Hadrian or Augustus had formerly been. The form was still the same,
> but the animating health and vigour were fled. The industry of the people was
> discouraged and exhausted by a long series of oppression. The discipline of the
> legions, which alone, after the extinction of every other virtue, had propped the
> greatness of the state, was corrupted by the ambition, or relaxed by the weakness,
> of the emperors. The strength of the frontiers, which had always consisted in
> arms rather than in fortifications, was insensibly undermined; and the fairest
> provinces were left exposed to the rapaciousness or ambition of the barbarians,
> who soon discovered the decline of the Roman empire.[54]

---

[53] *Ibidem*, p. 211, nn. 56, 58.    [54] *Ibidem*, pp. 211–12; the end of chapter 7.

We have left the mirror of princes and returned to the general history of decline and fall. There will be other grand conclusions like these paragraphs, which close Gibbon's seventh chapter; but a special character belongs to this passage, which ends the narrative that began with Commodus and is followed by two chapters on the condition of nations outside the empire. When narrative is resumed, it will be to recount the Persian and Gothic invasions and the anarchy of the 'thirty tyrants'.

It might almost be said that at this point in the volume of 1776, the explanation of the Decline and Fall is over, the narrative of the Decline and Fall about to begin. Gibbon has completed both the explanation and the narrative of the First Decline and Fall: the history of how the Augustan principate and the Antonine monarchy continued to fail to control the armies, the problem which had destroyed the republic and led to the creation of the principate itself. The earlier failure had led to the disintegration of a republic and its *libertas*; the second has begun to undermine a civil society, the civilisation of wealth and manners which had made the subjects of empire into something close to a nation. Under the Severi, the armies began to rule without honouring even the ghost of the senate; and as that ghost ceased to walk, the centre of government moved *alibi quam Romae* and was found wherever the successful army happened to be. As Rome and Italy lost even the semblance of political citizenship, the cosmopolis of manners was deprived of any will of its own, and the increasing burden of taxation is only the outward sign of a process in which manners are undermined by the absence of virtue, the organised will to maintain them.

It is worth remarking that this has been a secular process and narrative, at once classical and Enlightened; there has been no mention at all of the Christian religion. A new paradox, however, is about to appear in the organisation of Gibbon's history. In the remaining chapters of his first volume, we will begin to study the creation, first by Diocletian and then by Constantine, of a new kind of monarchy, and its first encounters with barbarism and religion. The narrative of these encounters, and of a Decline and Fall which must differ from the First, will occupy the five volumes of a history following that published in 1776, but for reasons we have not even begun to examine, the organisation of that history is to be very long delayed. The remainder of Volume 1 includes – but only includes – a narrative which is to bring us only to the verge of the new monarchy and its history. We must follow that narrative, as well as the encounter with barbarism that provides it with a context.

# CHAPTER 19

# The Illyrian recovery and the new monarchy

## (I)

The breakdown of the *gouvernement ambigu* – the disappearance of the senate as even an empty symbol of vanished republican legitimacy – is both cause and effect of a breakdown in the discipline of the legions. The next phase in the narrative is to be their progressive inability to resist or control increasingly massive incursions by those described as barbarians. In the eighth and ninth chapters of the *Decline and Fall*, Gibbon offers two *peintures* of the manners and customs of peoples so described, before returning to a narrative of their invasions and the ultimately if temporarily successful response of a sequence of strong soldier-emperors, who will reconstitute monarchy without the senate and prepare the new government of Diocletian and Constantine. This change in thematic pattern complicates the structure of Gibbon's narrative. We are at the end of the long story that began with Tiberius Gracchus; civic virtue, nearly extinct, no longer disciplines military virtue, and the latter is the victim of its own anarchy. It is not, however, extinct, and the age of the soldier-emperors is the last heroic age of the frontier legions; the military ethos described in chapter 1 dies hard. Their failure to resist the barbarians is easier to predict than to narrate, and is repeatedly postponed, perhaps to a Zosiman moment when all the blame may rest on Constantine.

There is the further problem of the barbarians themselves. Increasingly, as the narrative proceeds, they cease to hover outside the frontiers; they leave the wings and come upon the stage as actors. But the actions of barbarians do not lend themselves to classical narrative, since they are not the actions of individuals exercising lawful authority, so much as of hordes upon the move;[1] not armies but the migratory peoples described

---

[1] Womersley, 1994, 1, p. 252; last paragraph of ch. 9.

    Unless otherwise specified, all references in the notes to chapters 19 and 20 of this volume are to that text, and in order to avoid unnecessary repetition, only the page numbers are quoted for these two chapters.

by Machiavelli, bringing with them their social structure and their culture, which may become aggressive and transforming forces. *Peinture*, therefore, must merge into *écrit*; what they are becomes what they do; meanwhile, the narrative of what Romans do cannot altogether lose its classical structure. The *Decline and Fall* becomes an increasingly complex narrative from the point where Gibbon introduces the post-Severan period with two chapters on the manners and customs of barbarians.

These are the Persians, in chapter 8, and the forest Germans in chapter 9 (mutating into 'the Goths' in the first part of chapter 10). The Persians are 'barbarians' only in the classical sense that they are neither Greek nor Roman and are thought to obey masters rather than laws. If this is despotism it is part of their nature, not as with Romans for whom it is contrary to their nature. The Persians are a powerful and sophisticated people, practising a world religion and capable of military empire on a scale formidable to the Romans. It is not certain how they are to be situated in the quasi-evolutionary ladder of Enlightened stadial theory; but they are certainly not the horde of migratory pastoral warriors, situated somewhere between savagery and agriculture, to whom that theory attached the term 'barbarian' in its philosophical significance. The Germans of chapter 9 are 'barbarians' in this sense, as are the Goths, Franks and other invaders of the Roman provinces, and the 'Scythian' nomadic peoples like the Huns will appear behind them.

It follows that there are two ways of reading Gibbon's chapters on the 'barbarians'. One is to read them in the setting of Decline and Fall as it presently concerns us: the progressive loss of imperial control, especially in the west. Here the Persians figure as a rival empire, hardly 'barbaric' at all, which competes with the Romans for control over Mesopotamia, sometimes threatening their strongholds as far as Antioch; Gibbon's interest in military geography, an important component of his erudition, comes to the fore here. The Goths, Franks and other Germanic peoples figure differently, as an anarchic and anomic force on the move, with which the Romans fail in the end to cope; the Persians are similarly present, inasmuch as their armies bring about the failure and death of at least two emperors, Valerian and in a later volume Julian. But the dominant theme is the struggle of the Roman system to deal with the problems 'barbarians' present, and though ultimate failure is throughout predicted, the Illyrian narrative is one of success, and the catastrophe is deferred from AD 250 to 400. The equation of the empire with its decline threatens to distort the narrative, while keeping the Romans in the foreground.

It is with this narrative, however, that the present volume is concerned. The alternative treatment is to situate chapters 8 and 9–10 in the setting of Gibbon's increasing though never absent command of philosophical history, relating the successive stages of the history of the human mind and human society, together with 'the triumph of barbarism and religion'. In this setting the centrepiece of chapter 8 becomes his account of the Zoroastrian religion of the Persians,[2] gentile but not barbaric, and occupying an important place in his developing schemes for the history of both religion and philosophy. It may also be remembered that, in the grand narrative to which Gibbon may already have been looking forward, the Zoroastrian religion was doomed to be almost extinguished in its homeland by the rational monotheism of Islam. The barbarism of chapter 9, looking back to Tacitus and forward to Smith, plays its part in the history of society; the transhumant pastoralism of the forest Germans looks eastward to the shepherd stage of development and its recurrent invasions of Europe, westward to the settlement of barbarian and 'Gothic' invaders upon the free tenures which will make them crucial actors in European history. These great themes in Gibbon's writing may, however, be deferred while we pursue his narrative and enquire how the explanation of Decline and Fall, complete by AD 248, carries forward to its catastrophe a century and a half later, which Gibbon did not reach until 1781.

## (11)

From the reign of Augustus to the time of Alexander Severus, the enemies of Rome were in her bosom; the tyrants, and the soldiers; and her prosperity had a very distant and feeble interest in the revolutions that might happen beyond the Rhine and the Euphrates. But when the military order had levelled, in wild anarchy, the power of the prince, the laws of the senate, and even the discipline of the camp, the barbarians of the north and of the east, who had long hovered on the frontier, boldly attacked the provinces of a declining monarchy.[3]

Thus the opening of Gibbon's two chapters on Persian and German manners. When narrative is resumed, the opening runs:

From the great secular games celebrated by Philip to the death of the emperor Gallienus there elapsed (AD 248–268) twenty years of shame and misfortune. During that calamitous period every instant of time was marked, every province of the Roman world was afflicted by barbarous invaders and military tyrants,

---

[2] Pp. 216–21.    [3] P. 213; opening of chapter 8.

and the ruined empire seemed to approach the last and fatal moment of its dissolution. The confusion of the times, and the scarcity of authentic materials, oppose equal difficulties to the historian, who attempts to preserve a clear and unbroken thread of narration. Surrounded with imperfect fragments, always concise, often obscure, and sometimes contradictory, he is reduced to collect, to compare, and to conjecture: and though he ought never to place his conjectures in the rank of facts, yet the knowledge of human nature, and of the sure operation of its fierce and unrestrained passions, might, on some occasions, supply the want of historical materials.[4]

Conjectural history, as it came to be styled, is needed less to supply general patterns of social change than to fill gaps in the recorded narrative where this is deficient or neglected. The central problem of chapter 10 is to recount how the imperial war machine nearly collapsed for the reasons given, and how in spite of them it was rescued at the last moment by a series of military saviours. Who these were and where they came from is yet to be explained, but the answer will have to do with the frontiers and the barbarians. In chapter 9 the peoples beyond the Rhine have been depicted in a language heavily reliant upon Tacitus, and have appeared, as he showed them, more formidable in defending their forests than in attacking the provinces; though the Marcomannic war in the time of Marcus Aurelius, played down in the earlier account of his reign,[5] is now restored to its proper magnitude as the work of a

general conspiracy which . . . comprehended almost all the nations of Germany, and even Sarmatia, from the mouth of the Rhine to that of the Danube.[6]

We begin to look beyond the forests to the marshes east of them, and even to the brink of the steppe; European barbarism begins to enlarge the *Decline and Fall* to its full breadth as a history of Eurasia. Though we are told that the Germanic barbarians were constantly re-forming themselves into loose and fluid war-bands and confederacies,[7] it is now that we encounter, in language recalling Mexía,

that great people, who afterwards broke the Roman power, sacked the Capitol, and reigned in Gaul, Spain and Italy. So memorable was the part which they acted in the subversion of the Western empire, that the name of GOTHS is frequently but improperly used as a general appellation of rude and warlike barbarism,[8]

---

[4] P. 253; opening of chapter 10. For a modern historian's repetition of the same point, see Jones, 1986, 1, p. 23.
[5] P. 38; above, p. 428 this volume.
[6] P. 250; cf. p. 259, n. 22, where the 'conspiracy' becomes an effect of population pressure.
[7] P. 251.      [8] P. 255.

and their role in history may exceed its barbaric beginnings. Gibbon adds Jornandes[9] to Tacitus, and traces them from Scandinavia to Prussia[10] and then – growing more formidable as a military force – south and east to Sarmatia and encounter with

> the Sclavonic language . . . which has been diffused by conquest, from the confines of Italy to the neighbourhood of Japan.

> The Goths were now in possession of the Ukraine, a country of considerable extent and uncommon fertility, intersected with navigable rivers, which, from either side, discharge themselves into the Borysthenes; and interspersed with large and lofty forests of oaks. The plenty of game and fish, the innumerable bee-hives, deposited in the hollow of old trees and in the cavities of rocks, and forming, even in that rude age, a valuable branch of commerce, the size of the cattle, the temperature of the air, the aptness of the soil for every species of grain, and the luxuriancy of the vegetation, all displayed the liberality of Nature, and tempted the industry of man. But the Goths withstood all these temptations, and still adhered to a life of idleness, of poverty, and of rapine,[11]

disregarding this Virgilian setting as – we learn in a footnote[12] – the modern Cossacks still do. As Gibbon's horizon opens to include the continental history of barbarism, his language lessens its focus on the palace and the camp, and relies on the geographer and the traveller as well as the historian. The Goths traverse Roman Dacia and plunder the provinces south of the Danube. The emperor Decius, a worthy and not unvirtuous figure who has dreamed of restoring the powers of the *censor morum*[13] – we hear nothing of his reputation as a persecutor – is defeated and slain by them,[14] and his successor Gallus makes a disgraceful peace for which the soldiers kill him.[15] Valerian succeeds, and Gibbon acknowledges a need to divide his narrative into separate strands.[16] It would seem that the central European world is in motion, and as well as the Goths, it is necessary to record the formation of two powerful and lasting confederacies, the Franks and the Alemanni, who have achieved lasting identity and left their names to two great nations of modern Europe.[17] The Franks cross the Rhine, and raid as far as Spain and even Africa; a force of Alemanni penetrate the Alps and reach Ravenna, before they are repulsed by the praetorians under the command of a momentarily

---

[9] Gibbon does not seem to have owned a copy of the history of the Goths by a sixth-century historian whose name is now usually spelt 'Jordanes'. The above is Gibbon's invariable spelling. He thought the *De Rebus Goticis* an abridgement of a work by Cassiodorus, a Roman subject of the Gothic kingdom later established in Italy.

[10] Pp. 255–60. Gibbon encounters the problem of the historicity of Odin, which had interested him since 1764 (*EEG*, p. 281).

[11] P. 260.    [12] *Ibidem*, n. 28.    [13] Pp. 262–4.    [14] Pp. 264–5.    [15] P. 267.

[16] Pp. 268–9.    [17] Pp. 269–72.

virtuous senate (repressed by Gallienus the son and colleague of Valerian as soon as he hears of the episode).[18] This is as close as Gibbon comes to explaining, in this chapter, why barbarians have suddenly become so formidable and the imperial armies so weak. Perhaps we are looking at a moment when he is inclined to fall back from the decline of virtue, and prefer immoderate size, as an explanation of the decay of the empire; the sources of the Rhine and Danube were too near the passes into northern Italy.

While these disorders are going on, the Goths acquire a maritime, or at least an offshore capacity; they move into the Black Sea and take control of the kingdom of Bosphorus and a supply of flat-bottomed canoes. In these they infest the coasts of the Black Sea and the Sea of Marmora, sacking cities and enslaving the inhabitants; they pass the Hellespont and infest the Aegean – though, as Pedro Mexía had observed, it is getting a little hard to believe in the canoes by this time[19] – and their depredations extend to Ephesus and Athens.[20] In the midst of these disasters, the newly revived Sassanid empire of Persia goes on the offensive and subdues the kingdom of Armenia. Valerian marches to recover this ally and tributary, is taken prisoner and never returns.[21] The narrative now reverts to the Tacitean mode. The irresponsibility of Gallienus leads to an explosion of military pretenders; instead of Galba, Otho, Vitellius and Vespasian, the legendary 'thirty tyrants', reduced by Gibbon to a figure of nineteen – though the count obstinately comes out at twenty, including two women, Zenobia of Palmyra and Victoria in Gaul.[22] It is hard not to believe that Gibbon is using them to reduce the figure, though like Mexía before him he emphasises the 'manly' virtues which qualified each to rule.[23]

These are times of calamity: rebellions in Sicily, Alexandria and Isauria, a widespread plague and a famine, the last of which at least can be called 'the inevitable consequence of rapine and oppression'. There are signs of depopulation, which Gibbon tries to assess by means of an Enlightened use of what statistics he can find (the register of Alexandrians entitled to the distribution of corn).[24] This is perhaps the first indication that something is wrong with the imperial economy, but just as the

---

[18] P. 273.   [19] Above, p. 243 this volume.   [20] Pp. 274–82; narrated at length.
[21] Pp. 282–6. The narrative includes the surprise and sack of Antioch, and the repulse of the Persians from Emesa by the fanatical defenders of the local god. Gibbon does not say that this is the god of Elagabalus.
[22] P. 288.
[23] Above, p. 243 this volume; for Gibbon's use of the adjective, see Womersley, 1994, I, pp. 311 (Victoria), 313, 314 (Zenobia).
[24] P. 294.

defective histories of the time fail to provide Gibbon with general explanations of the barbarian invasions and the proliferation of warlords,
so there is something mystifying about the empire's sudden recovery.
Chapter II begins:

> Under the deplorable reigns of Valerian and Gallienus, the empire was op-
> pressed and almost destroyed by the soldiers, the tyrants and the barbarians. It
> was saved by a series of great princes, who derived their obscure origin from the
> martial provinces of Illyricum. Within a period of about thirty years, Claudius,
> Aurelian, Probus, Diocletian and his colleagues, triumphed over the foreign
> and domestic enemies of the state, re-established, with the military discipline,
> the strength of the frontiers, and deserved the glorious title of Restorers of the
> Roman world.[25]

The language is classical; *rem publicam restituerunt*. Rhetoric is still an
essential part of historiography, but the narrative should contain explanation. This sequence of saviours originates in circumstances both
obscure and suspicious, but has one or two features in common with the
glorious 'five good emperors'. The Illyrians are military men with few
pretensions to senatorial civility, and their time is spent in often desperate campaigning; but their conduct towards the senate, or its shadow,
lacks the brutality of Septimius Severus, and they report their actions
to the conscript fathers as if they still respected them. The parallel with
the Antonines fails at two points, or rather is never proposed. There
is no portrait of general prosperity to be painted, and – of far greater
significance – the sequence will end, not with another Commodus and
another military anarchy, but with the foundation by Diocletian of an
altogether new style of monarchy, having nothing in common with the
Augustan ambiguities. Remodelled and above all Christianised by Constantine, it is this whose subsequent history, of almost twelve centuries,
will constitute the Decline and Fall of Gibbon's future volumes.

Meanwhile there is a narrative of war to be recounted, the normal
employment of the historian – though Gibbon warns us that 'the general
design of this work' (he says nothing of the deficiencies of his sources)
'will not permit' a detailed relation of each reign.[26] What has conjectural
history to supply in its absence? The *imperatores* are Illyrians; that is, they
come from the recently Romanised provinces along the upper Danube,
where 'barbarian' pressure is strongest and the Alpine passes exposed.
Claudius eliminates the floating army of the Goths in a series of battles
in the lower Danubian region;

[25] P. 295.    [26] P. 303.

so considerable was the number of female captives, that every soldier obtained to his share two or three women. A circumstance from which we may conclude, that the invaders entertained some designs of settlement, as well as of plunder; since even in a normal expedition they were accompanied by their families,[27]

as was usual in Germanic or Gothic warfare. This was a coastwise *Volkerwänderung*, not a single-sex foray of vikings; and the old days of massive slave-hauling have briefly returned. Claudius nominates Aurelian as his successor, and we read that the generals preferred him to the dying emperor's brother. He has to deal with the frontier war in the setting of a plague of military pretenders, and his first step is to remove the settlements of Dacia from the north to the south bank of the Danube. Adam Smith must have approved Gibbon's suggestion that the prosperity and agriculture of the former province helped civilise the barbarians who would otherwise have plundered it; civil society can be an instrument of statecraft no less effective than war.[28] But an invasion of Alemanni has to be destroyed close to Rome, and it is an ominous sign that Aurelian finds it necessary to fortify the city, to which Gibbon's eye as a historian always returns.[29]

His remaining task is to eliminate the last two of the military usurpers, both of them, 'to complete the ignominy of Rome', women. Victoria in the far west is a 'mother of the camps',[30] a figure intelligible within the politics of the armies; but Zenobia in the far east is exceptional as a woman, as an Oriental, and as the sovereign of an independent state offering an alternative to Roman empire in the Greco-Syrian world – a second and more virtuous Cleopatra. Gibbon endeavours, not without success, to treat her with respect in all three capacities, and she may be the pre-eminent female figure in the whole *Decline and Fall*. Eighteenth-century Europe was acquainted with strong and effective empresses, and Gibbon has no difficulty in recognising Zenobia as one of the kind. He cannot, of course, resist being playful about her, or discussing her sexuality – though since her fertility entailed the production of heirs, she was right to control it as an instrument of state.[31] He describes as 'manly' (Mexía's *varonil*) the virtues and abilities she displays as a prince, but does not deny that she possessed them, or (with one exception) suggest that they were feigned; she can punish or pardon, she knows when to be frugal and when to be liberal; she annexes Egypt, and her role as protector of the Roman provinces in Asia becomes that of a rival. The problem of

[27] P. 302.   [28] Pp. 305–6.   [29] P. 310.   [30] P. 311.   [31] P. 313 and n. 55.

Gibbon's count of 'tyrants' may be resolved by supposing that Zenobia –
never proclaimed by mutinous legions – is not one of them.[32]

Aurelian marches against her, and is involved in encounters which
belong to the field of philosophical rather than classical history. Out of
'superstitious reverence', he spares the city of Tyana, the home two hundred and fifty years before of Apollonius the philosopher and wonder-
worker. Apollonius had been a figure of interest to deist moderns,[33] and
Gibbon inserts a memorably naughty footnote which nearly confounds
him with his contemporary Jesus Christ.[34] This story, like others, comes
down from the *Historia Augusta*, which Gibbon knows to be full of picturesque fictions; he is allowing both their fantasy and his philosophy to
supplement the narrative. Aurelian recovers Egypt and Syria, and be-
sieges Palmyra, a city Gibbon describes with the aid of modern travellers
and scholars.[35] Zenobia attempts escape, but is brought back, and 'as female fortitude is commonly artificial, so it is seldom steady or consistent',
denounces her own counsellors, including a certain Longinus, whom
Gibbon supposes to be the philosopher quoted at the end of chapter 2
and allows the death of a Stoic.[36] This passage when published aroused
the indignation of Suzanne Necker, who told Gibbon that female virtues
were not artificial. He replied that he had meant only physical courage
under the stress of war, and that women were designed to soften and
adorn the world, not to wage war in it. Mme Necker replied, in part,
that if Gibbon knew little about women, it was because he had not spent
enough time in polished conversation in the salons of Paris; he affably
agreed, and was the Neckers' guest for some months in 1777. Such are the
highlights of an exchange which might be explored in greater depth.[37]

Aurelian returns to Rome, and celebrates a triumph which Gibbon
describes at length, perhaps because it is nearly the last of its kind. In it are
led as human trophies Zenobia, loaded with golden chains and jewels,
and Tetricus – last of the western pretenders, who has survived by betraying his own legions – wearing the trousers peculiar to barbaric Gauls.
Contrary to ancient republican practice, both are allowed to survive their
ritual humiliation – Tetricus as a Roman senator, Zenobia as a Roman
matron.[38] Gibbon is telling us something about a change in manners,

---

[32] Pp. 314–15.
[33] Charles Blount's translation of his works had appeared in 1680. He also figures in orthodox
ecclesiastical histories which Gibbon consulted.
[34] P. 315, n. 63.     [35] Pp. 316–17.     [36] P. 319.
[37] *MW*, 11, pp. 176–80 (Necker to Gibbon), 186–90 (Gibbon to Necker), 193–5 (Necker); *EGLH*,
pp. 75, 83–6, 90–8; *Memoirs*, p. 158.
[38] Pp. 320–2.

though the abandonment of ancient severity can be regarded with mixed feelings. Due perhaps to his doubts about the *Historia Augusta*, he seems to be alternating between a benign and a darker narrative. Aurelian leaves Rome, after allegedly losing seven thousand men in putting down a rebellion of workers at the mint; Gibbon refuses to believe this story, and suggests that the senate, people and praetorians may have risen against him and he may have resumed the role of a tyrant conducting a blood-purge of the senate.[39] But when Aurelian is murdered by his own staff near Byzantium, the repentant conspirators report their own deed to the senate and ask it to elect an emperor. This unlikely tale – Gibbon insists that it is well documented[40] – takes up the opening pages of chapter 12. The choice falls upon Tacitus, who 'claimed his descent from the philosophic historian, whose writings will instruct the last generations of mankind', and is even compared to Numa Pompilius, the 'Sabine philosopher', who reigned as second king of Rome.[41] A better analogy would surely have been Pertinax, elected by the senate at the death of Commodus and soon after murdered by the praetorians; Tacitus lasts little longer, though the manner of his death is unknown.[42] Gibbon seems to have wanted to imagine the senate and army in a last blaze of good feeling, long after the ambiguity of their relationship has been exposed by Tiberius and swept aside by Severus. It is a fantasy, in which Tacitus the emperor figures in a sentimental history replacing a history of statecraft and action, and Tacitus the historian stands at the point of replacement. The former dies – significantly or not at Tyana – after possibly performing the role of Nerva in designating the trustworthy Probus to succeed him. This lesser Trajan clears Gaul of the Franks and pacifies most of Germany; he settles vast numbers of barbarians in various provinces, and attempts a wall like China's between the Rhine and the Danube;[43] but he demands too much of the legions in employing them on public works, and they murder him in a mutiny near Sirmium.[44] Like the assassins of Aurelian, they instantly repent and make an emperor of his lieutenant Carus, last of the Illyrian heroes and a senator as well as a soldier. 'In an age when the civil and military professions began to be' – only now began? – 'irrevocably separated from each other, they were united in the person of Carus', rough soldier though he likes to show himself.[45] He campaigns against the Persians, penetrates beyond the Tigris, but is killed, allegedly by lightning, in circumstances more

---

[39] Pp. 323–5.    [40] P. 328.    [41] Pp. 328, 329.
[42] For Pertinax, pp. 120–6 (chapter 4); for Tacitus, p. 334.
[43] Pp. 338–42.    [44] Pp. 346, 348.    [45] Pp. 346, 348.

than obscure. His sons succeed him – we may recall the death of Marcus Aurelius – but little more can be said of either than that the worse of the two, Carinus, celebrated games of uncommon magnificence in a Colosseum here described in detail.[46] From the intrigues of the camp which punctually ensue, there emerges as victor Diocletian, with whom a new order of things is to begin.

(III)

We are at the point of the crucial transformation which will bring to an end the first volume of the *Decline and Fall*: the termination of the Augustan principate which has been in anarchy since Septimius Severus and Philip the Arab, and whose ghosts have been contending with one another throughout the otherwise real achievements of the Illyrian restorers. Yet this does not mean that the roles prescribed by classical rhetoric have ceased to be of effect in either historiography or history; Diocletian, the son of a Dalmatian freedman who will put an end to the world of Augustus, is deliberately paralleled with that world's founder.

> The valour of Diocletian was never found inadequate to his duty, or to the occasion, but he appears not to have possessed the daring and generous spirit of a hero, who courts danger and fame, disdains artifice, and boldly challenges the allegiance of his equals. His abilities were useful rather than splendid – a vigorous mind improved by the experience and study of mankind; dexterity and application in business; a judicious mixture of liberality and economy, of mildness and rigour; profound dissimulation under the disguise of military frankness; steadiness to pursue his ends; flexibility to vary his means; and, above all, the great art of submitting his own passions, as well as those of others, to the interest of his ambition, and of colouring his ambition with the most specious pretences of justice and public utility. Like Augustus, Diocletian may be considered as the founder of a new empire. Like the adopted son of Caesar, he was distinguished as a statesman rather than as a warrior; nor did either of those princes employ force, whenever their purpose could be effected by policy.[47]

Like Augustus, again, Diocletian aims at stabilising a political system disordered by a long succession of competing soldiers; but instead of putting an end to a triumvirate it is his policy to establish a tetrarchy. He associates himself with the ferocious Maximian and both take the title of Augustus; but Diocletian is verbally identified with Jupiter and Maximian only with Hercules. The system is completed when each Augustus adopts a Caesar to succeed him; the purple is rendered collegiate to minimise

[46] Pp. 351–4.    [47] P. 359.

the effects of random proclamations by provincial armies. The Caesars are stationed on the Rhine and the Danube, the Augusti at Milan and Nicomedia; *alibi quam Romae* has become strategic necessity; but the latter are as constant campaigners as the former, and the modern reader suspects a regroupment of the legions between the frontiers and interior reserves. Gibbon seems to say nothing of this in his history of the wars of the tetrarchy. There is a peasant rebellion in Gaul, that of the Bagaudae, which permits both ancient and modern reflections; resembling that of the fourteenth-century Jacquerie, it moves Gibbon to suggest that 'very many of those institutions, referred by an easy solution to the feudal system, are derived from the Celtic barbarians'. He cites Caesar's account of the Gauls as divided into priests, nobles and commoners.

It was very natural for the plebeians, oppressed by debt or apprehensive of injury, to implore the protection of some powerful chief, who acquired over their persons and property the same absolute rights as, among the Greeks and Romans, a master exercised over his slaves. The greatest part of the nation was gradually reduced into a state of servitude; compelled to perpetual labour on the estates of the Gallic nobles, and confined to the soil, either by the real weight of fetters, or by the no less cruel and forcible restraints of the laws.[48]

The debate over the origins of serfdom and vassalage had been going on among French scholars since the sixteenth century,[49] and since at latest the fifteenth it had been a commonplace among English writers that the French peasants were so ground down by seigneurial and royal exactions that they were useless as soldiers and seldom rose in rebellion. Gibbon says nothing of either debate, and when the same oppressions produce the rising of the Bagaudae,

the ravages of the peasants equalled those of the fiercest barbarians. They asserted the natural rights of men, but they asserted those rights with the most savage cruelty.

Gibbon is borrowing directly from Voltaire, who in chapter cxxxi of the *Essai sur les Moeurs* asserted of the followers of Thomas Munzer in 1523: 'Ils réclamaient les droits du genre humain: mais ils les soutinrent en bêtes féroces.'[50] They are put down by the legions of Maximian.

So strong and uniform is the current of popular passions, that we might almost venture, from very scanty materials, to relate the particulars of this war; but we are not disposed to believe that the principal leaders, Aelianus and Amandus, were Christians, or to insinuate that the rebellion, as it happened in

---

[48] P. 363.    [49] Kelley, 1970.    [50] *NCG*, p. 140.

the time of Luther, was occasioned by the abuse of those benevolent principles of Christianity which inculcate the natural freedom of mankind.[51]

Gibbon was neither alluding to the American nor prognosticating the French revolution, and this is one of the very few allusions to Christianity before the narrative reaches the accession of Constantine. It is Enlightened in the sense that it praises religion as civility, instead of denouncing it as fanaticism. But contemporary parallels are also found in the usurpation of imperial authority in Britain by Carausius and after him by Allectus; a crisis of sea power in which we hear the voice both of the historian's militia experience and that of Gibbon's Jacobite forebears, responding with mixed feelings to the events of 1688 (and even 1588 and 1066). The somewhat precarious naval expedition sent by the Caesar Constantius

ventured to set sail with a side-wind and on a stormy day. The weather proved favourable to their enterprise. Under the cover of a thick fog they escaped the fleet of Allectus, which had been stationed off the Isle of Wight to receive them, landed in safety on the same part of the western coast, and convinced the Britons that a superiority of naval strength will[52] not always protect their country from a foreign invasion . . . The usurper had posted himself near London, to expect the formidable attack of Constantius, who commanded in person the fleet of Boulogne; but the descent of a new enemy required his immediate presence in the west. He performed this long march in so precipitate a manner that he encountered the whole force of the praefect with a small body of harassed and disheartened troops. The engagement was soon terminated by the total defeat and death of Allectus; a single battle, as it has often happened, decided the fate of this great island; and when Constantius landed on the shores of Kent, he found them covered with obedient subjects. Their acclamations were loud and unanimous; and the virtues of the conqueror may induce us to believe that they sincerely rejoiced in a revolution which, after a separation of ten years, restored Britain to the body of the Roman empire.[53]

We are reading words written by the Hampshire militia captain, in progress from Tory to Whig principles. An insecure dynasty in Britain cannot be defended on blue water alone, and even a loyal national militia may be insufficient without an expeditionary force which will meet the challenges on land in continental Europe. So much for England; for Rome, however, these are internal wars in far western provinces. The Caesars campaign on the Rhine and Danube, where they wisely

---

[51] P. 364.    [52] The choice of tense should be noted.
[53] P. 367. It had been the complaint of many Tory critics of the Glorious Revolution that William III had involved Britain in the wars of Europe beyond the point which was to her interest.

or unwisely settle large groups of barbarians within the frontiers. The Augusti take the lead in major operations in the east: a destructive reconquest of Egypt and Nubia, which moves Diocletian to ban and burn all books on the transmutation of metals –

It may be remarked that these ancient books, so liberally ascribed to Pythagoras, to Solomon, or to Hermes, were the pious frauds of more recent times . . . Philosophy, with the aid of experience, has at length banished the study of alchymy; and the present age, however desirous of riches, is content to seek them by the humbler means of commerce and industry[54] –

followed by a great Persian war, the result of a national revolt in Armenia directed against the Magian intolerance which has destroyed the solar cult of the deified kings. The Armenian hero Tiridates leads it, aided by a nomad adventurer whom the vengeance of the Chinese emperor has driven from Persia,[55] and the Roman decision to restore the Armenian kingship puts the imperial policy in contact with the history of central Asia. The treaty which ends the Persian war is among the few signed between the Romans and a literate enemy; it transfers five provinces beyond the Tigris to Roman control, and if, as scholars since Gibbon have believed, these were rather ceded to Armenia and garrisoned by Roman troops, he might see this as justifying Diocletian's adherence to 'the moderate policy of Augustus and the Antonines'[56] in avoiding further extensions of empire.

The arduous work of rescuing the distressed empire from tyrants and barbarians had now been completely achieved by a succession of Illyrian peasants. As soon as Diocletian entered into the twentieth year of his reign, he celebrated that memorable era, as well as the success of his arms, by the pomp of a Roman triumph . . . It was the last that Rome ever beheld. Soon after this period the emperors ceased to vanquish, and Rome ceased to be the capital for the empire.[57]

Diocletian's abandonment of the city needs to be dramatised as well as explained. Gibbon returns in imagination to his Capitoline starting-point and to the vivid emotions he had felt on his first visit to Rome, when 'each memorable spot where Romulus stood, or Tully spoke, or Caesar fell was at once present to my eye',[58] and embarks on one more of his grand elegies on republican legend in the midst of imperial decay.

[54] Pp. 372–3.   [55] Pp. 374–5.   [56] P. 380.   [57] Pp. 383, 384.   [58] *Memoirs*, p. 134.

The spot on which Rome was founded had been consecrated by ancient ceremonies and imaginary miracles. The presence of some god, or the memory of
some hero, seemed to animate every part of the city, and the empire of the world
had been promised to the Capitol. The native Romans felt and confessed the
power of this agreeable illusion. It was derived from their ancestors, had grown
up with their earliest habits of life, and was protected in some measure, by the
opinion of political utility. The form and the seat of government were intimately
blended together, nor was it esteemed possible to transport the one without destroying the other. But the sovereignty of the capital was gradually annihilated
in the extent of conquest; the provinces rose to the same level, and the vanquished nations acquired the name and privileges, without imbibing the partial
affections, of Romans. During a long period, however, the remains of the ancient
constitution and the influence of custom preserved the dignity of Rome.[59]

There is in fact no exorcising this *genius loci*; Cola di Renzo will be
affirming it in the last chapters of the *Decline and Fall*, and there is a sense
in which Diocletian is withdrawing from further competition with it and
hoping that it will wither in isolation.

The dislike expressed by Diocletian towards Rome and Roman freedom was
not the effect of momentary caprice, but the result of the most artful policy.
That crafty prince had framed a new system of imperial government, which
was afterwards completed by the family of Constantine; and as the image of the
old constitution was religiously preserved in the senate, he resolved to deprive
that order of its small remains of power and consideration. We may recollect,
about eight years before the elevation of Diocletian, the transient greatness and
the ambitious hopes of the Roman senate.[60]

The episode of the symbolically named Tacitus had displayed the unreal energy of an institution which had been nothing more than an image
of itself for over two centuries. Under the Julio-Claudians, the Flavians
and the Antonines, there had been a palace dynasty on the Palatine hill,
pretending to share power with the senate on the Capitol; a *gouvernement
ambigu*, compulsively driven by the search for legitimacy to pretend to
be what it was not and maintain images of republican legality which
substituted themselves for reality. When dynastic continuity lapsed, as
in the year 79, armies marched to Rome to instal new rulers in the
palace and extort from the senate a recognition it could not refuse but
no one else could give. When there were no more dynasties, as under the
post-Severan anarchy, armies were driven to confer the purple of themselves and once more march to Rome, or face provincial breakaway, in
the unending search for legitimacy. The Illyrian period had shown that

---

[59] P. 384.     [60] P. 386.

emperors and senators acting in the best of faith were locked in a hopeless relation, where one must extort what the other no longer had to give; the rhetorical structure of these chapters is valuable because it obliges us to suppose good faith in order to understand that it could no longer work. The original hypocrisy of Augustus was compelling his successors to act both sincerely and two-facedly and to fail in doing so. Diocletian and his colleagues were deciding to abandon pretence, and claim a new kind of legitimacy, as Severus had disdained to do; but they could do so only by abandoning the central sanctity;

and when they fixed their residence at a distance from the capital, they for ever laid aside the dissimulation which Augustus had recommended to his successors. In the exercise of the legislative as well as the executive power, the sovereign advised with his ministers, instead of consulting the great council of the nation. The name of the senate was mentioned with honour till the last period of the empire; the vanity of its members was still flattered with the honorary distinctions; but the assembly which had been so long the source, and so long the instrument of power, was respectfully suffered to sink into oblivion. The senate of Rome, losing all connection with the imperial court and the actual constitution, was left a venerable but useless monument of antiquity on the Capitoline hill.[61]

We may think of this as a search for honesty, since hypocrisy could be pursued only at the cost of ruinous civil wars; or as the substitution of an absolute for a corrupt mixed monarchy. But if what it meant was that Diocletian and his colleagues would no longer go to Rome and would reside instead in their administrative headquarters, by what apparatus of real and symbolic power would they be surrounded? The tetrarchy was more than a collegiate military dictatorship, a simple separation of the army from the magisterial structure; it was an attempt to escape from military virtue and its hopeless struggle to reunite itself with civic; and Gibbon instantly turns to consider how the emperor adopted the only other symbology of power available to a palace without a Capitol. He took to calling himself *dominus* or 'lord' in Latin, *basileus* or 'king' in Greek,[62] and to the ancient and universally recognised ritual of palace monarchy: personal sanctity and inaccessibility, protected by elaborate ceremony and a series of doorkeepers.

The pride, or rather the policy, of Diocletian, engaged that artful prince to introduce the stately magnificence of the court of Persia. He ventured to assure the diadem, an ornament detested by the Romans as the odious ensign

---

[61] P. 387.    [62] Pp. 387–8.

of royalty, and the use of which had been considered as the most desperate act of the madness of Caligula. It was no more than a broad white fillet set with pearls, which encircled the emperor's head. The sumptuous robes of Diocletian and his successors were of silk and gold; and it is remarked with indignation that even their shoes were studded with the most precious gems. The access to their sacred person was every day rendered more difficult by the institution of new forms and ceremonies. The avenues of the palace were strictly guarded by the various *schools*, as they began to be called, of domestic officers. The interior apartments were intrusted to the jealous vigilance of the eunuchs; the increase of whose numbers and influence was the most infallible symptom of the progress of despotism. When a subject was at length admitted to the imperial presence, he was obliged, whatever might be his rank, to fall prostrate on the ground, and to adore, according to the eastern fashion, the divinity of his lord and master.[63]

All this, of course, was as old in the Greco-Roman imagination, and its vision of 'oriental' kingship, as Deioces the Mede in Herodotus,[64] who had turned himself from a primitive king giving judgement in the open to the inhabitant of a forbidden city behind many-coloured concentric walls, from which he sent out written decisions and a swarm of agents to inform his secret counsels. It had deeply affected the ideas held of kingship, and the functions of this model of rule were as well known as its dangers.

Diocletian was a man of sense, who, in the course of private as well as public life, had formed a just estimate both of himself and of mankind; nor is it easy to conceive that in substituting the manners of Persia to those of Rome he was seriously actuated by so mean a principle as that of vanity. He flattered himself that an ostentation of splendour and luxury would subdue the imagination of the multitude; that the monarch would be less exposed to the rude licence of the people and the soldiers, as his person was secluded from the public view, and that habits of submission would insensibly be productive of sentiments of veneration. Like the modesty affected by Augustus, the state maintained by Diocletian was a theatrical representation; but it must be confessed that, of the two comedies, the former was of a much more liberal and manly character than the latter. It was the aim of the one to disguise, and the object of the other to display, the unbounded power which the emperors possessed over the Roman world.[65]

But liberal and manly behaviour, which is surely to act as the person one indeed is, is becoming inseparable from disguise, but not apparently from concealment. The liberal and manly Augustus was a hypocrite, because in pretending to be a citizen in the open forum he pretended he was not acting when in fact he was. Diocletian, never out of the role

[63] Pp. 388–9.   [64] Godley, 1926, I, pp. 126–31.   [65] P. 389.

in which his unlimited power was displayed, was never not acting and consequently never a hypocrite; yet in his case the essence of display was concealment. Augustus could go into the forum, openly and at the same time hypocritically; Diocletian could lay aside dissimulation by never going to Rome at all, but was obliged to remain inaccessible at the heart of his palace, encased within the role in which his power was displayed but he himself seldom seen. He was substituting rule by superstition for rule by hypocrisy. If power could appear in the public space only at the cost of role-playing and mask-wearing, we are not so far from the question of how Leviathan can represent our persons at all. And in the palace being created by Diocletian, a great deal of effective power must necessarily pass to those who control access to the sacred person, eunuchs included; as Gibbon reports Diocletian complaining[66] after he had with relief abdicated his hieratic role and returned to the authenticity of retirement. Their numbers multiply, as do their costs.

Ostentation was the first principle of the new system instituted by Diocletian. The second was division. He divided the empire, the provinces and every branch of the civil as well as military administration. He multiplied the wheels of the machine of government, and rendered its operation less rapid but more secure.[67]

Since he intended the tetrarchy to become a permanent institution

instead of a modest family of slaves and freedmen, such as had contented the simple greatness of Augustus and Trajan, three or four magnificent courts were established in the various parts of the empire, and as many Roman *kings* contended with each other and with the Persian monarch for the vain superiority of pomp and luxury. The number of ministers, of magistrates, of officers, and of servants, who filled the different departments of the state, was multiplied beyond the example of former times; and (if we may borrow the warm expression of a contemporary) 'when the proportion of those who received exceeded the proportion of those who contributed, the provinces were oppressed by the weight of tributes'.[68]

The contemporary is a Christian, Lactantius. Gibbon himself lived at a time in English politics when it could be contended that 'the influence of the crown has increased, is increasing, and ought to be diminished', and was to lose his near-sinecure with the Board of Trade to Burke's campaign for economical reform; but the economic fear which attended this alleged political corruption was not that of direct taxation, so much as of increased public debt. In Roman history 'from this period to the extinction of the empire', the crushing weight of 'particularly the land-tax

<hr/>

[66] Pp. 394–5.   [67] P. 389.   [68] Pp. 390–1.

and capitation' is repeatedly presented by historians 'as the intolerable and increasing grievance of their own times'.[69] Diocletian stands only at the beginning of this process, but:

> Whatever advantages and whatever defects might attend these innovations, they must be ascribed in a very great degree to the first inventor; but as the new frame of policy was gradually improved and completed by succeeding princes, it will be more satisfactory to delay the consideration of it till the season of its full maturity and perfection. Reserving, therefore, for the reign of Constantine a more exact picture of the new empire, we shall content ourselves with describing the principal and decisive outline, as it was traced by the hand of Diocletian.[70]

## (IV)

This is a crucial decision in the construction of the *Decline and Fall*, as must be considered further in the concluding chapter of this volume; but chapter 13 of the *Decline and Fall* itself ends with some passages of philosophical history which cannot pass unnoticed. Diocletian's decision to abdicate, and spend his remaining years in a palace (more correctly a villa) on the Dalmatian coast, sets the theme for what is left of this chapter. Gibbon describes the ruins of Spalato or Split – which he spells 'Spalatro' – from an imposing book by two English travellers,[71] but he adds:

> We are informed by a more recent and very judicious traveller that the awful ruins of Spalatro are not less expressive of the decline of the arts than of the greatness of the Roman empire in the time of Diocletian. If such was indeed the state of architecture, we must naturally believe that painting and sculpture had experienced a still more sensible decay. The practice of architecture is directed by a few general and even mechanical rules. But sculpture, and, above all, painting, propose to themselves the imitation not only of the forms of nature but of the characters and passions of the human soul. In those sublime arts the dexterity of the hand is of little avail unless it is animated by fancy and guided by the most correct taste and observation.
>
> It is almost unnecessary to remark that the civil distractions of the empire, the licence of the soldiers, the inroads of the barbarians, and the progress of despotism, had proved very unfavourable to genius, and even to learning. The succession of Illyrian princes restored the empire without restoring the sciences. Their military education was not calculated to inspire them with the love of letters; and even the mind of Diocletian, however active and capacious in business, was totally uninformed by study or speculation. The professions of law and physic are of such common use and certain profit that they will always

[69] *Ibidem.*    [70] Pp. 389–90.    [71] P. 397, n. 121.

secure a sufficient number of practitioners endowed with a reasonable degree of abilities and knowledge; but it does not appear that the students in those two faculties appeal to any celebrated masters who have flourished within that period. The voice of poetry was silent. History was reduced to dry and confused abridgements, alike destitute of amusement and instruction. A languid and affected eloquence was still retained in the pay and service of the emperors, who encouraged not any arts except those which contributed to the gratification of their pride or the defence of their power.[72]

It is the Tacitean generalisation with which Gibbon earlier closed his second chapter. The arts, liberty and virtue are necessary to one another and decline together. History, poetry and rhetoric are the arts of public speech, and flourish only where there is 'liberal and manly' counsel and citizenship; unlike the marginally more mechanical jurisprudence and physic, they cannot thrive in the climate of the palace, though in the military camps of the Illyrians even these declined. In the first of the two paragraphs quoted, it is further shown how the more polite and less political plastic arts – sculpture and painting are ranked above mechanical architecture – cannot thrive unless humans have the freedom to be what they are. Their function is to imitate nature, and human nature in particular, and in a political world where everything is becoming theatrical representation – the heirs of Augustus claiming to be what they are not, the heirs of Diocletian constantly playing the roles which are their only mode of being – there is little that is natural left to imitate. Even in his retirement from active business at Split, Diocletian would find no great art to patronise, because *negotium* and *otium* have ceased to support one another in a world increasingly unfree. We are among Longinus' pygmies, and the fierce giants are still some way off.

Gibbon proceeds, in a closing passage laden with significances that have yet to appear, to apply the same diagnosis to philosophy, another art dependent on free speech and the faithful observation of nature.

The declining age of learning and of mankind is marked, however, by the rise and rapid progress of the new Platonists. The school of Alexandria silenced those of Athens; and the ancient sects enrolled themselves under the banners of the more fashionable teachers, who recommended their systems by the novelty of their method and the austerity of their manners. Several of these masters – Ammonius, Plotinus, Amelius and Porphyry – were men of profound thought and intense application; but, by mistaking the true object of philosophy, their labours contributed much less to improve than to corrupt the human

[72] Pp. 397–8.

understanding. The knowledge that is suited to our situation and powers, the whole compass of moral, natural, and mathematical science, was neglected by the new Platonists; whilst they exhausted their strength in the verbal disputes of metaphysics, attempted to explore the secrets of the invisible world, and studied to reconcile Aristotle with Plato, on subjects of which both these philosophers were as ignorant as the rest of mankind. Consuming their reason in these deep but unsubstantial meditations, their minds were exposed to illusions of fancy. They flattered themselves that they possessed the secret of disengaging the soul from its corporeal prison; claimed a familiar intercourse with daemons and spirits; and, by a very singular revolution, converted the study of philosophy into that of magic. The ancient sages had derided the popular superstition; after disguising its extravagance by the thin pretence of allegory, the disciples of Plotinus and Porphyry became its most zealous defenders. As they agreed with the Christians in a few mysterious points of faith, they attacked the remainder of their theological system with all the fury of civil war. The Platonists would scarcely deserve a place in the history of science, but in that of the church the mention of them will very frequently occur.[73]

For the Christian Fathers the neo-Platonists could perceive spirit but not its union with matter in the Incarnation; but for Gibbon they are losing contact with history and reality. It does not seem to be an accident that he places them in the age of Diocletian, taking the place of the Stoic, Peripatetic and even Academic schools of the late republic and the principate. These had been philosophies for magistrates, practising *negotium* and *otium* in an age when actions and speech were free and things, especially *res publicae*, could be seen for what they were; even the gods as creations of the poetic imagination and the public judgement. The magistrate could take part in approved myths, rituals and performances, secretly despising the vulgar imagination but assured of who he was and what world he was attempting to shape; but as the republican and senatorial aristocracies lost control of their actions, and as the public world (where not shaped unthinkingly by the sword) became increasingly a series of theatrical performances, in which actors played roles instead of agents carrying out their business, problems of representation and reality became central, and contemplation, metaphysics and allegory usurped the intellect. Where Stoicism and Epicureanism had been philosophies for the forum and the villa, neo-Platonism was the intellectual pursuit of an empire ruled from sacred palaces. But this philosophy is contrasted no less directly with the 'human understanding', the 'knowledge suited to our situations', 'the whole compass of moral, natural and mathematical

[73]  Pp. 398–9; the closing paragraph of chapter 13.

science', of Locke and Enlightenment, and is therefore as antithetical to the new modernity as it was to classical antiquity. Together with its monastic and scholastic successors, the new Platonism will dominate the ten to fourteen centuries of 'modern history' that elapse while the descendants of the fierce giants are relearning the use of freedom, taste and science, and will make the history of philosophy part of the history of decline and fall, barbarism and religion. It belongs, however, less to the history of science than to the history of the Church, and is used by Gibbon to introduce the information that there is such a thing as the latter. He has said nothing of this so far, and our only hint that there are Christians abroad in the world of the Illyrian emperors is his use of Lactantius' *The Deaths of the Persecutors*.[74] We shall hear no more of the vast importance of neo-Platonism in the history of the church until chapter 21, when we are introduced to the great debates over the divine nature which oblige Constantine to convoke the Council of Nicaea. Chapters 15 and 16, which close the first volume of the *Decline and Fall* and conventionally dominate our reading of Gibbon's understanding of Christianity, are therefore to an important degree preliminary; aspects of the transition from the Roman decay to late antiquity, to the history of the Constantinean monarchy and the Christian church which Gibbon will be writing now the theses of Augustan principate and Antonine monarchy, of the severance of civic from military virtue and their mutual corruption, have ceased to be centrally significant. The history of barbarism has been introduced; the history of religion has only begun to appear, and Zoroaster and Plato are its prophets.

[74] Chapter 13, nn. 86, 91, 92, 93, 94, 103, 104, 107. Eusebius has also begun to appear (n. 53).

*Epilogue*

# CHAPTER 20

# The Constantinean moment

(I)

The fourteenth chapter of the *Decline and Fall* recounts the civil wars –
they are still wars among Roman citizens – between the members of
the college of emperors Diocletian has set up, which did not outlast
his abdication in 305. The narrative is continued to the moment when
Constantine is in sole control of the Roman world, having eliminated his
rivals, Maxentius in a battle at the gates of Rome in 312, and Licinius
in a naval battle on the Bosphorus and a siege of Byzantium in 323. At
this moment there occurs a profound breach in the continuity, both of
Roman history and of *The History of the Decline and Fall of the Roman Empire*.
The nature of this caesura will require close examination in the latter
part of this concluding chapter of *The First Decline and Fall*, but to reach it
we must first explore the narrative that arrives at the climactic moment.

A cycle of wars among commanding generals, leading to the establishment of a new unifying dynasty, challenges comparison with earlier
episodes of the same kind: the anarchy preceding the Illyrian succession, the wars at the death of Commodus leading to the triumph of the
Severi, the wars at the death of Nero that established the Flavians and
the nominative succession, even the wars of the triumvirates that ended
the republic and set up the principate. Constantine's victory by land and
sea in 323 may almost recall the *bellum Actiacum*, since it brings a new
system of government; though Augustus' victory was a triumph of west
over east, and Constantine's entailed a decisive shift of power from Italy
to the Hellespont. Nor do the wars of Diocletian's disintegrating tetrarchy indicate a change in the basis of power; the *imperatores* are merely
following out the logic of the *arcanum imperii*, which reveals that power
belongs to any army that can retain it. There is now scarcely the ghost
of the senate as an actor in the succession, and Diocletian's experiment
in sacred palace monarchy has failed to establish collegiality among his

lieutenants. How Constantine will control the armies from his new capital remains to be seen; the wait for Gibbon's first readers would prove a
long one.

This is not to say that chapter 14 merely chronicles the victories
and defeats of marching armies. Themes are present, and in one case
significantly absent. The chapter is to end with a distant prospect of
Constantine's removal of the empire's capital to the new city that bears
his name; the climax of both Tacitus' *arcanum* that emperors could be
made *alibi quam Romae* and Gibbon's Capitoline vision of the history of
a city deserted by its empire. Diocletian has established two capitals for
his Augusti, at Milan to watch the Alps and at Nicomedia to watch the
Persians,[1] while the Caesars their juniors based themselves at Mainz or
Trier on the Rhine, and at Sirmium or Naissus on the Danube. There
has occurred a decisive eastward shift of the balance of empire; it is casually observed that the Hellespont and Bosphorus 'flowed in the midst of
the Roman world'.[2] There is a progressive abandonment of Rome itself;
but that city is full of the ghosts of empire, and in the wars of 305–23 its
senate, people and praetorians more than once assert themselves. They
overthrow Severus and elect Maxentius; the formidable Galerius fails to
reduce them,[3] and when they find Maxentius a tyrant, it is the senate
and people who enlist the aid of Constantine in Gaul.[4] The battle of
the Milvian bridge in which Maxentius perishes is the last occasion on
which an army fights its way into Rome to elect an emperor, though the
senate, people and praetorians are now such shadowy figures that they
almost presage the medieval Romans, confronting Frederick Barbarossa
and his successors in a re-enactment of tragedy as farce. It is another
of those episodes not uncommon in Gibbon, when ghosts wage battle
because they cannot exorcise one another.

After the defeat of Maxentius, the victorious emperor passed no more than
two or three months in Rome, which he visited twice during the remainder of his
life, to celebrate the solemn festivals of the tenth and of the twentieth years of his
reign. Constantine was almost perpetually in motion to exercise the legions, or
to inspect the state of the provinces. Treves, Milan, Aquileia, Sirmium, Naissus
and Thessalonica, were the occasional places of his residence, till he founded a
NEW ROME on the confines of Europe and Asia.[5]

This strongly suggests the final departure of the *genius loci* from the
ancient city; but Gibbon has earlier given a material reason for the
senate and people's rebellion against Severus and Galerius. The latter

---

[1] Womersley, 1994, 1, pp. 384–5 (ch. 13).    [2] P. 417 (ch. 14).    [3] Pp. 409–12.
[4] P. 420.    [5] P. 429. The capital letters are Gibbon's; he rarely uses them.

had intended the abolition of the traditional immunity of Rome and its region from certain forms of taxation, which had survived the reforms of Caracalla,

and the officers of the revenue already began to number the Roman people, and to settle the proportion of the new taxes. Even when the spirit of freedom has been utterly extinguished, the tamest subjects have sometimes ventured to resist an unprecedented invasion of their property; but on this occasion the injury was aggravated by the insult, and the sense of private interest was quickened by that of national honour. The conquest of Macedonia, as we have already observed, had delivered the Roman people from the weight of personal taxes. Though they had experienced every form of despotism, they had now enjoyed that exemption near five hundred years; nor could they patiently brook the insolence of an Illyrian peasant, who from his distant residence in Asia, presumed to number Rome among the tributary cities of his empire.[6]

Little good does the resistance of senate, people and praetorians do them. Constantine's first action after the battle of the Milvian bridge in 312 is the final abolition of the praetorians.

By suppressing the troops which were usually stationed in Rome, Constantine gave the fatal blow to the dignity of the senate and people, and the disarmed capital was exposed without protection to the insults or neglect of its distant master. We may observe, that in this last effort to preserve their expiring freedom, the Romans, from the apprehension of a tribute, had raised Maxentius to the throne. He exacted that tribute from the senate under the name of a free gift. They implored the assistance of Constantine. He vanquished the tyrant, and converted the free gift into a perpetual tax.[7]

Gibbon describes how a graduated tax was imposed upon the senators as a class, whose heirs and families were subject to the same obligations; the passage immediately precedes that already quoted, on Constantine's indifference to Rome. The burden of taxation is already felt by the provincials of the empire at large; Gibbon has mentioned Constantine's remission of a tax he has probably himself imposed on the district of Autun, which is driving farmers to leave their fields uncultivated and take to the maquis as outlaws.[8] By the time we arrive at the end of the chapter and the final triumph of Constantine, over-taxation has advanced to the status of a principal cause of the Decline and Fall itself.

The successive steps of the elevation of Constantine, from his first assuming the purple at York, to the resignation of Licinius at Nicomedia, have been related with some minuteness and precision, not only as the events are in themselves

[6] P. 408.    [7] P. 429.    [8] P. 417.

interesting and important, but still more, as they contributed to the decline of the empire by the expence of blood and treasure, and by the perpetual increase, as well as of the taxes, as of the military establishment. The foundation of Constantinople, and the establishment of the Christian religion, were the immediate and memorable consequences of this revolution.[9]

(11)

Immediate results they may have been – by 'immediate' Gibbon did not necessarily mean 'instantaneous' – but Gibbon's readers in 1776 would have to wait five years to see these memorable consequences narrated and made the subjects of reflection. The two volumes that appeared in 1781 differed profoundly, in content, temper and structure, from that of 1776 as we have studied it so far. Their theme was the Roman empire as a Christian universal monarchy shaken from within and without, whose history, subsumed under the general title of *Decline and Fall*, covered the next eleven centuries and was to be related by Gibbon in a series of five volumes, appearing in 1781 and 1788. It could not be introduced without a close study of the legislation of Constantine and its consequences, and this theme is announced in the opening paragraphs of chapter 17,[10] which follow with thematic immediacy after the words last quoted; but between chapters 14 and 17 there intervene both a lapse of five years and the caesura imposed by chapters 15 and 16, which differ perplexingly in character both from those preceding and from those following them. It is with some consideration of the problems raised by their imposition that the present volume must conclude.

These two chapters deal with Christianity. Chapter 15 examines it as a socially expansive belief system, extending the numbers of its converts through a period beginning after the presumed lifetimes of the original twelve apostles and ending at the moment of Constantine's triumph. That is to say, it does not arrive at 'the establishment of the Christian religion', or the new problems of the relation between civil and ecclesiastical authority. These latter are mentioned in the first paragraph of chapter 17, opening volume 11 in 1781,[11] but not taken up until chapters 20 and 21. Chapter 15 (in 1776) lays great emphasis on the growing authority of Christian clergy in the first three centuries of their era,[12] and clearly indicates the division between civil and ecclesiastical authority,

---

[9] P. 445.     [10] *Decline and Fall*, vol. 11, ch. 17; Womersley, 1994, 1, p. 585.
[11] *Ibidem*: 'the division, unknown to the ancients, of civil and ecclesiastical affairs'.
[12] Pp. 482–97.

and their histories, which is to come. It cannot, however, be fully investigated until the 'establishment of the Christian religion' has taken effect, and Gibbon's narrative does not reach that moment until chapter 20, after a long study of Constantine's system of government, his life and death, and the reigns of his successors down to Julian.[3] Ecclesiastical history is being systematically postponed to a moment after civil history, and the history of the interactions between these histories is slow in preparation. Chapter 15, several years earlier, is in an important sense a pre-history, perhaps even a philosophical history of manners; it is a *peinture* of the primitive Christians, before the *écrit* of their active role in civil history – or 'history as well ecclesiastical as civil' – begins. This is a setting in which it will be necessary to consider the response to chapter 15 as a manifesto of Gibbon's evident unbelief; a setting arrived at by examining its place in the succession of the *Decline and Fall*'s volumes and chapters.

Chapter 16 is similarly retrospective. It is a history of the rise, progress and decline of the persecution of the Christians under the emperors, and is intended to set limits to the extent of persecution if not exactly to minimise it. This history of necessity begins with Nero and lasts until Galerius and Licinius; it is brought to an end when Licinius and Constantine oblige the emperor Maximin to call off the last of the imperially decreed persecutions.[4] It is a history that must be brought to an end before the effects of the establishment of Christianity can begin. To anticipate future argument, it may possibly be considered a philosophical history, derived from Hume, of the transition from a polytheist culture to a climate of opinion in which the phenomena of intolerance and tolerance could exist and make demands for the first time in history. One may further suggest, still tentatively, that what disturbed Gibbon's Christian readers was the substitution of this philosophical history for a Christian history, common ground to Eusebius, Tillemont and Bossuet, in which the carefully numbered ten general persecutions were signal moments in a divinely ordained sacred history, marking the sufferings and triumph of the church and stages on the way to the appearance of sacred monarchy and its empire.

Gibbon was no friend to Christian history, and was offering several kinds of Enlightened history to take its place. He was working towards the moment when civil and ecclesiastical history would exist in interaction and competition, but would not reach it until the establishment of

---

[3]  The themes of chapters 17, 18 and 19, in that order.     [4]  P. 576.

religion; when he did, he would confront the vast, and by no means easily focussed, question whether it continued the history of Decline and Fall or took its place. Chapters 15–16 in 1776, perhaps also 17–19 in 1781, occupy an interval, of five years duration in real time as Gibbon knew it, during which he was postponing the moment when ecclesiastical history would become relevant. But if chapter 15 is history of manners, and chapter 16 in part history of religion and philosophy, there is still, constitutive of history as Gibbon wrote it, the relation of a narrative; and here we face the fact that the narrative, as we have followed it through the first fourteen chapters of the *Decline and Fall*, reaches the victory of Constantine, the 'revolution' which will have the 'establishment' of Christianity as its 'consequence', without any mention of that religion, or any indication that it has played an active or passive role in history as so far recounted. Decius and Diocletian have been studied at length, without any word of the general persecutions with which they are credited; these will be examined in chapter 16.[5] Constantine's competition with his rivals has been narrated in detail, without any mention of the question whether the conduct or suspension of persecution played any part in its politics, or whether the support of Christians or pagans was an asset the competitors needed.[6] It is as if any history involving Christian actors or their values were situated in a different category from the history Gibbon is here recounting.

It is not that his authorities dictate this separation. Gibbon is by now using Christian historians: Lactantius, Eusebius himself, among moderns Le Nain de Tillemont;[7] but he employs them as authorities for events in civil history, and makes no mention of the Christian meanings they may have seen in them. He dismisses as hearsay of 'an obscure rhetorician' Lactantius' account of Diocletian's abdication as enforced by the threats of Galerius,[8] where a modern scholar thinks Lactantius a well-informed Christian counsellor whose evidence may be relied on.[9] In a later chapter he is to balance the Christian Eusebius against the pagan Zosimus,[20] but here Eusebius is scarcely allowed the role of a Christian historian. Only in one footnote does Gibbon mention the Christian reading of history, when he rejects both ancients and moderns

[5] For Decius, p. 555; Diocletian, pp. 562–70.
[6] For a modern interpretation of this matter, see Barnes, 1981.
[7] For Lactantius in ch. 14, see Womersley, 1994, III, p. 1232; for Eusebius, p. 1215; for Tillemont, p. 1268.
[8] Womersley, 1994, I, p. 401, n. 4.     [9] Barnes, 1981, p. 14.
[20] Womersley, 1994, I, p. 643, quoting the Gallican historian Claude Fleury.

who see divine judgement in the hideous deaths of the persecutors.[21] Constantine's victory at the Milvian bridge is related without mention of the cross seen in the sky or the words *in hoc signo vinces*;[22] this episode is discussed and dismissed at length in chapter 20,[23] when Constantine's motives are under examination, but is allowed no part in chapter 14, five years earlier.

That Gibbon did not believe in such prodigies is less than the point, which is that ecclesiastical history, even after it has begun to appear among his sources, is being rigorously excluded from the civil narrative and assigned to a different place in the architecture of the *Decline and Fall*. Gibbon will not notice, even to dismiss, histories which present events in civil history as presaging, or helping to bring about, the triumph of the church until he has completed a strictly civil narrative of the rise, the reign, and even the lifetime of Constantine; and only then will he reach the point where ecclesiastical history, now the narrative of ecclesiastical power and authority, has become of equal importance to the historian with the narrative of civil war and civil government. That point cannot be reached until the effects of the 'establishment' of the Christian religion have raised ecclesiastical authority to a height where it can not only affect the course of history, but impose a history of its own making. This will come about during the reign of Constantine, when he is obliged to attend the Council of Nicaea; but that is five years and five chapters away, and Gibbon is resolved to exhaust the resources of civil history before he turns to its ecclesiastical partner and opposite.

The result, as we stand at the end of chapter 14, is that the narration of 'the first decline and fall' is at last complete, and has been told in the discourse of civil history. It has been a history of *imperium et libertas*, of the separation of military from civil virtue, and the consequent decay of provincial culture and military discipline. The barbarians have appeared, but are less of a threat to Rome than 'the enemies in her bosom, the tyrants and the soldiers'; foreign invasion less of a threat than civil war. Ambitious but not irresponsible generals have attempted a solution as Augustus did; Diocletian's is an experiment in sacred monarchy. Constantine is a revolutionary figure in two ways: he re-creates sacred monarchy by building a new city which is its architectural embodiment, and he re-sacralises it by alliance with a new religion which will both sanctify it and challenge its authority. The causes of decline and fall

---

[21] P. 416, nn. 37, 38.    [22] Pp. 426–7.    [23] Pp. 735–44.

known to silver-age Romans and Florentine republicans are now superseded and a new history is to begin. It will be a history of Decline and
Fall only if the armies should continue to disintegrate; and an ominous
addition to the causes of decline has appeared, in the shape of an over-
taxation to pay for a military establishment, which will bring provincial
society to its collapse.

(III)

The argument so far has been that there is a hiatus between chapter 14
(1776) and chapter 17 (1781), where the history of Constantine's reign is
resumed; and another between chapter 14 and chapter 20, where there
begins the history of a new Rome in which civil and ecclesiastical authority co-exist and often compete. In each case, however, the gap is bridged
by the insertion of chapters 15 and 16, published in 1776 and completing
Gibbon's first volume. These two chapters deal, in widely differing ways,
with the history of Christianity before Constantine; before, that is, 'the
Church' – applying that term to the Christian community in the post-
apostolic period – had become 'established' and acquired an authority
able to compete with the civil. There is a sense in which Gibbon's history will develop its new momentum only from the point at which the
Church begins to acquire that authority; and if that point is placed at
the moment of its establishment by Constantine, the conclusion must
be that chapters 15 and 16 are prehistory rather than history. We have
already suggested how they may be placed in special sub-departments
of the arsenal of Enlightened historiography.

It is a problem, however, to determine what sort of history they are,
what place they occupy in the *Decline and Fall* as a whole, and what
Gibbon intended and effected by writing them and placing them where
he did. One should recall that there is no hint that they are coming in
the general preface of 1776, where Gibbon outlined his plans for the
first and future volumes.[24] Indeed, that preface contains no hint that the
history of the Church is going to form a major theme in the structure
of the *Decline and Fall*, though we may find it hard to believe that he did
not know it would. At the outset of chapter 17 (1781), he declares that
the historian must now take account of ecclesiastical authority as well
as civil; when and how did foreknowledge of this enter his mind as he
wrote?

---

[24] Pp. 2–3; *NCG*, pp. 372–4.

Gibbon tells us, concerning the composition of his first volume, that he found the three opening chapters peculiarly hard to write – perhaps because they were the first and he was still in search of his style; that Hume judged the narrative chapters from Commodus to Alexander Severus 'concise and superficial'; and that

the fifteenth and sixteenth Chapters have been reduced by three successive revisals from a large Volume to their present size; and they might still be compressed without any loss of facts or sentiments.[25]

Depending on the exact meaning to be attached to the words 'a large Volume', this suggests that the two chapters were hard to control, and that the difficulty may have arisen because they belonged neither to narrative nor to civil history, but introduced matter extraneous to either. They do not belong to the history of empire; they do not belong to the history of empire and church interacting. It is open to us to wonder how far back in his preparations Gibbon had planned to write them; when he came to see their subject-matter as a necessary part of his history. Our judgement is complicated by the circumstance that these chapters caused a furore, and have shaped a great many judgements of the work as a whole; even at the present day, our ideas about Gibbon's attitude to Christianity, and its role in the history of the Roman empire, are commonly based on our understandings of chapters 15 and 16. It can be argued that this is a mistake; that Christianity begins to play an active part in the *Decline and Fall* only with its establishment by Constantine, when ecclesiastical authority begins to interact with civil; and that chapters 15 and 16 are merely preliminary to that project, standing as we have argued at a point where ecclesiastical history is being introduced in order to be postponed. This if accepted would sharply modify our understanding of their place in Gibbon's history.[26]

Our thinking is further affected by Gibbon's remark on more than one occasion that there must have been some connexion between the rise of the Christian religion and the decline of the Roman empire.[27] With Machiavelli's remarks on the differences between Christian and civic virtue in mind, we look for signs that this connexion was a causal one; that Gibbon saw the Christians as fatally weakening the empire by their withdrawal from civic life in pursuit of other-worldly values. There are indeed moments when Gibbon seems to be intimating messages of this

[25] *Memoirs*, p. 156.
[26] For a further, but still tentative, statement of this position, see Pocock, 2000.
[27] *Memoirs*, p. 147.

kind. A study of the structure, and a tracing of the narrative, of his first volume produces, however, the counter-argument that chapters 1 through 14 provide a detailed narrative and explanation of the demoralisation of civic virtue and the decay of military discipline, in which Christianity has played no part and the causes are those with which the present volume has made us so familiar. Christianity is not the 'secret poison' described in chapter 2, and may even be its effect rather than its cause. There remains the question whether chapters 15 and 16, written as they may have been late in the composition of volume 1, have the intention or the effect of sending us back to chapters 1 through 14, and retrospectively altering our reading of them. Some have argued that something like this is the case.

It is possible to lean in a contrary direction. The successive crises of the pre-Christian empire can be, and have been, explained in pagan terms, as consequences of the decay of ancient Roman *virtus* and *libertas*; a decay occurring from within, narrated by authors both ancient and modern in a discourse of many centuries' standing. It can be argued that this explanation remains valid at the end of chapter 14, and that a reader in 1776 would be left expecting to weigh the success of Constantine's unprecedented attempts to deal with the problem (in which, by the way, the barbarians are playing a significant but not currently crucial part). The establishment of a new capital (and a new bureaucracy) is held out as a major theme of post-Constantinean history, and the ever-present and increasing menace of over-taxation has been mentioned as a further cause of future decline. The establishment of the Christian religion has also been mentioned; and chapters 15 and 16 massively inform the reader that the narrative is moving into a new key, in which the history of religion and the Church is to be dominant in ways that will not have surprised the reader, but are not presaged in Gibbon's preface; he has not told us, and may not have decided, how he is going to deal with it. The resolute exclusion of Christian historians from the narrative of Constantine's rise to power signals – the argument would continue – not only that his acquisition of empire is a secular, not a sacred process, but that the civil history of empire has been and remains valid and intelligible. It may further signal that the Christian narrative will be resumed only from the moment of that religion's establishment, and will be centrally concerned with the relation between ecclesiastical and civil authority. The effect of any such assumption would be to make chapter 15, and possibly chapter 16, anticipatory, looking forward to a future narrative rather than back to one already recounted; the test would come in chapter 16, where Gibbon must decide whether the persecuting emperors were dealing with Christianity as a serious threat to civil authority and its values, or in a larger sense finding themselves in a new climate where questions of tolerance and intolerance took on an importance they had not possessed before.

If the latter view were adopted, the significance of the two chapters would extend far beyond the question of the Decline and Fall as an effect for which causes are to be assigned, causes to which the growth of Christianity may have contributed. Their significance would become macrohistorical and almost metahistorical; they would be telling us for the first time that with the Constantinean moment and the coming of the Christians we are to enter on a new kind of history, in which the legislator is to confront the challenge of ecclesiastical authority – the item most emphasised by Gibbon – and the historian is to confront the Christian affirmation that there is a society and values transcending history altogether. Gibbon will never have much to say about Augustine, but may be thought of as engaged in an Enlightened reversal of his accomplishment. More immediately, it may be that chapters 15 and 16 begin the transformation of 'the decline and fall of the Roman empire' into 'the triumph of barbarism and religion'. The last-named forces – we are at this point concerned with the second – do not so much overthrow the empire as replace it by something different; a new kind of history, called by Gibbon 'modern' instead of 'ancient'.

To view the two chapters in this way is to set them aside from the narrative of the *Decline and Fall*, for which they provide a new context. To set them aside, however, is to suggest that they interrupt the narrative, whose resumption is postponed for five chapters and five years, and to raise questions about Gibbon's intentions and control of his project as he completed his first volume. Chapters 15 and 16 need to be considered in this light, as well as in the settings of ecclesiastical history and Enlightened philosophical history which they bring into conjunction and collision. This treatment, as well as the story of their impact and reception after volume 1 appeared in 1776, must be the subject of a future volume. For the present it can be asserted that the civil history of the Roman empire has been traced as a series of crises connecting the Augustan, Antonine, Severan and Illyrian periods, to the 'Constantinean moment' where it is about to be transformed; and that the history of the discourse in which this process was situated has been traced from Roman beginnings through the Christian millennium, to the point where we can see how the ancient problem of *libertas et imperium* was transformed into the Enlightened problems of ancient and modern, virtue and commerce, which supplied many of the meanings of Decline and Fall to Gibbon and his readers.

# Bibliography of works cited

EDITIONS PUBLISHED BEFORE 1900

Barbeyrac, Jean, 1728: *Traité de la Morale des Pères*. Amsterdam.

Beaufort, Louis, 1766: *La République Romaine, ou Plan General de l'Ancien Gouvernement de Rome, où on dévelope les différens ressorts de ce Gouvernement, l'influence qu'y avoit la Religion; la Souveraineté du Peuple, et la manière dont il l'exerçoit; quelle était l'autorité du Sénat et celle des Magistrats, l'administration de la Justice, les Prérogatives du Citoyen Romain, et les différentes conditions des sujets de ce vaste Empire*. La Haye/the Hague.

Biondo, Flavio, 1559: *Biondi Flavii Forliviensis de Roma triumphante lib. x priscorum scriptorum lectoribus utilissimi, ad totiusque Romanae antiquitatis cognitionem pernecessarii. Romae instauratae libri III. De origine ac gestis Venetorum liber. Italia illustrata, siue lustrata (nam uterque titulus doctis placet) in regiones seu prouincias diuisa XVIII. Historiarum ab inclinato Romano imperio decades III. Additis tribus pro argumentorum ratione indicibus nouis*. Basel, Frobenius.

Bossuet, Jacques-Benigne, 1788: *Discours sur l'Histoire Universelle, à Monseigneur le Dauphin; pour expliquer la suite de la Religion et les changemens des Empires. Nouvelle Edition*. Rouen.

Defoe, Daniel, 1698: *An Argument Showing that a Standing Army, with Consent of Parliament, is not Inconsistent with a Free Government*. London.

1726–27: *A General History of Discoveries and Improvements: in Useful Arts, particularly in the Great Branches of Commerce, Navigation, and Plantation, in all Parts of the Known World*. London.

Ferguson, Adam, 1799: *The History of the Rise, Progress and Termination of the Roman Republic. New Edition . . . revised and corrected*. Edinburgh.

Fletcher, Andrew, 1697–98: *A Discourse of Government in Relation to Militias*. Edinburgh and London.

Gordon, Thomas, 1722: *The Spirit of the Ecclesiastics of all Ages, as to the Doctrines of Morality, and more particularly the Spirit of the Ancient Fathers of the Church, Examin'd. By Mons. Barbeyrac, Professor of Laws and History in the University of Lausanne. Translated from the French by a Gentleman of Grays Inn. With a Preface by the Author of the Independent Whig*. London.

1728–31: *The Works of Tacitus, translated into English, with political discourses upon that author*. In two volumes, 1728 and 1731. London.

Hervey, John, Lord, 1734: *Ancient and Modern Liberty Stated and Compared*. London.

Hooke, Nathaniel, 1738: *The Roman History. From the Building of Rome to the Ruin of the Commonwealth*. London.

Jones, William, 1594: *Six Bookes of Civil Doctrine, written in Latine by Iustus Lipsius: which doe especially concerne Principalitie. Done into English by William Jones Gentleman*. London.

Lipsius, Justus, 1596: *De militia Romana libri quinque, commentarius in Polybium*. Antwerp.

 1599: *Admiranda, sive de magnitudine Romana*. Antwerp.

 1634: *Politicorum sive Civilis Doctrinae libri sex. Quid ad principatum maxime spectant*. Leyden.

Malvezzi, Virgilio, 1622: *Discorsi sopra Cornelio Tacito del marchese Virgilio Malvezzi al serenissimo Ferdinando II granduca Toscana*. Venice.

Mexía, Pedro, 1578: *Historia imperial y Cesarea, en la qual ensumma se contiene las vidas y hechos de todos los Cesares, Emperadores de Roma, desde Iulio Cesar hasta el Emperador Carlos Quinto, la qual compuso el magnifico cavallero Pedro Mexía, vezino de Sevilla*. Antwerp.

Middleton, Conyers, 1741: *The History of the Life of Marcus Tullius Cicero. In Two Volumes*. London: Printed for the Author.

Orosius, 1889: *Pauli Orosii Historiarum adversum paganos libri VII. Ex recognitione Caroli Zangemeister*. Leipzig: Teubner.

Pelloutier, Simon, 1741: *Histoire des Celtes, et particulièrement des Gaulois et des Germains, depuis les tems fabuleux, jusqu'à la Prise de Rome par les Gaulois*. Paris and the Hague.

Pertz, G. H., ed., 1868: *Monumenta Germaniae Historica Scriptorum Tomus XX*. Hanover, impensis bibliopoli aulici Hahniani.

Pius II, 1533: *Pii Pont. Max. Decadum Biondi Epitome*. Basel.

Tillemont, Louis Sebastien Le Nain, 1732–40: *Histoire des Empereurs et des autres princes qui ont regné durant les six premiers siècles de l'église, de leurs guerres contre les Juifs, des écrivains profanes, et des personnes les plus illustres de leurs temps*. Brussels.

Traheron, W., 1604: *The Historie of all the Romane Emperours, beginning with Caius Julius Caesar, and successively ending with Rodulph the Second now reigning . . . First collected in Spanish by Pedro Mexia, since enlarged in Italian by Lodovico Dolce and Girolamo Bardi, and now englished by W. T.]* London.

Trenchard, John, 1698: (With Walter Moyle). *An Argument Showing that a Standing Army is inconsistent with a Free Government and Absolutely Destructive to the Constitution of the English Monarchy*. London.

Valla, Lorenzo, 1543: *De Linguae Latinae Elegantia Libri Sex*. Cologne.

Wotton, William, 1701: *The History of Rome from the Death of Antoninus Pius to the Death of Severus Alexander*. London.

Wren, Matthew, 1657–58: *Considerations upon Mr. Harrington's Commonwealth of Oceana, restrained to the first part of the Preliminaries*. London.

Zosimus, 1648: *The New History of Count Zosimus, sometime advocate of the treasury of the Roman Empire. with the notes of the Oxford edition. In six books. To which is prefixed Leunclavius's Apology for the author. Newly Englished*. London.

## MODERN EDITIONS AND TRANSLATIONS
## OF CITED AUTHORS

Alexander, Sidney, 1969: (Trans. and ed.) *The History of Italy by Francesco Guicciardini*. New York: Collier.

Anselmo, Gian Mario, and Varotti, Carlo, 1992: (Eds.) *Niccolò Machiavelli: Le Grande Opere*. Turin: Bollati Boringhieri. Two volumes.

Barette, Paul, and Baldwin, Spurgeon, 1993: (Trans.) *Brunetto Latini: The Book of the Treasure*. New York: Garland.

Blythe, James M., 1997: (Trans.) *On the Government of Rulers: De Regimine Principum: Ptolemy of Lucca: with Portions Attributed to Thomas Aquinas*. Philadelphia: University of Pennsylvania Press.

Brown, Alison, 1994: (Trans.) *Francesco Guicciardini: Dialogue on the Government of Florence*. Cambridge: Cambridge University Press. *Cambridge Texts in the History of Political Thought*.

Bryce, J. C., 1985: (Ed.) *Adam Smith: Lectures on Rhetoric and Belles Lettres*. Indianapolis: Liberty Classics.

Busa, Roberto, 1980: (Ed.) *S. Thomae Aquinatis Opera Omnia, VII: aliorum medii aevii auctorum scripta* 61. Stuttgart-Bad Carnstatt. Flomann-Holzboog.

Cameron, Averil, and Hall, Stuart G., 1999: (Eds. and trans.) *Eusebius: The Life of Constantine*. Oxford: The Clarendon Press.

Campbell, R. H. and Skinner, A. S., 1981: (Eds.) *Adam Smith: An Inquiry into the Nature and Causes of the Wealth of Nations*. Indianapolis: Liberty Classics. Two volumes.

Canavan, Francis, 1999: (Ed.) *Selected Works of Edmund Burke: a New Reprint of the Payne Edition*. Indianapolis: Liberty Classics.

Carmody, Francis J., 1948: (Ed.) *Li Livres dou Tresor de Brunetto Latini*. Berkeley and Los Angeles: University of California Press. *University of California Publications in Modern Philology*, 22.

Coleman, Christopher B., 1993: (Ed. and trans.) *The Treatise of Lorenzo Valla on the Donation of Constantine*. Reprinted from an edition of 1922. Toronto: University of Toronto Press and Renaissance Society of America.

Dyson, R. W., 1998: (Trans.) *Augustine: The City of God Against the Pagans*. Cambridge: Cambridge University Press. *Cambridge Texts in the History of Political Thought*.

Elwin, W., and Courthope, W. J., 1967. (Eds.) *The Works of Alexander Pope (1881)*. New York: Garland Press.

Gewirth, Alan, 1951: (Trans.) *Marsilius of Padua: The Defensor Pacis*. Two volumes. New York, Columbia University Press.

Gilbert, Alan H., 1965: (Trans.) *Machiavelli: The Chief Works and Others*. Three volumes. Durham, NC: Duke University Press.

Godley, A. D., 1926: (Ed. and trans.) *Herodotus*. London: William Heinemann. *Loeb Classical Library*.

Graves, Robert, 1979: (Trans.) *Suetonius: The Twelve Caesars*. Harmondsworth: Penguin Books.

Grayson, Cecil and Margaret, 1965: (Eds. and trans.) *Francesco Guicciardini: Selected Writings*. London: Oxford University Press.

Griffiths, Gordon, Hankins, James, and Thompson, David, 1987: *The Humanism of Leonardo Bruni*. Binghamton: Center for Medieval and Renaissance Texts and Studies.

Hamilton, Walter, and Wallace-Hadrill, Andrew, 1986: (Eds. and trans.) *Ammianus Marcellinus: The Later Roman Empire*. Harmondsworth: Penguin Books.

Hamowy, Ronald, 1995: (Ed.) *Cato's Letters . . . by John Trenchard and Thomas Gordon*. Two volumes. Indianapolis: Liberty Classics.

Hankins, James, 2001: (Ed. and trans.) *Leonardo Bruni: History of the Florentine People: volume I, Books I–IV*. Cambridge, MA: Harvard University Press.

Holmes, Stephen, 1990: (Intro.) Thomas Hobbes: *Behemoth or The Long Parliament. Edited by Ferdinand Tönnies*. Chicago and London: University of Chicago Press.

Izbicki, Thomas, and Nederman, Cary, 2000: (Eds. and trans.) *Three Tracts on Empire*. Bristol: Thoemmes Press.

Jeudy, Colette, and Quillet, Jeannine, 1979: (Eds.) *Marsile de Padoue: Oeuvres Mineures*. Paris: Editions CNRS.

Klein, Milton M., 1963: (Ed.) *The Independent Reflector . . . by William Livingstone and Others*. Cambridge, MA: Harvard University Press.

Lowenthal, David, 1965: (Trans.) *Considerations on the Causes of the Greatness of the Romans and their Decline, by Montesquieu*. New York: The Free Press.

Mattingly, H., 1948: (Trans.) *Tacitus on Britain and Germany*. West Drayton: Penguin Books.

McCracken, G. E. et al., 1966: (Ed. with other translators) *Saint Augustine: the City of God Against the Pagans*. Cambridge, MA: Harvard University Press. Seven volumes. *Loeb Classical Library*.

McDonald, A. H., 1976: (Ed. with trans. by Henry Bettenson) *Livy: Rome and the Mediterranean*. Harmondsworth: Penguin Books.

Meek, R. L., Raphael, D. D., and Stein, P. G., 1982: (Eds.) *Adam Smith: Lectures on Jurisprudence*. Indianapolis: Liberty Classics.

Mierow, C. C., 1928: (Trans.) *The Two Cities: a Chronicle of Universal History to the Year 1146 AD, by Otto Bishop of Freising*. New York: Columbia University Press.

   1953: (Trans.) *The Deeds of Frederick Barbarossa, by Otto of Freising and his Continuator Rahewin*. New York: Columbia University Press. *Columbia Records in the History of Civilisation*.

Miller, Eugene, 1985: (Ed.) *David Hume: Essays Moral, Political, and Literary*. Indianapolis: Liberty Classics.

Moore, Clifford H., 1968: (Ed. and trans.) *Tacitus: the Histories I–III*. Cambridge, MA: Harvard University Press, *Loeb Classical Library*. (Reprint of 1925 edition).

Morrison, K. F., 1971: (Ed.) *Ferdinand Gregorovius: Rome and Medieval Culture. Selections from the History of the City of Rome in the Middle Ages*. Chicago: University of Chicago Press. *Classic European Historians*.

Mossner, E. C., and Ross, I. S., 1987: (Eds.) *The Correspondence of Adam Smith*. Indianapolis: Liberty Classics.

Nederman, Cary J., 1993: (Ed., with trans. by Fiona Watson) *Marsiglio of Padua: Writings on the Empire: Defensor Minor and De Translatio Imperii*. Cambridge: Cambridge University Press.

Nogara, Bartolomeo, 1927: (Ed.) *Scritti Inediti e Rari di Biondo Flavio*. Rome: Tipografia Poliglotta Vaticana.

Oz-Salzberger, Fania, 1995: (Ed.) *Adam Ferguson: An Essay on the History of Civil Society*. Cambridge: Cambridge University Press. *Cambridge Texts in the History of Political Thought*.

Paschoud, François, 1971: (Ed.) *Histoire nouvelle de Zosime*. Texte établi et traduit par François Paschoud. Paris.

Paton, W. R., 1923: (Ed. and trans.) *Polybius: the Histories*. London: William Heinemann. Loeb Classical Library.

Pocock, J. G. A., 1977: (Ed.) *The Political Works of James Harrington*. Cambridge: Cambridge University Press.

   1987a: (Ed.) *Edmund Burke: Reflections on the Revolution in France*. Indianapolis: Hackett Publications.

   1992: (Ed.) *Harrington: The Commonwealth of Oceana and A System of Politics*. Cambridge: Cambridge University Press. *Cambridge Texts in the History of Political Thought*.

Raimondi, Ezio, 1967: (Ed.) *Opere di Niccolo Machiavelli*. Milan: Ugo Marsia.

Ranum, Orest, 1976: (Ed., with trans. by Elborg Forster) *Jacques-Benigne Bossuet: Discourse on Universal History*. Chicago: University of Chicago Press. *Classic European Historians*.

Raymond, I. W., 1936: (Trans.) *Seven Books of History Against the Pagans: the Apology of Paulus Orosius*. New York: Columbia University Press. *Records in the History of Civilisation*.

Richter, Melvin, 1977: (selected translations) *The Political Theory of Montesquieu*. Cambridge: Cambridge University Press.

Robertson, John, 1997: (Ed.) *Andrew Fletcher: Political Works*. Cambridge: Cambridge University Press. *Cambridge Texts in the History of Political Thought*.

Rolfe, J. C., 1979: (Ed. and trans.) *Suetonius*. Cambridge, MA: Harvard University Press. *Loeb Classical Library*.

   1980: *Sallust*. Cambridge, MA: Harvard University Press. *Loeb Classical Library*.

Santini, Emilio, 1927: (Ed.) *Leonardi Aretini Historiarum Florentini Populi XII*. Bologna: Nicola Zanichelli. *Rerum Italicarum Scriptores, nuova edizione*.

Schlesinger, Alfred E., 1959: (Trans.) *Livy: Summaries, Fragments and Obsequies*. Cambridge, MA: Harvard University Press. *Loeb Classical Library*.

Seidel Menchi, Silvana, 1971: (Ed.) *Francesco Guicciardini: Storia d'Italia*. Turin: Einaudi.

Spongano, Raffaelle, 1951: (Ed.) *Francesco Guicciardini: Ricordi*. Florence: Sansoni.

Van den Heuvel, Jacques, 1961: (Ed.) *Voltaire: Mélanges*. Paris: Gallimard. *Bibliothèque de la Pléiade*.

Vickers, Brian, 1998: (Ed.) *Francis Bacon: The History of the Reign of King Henry VII and Selected Works*: Cambridge: Cambridge University Press. *Cambridge Texts in the History of Political Thought.*

Waley, P. J. and D. P., 1956: (Trans.) *Giovanni Botero: The Reason of State and The Greatness of Cities*. London: Routledge Kegan Paul.

Warmington, E. H., 1970: (Ed. with translations by others) *Tacitus: Agricola, Germania*. Cambridge, MA: Harvard University Press. *Loeb Classical Library.*

Weil, Françoise, and Courtney, Cecil, 2000: (Eds.) *Oeuvres Complètes de Montesquieu, 2: Considérations sur les causes de la grandeur des Romains et de leur décadence: Réflexions sur la monarchie universelle en Europe*. Oxford: Voltaire Foundation.

White, Horace, 1912–13: (Ed. and trans.; repr. 1991) *Appian's Roman History, vol I; vols. III and IV: The Civil Wars*. Cambridge, MA: Harvard University Press. *Loeb Classical Library.*

Williamson, G. A., 1965: (Trans.) *Eusebius: The History of the Church*. Harmondsworth: Penguin Books.

## MONOGRAPHS, ARTICLES AND DISSERTATIONS

Arendt, Hannah, 1958: *The Human Condition*. Chicago: University Press of Chicago.

Armitage, David, 1998: (Ed.) *Theories of Empire, 1450–1800*. Aldershot: Ashgate.
2000: *The Ideological Origins of the British Empire*. Cambridge: Cambridge University Press.

Armitage, David, Himy, Armand, and Skinner, Quentin, 1995: (Eds.) *Milton and Republicanism*. Cambridge: Cambridge University Press.

Badian, Ernst, 1972: *Publicans and Sinners*. Ithaca: Cornell University Press.

Bailyn, Bernard, 1967: *The Ideological Origins of the American Revolution*. Cambridge, MA: Harvard University Press.

Baker, David J., 1997: *Between Nations: Shakespeare, Spenser, Marvell and the Question of Britain*. Stanford: Stanford University Press.

Baldini, A. Enzo, 1992: (Ed.) *Botero e la Ragion di Stato: atti del convegno in memoria di Luigi Firpo, Torino 8–10 marzo 1990*. Florence: Olschki.

Ball, Terence et al., 1987: (Eds.) *Political Innovation and Conceptual Change*. Cambridge: Cambridge University Press.

Baridon, Michel, 1971: 'Une lettre inédite d'Edward Gibbon à Jean-Baptiste-Antoine Suard', *Études Anglaises*, XXIV, i, pp. 80–7.

Barnes, Timothy D., 1981: *Constantine and Eusebius*. Cambridge, MA: Harvard University Press.

Baron, Hans, 1955a: *The Crisis of the Early Italian Renaissance: Civic Humanism and Republican Liberty in an Age of Classicism and Tyranny*. Princeton: Princeton University Press. Two volumes.
1955b: *Humanistic and Political Literature in Florence and Venice at the Beginning of the Quattrocento: Studies in Criticism and Chronology*. Cambridge, MA: Harvard University Press.
1966: *Crisis*, one-volume edition. Princeton: Princeton University Press.

1968: *From Petrarch to Leonardo Bruni: Studies in Humanistic and Political Literature.* Chicago: Newberry Library and University of Chicago Press.

1988: *In Search of Florentine Civic Humanism: Essays on the Transition from Medieval to Modern Thought.* Two volumes. Princeton: Princeton University Press.

Belligni, Eleonora, 1999: *Lo Scacco della Prudenza: precettistica politica ed sperienza storica in Virgilio Malvezzi.* Florence, L. S. Olschki.

Berlin, Isaiah, 1958: *Two Concepts of Liberty.* Oxford: Oxford University Press.

1990: *The Crooked Timber of Humanity: Chapters in the History of Ideas.* London: John Murray.

1997: *The Proper Study of Mankind: an Anthology of Essays.* Edited by Henry Hardy and Roger Hausheer. London: Chatto and Windus.

Bernal, Martin, 1987: *Black Athena: the Afro-Asiatic Roots of Classical Civilisation.* London: Free Association Books.

Bireley, Robert, 1990: *The Counter-Reformation Prince: Anti-Machiavellianism or Catholic Statecraft in Early Modern Europe.* Chapel Hill: University of North Carolina Press.

Bosbach, Franz, 1988: *Monarchia Universalis: ein politischer Leitbegriff der frühen Neuzeit.* Göttingen.

Bouwsma, William J., 1968: *Venice and the Defense of European Liberty: Renaissance Values in the Age of the Counter-Reformation.* Berkeley and Los Angeles: University of California Press.

Bowersock, G. W., 1977: 'Gibbon on Civil War and Rebellion in the Decline of the Roman Empire', in Bowersock, Clive and Graubard, 1977, pp. 27–35.

Bowersock, G. W., Clive, John, and Graubard, Stephen, 1977: (Eds.) *Edward Gibbon and the Decline and Fall of the Roman Empire. Daedalus*, vol. 105, 3; subsequently published, Cambridge, MA: Harvard University Press.

Bowersock, G. W., Brown, Peter, and Grabar, Oleg, 1999: (Eds.) *Late Antiquity: A Guide to the Post-Classical World.* Cambridge, MA and London: the Belknap Press of Harvard University Press.

Brading, D. A., 1991: *The First America: the Spanish Monarchy, Creole Patriots, and the Liberal State, 1492–1867.* Cambridge: Cambridge University Press.

Brewer, John, 1989: *The Sinews of Power: War, Money and the English State, 1688–1783.* New York: Knopf.

1997: *The Pleasures of the Imagination: English Culture in the Eighteenth Century.* New York: Farrar, Straus, Giroux.

Brezzi, Paolo, and Lorch, Maristella, 1984: (Eds.) *Umanesimo a Roma nel Quattrocento.* Rome: Istituto di Studi Romani, and New York: Barnard College.

Brown, Peter, 1967: *Augustine of Hippo: a Biography.* Berkeley and Los Angeles: University of California Press.

Brown, Stewart, 1997: (Ed.) *William Robertson and the Expansion of Empire.* Cambridge: Cambridge University Press.

Browning, Reed, 1982: *Political and Constitutional Ideas of the Court Whigs.* Baton Rouge: Louisiana State University Press.

Bulletta, Silvia, 1995: *Virgilio Malvezzi e la storiografia classica.* Milan: Istituto di Propaganda Libraria.

Burke, Peter, 1991: 'Tacitus, Scepticism and Reason of State', in Burns, 1991, pp. 479–98.

Burns, J. H. 1988: (Ed.) *The Cambridge History of Medieval Political Thought, c. 350–c. 1450*. Cambridge: Cambridge University Press.

1991: (Ed., with the assistance of Mark Goldie) *The Cambridge History of Political thought, 1450–1700*. Cambridge: Cambridge University Press.

1992: *Lordship, Kingship and Empire: the Idea of Monarchy, 1400–1525*. Oxford: the Clarendon Press.

Champion, J. A. I., 1992: *The Pillars of Priestcraft Shaken: the Church of England and its enemies, 1660–1730*. Cambridge: Cambridge University Press.

Church, W. F., 1972: *Richelieu and Reason of State*. Princeton: Princeton University Press.

Collini, Stefan, Whatmore, Richard, and Young, B. W., 2000: (Eds.) *History, Religion and Culture: British Intellectual History, 1750–1950*. Cambridge: Cambridge University Press.

Conrad, F. W., 1988: 'A Preservative Against Tyranny: the Political Theology of Sir Thomas Elyot', Ph.D. dissertation, Johns Hopkins University.

Craddock, Patricia, 1987: *Edward Gibbon: a Reference Guide*. Indexed by Patricia B. Craddock and Margaret Craddock Huff. Boston: G. K. Hall.

Darnton, Robert, 1979: *The Business of Enlightenment: a Publishing History of the Encyclopédie, 1775–1800*. Cambridge, MA: the Belknap Press of Harvard University Press.

Davis, Charles T., 1957: *Dante and the Idea of Rome*. Oxford: Oxford University Press.

1974: 'Ptolemy of Lucca and the Roman Republic', *Proceedings of the American Philosophical Society*, CXVIII, 1, pp. 30–50.

DeGrazia, Sebastian, 1989: *Machiavelli in Hell*. Princeton: Princeton University Press.

Dickson, P. G. M., 1967: *The Financial Revolution in England: a Study in the Development of Public Credit*. London: Macmillan.

Donaldson, Peter, 1988: *Machiavelli and Mystery of State*. Cambridge: Cambridge University Press.

Dorey, T. A., 1969: (Ed.) *Tacitus*. London: Routledge & Kegan Paul.

Duke, A. C., and Tamse, C. A., 1985: (Eds.) *Clio's Mirror: Historiography in Britain and the Netherlands*. Zutphen: De Walburg Press.

Dunn, John, 1969: 'The Politics of Locke in England and America in the Eighteenth Century', in John W. Yolton (ed.), *John Locke: Problems and Perspectives*. Cambridge: Cambridge University Press, pp. 45–80.

1990: (Ed.) *The Economic Limits to Modern Politics*. Cambridge: Cambridge University Press.

Eckstein, Arthur M., 1995: *Moral Vision in the Histories of Polybius*. Berkeley and Los Angeles: University of California Press.

Elliott, John H., and Brockliss, Laurence B., 1999: (Eds.), *The World of the Favourite*. New Haven: Yale University Press.

Ellis, Harold A., 1988: *Boulainvilliers and the French Monarchy: Aristocratic Politics in Early Eighteenth-Century France*. Ithaca: Cornell University Press.

Erasmus, H. J., 1962: *The Origins of Rome in Historiography from Petrarch to Perizonius*. Assen: Van Gorcum.

Erskine-Hill, Howard, 1983: *The Augustan Ideal in English Literature*. London: Edward Arnold.

Ferguson, Arthur B., 1979: *Clio Unbound: Perceptions of the Social and Cultural Past in Renaissance England*. Durham, NC: Duke University Press.

Fernandez-Santamaria, J. A., 1977: *The State, War and Peace: Spanish Political Thought in the Renaissance*. Cambridge: Cambridge University Press.

Ferrill, Arther, 1986: *The Fall of the Roman Empire: the Military Explanation*. London: Thames and Hudson.

Folz, Robert, 1969: *The Concept of Empire in Western Europe from the Fifth Century to the Fourteenth Century*. London: Edward Arnold (translated from the French by Sheila Ann Ogilvie.)

Fontana, Biancamaria, 1991: *Benjamin Constant and the Post-Revolutionary Mind*.

Foot, Michael, 1957: *The Pen and the Sword*. London: Macgibbon and Kee.

Ford, Franklin L., 1953: *Robe and Sword: the Regrouping of the French Aristocracy after Louis XIV*. Cambridge, MA: Harvard University Press.

Fukuda, Arihiro, 1997: *Sovereignty and the Sword: Harrington, Hobbes and Mixed Government in the English Civil Wars*. Oxford: the Clarendon Press.

Gabba, Emilio, 1956: *Appiano e la storia delle guerre civili*. Florence: La Nuova Italia.

Gay, Peter, 1966: *The Enlightenment: an Interpretation. Vol. I: The Rebirth of Modern Paganism*. New York: Knopf.

Gentles, Ian, 1992: *The New Model Army in England, Ireland and Scotland, 1645–1653*. Oxford: Blackwell.

Gilbert, Felix, 1977: *History: Choice and Commitment*. Cambridge, MA: the Belknap Press of Harvard University Press.

Gilmore, M. P., 1941: *Argument from Roman Law in Political Thought, 1200–1600*. Cambridge, MA: Harvard University Press.

Goldie, Mark, 1987: 'The Civil Religion of James Harrington', in Pagden, 1987, pp. 197–222.

　　1993: 'Priestcraft and the Birth of Whiggism', in Phillipson and Skinner, 1993, pp. 209–31.

Gould, Eliga H., 2000: *The Persistence of Empire: British Political Culture in the Age of the American Revolution*. Chapel Hill: University of North Carolina Press.

Haitsma Mulier, E. O. G., 1980: *The Myth of Venice in Dutch Republican Thought*. Assen: Van Gorcum.

Hale, J. R. 1968: 'The End of Florentine Liberty', in Rubinstein, 1968, pp. 501–4.

Hamowy, Ronald, 1990: '*Cato's Letters*, John Locke and the Republican Paradigm', *History of Political Thought*, XI, pp. 273–94.

Hankins, James, 1995: 'The "Baron Thesis" after Forty Years and some Recent Studies of Leonardo Bruni', *Journal of the History of Ideas*, LVI, 2, pp. 309–38.

2000: (Ed.) *Renaissance Civic Humanism: Reappraisals and Reflections*. Cambridge: Cambridge University Press.

Hay, Denys, 1952: *Polydore Vergil*. Oxford: the Clarendon Press.

1959: 'Flavio Biondo and the Middle Ages', *Proceedings of the British Academy*, XLV, pp. 97–125.

Headley, John M., 1997: *Church, Empire and World*. Aldershot: Ashgate.

Helgerson, Richard, 1992: *Forms of Nationhood: the Elizabethan Writing of England*. Chicago: University of Chicago Press.

Hoak, Dale, and Feingold, Mordechai, 1996: (Eds.) *The World of William and Mary: Anglo-Dutch Perspectives on the Revolution of 1688–89*. Stanford: Stanford University Press.

Holmes, Stephen, 1984: *Benjamin Constant and the Making of Modern Liberalism*. New Haven: Yale University Press.

Hont, Istvan, 1990: 'Free Trade and the Economic Limits to National Politics: Neo-Machiavellian Political Economy Reconsidered', in Dunn, 1990, pp. 41–120.

Hont, Istvan, and Ignatieff, Michael, 1983: (Eds.) *Wealth and Virtue: the Shaping of Political Economy in the Scottish Enlightenment*. Cambridge: Cambridge University Press.

Jones, A. H. M., 1986: *The Later Roman Empire: a Social, Economic and Administrative Survey*. Two volumes. Baltimore: The Johns Hopkins University Press.

Kagan, Richard, 1999: 'The Emperor's Chronicles', in Pedro Navasues Palacio (ed.), *Carolus V Imperator*. Madrid: Editores Lunwerg.

Kelley, Donald R., 1970: *The Foundations of Modern Historical Scholarship*. Princeton: Princeton University Press.

1990: *The Human Measure: Social Thought in the Western Legal Tradition*. Cambridge, MA: Harvard University Press.

1991a: *Versions of History from Antiquity to the Enlightenment*. New Haven: Yale University Press.

1991b. *Renaissance Humanism*. Boston: Twayne Publishers.

1993: 'Tacitus Noster: the *Germania* in the Renaissance and Reformation', in Luce and Woodman, 1993, pp. 152–67.

1998: *Faces of History: Historical Enquiry from Herodotus to Herder*. New Haven: Yale University Press.

Kendrick, T. D., 1950: *British Antiquity*. London: Methuen.

Keohane, N. O., 1980: *Philosophy and the State in France: the Renaissance to the Enlightenment*. Princeton: Princeton University Press.

Kishlansky, Mark A., 1979: *The Rise of the New Model Army*. Cambridge: Cambridge University Press.

Koebner, Richard, 1961: *Empire*. Cambridge: Cambridge University Press.

Leites, Edmund, 1988: (Ed.) *Conscience and Casuistry in Early Modern Europe*. Cambridge: Cambridge University Press.

Levine, Joseph M., 1987: *Humanism and History: Origins of Modern English Historiography*. Ithaca: Cornell University Press.

1991: *The Battle of the Books: History and Literature in the Augustan Age*. Ithaca: Cornell University Press.

1999a: *The Autonomy of History: Truth and Method from Erasmus to Gibbon*. Chicago: University of Chicago Press.

1999b: *Between the Ancients and the Moderns: Baroque Culture in Restoration England*. New Haven: Yale University Press.

Lloyd, Howell A., 1994: (Ed.) *Charles Loyseau: A Treatise of Orders and Plain Dignities*. Cambridge: Cambridge University Press. *Cambridge Texts in the History of Political Thought*.

Luce, T. J., and Woodman, A. J., 1993: (Eds.) *Tacitus and the Tacitean Tradition*. Princeton: Princeton University Press.

Maffei, Domenico, 1964: *La Donazione di Costantino nei giuristi medievali*. Milan: Giuffré.

Mansfield, Harvey C., 1979: *Machiavelli's New Modes and Orders: a Study of the Discourses on Livy*. Ithaca: Cornell University Press.

1996: *Machiavelli's Virtue*. Chicago: University of Chicago Press.

2000: 'Bruni and Machiavelli on Civic Humanism', in Hankins, 2000, pp. 223–46.

Markus, R. A., 1970: *Saeculum: History and Society in the Theology of St. Augustine*. Cambridge: Cambridge University Press.

Matthews, John, 1989: *The Roman Empire of Ammianus*. Baltimore: the Johns Hopkins University Press.

Mayhew, Robert, 2000: *Enlightenment Geography: the Political Languages of British Geography, 1650–1850*. London: Macmillan/New York: St Martins.

Mazzocco, Angelo, 1982: 'Rome and the Humanists: the Case of Biondo Flavio', in Ramsey, 1982, pp. 185–96.

1984: 'Decline and Rebirth: Bruni and Biondo', in Brezzi and Lorch, 1984, pp. 249–66.

McCuaig, William, 1989: *Carlo Sigonio: the Changing World of the Late Renaissance*. Princeton: Princeton University Press.

McLaren, A. N., 1999: *Political Culture in the Reign of Elizabeth I: Queen and Commonwealth, 1558–1585*. Cambridge: Cambridge University Press.

Meinecke, Friedrich, 1957: *Machiavellism*. (English translation of *Der Idee der Staatsräson*, 1924). London: Routledge & Kegan Paul.

Mellor, Ronald, 1995: (Ed.) *Tacitus: the Classical Heritage*. New York: Garland Publishing.

Mendle, Michael A., 2001: (Ed.) *The Putney Debates of 1647: the Army, the Levellers and the English State*. Cambridge: Cambridge University Press.

Miller, Peter N., 2000: *Peiresc's Europe: Learning and Virtue in the Seventeenth Century*. New Haven: Yale University Press.

Molho, Anthony, and Tedeschi, John A., 1971: (Eds.) *Renaissance Studies in Honour of Hans Baron*. De Kalb: Northern Illinois University Press.

Momigliano, Arnaldo, 1963: (Ed.) *Paganism and Christianity in the Fourth Century*. Oxford: the Clarendon Press.

1977: *Essays in Ancient and Modern Historiography*. Middletown: Wesleyan University Press.

1990: *The Classical Foundations of Modern Historiography: the Sather Classical Lectures, 1961–62*. Berkeley and Los Angeles: University of California Press.

Mommsen, Theodore E., 1959: *Medieval and Renaissance Studies*. Ithaca: Cornell University Press.

Morford, Mark, 1991: *Stoics and Neostoics: Rubens and the Circle of Lipsius*. Princeton: Princeton University Press.

Muldoon, James, 1999: *Empire and Order: the Concept of Empire, 800–1800*. London: Macmillan/New York: St Martins.

Neveu, Bruno, 1968: *Un Historien à l'école de Port-Royal: Sébastien le Nain de Tillemont, 1637–1698*. The Hague: Martinus Nijhoff. *Archives internationales d'histoire des idées*, XV.

Norbrook, David, 1998: *Writing the English Republic: Poetry, Rhetoric and Politics, 1627–1660*. Cambridge: Cambridge University Press.

O'Brien, Karen, 1997: *Narratives of Enlightenment: Cosmopolitan History from Voltaire to Gibbon*. Cambridge: Cambridge University Press.

Oestreich, Gerhard, 1982: *Neostoicism and the Early Modern State*. (Ed. Brigitta Oestreich and H. G. Koenigsberger; trans. David McLintock) Cambridge: Cambridge University Press.

Pagden, Anthony, 1987: (Ed.) *The Languages of Political Theory in Early Modern Europe*. Cambridge: Cambridge University Press.

1995: *Lords of All the World: Ideologies of Empire in Spain, Britain, and France, c. 1500–c. 1800*. New Haven: Yale University Press.

Parel, Antony J., 1992: *The Machiavellian Cosmos*. New Haven: Yale University Press.

Parker, Geoffrey, 1972: *The Army of Flanders and the Spanish Road, 1567–1659*. Cambridge: Cambridge University Press.

1988: *The Military Revolution and the Rise of the West, 1500–1800*. Cambridge: Cambridge University Press.

Parsons, Jotham, 2001: 'Money and Sovereignty in Early Modern France', *Journal of the History of Ideas*, LXII, i, pp. 59–80.

Pelikan, Jaroslav, 1987: *The Excellent Empire: the Fall of Rome and the Triumph of the Church*. San Francisco: Harper and Row.

Peltonen, Markku, 1995: *Classical Humanism and Republicanism in English Political Thought, 1570–1640*. Cambridge: Cambridge University Press.

1996: (Ed.) *The Cambridge Companion to Francis Bacon*. Cambridge: Cambridge University Press.

Phillips, Mark S., 2000: *Society and Sentiment: Genres of Historical Writing in Britain, 1740–1820*. Princeton: Princeton University Press.

Phillipson, Nicholas, and Skinner, Quentin, 1993: (Eds.) *Political Discourse in Early Modern Britain*. Cambridge: Cambridge University Press.

Pincus, Steven C. A., 1995: 'The English Debate over Universal Monarchy', in Robertson, 1995, pp. 37–62.

1996: *Protestantism and Patriotism: Ideologies and the Making of English Foreign Policy, 1650–1688*. Cambridge: Cambridge University Press.

Pocock, J. G. A., 1975: *The Machiavellian Moment: Florentine Political Thought and the Atlantic Republican Tradition*. Re-issued 2003. Princeton: Princeton University Press.

    1985: *Virtue, Commerce and History: Essays on Political Thought and History, Chiefly in the Eighteenth Century*. Cambridge: Cambridge University Press.

    1987b: *The Ancient Constitution and the Feudal Law: a Reissue with a Retrospect*. Cambridge: Cambridge University Press.

    1996: 'Standing Army and Public Credit: the Institutions of Leviathan', in Hoak and Feingold, 1996, pp. 87–103.

    2000: 'Gibbon and the Primitive Church', in Collini, Whatmore and Young, 2000, pp. 48–68.

Rahe, Paul A., 1992: *Republics Ancient and Modern*. Two volumes. Chapel Hill: University of North Carolina Press.

    2000: 'Situating Machiavelli', in Hankins, 2000, pp. 270–308.

Ramsey, P. A., 1982: (Ed.) *Rome in the Renaissance: the City and the Myth*. Binghamton: State University of New York Press.

Ranum, Orest, 1980: 'D'Alembert, Tacitus and the Political Sociology of Despotism', *Transactions of the Fifth International Congress on the Enlightenment*, pp. 547–58. Oxford: Oxford University Press.

Raskolnikoff, Mouza, 1992: *Histoire Romaine et Critique Historique dans l'Europe des Lumières*. Rome: Ecole Française de Rome/Strasbourg: l'Université des Sciences Humaines de Strasbourg.

Richardson, J. S., 1992: '*Imperium Romanum*: Empire and the Language of Power', in Armitage, 1992, pp. 1–10.

Ricuperati, Giuseppe, 1999: 'Jacques-Bénigne Bossuet et l'histoire universelle', *Storia della Storiografia*, XXXV, pp. 27–62.

Ridolfi, Roberto, 1976: *The Life of Francesco Guicciardini* (trans. Cecil Grayson). London: Routledge & Kegan Paul.

Robbins, Caroline, 1959: *The Eighteenth-Century Commonwealthman: Studies in the Transmission, Development and Circumstance of English Liberal Thought from the Restoration of Charles II until the War with the Thirteen Colonies*. Cambridge, MA: Harvard University Press.

Robertson, John, 1985: *The Militia Issue and the Scottish Enlightenment*. Edinburgh: John Donald.

    1993: 'Universal Monarchy and the Liberties of Europe: David Hume's Critique of an English Whig Doctrine', in Phillipson and Skinner, 1993, pp. 349–76.

    1995: (Ed.) *A Union for Empire: Political Thought and the Union of 1707*. Cambridge: Cambridge University Press.

Rogers, G. A. J., and Sorell, Tom, 2001: (Eds.) *Hobbes and History*. London: Routledge.

Rogers, Pat, 1997: 'Gibbon and the Decline and Growth of the Club', in Womersley, 1997a, pp. 105–20.

Roller, Matthew B., 2001: *Constructing Autocracy: Aristocrats and Emperors in Julio-Claudian Rome*. Princeton: Princeton University Press.

Ross, Ian Simpson, 1995: *The Life of Adam Smith*. Oxford: the Clarendon Press.

Rostovtseff, Michael, 1926: *The Social and Economic History of the Roman Empire*. Oxford: the Clarendon Press.

Rowland, Ingrid, 1998: *The Culture of the High Renaissance: Ancients and Moderns in Sixteenth-Century Rome*. Cambridge: Cambridge University Press.

Rubinstein, Nicolai, 1968: (Ed.) *Florentine Studies: Politics and Society in Renaissance Florence*. London: Faber and Faber.

Schellhase, Kenneth, 1976: *Tacitus in Renaissance Political Thought*. Chicago: University of Chicago Press.

Schiavone, Aldo, 2000: *The End of the Past: Ancient Rome and the Modern West*. (Trans. Margery J. Schneider.) Cambridge, MA: Harvard University Press.

Schwoerer, Lois G., 1974: *No Standing Armies! the Anti-Army Ideology in Seventeenth-Century England*. Baltimore: the Johns Hopkins University Press.

Skinner, Quentin, 1978: *The Foundations of Modern Political Thought. Volume One: the Renaissance. Volume Two: the Age of Reformation*. Cambridge: Cambridge University Press.

1990: 'Machiavelli's *Discorsi* and the Pre-humanist Origins of Republican Ideas,' in Bock, Gisela, Skinner, Quentin, and Viroli, Maurizio (eds.), *Machiavelli and Republicanism*. Cambridge: Cambridge University Press, pp. 121–41.

1996: *Reason and Rhetoric in the Philosophy of Hobbes*. Cambridge: Cambridge University Press.

Smalley, Beryl, 1971: 'Sallust in the Middle Ages', in R. R. Bolgar (ed.), *Classical Influences on European Culture, AD 500–1500*. Cambridge: Cambridge University Press, pp. 165–94.

Soll, Jacob, 1997: 'Amelot de la Houssaye and the Tacitean Tradition', *Translation and Literature*, VI, 2, pp. 186–202.

2000: 'Amelot de la Houssaye's Tacitus', *Journal of the History of Ideas*, LXI, 2, pp. 167–87.

Stockton, David, 1979: *The Gracchi*. Oxford: the Clarendon Press.

Struever, Nancy S., 1970: *The Language of History in the Renaissance: Rhetoric and Historical Consciousness in Florentine Humanism*. Princeton: Princeton University Press.

Syme, Ronald, 1939: *The Roman Revolution*. Oxford: the Clarendon Press.

Syme, Ronald, 1958: *Tacitus*. Two volumes. Oxford: the Clarendon Press.

Toffanin, Giuseppe, 1921: *Machiavelli e il Tacitismo*. Padua: Draghi.

Tuck, Richard, 1993: *Philosophy and Government, 1572–1651*. Cambridge: Cambridge University Press.

Viroli, Maurizio, 1992: *From Politics to Reason of State: the Acquisition and Transformation of the Language of Politics, 1250–1600*. Princeton: Princeton University Press.

Volpilhac-Auger, Catherine, 1985: *Tacite et Montesquieu*. Oxford: the Voltaire Foundation.

1993: *Tacite en France de Montesquieu à Chateaubriand*. Oxford: the Voltaire Foundation.

Walbank, F. W., 1972. *Polybius*. Berkeley and Los Angeles: University of California Press.

1979. *A Historical Commentary on Polybius*. Oxford: the Clarendon Press. Three volumes.

Weinbrot, Howard K., 1978: *Augustus Caesar in 'Augustan' England: the Decline of a Classical Norm*. Princeton: Princeton University Press.

1993a: *Britannia's Issue: the Rise of British Literature from Dryden to Ossian*. Cambridge: Cambridge University Press.

1993b: 'Politics, Taste and National Identity: Some Uses of Tacitism in Eighteenth-Century Britain', in Luce and Woodman, 1993, pp. 168–84.

Williamson, Arthur, 1979: *Scottish National Consciousness in the Age of James VI*. Edinburgh: John Donald.

Wirszubski, Ch., 1950: *Libertas as a Political Idea at Rome during the Late Republic and Early Principate*. Cambridge: Cambridge University Press.

Womersley, David, 1988: *The Transformation of the Decline and Fall of the Roman Empire*. Cambridge: Cambridge University Press.

1997a: (Ed.) *Edward Gibbon; Bicentenary Essays*. Oxford: the Voltaire Foundation.

1997b: (Ed.) *Religious Scepticism: Contemporary Responses to Gibbon*. Bristol: Thoemmes Press.

Woolrych, Austin, 1987: *Soldiers and Statesmen: the General Council of the Army and its Debates, 1647–48*. Oxford: the Clarendon Press.

Wright, Johnson Kent, 1997: *A Classical Republican in Eighteenth-Century France: the Political Thought of Mably*. Stanford: Stanford University Press.

Zagorin, Perez, 1998: *Francis Bacon*. Princeton: Princeton University Press.

Zhang, Zhizhong, 1993: 'From Cosimo the *Pater Patriae* to Cosimo the Grand Duke: the Images of the Medici as seen by Machiavelli, Guicciardini and Vettori'. Ph.D. dissertation: Johns Hopkins University.

# *Index*